The Archaeology of the South-West Reinforcement Gas Pipeline, Devon: Investigations in 2005–2007

The Archaeology of the South-West Reinforcement Gas Pipeline, Devon: Investigations in 2005–2007

by
Andrew Mudd and Stuart Joyce

with major contributions from

Henrietta Quinnell, Sarah Cobain, E.R. McSloy, David Starley, Angela Aggujaro, Susan Watts and John Allan

and other contributions from

Michael Allen, Peter Davenport, Jonny Geber, Harriet Jacklin, Roger T. Taylor, Victoria Taylor and Sylvia Warman

Principal illustrator Lorna Gray
with contributions from Lucy Martin

Cotswold Archaeology Monograph No. 6
Cirencester 2014

Cotswold Archaeology Monograph No. 6

Published by Cotswold Archaeology
Copyright © Authors and Cotswold Archaeology 2014
Building 11, Kemble Enterprise Park, Cirencester, Gloucestershire GL7 6BQ

All rights reserved. No part of this publication may be reproduced, stored in a retrieval system, or transmitted in any form or by any means, electronic, photocopying, recording or otherwise, without the prior permission of the copyright owner.

ISBN 978-0-9553534-7-5

The following images are supplied to Cotswold Archaeology for use in this publication volume:
Fig. 2.26: Frame DAP BS.10A 11 July 1984, Frances Griffith, Devon County Council; Fig. 3.12: Frame DAP VL.04 7 July 1992, Bill Horner, Devon County Council; Fig. 4.12: Frame DAP JM.8 11 Jan 1988, Frances Griffith, Devon County Council; © Devon County Council.
Fig. 2.29: RAF/3G/TUD/UK/223 fr. 5113 12 July 1946, English Heritage (NMR) RAF photography library ref. 430.

Mapping in Figs 1.1–1.7, 2.1, 2.3, 2.6, 2.9, 2.11, 2.13, 2.15, 2.17, 2.21, 2.23, 2.25, 2.30, 3.1, 3.3, 3.6, 3.8, 3.10, 3.13, 3.19, 3.20, 3.26, 3.29, 4.1–2, 4.5, 4.11, 4.14, 4.21, 4.22, 5.1, 5.3, 5.4, 5.6, 5.7, 5.9 and 5.10 is reproduced from the Ordnance Survey on behalf of the controller of Her Majesty's Stationery Office, © Crown Copyright Cotswold Archaeology Ltd 100002109.

Cropmark plots in Figs 2.23 and 3.10 are based on Devon County Council aerial photographic refs DAP BS.10A-12, FE.09-10, MH.07-09, RG.01-02, VL.03-06. Cropmark plot on Fig. 5.3 based upon English Heritage (NMR) aerial photographic library ref. 13550.

Geophysical survey greyscale and interpretative plots in Figs 2.11, 2.13, 2.17, 2.23, 3.3, 3.13, 4.11, 5.1 and 5.9-10 reproduced from Archaeological Surveys 2006a–c and 2007.

Geological information in Figs 2.41–2.44 courtesy of British Geological Survey (BGS 1974a–b, 1976 and 1995).

Front cover: View west along the Fishacre to Choakford pipeline route north of Fursdon, Staverton
Back cover: Roman enclosure at Billany Farm; Beaker pottery from Springfield; Medieval hearth at Exwell Barton

Cover design by Lucy Martin, Cotswold Archaeology
Produced by Past Historic, Kings Stanley, Gloucestershire
Printed by Short Run Press, Exeter

CONTENTS

List of Illustrations	vi
List of Tables	x
Acknowledgements	xii
Summary	xiii
Resumé	xiv
Zusammenfassung	xv

Chapter 1   Introduction
Project Background	1
Location and topography	4
Archaeological character	11
Content and structure of report	12

Chapter 2   Earlier Prehistoric Period
Introduction	15
Site descriptions by Stuart Joyce and Andrew Mudd	15
Neolithic and Bronze Age pottery by Henrietta Quinnell, with petrographic comment by Roger T. Taylor	45
Worked flint and chert by E.R. McSloy	55
Other worked and utilised stone by Susan Watts, with geological identification by Roger T. Taylor	63
Bronze pin from Crablake Farm, Exminster by E.R. McSloy	66
Plant macrofossils and charcoal by Sarah Cobain	66
Cremated human remains from Salston B, Ottery St Mary by Harriet Jacklin	76
Radiocarbon dating by Andrew Mudd	77

Chapter 3   Later Prehistoric and Roman Periods
Introduction	79
Site descriptions by Stuart Joyce and Andrew Mudd	79
Later Iron Age pottery by Henrietta Quinnell	105
Roman pottery by E.R. McSloy and Angela Aggujaro	106
Worked and utilised stone by Susan Watts, with geological identification by Roger T. Taylor	110
Other artefacts by E.R. McSloy	114
Metalworking by David Starley	115

Plant macrofossils and charcoal by Sarah Cobain	121
Radiocarbon dating by Andrew Mudd	130

Chapter 4   Medieval and Later Periods
Introduction	131
Site descriptions by Stuart Joyce and Andrew Mudd	131
Medieval and later pottery by John Allan, with a contribution from Roger T. Taylor	148
Flemish bricks by John Allan	155
Worked and utilised stone by Susan Watts, with geological identification by Roger T. Taylor	155
Other artefacts by E.R. McSloy	155
Plant macrofossils and charcoal by Sarah Cobain	156
Animal bones and sea shells by Jonny Geber, with Sylvia Warman and Victoria Taylor	166
Radiocarbon dating by Andrew Mudd	166

Chapter 5   Enclosures and Field Systems
Introduction	167
Undated ditches of possible prehistoric or Roman date by Stuart Joyce and Andrew Mudd	167
Medieval and later ditches and boundaries by Stuart Joyce and Andrew Mudd	173

Chapter 6   Discussion
Introduction	177
Mesolithic (9500 to 4000 BC)	177
Early Neolithic (4000 to 3300 BC)	180
Middle to Late Neolithic (3300 to 2400 BC)	180
Early Bronze Age (2400 to 1800 BC)	182
Middle Bronze Age (1800 to 1300 BC)	184
Iron Age and Roman (400 BC to AD 400)	186
Post-Roman and Medieval (AD 400 to 1500)	191
Concluding remarks	193

Appendix Technical methodologies	193
References	195
Index	205

List of Illustrations

1.1	Site locations. Scale 1:300,000	2
1.2	Ottery St Mary to Aylesbeare; site locations. Scale 1:30,000	5
1.3	Aylesbeare to Kenn; site locations. Scale 1:30,000	6
1.4	Aylesbeare to Kenn; site locations. Scale 1:30,000	7
1.5	Fishacre to Choakford; site locations. Scale 1:30,000	8
1.6	Fishacre to Choakford; site locations. Scale 1:30,000	9
1.7	Fishacre to Choakford; site locations. Scale 1:30,000	10
2.1	Pixies' Parlour (Site 4); plan of excavated features. Scales 1:250 and 1:10,000	16
2.2	Pixies' Parlour (Site 4); sections 1, 2 and 3 through feature 3.04.096. Scale 1:50	17
2.3	Croft Cottages (Site 20); plan of excavated features. Scales 1:200 and 1:10,000	18
2.4	Croft Cottages (Site 20); plan of linear feature 8.02.004. Scale 1:50	18
2.5	Croft Cottages (Site 20); section 4 through linear feature 8.02.004. Scale 1:20	19
2.6	Hems Valley (Site 17); plan of excavated features. Scales 1:250 and 1:10,000	19
2.7	Hems Valley (Site 17); sections 5 to 8 through pits. Scale 1:20	21
2.8	Hems Valley (Site 17); view of pit 2.02.006, looking south-east. Scale 0.4m	21
2.9	Moore Farm (Site 28); plan of excavated features. Scales 1:200, 1:2000 and 1:10,000	22
2.10	Moore Farm (Site 28); sections 9 and 10 through ditches. Scale 1:20	23
2.11	Salston B (Site 6); plan of geophysical anomalies and excavated features. Scales 1:500, 1:2000 and 1:10,000	25
2.12	Salston B (Site 6); Early Bronze Age cremation pit 205.004, looking west. Scale 0.4m	26
2.13	Springfield (Site 31); plan of geophysical anomalies and excavated features. Scales 1:2000 and 1:10,000	26
2.14	Springfield (Site 31); Beaker pit 24.03.060, looking north. Scale 0.6m	27
2.15	Land East of Broad Oak (Site 7); plan showing extract from 1845 Tithe Map and excavated features. Scales 1:2000 and 1:10,000	28
2.16	Land East of Broad Oak (Site 7); sections 11 to 16. Scales 1:20 and 1:50	29
2.17	South-East of Broad Oak (Site 8); plan of geophysical anomalies and excavated features. Scales 1:500, 1:1500 and 1:10,000	30
2.18	South-East of Broad Oak (Site 8); sections 17 to 20. Scale 1:50	31
2.19	South-East of Broad Oak (Site 8); excavation of ditch 5.01.020 in progress, looking east	31
2.20	South-East of Broad Oak (Site 8); ditch 5.01.20, looking south-west. Scale 1m	32
2.21	Crablake Farm (Site 15); plan of excavated features. Scales 1:200, 1:2000 and 1:10,000	33
2.22	Crablake Farm (Site 15); the Trevisker pot *in situ* in pit 14.09.003, looking south-east. Scale 0.5m	34
2.23	Hood Ball (Site 21); plan of geophysical anomalies, cropmarks and excavated features. Scales 1:200, 1:2000 and 1:10,000	36
2.24	Hood Ball (Site 21); pit 12.05.009, looking north-west. Scale 0.2m	37
2.25	Hood Quarry (Site 23); plan of cropmarks and excavated features. Scales 1:1000 and 1:10,000	37
2.26	Hood Quarry (Site 23); aerial photograph showing cropmarks and location of excavation. Ditch 13.03.004 runs from the southern end of the trench through and beyond Hood Copse (Devon County Council Ref. DAP BS.10A)	38
2.27	Hood Quarry (Site 23); sections 21 and 22. Scale 1:50	39
2.28	Hood Quarry (Site 23); ditch 13.03.004, looking east. Scale 1m	39

2.29	Hood Quarry (Site 23); aerial photograph showing cropmarks (NMR ref. RAF/3G/TUD/UK/223)	40	2.47	Stones from Hems Valley (Site 17) pit 2.02.004. Clockwise from top left: rubbing stone of vesicular lava (S2); rubbing stone of volcanic tuff (S1) cobble of porphyritic lava; cobble of porpyritic lava	65
2.30	Beneknowle (Site 30); plan showing excavated features. Scales 1:50, 1:1250 and 1:10,000	42			
2.31	Beneknowle (Site 30); sections 23 to 26. Scale 1:50	43	2.48	Stone from Hems Valley (Site 17) pit 2.02.006. Rubbing stone of volcanic tuff (S3)	65
2.32	Beneknowle (Site 30); terraced structure 21.06.008, looking west. Scale 1m	43	2.49	Stone from Hems Valley (Site 17) pit 2.02.016. Cobble of fine-grained sandstone	66
2.33	Pixies' Parlour (Site 4); Early Neolithic pottery. Top row: bodysherds showing white inclusions of vein quartz added to granite-derived fabric (Fabric VQ1). Bottom left: bodysherd of clay with ?limestone voids (Fabric IV.1). Bottom right: rimsherd from carinated bowl in Permian breccia-derived fabric (Fabric PB.1)	46	2.50	Bronze pin shaft from Crablake Farm (Site 15) pit 14.09.007. Scale 1:1	66
			3.1	Slade Farm (Site 2); plan of pit 2.03.004. Scales 1:50 and 1:10,000	79
			3.2	Slade Farm (Site 2); section 27 through pit 2.03.004. Scale 1:20	80
			3.3	Pixies' Parlour (Site 4); plan of geophysical anomalies and (A) Roman and later features. Scales 1:250, 1:1250, 1:10,000	81
2.34	Late Neolithic Grooved Ware from Moore Farm, Harberton (Site 28), pit 18.12.018. Scale 1:2	49	3.4	Pixies' Parlour (Site 4); sections 28 to 31 through ditch 3.04.004. Scale 1:50	82
2.35	Late Neolithic Grooved Ware from Moore Farm, Harberton (Site 28), ditch 18.12.049. Scale 1:2	50	3.5	Pixies' Parlour (Site 4); excavating ditch 3.04.004, looking west	82
2.36	Beaker sherds from Springfield (Site 31), pit 24.03.060	51	3.6	Exwell Barton Iron Age ditches (Site 14); plan of excavated features. Scales 1:500 and 1:10,000	83
2.37	Early Bronze Age Beaker from Springfield (Site 31), pit 24.03.060. Scale 1:2	51	3.7	Exwell Barton Iron Age ditches (Site 14); sections 32 to 34. Scale 1:50	84
2.38	Trevisker Ware pot from Crablake Farm (Site 15), pit 14.09.003, conserved	53	3.8	Barton Hill Cross (Site 19); transcription of 1838 Tithe Map, showing excavated features. Scales 1:1250 and 1:10,000	85
2.39	Crablake Farm (Site 15); upper decorated sherds from vessel in pit 14.09.003	53			
2.40	Middle Bronze Age Trevisker Ware pottery. Scales 1:3 and 1:2	53	3.9	Barton Hill Cross (Site 19); sections 35 to 38. Scale 1:50	86
2.41	Ottery St Mary to Aylesbeare (OTA) flint distribution in relation to geology. Scale 1:50,000	56	3.10	Lower Velwell (Site 22); plan of cropmarks and excavated features. Scales 1:1250 and 1:10,000	87
2.42	Aylesbeare to Kenn (ATK) flint distribution in relation to geology. Scale 1:50,000	57	3.11	Lower Velwell (Site 22); plan of furnaces. Scale 1:20	88
			3.12	Lower Velwell (Site 22); aerial photograph showing cropmarks. (Devon County Council Ref. DAP VL.04)	89
2.43	Fishacre to Choakfoard (FTC) flint distribution in relation to geology. Scale 1:50,000	60			
2.44	Fishacre to Choakford (FTC) flint distribution in relation to geology. Scale 1:50,000	61	3.13	Billany Farm (Site 24); plan of geophysical anomalies and excavated features. Scales 1:1000 and 1:10,000	90
2.45	Worked flint and chert. Scale 2:3	63	3.14	Billany Farm (Site 24); plan of excavated features. Scale 1:250	91
2.46	Stones from Hems Valley (Site 17), pit 2.02.010. A. clockwise from top left: cobble of vesicular lava; cobble of porphyritic lava; burnt volcanic tuff; cobble of porphyritic lava with one flat side (S4). B. top to bottom; sandstone cobble, sandstone cobble, lava cobble	64	3.15	Billany Farm (Site 24): initial trench through terrace 14.01.107, looking east. Scale 1m	92
			3.16	Billany Farm (Site 24); ditch 14.01.105, looking north-east. Scale 1m	92
			3.17	Billany Farm (Site 24); ditch 14.01.106, looking west. Scale 1m	93

3.18	Billany Farm (Site 24): sections 39 and 40. Scale 1:50	93	4.8	Lower Nutwell (Site 12); view of cobbles 12.01.019 and plinth 12.01.010, looking south-west. Scale 1m	136
3.19	Dun Cross (Site 25); plan of excavated features, showing burnt areas. Scales 1:250 and 1:10,000	94	4.9	Lower Nutwell (Site 12); bricks 12.01.029 and cobbles 12.01.019, looking north-west. Scale 1m	136
3.20	Tigley A (Site 26); excavated features on transcription of 1842 Tithe Map. Scales 1:125, 1:2000 and 1:10,000	95	4.10	Lower Nutwell (Site 12); extract from 1849 Tithe Map showing cob building. Scale 1:2500	137
3.21	Tigley A (Site 26); sections 41, 42 and 43. Scale 1:20	96	4.11	White House (Site 13); plan of excavated features, showing geophysical survey results. Scales 1:2000 and 1:10,000	138
3.22	Tigley A (Site 26); furnace cluster, pre-excavation, looking south-east. Scales 0.5m and 1m	96	4.12	White House (Site 13); aerial photograph of earthworks showing location of excavated area, looking south-east (Devon County Council Ref. DAP JM.08)	139
3.23	Tigley A (Site 26); furnaces, looking north. Scale 0.5m	97
3.24	Tigley A (Site 26); section 41, looking west. Scale 1m	97	4.13	White House (Site 13); trackway 12.12.004, looking west. Scale 1m	140
3.25	Tigley A (Site 26); furnace 16.07.008, looking north. Scale 0.5m	98	4.14	Exwell Barton medieval settlement (Site 14); plan showing transcription from 1838 Tithe Map and First Edition Ordnance Survey map of 1890–1, and excavated features. Scales 1:2000 and 1:10,000	140
3.26	Springfield (Site 31); plan of excavated features. Scales 1:2500 and 1:10,000	100
3.27	Springfield (Site 31); plan of excavated features. Scale 1:1000	101	4.15	Exwell Barton medieval settlement (Site 14); phased plan of excavated features. Scale 1:1000	141
3.28	Springfield (Site 31); view of oven 24.03.036, looking south-east. Scale 1m	103	4.16	Exwell Barton medieval building (Site 14); plan of excavated features. Scale 1:100	142
3.29	Filham House (Site 34); plan of excavated features. Scales 1:250 and 1:10,000	104	4.17	Exwell Barton medieval building (Site 14); hearth 13.02.132, looking north-east. Scale 1m	143
3.30	Roman pottery from Billany Farm (Site 24) and Springfield (Site 31). Scale 1:4	109	4.18	Exwell Barton medieval settlement (Site 14); plan and sections of sunken-floored building 13.02.272. Scales 1:50 and 1:25	144
3.31	Quern fragments from Billany Farm (Site 24). Scale 1:4	112
3.32	Stone mould for pewter dish from Springfield (Site 31). Site 1:2	114	4.19	Exwell Barton medieval settlement (Site 14); view of hearth 13.02.203 (far) and oven 13.02.273 (near), looking north-west. Scale 0.5m	145
3.33	Stone mould for pewter dish from Springfield (Site 31)	114
3.34	Roman glass beads. Scale 1:1	114	4.20	Exwell Barton medieval settlement (Site 14), sunken-floored building 13.02.272, looking south-west. Scale 1m	146
4.1	Tigley B (Site 27); plan of pit 16.08.020. Scales 1:100 and 1:10,000	131
4.2	Coldharbour (Site 1); extract from 1845 Tithe Map, showing excavated feature. Scales 1:4000 and 1:10,000	132	4.21	Bluepost (Site 29); plan of pit 19.07.004. Scales 1:50 and 1:10,000	147
4.3	Salston A (Site 5); location on extract from 1845 Tithe Map. Scale 1:7500	133	4.22	Forder Cross (Site 32); extract from 1843 Tithe Map, showing excavated features. Scales 1:2000 and 1:10,000	148
4.4	Salston A (Site 5); excavation in progress, looking west. Scales 1m	133
4.5	Lower Nutwell (Site 12); plan of building. Scales 1:100 and 1:10,000	135	4.23	Forder Cross (Site 32); sections 46 to 50. Scales 1:20 and 1:50	149
4.6	Lower Nutwell (Site 12); view of building, looking west. Scale 1m	135	4.24	Medieval and later pottery. Scale 1:4	152
4.7	Lower Nutwell (Site 12); view of interior of wall 12.01.006, looking north-west. Scale 1m	136	4.25	Post-medieval pottery. Scale 1:4	153

4.26	Iron whittle-tang knife from Exwell Barton (Site 14), pit 13.02.161. Scale 1:1	156	
4.27	Post-medieval bead from Tigley B (Site 27), ditch 16.08.006. Scale 1:1	156	
5.1	Knightstone Farm (Site 3); geophysical anomalies and excavated features on transcription of 1845 Tithe Map. Scales 1:2000 and 1:10,000	167	
5.2	Knightstone Farm (Site 3); sections 51 to 53. Scale 1:50	168	
5.3	New Nutwalls (Site 9); excavated features on transcription of 1841 Tithe Map. Scales 1:1250 and 1:10,000	169	
5.4	The Nutwell Lodge (Site 11); excavated features on transcription of 1849 Tithe Map. Scales 1:1250, 1:5000 and 1:10,000	170	
5.5	The Nutwell Lodge (Site 11); sections 54 and 55. Scale 1:50	170	
5.6	Soloman's Farm (Site 16); excavated features on transcription of 1838 Tithe Map	171	
5.7	Moothill Cross (Site 18); excavated features on transcription of 1842 Tithe Map. Scales 1:1250 and 1:10,000	172	
5.8	Moothill Cross (Site 18); section 56. Scale 1:50	172	
5.9	Wood Farm (Site 33); plan of geophysical anomalies and excavated features. Scales 1:2000 and 1:10,000	173	
5.10	Hogsbrook Farm (Site 10); extract from 1849 Tithe Map, showing excavated features. Scales 1:2500 and 1:10,000	174	
6.1	Radiocarbon dates calibrated using OXCal 4.1.7 (Bronk Ramsey 2009) and the Incal09 dataset (Reimer *et al.* 2009). Distributions in blue are for samples which were redeposited in their contexts and/or consisted of old wood; distributions in red are for samples which were intrusive in their contexts	178	
6.2	Percentage of wild food, cultivated crops and weed species	182	
6.3	Broad characterisation of charcoal species fragments identified from the Neolithic to post-medieval periods	183	
6.4	Full analysis of charcoal species identified from the Neolithic to medieval periods	183	

List of Tables

1.1	Sites investigated along the pipeline corridors	3
1.2	Periods represented on the main sites described	13
2.1	Radiocarbon dates from Pixies' Parlour, Site 4 (OTA 3.04)	17
2.2	Radiocarbon dates from Hems Valley, Site 17 (FTC 2.02)	20
2.3	Radiocarbon dates from Moore Farm, Site 28 (FTC 18.12)	23
2.4	Radiocarbon dates from Salston B, Site 6 (OTA 4.01)	24
2.5	Radiocarbon dates from Land East of Broad Oak, Site 7 (OTA 4.10)	29
2.6	Radiocarbon date from South-East of Broad Oak, Site 8 (OTA 5.01)	32
2.7	Radiocarbon dates from Crablake Farm, Site 15 (ATK 14.09)	34
2.8	Radiocarbon dates from Hood Ball, Site 21 (FTC 12.05)	35
2.9	Radiocarbon dates from Hood Quarry, Site 23 (FTC 13.03)	41
2.10	Radiocarbon dates from Beneknowle, Site 30 (FTC 21.06)	44
2.11	Radiocarbon dates from Filham House, Site 34 (FTC 33.01)	45
2.12	Early Neolithic ceramics: sherd numbers with weight in grammes	46
2.13	Middle and Late Neolithic ceramics: sherd numbers with weight in grammes	47
2.14	Middle Bronze Age ceramics: sherd numbers with weight in grammes	52
2.15	Pixies' Parlour, Site 4 (OTA 3.04): worked lithics from Early Neolithic Pit Group 3.04.096. All material flint except where stated. Pri. = primary, Sec. = secondary, Tert. = tertiary	58
2.16	Hems Valley, Site 17 (FTC 2.02): worked flint from Middle Neolithic pit groups. Pri. = primary, Sec. = secondary, Tert. = tertiary	59
2.17	Filham House, Site 34 (FTC 33.01): worked flint from Middle Bronze Age Pit 33.01.006. Pri. = primary, Sec. = secondary, Tert. = tertiary	62
2.18	Hems Valley, Site 17 (FTC 2.02): cobbles and stone fragments from Middle Neolithic pits	64
2.19	Neolithic plant macrofossil identifications; Hems Valley (Site 17)	67
2.20	Neolithic plant macrofossil identifications; Hems Valley (Site 17) and Moore Farm (Site 28)	67
2.21	Neolithic charcoal identifications (broad characterisation): Hems Valley (Site 17) and Moore Farm (Site 28)	68
2.22	Neolithic charcoal identifications (full analysis): Hems Valley (Site 17) and Moore Farm (Site 28)	68
2.23	Bronze Age charcoal identifications (broad characterisation): Pixies' Parlour (Site 4), Land East of Broad Oak (Site 7), Crablake Farm (Site 15)	69
2.24	Bronze Age charcoal identifications (full analysis): Salston B (Site 6), Hood Ball (Site 21), Beneknowle (Site 30)	69
2.25	Bronze Age plant macrofossil identifications: Crablake Farm (Site 15), Hood Ball (Site 21), Beneknowle (Site 30), Filham House (Site 34)	70
2.26	Bronze Age charcoal identifications (broad characterisation): Hood Ball (Site 21) and Filham House (Site 34)	72
2.27	Cremation burial from Salston B, Site 9 (pit 205.004). (Total bone weight 767g)	76
3.1	Radiocarbon dates from Slade Farm, Site 2 (OTA 2.03)	80
3.2	Radiocarbon date from Exwell Barton, Site 14 (ATK 13.02)	84
3.3	Radiocarbon date from Lower Velwell, Site 22 (FTC 12.05w)	88
3.4	Radiocarbon dates from Billany Farm, Site 24 (FTC 14.01)	94
3.5	Radiocarbon dates from Dun Cross, Site 25 (FTC 16.01)	94
3.6	Radiocarbon dates from Tigley A, Site 26 (FTC 16.07)	98
3.7	Radiocarbon date from Springfield, Site 31 (FTC 24.03)	103

3.8	Later Iron Age ceramics; sherd numbers with weight in grammes	106	3.22	Roman plant macrofossil identifications; Springfield (Site 31)	126
3.9	Roman pottery summary; Billany Farm (Site 24) and Springfield (Site 31)	107	4.1	Radiocarbon date from Tigley B, Site 27 (FTC 16.08)	132
3.10	Roman pottery forms; Billany Farm (Site 24) and Springfield (Site 31)	109	4.2	Radiocarbon date from Bluepost, Site 29 (FTC 19.07)	147
3.11	Pixies' Parlour (Site 4); worked and utilised stone	110	4.3	Total quantities of pottery from the Exwell Barton medieval settlement (Site 14)	150
3.12	Lower Nutwell (Site 12); worked and utilised stone	110	4.4	Early medieval plant macrofossil identifications; Tigley B (Site 27) and Moore Farm (Site 28)	157
3.13	Billany Farm (Site 24) and Springfield (Site 31); worked and utilised stone from Romano-British contexts	111	4.5	Early medieval charcoal identifications (broad characterisation); Tigley B (Site 27) and Moore Farm (Site 28)	157
3.14	SEM-based analysis of metallurgical samples. Mineral composition (%) from Tigley A (Site 26) and Lower Velwell (Site 22)	115	4.6	Medieval plant macrofossil identifications; Coldharbour (Site 1) and Exwell Barton (Site 14)	158
3.15	Origin of metalworking residues by mass (in grammes)	118	4.7	Medieval plant macrofossil identifications; Exwell Barton (Site 14) and Bluepost (Site 29)	159
3.16	Iron Age plant macrofossil identifications; Slade Farm (Site 2), Pixies' Parlour (Site 4), Crablake Farm (Site 15)	121	4.8	Medieval charcoal identifications (broad characterisation); Coldharbour (Site 1), Exwell Barton (Site 14), Bluepost (Site 29)	161
3.17	Iron Age charcoal identifications (full analysis); Slade Farm (Site 2) and Tigley A (Site 26)	122	4.9	Medieval charcoal identifications (full analysis); Exwell Barton (Site 14)	162
3.18	Iron Age charcoal identifications (broad characterisation); Exwell Barton (Site 14), Crablake Farm (Site 15) and Tigley A (Site 26)	123	4.10	Post-medieval plant macrofossil identifications; Pixies' Parlour (Site 4) and Exwell Barton (Site 14)	163
3.19	Roman charcoal identifications (broad characterisation); Pixies' Parlour (Site 4), Billany Farm (Site 24), Springfield (Site 31)	124	4.11	Post-medieval charcoal identifications (broad characterisation); Pixies' Parlour (Site 4)	163
3.20	Roman plant macrofossil identifications; Billany Farm (Site 24)	125	6.1	Key to scheme-wide radiocarbon dating plot	179
3.21	Roman charcoal identifications (full analysis); Billany Farm (Site 24) and Dun Cross (Site 25)	125			

Acknowledgements

None of the work undertaken and reported upon here would have been possible without the financial support of National Grid through their principal contractor Laing O'Rourke. The success of the project is due in large part to their commitment to the archaeological objectives of this nationally important pipeline scheme. The fieldwork was managed for Cotswold Archaeology (CA) by Mark Collard and co-ordinated in the field by Stuart Joyce, aided by CA project staff who took charge of individual site excavations and watching briefs. Following fieldwork, Stuart Joyce also undertook the site analyses and reporting. The post-excavation programme was managed initially by Annette Hancocks and later by Andrew Mudd. Individual authors are acknowledged in the report. Their work was built upon a foundation of finds and soils assessment undertaken by CA staff and external contributors. Materials assessments were undertaken by Wendy Carruthers (plant macrofossils), Dana Challinor (wood charcoal), Victoria Taylor (fired clay, ceramic building materials and metals) and Sylvia Warman (animal bone). X-rays and metalwork cleaning were undertaken by Karen Barker Antiquities Conservation Service.

Gratitude is extended to Bill Horner, County Archaeologist, Devon County Council, for monitoring and advice during fieldwork, and comments on the assessment report. CA is also extremely grateful to Dr Joshua Pollard and Professor Stephen Rippon for reviewing a draft of this report, and for Stephen Rippon's suggestions for situating the project's findings within the themes of current landscape research in the South West. The aerial photographs consulted during the course of work were supplied by Devon County Council and English Heritage (National Monuments Record). The Woodbury Tithe Map reproduced as Figures 4.10, 5.4 and 5.10 was kindly supplied by Devon Record Office, and we are grateful for the opportunity to use the other maps held by them. Frances Healy produced the scheme-wide radiocarbon plot shown in Figure 6.1. Most illustrations were drawn by Lorna Gray. Jane Read produced the illustrations of the prehistoric and medieval pottery (Figures 2.34, 2.35, 2.37, 2.40 and 4.24–4.25). The conservation of the Trevisker vessel was undertaken by staff at the Royal Albert Memorial Museum, Exeter. Photographs of the Beaker and Trevisker pottery in Figures 2.36, 2.38 and 2.39 were taken by Henrietta Quinnell. Other photographs were taken by Cotswold Archaeology staff. Radiocarbon dating was undertaken by Rafter Radiocarbon Dating Laboratory, Lower Hutt, New Zealand, and Scottish Universities Environmental Research Centre, East Kilbride, Scotland. Mike Allen would like to thank Alan Clapham for his examination of the faecal pellets and his fruitful discussion and comments. E.R. McSloy is grateful to David Dungworth of English Heritage for examining the medieval iron knife and Bronze Age pin.

The text was edited by Martin Watts and Karen Walker and copyedited by Helen Kemp. Translations of the summary were undertaken by Anne Roussel and Jörn Schuster.

Summary

Between April 2005 and October 2007 archaeological investigations were undertaken by Cotswold Archaeology at the request of Laing O'Rourke on behalf of National Grid along three sections of natural gas pipeline in East and South Devon. These sections, running south of Exeter and east of Plymouth, were from Ottery St Mary to Aylesbeare, from Aylesbeare to Kenn, and from Fishacre to Choakford. The total length amounted to 56km. Archaeological remains from 88 plots were examined by excavation, and the results from over thirty sites are presented in this report. The project has added substantially to the density and distribution of activity for most periods which in many respects supports the emerging patterns in the south-west peninsula.

Mesolithic finds were sparse, but of great interest were 13 earlier prehistoric sites including relatively rare Early, Middle and Late Neolithic sites, two Early Bronze Age/Beaker features, and significant evidence for Middle Bronze Age settlement and land division. Early Neolithic flintwork and pottery in six different fabrics came from a pit at Pixies' Parlour, Ottery St Mary (Site 4), and a section of Early Neolithic ditch was discovered at Croft Cottages, Staverton (Site 20). Pits containing Middle Neolithic Peterborough Ware and deposits of stones were found in the Hems Valley, Staverton (Site 17), while Late Neolithic Grooved Ware pits associated with a curving ditch at Moore Farm, Harberton (Site 28), were dated by radiocarbon for the first time in Devon. Sherds of All-Over-Cord Beaker from a pit near a round barrow at Springfield, Ugborough (Site 31), are the first of this Beaker type in the county. An unaccompanied cremation burial from Salston B, Ottery St Mary (Site 6), dated to the Early Bronze Age, was the only human remains encountered on the entire project. A variety of evidence for Middle Bronze Age occupation included a group of pits containing Trevisker Ware (including a semi-complete vessel) at Crablake Farm, Exminster (Site 15), and pits with only charred plant remains at Hood Ball, Rattery (Site 21), both sites probably relating to settlement of some form. Part of a Middle Bronze Age terraced building at Beneknowle, Diptford (Site 30), appears to be of a type hitherto found only in Cornwall, and the range of charred plants from burning within it is currently unique in Devon. Middle Bronze Age ditches near Broad Oak, Ottery St Mary (Sites 7 and 8), support emerging indications of land division in the Otter Valley at this time, while in South Devon there are indications, from a large rectilinear ditch at Hood Quarry, Dartington (Site 23), of extensive land division tentatively dated to the Middle Bronze Age.

The apparent absence of sites of Early Iron Age date conforms to the regional pattern, but Middle/Later Iron Age sites included a group of iron-smelting furnaces at Tigley A, Dartington (Site 26), and scattered evidence of settlement elsewhere. The furnaces are securely dated by radiocarbon to the 3rd to 4th centuries BC, and are of an unstandardised non-slag-tapping shaft form, probably using local ore. They were not associated with settlement, and the fragmentary evidence from pits and gullies at a number of other sites, such as Slade Farm, Ottery St Mary (Site 2), Crablake Farm, Exminster (Site 15), Barton Hill Cross, Littlehempston (Site (Site 19), Springfield, Ugborough (Site 31) and Filham House, Ugborough (Site 34), appear typical of the materially poor, unenclosed settlements of this period.

Parts of two Roman settlements were examined, a hillslope enclosure at Billany Farm, Dartington (Site 26), and an open settlement at Springfield, Ugborough (Site 31), while a penannular gully and enclosure ditch at Pixies' Parlour, Ottery St Mary (Site 4), both virtually devoid of material, appear likely to have been of Roman date. The Billany Farm enclosure produced rare evidence of flax cultivation. The evidence for pewter manufacture and iron smelting at Springfield in the later Roman period is also rare, and like the Iron Age furnaces at Tigley (and another pair of ironworking furnaces at Lower Velwell, Rattery (Site 22), of likely Iron Age or Roman date) add to the small but growing body of evidence for early metalworking in the region.

Early medieval remains were sparse but three pits (at Pixies' Parlour, Tigley B, Harberton (Site 27) and Moore Farm) without diagnostic finds, yielded radiocarbon dates in the 5th to 7th centuries, suggesting that aceramic and artefact-poor occupation may be identified more widely. Part of a 12th/14th-century medieval settlement with a house and sunken outbuilding was examined at Exwell Barton, Powderham (Site 14), one of the very few instances in the county that a rural settlement of this period has been excavated away from Dartmoor. The sunken outbuilding appears to have been a corn drying building or bakehouse and yielded prolific quantities of charred oats and rye, a typical mixed assemblage for the South West. The building form appears unique so far in the region. Cereals also came from apparently isolated medieval pits at Bluepost, Harberton (Site 29), and Coldharbour, Ottery St Mary (Site 1), and it appears that crops were sometimes burnt in non-domestic situations. Post-medieval sites included an agricultural cob building of probable 18th-century date at Lower Nutwell, Woodbury (Site 12).

The material remains from the project included significant assemblages of Neolithic and Bronze Age pottery, flintwork and stone, and groups of Roman and medieval pottery. Bone was largely absent due to the acidic nature of the soils, but charred plant remains provide important economic and environmental evidence for all periods, and have been used to obtain over fifty radiocarbon dates. Overall economic trends include notably similar food remains in the Neolithic and Bronze Age (dominated by hazelnuts), while the contribution of cereals is not really marked until the Iron Age and continues thereafter. The changing environment is signalled by an increasing diversity of types of wood used for fuel from the early prehistoric through to the medieval period, with hedgerow species particularly prevalent from the Iron Age, and gorse becoming far more common after the Roman period.

Résumé

Entre avril 2005 et octobre 2007 Cotswold Archeology, sur la demande de Laing O'Rourke et de la part de National Grid, a entrepris des fouilles archéologiques le long de 3 pipelines de gaz naturel dans le Devon est et sud. Ces sections qui longent le sud d'Exeter et l'est de Plymouth vont de Ottery St Mary à Aylesbeare, de Aylesbeare à Kenn, et de Fishacre à Choakford. La longueur totale est de 56 km. Les traces archéologiques provenant de 88 parcelles ont été étudiées, et ce rapport contient les résultats de plus de 30 sites. Le projet a donné beaucoup de poids à la densité et à la distribution de l'activité humaine pour la plupart des périodes, et à de nombreux égards il soutient les modèles qui émergent de la péninsule du sud-ouest.

Les découvertes mésolithiques se sont faites rares mais néanmoins 13 sites de la Protohistoire, y compris les sites relativement rares du Néolitique ancien, moyen et final, deux particularités de l'Age du Bronze ancien/ du Gobelet et d'importants indices d'occupation humaine et de division des terres datant de l'Age du Bronze moyen, se sont révélés très importants. Le travail de la pierre et les poteries faites avec 6 matériaux différents, datant du Néolithique ancien, provenaient d'un trou à Pixie's Parlour, Ottery St Mary (site 4), et la section d'un fossé datant du Néolithique ancien a été retrouvée à Croft Cottages, Staverton (site 20).

Dans la vallée Hems, Staverton (site 17) des trous contenaient des poteries du style Peterboroug Ware et des gisements de pierre. En même temps pour la première fois dans le Devon des trous contenant des poteries du style Grooved Ware, datant du Néolitique supérieur et associés à un fossé arqué de la ferme Moore à Harberton (site 28) ont été datés par radiocarbone. Des tessons de gobelets du style All-Over-Cord, provenant d'un trou près d'un tumulus rond à Springfield, Ugborough (site 31) sont les premiers à être découverts dans le comté. A Salston B, Ottery St Mary (site 6) la sépulture d'un seul corps incinéré et datant de l'Age du Bronze ancien, sont les seuls restes humains retrouvés pendant tout ce projet. Un nombre d'indices différents concernant l'occupation humaine à l'Age du Bronze moyen comprenait un ensemble de trous contenant des poteries du style "Trevisker Ware" (y compris un récipient à moitié complet) sur la ferme Crablake, Exminster (site 15) ainsi que des trous à Hood Ball, Rattery (site 21) qui ne contenaient que des traces de végétaux carbonisées. Ces deux sites s'identifiaient sans doute à une sorte de communauté humaine. A Beneknowle, Diptford (site 30) la partie d'un batiment adjacent, datant de l'Age du Bronze moyen semble être d'un type particulier, jusqu'ici trouvé seulement en Cornouailles et la gamme de végétaux carbonisés par le feu dans cette région est pour le moment unique au Devon. Les fossés de l'Age du Bronze moyen près de Broad Oak, Ottery St Mary (sites 7 et 8) confirment les indices récemment trouvés, indiquant à cette époque une division des terres dans la vallée Otter, tandis que dans le Devon sud les indices provenant d'un grand fossé rectiligne à Hood Quarry, Dartington (site 23) indiquent une vaste division des terres qui pour le moment daterait de l'Age du Bronze moyen.

L'absence manifeste de sites datant de l'Age du Fer inférieur est conforme au modèle régional, mais les sites de l'Age du Fer moyen et supérieur comprennaient un ensemble de hauts-fourneaux à Tingley A, Dartington, (site 26) et des indications de sédentarisation dispersées ailleurs. Les hauts-fourneaux ont été bien datés par radiocarbone, sont du IIIème et du IVième siècle avant notre ère et sont hors norme, avec une forme de puits de martelage sans scories qui utilisait probablement les minérais de la région. Ils n'appartenaient pas à une communauté humaine et les preuves partielles provenant des trous et des sillons situés sur un nombre sites, tels que Slade Farm, Ottery St Mary (site 2), Crablake Farm, Exminster (site 15), Barton Hill Cross, Littlehempston Site (site 19), Springfield, Ugborough (site 31), et Filham House, Ugborough (site 34), semblent être des exemples typiques pour cette période: des batiments pauvres en matériaux et pas clôturées.

Plusieurs parties de deux communautés romaines ont été fouillées: une enceinte sur le versant de la colline à

Billany Farm, Dartington (site 26) et une communauté non-cloturée à Springfield, Ugorough (site 31), quoique le sillon quasiment circulaire et le fossé d'enceinte de Pixies' Parlour, Ottery St Mary (site 4), qui sont tous les deux pratiquement dépourvus de matériaux, semblent probablement dater de l'ère romaine.

Le terrain de Billany Farm nous a donné de rares preuves de la culture du lin. Les traces de fabrication de l'étain et de l'extraction du fer à Springfield à l'ère romaine ultérieure sont rares, telles que les fonderies de Tigley (plus les deux autres hauts-fourneaux sidérurgiques de Lower Velwell, Rattery (site 22) datant sans doute de l'Age du Fer ou de l'ère romaine. Tout cela s'ajoute à l'accumulation des preuves du travail des métaux dans la région.

Les vestiges du début du Moyen-Age étaient rares mais 3 trous (à Pixies' Parlour, à Tigley Bet à Harberton (site 27) et sur la ferme Moore) ont produit des datations par radiocarbone, sans avoir fait d'examen complémentaire, du VIème et du VIIème siècle, supposant un manque d'artefact et de céramique, on peut identifier une occupation humaine plus étendue. Une partie d'une communauté médiévale du XIIième / XIVième siècle contenant une maison et une dépendance en contre-bas, a été étudiée à Exwell Barton, Powderham (site 14), un des rares exemples dans le comté d'une communauté de cette période qui a été fouillée loin de Dartmoor. Le bâtiment en contre-bas auraient servi de séchoir à blé ou de four dans lequel on a retrouvé d'énormes quantités de flocons d'avoine et de seigle carbonisés, un mélange typique pour le sud-ouest.

Jusqu'à présent la forme du batiment semble être unique pour la région. D'autre part des céréales provenaient des trous du Moyen-Age de Bluepost, Harberton (site 29) et de Coldharbour, Ottery St Mary (site 1) qui étaient apparemment isolés et il semblerait que les récoltes n'étaient pas toujours brûlées dans un contexte familial. Après le Moyen-Age à Lower Nutwell, Woodbury (site 12) les sites comprenaient un batiment agricole en torchis datant sans doute du XVIIIième siècle.

Les traces matérielles du projet font partie d'importantes collections de poteries, d'objets en pierre taillée et en silex du Néolithique et de l'Age du Bronze ainsi que différentes sortes de poteries de la période romaine et médiévale.

Les restes osseux ont pratiquement disparu, ceci dû à l'acidité des sols, mais les traces végétales carbonisées fournissent d'importants indices sur l'économie et l'environnement pour toutes les périodes, et ont permis d'obtenir plus de 50 datations par radiocarbone. Les traces de nourritures semblables font partie des grandes tendances économiques du Néolitique et de l'Age du Bronze, ceux-ci étant dominés par la noisette, tandis que les céréales avant l'Age du Fer ne contribuent à l'économie qu'en faible partie, mais depuis, leur role est constant. Les changements de l'environnement sont marqués par une diversité de plus en plus variée des différents types de bois utilisés comme combustible, à partir de la Protohistoire jusqu'au Moyen-Age, avec des espèces de haies particulièrement répandues dès l'Age du Fer et des ajoncs qui apparaissent de plus en plus fréquemment après l'ère romaine.

Traduction: Anne Roussel

Zusammenfassung

Zwischen April 2005 und Oktober 2007 hat Cotswold Archaeology für Laing O'Rourke im Auftrag von National Grid den Verlauf von drei Teilabschnitten einer Naturgaspipeline in Ost- und Süd-Devon archäologisch untersucht. Diese südlich von Exeter und östlich von Plymouth gelegenen Abschnitte mit einer Gesamtlänge von 56km verliefen von Ottery St Mary nach Aylesbeare, von Aylesbeare nach Kenn, und von Fishacre nach Choakford. Auf 88 Fundstellen wurden archäologische Befunde durch Ausgrabungen untersucht. In diesem Band werden die Ergebnisse von über 30 Fundplätzen vorgelegt. Durch das Projekt hat sich die Fundstellendichte und –verbreitung für die meisten Perioden bedeutend erweitert, wodurch in vielerlei Hinsicht die sich immer mehr abzeichnenden Fundmuster auf der Halbinsel im Südwesten Englands untermauert werden.

Es fanden sich nur wenige Funde mesolithischer Zeitstellung, von größerer Bedeutung waren hingegen dreizehn vorgeschichtliche Fundplätze, darunter relative seltene früh-, mittel- und spätneolithische Bodendenkmale, zwei becher-/frühbronzezeitliche Befunde sowie bedeutende Hinweise für mittelbronzezeitliche Besiedlung und Flurparzellierung. Frühneolithische Feuersteingegenstände und Keramik aus sechs verschiedenen Warenarten stammen aus einer Grube bei Pixies' Parlour, Ottery St Mary (Fundplatz 4), und bei Croft Cottages, Staverton (Fundplatz 20), wurde ein neolithischer Grabenabschnitt entdeckt. Gruben, die mittelneolithische Peterborough Ware-Keramik und Steindeponierungen enthielten, fanden sich im Hems Valley, Staverton (Fundplatz 17), während bei Moore Farm, Harberton (Fundplatz 28), gelegene spätneolithische Grooved Ware-Keramik Gruben, die in Verbindung mit einem gewundenen Graben zu sehen sind, erstmals in Devon radiokarbondatiert werden konnten. Scherben totalschnurverzierter Becherkeramik (All-Over-Cord Beaker) aus einer Grube in der Nähe eines Rundhügels bei Springfield, Ugborough (Fundplatz 31), sind die ersten bislang in der Grafschaft gefundenen Scherben dieser Becherart. Eine beigabenlose Brandbestattung der frühen Bronzezeit bei Salston B, Ottery St Mary (Fundplatz 6), enthielt die einzigen während des gesamten Projekts gefundenen menschlichen Überreste. Zu den diversen

Hinweisen auf mittelbronzezeitliche Besiedlung gehört u.a. eine Gruppe von Gruben bei Crablake Farm, Exminster (Fundplatz 15), die Trevisker Ware-Keramik (darunter ein zur Hälfte erhaltenes Gefäß) enthielten, sowie Gruben mit verkohlten Pflanzenresten bei Hood Ball, Rattery (Fundplatz 21); beide Fundplätze sind wahrscheinlich als Hinweise auf Siedlungen zu interpretieren. Ein terrassiertes Gebäude der mittleren Bronzezeit bei Beneknowle, Diptford (Fundplatz 30), scheint zu einem bislang nur in Cornwall gefunden Typ zu gehören. Das Spektrum der durch Feuer innerhalb dieses Gebäudes verkohlten Pflanzenreste ist für Devon bislang einzigartig. Mittelbronzezeitliche Gräben in der Nähe von Broad Oak, Ottery St Mary (Fundplätze 7 und 8), liefern weitere Beispiele für die in diesem Zeitraum vermehrt auftretenden Hinweise auf Flurparzellierung im Otter Valley, während in Süd-Devon eine große rechteckige Grabenanlage bei Hood Quarry, Dartington (Fundplatz 23), auf ausgedehnte, wohl mittelbronzezeitliche Parzellierung hinweist.

Das scheinbare Fehlen früheisenzeitlicher Fundstellen entspricht dem regionalen Bild, hingegen fanden sich Fundplätze der mittleren/späteren Vorrömischen Eisenzeit in Form einer Gruppe von Rennfeueröfen zur Eisenherstellung bei Tigley A, Dartington (Fundplatz 26), sowie andernorts als vereinzelte Hinweise auf Besiedlung. Die durch Radiokarbondatierung sicher in das 4. bis 3. Jahrhundert v. Chr. datierten Öfen gehören zu einer nicht-standardisierten Schaftform ohne Schlackenabstich, in denen vermutlich lokales Erz verarbeitet wurde. Sie lagen nicht in der Nähe von Siedlungen. Die wenigen Funde aus Gruben und Abflussgräben von einer Reihe anderer Fundplätze, u.a. Slade Farm, Ottery St Mary (Fundplatz 2), Crablake Farm, Exminster (Fundplatz 15), Barton Hill Cross, Littlehempston (Fundplatz 19), Springfield, Ugborough (Fundplatz 31) und Filham House, Ugborough (Fundplatz 34), scheinen für die fundarmen, offenen Siedlungen dieser Periode typisch zu sein.

Es wurden Teilbereiche zweier Siedlungen der Römischen Kaiserzeit untersucht: eine Einfriedung in Hanglage bei Billany Farm, Dartington (Fundplatz 26), sowie eine offene Siedlung bei Springfield, Ugborough (Fundplatz 31), während bei Pixies' Parlour, Ottery St Mary (Fundplatz 4), ein offener Ringgraben und ein Umfassungsgraben – beide nahezu fundleer – wahrscheinlich ebenfalls kaiserzeitlicher Datierung sind. In der Einfriedung bei Billany Farm fanden sich seltene Anzeichen für Flachsanbau. Die bei Springfield gefundenen späterkaiserzeitlichen Hinweise auf Zinnverarbeitung und Eisenverhüttung sind ebenfalls selten, aber wie die eisenzeitlichen Öfen bei Tigley (sowie zwei weitere, wahrscheinlich eisen- oder kaiserzeitliche Rennfeueröfen bei Lower Velwell, Rattery (Fundplatz 22)), sind sie weitere Beispiele für die kleine aber stetig wachsende Anzahl von Belegen für frühe Metallverarbeitung in der Region.

Es wurden kaum frühmittelalterliche Funde oder Befunde gemacht, aber drei Gruben (bei Pixies' Parlour, Tigley B, Harberton (Fundplatz 27) und Moore Farm) ohne diagnostische Funde lieferten Radiokarbondatierungen des 5. bis 7. Jahrhunderts n. Chr., was nahelegt, dass akeramische und fundarme Besiedlung vielleicht weiter verbreitet ist als bislang angenommen. Ein Teil einer mittelalterlichen Siedlung des 12./14. Jahrhunderts mit Haus und Nebengebäude mit tiefergelegtem Boden wurde bei Exwell Barton, Powderham (Fundplatz 14), untersucht. Damit bot sich hier eine der für die Grafschaft seltenen Gelegenheiten, eine ländliche Siedlung außerhalb des Dartmoor auszugraben. Das Nebengebäude mit tiefergelegtem Boden scheint eine Getreidedarre oder ein Backhaus gewesen zu sein, denn es fanden sich große Mengen verkohlten Hafers und Roggens, eine für den Südwesten typische Fundvergesellschaftung. Die Gebäudeform ist in der Region bislang einzigartig. Darüber hinaus wurde Getreide auch in scheinbar isoliert gelegenen, mittelalterlichen Gruben bei Bluepost, Harberton (Fundplatz 29), und Coldharbour, Ottery St Mary (Fundplatz 1) angetroffen; es scheint, dass Getreide bisweilen auch in nicht-häuslichen Zusammenhängen verbrannt werden konnte. Unter den frühneuzeitlichen Fundplätzen ist ein landwirtschaftliches Lehmgebäude bei Lower Nutwell, Woodbury (Fundplatz 12) zu nennen, dass wahrscheinlich ins 18. Jahrhundert datiert.

Zu den während des Projekts gefundenen materiellen Hinterlassenschaften gehören u.a. wichtige Fundkomplexe neolithischer und bronzezeitlicher Keramik, Feuerstein- und Steingeräte, sowie kaiserzeitliche und mittelalterliche Keramik. Knochen hat sich auf Grund der sauren Böden größtenteils nicht erhalten. Demgegenüber haben verkohlte Pflanzenreste für alle Perioden wichtige Ergebnisse zu Wirtschaft und Umwelt geliefert und darüber hinaus mehr als 50 Radiokarbondatierungen ermöglicht. Zusammenfassend lässt sich zu den wirtschaftlichen Trends sagen, dass Nahrungsreste des Neolithikums und der Bronzezeit eine recht ähnliche Zusammensetzung haben (mit einer Dominanz von Haselnuss), wohingegen Getreide erst ab der Vorrömischen Eisenzeit an Bedeutung gewinnt. Der Wandel des Naturraums wird durch eine vom Neolithikums bis ins Mittelalter zunehmende Diversität der als Brennholz genutzten Holzarten signalisiert, wobei ab der Eisenzeit vor allem Heckensträucher vorherrschen und Ginster nach der Römischen Kaiserzeit häufiger vorkommt.

Übersetzung: Jörn Schuster

Chapter 1
Introduction

This report presents the results of the fieldwork carried out by Cotswold Archaeology (CA) along three sections of natural gas pipeline in East and South Devon forming part of the National Grid South-West Reinforcement Project. These pipelines ran between Ottery St Mary and Aylesbeare (10km), Aylesbeare and Kenn (16km), and Fishacre and Choakford (30km). The first two sections in East Devon formed an almost continuous length of pipeline between them east and south of Exeter (Fig. 1.1). The terminal at Kenn was separated by a distance of 25km from the section in South Devon, which started at Fishacre Barton, north of Totnes and ran to the south of Dartmoor almost as far as Plymouth. These pipelines had impacts on a range of archaeological sites dating from the Early Neolithic to the 18th century, and resulted, in particular, in a contribution to information on the nature and density of sites in the prehistoric period in these parts of Devon.

Project background

Consideration and planning of the pipeline schemes go back a number of years. In 2001 Cotswold Archaeology carried out preliminary field surveys, including fieldwalking on arable land and two areas of geophysical survey, in connection with an earlier consideration of the Fishacre–Choakford section of pipeline (CA 2001; Stratascan 2001). This proposed route partly coincided with that of the eventual scheme. In April 2005 CA was commissioned by Laing O'Rourke, on behalf of National Grid, to undertake Archaeology and Heritage Surveys of all three lengths of pipeline. The Archaeology and Heritage Surveys formed part of the Archaeology and Cultural Heritage chapters of the relevant Environmental Statements (ESs), produced to meet the requirements of *The Public Gas Transporter Pipeline Works (Environmental Impact Assessment) Regulations 1999*. The surveys comprised Desk-Based Assessments (DBAs) and Archaeological Field Reconnaissance Surveys (AFRSs), the results of which were presented in three reports each of three volumes (CA 2005a, 2005b, 2006).

The Archaeology and Heritage Surveys identified a number of locations with known or suspected archaeological remains and estimated that there were about 45 sites with the potential to suffer impacts during pipeline construction (11 regarded as being at high risk and 34 at moderate risk). In addition, the ESs recognised that, because of the lack of systematic archaeological prospection, there was the potential for as yet unidentified sites to lie along the lengths of the pipelines. Consequently, a staged approach to further archaeological investigation was undertaken to determine the impact of construction of the pipelines on archaeological sites and to devise appropriate mitigation for any archaeological remains found. These investigations comprised archaeological geophysical surveys, earthwork surveys and trial trenching ahead of construction. The geophysical surveys (Archaeological Surveys 2006a, 2006b, 2006c, 2007) were targeted on cropmarks and other areas of archaeological potential identified in the Archaeology and Heritage Surveys. Subsequent trial trenching investigated anomalies of archaeological potential identified from the geophysical surveys. These evaluations had the limited aims of providing data on the date, character, quality and extent of archaeological deposits in order to inform subsequent mitigation, decisions about which were made in consultation with Devon County Council Archaeology Service (DCCAS) and National Grid's Archaeological Adviser, Linda Bonnor. They did not result in independent reports.

Consent to construct the pipeline was granted in April 2006 by the Secretary of State for Trade and Industry subject to the implementation of a programme of archaeological work to be agreed with DCCAS. A number of sites were identified as requiring archaeological excavation ahead of construction, which was carried out in accordance with Written Schemes of Investigation (WSIs) approved by DCCAS. Elsewhere,

2 *The Archaeology of the South-West Reinforcement Gas Pipeline, Devon: Investigations in 2005–2007*

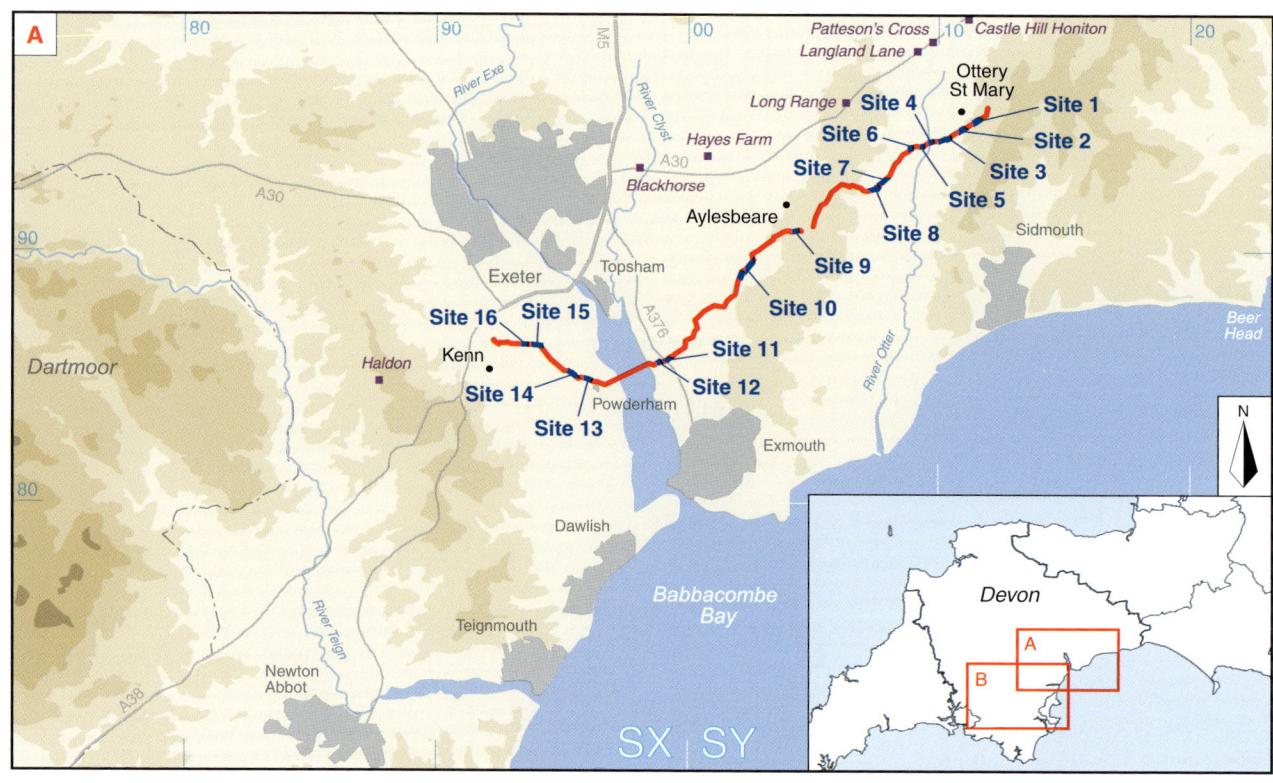
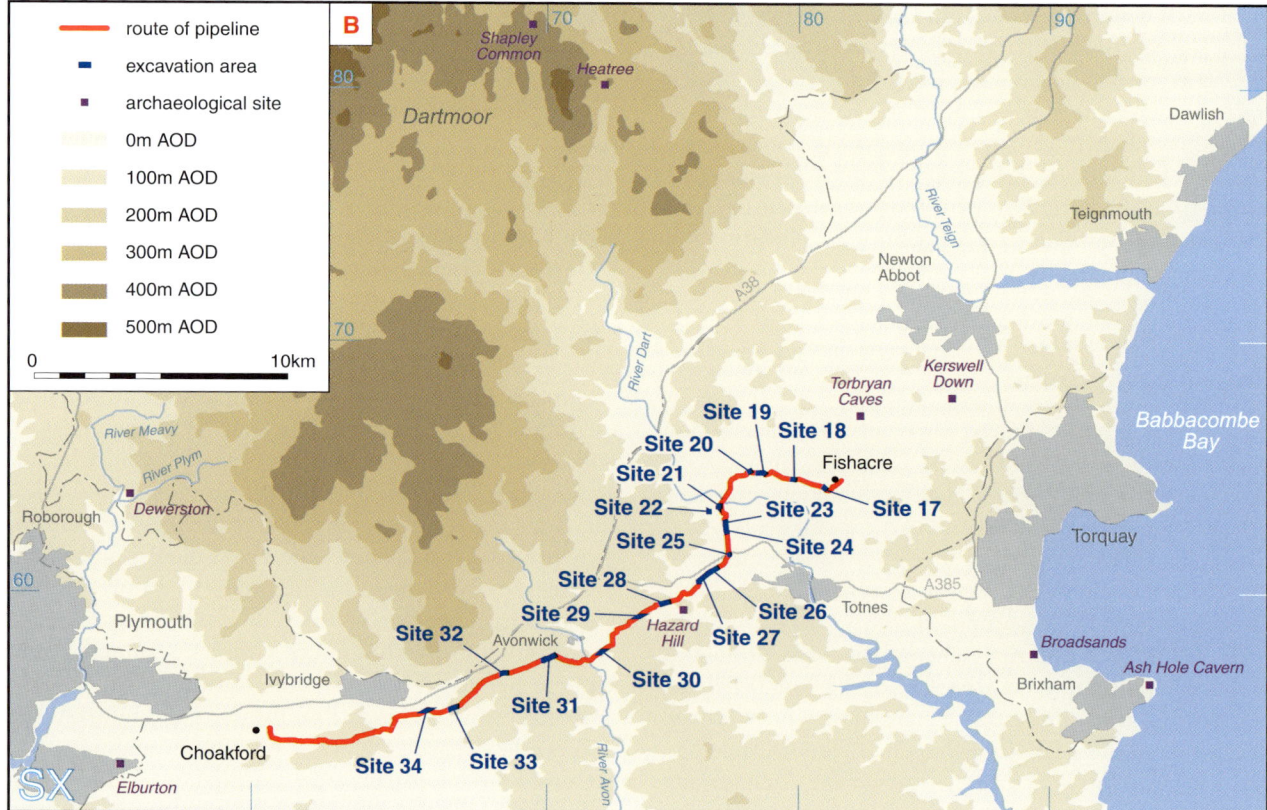

Fig. 1.1   Site locations. Scale 1:300,000

Table 1.1: Sites investigated along the pipeline corridors

Site No.	Plot No.	Name	Archaeology Date/type	Excavation	Evaluation	Watching Brief	Geophysical Survey
1	OTA 1.03	**Coldharbour**	Medieval pit	-	-	✓	-
2	OTA 2.03	**Slade Farm**	Iron Age pit	-	-	✓	-
3	OTA 2.06/3.01	**Knightstone Farm**	?early boundary ditches	-	✓	-	✓
4	OTA 3.04	**Pixies' Parlour**	Neolithic pit, Roman enclosure & others	✓	✓	-	✓
5	OTA 3.07	**Salston A**	Post-medieval brick clamp	-	-	✓	-
6	OTA 4.01	**Salston B**	Bronze Age cremation & other features	✓	✓	-	✓
7	OTA 4.10	**Land East of Broad Oak**	Bronze Age ditches, undated ditches	-	-	✓	-
8	OTA 5.01/5.02	**Land South-East of Broad Oak**	?Bronze Age ring-ditch & other features	✓	✓	✓	✓
9	ATK 0.03	**New Nutwalls**	Undated curvilinear ditch and undated ditch	-	-	✓	-
10	ATK 4.04 & 4a.01	**Hogsbrook Farm**	Undated ditches	-	-	✓	-
11	ATK 11.04	**The Nutwell Lodge**	Undated ditch and ?circular ditch	-	-	✓	-
12	ATK 12.01	**Lower Nutwell**	Post-medieval cob building	-	✓	-	✓
13	ATK 12.12	**White House**	Undated trackway and ditch terminus	-	✓	✓	✓
14	ATK 13.02	**Exwell Barton**	?Iron Age ditch, medieval house and kitchen	✓	✓	✓	-
15	ATK 14.09	**Crablake Farm**	Bronze Age pits, Iron Age ditch	-	-	✓	✓
16	ATK 15.02	**Soloman's Farm**	Undated rectilinear ?enclosure ditch & four-post structure	-	-	✓	-
17	FTC 2.02	**Hems Valley**	Neolithic pits	-	-	✓	-
18	FTC 4.02	**Moothill Cross**	Undated curvilinear ?enclosure ditch	-	-	✓	-
19	FTC 7.01	**Barton Hill Cross**	Iron Age/Roman settlement	-	-	✓	-
20	FTC 8.02	**Croft Cottages**	Neolithic ditch	-	-	✓	-
21	FTC 12.05	**Hood Ball**	Bronze Age pits	-	-	✓	✓
22	FTC 12.05w	**Lower Velwell**	?Iron Age/ Roman furnaces	-	-	✓	-
23	FTC 13.03	**Hood Quarry**	?Bronze Age and ?Roman ditches	✓	✓	-	✓
24	FTC 14.01	**Billany Farm**	Roman enclosure	✓	✓	-	✓
25	FTC 16.01	**Dun Cross**	Roman pits	-	-	✓	-
26	FTC 16.07	**Tigley A**	Iron Age iron smelting furnaces	-	-	✓	-

Table 1.1 (cont.): Sites investigated along the pipeline corridors

Site No.	Plot No.	Name	Archaeology Date/type	Excavation	Evaluation	Watching Brief	Geophysical Survey
27	FTC 16.08	Tigley B	6th/7th-century pit	-	-	✓	-
28	FTC 18.12 & 18.13	Moore Farm	Mesolithic pit. Neolithic ditches and pits	-	-	✓	-
29	FTC 19.07 & 19.08	Bluepost.	Medieval pit & undated pit	-	-	✓	-
30	FTC 21.06	Beneknowle	Bronze Age building	-	-	✓	-
31	FTC 24.02 to 24.05	Springfield	Beaker pit & Roman settlement	✓	✓	✓	✓
32	FTC 26.01	Forder Cross	?Medieval curving ditches and pits	-	-	✓	-
33	FTC 31.05 to 31.07	Wood Farm	?prehistoric ditches	-	-	✓	✓
34	FTC 33.01 & 33.02	Filham House	Bronze Age pit, Iron Age ?hearths	-	-	✓	✓

topsoil removal as part of construction works was monitored by an attending archaeologist as a watching brief, also governed by approved WSIs, which also covered cases where deeper soil removal was required to reach archaeological levels. The watching briefs included the recording of all breached hedgerows. The mitigation excavations were undertaken on nine defined areas, while the scheme-wide watching briefs resulted in the discovery and recording of a large number of other sites/features. In each case archaeological excavation and recording was carried out to similar sampling levels and standards. A summary of mitigation measures is presented in Table 1.1. All parcels of land were identified by the pipeline section code: OTA (Ottery St Mary to Aylesbeare), ATK (Aylesbeare to Kenn) and FTC (Fishacre to Choakford), and a unique code (Plot no.) allocated by Laing O'Rourke. For this publication sites containing significant features are designated by name, parish and a unique number in sequence from east to west (Figs 1.2–1.7); but for less significant sites plot numbers only are used. Site names reflect only nearby mapped places and features, and confer no implication of land ownership.

Location and topography

The pipelines crossed the distinctive landscapes of East and South Devon. Although part of the Aylesbeare to Kenn pipeline lay on the western side of the Exe estuary (and in Teignbridge rather than East Devon district), the combined Ottery St Mary to Kenn section of the route is here labelled East Devon for convenience. The character of the landscape on both sides of the Exe is similar, deriving from the sandy geologies of Greensand, Aylesbeare Mudstone and Dawlish Sandstones to the east of the Exe, and the Permian Breccias to the west.

The land lies within the eastern Devon lowlands *pays* characterised by varied but generally well-drained soils that have been agriculturally productive in historical times (Rippon 2012, 26–34 and 50, fig. 2.10). The Ottery St Mary to Aylesbeare pipeline begins approximately 1km east of Ottery St Mary (SY 1210 9581), at the foot of the wooded Greensand ridge of East Hill, from where it runs south-west, crossing the River Otter 500m to the south of the town (Fig. 1.2). It continues in a south-westerly direction, before turning to run west, then north-west, to pass between West Hill and Higher Metcombe. Thereafter the route runs south-west terminating *c.* 500m south-east of the village of Aylesbeare (SY 0458 9069). The Aylesbeare to Kenn pipeline commences approximately 500m south of Aylesbeare (SY 0455 9086) and, after running west for just over 1km, continues generally south-west passing east of Woodbury Salterton until the Exe estuary, 1km south of Exton (Fig. 1.3). The route crosses under the Exe at Powderham Sand, recommencing on the western side of the estuary just north of the village of Powderham (Fig. 1.4). From there the route runs north of the Powderham plantations, turns and runs west for 2km, terminating approximately 1km north of Kenn (SX 9232 8645). The landscape is characterised by plateaux cut by steep valleys, of which the Otter is the principal one east of the Exe, and the Kenn to the west. The area, while overwhelmingly agricultural, has natural lowland heaths and plantations of conifer. The pipeline stops short of the dominant Haldon Ridge, formerly heathland and now planted with coniferous forest.

The South Devon pipeline begins north of Totnes at Fishacre Above Ground Installation (AGI) (SX 2817 0645) and terminates about 10km from Plymouth at Choakford AGI (SX 2589 0546). It lies within a steeply undulating landscape resulting from networks of small

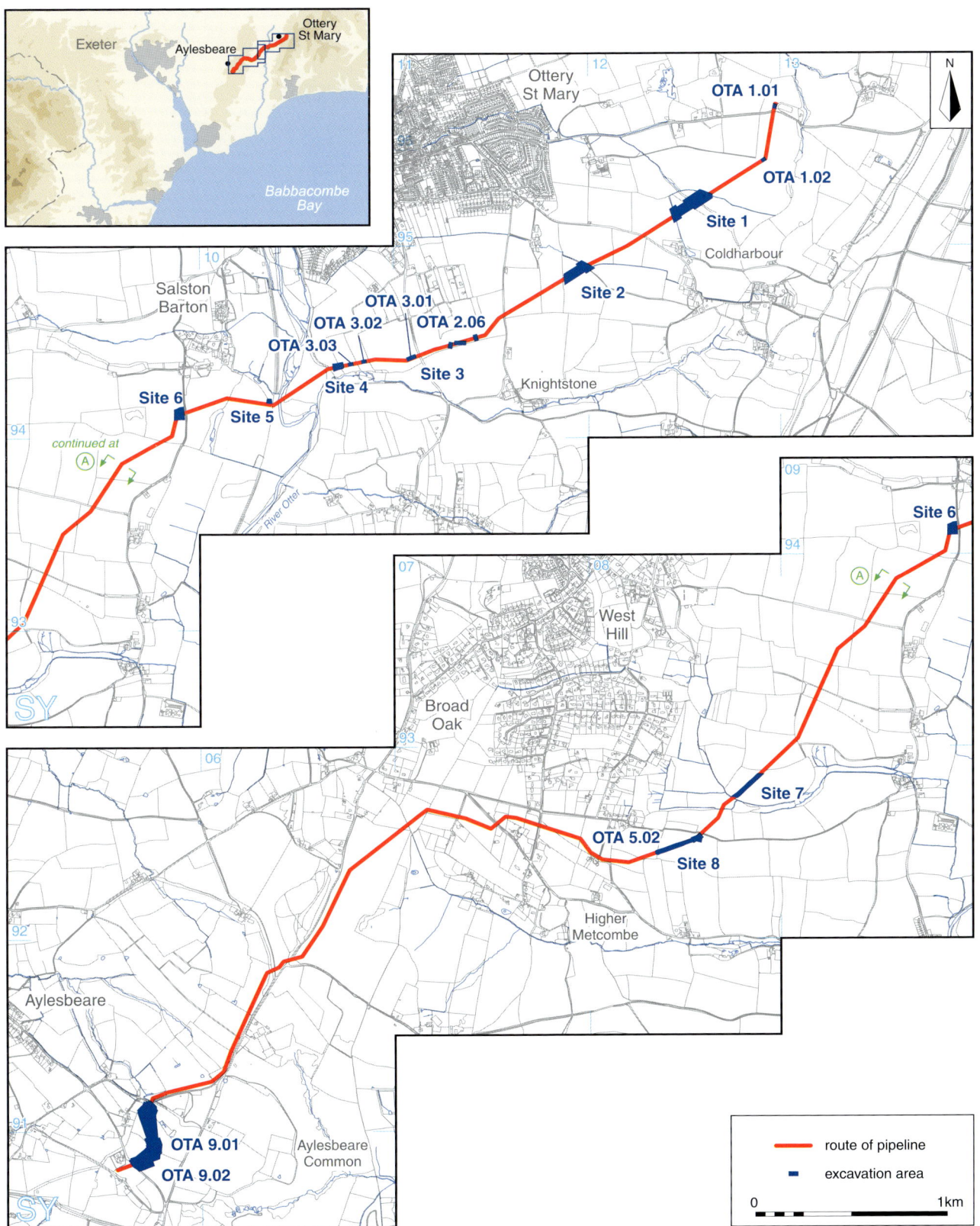

Fig. 1.2 Ottery St Mary to Aylesbeare; site locations. Scale 1:30,000

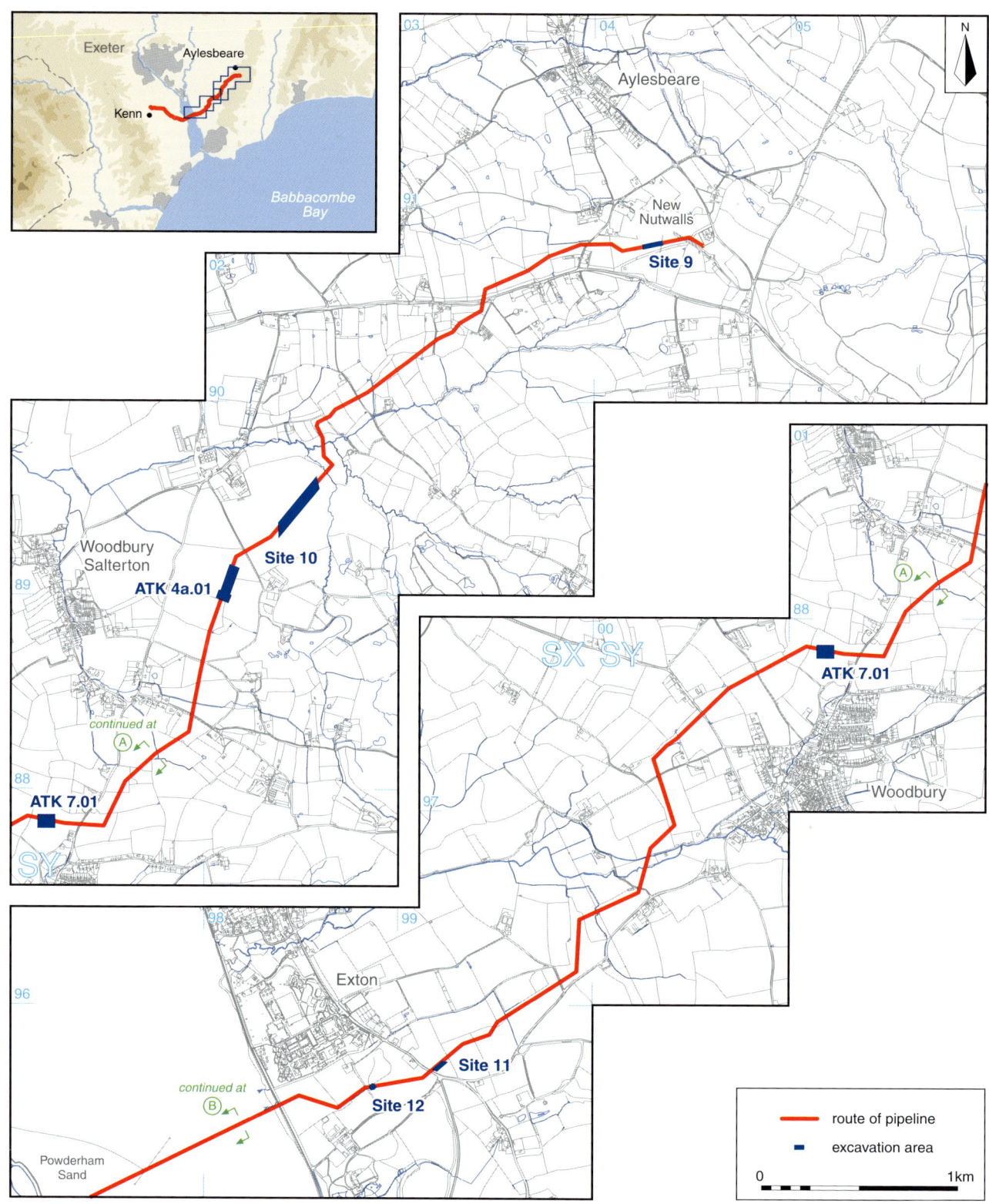

Fig. 1.3   Aylesbeare to Kenn; site locations. Scale 1:30,000

Introduction 7

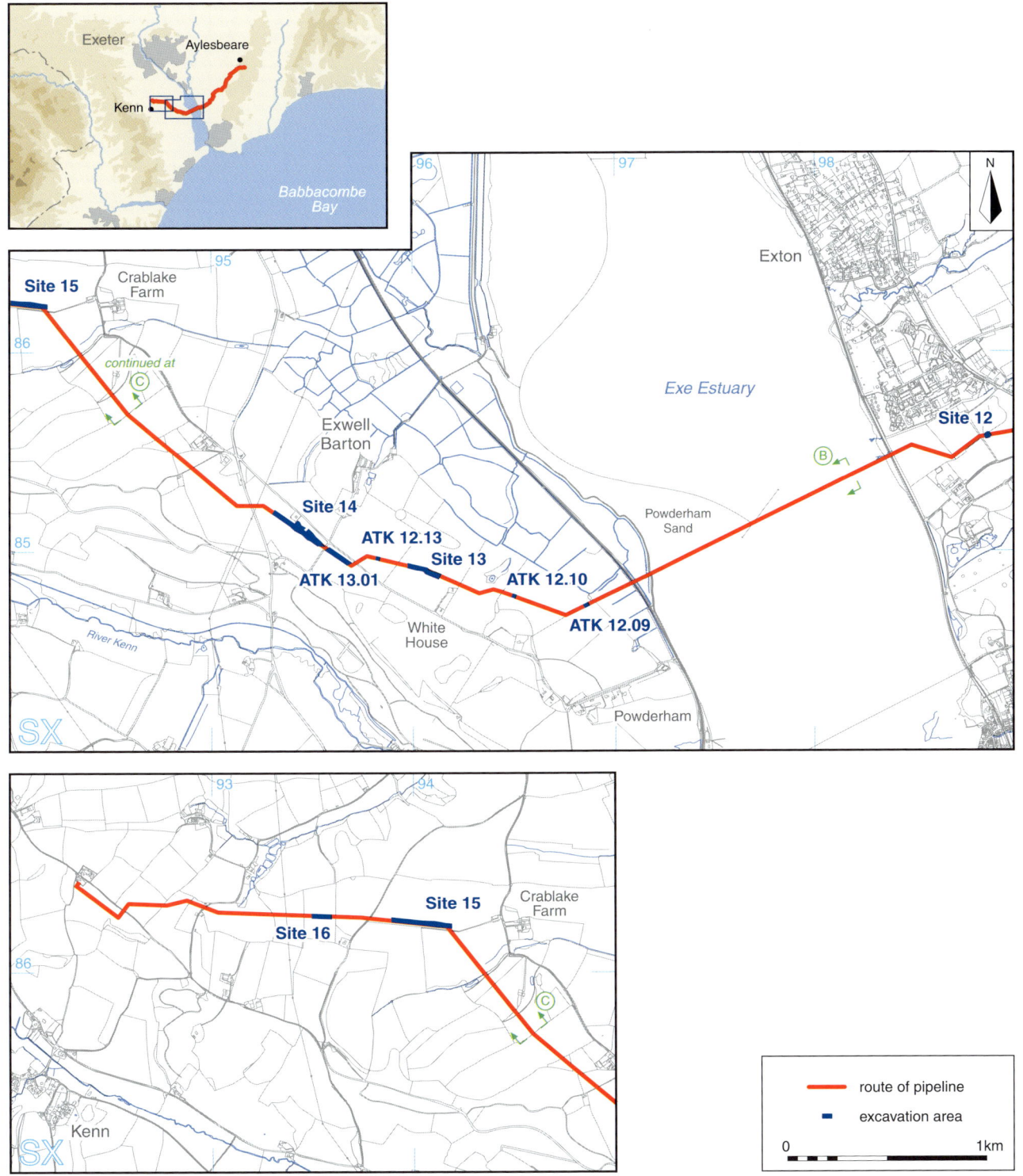

Fig. 1.4   Aylesbeare to Kenn; site locations. Scale 1:30,000

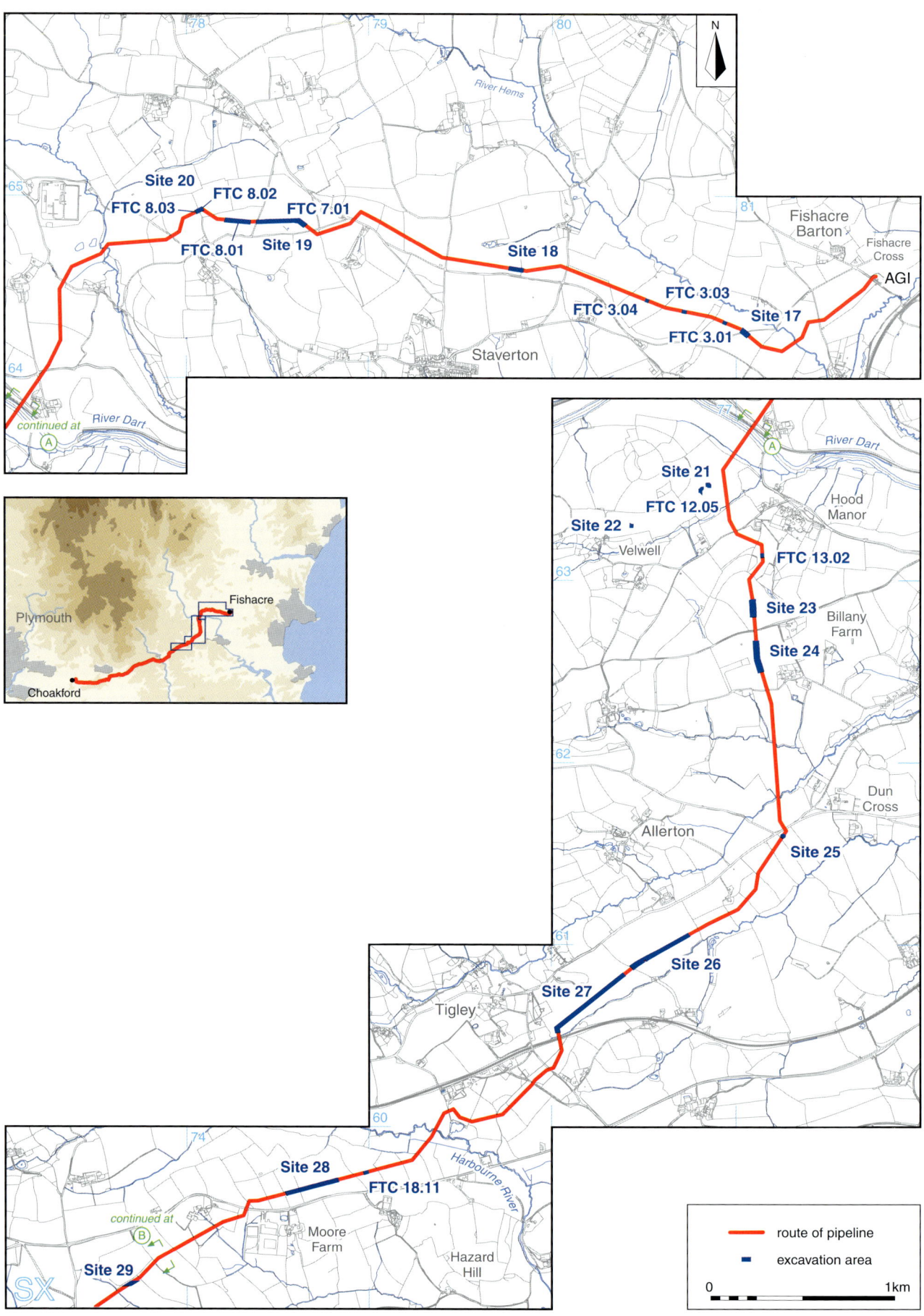

Fig. 1.5   Fishacre to Choakford; site locations. Scale 1:30,000

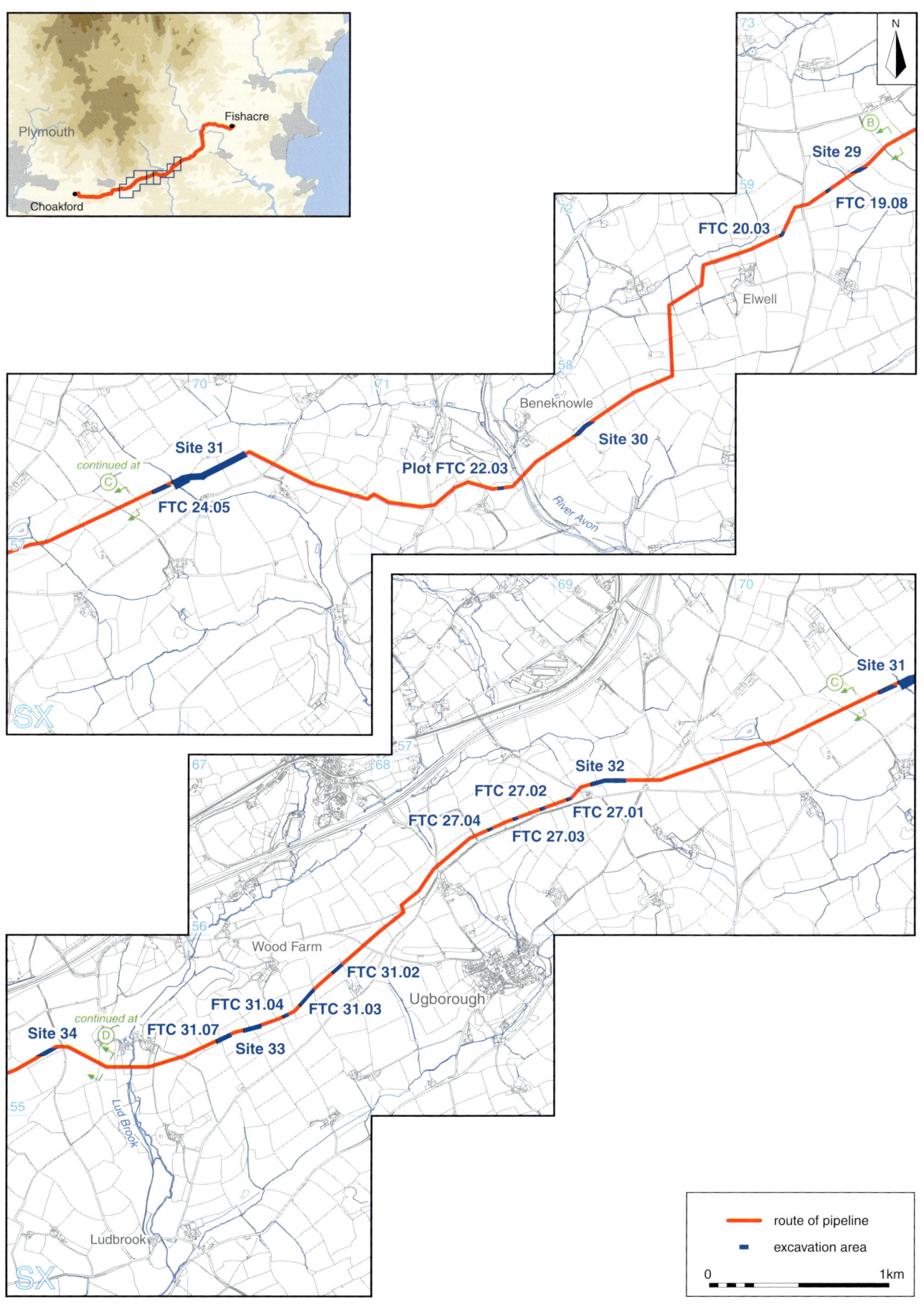

Fig. 1.6   Fishacre to Choakford; site locations. Scale 1:30,000

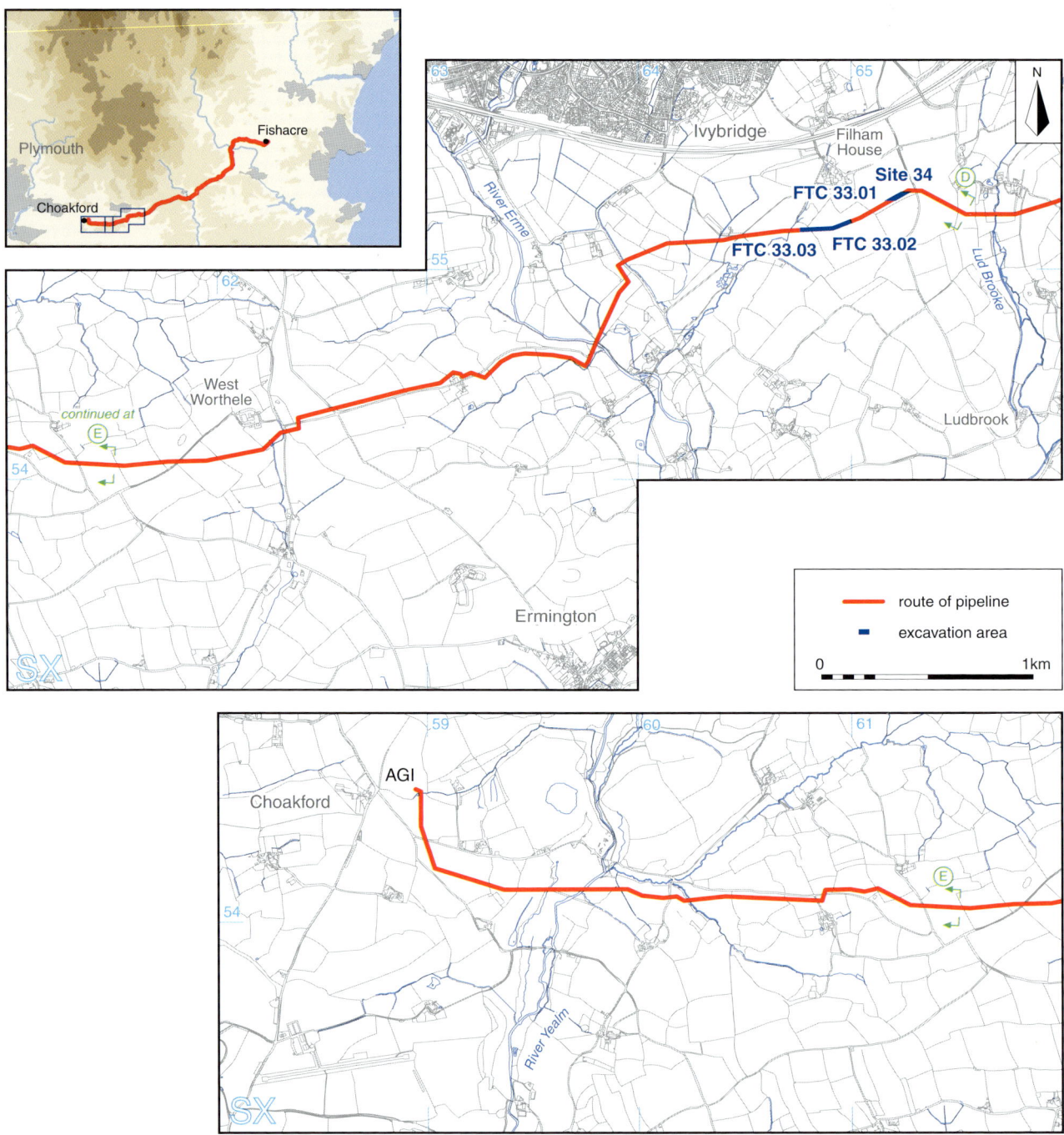

Fig. 1.7 Fishacre to Choakford; site locations. Scale 1:30,000

streams draining into the rivers Dart, Avon and Erme. West of the River Erme the land is lower and flatter. The underlying geology is complex and comprises mainly slate weathering to a fragmented shillet, with igneous intrusions that form the Devonian volcanic belt. This is within the *pays* of the Culm Measures, traditionally poor farmland of 'cold' acidic soils and historically having an emphasis on livestock rearing (Rippon 2012, 49–50, and fig. 2.10). The agricultural landscape today comprises a patchwork of often small fields and scattered farmsteads and hamlets, and is dominated by the mass of Dartmoor on the northern skyline. From Fishacre Barton the pipeline runs westward to the north of Staverton and then turns to run southward, passing west of Hood Manor and east of Allerton (Fig. 1.5). The route then turns on a south-westerly alignment to the River Avon, south of Avonwick village near Beneknowle (Fig. 1.6). The south-westerly alignment continues, running north of Ugborough and south of Ivybridge (Fig.1.7). The westerly alignment then runs to its termination beyond the River Yealm at Choakford.

Archaeological character

The pipeline investigations in both East and South Devon lie in the agricultural lowlands of the county where archaeological remains are less visible than those the uplands of Dartmoor, and less often brought to light by development than those of the urban centres and hinterlands of Plymouth, Exeter and other towns. Research-oriented programmes of fieldwork have been patchy, and the results of aerial survey, while locally important, have been variable (Griffith 1994, 87). For these reasons the archaeological character of the pipeline routes, prior to the present project, were comparatively little studied or understood. In many ways the baseline for the archaeology of East Devon was provided by the discoveries made in relation to the A30 Honiton to Exeter road improvement in the 1990s (Fitzpatrick *et al.* 1999) even though this report is now more than a decade old. For South Devon there was no comparable body of information and discoveries have been more piecemeal. The collective review of the archaeology of Dartmoor in the mid-1990s (Griffiths 1994) provides much comparative material for both moor and off-moor studies. At that time, the archaeology of the rest of Devon was very much a poor relation (Griffith 1994). Since then there has been a huge collective effort towards summarising the archaeological resource of the South West and signposting directions for future research (Webster 2008a). This has been of enormous benefit to archaeologists working in the region, but has also emphasised how our understanding of lowland Devon, while gradually increasing, lags behind that of the counties to the east (Dorset, Somerset and Wiltshire in particular) and also to some extent Cornwall to the west.

The Palaeolithic in Devon is represented, most significantly, by the nationally important cave sites in South Devon, including Kent's Cavern, Pixies' Hole, Windmill Cave and Three Holes Cave (Hosfield *et al.* 2008, 31–40), although the river gravels have yielded sporadic finds of handaxes in less useful contexts (Fitzpatrick 1999, 213). The Mesolithic period has been largely encountered though scatters of diagnostic flintwork. The most contextually useful collections have come from the uplands where they are sometimes associated with episodes of burning, and it appears that hunter-gatherers manipulated the environment for exploiting wild herds (Hosfield *et al.* 2008, 53). Coastal sites at this time suggest the seasonal exploitation of seafood, and it is possible that upland and coastal sites were occupied by the same mobile groups (ibid.). It has been noted that flint scatters are often multi-period, but the extent to which this implies a continuity of patterns of activity into the Neolithic and Bronze Age is not at all clear (Fitzpatrick 1999, 213).

From the Neolithic period, discoveries of isolated or small groups of pits, with or without deliberate deposits of material, have been the archaeological norm and other types of site are not well defined (ibid.). Hembury is the best understood Early Neolithic causewayed enclosure in the county and one of the few defined Neolithic monuments, and while others at Raddon Hill (Gent and Quinnell 1999a) and perhaps Membury (Tingle 2006) can now be added to the list, the distribution is sparse and eastern. The form of hilltop sites in South Devon at Haldon (Willock 1936; Gent and Quinnell 1999b) and Hazard Hill (Houlder 1963) is uncertain and they may have more in common with the tor enclosures of Cornwall, although the nature and date of putative examples in Devon (e.g. Whittor, Peter Tavy) are uncertain (Quinnell 1994a, 53). Early Neolithic long barrows are rare in Devon (Whittle *et al.* 2011b, 476–8, fig. 10.1) and their presence on Dartmoor, where the preservation of early prehistoric earthworks is generally exceptional, is still debatable (Quinnell 1994a, 50–1). Neolithic monuments are now more widely recognised in the east and centre of the county; the long enclosure and possible cursus at Castle Hill, Honiton, provide an example of a group of monuments found widely in Britain but showing a huge variety of form. Comparative sites lie for the most part further east without there being any regional type (Fitzpatrick 1999, 213–15) although a ceremonial complex at Nether Exe includes similar types of monument and numerous ring-ditches nearby, and that in the Bow–North Tawton area in mid Devon includes at least two long enclosures and a henge (Griffith 1985). In most of Devon the nature of monumentality in the later Neolithic and Bronze Age is largely unknown. Dartmoor has a range of stone circles, rows, round cairns and barrows, which are poorly dated but fall generally within the later Neolithic and earlier Bronze Age (Quinnell 1994a). These are on a smaller scale than monuments further east, and in the lowlands similar features may have been largely lost to later cultivation and in any case may have left only traces of posthole/socket patterns difficult to detect through archaeological prospection. Ring-ditches are now fairly common throughout the county but dating is often insecure, and the frequent absence of bone due to acid soils in most parts of Devon means that little information on mortuary practices is available for this, or any other, period.

The Middle Bronze Age saw the establishment of field systems in some parts of Devon, most clearly on Dartmoor but now also evident in parts of East Devon at Hayes Farm, Clyst Honiton (Barber 2000), Castle Hill and Patteson's Cross, west of Honiton (Fitzpatrick *et al.* 1999), and suggested for South Devon at Kerswell Down near Kingskerswell (Quinn 1995). There is continuing difficulty with characterising the range of Bronze Age settlement in the county (Griffith 1994, 94), which clearly includes enclosures and roundhouses on Dartmoor, but elsewhere may not display clear boundaries or structures. In East Devon the forms of settlements appear similar to those in Dorset and Wiltshire, with posthole buildings and fields evident at

Patteson's Cross, although the posthole groups within the field system at Castle Hill showed no clear evidence of domestic structures (Fitzpatrick *et al.* 1999, figs 6, 28). Pits containing Trevisker pottery or other datable remains may represent settlement-related occupation (Quinnell, in prep.) or activities of a funerary or ritual character.

The Iron Age in Devon is dominated by the evidence for enclosures of varying size (Griffith 1994, 93), many of them small and on slopes rather than hilltops, and probably designed for livestock management (Fox 1952). Little, however, is known about their date and they may span a considerable time range (Fitzpatrick 2008, 130), that at Holworthy Farm, North Devon, having both Middle Bronze Age and Iron Age dating (Green 2009), and one at Rudge in Mid Devon apparently Early Roman (Todd 1998). Large, defended hillforts lie mostly in East Devon (Hembury, Woodbury Castle, Dumpdon, Blackbury Castle) and are similar to, although smaller than, those in Somerset and Dorset (Fitzpatrick 1999, 218–19; Rippon 2012, fig. 14.7). The Iron Age in Devon as a whole, however, is poorly defined because of the shortage of ceramics from the Late Bronze Age to Middle (or Later) Iron Age, and it is thought possible that Devon was aceramic in the century before the Roman conquest (Quinnell 1994b, 78). As elsewhere, the plateau in the radiocarbon calibration curve during the Iron Age is unhelpful in refining chronology. The settlements west of Honiton at Blackhorse, Long Range and Langland Lane appear to have been unenclosed (at least initially at Blackhorse) and were identified principally by the presence of pen-annnular gullies (Fitzpatrick 1999, 219). This may be typical of the situation elsewhere, although this is essentially unknown at present (Fitzpatrick 2008, 130). Similar but very slight remains of a timber roundhouse were excavated at Gold Park, Shapley Common, Dartmoor, set among fields and a trackway of Bronze Age origin (Gibson 1992). It does not seem that fields or other land division was characteristic of the Iron Age or even the Roman period in Devon, in contrast with other parts of the country, or at least they have left little archaeological trace (Rippon 2008, 118–19).

Roman rural settlement is not well known and no complete settlement plans have been recovered (Holbrook 2008, 153). The region immediately to the east (Dorset, Somerset and Gloucestershire) has a high density of villas, but this does not extend into Devon where the character of the *civitas* of the Dumnonii may have been different and, in common with the Iron Age, apparently included a relatively low level of material culture. Romano-Celtic temples are not known in Devon, and with the general absence of bone there is little that can be said about burial rites. The Roman military presence is seen largely as controlling the exploitation of minerals (the Dartmoor and Exmoor fringes) and securing the Bristol Channel, but this does not seem to have been a long-term interest and there is little evidence of the military after the 1st century AD (Holbrook 2008, 160–1).

In the immediate post-Roman period, the South West had a distinctive character not directly affected by Anglo-Saxon incursions until the 6th century and later (Webster 2008b, 169). Archaeological evidence is sparse everywhere because of the lack of chronologically diagnostic artefacts, and understanding of the period has relied on relatively few excavations, particularly those of 'elite' sites with imported pottery and metalwork, none of which listed by Webster lie in Devon. Pottery from the eastern Mediterranean has been found at a few sites on the south coast (Bantham at the mouth of the Avon, and Mothecombe near the mouth of the Erme) and there was also occupation at Wembury (Webster 2008b, 179). The most easterly occurrence of Mediterranean imports at this time is at High Peak near Sidmouth (Rippon 2012, 303). The form of settlements is not clear, but the large oval ditched enclosure at Hayes Farm, Clyst Honiton (Simpson *et al.* 1989) may be one type. The modern character of the county, with its urban hierarchy, settlement patterns and field systems belongs with the later Saxon to Norman Conquest period, between the 8th and 11th centuries (Rippon and Croft 2008, 195). It has been characterised as a landscape of early field enclosure, with fossilised cropping units frequently incorporated into later hedgebank boundaries from the 13th century onwards (Turner 2007, 28–48). Later developments in the medieval period saw an increasing population and the expansion of arable cultivation, sometimes into apparently marginal upland, until here, as elsewhere in the country, there was a contraction and abandonment of some settlements in the later medieval period, most clearly visible on Dartmoor (Rippon and Croft 2008, 196–7).

Content and structure of report

The archaeological results from all three sections of pipeline were drawn together in an assessment report (CA 2010) that included recommendations for detailed analysis and the present publication. The assessment recognised that the project, undertaken in a narrow corridor of investigation, had produced a large number of minor and undated features and a smaller number of more valuable but essentially poorly defined sites. It is pertinent to make the point that discoveries made as a consequence of this type of development, where considerable efforts are made to mitigate its effects by avoidance of archaeological sites, are records of what, for the most part, remain to be found once the known archaeology has been accounted for. This strategy resulted in a great deal of scattered information which is difficult to put into context or discuss meaningfully. It was therefore not desirable to publish a detailed record of everything and, indeed, few of the sites on their own would justify lengthy treatment. At the same time, the value of the project lies in the cumulative gain of (for the most part) low-grade information, which deserves presentation and integration with the other findings and, where possible, with emerging themes in the archaeology of the region. The assessment also identified a lack of large quantities of finds, making the dating and characterisation of sites difficult in many cases. Bone was almost completely absent due to the acid soils, but charred plant remains were reasonably common and sometimes of good quality. An extensive suite of radiocarbon dates has been obtained to provide dating for the range of features found, to confirm pottery dating for some and to acquire baseline dating information for others. All radiocarbon dates are quoted at 95% confidence unless stated otherwise. Quotations in the text are sometimes described as 'in the range' to avoid repeating the details of each intersection on the calibration curve. The detail of each date is tabulated.

The results of the archaeological work include significant new information on a range of periods for each of the pipeline sections (Table 1.2). Of particular significance are 13 Neolithic and Bronze Age sites:

Table 1.2: Periods represented on the main sites described

Site No.	Name	Mesolithic	Neolithic	Bronze Age	Iron Age	Roman	Early Medieval	Medieval / post-Med
1	Coldharbour	-	-	-	-	-	-	✓
2	Slade Farm	-	-	-	✓	-	-	-
3	Knightstone Farm	-	-	?	-	?	-	-
4	Pixies' Parlour	?	✓	✓	✓	✓	✓	✓
5	Salston A	-	-	-	-	-	-	✓
6	Salston B	-	-	✓	-	-	-	-
7	Land East of Broad Oak	-	-	✓	-	-	-	-
8	Land SE of Broad Oak	-	-	✓	-	-	-	-
9	New Nutwells	-	-	?	?	-	-	-
10	Hogsbrook Farm	-	-	-	-	-	-	✓
11	The Nutwell Lodge	-	-	?	?	-	-	-
12	Lower Nutwell	-	-	-	-	-	-	✓
13	White House	-	-	-	-	-	-	✓
14	Exwell Barton	-	-	-	?	?	-	✓
15	Crablake Farm	-	-	✓	✓	-	-	-
16	Soloman's Farm	-	-	-	?	?	-	-
17	Hems Valley	-	✓	-	-	-	-	-
18	Moothill Cross	-	-	-	?	?	-	-
19	Barton Hill Cross	-	-	-	✓	✓	-	-
20	Croft Cottages	-	✓	-	-	-	-	-
21	Hood Ball	-	-	✓	-	-	-	-
22	Lower Velwell	-	-	-	?	?	-	-
23	Hood Quarry	-	-	✓	-	✓	-	-
24	Billany Farm	-	-	-	-	✓	-	-
25	Dun Cross	-	-	-	-	✓	-	-
26	Tigley A	-	-	-	✓	-	-	-
27	Tigley B	-	-	-	-	-	✓	-
28	Moore Farm	✓	✓	-	-	-	✓	-
29	Bluepost	-	-	-	-	-	-	✓
30	Beneknowle	-	-	✓	-	-	-	-
31	Springfield	-	-	✓	✓	✓	-	-
32	Forder Cross	-	-	-	-	-	-	?
33	Wood Farm	-	-	?	?	?	-	-
34	Filham House	-	-	✓	✓	-	-	-

- Neolithic pits and small features at Pixies' Parlour, Ottery St Mary (Site 4), Hems Valley Staverton (Site 17), Croft Cottages (Site 20) and Moore Farm (Site 28);
- Beaker/Bronze Age pits at Pixies' Parlour (Site 4), Crablake Farm, Exminster (Site 15), Hood Ball, Rattery (Site 21), Springfield, Ugborough (Site 31) and Filham House, Ugborough (Site 34);
- a Bronze Age cremation pit at Salston B, Ottery St Mary (Site 6);
- Middle Bronze Age ditches on land east of Broad Oak (Site 7), near a ring-ditch south-east of Broad Oak (Site 8, both Ottery St Mary) and probably also at Hood Quarry, Dartington (Site 23);
- a terraced building at Beneknowle, Diptford (Site 30) radiocarbon dated to the Middle Bronze Age.

There were ten sites with features of Iron Age or Roman date. These included:

- parts of settlements at Pixies' Parlour (Site 4), Barton Hill Cross, Littlehempston (Site 19), Billany Farm, Dartington (Site 24) and Springfield, Ugborough (Site 31);
- ditches at Exwell Barton, Powderham (Site 14) perhaps representing peripheral field boundaries;
- possible settlement features at Crablake Farm (Site 15);
- iron smelting furnaces at Tigley A, Harberton (Site 26);
- a pit at Slade Farm, Ottery St Mary (Site 2) and burnt features at Filham House, Ugborough (Site 34).

Medieval sites were rare, but comprised:

- part of a settlement at Exwell Barton, Powderham (Site 14) with a dwelling and a building with a sunken floor;
- the remains of an 18th-century cob building at Lower Nutwell, Woodbury (Site 12);
- traces of an 18th-century brick clamp at Salston A, Ottery St Mary (Site 5).

A large proportion of the undated ditches are likely to have been medieval and later agricultural features, although others are possibly prehistoric. There has been some attention paid to comparing the locations and alignments of undated ditches with the earliest mapped evidence for field boundaries (mainly from tithe maps of the earlier 19th century) in order to assess their likely date. Extensive use has been made of this source but a full landscape analysis using documentary and field evidence to examine the wider setting and relationships between landscape features, as exemplified by the survey of Bodmin Moor (Johnson and Rose 1994), was beyond the scope of this project.

The presentation of the results is within a chronological framework, commencing with the Earlier Prehistoric period (Chapter 2) which encompasses the Mesolithic through to the Middle/Late Bronze Age. This is further divided into subdivisions reflecting different pottery traditions and their long chronologies. Within this framework the site narratives follow the route from east to west. The associated finds and environmental evidence follow these narratives. This is followed by the Later Prehistoric and Roman periods (Chapter 3), covering the period 400 BC to AD 400 and forming a convenient unit because of the difficulties of determining the chronological range of handmade Iron Age pottery, which may have extended into the 1st century AD, probably overlapping with Roman wares. In the Medieval and Later chapter (Chapter 4) there is slight evidence for post-Roman (Early medieval) activity from radiocarbon dates. The bulk of the chapter, however, is devoted to the unexpected discovery of part of a medieval settlement or farmstead at Exwell Barton. There were a few later finds of interest, principal among them being the cob agricultural building at Lower Nutwell. There is a brief resumé of undated features in Chapter 5.

All specialist reports have been edited for this publication and the more involved technical methodologies (charred plant macrofossils, metalworking debris and cremated bone) are presented collectively in an appendix. The full reports and supporting information are available in the site archive. The archive and, subject to the agreement of the legal landowners, the artefacts will be deposited with the Royal Albert Memorial Museum, Exeter, under the following accession numbers: Ottery St Mary to Aylesbeare (OTA06) – RAMM 518/2006; Aylesbeare to Kenn (ATK06) – RAMM 172/2008; and with the Plymouth City Museum and Art Gallery, Fishacre to Choakford (FTC06) – AR 2007.2.

Chapter 2
Earlier Prehistoric Period

Introduction

This chapter describes the evidence recovered from 13 earlier prehistoric sites (Table 1.2; Figs 1.2–1.7). The Mesolithic is represented by one dated feature at Moore Farm, Harberton, in South Devon (Site 28; Fig. 1.5) and a scatter of superficial and redeposited flintwork from both the East and South Devon sections of the route. There were two sites with features containing Early Neolithic pottery; a pit at Pixies' Parlour, Ottery St Mary (Site 4), and a possible ditch terminal at Croft Cottages, Staverton (Site 20). Rare finds of Middle Neolithic Peterborough Ware together with a deposit of stones and flints came from a group of pits at Hems Valley, Staverton (Site 17). There was Grooved Ware from Late Neolithic pits at Moore Farm, Harberton (Site 28), the first time this pottery has been dated by radiocarbon in Devon. The Early Bronze Age is represented by two features: a pit containing several sherds of All-Over-Cord Beaker (the first of this type from Devon) near the large round barrow at Springfield, Ugborough (Site 31), and a cremation burial west of the Otter Valley at Salston B, Ottery St Mary (Site 6), dated by radiocarbon and the only human remains found on the project. The number of new Middle Bronze Age sites discovered (eight) is remarkable. They came from both the southern and eastern parts of the route and include part of a terraced building at Beneknowle, Diptford (Site 30); pits with and without Trevisker Ware pottery at Pixies' Parlour, Ottery St Mary (Site 4), Crablake Farm, Exminster (Site 15), Hood Ball, Rattery (Site 21) and Filham House, Ugborough (Site 34); and evidence of land boundaries east of Broad Oak, Ottery St Mary (Site 7) and at Hood Quarry, Dartington (Site 23). A ring-ditch south-east of Broad Oak, Ottery St Mary (Site 8) is insecurely dated but considered likely to be Bronze Age as well. There was no indication of activity after about 1000 BC until the Middle Iron Age from about 400 BC (Chapter 3).

Site descriptions
Stuart Joyce and Andrew Mudd

Mesolithic (9500–4000 BC)

The only site to contain an identified Mesolithic feature lay in South Devon at Moore Farm on an east-facing slope south of the Harbourne River in the parish of Harberton (Site 28; Fig. 2.9). Archaeological features here comprised mainly a scatter of small pits with Late Neolithic dating evidence (below).

Pit 18.12.043 was only partially revealed; it was 0.7m wide and 0.25m deep, extending to the north beyond the limit of the site. The profile was broadly symmetrical with stepped sides and a slightly concave base. The charcoal-rich fill was mid red-brown silty clay containing mainly oak wood but also hazelnut shell in small quantities. A single radiocarbon determination on a hazelnut shell produced a date of 5017–4847 cal. BC (NZA-36267), placing it within the Late Mesolithic (Table 2.3). This may suggest that a number of undated pits are of a similar date, although it is also possible that the hazelnut was residual within a Neolithic pit. Isolated finds of worked flint from diagnostic tool forms, or showing technological traits attributable to the Mesolithic period, were identified from six plots: Site 4 (Pixies' Parlour, Ottery St Mary), OTA 09.01 (south-east of Aylesbeare), Site 14 (medieval house, Exwell Barton), FTC 8.01 (east of Croft Cottages, Staverton), Site 21 (Hood Ball, Rattery), and Site 34 (south of Filham House, Ugborough) (Figs 1.2–1.7). These consisted of a small number of blades/bladelets and microliths recovered from unstratified or residual contexts. It is possible that some less diagnostic pieces from the assemblage from Pixies' Parlour are also Mesolithic rather than earlier Neolithic, although this cannot be determined with any certainty.

The scale and nature of Mesolithic activity along the pipeline route is difficult to ascertain from these finds. The fact that no surface collection surveys were

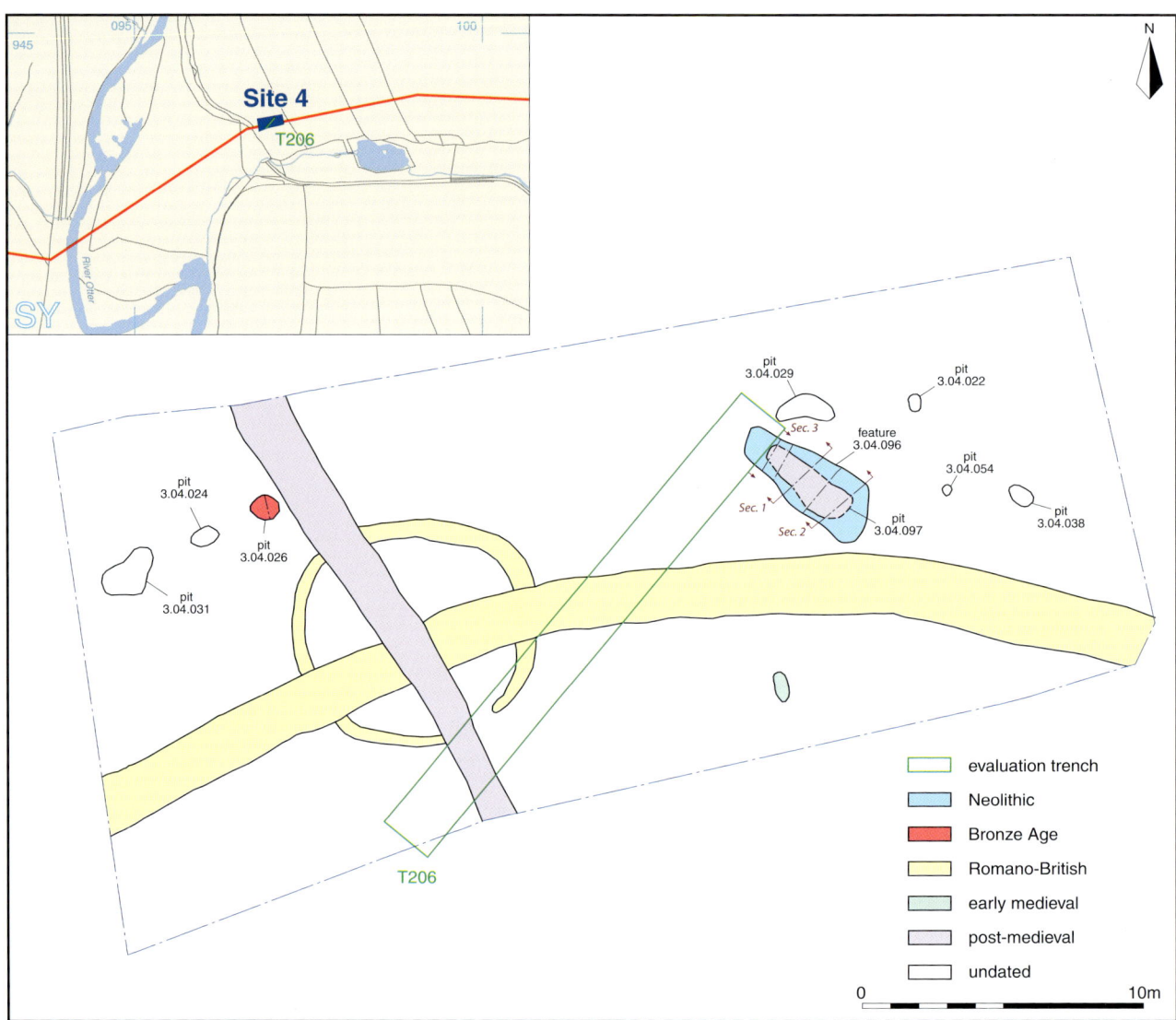

Fig. 2.1 Pixies' Parlour (Site 4); plan of excavated features. Scales 1:250 and 1:10,000

undertaken in 2005–6, and only a small section of the Fishacre–Choakford pipeline was investigated by this means in 2001, makes it undoubtedly the case that evidence of Mesolithic (and later) activity contained exclusively within the ploughsoil has not been recorded. The flintwork from this and later periods is discussed below and the distributions plotted on Figures 2.41–2.44. The fieldwalking finds came from Site 17 and plots 3.03, 3.04, 7.01, 27.02, 27.03 and 27.04 of the Fishacre–Choakford pipeline.

Early Neolithic (4000–3300BC)

East Devon

Site 4: Pixies Parlour, Ottery St Mary
The site lies on a spur overlooking the confluence of a stream to the south with the floodplain of the River Otter, which runs about 200m to the west (Figs 1.2, 2.1). The underlying geology, mapped as Otter Sandstone Formation, was found to be a moderately compact silty sand. The site is known for superficial finds of prehistoric flintwork, the collection of 27 Mesolithic blades, three scrapers and four other pieces from the area having been noted previously (DHER ref. SY09SE/1). The entire stretch of pipeline route from Knightstone Lane (OTA 2.06, Fig. 1.2) to Pixies' Parlour was the subject of geophysical survey, resulting in the discovery of a substantial curving ditch in this field (Fig. 3.3). It was this ditch that prompted the evaluation and subsequent set-piece excavation in this field and the identification of significant Iron Age and Roman features. However, it was the earlier prehistoric finds, in the form of flintwork (Fig. 2.45 nos 1–5) and Early Neolithic pottery, which comprised the majority of the archaeological material recovered. The more limited evidence for Middle Bronze Age activity is described later, and the Iron Age/Roman features in Chapter 3.

Located in the east of the site was large sub-oval

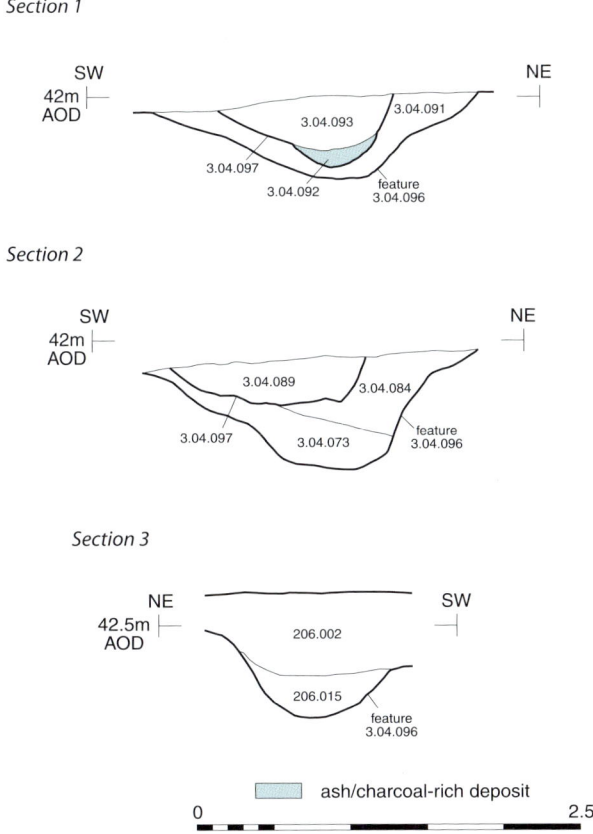

Fig. 2.2 Pixies' Parlour (Site 4); sections 1, 2 and 3 through feature 3.04.096. Scale 1:50

An interpretation of these intercutting features is shown in Figures 2.1 and 2.2 (sections 1 and 2) where deposit 3.04.092 is interpreted as occupying the later pit 3.04.097. An alternative view, that this large and only moderately abraded assemblage of Neolithic pottery, with a considerable group of associated flintwork, was entirely redeposited in a post-medieval pit, seems less likely.

The feature examined in T206 would appear to have been part of the original Neolithic feature as the fill, 206.015 (Fig. 2.2, section 3), a grey-brown sandy silt, contained 45 sherds of Early Neolithic pottery in a variety of fabrics, and 56 pieces of worked flint of less diagnostic but broadly comparable date. Six sherds of pottery and four pieces of flint came from the upper fill of the middle section (Fig. 2.2, section 2, fill 3.04.089), and a further six sherds from upper fill in the southern section (Fig. 2.2, section 1, fill 3.04.093) but these seem to have been redeposited in the later cut in both sections. The secondary fill, 3.04.084, in the middle section consisted of a mixed clay silt and sandy silt deposit and would seem to be within the original feature. A consideration of the overall size, form and fills of the Early Neolithic feature suggests it might have been a tree-throw hole that received a considerable quantity of cultural material from activity immediately nearby. There is nothing intrinsic to the material or its position to suggest a 'placed' deposit. The worked flint, which is in sharp condition and includes knapping debris, shows evidence of soft-hammer technology and includes a higher proportion of blades (27%) than any other stratified group on the project, suggesting that it is of contemporaneous date (Table 2.15).

The occurrence of such a wide range of pottery fabrics within a single early prehistoric feature is without parallel in Devon (Fig. 2.33; Quinnell, this report) and is of considerable significance as the material is considered to be mostly within its primary context. Further evidence for Early Neolithic activity from this site comes from a possible broken or unfinished leaf-shaped arrowhead recovered from Roman ditch 3.04.004 (Fig. 2.45, no. 4).

Livermore Farm, Aylesbeare (OTA 9.02; Fig. 1.2)

A residual sherd of Early Neolithic pottery in a vein quartz fabric was retrieved from a field boundary ditch. This is a tiny sherd but suggests the presence of

feature 3.04.096, which was initially examined within evaluation trench T206 and then during full excavation (Fig. 2.1). It was 5m long, 2m wide and 0.75m deep, with an irregular and slightly asymmetrical profile and a concave base (Fig. 2.2). The feature as a whole contained 57 sherds (229g) of Earlier Neolithic pottery and 56 pieces of worked flint, but there is difficulty in determining the form of the original Neolithic feature since it appears from carbonised plant remains from charcoal-rich deposit 3.04.092, which were not Neolithic in character and returned a 16th/17th-century radiocarbon date, that a much later pit had been cut into this feature (Table 2.1, NZA-36306).

Table 2.1: Radiocarbon dates from Pixies' Parlour, Site 4 (OTA 3.04)

Feature	Context	Lab No.	Material	δ ^{13}C	Radiocarbon Age	Calibrated Age 95%	Calibrated Age 68%
Pit 03.04.036	03.04.037	NZA 36659	Barley grain (*Hordeum vulgare*)	-21.4‰	1351 ± 25 yr BP	642–92 AD (91.6%) plus 750–63 AD (3.3%)	653–74 AD (67.5%)
Pit 03.04.097	03.04.092	NZA 36306	Emmer/spelt wheat (*Triticum dicoccum/spelta*)	-23.5‰	274 ± 20 yr BP	1523–74 AD (36.1%) plus 1628–64 AD (58.6%)	1529–43 AD (17.9%) plus 1635–56 AD (50.8%)

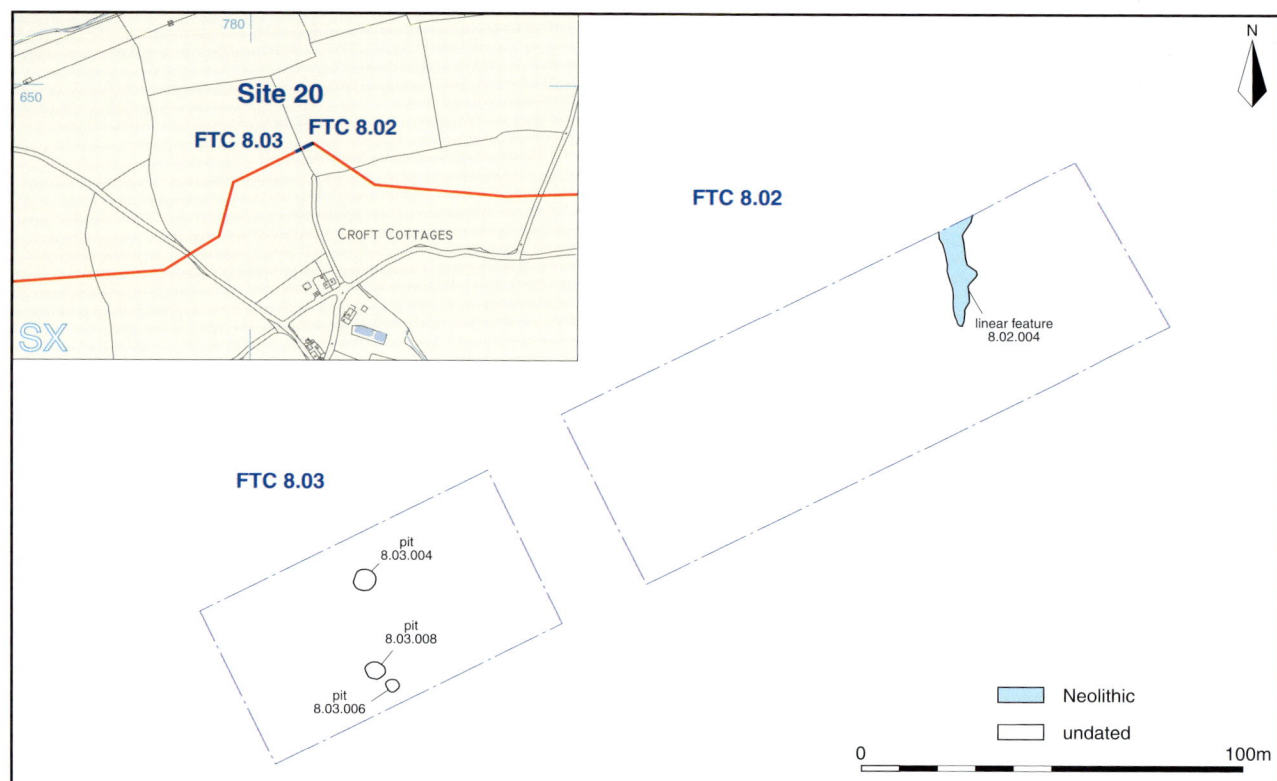

Fig. 2.3 Croft Cottages (Site 20); plan of excavated features. Scales 1:200 and 1:10,000

an Early Neolithic feature in the vicinity. There was no significant flintwork from this plot which lies on a south-facing slope on Aylesbeare Mudstone. The plot had been stripped to a width of 50m and, other than the field boundary ditches, revealed just two small pits without finds.

South Devon

Site 20: Croft Cottages, Staverton

The site is located on flat ground on a westerly projecting ridge. A single irregularly shaped north/south-orientated linear feature, 8.02.004, was identified within the 5m-wide strip (Fig. 2.3). The single fill, 8.02.005, contained six joining sherds (13g) of an Early Neolithic carinated bowl. The feature was 0.74m wide and 0.4m deep with 3m length lying within the excavation area. In plan it was somewhat irregular and the longitudinal profile was also irregular, although the cross profile was less so (Figs 2.4, 2.5). This was the only linear feature of this period from the project although there is a possibility that the pottery was redeposited. It is not clear what kind of site this feature related to; it may have been an elongated pit resulting from activity such as tree clearance, although it is possible that it was a segment of an interrupted ditched boundary or enclosure. The wider picture is unclear although a vertical aerial photograph shows faint concentric curvilinear markings (cropmarks or soil marks) on the western edge of FTC 8.02 which may be relevant (NMR library ref. 543).

No other prehistoric features were identified, but three undated pits, 8.03.004, 8.03.006 and 8.03.008, 15m to the south-west (in FTC 8.03) may be related. These were all circular in plan with steep sides and flat bases,

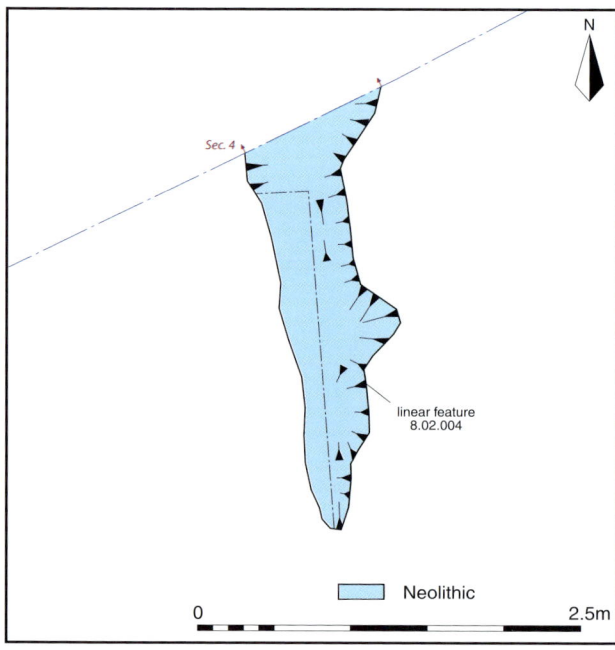

Fig. 2.4 Croft Cottages (Site 20); plan of linear feature 8.02.004. Scale 1:50

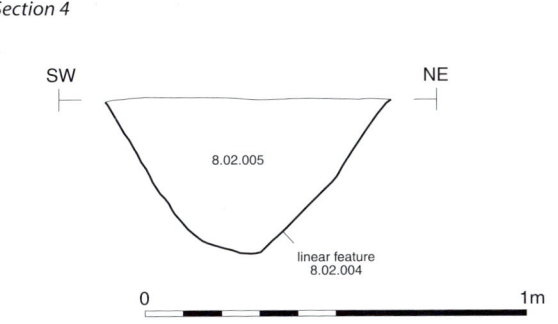

Fig. 2.5 Croft Cottages (Site 20); section 4 through linear feature 8.02.004. Scale 1:20

containing a clay silt fill. An obliquely blunted bladelet from FTC 8.01, recovered during topsoil removal, suggests that this ridge saw Mesolithic activity, while further residual, but less datable, prehistoric flintwork came from FTC 7.01 to the east (Fig. 2.43).

Middle to Late Neolithic (3300–2400 BC)

South Devon

Site 17: Hems Valley, Staverton

The plot is on flat land within the low-lying valley of the River Hems, which runs approximately 100m to the north (Fig. 2.6). Fieldwalking in 2001 recovered eight worked flints, including a fabricator and a scraper of probable Late Neolithic or Early Bronze Age date (Fig. 2.43). At the centre of the site was a spatially discrete group of six pits cutting the shillet substrate.

Pit 2.02.004 was sub-circular in plan, 0.83m long, 0.78m wide and 0.18m deep (Fig. 2.7, section 5). The single orange-brown silty fill, 2.02.005, contained 32 sherds of probable Peterborough Ware pottery, including a pointed rim and bodysherds with incised zig-zag and close-spaced parallel lines and comb-impressed decoration. In addition, eight pieces of worked flint, two rubbing stones and four pieces of burnt volcanic tuff were recovered. One of the rubbing stones was also

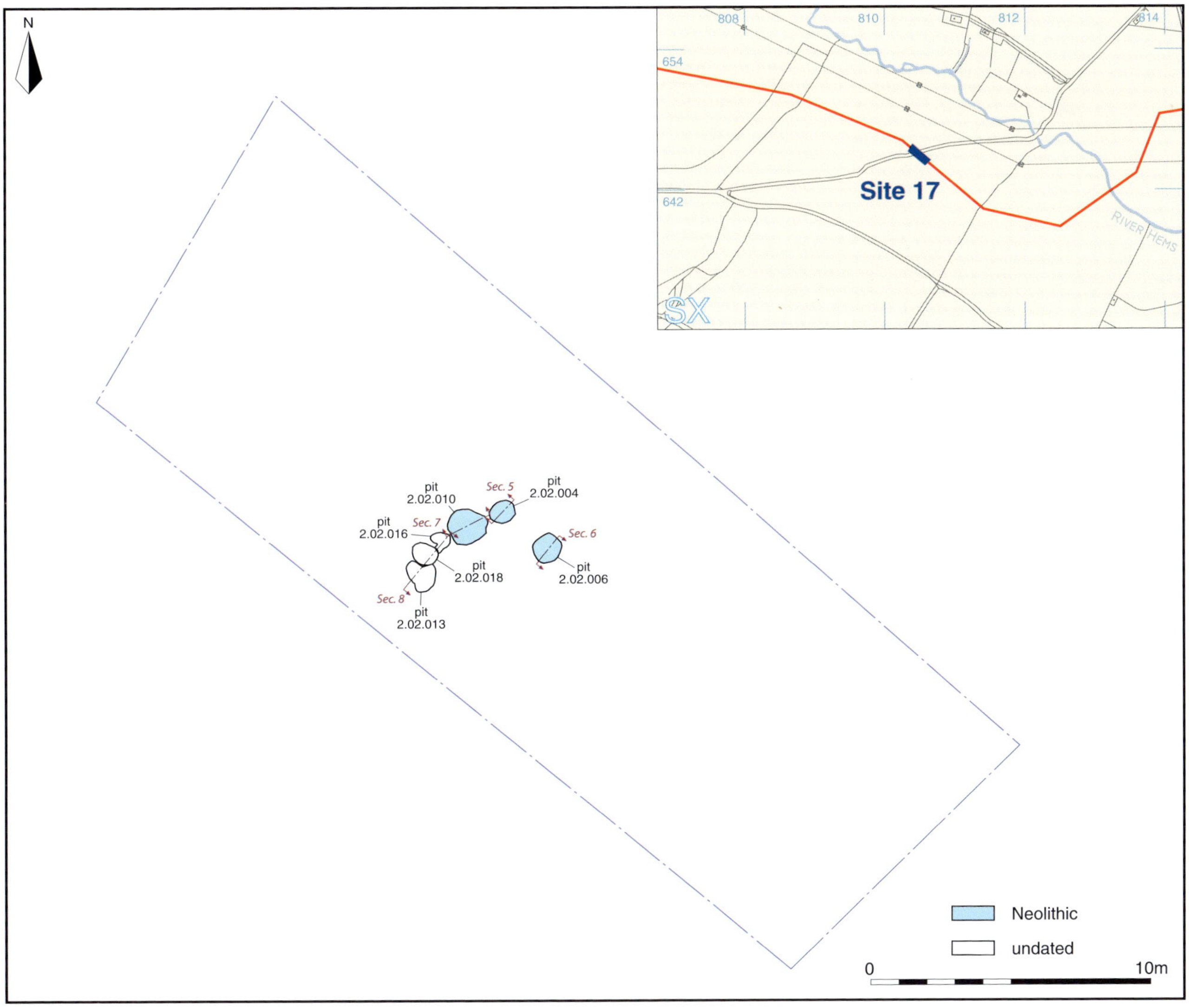

Fig. 2.6 Hems Valley (Site 17); plan of excavated features. Scales 1:250 and 1:10,000

Table 2.2: Radiocarbon dates from Hems Valley, Site 17 (FTC 2.02)

Feature	Context	Lab No.	Material	δ ^{13}C	Radiocarbon Age	Calibrated Age 95%	Calibrated Age 68%
Pit 02.02.004	02.02.005	NZA 36262	Hazelnut shell (*Corylus avellana*)	-22.6‰	4446 ± 20 yr BP	3325–3218 BC (34.3%) plus 3174–3158 BC (2.9%) plus 3120–3018 BC (57.9%)	3306–3302 BC (1.5%) plus 3263–3240 BC (16.5%) plus 3103–3079 BC (17.0%) plus 3067–3024 BC (33.4%)
Pit 02.02.006	02.02.007	NZA 36263	Hazelnut shell (*Corylus avellana*)	-23‰	4431 ± 20 yr BP	3311–3292 BC (2.0%) plus 3285–3273 BC (1.2%) plus 3263–3237 BC (9.4%) plus 3108–3006 BC (76.4%) plus 2983–2931 BC (5.8%)	3095–3022 BC (67.9%)
Pit 02.02.010	02.02.011	NZA 32773	Hazel charcoal (*Corylus avellana*)	-26.1‰	4495 ± 25 yr BP	3339–3095 BC (94.9%)	3331–3306 BC (11.4%) plus 3302–3263 BC (17.4%) plus 3240–3212 BC (13.2%) plus 3186–3154 BC (14.4%) plus 3128–3103 BC (11.2%)
Pit 02.02.010	02.02.011	NZA 36264	Hazelnut shell (*Corylus avellana*)	-24.8‰	4458 ± 20 yr BP	3327–3215 BC (51%) plus 3181–3156 (6.7%) plus 3123–3079 (19.0%) plus 3068–3024 (18.0%)	3264–3236 BC (11.1%) plus 3287–3272 BC (7.2%) plus 3264–3236 BC (20.3%) plus 3167–3163 BC (1.6%) plus 3108–3085 BC (13.6%) plus 3058–3028 BC (14.5%)

of volcanic tuff, while the other was of vesicular lava (Fig. 2.47). The charred plant remains were dominated by hazelnut shells (Table 2.19, sample 290), one of which produced a radiocarbon date of 3325–3018 cal. BC (NZA-36262) (Table 2.2).

Pit 2.02.010 was more substantial, 1.2m in diameter and 0.5m deep (Fig. 2.7, section 7). The main fill, 2.02.011, of grey brown clay silt, overlay a lens of charcoal and hazelnut shell at the base of the pit (2.02.012), from which a radiocarbon determination (on hazel charcoal) returned a date of 3339–3095 cal. BC (NZA-32773). A second radiocarbon determination, on hazelnut shell, produced a date of 3327–3024 cal. BC (NZA-36264), confirming the original date. Fill 2.02.011 contained 17 sherds of Neolithic pottery, which in view of the dating can be defined as Peterborough Ware, including decorated pieces. It also contained 21 pieces of worked flint (including end scrapers/retouched flakes, and core reused as a hammer stone), and seven large pieces of stone (Fig. 2.46). A pebble of porphyritic lava had been utilised as a rubbing stone. This pebble, and the five unworked pebbles, are likely to have come from the nearby headwaters of the River Hems (Watts, this report).

Pit 2.02.006 was 0.90m wide and 0.26m deep (Figs 2.7, section 6, and 2.8). The charcoal-rich primary fill (2.02.007) contained several stones including a long, narrow pebble of volcanic tuff of unknown purpose, worn smooth along both long edges, (Fig. 2.48). Hazelnut shell (from sample 292), yielded a radiocarbon date of 3311–2931 cal. BC (NZA-36263). The upper fill, 2.02.008, contained ten sherds of similar Neolithic pottery, as well as a burnt denticulate on a blade/long

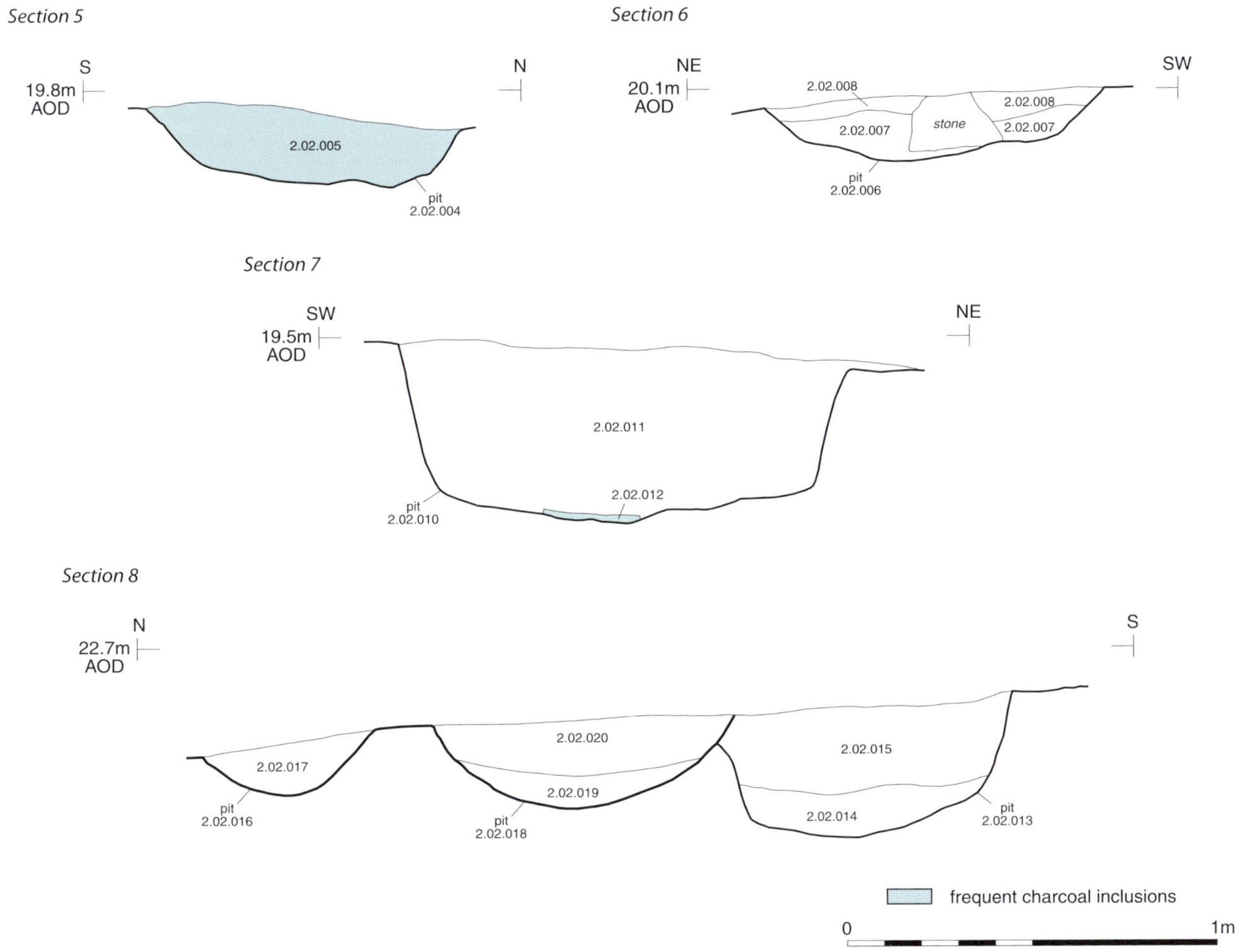

Fig. 2.7   Hems Valley (Site 17); sections 5 to 8 through pits. Scale 1:20

Fig. 2.8   Hems Valley (Site 17); view of pit 2.02.006, looking south-east. Scale 0.4m

flake (Fig. 2.45, no. 9). A small fragment of burnt stone may have derived from a hearth.

Soil samples from these pits were dominated by fragments of hazelnut shell and large fragments of charcoal, mostly identified to hazel or less specifically hazel/alder, with some oak also present (Tables 2.19–2.20). However, virtually no cereal remains were recovered, which suggests temporary or seasonal occupation, or a more permanent settlement engaged in very small-scale arable cultivation.

It is likely that pits 2.02.013, 2.02.016 and 2.02.018 were also Neolithic by association, although they were not datable. Pit 2.02.013 was oval in plan and was 1.2m long, 0.8m wide and 0.35m deep. It had relatively steep, symmetrical sides and a slightly concave base. Its secondary fill (2.02.015) contained worked flint, including a combined denticulate/end scraper on a blade-like flake (Fig. 2.45, no.10), and some amorphous fragments of fired clay. Pit 2.02.016 was 0.7m long, 0.45m wide and 0.15m deep, and its fill, 2.02.017, contained one piece of worked flint. Both pits were cut by pit 2.02.018 which was 0.92m long, 0.75m wide and 0.26m deep. Its secondary fill, 2.02.020, contained five pieces of undiagnostic worked flint. The worked flint from these pits cannot be dated intrinsically, but it does not contradict the Middle Neolithic dating of the pottery and radiocarbon determinations.

None of the pits showed evidence of use prior to backfilling, or erosion of the sides or base. All but pit 2.02.016 displayed steep sides with clean sculpted shapes. The flint recovered from the pits was unabraded and in sharp condition, which, together with the

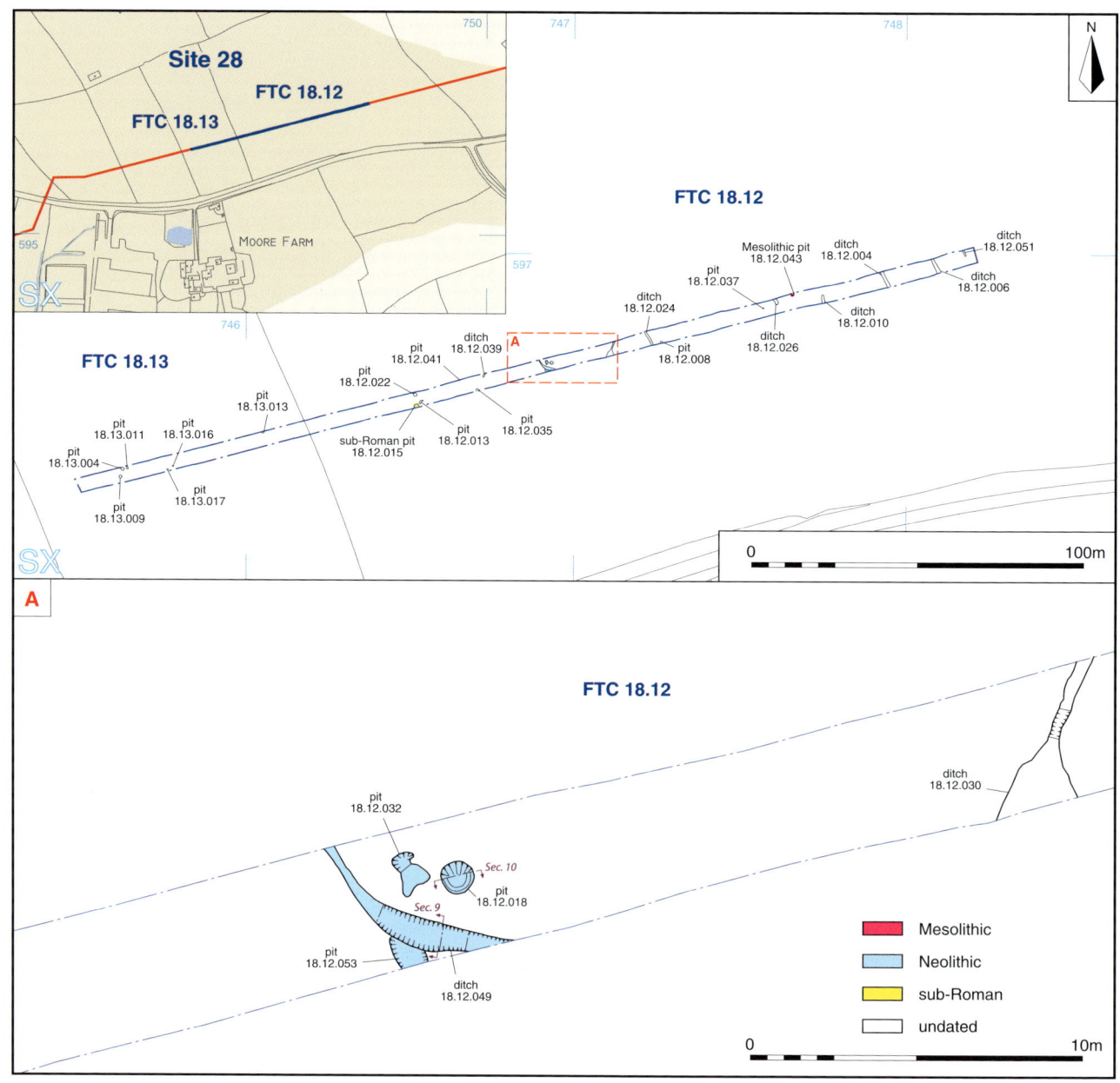

Fig. 2.9 Moore Farm (Site 28); plan of excavated features. Scales 1:200, 1:2000 and 1:10,000

presence of small removals or shatter spalls and chips, is suggestive of a discrete assemblage.

Site 28: Moore Farm, Harberton
The site lies at approximately 115m AOD, on a gentle east-facing ridge, above and approximately 0.5km south of the River Harbourne (Fig. 2.9). There was a large number of small undated pits and sections of ditch in this plot, all cutting the natural shillet substrate. A pit containing predominantly oak charcoal and hazelnut shell (pit 18.12.043) returned a Mesolithic radiocarbon date (see above). The Neolithic period was represented by three pits and a curvilinear ditch, some containing Late Neolithic Grooved Ware pottery, but other undated features may have been of a similar date.

Pit 18.12.032 was irregular, *c.* 1.1m long and 0.45m wide, with a depth of 0.18m. The single, yellow-brown silty clay fill, 18.12.033, contained 46 sherds of undecorated and much abraded Grooved Ware pottery in gabbroic fabric, and also a fragment of oyster shell. Next to this was pit 18.12.018, which had a diameter of 1m and a depth of 0.25m (Fig. 2.10, section 10). The yellow-brown primary fill, 18.12.019, contained eight sherds of Grooved Ware pottery. The secondary fill, 18.12.020, comprised charcoal-rich, red-brown silt containing 50 sherds of Grooved Ware pottery. A soil sample contained frequent hazelnut shell, but no

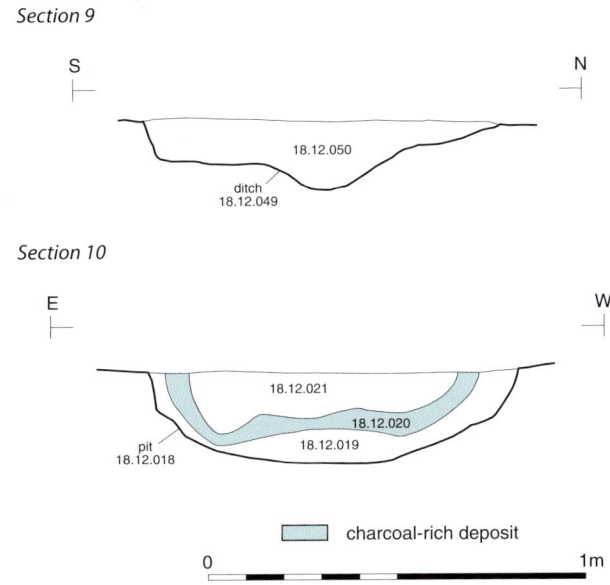

Fig. 2.10 Moore Farm (Site 28); sections 9 and 10 through ditches. Scale 1:20

other charred remains (Table 2.21, sample 301). A radiocarbon sample returned a date in the range 2860–2579 cal. BC (NZA 36265), conforming to the pottery identification (Table 2.3). The tertiary fill of red-brown

Table 2.3: Radiocarbon dates from Moore Farm, Site 28 (FTC 18.12)

Feature	Context	Lab No.	Material	δ ^{13}C	Radiocarbon Age	Calibrated Age 95%	Calibrated Age 68%
Pit 18.12.015	18.12.017	NZA 36703	Wheat cf emmer (*Triticum* cf *dicoccum*)	-24.1‰	1619 ± 20 yr BP	395–468 AD (59.6%) plus 479–534 AD (35.6%)	405–36 AD (43.8%) plus 490–509 AD (16.2%) plus 518–29 AD (8.5%)
Pit 18.12.018	18.12.020	NZA 36265	Hazelnut shell (*Corylus avellana*)	-23.4‰	4120 ± 20 yr BP	2860–2806 BC (26.5%) plus 2756–2717 BC (15.6%) plus 2704–2579 BC (52.8%)	2850–2828 BC (12.7%) plus 2821–2811 BC (6.0%) plus 2742–2725 BC (9.0%) plus 2694–2625 BC (40.5%)
Pit 18.12.043	18.12.044	NZA 36267	Hazelnut shell (*Corylus avellana*)	-27.2‰	6046 ± 25 yr BP	5017–4847 BC (95.0%)	4993–4930 BC (59.5%) plus 4921–4909 BC (8.0%) plus 4860–4859 BC (0.7%)
Pit 18.12.053	18.12.054	NZA 36266	Hazelnut shell (*Corylus avellana*)	-26‰	4117 ± 20 yr BP	2859–2807 BC (26.1%) plus 2754–2718 BC (13.8%) plus 2702–2579 BC (55.0%)	2849–2811 BC (21.2%) plus 2740–2727 BC (6.5%) plus 2693–2684 BC (4.5%) plus 2678–2622 BC (35.8%)

silt (18.12.021) contained another 20 sherds of Grooved Ware pottery. To the south-west, pit 18.12.053 extended beyond the southern limit of excavation. It was 0.75m wide and 0.2m deep, with a symmetrical U-shaped profile. Abundant hazelnut shell fragments came from its single fill 18.12.054 (Table 2.21, sample 310), one of which returned a radiocarbon date of 2859-2579 cal. BC (NZA-36266). The pit was cut by curvilinear gully 18.12.049, which was 0.95m wide and 0.17m deep with an irregular profile that may indicate recutting (Fig. 2.10, section 9). Its single fill, 18.12.050, was a compact clay-silt, containing 44 sherds of Grooved Ware pottery from two separate vessels. Pit 18.12.015 yield a late/sub-Roman radiocarbon date from a grain of wheat (below).

In the adjacent plot to the west (Fig. 2.9), undated pit 18.13.004 was 1m long, 0.94m wide and 0.28m deep. It contained frequent wood charcoal and hazelnut shells (Tables 2.20, 2.21, samples 305 and 306), suggesting an early prehistoric date. No dating evidence was recovered from pits 18.13.009, 18.13.011, 18.13.013 and 18.13.017, which may also belong to the prehistoric period.

The wider context of these Neolithic features is difficult to evaluate. Ditch 18.12.30 forms a slightly irregular curvilinear ditch, not dissimilar to ditch 18.12.049, with which it may have formed a single feature lying on the arc of a circle about 25m in diameter. It is possible that it formed a ring-ditch, which, although of rather early date, is not unlikely in the late Neolithic context of the variety of circular monuments in the region, including round barrows and 'hengiform' enclosures (Webster 2008a, 97). Aerial photography (NMR library ref. 12637) has partially revealed a double-ditched subrectangular enclosure to the east, within plot 18.11, and further sub-rectangular fields or enclosures can be seen to the north of plots 18.12 and 18.13, but their morphology suggests a Roman date rather than anything earlier.

Early Bronze Age/Beaker (2400–1800 BC)

East Devon

Site 6: Salston B, Ottery St Mary
The site lies south of Ottery St Mary at approximately 50m AOD on flat ground on the margin of the valley of the River Otter (Fig. 2.11). The initial interest in the site was the presence of three ditches identified on the geophysical survey, but a trial trench targeted on two of these ditches found a pit (205.004), about 0.5m in diameter and 0.22m deep, containing cremated human bone and charcoal identified as mostly oak (Fig. 2.12). The burial was that of an adult woman and a radiocarbon date on the bone itself produced a date in the range 1948–1772 cal. BC (NZA-36660). A second radiocarbon determination from the same fill (sample 64), obtained from alder charcoal, produced a date of 2137–1975 cal. BC (NZA-36711), the slightly earlier result probably due to dating old wood (Table 2.4). These dates place the burial within the Early Bronze Age.

None of the other features in the excavation area appear to have been associated with this burial. A number of pits, ranging in size from 1.1m to 1.4m in diameter, were larger than the cremation pit and without burnt remains, while pit 4.01.047 was rectangular and measured 2.5m long and 1.3m wide. There were also two undated ditches, 4.01.004 and 4.01.006, which cannot be attributed to the early historical field pattern and may have been early features. Curvilinear ditch 4.01.004 was between 0.8m and 1.7m wide and 0.25m to 0.45m deep with moderately sloping sides and a concave base. Ditch 4.01.006 was between 0.45 and 0.9m wide and 0.2m and 0.32m deep.

South Devon

Site 31: Springfield, Ugborough
The site lies at approximately 140m AOD, situated just off the crest of a hill, on a south facing slope. The pipeline corridor was diverted immediately south of an extant round barrow which is assumed to be Bronze Age and has one of the largest mounds in Devon (Scheduled Monument 33756; Fig. 2.13). Most of the

Table 2.4: Radiocarbon dates from Salston B, Site 6 (OTA 4.01)

Feature	Context	Lab No.	Material	δ ^{13}C	Radiocarbon Age	Calibrated Age 95%	Calibrated Age 68%
Cremation 205.004	205.012	NZA 36660	Cremated bone (long bone)	-22.6‰	3542 ± 25 yr BP	1948–1863 BC (60.4%) plus 1848–1772 BC (34.6%)	1927–1876 BC (49.1%) plus 1839–1823 BC (11.2%) plus 1793–1781 BC (7.4%)
Cremation 205.004	205.012	NZA 36711	Alder charcoal (*Alnus glutinosa*)	-26.6‰	3675 ± 25 yr BP	2137–1975 BC (95%)	2130–2082 BC (41.1%) plus 2055–2022 BC (25.1%) plus 1987–1983 (2.2%)

Earlier Prehistoric Period 25

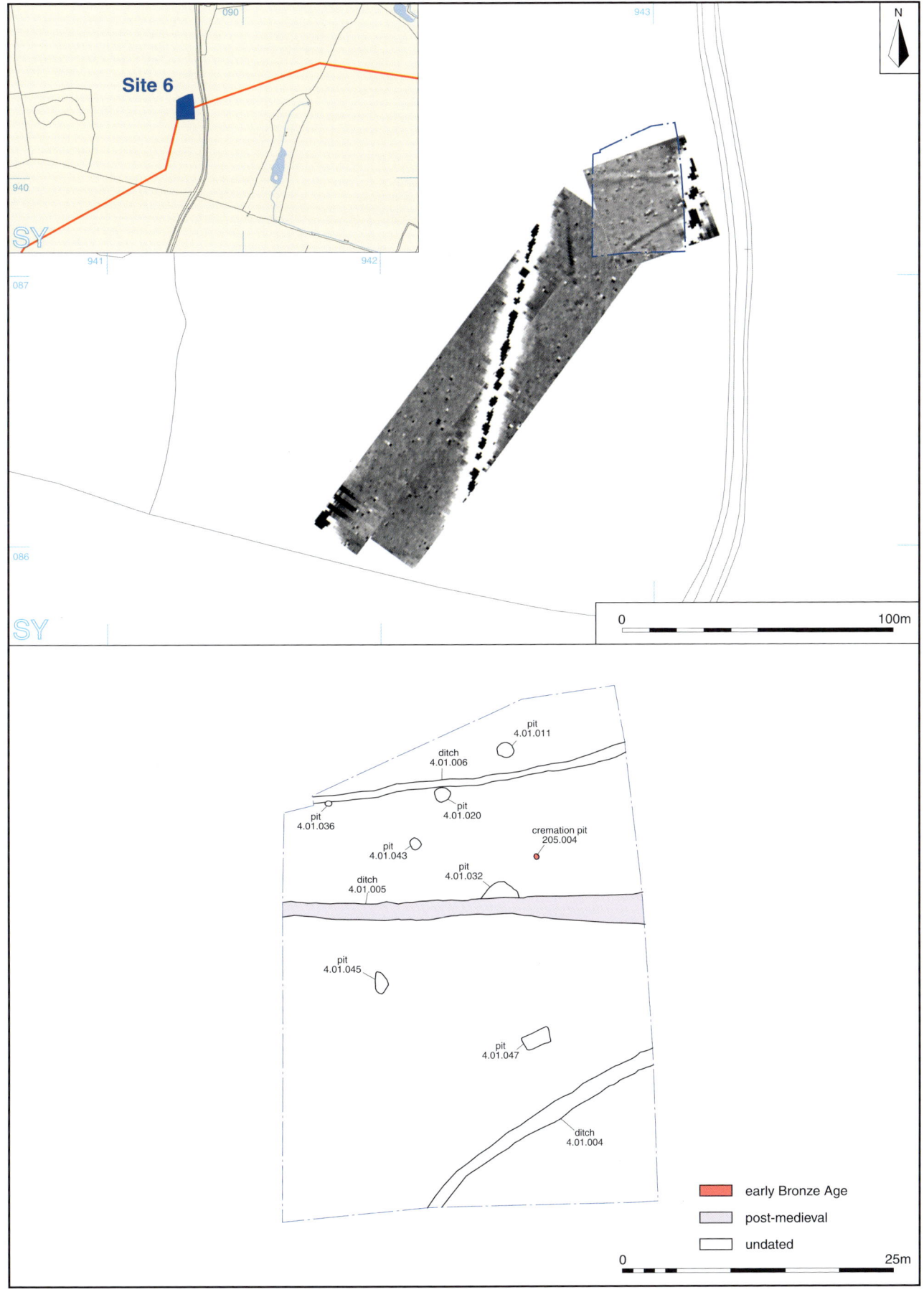

Fig. 2.11 Salston B (Site 6); plan of geophysical anomalies and excavated features. Scales 1:500, 1:2000 and 1:10,000

Fig. 2.12 Salston B (Site 6); Early Bronze Age cremation pit 205.004, looking west. Scale 0.4m

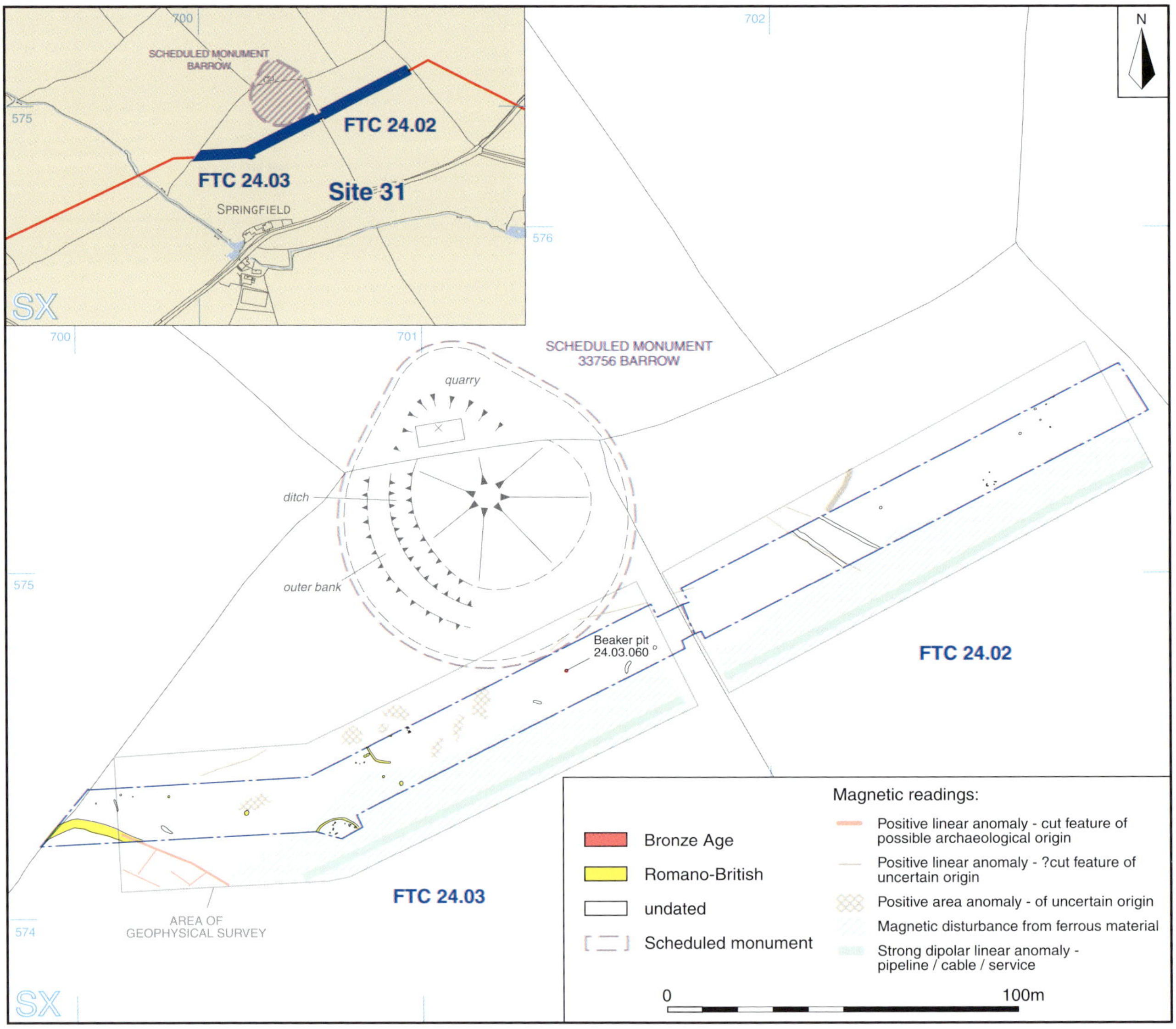

Fig. 2.13 Springfield (Site 31); plan of geophysical anomalies and excavated features. Scales 1:2000 and 1:10,000

Fig. 2.14 Springfield (Site 31); Beaker pit 24.03.060, looking north. Scale 0.6m

archaeological remains within this excavated site relate to an extensive but ill-defined Romano-British settlement, which is dealt with in Chapter 3. However, a single pit, 24.03.060, contained Beaker remains.

The Beaker pit was 0.78m in diameter and 0.14m deep (Fig. 2.14). The primary fill, 24.03.061, contained 40 sherds of All-Over-Cord (AOC) decorated Beaker pottery, the secondary fill (24.03.062) contained eight sherds and the upper fill (24.03.063) four sherds, all from the same vessel (Figs 2.36, 2.37). No conjoining sherds were present and the sherds were abraded, suggesting their deposition in a secondary context. Notwithstanding the loss of a proportion of the pit and its contents through later truncation, it is likely that only some sherds from the vessel had been buried. This is the first recorded instance of AOC pottery to be found in Devon or Cornwall and as such is of regional significance. There were no associated artefacts or burnt remains and the reason for the presence of this pit remains obscure. Likewise, there was no opportunity to provide independent dating of the Beaker, which can only be placed in the broad range of *c.* 2500–2000 BC.

The relationship between the barrow and the Beaker pit cannot be advanced much further on current evidence, although the Beaker can be seen to have lain on the long axis of the barrow as it currently exists, about 15m south of the projected line of the ditch (Fig. 2.13). The barrow was not surveyed in the present works and the dimensions are based upon the description in the schedule (undertaken in 1999) which states that it measures 47m wide, 62m long and 3m high (English Heritage 2001). There is damage caused by a quarry on its northern side containing a building, and a low waste tip on the barrow's eastern side. Nonetheless, the oval form of the barrow is thought to be original. The barrow shows traces of an encircling ditch, 6m wide and 0.2m deep, on its western side, together with an apparent outer bank. It is classified as a 'bowl barrow' (the most commonly occurring type) although the oval or elliptical shape and outer bank would make it atypical.

Middle Bronze Age (1800–1200 BC)

East Devon

Site 4: Pixies' Parlour, Ottery St Mary
While most of the prehistoric interest from this site lies in the Early Neolithic assemblage from pit 3.04.096, Middle Bronze Age material was also recovered in small quantities. Pit 3.04.026, which was 0.75m in diameter and 0.17m deep, lay in the western part of the site (Fig. 2.1). Above a sterile primary orange-brown sandy silt (3.04.027) the secondary grey-brown fill, 3.04.028, contained one sherd of grog-tempered, probably Middle Bronze Age, pottery associated with oak and hazel charcoal. Two further sherds of pottery in a grogged fabric, and again of probable Middle Bronze Age date, came from the Roman curvilinear ditch 3.04.004. It is possible that some of the undated pits on this site were also of Bronze Age date. Pit 3.04.024 was oval in plan, with a symmetrical profile and a flat base, while pit 3.04.031 was kidney shaped, with moderately sloping symmetrical sides and a slightly irregular base. Some of the worked flint from superficial and redeposited contexts may also be of this date, but no diagnostic artefacts were recovered.

Site 7: Land East of Broad Oak, Ottery St Mary
The site lies at approximately 60m AOD on a south-facing slope above the curve of a small tributary of the River Otter (Fig. 2.15). The 6m-wide topsoil strip across this large field revealed five ditches and two shallow pits cut into the pebbly sandstone substrate. Three ditches, while without dating evidence, appear likely to be

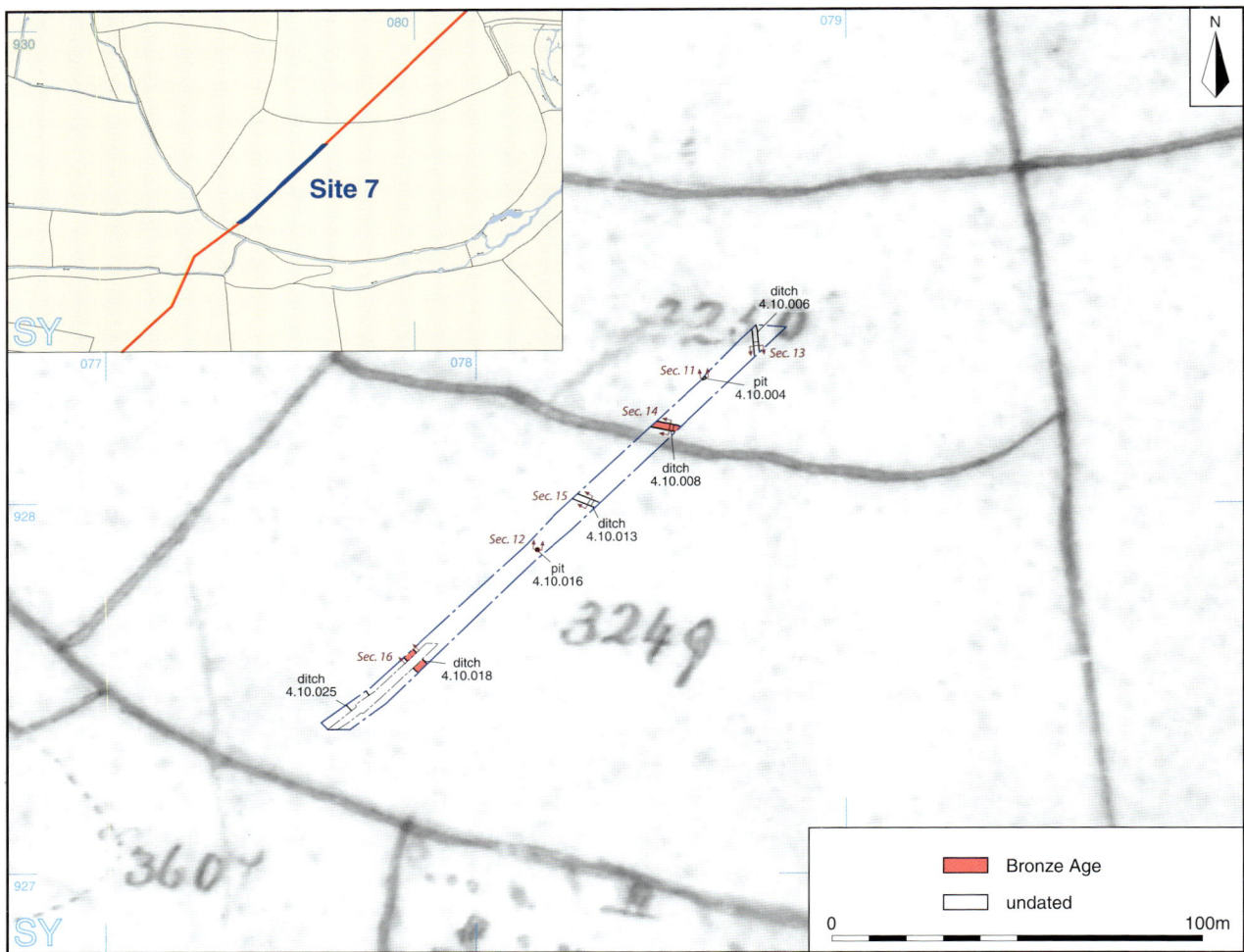

Fig. 2.15 Land East of Broad Oak (Site 7); plan showing extract from 1845 Tithe Map and excavated features. Scales 1:2000 and 1:10,000

medieval or later in date. The other two ditches appear to be rather older.

At the centre of the site was east/west-orientated ditch 4.10.008, 1.9m wide and 0.75m deep. The sides were steeply sloping, and the northern edge had a stepped profile suggestive of slumping or recutting, while the base was broad and flat (Fig. 2.16, section 14). The primary fill, 4.10.009, was sand, derived from natural silting soon after construction. Deposit 4.10.010, similarly comprising friable coarse sand, represents a second phase of natural deposition that also appears to have been relatively rapid as the steep edges were maintained. The third fill, 4.10.011, was a compact clay-silt and may have occupied a recut. It may have been associated with activity close to the ditch as it contained 13 sherds, some conjoining, from a plain Trevisker vessel in Exeter volcanic fabric, datable to the Middle Bronze Age. The upper fill, 4.10.012, derived from gradual erosion of surrounding topsoil/subsoil deposits, contained six sherds of Middle Bronze Age pottery that may have been redeposited.

Evidence of Bronze Age activity in this plot is supported by six sherds of grog- and rock-tempered pottery from pit 4.10.016. The pit was 0.8m in diameter and 0.21m deep (Fig. 2.16, section 12). A soil sample from fill 4.10.17 contained mainly oak charcoal, which returned a radiocarbon date of 3637–3519 cal. BC (NZA-36714), suggesting that the charcoal was residual (Table 2.5). Pit 4.10.004 lay approximately 50m north-west of pit 4.10.016. It was 0.88m long and 0.78m wide but just 70mm deep, suggesting a degree of later truncation (Fig. 2.16, section 11). Ash charcoal from the single charcoal-rich silty sandy fill, 4.10.005, produced a radiocarbon date of 1308–1128 cal. BC (NZA-36373), compatible with the pottery dating from pit 4.10.016 and ditch 4.10.008.

Ditch 4.10.018 had a similar steep-sided and flat-based profile to ditch 4.10.008, although at 3.5m wide and 1.5m deep it was almost twice the size (Fig. 2.16, section 16). While the upper fill (4.10.023) yielded a small potsherd of probable Roman date, this is not good dating evidence for the origin of the ditch which, because of its character and non-modern origin, may well be Bronze Age. The primary fill (4.10.019) was a sterile sand and above that was a thick deposit of silty sand with occasional flecks of charcoal (4.10.020). A soil sample from this deposit retrieved only small charcoal unsuitable

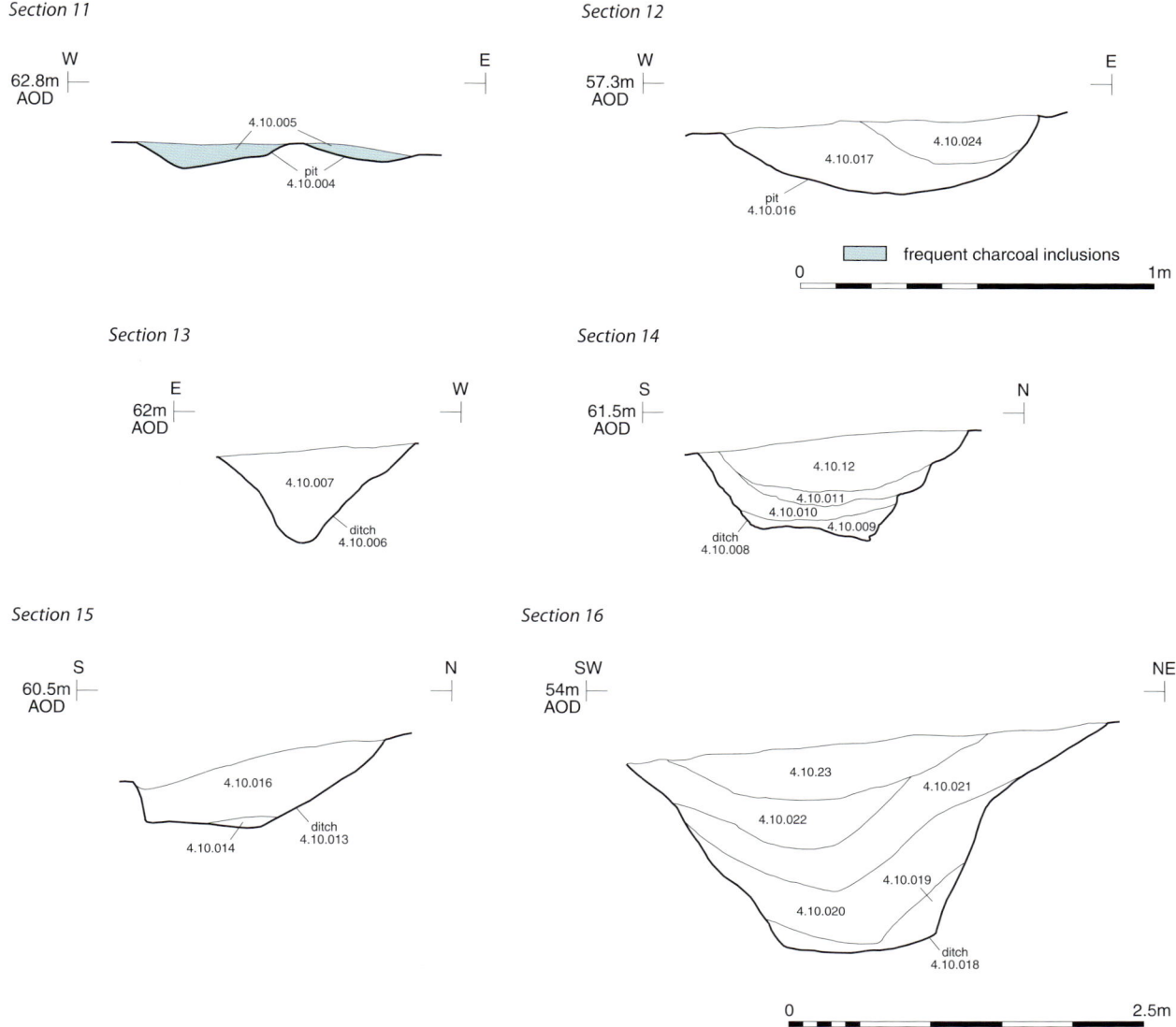

Fig. 2.16 Land East of Broad Oak (Site 7); sections 11 to 16. Scales 1:20 and 1:50

for radiocarbon dating. The upper deposits, filling a broad weathering cone, can be assumed to have accumulated over a considerable time span and it seems possible that the ditch was finally levelled by Roman ploughsoil.

It is not possible to attribute the remaining ditches to any particular period. Indeed many of them were probably reused over a considerable period of time. However, ditch 4.10.013 lay 25m to the south of, and on a similar alignment to Bronze Age ditch 4.10.008, and it is possible that it had a similar origin. It had a

Table 2.5: Radiocarbon dates from Land East of Broad Oak, Site 7 (OTA 4.10)

Feature	Context	Lab No.	Material	δ ^{13}C	Radiocarbon Age	Calibrated Age 95%	Calibrated Age 68%
Pit 04.10.004	04.10.005	NZA 36373	Ash charcoal (*Fraxinus excelsior*)	-24.3‰	2990 ± 20 yr BP	1308–1128 BC (95.0%)	1289–1278 BC (5.9%) plus 1269–1194 BC (59.2%) plus 1138–1133 BC (2.9%)
Pit 04.10.016	04.10.017	NZA 36714	Oak charcoal (heartwood) (*Quercus robur/petraea*)	-25.7‰	4776 ± 25 yr BP	3637–3519 BC (95.2%)	3633–3627 BC (6.7%) plus 3585–3528 BC (61.0%)

similar asymmetrical profile and broad, flat base (Fig. 2.16, section 15). The primary fill, 4.10.014, was a sand, similarly derived from natural silting soon after con-struction. The upper fill, 4.10.016, was a grey-brown silty sand. In contrast, north/south-orientated ditch 4.10.006, while 1.38m wide and 0.7m deep, had a v-shaped symmetrical profile and a single, stony fill, 4.10.007, which appeared to be a deliberate deposit. It is likely that this ditch had a later origin although it does not coincide with a field boundary on the tithe map. The broad, shallow ditch 4.10.025 (1.6m wide but just 0.15m deep) may have been a furrow and is therefore likely to be relatively modern.

Site 8: Land South-East of Broad Oak, Ottery St Mary
The site lies at approximately 67m AOD on relatively flat land at the base of an east-facing slope. The geology is Triassic Upper Sandstone. Aerial photography had identified a group of three possible ring-ditches on the northern edge of this plot (NMR library ref. 13310), although the pipeline was to affect part of only the northern one. The geophysical survey of the pipeline easement identified part of this ring-ditch lying immediately adjacent to a former double-ditched field boundary (Fig. 2.17). This was evaluated by trial trenching before soil stripping of an area 39m long by 11m wide was carried out, and the area then subject to archaeological excavation (Fig. 2.19).

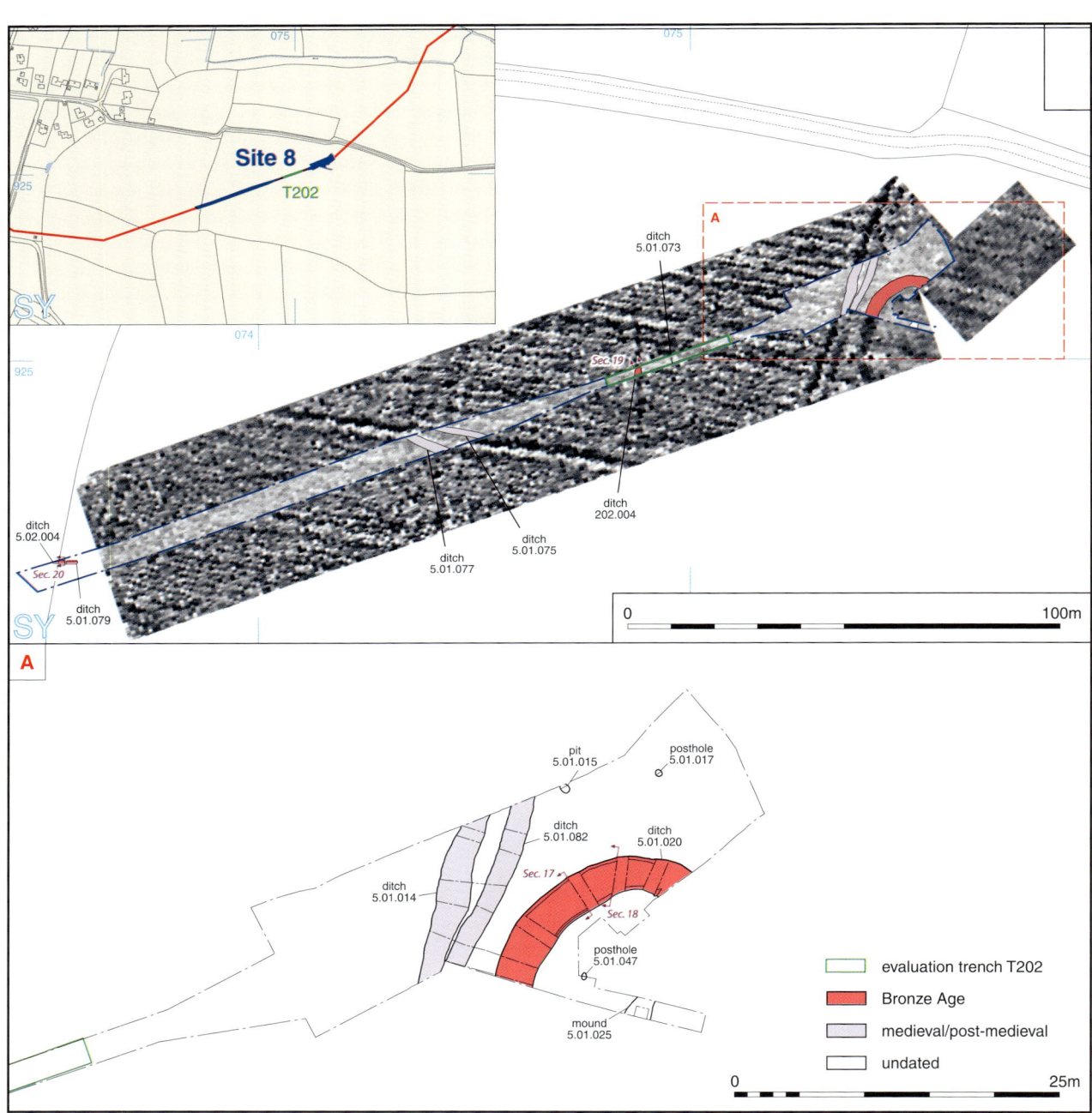

Fig. 2.17 South-East of Broad Oak (Site 8); plan of geophysical anomalies and excavated features. Scales 1:500, 1:1500 and 1:10,000

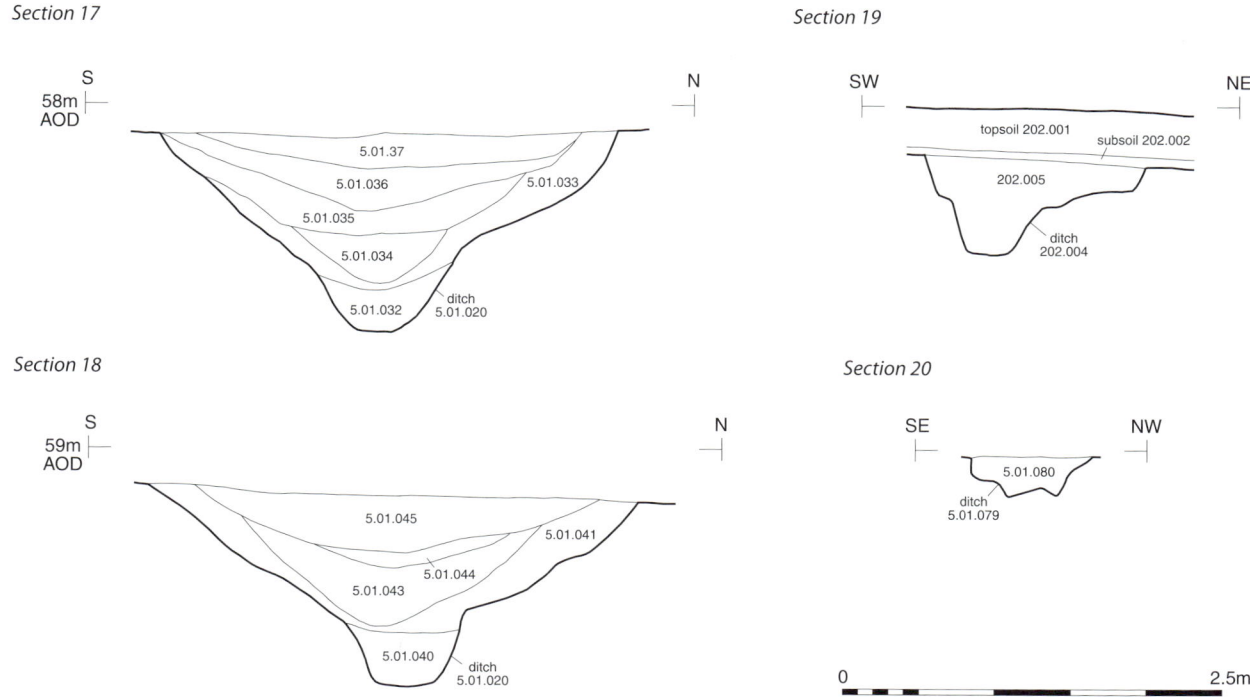

Fig. 2.18 South-East of Broad Oak (Site 8); sections 17 to 20. Scale 1:50

Fig. 2.19 South-East of Broad Oak (Site 8); excavation of ditch 5.01.020 in progress, looking east

Soil stripping revealed part of a ring-ditch, 5.01.020, between 2.5m and 3.3m wide, and up to 1.65m deep. The complete circuit can be projected to have been about 18m across internally. The excavation of five sections through the ditch showed a similar ditch profile and sequence of fills. The rounded base contained a thick deposit of primary sandy fill, 5.01.040. Thereafter, the ditch appears to have been left open to weather as the edges stabilised at a shallower angle (Fig. 2.18, sections 17, 18). A sequence of four or five later, equally sterile, fills suggests a long period of natural silting. The secondary fill, 5.01.041, was a silty sand derived

Fig. 2.20 South-East of Broad Oak (Site 8); ditch 5.01.020, looking south-west. Scale 1m

from gradual silting while tertiary fill, 5.01.043, was a gleyed deposit of pale, bluish silty clay, presumably laid down gradually and influenced by waterlogging (Fig. 2.20). The fourth deposit, 5.01.044, was a dark sediment, possibly a former turf, suggesting a period of stabilisation before the final deposit, 5.01.045, possibly deposited by ploughing. Three soil samples (from deposits 5.01.050, 5.01.059 and 5.01.043) contained very little. A sample of oak charcoal, recovered from the primary fill 5.01.059, gave a radiocarbon date in the range 3973–3803 cal. BC (NZA-36704), but this appears more likely to have been redeposited from the original land surface than to relate to activity contemporary with the ditch (Table 2.6). Within the area delineated by ring-ditch 5.01.020, mound material, up to 0.42m thick, was also identified. Deposits 5.01.025 and 5.01.026 consisted of redeposited natural sand, most likely excavated from towards the base of the encircling ditch. Between these two layers was a deposit of charcoal-rich sandy silt. Layer 5.01.069/070 was only partially revealed immediately within the arc of the ring-ditch. It seemed to overlie the mound deposits and may have formed a covering topsoil but it remains possible that it represents a buried topsoil beneath the mound. These relationships were not further investigated as the majority of the area within the ring-ditch lay outside of the pipeline corridor. Lithics from deposit 05.01.025 comprised a flake and possible utilised blade, which are consistent with Neolithic/Early Bronze Age flint-working but do not themselves confirm the date of the monument. A further 25 pieces of worked flint from subsoil or topsoil comprised mostly flake debitage, although three scrapers, a retouched flake and a broken fragment from a plano-convex knife were also recovered (McSloy, below).

Undated features consisting of two postholes (5.01.047 and 5.01.017) and a pit (5.01.015) also lay within the stripped area. Pit 5.01.015 and posthole 5.01.017 cut the natural substrate and were sealed by subsoil. Posthole 5.01.047 cut the subsoil and was sealed by topsoil, indicating that it post-dated the ring ditch and mound.

Table 2.6: Radiocarbon date from South-East of Broad Oak, Site 8 (OTA 5.01)

Feature	Context	Lab No.	Material	$\delta^{13}C$	Radiocarbon Age	Calibrated Age 95%	Calibrated Age 68%
Ring-ditch 05.01.020	05.01.059	NZA 36704	Oak charcoal (heartwood) (*Quercus robur/petraea*)	-25.4‰	5117 ± 25 yr BP	3973–3925 BC (45.3%) plus 3917–3914 BC (0.5%) plus 3875–3803 BC (48.7%)	3965–3939 BC (37.0%) plus 3855–3841 BC (13.0%) plus 3838–3817 BC (18.3%)

An east/west-orientated ditch terminus, 5.01.079, was identified at the south-western end of the site. It was 0.8m wide and 0.25m deep with an irregular profile perhaps suggesting recutting (Fig. 2.18, section 20). This feature continued into plot 5.02 (as ditch 5.02.004), and contained a single sherd of probable Middle Bronze Age pottery in grogged fabric. Ditch 202.004 in trench T202 was shown on the geophysical plot running north/south. It was 0.65m deep with steep sides and a flat base, but the overall width of 1.4m included a shallower ledge on the eastern side (Fig. 2.18, section 19). Both ditches appear to relate to pre-modern land division, but it is not known whether they are of the same date or whether they are prehistoric. The Bronze Age pottery is abraded and may have been redeposited. There are ditches in the field diagonally to the north-west on a different alignment to the tithe map field boundaries, and it is possible that there was widespread prehistoric or Roman land division here, although any of these ditches could have been dug for reasons other than field demarcation and may be more recent.

Site 15: Crablake Farm, Exminster

A group of five shallow pits was found on an east-facing slope in the eastern part of this plot at approximately 38m AOD (Fig. 2.21). They were initially thought to

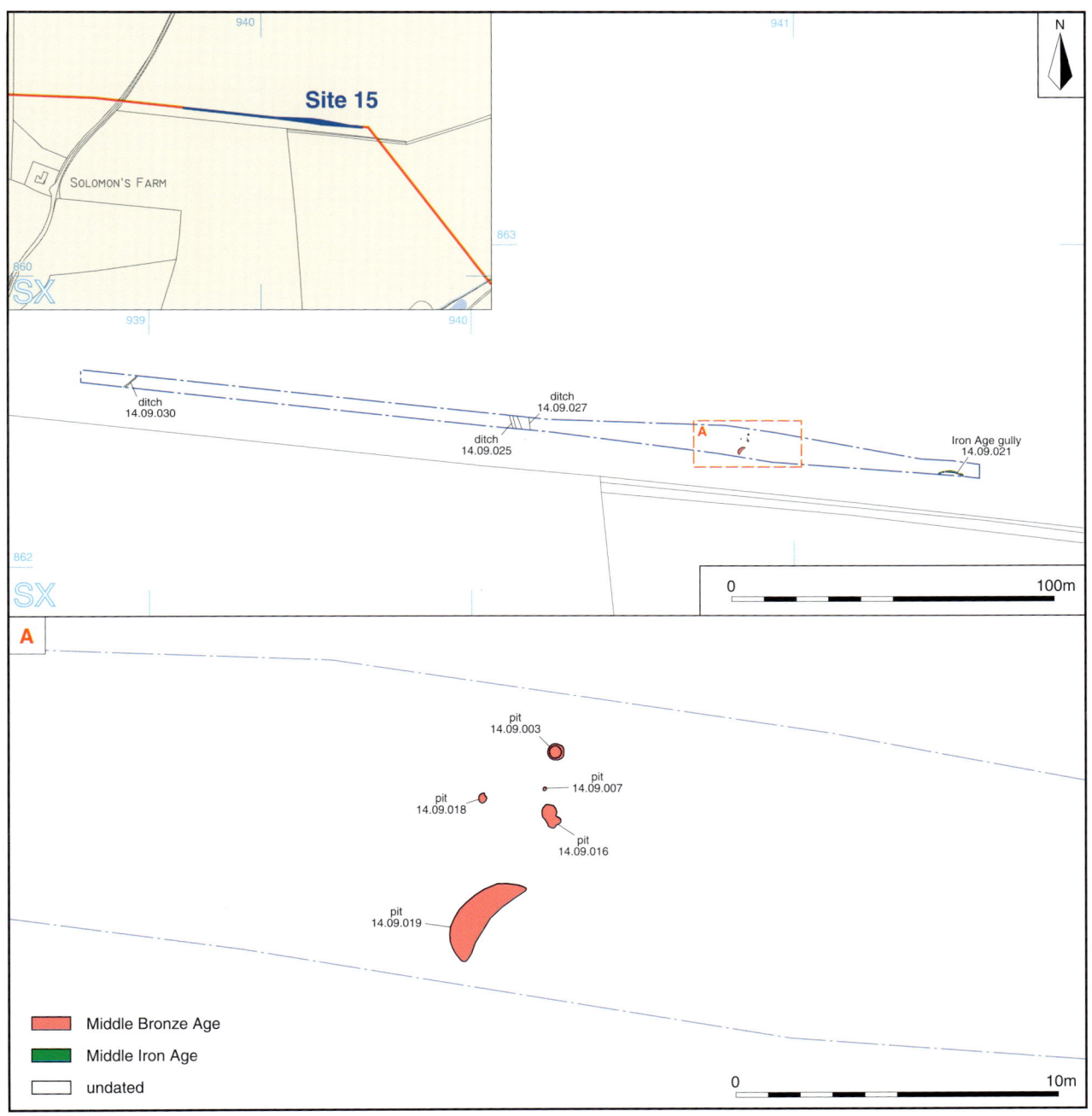

Fig. 2.21 Crablake Farm (Site 15); plan of excavated features. Scales 1:200, 1:2000 and 1:10,000

Fig. 2.22 Crablake Farm (Site 15); the Trevisker pot in situ in pit 14.09.003, looking south-east. Scale 0.5m

be cremation pits but soil samples yielded no cremated bone and only small quantities of charcoal, so the function of the pits is not clear.

Pit 14.09.018 was 0.23m in diameter and 60mm deep. The single fill, 14.09.020, contained five joining sherds of Early to Middle Bronze Age Trevisker-style pottery in Exeter volcanic fabric with cord-impressed decoration. A radiocarbon date from oak heartwood produced a date of 2027–1910 cal. BC (NZA-36377), but this only provides a *terminus post quem* as there is undoubtedly an old-wood offset which could amount to several hundred years (Table 2.7).

Pit 14.09.003 was 0.51m wide and 0.24m deep. The fill (14.09.005/14.09.006) contained about one eighth of a Trevisker vessel (14.09.004), which was lifted in a block (Figs 2.22, 2.38). The vessel is very similar in form to the Trevisker style pottery from pit 14.09.018. Gorse/broom charcoal from this pit (sample 207) returned a radiocarbon date of 367–201 cal. BC (NZA-32777) (Table 2.7). This is a relatively late date and it is probable that the charcoal was intrusive within this feature. The Trevisker pot did not include a base or rim so it was never a complete *in situ* vessel. It did, however, fill most of the pit and it seems that the pit was dug to receive it.

South of pit 14.09.003 was pit 14.09.016, which was 0.7m in length, 0.4m wide and 30mm deep. It was excavated in quadrants (numbered separately), the single fill containing 14 bodysherds of Middle Bronze Age pottery in Exeter volcanic fabric, one piece of worked flint and small quantities of charcoal and charred cereal grains. A sample of hazel charcoal from soil sample

Table 2.7: Radiocarbon dates from Crablake Farm, Site 15 (ATK 14.09)

Feature	Context	Lab No.	Material	δ ^{13}C	Radiocarbon Age	Calibrated Age 95%	Calibrated Age 68%
Pit 14.09.003	14.09.006	NZA 32777	Gorse/broom charcoal (*Ulex spp/Cytisus spp*)	-24.2‰	2212 ± 25 yr BP	367–201 BC (94.9%)	357–346 BC (7.4%) plus 315–275 BC (26.3%) plus 257–206 BC (34.0%)
Pit 14.09.016	14.09.009	NZA 32772	Hazel charcoal (*Corylus avellana*)	-25.9‰	3295 ± 25 yr BP	1627–1504 BC (95.0%)	1607–1567 BC (38.2%) plus 1561–1529 BC (30.3%)
Pit 14.09.016	14.09.011	NZA 36376	Barley grain (*Hordeum vulgare*)	-23.5‰	3207 ± 20 yr BP	1510–1431 BC (95.3%)	1495–1451 BC (67.9%)
Pit 14.09.018	14.09.020	NZA 36377	Oak charcoal (heartwood) (*Quercus robur/petraea*)	-26.1‰	3611 ± 20 yr BP	2027–1910 BC (95.0%)	2015–1994 BC (21.4%) plus 1979–1938 BC (45.9%)
Ring-ditch 14.09.021	14.09.023	NZA 36268	Barley grain (*Hordeum vulgare*)	-21.4‰	2102 ± 15 yr BP	176–53 BC (94.9%)	166–99 BC (68.0%)
Ring-ditch 14.09.021	14.09.023	NZA 36378	Barley grain (*Hordeum vulgare*)	-22.4‰	2140 ± 20 yr BP	347–313 BC (13.5%) plus 206–95 BC (81.5%)	336–329 BC (4.0%) plus 202–160 BC (54.3%) plus 130–117 BC (9.2%)

203 (deposit 14.09.009) returned a radiocarbon date of 1627–1504 cal. BC (NZA-32772); a second sample (205) produced a date of 1510–1431 cal. BC (NZA-36376). These dates are not statistically similar but are in the expected range as indicated by the pottery (Table 2.7).

To the south of this was elongated pit 14.09.019, which was 2.83m long, 0.98m wide and 0.15m deep. The single fill of yellow-brown silty sand, 14.09.013, contained a rim sherd of Trevisker-type Middle Bronze Age pottery (Fig. 2.40, no. 8). To the north of pit 14.09.016 was the severely truncated base of pit 14.09.007, which contained a bronze object, possibly a fragment of a pin shaft in poor condition (Fig. 2.50).

Other sites

In addition to the sites described above, a moderately abraded base angle in Exeter volcanic fabric of Trevisker character was recovered from subsoil at Hogsbrook Farm (Site 10) on the eastern side of the Exe (Fig. 1.3). In plot ATK 12.13 on the western side (Fig. 1.4), two abraded bodysherds in rock, vein quartz and grog fabric were recovered from topsoil. The thickness and general finish of the sherds suggests Middle Bronze Age activity. Finds from both plots indicate Middle Bronze Age activity in the vicinity about which little more can be said.

South Devon

Site 21: Hood Ball, Rattery

The site lies at approximately 29m AOD, on gently sloping land at the base of the south-east facing slope of Hood Ball, a dominant local hill. Two areas to the west of the pipeline were stripped of overburden in preparation for use as storage areas (Fig. 2.23). Seven pits were identified. These were similar in form, between 0.3m and 0.6m wide and between 0.12m and 0.38m deep, with single, dark, charcoal-rich fills (Fig. 2.24). Soil samples from five of the pits contained burnt material consisting of a small quantity of cereal grains, a fragment of sloe or plum stone, a hazelnut shell fragment and mixed wood charcoal (Tables 2.24, 2.25 and 2.26). The lack of any cremated bone and the palaeobotanical evidence for food preparation suggests that these features represent the remains of domestic occupation, although none of the pits seem appropriate either as structural elements or as facilities for storage. Radiocarbon dates from three pits were broadly consistent, placing this pit group firmly within the Middle Bronze Age (Table 2.8).

The wider context of these pits remains to be examined. Rectangular enclosures and linear cropmarks lie to the west of the site and, while these are as yet undated, a Roman date appears more likely than a Bronze Age

Table 2.8: Radiocarbon dates from Hood Ball, Site 21 (FTC 12.05)

Feature	Context	Lab No.	Material	δ ^{13}C	Radiocarbon Age	Calibrated Age 95%	Calibrated Age 68%
Pit 12.05.004	12.05.005	NZA 36510	Hazelnut shell (*Corylus avellana*)	-25.2‰	3097 ± 55 yr BP	1493–1214 BC (95.0%)	1428–1306 BC (68.3%)
Pit 12.05.004	12.05.007	NZA 36260	Hazel charcoal (*Corylus avellana*)	-22.7‰	3021 ± 20 yr BP	1379–1334 BC (20.3%) plus 1321–1211 BC (74.7%)	1367–1356 BC (7.0%) plus 1313–1258 BC (55.3%) plus 1227–1219 BC (4.9%)
Pit 12.05.004	12.05.007	NZA 36261	Hawthorn/rowan/ crab apple charcoal (*Crateagus monogyna/ Sorbus spp/Malus sylvestris*)	-26.6‰	3099 ± 20 yr BP	1425–1366 BC (64.1%) plus 1359–1313 BC (31.0%)	1412–1378 BC (51.2%) plus 1334–1320 BC (16.5%)
Pit 12.05.009	12.05.015	NZA 36174	Barley grain (*Hordeum vulgare*)	-24.9‰	2985 ± 30 yr BP	1368–1348 BC (2.4%) plus 1314–1121 BC (92.7%)	1288–1279 BC (4.0%) plus 1268–1190 BC (50.6%) plus 1175–1159 BC (7.3%) plus 1142–1130 BC (6.5%)
Pit 12.05.011	12.05.12	NZA 36173	Rye grain (*Secale cereale*)	-22.1‰	2998 ± 30 yr BP	1371–1341 BC (6.7%) plus 1316–1127 BC (88.4%)	1306–1194 BC (65.4%) plus 1138–1133 BC (2.3%)

Fig. 2.23 Hood Ball (Site 21); plan of geophysical anomalies, cropmarks and excavated features. Scales 1:200, 1:2000 and 1:10,000

Fig. 2.24 Hood Ball (Site 21); pit 12.05.009, looking north-west. Scale 0.2m

one (Fig. 2.23, inset). Less distinct cropmarks on the western edge of the current plot are less easy to evaluate, but appear to include at least one enclosure (DCC: DAP FE.10; DAP VL.05). Geophysical survey of the pipeline route seems to show the corner of a further rectilinear enclosure lying partially within the easement and extending eastwards (Fig. 2.23). This was investigated by a trial trench, but no features were identified, which is puzzling given the clear magnetic signal.

Site 23: Hood Quarry, Dartington

Geophysical survey confirmed the location of a large east/west linear feature, which had been identified from cropmarks, running in a straight line for over 450m (Figs. 2.25, 2.26). The feature was located just off the crest of the hill, on a north-facing slope at approximately 100m AOD. The underlying geology of Devonian Slate was seen to comprise a clayey mudstone.

A trial trench confirmed the presence of a substantial

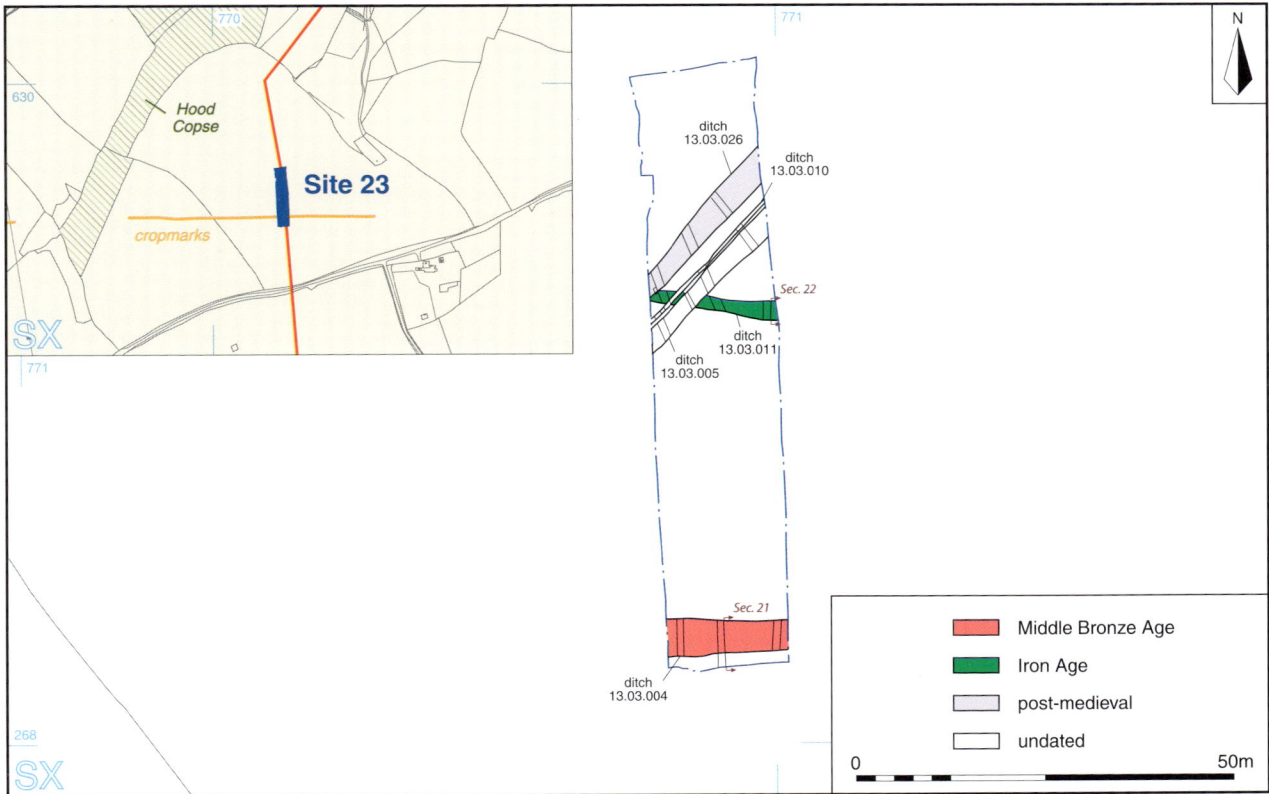

Fig. 2.25 Hood Quarry (Site 23); plan of cropmarks and excavated features. Scales 1:1000 and 1:10,000

Fig. 2.26 Hood Quarry (Site 23); aerial photograph showing cropmarks and location of excavation. Ditch 13.03.004 runs from the southern end of the trench through and beyond Hood Copse (Devon County Council Ref. DAP BS.10A)

ditch, the fill of which contained one sherd of granitic pottery of probable Iron Age date and two pieces of worked flint. The feature was not fully excavated at that stage. Subsequent excavation revealed a large east/west-orientated ditch, 13.03.004, corresponding to the features seen through aerial photography and geophysical survey. Three complete sections were excavated through it which showed similar profiles and deposits. The ditch was 5m wide and 1.85m deep with a shallow, slightly asymmetrical, profile that probably reflects the natural slope of the ground. The primary fill (Fig. 2.27, section 21, 13.03.051) was derived from initial silting, probably soon after construction. It yielded very little and three soil samples contained only traces of charcoal. A secondary phase of silting (13.03.052) was similarly without finds and probably represents a longer period of natural silting within the open ditch. This was overlain by a stony deposit (13.03.053) largely confined to the southern side. This probably relates to an episode of bank collapse, which, in view of the sharp change in the nature of the fill, may have been a deliberate attempt to level the ditch and may indicate the initial disuse phase of the feature. Orange-brown gravelly clay deposit 13.03.054, derived from natural silting, would represent infilling following abandonment. The uppermost fill, occupying a wide, eroded depression in the top of the ditch, derived from natural accumulation over the long term (Fig. 2.28).

A radiocarbon measurement on hawthorn/rowan/crab apple charcoal from the primary fill of the ditch (13.03.045, n.i.) produced a date of 3766–3652 cal. BC (NZA-36532). This date in the Early Neolithic is considered unlikely to reflect the date of the deposit and the charcoal is likely to have been redeposited. Ash charcoal from primary fill 13.03.051 returned a radiocarbon date of 1433-1315 cal. BC (NZA-36528), putting it in the Middle Bronze Age (Table 2.9). While the carbon sample does not have the integrity one would wish, at face value this appears to be the likely date of the feature.

The geophysical survey also indicated the presence of another ditch about 40m downhill to the north. Three sections showed that this east/west-orientated ditch, 13.03.011, measured 2.36m wide and 1.25m

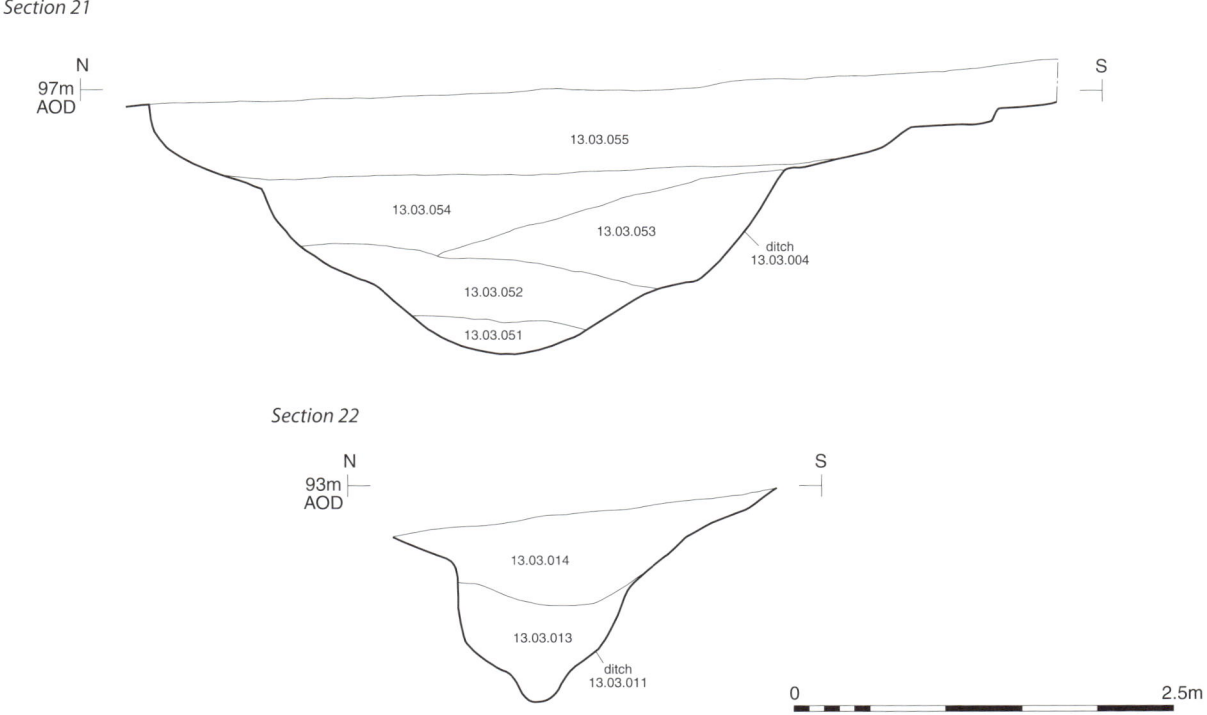

Fig. 2.27 Hood Quarry (Site 23); sections 21 and 22. Scale 1:50

Fig. 2.28 Hood Quarry (Site 23); ditch 13.03.004, looking east. Scale 1m

deep (Fig. 2.27, section 22). It has a steep-sided lower profile which included a slot in the base and a much shallower upper profile. The lower fill (13.03.013), consisting of clay-silt with schist fragments, occupied the body of the ditch, the lack of erosion on the sides suggesting that it had filled in rapidly. There were no finds and three soil samples yielded little except some modern material which was probably intrusive from the recent field boundary ditches here. The secondary fill (13.03.014) occupied the upper weathering cone and probably accumulated gradually after the largely infilled ditch had attained stability. It contained a single tiny sherd of Black-Burnished Ware pottery of a broad Roman date, but this may well have post-dated the ditch's construction. Radiocarbon dates obtained from hawthorn charcoal and a vetch seed, recovered from sample 3 (deposit 10.09), the sole deposit identified during the evaluation phase, returned dates in the ranges 1406–1269 cal. BC (NZA-36526) and 387–208 cal. BC (NZA-36527) respectively. The dates are incompatible and the first sample is likely to have been redeposited from earlier occupation here.

While there was an initial preconception that ditches 13.03.004 and 13.03.011 formed two sides of an enclosure, a consideration of their form and dating against the wider picture provided by the cropmarks suggests that they are not directly related. The ditches are on slightly different alignments and cropmarks show that there are partial patterns of enclosures to the north and west with which ditch 13.03.011 is more likely to be associated (Fig. 2.26). On grounds of morphology and density these are more likely to be Iron Age or Roman than any earlier. In contrast, ditch 13.03.004 is a singular feature apparently having no association with the other cropmarks.

Subsequent inspection of vertical aerial photographs

Fig. 2.29 Hood Quarry (Site 23); aerial photograph showing cropmarks (NMR ref. RAF/3G/TUD/UK/223)

Table 2.9: Radiocarbon dates from Hood Quarry, Site 23 (FTC 13.03)

Feature	Context	Lab No.	Material	δ¹³C	Radiocarbon Age	Calibrated Age 95%	Calibrated Age 68%
Ditch 13.03.004	13.03.045	NZA 36532	Hawthorn/rowan/ crab apple charcoal (*Crateagus monogyna/ Sorbus* spp/*Malus sylvestris*)	-27‰	4933 ± 25 yr BP	3766–3652 BC (95.1 %)	3746–3743 BC (2.2%) plus 3711–3656 BC (65.1%)
Ditch 13.03.004	13.03.051	NZA 36528	Ash charcoal (*Fraxinus excelsior*)	-25‰	3114 ± 20 yr BP	1433–1370 BC (80.2%) plus 1342–1315 BC (14.7%)	1425–1384 BC (69.4%) plus 1325–1324 BC (0.9%)
Ditch 13.03.009	10.09	NZA 36526	Hawthorn pip (*Crateagus monogyna*)	-26.3‰	3067 ± 20 yr BP	1406–1290 BC (93.1%) plus 1277–1269 BC (1.9%)	1388–1366 BC (22.2%) plus 1359–1312 BC (46.5%)
Ditch 13.03.009	10.09	NZA 36527	cf Vetch (*Vicia* spp)	-26‰	2246 ± 20 yr BP	387–349 BC (32.3%) plus 302–208 BC (62.7%)	380–355 BC (26.0%) plus 283–253 BC (28.7%) plus 248–232 BC (13.7%)

appears to show ditch 13.03.004 turning to the south-west and then again to the south (Fig. 2.29; NMR library ref. 430). While the ditch can be traced no further at present, the evidence suggests that there is a very large linear boundary here. There was no evidence of the ditch in the pipeline easement further south, but if it had continued round to the south, perhaps now under modern hedgerows, it may have originally enclosed the top of the hill, which at up to 1km long and 0.5km wide would represent an enclosed area of about 50 hectares.

Site 30: Beneknowle, Diptford
The site lies on the hillside above the River Avon, east of Beneknowle and about 1km south-east of Avonwick (Fig. 2.30). Stripping of the 5m-wide easement revealed three features: a pit, later recognised as a terraced structure, 21.06.008, a nearby ditch 21.06.004 and, further down slope to the south-west, another ditch 21.06.006. The terraced structure occupied gently sloping ground at the north-western end of the site at approximately 123m AOD. It comprised a partly revealed subrectangular pit, with a shallow ramp protruding on the south-east side (Fig. 2.32). Its north-west/south-east dimension remains unknown but its revealed width was 4.5m and it reached a maximum depth of 0.7m on its eastern side where it had been cut most deeply so as to achieve a level floor.

The terraced area was quite sharply defined with vertical edges and a more or less traceable peripheral gully which seems to have been an original feature (Fig. 2.31). Also original to the feature was a probable posthole, 21.06.014, which contained around its sides several edge-set slate stones, almost certainly *in situ* post-packing. There were edge-set stones elsewhere within the peripheral gully as well as loose stones higher up in the fills, suggesting that the pit had been stone-lined. The post appears to have been deliberately removed and backfilled with clean soil 21.06.016. A similar clean deposit, 21.06.009, infilled the edges of the pit. A charcoal-rich, firm deposit, 21.06.010, covered the floor surface and sealed all previous deposits and the floor of the pit. While it is possible that this was an occupation deposit, its uniform nature and extent up the sides of the pit suggests that it represents an event relating to the final phase of the building, such as the burning of the structure or material within it. Later deposits 21.06.011 and 21.06.012 on the eastern side of the pit comprised mid-brown clay-silts with frequent shale fragments, while the main fill of the pit 21.06.013 was a dark orange-brown clay silt. The uniform, unsorted nature of this fill suggests it may well have been a deliberate backfill of the abandoned structure.

An overall interpretation of the structure is that it occupied a cut terrace that was originally stone-lined, presumably to retain the material into which it had been cut. This lining included packing around a door-post on the south-western side of the entrance, and there was presumably also a similar arrangement for the north-eastern door-post, although the 'gully' and stone here was not readily interpreted as a post-setting. Interestingly, there seems also to have been a stone lining forming the threshold between the access ramp and the building. While the door-posts were probably wooden, there is no indication of how the rest of the superstructure was constructed. The fact that the stone lining was not generally preserved suggests that the

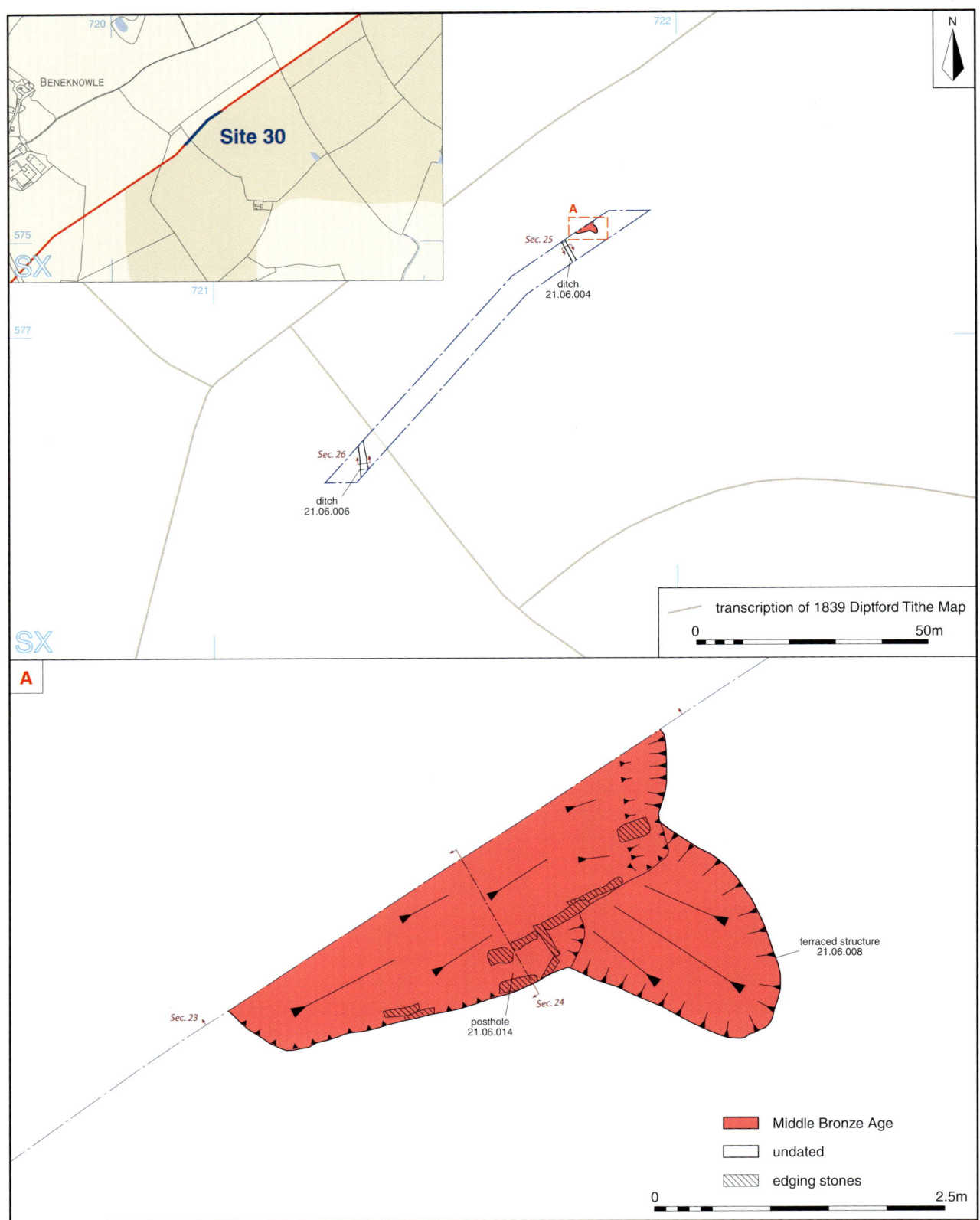

Fig. 2.30 Beneknowle (Site 30); plan showing excavated features. Scales 1:50, 1:1250 and 1:10,000

structure was dismantled after use and most of the stones removed. The subsequent filling is therefore likely to relate to an abandonment phase. The charcoal-rich layer 21.06.010 overlay the floor in the central area and must have been deposited shortly after the structure fell into disuse (Fig. 2.31, sections 23, 24). The analysis of this material showed that it included a vast range of crops and wild plant species, with fat hen/goosefoot, cleavers,

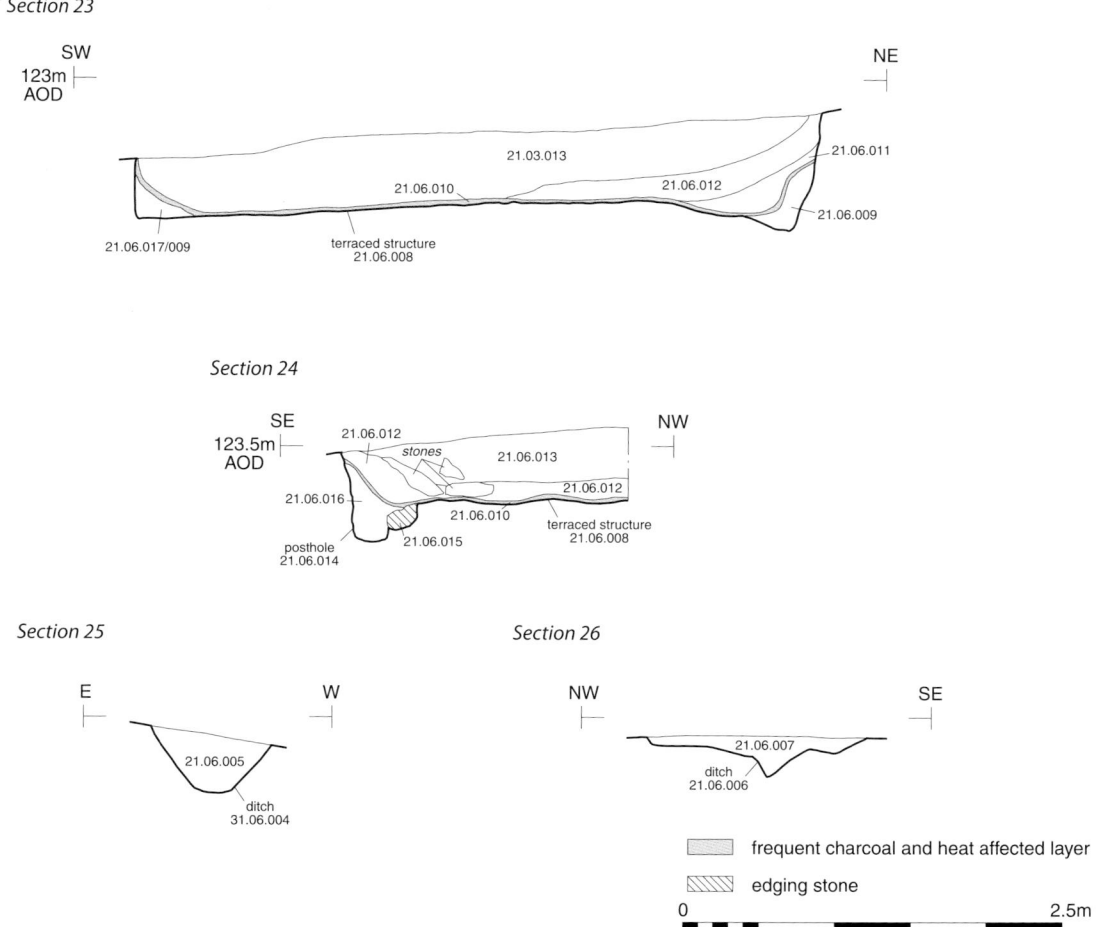

Fig. 2.31 Beneknowle (Site 30); sections 23 to 26. Scale 1:50

Fig. 2.32 Beneknowle (Site 30); terraced structure 21.06.008, looking west. Scale 1m

Table 2.10: Radiocarbon dates from Beneknowle, Site 30 (FTC 21.06)

Feature	Context	Lab No.	Material	$\delta^{13}C$	Radiocarbon Age	Calibrated Age 95%	Calibrated Age 68%
SFB 21.06.008	21.06.010	SUERC-35996 GU-24835	Vetch seeds (*Vicia* spp)	-24.1‰	3010 ± 30 yr BP	1390–1120 BC (95.4%)	1370–1350 BC (7.1%) plus 1320–1210 BC (61.1%)
SFB 21.06.008	21.06.010	NZA 32775	Barley grain (*Hordeum vulgare*)	-25.3‰	3021 ± 25 yr BP	1385–1194 BC (94.8%)	1369–1346 BC (13.2%) plus 1314–1257 BC (48.8%) plus 1229–1218 BC (6.5%)
SFB 21.06.008	21.06.010	NZA 36308	Hazelnut shell (*Corylus avellana*)	-25.5‰	4200 ± 25 yr BP	3342–3097 BC (95.0%)	3334–3308 BC (11.7%) plus 3296–3282 BC (5.9%) plus 3274–3263 BC (5.0%) plus 3238–3209 BC (13.7%) plus 3190–3151 BC (17.5%) plus 3135–3104 BC (13.7%)

vetch, ribwort plantain and black bindweed particularly common. Oats and barley were among the cereal, while blackberry and raspberry are also likely to have been food items. The wood charcoal was also diverse, with oak the most common (Tables 2.24, 2.25, Sample 313). It is possible that the carbonised remains represent material stored in the building during a conflagration, and also may include burnt debris from the building itself. The well-defined, undisturbed nature of this burnt layer, and the lack of erosion to the pit edges, suggests that the pit was backfilled fairly shortly afterwards.

There were no artefacts from any of the fills. A radiocarbon measurement on a charred barley grain yielded a date of 1385–1194 cal. BC (NZA-32775). A second measurement on a charred hazelnut shell yielded a date of 3342–3097 cal. BC (NZA-36308). A third on vetch seeds returned a date of 1390–1120 cal. BC (SUERC-35996), which is virtually identical to the first date and strongly suggests that the building dates to the Middle Bronze Age (Table 2.10).

Ditch 21.06.004 was 0.8m wide and 0.4m deep with moderately steep sides. It was without finds. It was 3m south-west of the Middle Bronze Age structure but this location may be coincidental. It is on a similar alignment to the current field boundary to the west, and may be a former subdivision of this field. Ditch 21.06.006, was relatively broad and shallow (0.3m) with an irregular base. It may be a furrow or drain although it ran obliquely to the field boundary to the north and may pre-date it. The irregular, curving pattern of fields in this area, partly preserved in the modern landscape, suggests that the layout may have been conditioned by pre-medieval land arrangements (Fig. 2.30).

Site 34: Filham House, Ugborough (FTC 33.01)

The site comprised a single pit located at *c.* 66m AOD on flat land between Lud Brook to the east and the valley of the River Erme to the west (location on Figs 1.7 and 3.29). Pit 33.01.006 was 0.77m long, 0.65m wide and 0.16m deep. The fills, 33.01.007 and 33.01.008, contained frequent wood charcoal mostly identified as oak and hazel, but were dominated by charred hazelnut shells (Table 2.25, samples 316 and 317) and 34 pieces of worked flint, suggestive of an earlier prehistoric date. The sharp condition of the flint and common presence of small debitage suggests a stratified assemblage. A single long flake contained a small area of abrupt retouch, which with other pieces shows signs of utilisation as cutting pieces. Most pieces are flakes struck with a hard hammer, characteristics consistent with the Late Neolithic or Bronze Age. Paired samples of a sloe stone and a barley grain produced radiocarbon dates in the ranges 1379–1208 cal. BC (NZA-36307) and 1404–1215 cal. BC (NZA-36172) respectively, dating activity to the Middle Bronze Age (Table 2.11).

Table 2.11: Radiocarbon dates from Filham House, Site 34 (FTC 33.01)

Feature	Context	Lab No.	Material	δ ^{13}C	Radiocarbon Age	Calibrated Age 95%	Calibrated Age 68%
Pit 33.01.006	33.01.007	NZA 36307	Blackthorn pip (*Prunus spinosa*)	-25.6‰	3018 ± 20 yr BP	1379–1333 BC (17.7%) plus 1321–1208 BC (77.4%)	1366–1359 BC (4.1%) plus 1313–1257 BC (55.4%) plus 1230–1217 BC (8.6%)
Pit 33.01.006	33.01.007	NZA 36172	Barley grain (*Hordeum vulgare*)	-26.2‰	3045 ± 30 yr BP	1404–1255 BC (90.8%) plus 1233–1215 (3.9%)	1378–1334 BC (33.5%) plus 1321–1286 BC (25.5%) plus 1282–1267 BC (9.5%)

Neolithic and Bronze Age pottery

Henrietta Quinnell, with petrographic comment by Roger T. Taylor

Material is described in accordance with the conventions recommended by the Prehistoric Ceramics Research Group (2010). Terms for abrasion follow a slightly adapted version of Sorenson (1996). Colour definitions follow Munsell (1975).

Very fresh	Sorenson Grade 1, hardly ever applicable
Fresh	Colour of core slightly patinated but unaltered surfaces with sharp corners and edges
Moderate abrasion	Core colour patinated, some definition in the sharpness of corners lost
Abraded	Core colour patinated, slight rounding of corners and slight erosion of surfaces
High abrasion	Colour patinated, rounding of corners and of sherd outline, surfaces somewhat eroded

The fabrics are described at the beginning of each period section below. Petrological comment has been provided from microscopy of selected samples. Nine thin-sections were prepared and TS numbers are indicated for fabrics where relevant. P-numbers refer to individual sherds and sherd groups, some of which are illustrated.

Early Neolithic
Fabrics

GN.1 Granite-derived fabric, moderate coarse inclusions, some up to 2mm, of quartz, altered feldspar, biotite, slate fragments and rock, possibly hornfels. Source somewhere just off the Dartmoor Granite.

GN.2 Granite-derived fabric, moderate coarse inclusions of quartz, altered white feldspar, biotite and sparse slate fragments. Source somewhere just off the granite. (TS 7).

PB.1 Permian Breccia fabric, sparse medium inclusions, quartz, some fresh feldspar with cleavage planes, flake of muscovite mica *c.* 2mm; also isolated grain of polished quartz. The polished quartz indicates an estuarine source, most probably the Exe Valley with remote input from Permian breccias.

CH.1 Upper Greensand-derived fabric. Sparse very coarse angular white chert inclusions in a matrix with abundant ferruginous pellets, occasional polished and unpolished quartz grains: the chert, polished quartz and matrix all derive from the Upper Greensand.

CH.2 Upper Greensand-derived fabric. Sparse coarse inclusions of chert, both white and brown, and well-rounded quartz including polished grains.

IV.1 Plain clay with rounded voids of uncertain origin: fabrics of this type have been associated with limestone temper which has dissolved out.

VQ.1 Sparse coarse vein quartz added to a granite-derived fabric containing altered feldspar, biotite and quartz. Both vein quartz and matrix clay fabric local to Croft Cottages and the area just off the Darmoor Granite.

East Devon

Site 4: Pixies' Parlour pits (Table 2.12)

Feature 3.04.096

The feature (including intrusive pit 3.04.097) contained 57 sherds, 229g, in six fabrics, moderately abraded, many with noticeable inclusions of chert (Fabric CH.1), and including parts of rims of two carinated bowls P1 and P2.

P1 (not illus.) primary fill 206.015. Rim sherd from carinated bowl. Fabric GN.1 reduced (5YR4/1) dark grey, slightly everted, with burnish on interior. See Laidlaw 1999, fig. 79 nos 1, 3 from Long Range, West Hill.

P2 (not illus.) primary fill 206.015. Rim sherd from carinated bowl. Fabric PB.1 reduced (5YR4/1) dark grey, slightly everted, with burnish on interior.

Comment

Both the fabrics and the carinated bowl sherds are characteristic of the Early Neolithic in Devon (Fig. 2.33). The noticeable white inclusions, of chert in fabrics CH.1 and CH.2, and of vein quartz in VQ.1, are very much an Early Neolithic feature. The recent publication of an Early Neolithic pit assemblage from Wayland's, Tiverton,

Table 2.12: Early Neolithic ceramics: sherd numbers with weight in grammes

Context No.	Feature	Sherds	Wt	Ref.	Fabric
Pixies' Parlour, Site 4, Pit 3.04.096/097					
206.015	Primary fill, pit 3.04.096	1	4	P1	GN.1 granite-derived
		3	12	P2	PB.1 Permian breccia-derived
		20	102	-	CH.1 Upper Greensand with chert
		10	33	-	IV.1 fabric with voids
		5	14	-	GN.2 granite derived
		6	22	-	CH.2 Upper Greensand with chert
3.04.089	Upper fill, pit 3.04.096	1	9	-	PB.1 Permian breccia-derived
		2	3	-	CH.1 Upper Greensand with chert
		5	23	-	CH.2 Upper Greensand with chert
3.04.093	Fill, pit 3.04.097	6	7	-	CH.1 Upper Greensand with chert
Total		**57**	**229**		
Livermore Farm, Plot OTA 9.02.012					
9.02.012	Surface find from ditch 9.02.011	1	2	-	CH.1 Upper Greensand with chert
Croft Cottages, Site 20, ditch					
8.02.005	Fill, ditch terminal 8.02.004	6	13	P3	VQ.1 vein quartz in granite-derived matrix

Fig. 2.33 Pixies' Parlour (Site 4); Early Neolithic pottery. Top row: bodysherds showing white inclusions of vein quartz added to granite-derived fabric (Fabric VQ1). Bottom left: bodysherd of clay with ?limestone voids (Fabric IV.1). Bottom right: rimsherd from carinated bowl in Permian breccia-derived fabric (Fabric PB.1)

discussed another four Devon sites with single, or groups of, pits containing Early Neolithic ceramics (Leverett and Quinnell 2010). The pit at Long Range contained three closely related sandy fabrics (Laidlaw 1999) but no other Devon pit has such a wide range of fabrics as Pixies' Parlour. It is probable that Fabrics CH.1, CH.2 and IV.1 at Pixies' Parlour were sourced fairly locally but the granite-derived Fabrics GN.1 and GN.2 probably came from the vicinity of Dartmoor and the breccia-derived fabric PB.1 from the Exeter area. Feature 3.04.096 contained an assemblage of Early Neolithic flintwork. The presence of fabrics deriving from the Exmoor area in the Wayland's, Tiverton, pit indicates the occasional sourcing of pottery from some distance (Leverett and Quinnell 2010) as does the well-known occurrence of Lizard gabbroic pottery on Devon Early Neolithic sites.

Carinated bowls are generally considered to be among the earliest forms of Neolithic pottery to occur in Britain (Sheridan *et al.* 2008, 18) but occur frequently on causewayed and tor enclosure sites dating for several centuries from *c.* 3700 cal. BC (Whittle *et al.* 2011, Chapter 10). The assemblage from Carn Brea in Cornwall provides the best published range of comparanda from Cornwall or Devon (Smith 1981, figs 67–8). Radiocarbon determination NZA-36306 from pit 3.04.097, calibrating to AD 1523–1664, was of no assistance in determining Neolithic chronology (Table 2.1) and this appears to have been an intrusive pit (see Chapter 4). The elongated shape of the feature is most unusual for Neolithic pits (Leverett and Quinnell 2010).

Plot OT/A 9.02: surface find (Table 2.12)

A surface find from field boundary ditch 9.02.011 (context 9.02.012) is a small moderately abraded sherd of Early Neolithic fabric similar to Pixies' Parlour Fabric CH.1.

South Devon

Site 20: Croft Cottages, Staverton (Table 2.12)

Linear feature 8.02.004

P3 (not illus.) 8.02.005 fill of a possible ditch terminal 8.02.004 with six conjoining moderately abraded sherds. The fabric VQ.1 with vein quartz inclusions is typical Early Neolithic and the sherds come from neck of a carinated bowl (see Smith 1981, figs 67–8). The micaceous fabric is probably based on granite-derived clay from the Dart valley which runs within a kilometre of the site, with added crushed vein quartz from a dyke rather closer to Dartmoor.

Middle Neolithic Peterborough Ware (Table 2.13)

Fabrics

QU.1 Plain clay fabric with rare rounded quartz grains. Local clay sourced in the Ottery St Mary area.

VQ.2 Sparse mainly vein quartz, small slate fragments, and a little limonite. Components vary slightly in different sherds. Probably a stream source local to the area of Hems Valley.

East Devon

Site 2: Slade Farm, Ottery St Mary

Pit 2.03.004

From fill 2.03.005, seven sherds moderate abrasion fabric QU.1 generally reduced (5YR4/1) dark grey, with sparse, ?ferruginous inclusions. Three of these sherds (P4 not illus.) have abraded traces of close-set fingernail impressions on an oxidised exterior (5YR6/4) light reddish brown and a somewhat laminated fracture. The close-set pattern of impressions suggests the Mortlake style, within the

Table 2.13: Middle and Late Neolithic ceramics: sherd numbers with weight in grammes

Context No.	Feature	Sherds	Wt	Ref.	Fabric
Slade Farm, Site 2, pit					
2.03.005	Fill, pit 2.03.004	7	42	P4	QU.1 rare rounded quartz
Hems Valley, Site 17, pits					
2.02.005	Fill, pit 2.02.004	22	95	P5	VQ.2 sparse vein quartz, limonite and slate
2.02.008	Fill, pit 2.02.006	10	12	P6	VQ.2
2.02.011	Fill, pit 2.02.010	12	65	P7	VQ.2
		5	17	P8	VQ.2
Total		**49**	**189**		
Moore Farm, Site 28, pits and ditch					
18.12.019	Primary fill, pit 18.12.018	8	59	P9	VQ.3 vein quartz added to micaceous clay
18.12.020	Secondary fill, pit 18.12.018	5	21	P10	QU.2 sparse quartz
		2	8	-	GR.1 grog in local clay
		20	27	P9 part	VQ.3
		6	23	P12a part?	QU.3 sparse quartz, slate, feldspar
		17	43	P12b	QU.3
18.12.021	Upper fill, pit 18.12.018	9	15	P9 part	VQ.3
		1	20	P11	QU.3
		4	16	P10 part?	QU.2
		6	39	P12a	QU.3
18.12.033	Fill, pit 18.12.032	46	500	P13	GA.1 Gabbroic
18.12.054	Fill, pit 18.12.053	3	3	-	QU.3
18.12.055	Fill, ditch 18.12.049	44	560	P14, P15	VQ.3
Total		**171**	**1334**		

Middle Neolithic Peterborough tradition. The other sherds are not oxidised, are rather harder and have a more even fracture. In view of the three radiocarbon determinations from this pit (NZA-36305 calibrating to 388–208 BC, NZA-36320 calibrating to 388–212 BC and NZA-36304, calibrating to 392–212 BC) it seems probable that the pit and the sherds with the more even fracture belong in the Iron Age, with P4 being redeposited.

Comment
Peterborough ceramics are rare in Devon and generally occur as single finds or in small assemblages. The Mortlake sherd from the foreshore at Westward Ho! has similar fingernail decoration to P4 (Quinnell 2007, fig. 1). The most significant assemblage, some 146 mainly Mortlake sherds, 1.36kg, comes from the ditches of an oblong enclosure at Castle Hill, Honiton (Laidlaw and Mepham 1999, fig. 23). Other East Devon material comes from Beer, from Topsham, and from an unpublished site near the Sidmouth Donkey Sanctuary (Quinnell 2008). Of all these, only the sherds from Topsham appear to come from pits.

South Devon

Site 17: Hems Valley, Staverton
The 49 sherds (189g), in this assemblage are all highly abraded and of small size. They are of all of fabric VQ.2 with a little variation in components and all probably from the broad area of the site.

Pit 2.02.004
P5 (not illus.) 2.02.005 fill of pit 2.02.004. Sixteen sherds fabric VQ.2 reduced (5YR4/1) dark grey, appear come from one vessel with a pointed rim (as P12b, Fig. 2.34 no.1) and finely incised zig-zag and close-spaced parallel lines: some of the parallel lines are only 1.5mm apart, the zig-zags 4mm apart. The rim has a small internal facet with small slanting parallel incisions, possibly fingernail. Also six sherds in fabric VQ.2 probably from two separate vessels with very abraded incisions.

Pit 2.02.006
P6 (not illus.) 2.02.08 fill of pit 2.02.006. Ten sherds including a small flat-topped rim; reduced (5YR4/1) dark grey, VQ.2 fabric.

Pit 2.02.010
P7 (not illus.) 2.02.011 fill of pit 2.02.010. Twelve sherds including base angle with abraded incised decoration: VQ.2 fabric generally oxidised (5YR6/4) light reddish brown.

P8 (not illus.) 2.02.011 fill of pit 2.02.010. Five sherds with pattern of very fine incised lines: VQ.2 fabric, oxidised exterior (5YR6/4) reddish brown, interior reduced (5YR5/1) grey.

Comment
The form of the two rims present, P5 and P6, and the style of the decoration are consistent with Grooved Ware (Longworth 1971) and so provided a Grooved Ware attribution of the pottery on assessment. Pit 2.02.004 has radiocarbon determination NZA-36262 calibrating to 3120–3018 BC (57.9%). Pit 2.02.006 has determination NZA-36263 calibrating to 3108–3006 BC (76.4%). Pit 2.02.010 has NZA-36264, calibrating to 3327–3024 BC, and NZA-32773, calibrating to 3339–3095 BC (both 95% probability). These dates form a tight group in the late fourth millennium BC, rather earlier than dates on Grooved Ware elsewhere which suggest 3000/2900 cal. BC as a likely start for the ceramic style (Cleal 1999, 7). The dates are far more appropriate for Peterborough Ware. It should be noted that the abraded state of the sherds suggests that they had been around for a while before deposition in the pits, and are, if anything, earlier than the date range indicated. Both pits 2.02.006 and 2.02.010 produced a little flintwork.

The pottery from the Hems Valley pits is likely to have Peterborough Ware affinities, with the presence of a basal angle suggesting that some sherds at least should belong to the Fengate sub-group. This sub-group also probably provides some stylistic analogies for the use of fine incisions on P5 (Smith 1965, fig. 34 and p.78). It is now well recognised that the various sub-groups of Peterborough Ware are broadly contemporary and not chronological (Gibson and Kinnes 1997). Some Peterborough Ware sherds from sites in Devon have been considered to have Fengate affinities, notably a rim from Broadsands Chambered Tomb in Torbay (Sheridan *et al.* 2008, fig. 4 no. 3), a rim from the oblong enclosure which produced Mortlake sherds at Castle Hill, Honiton (Laidlaw and Mepham 1999, fig. 23 no. 4), and at least one sherd from Topsham (Smith 1975). A recent national review of the radiocarbon determinations associated with the Fengate sub-group suggests that this was current between 3350 and 2900 cal. BC (Peter Marshall, quoted in Sheridan *et al.* 2008, 16), dating which suits the Hems Valley pits very well.

Late Neolithic Grooved Ware (Table 2.13)

Fabrics

VQ.3 Moderate angular vein quartz up to 6mm: some smaller quartz grains, mica and micaceous slate fragments in matrix. Probably both clay and vein quartz source from the Moore Farm area. (TS3, 6)

QU.2 Plain clay with sparse quartz probably from the Moore Farm area. (TS4)

QU.3 Clay matrix with sparse quartz, altered feldspar and rounded slate fragments, probably from a stream in the Moore Farm area. (TS5)

GR.1 Moderate coarse grog inclusions in clay matrix with some subangular quartz and mica fragments, probably from the Moore Farm area.

GA.1 Gabbroic. The components of feldspar, amphibole, quartz and magnetite are entirely typical of Lizard gabbroic clays. (TS2)

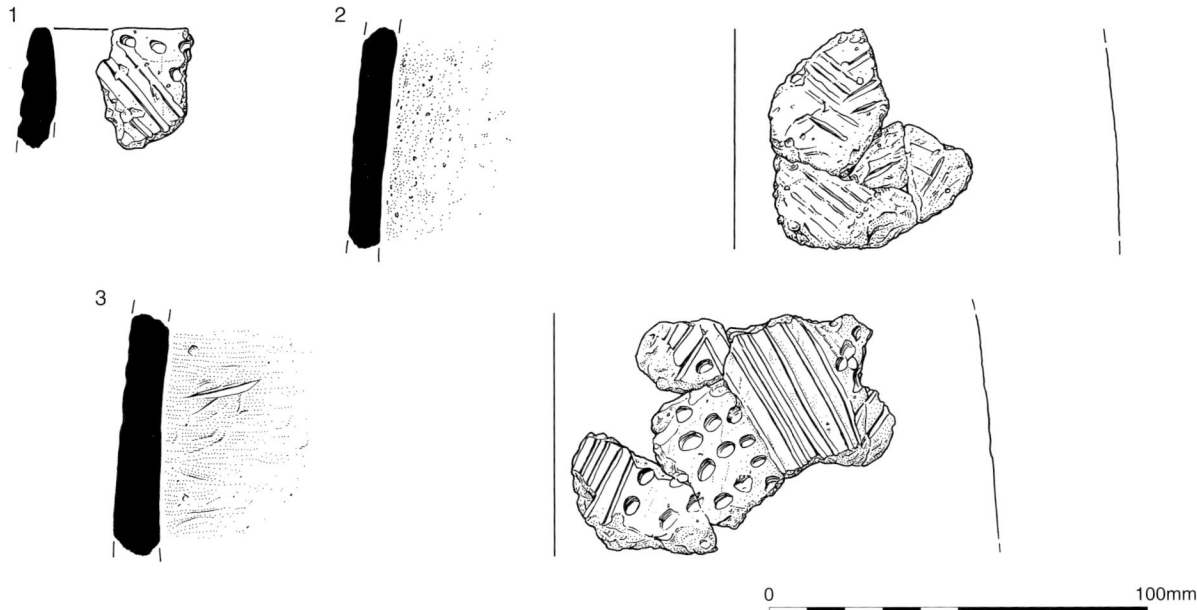

Fig. 2.34 Late Neolithic Grooved Ware from Moore Farm, Harberton (Site 28), pit 18.12.018. Scale 1:2

South Devon

Site 28: Moore Farm, Harberton, Grooved Ware pits and ?ring-ditch

Three pits and part of a possible ring-ditch produced an assemblage of 171 sherds weighing 1334 grammes. A minimum of nine vessels and five fabrics are present. Four of the fabrics are probably of local origin with some overlap between them, the fifth represents the first known instance of Lizard gabbroic fabric in a Late Neolithic context in Devon. Most of the sherds are soft and abraded. In view of the presence of a number of conjoins on abraded sherds much of the abrasion may be due to bioturbation factors.

Pit 18.12.018

P9 (not illus.) 18.12.019 primary fill. Eight abraded sherds in VQ.3 fabric. Oxidised (5YR5/8) yellowish red, with (5YR4/1) dark grey interior. Base angle and lower vessel wall sherds with decoration of very fine incised lines. Twenty small sherds from this vessel in overlying 18.12.020 and a further nine in uppermost fill 18.12.021.

P10 (Fig. 2.34 no.2) 18.12.020 middle fill. Five abraded sherds, hard QU.2 fabric reduced (5YR4/1) dark grey from girth of vessel *c.* 200mm in diameter. Chevron decoration in fine incised lines. Four sherds from P10 in overlying fill 18.12.021. Another vessel is represented in this context by two abraded sherds in a fabric with grog GR.1, oxidised (5YR6/4) light reddish yellow to reduced (6/1) light grey.

P11 (not illus) 18.12.021 upper fill. Abraded incised sherd in fabric QU.3 oxidised (5YR5/6) yellowish red, with (5YR4/1) dark grey interior.

P12a (Fig. 2.34 no.3) 18.12.021 upper fill. Six bodysherds abraded in fabric QU.3 oxidised (5YR5/6) yellowish red with some reduction in interior (5YR5/3) reddish brown. These come from the girth of large vessel *c.* 220mm in diameter, exterior decorated with a complex design of incised lines and stab-and-drag marks. Also six sherds from middle fill 18.12.20.

P12b (Fig. 2.34 no. 1) 18.12.020 middle fill. Flat-topped rim with incised lines and stab-and-drag marks below, probably from P12a. Sixteen sherds, some decorated, from upper part of vessel. Fabric as P12a but rather more reduced (5YR5/2) reddish grey.

Pit 18.12.032

P13 (not illus.) 18.12.033 fill. Forty-six sherds, abraded, of soft gabbroic fabric GA.1 with common coarse inclusions especially of feldspar. Surfaces oxidised (5YR5/3) yellowish red with reduced core (5YR4/1) dark grey. These come from lower wall and base of one vessel. One sherd less abraded that the remainder preserves remnants of stab-and-drag decoration.

Pit 18.12.053

Fill 18.12.054 contains three undecorated sherds in a fabric similar to P12a, one with part of a groove.

Ditch 18.12.049

P14 (Fig. 2.35 no. 4) 18.12.55, fill. Flat-topped rim with horizontal grooves below. Non-joining bodysherds from vessel girth show more elaborate incised decoration below. Open fabric VQ.3, slightly oxidised throughout (5YR4/3) dark reddish gray. P14 and P15 are represented by the 44 sherds of similar fabric from the ditch and were initially considered as one vessel. Some were moderately abraded but some fresh, indicating that not all the sherds present were retrieved.

P15 (Fig. 2.35 no. 5) 18.12.55, fill. Parts of the girth and base angle section of a large vessel maximum surviving diameter *c.* 280mm fabric VQ.3. This vessel is too

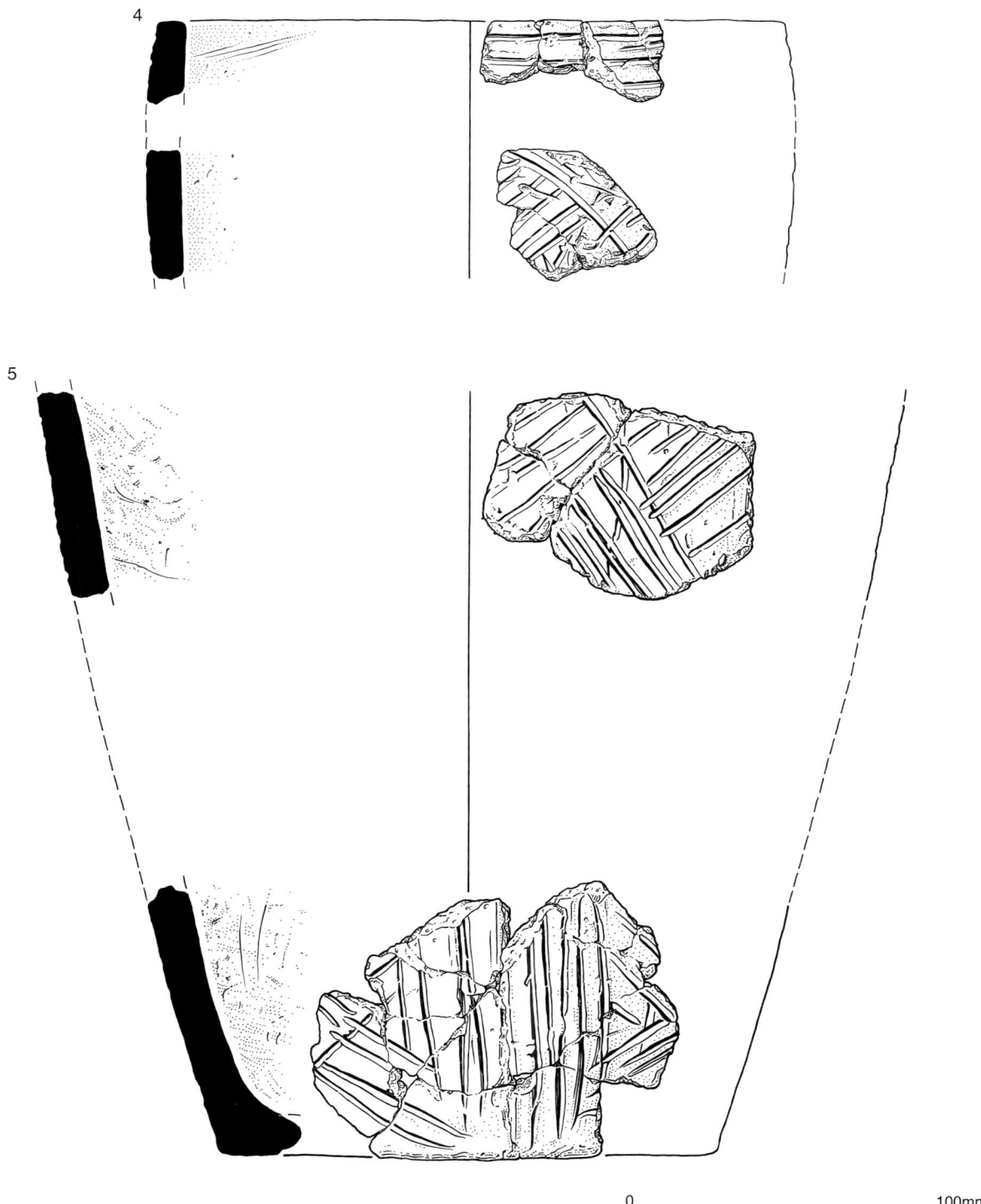

Fig. 2.35 Late Neolithic Grooved Ware from Moore Farm, Harberton (Site 28), ditch 18.12.049. Scale 1:2

large for P14 to be its rim but the decoration of the two is remarkably similar. P15 is markedly oxidised on the exterior (5YR6/6) reddish yellow, but the interior is reduced (5YR3/1) very dark grey.

Comment
The general character of this assemblage suggests that it belongs broadly in the Durrington Walls sub-group of Grooved Ware (Longworth 1971). Radiocarbon determinations NZA-36265, calibrating to 2860–2579 BC, from pit 18.12.018, and NZA-36266, calibrating to 2859–2579 BC, from pit 18.12.053, are remarkably similar and belong in the earlier part of Grooved Ware chronology, now established for southern Britain as between 2900 and 2100 cal. BC, with some doubts

about the later two centuries (Garwood 1999, 152). Date NZA-36267 from pit 18.12.043 indicates inclusion of some material of Mesolithic date and has no associated pottery.

These are the first dates for Grooved Ware from Devon to be published. Only one Devon site with Grooved Ware was included in a gazetteer published in 1999, that at Three Holes Cave, Torbryan (Rosenfeld 1964; Longworth and Cleal 1999, no. 59), although a number of other sites are now known. At least one Grooved Ware vessel has been recognised by the author among the unpublished material from Ash Hole Cavern, Torbay. The other sites are represented by pits, and thus provide closer contextual parallels to the Moore Farm site. Pits at Digby on the outskirts of Exeter have produced a small group of vessels (Quinnell, in prep.) and there were a group of three pits at Bow, Mid Devon (Brown 2003). Two pits at the Royal Naval Stores Depot at Topsham produced sherds, the group from one of these restoring to a single vessel with associated radiocarbon dates broadly similar to those from Moore Farm (Steinmetzer and Quinnell, forthcoming). A recent find, possibly residual, from features associated with a ring-ditch at Cowick Lane, Exeter, contained a sherd from a bowl with applied vertical strips. A total of seven sites with Grooved Ware sherds, four from a pit or pits, are therefore now known from Devon. They all appear to belong broadly in the Durrington Walls Grooved Ware sub-group.

Beaker/Early Bronze Age

Fabric

GN.3   Granite-derived fabric, with common quartz, biotite mica and altered feldspar. Probable local stream source, with stream sand added to matrix clay. (TS1)

South Devon

Site 31: Beaker pit by Springfield Barrow (FTC 24.03)

Pit 24.03.060

P16   (Figs 2.36, 2.37 no. 6). Fifty-two sherds weighing 178g are from the same vessel, a fine granite-derived fabric, oxidised throughout (5YR6/4) light reddish brown. The fabric could have been sourced in the Avon valley some 2km to the east. The sherds come from three contexts in pit 24.03.060: 24.03.061 primary fill 40 sherds (150g), 24.03.62 second fill 8 sherds (16g), 24.03.63 upper fill 4 sherds (12g). A single plain sherd (6g) in subsoil 24.03.002 is of the same fabric but thickness suggests a second vessel. No conjoins are present and sherds are abraded. No rim is present, although some sherds show a slight thickening from just below the rim: most of base missing; base (angle) sherds occur in two upper levels. It is likely that only some sherds from a vessel had been buried, a frequent practice in Devon (Quinnell 2003).

Comment

Decoration is of impressed cord closely set and covering the whole vessel, in the style known as All-Over-Cord or AOC. Vessels with AOC decoration frequently have a slight carination in their vessel wall and this is present here (Clarke 1970, 281). The style is found both on the continent and as possibly the earliest style in Britain (Needham 2005, passim); a likely date range runs from the 25th century BC down the remainder of the 3rd millennium BC. This is the first AOC Beaker to be found in either Devon or Cornwall, the south-west peninsula being an area where the use of Beakers appears to have been adopted comparatively late (Quinnell 2003; Jones and Quinnell 2006). Comparatively few Beakers were deposited beneath cairns and barrows and none of these barrow finds can be demonstrated to belong to early phases of Beaker use. It is likely that pit 24.03.060, perhaps part of a broad spread, marks a significant

Fig. 2.36 Beaker sherds from Springfield (Site 31), pit 24.03.060

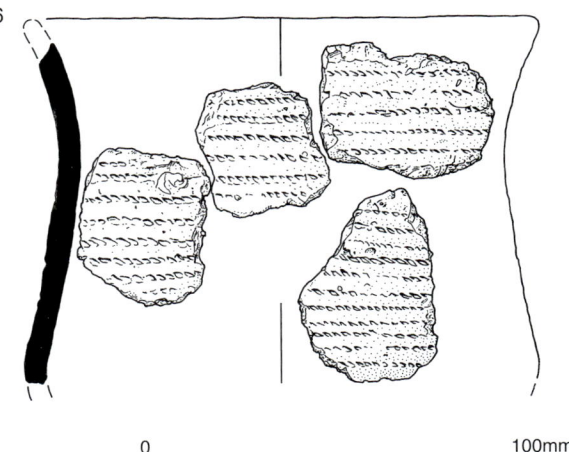

Fig. 2.37 Early Bronze Age Beaker from Springfield (Site 31), pit 24.03.060. Scale 1:2

locale later chosen for the building of the barrow in the Early Bronze Age.

Middle Bronze Age (Table 2.14)

Fabrics

GR.2   Sparse grog, chert and rounded quartz grains, probably fairly local to Pixies' Parlour.

GR.3   Sparse grog and quartz inclusions including a substantial chunk of vein quartz. Some fine mica and rounded quartz in the matrix. Probably fairly local to Pixies' Parlour.

RO.1   Common inclusions: rock fragments: basalt fragments with plagioclase feldspar laths set in a matrix of brown decomposed pyroxene, 0.2–4.5mm; quartz: angular to sub-rounded grains 0.05-0.2mm. Matrix: quartz common less than 0.05mm. A basaltic rock-tempered fabric with fragments derived from the Exeter Volcanic Rocks which are distributed around the Exeter district with the nearest potential source for this site being around Killerton (examination of TS8, 9).

East Devon

Site 4: Pixies' Parlour

Pit 03.04.026 contained a moderately abraded thick sherd in grogged fabric GR.2 in secondary fill of pit 3.04.026. This is oxidised (5YR6/4) light reddish brown. Two similar sherds were redeposited in layer 3.04.061 in ditch 03.04.004. This grogged fabric is common on Middle Bronze Age sites in East Devon, for example at Castle Hill, Honiton (Laidlaw and Mepham 1999, 45) and has not been identified locally in sites of a subsequent date.

Site 7: Land East of Broad Oak

Ditch 4.10.008

P17   (Fig. 2.40, no. 7) third fill 4.10.11 of ditch 4.10.008. Eleven fresh sherds, some conjoining, of undecorated vessel with simple out-turned rim in Exeter Volcanic fabric RO.1 generally reduced (5YR4/2) dark reddish grey. Internal rim diameter 140mm. The form of this vessel is typically Middle Bronze Age Trevisker (e.g. Laidlaw and Mepham 1999. fig. 58, no. 3, Castle Hill). This form is frequent in the larger assemblages found on Cornish sites such as Trethellan (Woodward and Cane 1991) but undecorated versions appear more common in Devon than in Cornwall. Two sherds from another vessel of this form in a finer version of the same fabric from this context and a further six sherds from fourth fill 4.10.12 of ditch 4.10.008.

Pit 4.10.016

Fill 4.10.017 contained six moderately abraded sherds of Middle Bronze Age fabric with grog GR.3.

Table 2.14: Middle Bronze Age ceramics: sherd numbers with weight in grammes

Context No.	Feature	Sherds	Wt	Ref.	Fabric
Pixies' Parlour, Site 4					
3.04.028	Secondary fill, pit 3.04.026	1	25	-	GR.2 grog, chert, quartz
3.04.061	Layer in ditch 3.04.004	2	38	-	GR.2
Total		3	63		
East of Broad Oak, Site 7					
4.10.011	Third fill, ditch 4.10.008	13	228	P17	RO.1 Exeter volcanic
4.10.012	Fourth fill, ditch 4.10.008	6	14	-	RO.1 Exeter volcanic
4.10.017	Primary fill, pit 4.10.016	6	20	-	GR.3 grog, vein quartz
Total		25	262		
South-East of Broad Oak, Site 8					
5.02.005	Fill, ditch 5.02.004	1	10	-	GR.2 grog, chert, quartz
Hogsbrook Farm, Site 10, surface find					
4a.01.02	Subsoil	1	26	-	RO.1 Exeter volcanic
Plot ATK 12.13 surface find					
12.13.001	Subsoil	2	21	-	RO.1 Exeter volcanic
Crablake Farm, Site 15					
14.09.004	Fill, pit 14.09.003	46	2980	P18	RO.1 Exeter volcanic
14.09.020	Fill, pit 14.09.018	5	117	P19	RO.1 Exeter volcanic
14.09.013	Fill, pit 14.09.019	1	19	P20	RO.1 Exeter volcanic
14.09.008/9	Fills, pit 14.09.016	14	72	-	RO.1 Exeter volcanic
Total		66	3188		

Site 8: South-east of Broad Oak
Ditch terminal 5.02.004 (fill 5.02.005) contained one abraded sherd of probable Middle Bronze Age grogged fabric GR.2.

Site 10: Plot 4a.01, surface find
Subsoil 4a.01.002 produced a moderately abraded base angle in Exeter Volcanic fabric RO.1, probably of Trevisker, Middle Bronze Age, affinities.

Plot ATK 12.13 surface finds
Topsoil 12.13.001 produced two abraded thick body-sherds RO.1 fabric; the thickness and general finish of the sherds suggests a Middle Bronze Age date.

Site 15, Crablake Farm, Exminster: domestic site with pits
An assemblage of 66 sherds, weighing 3188g, came from four pits. Most of this is represented by the large lower wall of P18 which had been buried *in situ* but had cracked into sherds. All the sherds appeared to be of a similar fabric Exeter Volcanic RO.1.

Pit 14.09.003

P18 (Figs 2.38, 2.39, 2.40, no. 9) fill 14.09.004 of pit 14.09.003. Parts of a Trevisker vessel in Exeter Volcanic fabric RO.1 lifted in a block of soil and subsequently excavated. Fabric breaks fairly fresh. After treatment most of the vessel present belonged to a complete circuit from the lower part of the vessel, 390mm across at the top, 300mm at the bottom and *c.* 155mm high. Three sherds possibly came from the decorated upper part of the vessel and indicated that this had cord impressions, double parallel twist, rather irregular, with an infilled chevron design: thickening at the base of one of these sherds indicated that the vessel may have had lugs. However the decorated

Fig. 2.38 Trevisker Ware pot from Crablake Farm (Site 15), pit 14.09.003, conserved

Fig. 2.39 Crablake Farm (Site 15); upper decorated sherds from vessel in pit 14.09.003

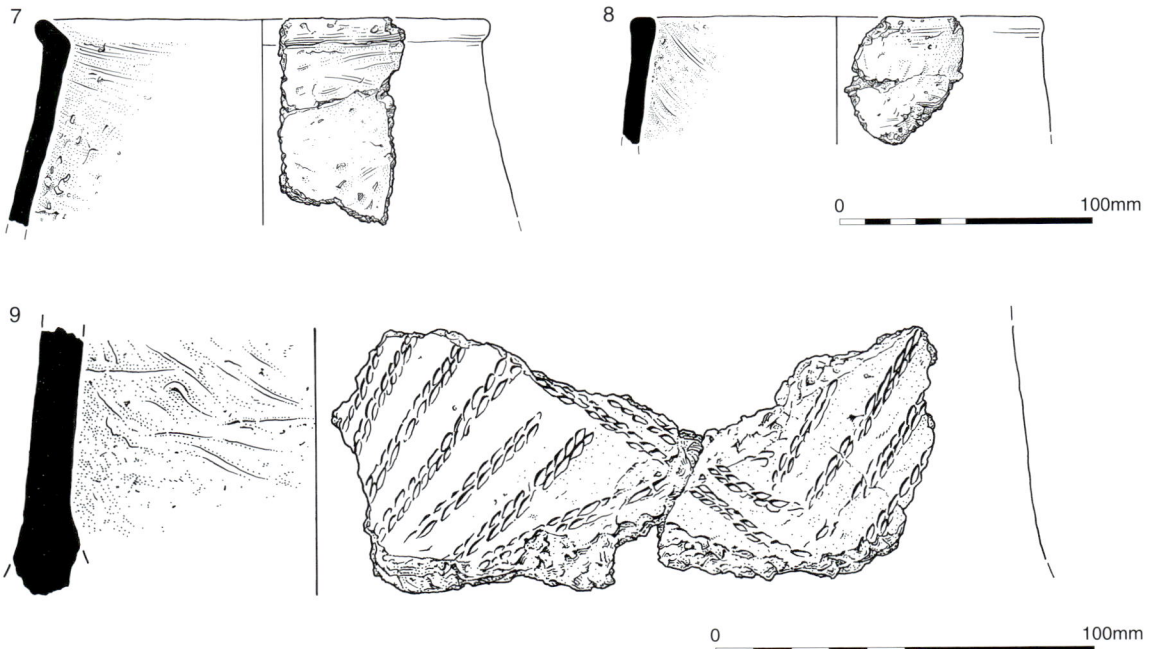

Fig. 2.40 Middle Bronze Age Trevisker Ware pottery. Scales 1:3 and 1:2

sherds appear to be from a vessel of smaller diameter than the restored lower section, but distortion of the latter makes any definite attribution to two separate vessels difficult. No part of a rim was present. The fabric was fairly evenly fired and oxidised (5YR5/6) yellowish red. Given the general shape and proportions of Trevisker vessels, it is probable that the vessel would originally have been 450–500mm high and that about one eighth only was present in pit 14.09.003. The complete circuit was buried level with the upper part on the original vessel uppermost; the three decorated sherds appear to have been deposited just above this circuit. The burial of these pieces is strongly reminiscent of structured depositional practices associated with some Trevisker wares; most notable among recent finds is that of sherds from a vessel buried in the infill of a house at Boden in the Helford River area of Cornwall (Quinnell forthcoming (a), P1). Radiocarbon determination NZA-32777, calibrating to 367–201 BC, was obtained from Ulex/cytisus charcoal from the pit but is assumed to be intrusive.

Pit 14.09.018

P19 (not illus.) fill 14.9.020. Sherds from vessel in moderately abraded Exeter Volcanic RO.1 fabric. This appears to have had a large oval lug situated on a girth at least 300mm in diameter. Sherds generally reduced (5YR4/1) dark grey but with oxidised surfaces (5YR6/6) reddish yellow. The lug remnants and other sherds are decorated with parallel twist double cord impressed lines which are entirely characteristic of Trevisker. Radiocarbon determination NZA-36377, calibrating to 2027–1910 BC, came from oak heartwood from this pit.

Pit 14.09.019

P20 (Fig. 2.40, no. 8) fill 14.09.013. Flat-topped rim 140mm internal diameter with slight expansion fabric RO.1. Reduced (5YR4/1) dark grey with oxidised patches (5YR5/3) reddish brown on exterior. Probably from an undecorated vessel. Sherds fairly fresh. Similarity of fabric suggests this may be of the same date as sherds in 14.09.008. A common Trevisker form (see Laidlaw and Mepham 1999, fig. 24 nos 15, 17 from Castle Hill).

Pit 14.09.016

Fills 14.09.008/9. Fourteen body moderately abraded sherds fabric RO.1, generally reduced (5YR3/1) very dark grey but with oxidised exterior (5YR5/6) yellowish red. *Corylus* charcoal from this pit provided a radiocarbon date of 1627–1504 cal. BC (NZA-32772); a second date from this pit was 1510–1431 cal. BC (NZA-36376) (Table 2.7).

Comment

The fabrics from these pits appear similar, with rock inclusions apparently of volcanic character: three out of the four have parts of vessels with Trevisker affinities. Basalt volcanic rock from the Exeter area, Fabric RO.1, was the only fabric present through the probably long use of Site 15 and was also found at Site 7 and Site 10. It has previously been recorded on three Middle Bronze Age Devon sites. This fabric forms some 17% of the assemblage at Castle Hill, Honiton (Laidlaw and Mepham 1999, table 4). A few sherds were found at Hayes Farm just east of Exeter (Woodward and Williams 1989). The majority of the small assemblage from hut circles at Heatree, Manaton, on the east side of Dartmoor also had Exeter Volcanic inclusions (Quinnell 1991, 22). These inclusions are of similar material to than identified in Middle Iron Age fabrics of Group 6 by Peacock (1969). Thus Exeter Volcanic fabric (RO.1) has now been found at six sites spread across Devon, from East Dartmoor eastwards to Honiton, in the Middle Bronze Age and obviously had long use as a regional fabric source.

Recent work (Quinnell, forthcoming b) is demonstrating that pits with Trevisker ceramics broadly assigned to the Middle Bronze Age, so far found but not published on at least ten sites in Devon, may the remnants of occupation activity. Date NZA-36377, 2017–1910 cal. BC, from pit 14.09.18 is the earliest radiocarbon determination for Trevisker pottery in Devon, from an apparent domestic rather than funerary context. However, as it is on heartwood it can only be regarded as a *terminus post quem*. Dates 1627–1504 cal. BC (NZA-32772) and 1510–1431 cal. BC (NZA-36376) from pit 14.09.16 are not statistically similar. The later date is much more in keeping with those from Trevisker settlement contexts in Devon. The dates as a group suggest intermittent use of the site involving Trevisker pottery over much of the earlier 2nd millennium BC.

Catalogue (Figs 2.34, 2.35, 2.37, 2.40)

1   Grooved Ware. Flat-topped rim with incised lines and stab-and-drag marks below, probably from vessel P12a. Fabric QU.3, vessel P12b. Moore Farm (Site 28), fill 18.12.020 of pit 18.12.018

2   Grooved Ware. Abraded sherds with fine incised chevron decoration. Fabric QU.2, vessel P10. Moore Farm (Site 28), fills 18.12.020 and 18.12.021 of pit 18.12.018

3   Grooved Ware. Large, 220mm diameter, vessel with complex incised and stab-and-drag decoration. Fabric QU.3, vessel P12a. Moore Farm (Site 28), fills 18.12.020 and 18.12.021 of pit 18.12.018

4   Grooved Ware. Flat-topped rim with horizontal grooves below. Fabric VQ.3, vessel P14. Moore Farm (Site 28), fill 18.12.055 of ditch 18.12.049

5   Grooved Ware. Body and base angle of large, 280mm diameter, vessel. Fabric VQ.3, vessel P15. Moore Farm (Site 28), fill 18.12.055 of ditch 18.12.049

6   Beaker bodysherds decorated with impressed cord. Fabric GN.3, vessel P16. Fills 24.03.061, 24.03.062 and 24.03.063 of pit 24.03.060

7   Trevisker Ware. Undecorated vessel with out-turned rim and internal diameter of 140mm. Fabric RO.1, vessel P17. Land East of Broad Oak (Site 7), fill 14.10.011 of ditch 14.10.008

8   Trevisker Ware. ?Undecorated vessel with flat-topped rim and internal diameter of 140mm. Fabric RO.1, vessel P20. Crablake Farm (Site 15), fill 14.09.013 of pit 14.09.019

9   Trevisker Ware. Sherds decorated with double parallel twist cord impressions and infilled chevron design. Thickening at the base of one of the sherds indicates that the vessel may have had lugs. Fabric RO.1, vessel P18. Crablake Farm (Site 15), fill 14.09.004 of pit 14.09.003

Worked flint and chert

E.R. McSloy

A total of 659 (5635g) pieces of worked flint and chert, together with 36 pieces of unworked/heat-affected flint, was recovered from excavation and trench evaluation. An additional 32 pieces were recovered from fieldwalking undertaken in 2001 along part of the South Devon route, 29 of these relating to plots included in the final choice of route (Site 17 and plots 3.03, 3.04, 7.01, 27.02, 27.03 and 27.04). The majority of material was hand-collected, with 54 pieces retrieved from bulk soil samples. Recording consists of quantification (count) by raw material and 'class' and, where appropriate, a note of cortex, burning, any patination and post-depositional damage. Additional recording undertaken for the stratified groups includes recording of flint colour, cortex coverage, source and hammer-mode where this was determinable.

A relatively small proportion of the assemblage consists of probable stratified groups: from Pixies' Parlour, Ottery St Mary (Site 4), for which Early Neolithic dating is supported by associated pottery, and from Hems Valley, Staverton, and Filham House, Ugborough (Sites 17 and 34), which date to later in the Neolithic and Bronze Age respectively. Among the remainder of the assemblage there are indications from diagnostic tool forms or technological traits for dating spanning the Mesolithic to Early/Middle Bronze Age.

A total of 60 pieces with secondary working was identified and a further 13 pieces which had been utilised, probably as cutting implements. The bulk of the remainder comprises waste flakes or blades and cores/core fragments. There are three hammerstones, all of which have been adapted to this use from cores (Fig. 2.45, no. 11).

Condition

The condition of the lithics is mixed; high levels of edge damage and breakage were recorded among unstratified or redeposited groups including material from the fieldwalking survey. For the excavated groups from Pixies' Parlour (Site 4), Hems Valley (Site 17) and Filham House (Site 34), breakage was less and their condition commonly recorded as 'sharp'. A very small proportion of the flint overall (five pieces) exhibited patination, typically as a deep white discolouration. In such cases importation from chalky soils well to the east is likely.

Raw material

Raw material comprises primarily flint (686 pieces) of varying colour and quality and nine pieces of chert. The chert is mainly of coarse-grained brown or grey/greenish type and probably comes from the Upper Greensand of the Blackdown Hills. A greensand chert core from Pixies' Parlour (redeposited in the Roman penannular ditch) exhibits a very worn cortex and was clearly from a derived source.

The flint ranges in colour from dark grey, through mid or mottled greys and pale grey; though with the majority across the area tending to darker greys. Also notable are 14 pieces of red-banded (iron-stained) flint noted from Pixies' Parlour (Site 4) and a field to the east (OTA 3.02). This distinctive material was selected for a utilised flake/long blade (Fig. 2.45 no. 3) and a scraper from the same site. Similar material was noted from Castle Hill, west of Honiton, Devon (Bellamy 1999, 37), where it was thought possibly to come from a clay-with-flints source.

Indications of flint source, based on the character and degree of wear to the cortex, suggests exploitation of both primary chalk and derived sources. Where this was systematically measured among the 'stratified' groups, flint from primary sources is most common in the proportion 3:1. In most instances the cortex is moderately thick and buff in colour. The most likely source would be the coastal chalk sources of east Devon such as those in the region of Beer Head, or possibly the inland sources among the Blackdown Hills described by Newberry (2002).

A lesser quantity of material with heavily worn cortex was probably collected from eroded sources which might include beach sources to the south and south-east, or possibly the 'Bovey and Decoy Basins' to the south described by Newberry (2002, 17–19). Such material appeared to be notably abundant among the unstratified groups collected from the Fishacre to Choakford section. Much of this 'derived' flint is of reduced quality with flaws relatively common, suggesting that raw material was at times difficult to obtain or perhaps that quality was less of an imperative.

Lithic assemblages

Quantities of flint or chert were recovered from 66 divisions across the length of the three pipelines. Figures 2.41–2.44 provide a summary of the distribution of lithics from the whole route, where fewer than ten flints are represented by single symbols. The larger site groups (>10 pieces) are shown as pie charts and described separately below. Tables 2.15–2.17 provide more detail on the stratified groups.

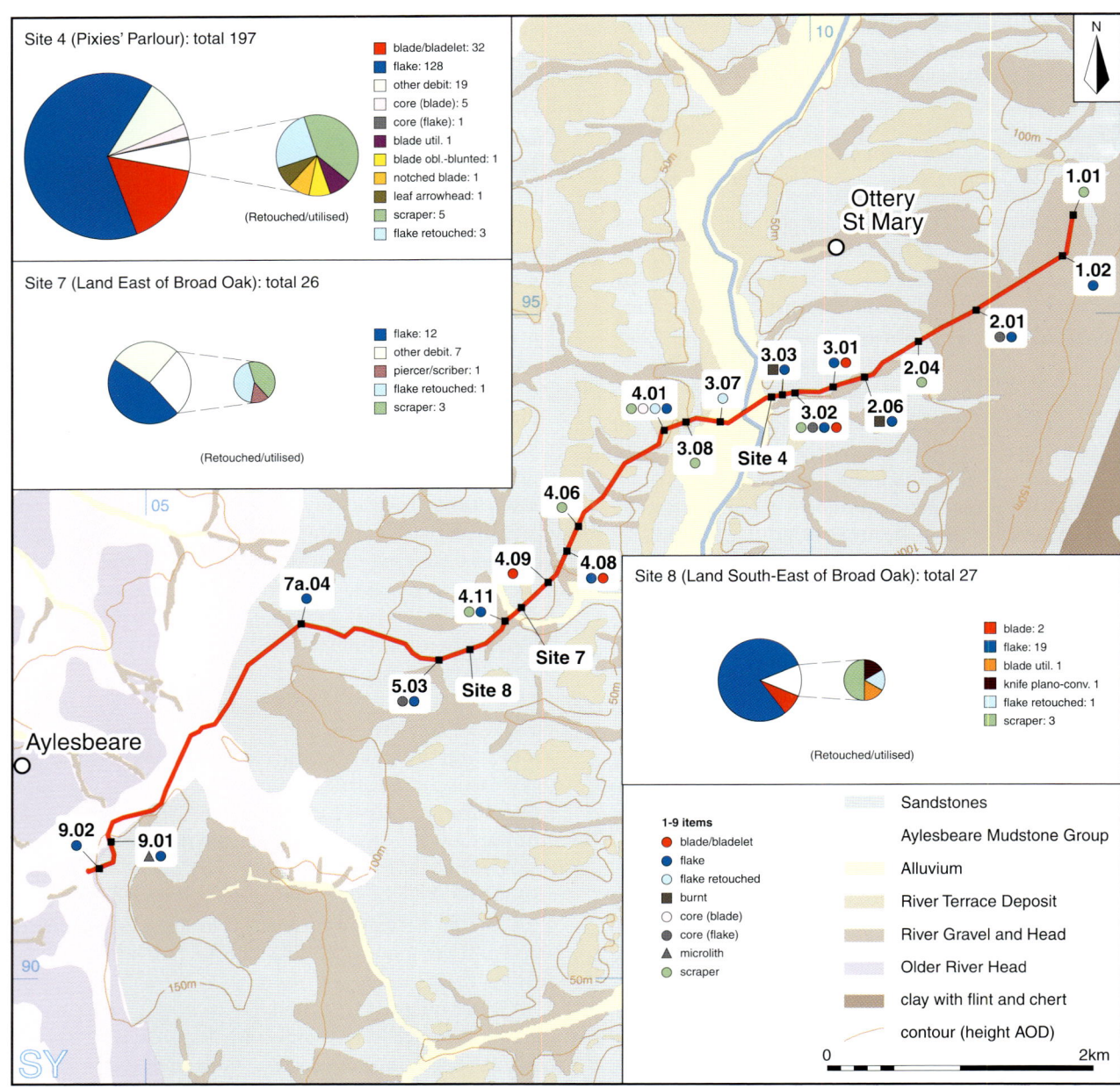

Fig. 2.41 Ottery St Mary to Aylesbeare (OTA) flint distribution in relation to geology. Scale 1:50,000

East Devon

East of Pixies' Parlour (Plot OTA 3.02)

A small group of 11 pieces was recovered, including two scrapers. The material derived from topsoil and subsoil deposits and there were no further indications of early prehistoric activity. Raw material comprises unpatinated grey flint.

Pixies' Parlour (Site 4)

This site produced a comparatively large group of worked lithics (197 pieces) including nine pieces with secondary working and a further eight utilised pieces (Fig. 2.41). The lithics from feature 03.04.096, and other pieces of Early Neolithic date are considered below. Limited evidence for Middle Bronze Age activity was also apparent in the form of pottery from pit 3.04.026 (fill 3.04.028) and Roman ditch 3.04.004 (fill 03.04.061). No lithics were recovered from either feature.

A number of blades/bladelets, a plunging rejuvenation flake in chert (Fig. 2.45. no. 2), a possible core-tablet type rejuvenation flake and an obliquely-blunted bladelet (Fig. 2.45. no. 1) are possible indications of Mesolithic activity, although this material is redeposited. Several scrapers are present including a large discoidal piece (Fig. 2.45. no. 5), which might reasonably belong to the Neolithic or later periods. The bulk of the remainder comprises unretouched flakes/chips, flake core fragments and shatter pieces. Based on characteristics of flake removals, which tend to 'squat' proportions

Earlier Prehistoric Period 57

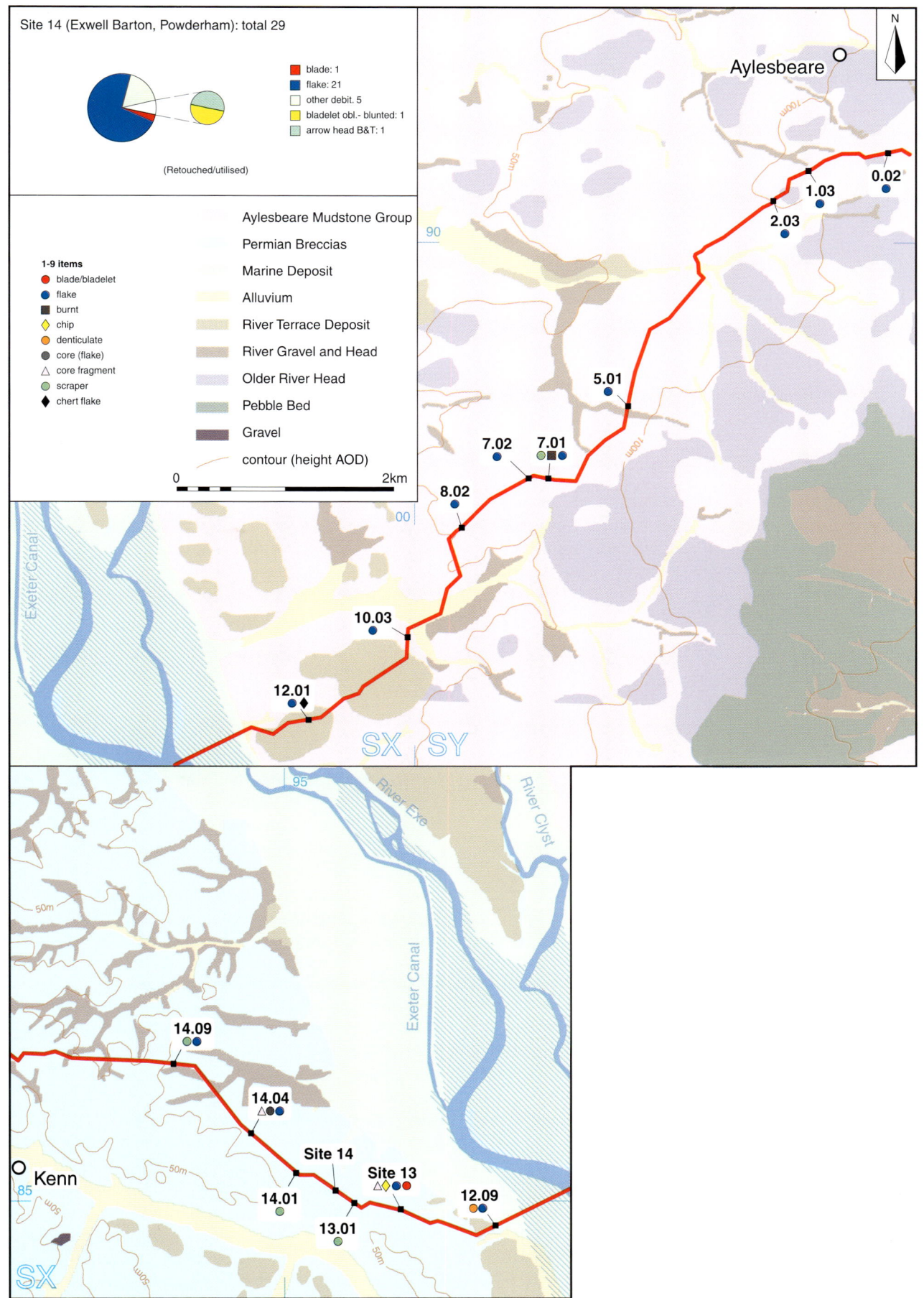

Fig. 2.42 *Aylesbeare to Kenn (ATK) flint distribution in relation to geology. Scale 1:50,000*

Table 2.15: Pixies' Parlour, Site 4 (OTA 3.04): worked lithics from Early Neolithic Pit Group 3.04.096. All material flint except where stated. Pri. = primary, Sec. = secondary, Tert. = tertiary

Material	Class	Pri.	Sec.	Tert.	Total
chert	blade	-	-	1	1
flint	blade	-	3	2	5
	blade utilised broken	-	2	3	5
	bladelet	-	1	3	4
	chip/shatter	-	-	6	6
	core fragment	-	-	1	1
	flake	1	8	23	32
	flake crested	-	1	-	1
Total		1	15	39	55

and are mostly hard-hammer struck, a proportion at least probably relates to the later (Bronze Age) activity from the site. Flake (and blade) removals are primarily tertiary or secondary, suggesting that initial reduction was undertaken elsewhere.

Early Neolithic material
A group of 56 pieces, all of flint except one piece of chert, was associated with Early Neolithic feature 03.04.096 (Table 2.15). Fifteen removals from this group are of blade proportions, with length/breadth ration of 2:1 or greater. Blade/bladelet length was in the range 22–48mm. A significant proportion of the removals exhibit evidence for platform preparation in the form of abrasion close to the butt, on the dorsal side. Many, it appears, were struck with a 'soft' hammer, resulting in diffuse bulb and lipped butt. The sharp condition of the removals from this deposit and prevalence of blades/long flakes, including a crested piece, suggests a proportion at least of the lithics from this deposit are stratified and of Early Neolithic date.

The bulk of the remainder of the worked flint is re-deposited, mostly in Romano-British deposits. Tools of Early Neolithic form are confined to broken or unfinished leaf-shaped arrowhead (Fig. 2.45 no. 4) from Roman ditch 3.04.004 (deposit 03.04.011). A large (90mm) utilised blade/long flake (Fig. 2.45 no. 3) from penannular ditch 3.04.045 may also be of this date.

Land East of Broad Oak (Site 7)
A small group of 26 pieces of worked flint was recovered mainly from subsoil deposit 04.10.002, possible Bronze Age ditch 4.10.018 (fill 04.10.023) or undated deposits (Fig. 2.41). A single flake was recovered in association with pottery of Middle Bronze Age type (pit 4.10.016, fill 04.10.017). There are five pieces identified with secondary working comprising three scrapers, a flake with knife-like retouch and an unusual tool from a flake with abrupt retouch forming a right-angle and described as a piercer/scriber. The remainder consists of flakes or broken flakes and the group as a whole would be consistent with Late Neolithic/Early or Middle Bronze Age flintworking.

Land South-East of Broad Oak (Site 8)
A total of 27 pieces was associated with this division (Fig. 2.41). No pottery of earlier prehistoric date was recovered, although a small part of the recovered lithics (a flake and possible utilised blade) derived from deposits internal to the ring-ditch and interpreted as mound material (deposit 05.01.025). The remainder of the worked flint derives from subsoil or topsoil deposits and some pieces are abraded. There are five pieces with secondary working: three scrapers, a retouched flake and a broken fragment from a plano-convex knife. The remainder consists of flake debitage and the group taken together would be consistent with Late Neolithic/Early or Middle Bronze Age flintworking.

Other
Smaller groups of lithics (between one and nine pieces) were recovered along the length of the Ottery St Mary to Aylesbeare section. The majority consists of unutilised removals or other debitage, about which little meaningful can be said. Of individual note is a single Mesolithic piece, a geometric microlith (Fig. 2.45 no. 6) from Plot OTA 9.01.

Deepway Farm, Woodbury (ATK 7.01)
A group of 19 pieces of worked flint was recovered, all deriving from topsoil or subsoil deposits and mostly abraded (Fig. 2.42). Identifiable tools consist of three scrapers including a small 'button' scraper. Similar small scrapers are commonly ascribed Late Neolithic/Early Bronze Age dating. The flake removals are broad and squat, a characteristic of Late Neolithic and later flint-working, although likely also to be affected by properties of the available raw materials.

White House, Powderham (Site 13)
A small group of seven pieces including flakes, a blade and a flake core fragment was recovered from topsoil and subsoil deposits. No tools or other notable pieces were present.

Exwell Barton, Powderham (Site 14)
A group of 29 pieces was recovered, the majority clearly residual from medieval deposits (Fig. 2.42). Limited evidence for Mesolithic activity is in evidence in the form of an obliquely blunted bladelet from within the medieval house (Fig. 2.45 no. 7) and a broken bladelet from the backfill of the sunken outbuilding. The remainder consists of flakes/chips and, exceptionally, a very finely worked barbed and tanged arrowhead (Fig. 2.45 no. 8), from subsoil. This item has suffered damage

to its tang and one barb, which precludes attribution to Green's typology with certainty (Green 1980), but is made with regular convex longer edges and shallow invasive retouch extending over both faces. It certainly belongs with Green's 'fancy' group and the (slightly) concave base would be consistent with it being of Green Low type (ibid., fig. 46). Its large size and high quality may suggest it is a disturbed grave find (Devaney 2005) and it almost certainly dates early in the Early Bronze Age, probably before c. 2000 BC.

Other
The remaining portion of the recovered lithics represents topsoil/subsoil-derived material occurring as single flints or up to three pieces from each division. There are few tools; a denticulate on a blade from Lower Nutwell, Site 12 (ATK 12.01) is representative of implements most common from the Mesolithic and Neolithic periods and a small, discoidal 'button' scraper from south-east of Site 14 (ATK 13.01) may date to the Early Bronze Age. The majority comprises flake debitage which is not datable in isolation or otherwise of significance.

South Devon

Hems Valley, Staverton (Site 17)
A total of 78 pieces was recovered from excavation, including four pieces with secondary working, three utilised pieces and two hammerstones, both from cores (Fig. 2.43). The assemblage derives primarily from series of six pits containing Middle Neolithic Peterborough Ware. An additional eight pieces, mainly flakes, were recovered from fieldwalking in 2001. Single examples of scraper, retouched flake and a fragment from a fabricator were recorded. The latter, which may be contemporary with the Middle Neolithic activity described below, consists of a short, square-ended portion with bi-facial working and with possible wear from use.

Middle Neolithic material
A total of 64 pieces was recovered from the Middle Neolithic pits (Table 2.16). The presence of small spalls and chips and the overall sharp condition of the flint is suggestive of a stratified group. In colour, raw material, overall character and condition, the flint from this group is consistent. The majority comprises secondary or tertiary flakes in good quality dark grey or grey flint, most of which probably came from primary (chalk) source. Where this can be assessed (13 pieces), removals are all hard-hammer struck. The flake removals exhibit 'squat' proportions (length/breadth ratio near to 1:1) with no evidence for platform preparation.

Identifiable tools from the pits are limited to a denticulate on a blade/long flake from pit 02.02.006 (Fig. 2.45 no. 9), a combined denticulate/end scraper on a blade-like flake from pit 02.02.013 (Fig. 2.45 no. 10) and end scrapers/retouched flakes from pit fill 02.02.010. None of the tools are exclusively of the

Table 2.16: Hems Valley, Site 17 (FTC 2.02): worked flint from Middle Neolithic Pit Groups. Pri. = primary, Sec. = secondary, Tert. = tertiary

Class	Pri.	Sec.	Tert.	Total
blade	-	1	-	1
flake	3	4	31	38
scraper end	-	1	-	1
scraper/denticulate	-	-	1	1
denticulate	-	-	1	1
retouched frag	-	-	1	1
shatter/chip	1	1	17	19
flake core	-	-	1	1
core fragment	-	-	1	1
Total	**4**	**7**	**52**	**64**

Middle/Later Neolithic and, though not unknown, denticulates are uncommon finds from this period. A hammerstone from the largest pit 02.02.010 (Fig. 2.45 no. 11) is a reuse of a core in a dense pale grey flint. It is of cylindrical form with long flake/blade removals from two platforms and in its original use might have dated to the Mesolithic or Early Neolithic.

Springfield, Ugborough (Site 31)
A group of 50 pieces was recovered; for the most part redeposited within Romano-British deposits or from subsoil horizons (Fig. 2.44). No material came from pit 24.03.060, a feature containing Beaker pottery. A distinctive aspect of the lithics from this site division is the raw material, which is of indifferent quality and obtained mainly from derived sources (above). There are a small number of blades/bladelets with evidence for platform preparation, bladelet cores and one core tablet, which are indications of some Mesolithic activity. The bulk of the flint comprises flake removals, a number of which are fully cortical and which are commonly broad, squat and irregular. The overall crudeness of the flake debitage, while in part an effect of the raw material, may be an indication of relatively late dating (Bronze Age). Further indications of this are among the tools, which include two piercers, implements which are frequently recorded in the Early to Middle Bronze Age toolkit, and a number of miscellaneous retouched pieces.

Filham House, Ugborough (Site 34, FTC 33.01)
Excepting four flakes recovered as unstratified material, the flint derived from the fills of pit 33.01.006. Radiocarbon determinations from this feature indicate a Middle Bronze Age date (Table 2.11).

The lithics from pit 33.01.006 comprised 33 pieces including 13 pieces (mainly small chips) recovered from a bulk soil sample (Table 2.17). The group mainly consists of unutilised flake removals, most with

60 *The Archaeology of the South-West Reinforcement Gas Pipeline, Devon: Investigations in 2005–2007*

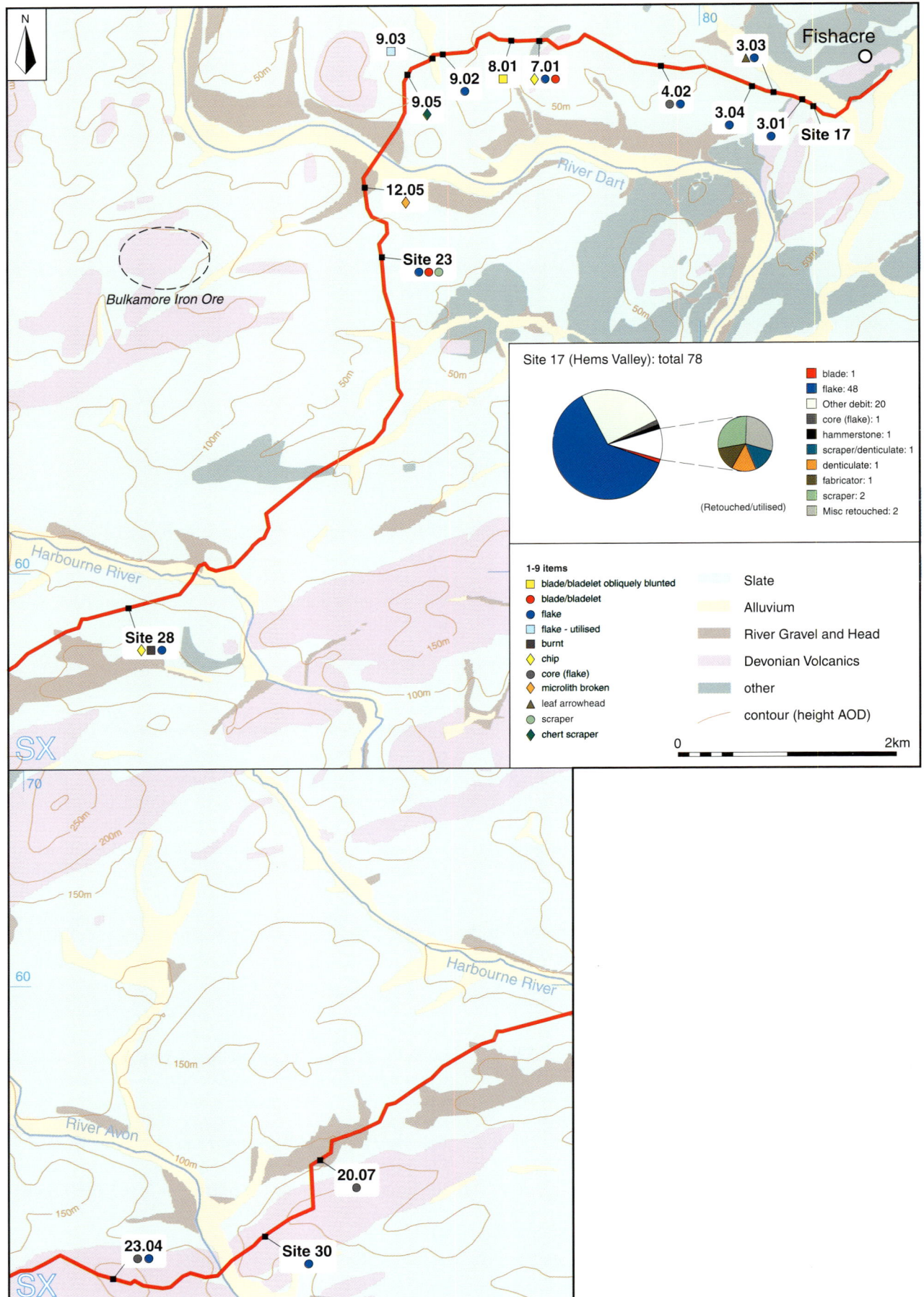

Fig. 2.43 Fishacre to Choakfoard (FTC) flint distribution in relation to geology. Scale 1:50,000

Earlier Prehistoric Period 61

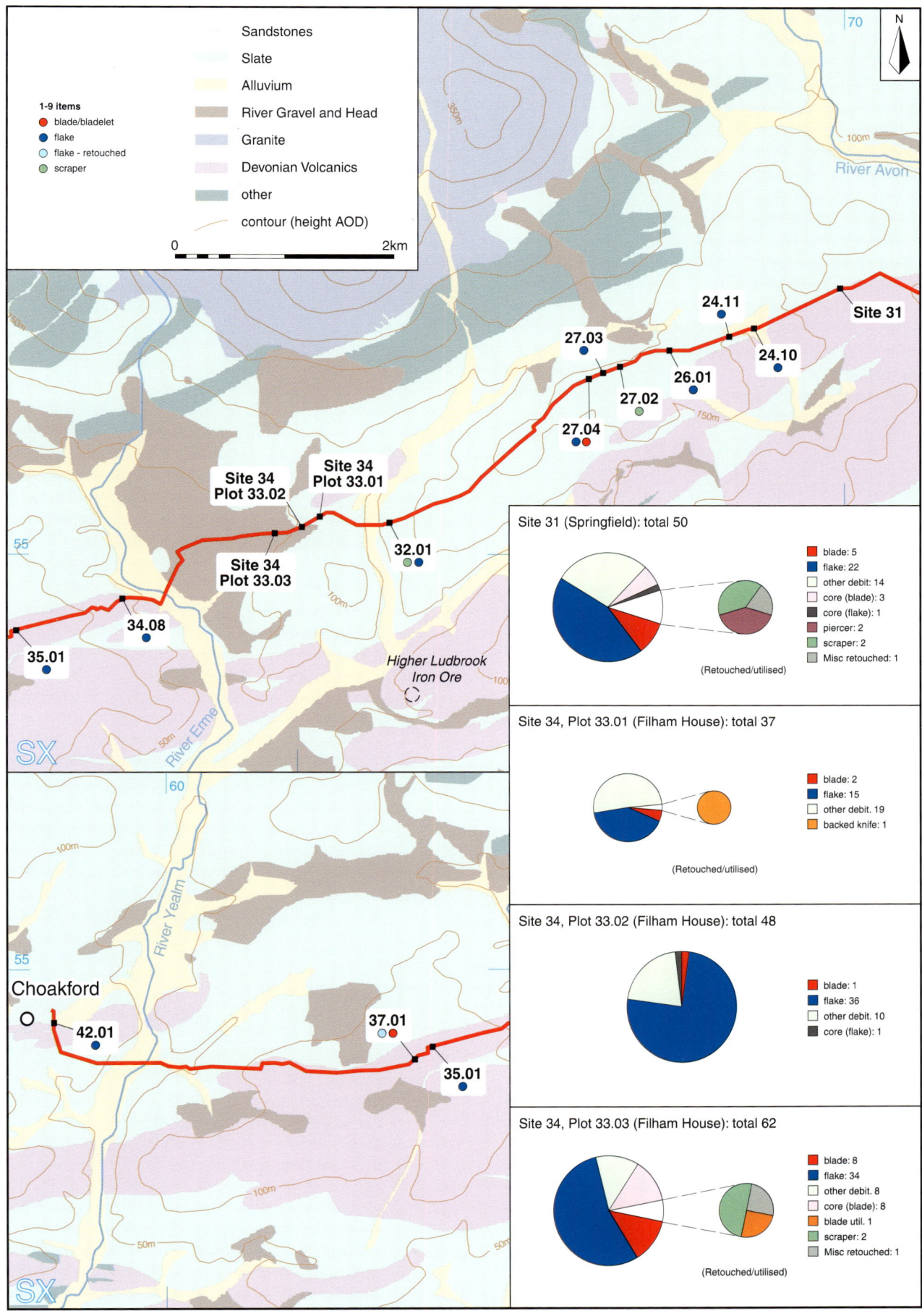

Fig. 2.44 Fishacre to Choakford (FTC) flint distribution in relation to geology. Scale 1:50,000

Table 2.17: Filham House, Site 34 (FTC 33.01): worked flint from Middle Bronze Age Pit 33.01.006. Pri. = primary, Sec. = secondary, Tert. = tertiary

Class	Pri.	Sec.	Tert.	Total
blade	-	-	2	2
flake	-	-	11	11
backed knife	-	1	-	1
chip/shatter	1	-	19	20
Total	**1**	**1**	**32**	**34**

indications of hard hammer percussion and with no evidence for platform preparation. Included is a single retouched piece (Fig. 2.45 no. 12) which consists of a long flake with a small area of retouch to one of its longer edges and indications of use as a cutting piece on two edges. A further two pieces appear to have been utilised for cutting. The flint debitage is mainly in sharp condition and most are secondary or tertiary flakes/chips in good quality grey flint. An exception is a bladelet in pale grey flint which might be a residual Mesolithic piece.

Filham House, Ugborough (Site 34, FTC 33.02)
Material from this plot (48 pieces in total) was recovered from subsoil or colluvial deposits, a 'spread' (33.02.006) containing possible Iron Age pottery, and from undated pit 33.02.004 (one flake). The assemblage comprises entirely flakes or other debitage with no secondary working or evidence for utilisation (Fig. 2.44). Based on observations of technology, the majority of the material probably relates to the Late Neolithic/Bronze Age periods.

South-west of Filham House, Ugborough (Site 34, FTC 33.03)
All material (62 pieces) was unstratified or recovered from subsoil horizons and was commonly abraded. There are a few possible Mesolithic or early Neolithic pieces in the form of blades and worked-down bladelet cores. Among the blades are clearly soft-hammer struck examples in good quality pale grey flint. The raw material is varied; most abundant is a paler or mid grey, commonly coarse-textured, flint with very worn cortex suggesting a derived source. As with the group from Springfield (Site 31) the properties of this raw material may have contributed to the thick, squat proportions of most removals. Tools are restricted to scrapers and miscellaneous retouched pieces and the 'feel' for this group is that most is relatively late, probably within the Bronze Age.

Other
In addition to the group of eight pieces noted above in association with Site 17, a total of 24 pieces of worked flint were recovered from fieldwalking: from plots 3.03, and 3.04 in the Hems valley; plot 7.01 at Barton Hill Cross, Littlehempston; and plots 27.02, 27.03 and 27.04 between Forder Cross and Hillhead Cross, Ugborough (Figs 2.43, 2.44). Most groups comprise flakes only. The largest group, from plot 3.03, comprised 11 pieces, including arrowheads of leaf-shaped and barbed and tanged form. The leaf arrowhead, an early Neolithic form, is relatively crude, being asymmetric and with invasive retouch not extending over the whole ventral. It conforms most closely to Green's Type 4C (Green 1980, fig. 29). The (Early/Middle Bronze Age) barbed-and-tanged arrowhead is also of crude manufacture and can be classified as of Green's Sutton A type (ibid., fig. 45).

Most of the remaining flint from this route must be representative of well-dispersed background prehistoric activity. A broken section from a bladelet with one blunted edge from Hood Ball, Rattery (Site 21, pit 12.05.009), probably represents a geometric microlith of Mesolithic type (Fig. 2.45 no. 13). The pit is dated to the Middle Bronze Age by radiocarbon and the flint must be residual. At Hood Quarry (Site 23) a scraper was recovered from the trial trench through the probable Bronze Age ditch 13.03.004 (Fig. 2.45 no. 14)

Catalogue (Fig. 2.45)

1	Blade, obliquely blunted at proximal. Grey flint. Site 4. Subsoil 03.04.002
2	'Plunging' core rejuvenation flake. Grey flint. Site 4. Pit 3.04.096, fill 206.009
3	Long flake/blade; utilised. Grey flint. Site 4. Ditch 3.04.045 (fill 206.007)
4	Broken leaf-shaped arrowhead or knife. On blade with partial bifacial retouch. Point broken. Possibly Type 2C (as Green 1980, fig. 28/Type 2C/e).Grey flint. Site 4. Ditch 3.04.004 (fill 03.04.011)
5	Discoidal scraper. Red-stained grey flint. Site 4. Redeposited in pit 3.04.097, fill 03.04.089
6	Geometrical microlith. Grey flint. OTA 9.01 subsoil 9.01.002
7	Bladelet, obliquely blunted at proximal end. Grey flint. Site 14. Floor 13.02.194
8	'Fancy' type barbed and tanged arrowhead. Very fine shallow invasive retouch over both surfaces. Dark grey flint Probably Green Low type; (as Green 1980, fig. 46/f). Length 38mm; width 34mm; thickness 4mm. Site 14. Subsoil 13.02.002
9	Denticulate on blade/long flake. Burnt flint. Site 17. Pit 2.02.006, fill 2.02.008
10	Endscraper/denticulate on long cortical flake. Dark grey flint. Site 17. Pit 2.02.013, fill 2.02.015
11	Hammerstone from opposed-platform cylindrical core. Pale grey flint. Site 17. Pit 02.02.010, fill 02.02.011
12	Partially 'backed' knife on long flake. Dark grey flint. Site 34. Pit 33.01.006, fill 33.01.007
13	Broken geometric microlith(?). Grey flint. Site 21.Pit 12.05.009, fill 12.05.010
14	Scraper of Greensand chert ?thermal flake. Site 23. Ditch 13.03.004, fill 905

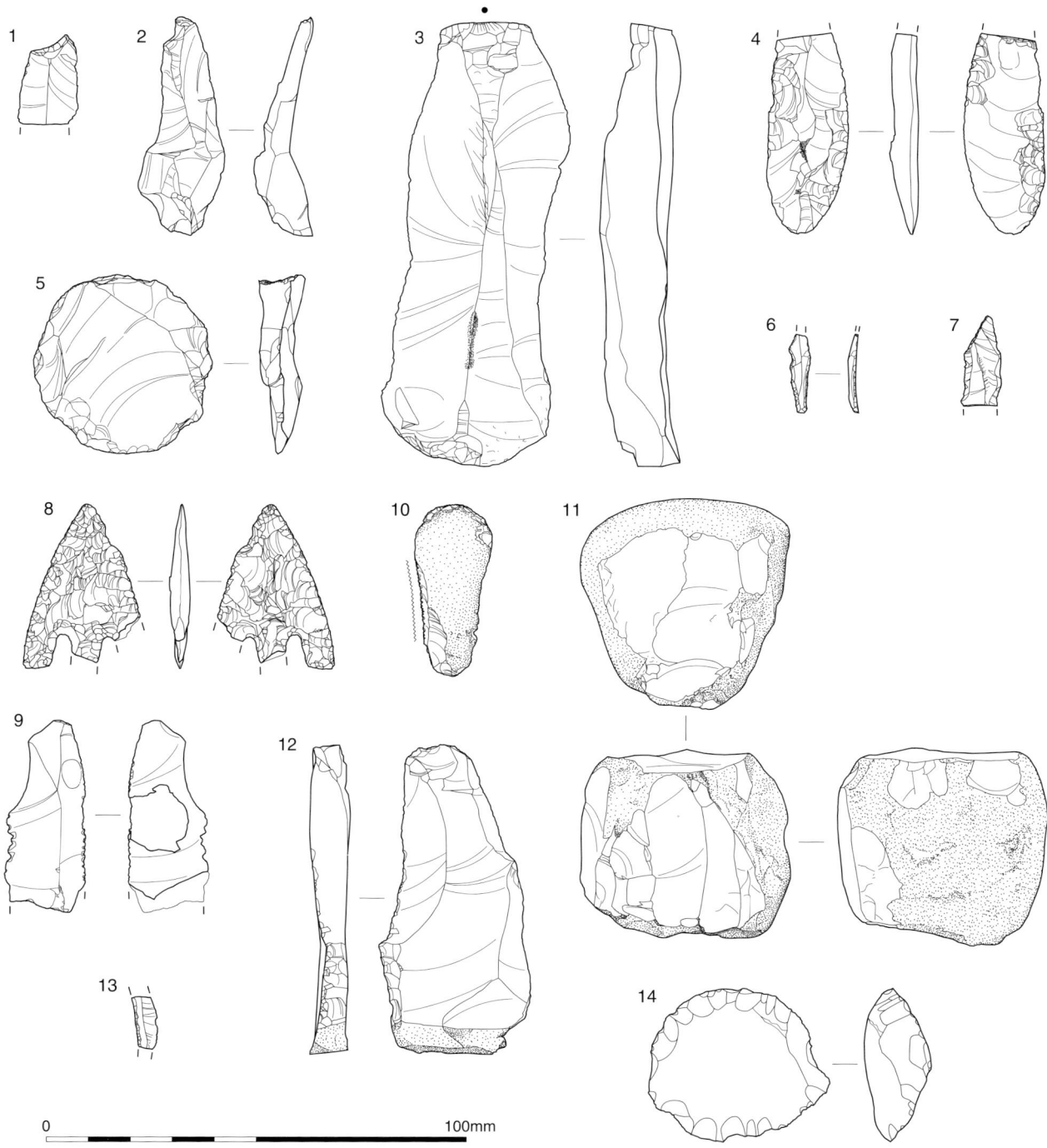

Fig. 2.45 Worked flint and chert. Scale 2:3

Other worked and utilised stone

Susan Watts, with geological identification by Roger T. Taylor

South Devon

Hems Valley, Staverton, Site 17

Neolithic rubbing stones and cobbles

Nineteen cobbles and fragments of porphyritic lava, volcanic tuff, sandstone and siltstone were recovered from four of a group of six Middle Neolithic pits (Table 2.18; Figs 2.46–2.49. Of these, three cobbles (S1, S2 and S4) appear to have been utilised as rubbing stones and another, a long, narrow cobble (S3) has been worn smooth along both long edges. A number of the other unworked cobbles are also likely to have been especially collected, perhaps for intended use, probably from the headwaters of the River Hems. It is also noticeable that the five fragments of local volcanic tuff are burnt, suggesting they derived from a hearth.

Table 2.18: Hems Valley, Site 17 (FTC 2.02): cobbles and stone fragments from Middle Neolithic pits

Pit	Context	Stone Artefact
2.02.004	Fill 2.02.005	4 fragments of local volcanic tuff, burnt (29g)
2.02.004	Fill 2.02.005	Sub-angular fragment of local volcanic tuff (see description) (S1)
2.02.004	Fill 2.02.005	2 river cobbles of porphyritic lava (206g + 242g)
2.02.004	Fill 2.02.005	River cobble of vesicular and porphyritic lava (see description) (S2)
2.02.006	Fill 2.02.007	Elongated cobble of local foliated volcanic tuff (see description) (S3)
2.02.006	Fill 2.02.008	Small fragment of local volcanic tuff, burnt (2g)
2.02.010	Fill 2.02.012	Fragment of local siltstone (8g)
2.02.010	Fill 2.02.011	3 cobbles of porphyritic lava (400g + 235g + 382g), 1 fragment of local volcanic tuff, burnt (343g), and 1 cobble of vesicular lava (270g)
2.02.010	Fill 2.02.011	Fragment of lava (333g)
2.02.010	Fill 2.02.011	Cobble of porphyritic lava (see description) (S4)
2.01.010	Fill 2.02.011	Local elongated cobble of fine-grained laminated sandstone (206g)
2.02.016	Fill 2.02.017	Elongated cobble of fine-grained local sandstone (336g)

Few cobble tools are currently known from Neolithic sites in the South West. At Portscatho, Cornwall, a water-worn cobble rubbing stone was found in one of a cluster of four Early Neolithic pits (Jones and Reed 2006, 4, 11), and another was recovered from one of a group of ten Early Neolithic pits at Tregarrick Farm, Roche, Cornwall (Quinnell and Taylor 2002–3, 123). At Tremough, also in Cornwall, a cobble grinding tool was found in one of the later Neolithic pits but none were recovered from the Early Neolithic pits (Gossip and Jones 2007, 6, 8). In Devon, a cobble rubbing stone was found in an Early Neolithic tree-throw pit at Waylands, Tiverton (Leverett and Quinnell 2010, 10). As in Hems Valley, several unworked cobbles were also found at Portscatho, Tregarrick Farm and in the later Neolithic pits at Tremough. Nevertheless the assemblage from Hems Valley adds significantly to the number of cobbles, both worked and unworked, recovered from Neolithic sites in Devon and Cornwall.

Many Neolithic pits are now thought to have been

Fig. 2.46 Stones from Hems Valley (Site 17), pit 2.02.010. A. clockwise from top left: cobble of vesicular lava; cobble of porphyritic lava; burnt volcanic tuff; cobble of porphyritic lava with one flat side (S4). B. top to bottom; sandstone cobble, sandstone cobble, lava cobble

dug specifically for the purpose of being infilled with a mixture of artefacts, soil and other material, possibly as part of a formalised 'clearing up' procedure related to the occupation or leaving of a site. Such sites may have been routinely revisited, accounting perhaps for the development of pit groups. The various contents of the pits may have had specific social or symbolic significance and have been chosen in response to local traditions and conditions (Jones and Reed 2006, 21; Gossip and Jones 2007, 29; Thomas 1999, 64–74; Pollard 2001, 322–8; Leverett and Quinnell 2010, 10). In view of this, it may be significant that only four of the six pits at Hems Valley produced cobbles. At Tregarrick Farm, cobbles were only found in two out of ten pits, while at Portscatho they derived from two out of four pits, and at Tremough from three out of eight pits (Cole and Jones 2002–3, 112; Jones and Reed 2006, 4, 11; Gossip and Jones 2007, 8). All the cobbles and stone fragments, both worked and unworked, therefore, may be considered as structured deposits, in that all were especially selected for deposition in a particular pit at a particular time.

Catalogue

S1. (Fig. 2.47, top right) Subangular fragment of local volcanic tuff. Appears to have been used as a rubbing stone with one flat, possibly worn side. The opposite side may also have been used, although one half is higher than the other. The stone would have been used one-handed. L10.21cm/W6.63cm/Th5.34cm. Weight 352g. Pit 2.02.004, fill 2.02.005

S2. (Fig. 2.47, top left) River cobble of vesicular and porphyritic lava with one flat side utilised as a rubbing stone. The rubbing stone would have been used one-handed and appears to have finger grips in the side. L9.09cm/W7.78cm/W3.65cm. Weight 307g. Pit 2.02.004, fill 2.02.005

S3. (Fig. 2.48) Utilised elongated flat, narrow cobble of local foliated volcanic tuff. The surviving end of the cobble, which is broken, is rounded and the thin side edges have been rubbed or worn smooth. L9.23cm/W4.00cm/Th1.97cm. Weight 118g. Pit 2.02.006, fill 2.02.007

S4. (Fig. 2.46A, bottom left) Cobble of porphyritic lava with one flat side. Possibly used as a one-handed rubbing stone. L9.17cm/W6.26cm/Th2.93cm. Weight 234g. Pit 2.02.010, fill 2.02.011

Fig. 2.47 Stones from Hems Valley (Site 17) pit 2.02.004. Clockwise from top left: rubbing stone of vesicular lava (S2); rubbing stone of volcanic tuff (S1); cobble of porphyritic lava; cobble of porpyritic lava

Fig. 2.48 Stone from Hems Valley (Site 17) pit 2.02.006. Rubbing stone of volcanic tuff (S3)

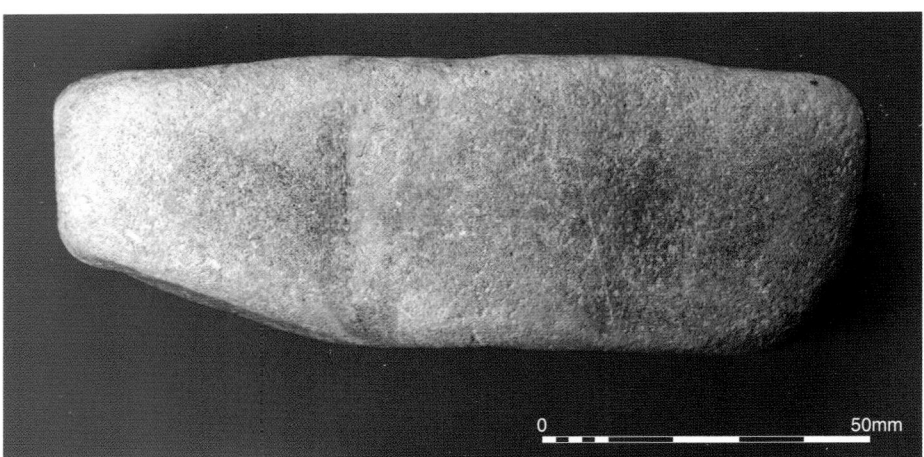

Fig. 2.49 Stone from Hems Valley (Site 17) pit 2.02.016. Cobble of fine-grained sandstone

Bronze pin from Crablake Farm, Exminster

E.R. McSloy

The only prehistoric metal item of note was a fragment of a bronze pin shaft from Crablake Farm, Exminster (Site 15, Fig. 2.21). The item was examined by x-ray fluorescence (XRF) analysis by David Dungworth whose report is retained in archive. The dating of this object to the Middle Bronze Age is indicated by associations of Trevisker Ware and radiocarbon dates from adjacent pits. The pin is highly corroded, with little or original surface remaining. There is the suggestion of decorative twisting at one end. XRF analysis indicated use of a tin bronze. The absence of zinc is consistent with prehistoric manufacture although absence of any trace elements (nickel, arsenic, antimony, etc.) is unusual (Dungworth 2011b).

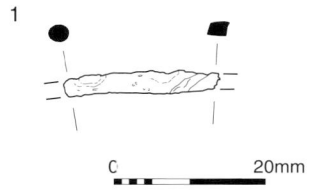

Fig. 2.50 Bronze pin shaft from Crablake Farm (Site 15) pit 14.09.007. Scale 1:1

Catalogue (Fig. 2.50)
1   Copper alloy; possibly part short section from the shaft of a pin. Surviving length 20mm; max. diam. 3.5mm. Site 15, pit 14.09.007, fill 14.09.032

Plant macrofossils and charcoal

Sarah Cobain

Results of assessment and analysis

On the whole the samples of plant macrofossils and charcoal were well preserved and offer a relatively rare opportunity to examine activities undertaken during the Neolithic and Bronze Age periods in Devon. This section summarises the results from the assessed and analysed botanical samples. The detailed results of analysis are presented in Tables 2.19–2.26. SS refers to soil sample number.

Mesolithic

South Devon

Moore Farm, Harberton (Site 28)
Pit 18.12.043 contained a small quantity (five fragments) of carbonised hazelnut shells, one of which returned a late Mesolithic radiocarbon date (Table 2.3). The charcoal from this feature was too small to identify and was not analysed. The remains appear to represent discarded domestic waste.

Neolithic

South Devon

Hems Valley, Staverton (Site 17)
The fills of the Middle Neolithic pits (Table 2.19, SS 290–295, and Table 2.20, SS 296 and SS 298) were dominated by large quantities of carbonised hazelnut shells. Pit 2.02.016 also contained a single vetch/vetchlings seed, pit 2.02.013 contained carbonised barley and indeterminate cereal grains and pit 2.02.006 a possible carbonised barley grain. Charcoal from fill 2.02.007 of pit 2.02.006 was fully analysed and was dominated by alder/hazel and hazel fragments with a moderate amount of oak and a single hawthorn/rowan/crab apple fragment identified (Table 2.22, SS 292). The broad characterisation of charcoal from pits 2.02.004, fill 2.02.008 of pit 2.02.006 and pit 2.02.010 mirrored this trend and consisted dominantly of alder/hazel and hazel charcoal fragments (Table 2.21).

Moore Farm, Harberton (Site 28)
The plant macrofossil assemblages from Late Neolithic pits 18.12.018 and 18.12.053 (Table 2.20, SS 301, SS 310), like those from Hems Valley, were dominated by carbonised hazelnut shells, and pit 18.12.053 contained a single carbonised crab apple pip. The charcoal from pit 18.12.018 was fully analysed and, like Hems Valley, was dominated by alder/hazel and hazel charcoal with a small amount of oak (Table 2.22). The broad characterisation of charcoal from pit 18.12.053 follows this trend with a small amount of ash charcoal additionally identified (Table 2.21).

Two samples were retrieved from the second fill 18.13.006 and third fill 18.13.007 of pit 18.13.004 (Table 2.20, SS 305, SS 306) which contained moderate volumes of carbonised hazelnut

Table 2.19: Neolithic plant macrofossil identifications: Hems Valley (Site 17)

Habitat Codes: A = Arable weed; D = Opportunistic weed from a disturbed environment; DC = Opportunistic weed but may have been consumed; P = Grassland species (possible pasture); E = Economic species (plants deliberately cultivated for economic use); H = Heathland species; HSW = Hedgerow, scrub, woodland species; M = Marsh/wetland species; WF = Wild Food
Identifications: * = modern; hw = heartwood (old wood); sw = sapwood (young wood)

Habitat code			Site	17	17	17	17	17	17
			Context number	02.02.005	02.02.007	02.02.008	02.02.011	02.02.014	02.02.015
			Feature number	02.02.004	02.02.006	02.02.006	02.02.010	02.02.013	02.02.013
			Sample number	290	292	291	293	294	295
			Sample volume (L)	39	16	8	30	16	14
			Flot volume (ml)	223	112	85	77	21	33
	Family	Species	Common Name						
D	Amaranthaceae	*Chenopodium album*	Fat hen *	-	-	1	1	-	-
WF/ HSW	Betulaceae	*Corylus avellana*	Hazelnut	5001	1537	607	974	72	25
D	Caryophyllaceae	*Stellaria media*	Common chickweed *	-	-	1	-	-	-
E	Poaceae	*Avena spp*	Oat	-	-	-	-	-	-
E		*Hordeum vulgare*	Hulled barley	cf 1	-	-	-	1	-
E		*Triticum dicoccum/ spelta*	Emmer/spelt wheat	-	-	-	-	-	-
E		Poaceae	Indet. cereal grain	-	-	-	-	1	-
D	Polygonaceae	*Fallopia convolvulus*	Black-bindweed *	-	1	-	-	-	-
DC			Tuber spp	cf 1	-	-	-	-	-
			Total macrofossils identified	5003	1538	609	975	74	25

Table 2.20: Neolithic plant macrofossil identifications: Hems Valley (Site 17) and Moore Farm (Site 28). (For Key see Table 2.19)

Habitat code			Site	17	17	28	28	28	28
			Context number	02.02.017	02.02.019	18.12.020	18.12.054	18.13.006	18.13.007
			Feature number	02.02.016	02.02.018	18.12.018	18.12.053	18.13.004	18.13.004
			Sample number	298	296	301	310	305	306
			Sample volume (L)	9	8	15	28	26	27
			Flot volume (ml)	40	12	275	330	98	269
	Family	Species	Common Name						
D	Amaranthaceae	*Chenopodium album*	Fat hen *	-	-	-	1	1	6
WF/ HSW	Betulaceae	*Corylus avellana*	Hazelnut	144	54	435	154	35	53
DC	Fabaceae	*Vicia spp/ Lathyrus spp*	Vetch/ vetchlings	1	-	-	-	-	-
WF/ HSW	Rosaceae	*Malus sylvestris*	Crab apple	-	-	-	1	-	-
			Total macrofossils identified	145	54	435	156	36	59

Table 2.21: Neolithic charcoal identifications (broad characterisation): Hems Valley (Site 17) and Moore Farm (Site 28) (For Key see Table 2.19).

			Site	17	17	17	28	28
			Context number	02.02.005	02.02.008	02.02.011	18.12.054	18.13.007
			Feature number	02.02.004	02.02.006	02.02.010	18.12.053	18.13.004
			Sample number	290	291	293	310	306
			Sample volume (L)	39	8	30	28	17
Family	Species		Common Name					
Betulaceae	*Alnus glutinosa*	Alder	-	-	-	-	-
	Alnus glutinosa/ Corylus avellana	Alder/ hazel	7	4	10	6	3
	Corylus avellana	Hazel	12	5	8	7	13
Fagaceae	*Quercus robur/petraea*	Sessile/pedunculate oak	-	6	1	-	2
	Quercus robur/petraea hw	Sessile/pedunculate oak h/w	1	1	-	4	2
	Quercus robur/petraea sw	Sessile/pedunculate oak s/w	-	-	1	-	-
Oleaceae	*Fraxinus excelsior*	Ash	-	-	-	3	-
Rosaceae	*Crataegus monogyna/ Sorbus spp/Malus sylvestris*	Hawthorn/ rowan/ crab apple	-	4	-	-	-
	Prunus avium/padus	Wild/bird cherry	-	-	-	-	-
	Prunus spinosa	Blackthorn/sloe	-	-	-	-	-
		Total fragments identified	**20**	**20**	**20**	**20**	**20**

Table 2.22: Neolithic charcoal identifications (full analysis): Hems Valley (Site 17) and Moore Farm (Site 28)

		Site	17	28
		Context number	02.02.007	18.12.020
		Feature number	02.02.006	18.12.018
		Sample number	292	301
		Sample volume (L)	16	15
Family	Species	Common Name		
Betulaceae	*Alnus glutinosa/Corylus avellana*	Alder/hazel	33	61
	Corylus avellana	Hazel	16	35
Fagaceae	*Quercus robur/petraea*	Sessile/pedunculate oak	23	2
	Quercus robur/petraea hw	Sessile/pedunculate oak h/w	6	2
	Quercus robur/petraea sw	Sessile/pedunculate oak s/w	1	-
Rosaceae	*Crataegus monogyna/ Sorbus spp/Malus sylvestris*	Hawthorn/ rowan/crab apple	1	-
		Total fragments identified	**80**	**100**

shells, although these are recorded in much lower volumes than from Hems Valley. The charcoal from fill 18.13.007 was broadly characterised and, like the others, was dominated by alder/hazel and hazel fragments with smaller quantities of oak (Table 2.21).

Bronze Age

East Devon

Pixies' Parlour, Ottery St Mary (Site 4)
The charcoal from pit 03.04.026 (Table 2.23 SS 66) was broadly characterised and consisted dominantly of oak with a small amount of alder/hazel identified. There were no plant macrofossils identified. This pit was initially described as a possible cremation pit, although no cremated bone was recovered. As with the cremation pit at Salston B, Ottery St Mary (Site 6), described below, cremation pits are typically dominated by oak charcoal with smaller quantities of other species. The charcoal from this pit follows this trend, although oak may dominate in non-cremation contexts such as some of the Bronze Age pits at Crablake Farm, Exminster (Site 15)

Salston B, Ottery St Mary (Site 6)
The charcoal from fill 205.012 of pit 205.004 (Table 2.24, SS 63) was fully analysed and consisted dominantly of oak, with smaller amounts of alder and alder/hazel. This material was most likely firing debris from the cremation pyre.

Table 2.23: Bronze Age charcoal identifications (broad characterisation): Pixies' Parlour (Site 4), Land East of Broad Oak (Site 7) and Crablake Farm (Site 15). (For Key see Table 2.19)

Family	Species	Common Name	Site	4	7	15	15	15	15
		Context number		03.04.028	04.10.017	14.09.009	14.09.009	14.09.009	14.09.006
		Feature number		03.04.026	04.10.016	14.09.016	14.09.016	14.09.016	14.09.003
		Sample number		66	213	203	204	205	207
		Sample volume (L)		5	6	4	3	4	4
Betulaceae	*Alnus glutinosa/Corylus avellana*	Alder/hazel		3	1	11	2	-	-
	Corylus avellana	Hazel		-	-	-	-	-	-
Fabaceae	*Ulex* spp/*Cytisus* spp	Gorse/broom		-	-	3	3	-	3
Fagaceae	*Quercus robur/petraea*	Sessile/pedunculate oak		16	-	6	12	-	7
	Quercus robur/petraea hw	Sessile/pedunculate oak h/w		1	19	-	-	5	-
	Quercus robur/petraea sw	Sessile/pedunculate oak s/w		-	-	-	-	-	-
Oleaceae	*Fraxinus excelsior*	Ash		-	-	-	-	-	-
Rosaceae	*Crataegus monogyna/Sorbus* spp/*Malus sylvestris*	Hawthorn/rowan/crab apple		-	-	-	-	-	-
Rosaceae	*Prunus avium/padus*	Wild/bird cherry		-	-	-	2	-	-
	Prunus spinosa	Blackthorn/sloe		-	-	-	-	-	-
Salicaceae	*Salix* spp/*Populus* spp	Willow/poplar		-	-	-	1	-	-
		Total fragments identified		**20**	**20**	**20**	**20**	**5**	**10**

Table 2.24: Bronze Age charcoal identifications (full analysis): Salston B (Site 6), Hood Ball (Site 21), Beneknowle (Site 30). (For Key see Table 2.19)

Family	Species	Common Name	Site	6	21	21	30
		Context number		205.012	12.05.014	12.05.016	21.06.010
		Feature number		205.004	12.05.013	12.05.013	21.06.008
		Sample number		63	225	226	313
		Sample volume (L)		6	8	6	22
Betulaceae	*Alnus glutinosa*	Alder		8	19	17	4
	Alnus glutinosa/Corylus avellana	Alder/hazel		3	72	54	19
	Corylus avellana	Hazel		-	-	5	2
Fagaceae	*Quercus robur/petraea*	Sessile/pedunculate oak		4	-	-	3
	Quercus robur/petraea hw	Sessile/pedunculate oak h/w		54	-	-	54
	Quercus robur/petraea sw	Sessile/pedunculate oak s/w		-	-	-	3
Oleaceae	*Fraxinus excelsior*	Ash		-	6	3	-
Rosaceae	*Crataegus monogyna/Sorbus* spp/*Malus sylvestris*	Hawthorn/rowan/crab apple		-	-	-	15
Salicaceae	*Salix* spp/*Populus* spp	Willow/poplar		-	3	21	-
		Total fragments identified		**69**	**100**	**100**	**100**

Land East of Broad Oak, Ottery St Mary (Site 7)

Primary fill 04.10.017 taken from Middle Bronze Age pit 04.10.016 was broadly characterised and was dominated by oak (Table 2.23, SS 213).

Crablake Farm, Exminster (Site 15)

Three soil samples were taken from Middle Bronze Age pit 14.09.016 (Tables 2.25 and 2.23). Fill 14.09.009 (Table 2.25, SS 203) contained carbonised indeterminate cereal grains and

Table 2.25: Bronze Age plant macrofossil identifications: Crablake Farm (Site 15), Hood Ball (Site 21), Beneknowle (Site 30), Filham House (Site 34). (For Key see Table 2.19)

Habitat code	Family	Species	Common Name	Site 15	Site 15	Site 15	Site 21	Site 21	Site 21	Site 21	Site 30	Site 34	Site 34	Site 34
			Context number	14.09.009	14.09.009	14.09.016	12.05.007	12.05.015	12.05.012	12.05.011	21.06.010	33.01.006	33.01.007	33.01.008
			Feature number	14.09.016	14.09.016	14.09.016	12.05.004	12.05.009	12.05.011	12.05.011	21.06.008	33.01.006	33.01.006	33.01.006
			Sample number	203	205	235	229	228	313	316	317			
			Sample volume (L)	4	3	7	25	6	16	8	3			
			Flot volume (ml)	15	10	28	66	48	185	776	104			
D	Amaranthaceae	*Chenopodium album*	Fat hen *	-	-	-	-	-	-	6	-	-	-	-
DC		*Chenopodium* spp	Fat hen/goosefoot	-	-	-	-	-	130	-	-	-	-	-
M	Apiaceae	*Apium nodiflorum*	Fool's-water-cress	-	-	-	-	-	6	-	-	-	-	-
D		*Hieracium* spp	Hawkweeds	-	-	-	-	-	10	-	-	-	-	-
WF	Betulaceae	*Corylus avellana*	Hazelnut	-	-	-	1	-	1	2006	298	-	-	-
DC	Brassicaceae	*Brassica/Sinapis* spp	Mustard/cabbage/charlock	-	-	-	-	-	37	-	-	-	-	-
P	Fabaceae	*Medicago lupulina*	Black medick	-	-	-	-	-	3	-	-	-	-	-
HSW/H		*Ulex* spp/*Prunus spinosa*	Gorse/blackthorn spines	-	-	-	-	-	1	-	-	-	-	-
DC		*Vicia* spp/*Lathyrus* spp	Vetch/vetchlings	-	-	-	-	-	102	-	-	-	-	-
P	Lamiaceae	*Prunella vulgaris*	Self heal	-	-	-	-	-	2	-	-	-	-	-
D	Plantaginaceae	*Plantago major*	Greater plantain	-	-	-	-	-	47	-	-	-	-	-
E	Poaceae	*Avena* spp	Oat	-	-	-	-	-	3	-	-	-	-	-
E		*Hordeum vulgare*	Hulled barley	-	2	-	-	3	1	5	-	-	-	-
E		*Secale cereale*	Rye	-	1	-	-	1	-	1	-	-	-	-
E		*Triticum aestivum*/*triticum/durum*	Bread-type wheat	-	-	-	-	-	-	-	-	-	-	-
E		*Triticum dicoccum/spelta*	Emmer/spelt wheat	-	-	-	-	2	-	-	-	-	-	-
E		Poaceae	Indet. cereal grain	2	-	-	1	-	1	2	-	-	-	-
E		Poaceae	Cereal chaff – culm node	-	-	-	-	-	-	2	-	-	-	-
E		Poaceae	Cereal chaff – Palea	-	-	-	-	-	1	-	-	-	-	-
D		Poaceae	Grass	-	-	-	-	-	4	1	-	-	-	-
D	Polygonaceae	*Fallopia convolvulus*	Black-bindweed	-	-	-	-	-	42	-	-	-	-	-

Earlier Prehistoric Period 71

Habitat code	Family	Species	Common Name	Site	15	15	21	21	21	21	30	34	34
			Context number		14.09.009	14.09.009	12.05.007	12.05.015	12.05.012	21.06.010	21.06.008	33.01.007	33.01.008
			Feature number		14.09.016	14.09.016	12.05.004	12.05.009	12.05.011	21.06.008	33.01.006	33.01.006	
			Sample number		203	205	235	229	228	313	316	317	
			Sample volume (L)		4	3	7	25	6	16	8	3	
			Flot volume (ml)		15	10	28	66	48	185	776	104	
DC		*Rumex* spp	Dock		-	-	-	-	-	17	-	-	
DC		*Rumex acetosa*	Common sorrel		-	-	-	-	-	1	-	-	
DC		*Rumex conglomeratus*	Clustered dock		-	-	-	-	-	1	-	-	
P	Ranunculaceae	*Ranunculus repens*	Buttercup		-	-	-	-	-	3	-	-	
WF	Rosaceae	*Prunus* spp	Cherry spp pip		-	-	-	-	1	-	-	-	
WF		*Rubus fruticosus*	Blackberry		-	-	-	-	-	5	-	-	
WF		*Rubus ideaus*	Raspberry		-	-	-	-	-	1	-	-	
WF		*Rubus saxatilis* sect *Glandulosus*	Stone bramble		-	-	-	-	-	3	-	-	
A	Rubiaceae	*Galium aparine*	Cleavers		1	-	-	-	-	105	2	-	
D	Solanaceae	*Solanum nigrum*	Black nightshade		-	-	-	-	-	2	-	-	
			Total macrofossils identified		3	3	2	6	3	539	2015	298	

Table 2.26: Bronze Age charcoal identifications (broad characterisation): Hood Ball (Site 21) and Filham House (Site 34). (For Key see Table 2.19)

Site		21	21	21	21	21	21	21	34	34
Context number		12.05.010	12.05.012	12.05.015	12.05.023	12.05.005	12.05.020	12.05.021	33.01.007	33.01.008
Feature number		12.05.009	12.05.011	12.05.009	12.05.019	12.05.004	12.05.019	12.05.019	33.01.006	33.01.006
Sample number		227	228	229	231	233	237	238	316	317
Sample volume (L)		6	6	23	6	26	6	8	48	3
Family	Species	Common Name								
Betulaceae	*Alnus glutinosa/Corylus avellana*	Alder/hazel	-	4	-	-	9	-	7	4	10
	Corylus avellana	Hazel	-	2	-	-	11	1	-	3	3
Fabaceae	*Ulex* spp/*Cytisus* spp	Gorse/broom	-	-	-	-	-	-	-	-	-
Fagaceae	*Quercus robur/petraea*	Sessile/pedunculate oak	1	-	-	9	-	-	3	7	5
	Quercus robur/petraea h/w	Sessile/pedunculate oak h/w	-	-	-	9	-	3	-	4	1
	Quercus robur/petraea s/w	Sessile/pedunculate oak s/w	-	-	-	-	-	-	-	-	1
Oleaceae	*Fraxinus excelsior*	Ash	11	14	20	1	-	15	6	1	-
Rosaceae	*Crataegus monogyna/Sorbus* spp/*Malus sylvestris*	Hawthorn/rowan/crab apple	-	-	-	1	-	1	4	-	-
Rosaceae	*Prunus avium/padus*	Wild/bird cherry	-	-	-	-	-	-	-	-	-
	Prunus spinosa	Blackthorn/sloe	-	-	-	-	-	-	-	1	-
Salicaceae	*Salix* spp/*Populus* spp	Willow/poplar	-	-	-	-	-	-	-	-	-
	Total fragments identified		12	20	20	20	20	20	20	20	20

a carbonised cleavers seed. Fill 14.09.011 (SS 205) contained carbonised barley and bread wheat cereal grains. Fill 14.09.010 (SS 204) contained no plant macrofossil material. The charcoal from the three fills of this pit was broadly characterised and consisted of alder/hazel, gorse/broom, oak, cherry and willow/poplar. The cereal remains and cleavers, which is an arable weed, provides evidence for cereal processing nearby. The charcoal from fill 14.09.006 of pit 14.09.003 (Table 2.23, SS 207) was broadly characterised and contained small amounts of gorse/broom and oak charcoal fragments, although gorse/broom charcoal returned an Iron Age radiocarbon date and is most likely intrusive (Table 2.7).

South Devon

Hood Ball, Rattery (Site 21)
Middle Bronze Age pit 12.05.011, fill 12.05.012 contained carbonised barley and rye cereal grains, and a fragment of a carbonised cherry pip (Table 2.25, SS 228). Pit 12.05.009 contained carbonised barley, emmer/spelt and indeterminate cereal grains (SS 229). Pit 12.05.004 contained an indeterminate cereal grain and carbonised hazelnut shell (SS 235).

Two samples of charcoal from pit 12.05.013 were fully analysed and contained large amounts of alder/hazel and alder charcoal and smaller amounts of ash and willow/poplar (Table 2.24, SS225 and SS 226). The broadly characterised charcoal from pits 12.05.009, 12.05.011, 12.05.009, 12.05.004, 12.05.019 consisted of larger amounts of ash together with alder, hazel, alder/hazel, oak and hawthorn/rowan/crab apple fragments (Table 2.26). The large amounts of alder and willow/poplar are probably associated with fuel collected from the floodplain of the nearby River Dart. This material is again indicative of burnt discarded domestic and cereal processing.

Beneknowle, Diptford (Site 30)
The sample from fill 21.06.010 of the Bronze Age terraced building (21.06.008) contained a very rich assemblage of plant macrofossil material (Table 2.25, SS 313). It contained evidence of crops including oat, barley, culm nodes and paleas and arable weeds such as cleavers; opportunistic weeds including large numbers of fat hen/goosefoot, black-bindweed and ribwort plantain seeds, moderate numbers of mustard/cabbage/charlock; grassland species indicating possible hay including black medick and self heal and hedgerow and woodland species indicated by gorse/blackthorn spines, hazelnut and brambles. There is also evidence of plants from wet areas, such as fool's-water-cress, and carbonised water-vole faecal pellets. The plant macrofossil and faecal pellet identifications (Allen, below) indicate that the organic material had been collected from a variety of habitats. The large numbers of vetch seeds, together with cereal remains, hay and brambles suggest that this may have been a collection of fodder which was later burnt. The charcoal was fully analysed and a large quantity was identified as oak with smaller quantities of alder, hazel and hawthorn/rowan/crab apple (Table 2.24). It is possible that this represents part of a burnt timber structure, but the charcoal fragments are too small to be certain.

Filham House, Ugborough (Site 34)
Middle Bronze Age pit 33.01.006 contained large numbers of carbonised hazelnut shells from both primary fill 33.01.007 and secondary fill 33.01.008 (Table 2.25, SS 316, SS 317). Fill 33.01.007 also contained carbonised cleavers, grass and modern fat hen seeds. The charcoal from these two fills was broadly characterised and consisted of alder/hazel, hazel, oak and blackthorn fragments (Table 2.26).

Charred small mammal/rodent faecal pellets from Beneknowle, Diptford (Site 30)

Michael J. Allen

Six sub-cylindrical charred items were recovered from Sample 313, context 21.06.010, of Bronze Age terraced structure 21.06.008. The pellets were investigated under a stereo binocular microscope at ×10 - ×40 magnifications and examined for gross morphology and compared with a number of rodent and small mammal droppings. The contents of two were visually inspected for identifiable food remains.

The charred pellets are faecal droppings. They are sub-cylindrical with blunt ends and average 5.5mm by 3.3mm in size. Given shrinkage on charring (due to the original water content) we might expect 30–50% reduction in size, indicating they originally may have been approximately 7.2–11mm by 4.3–6mm. The pellets are too spherical for squirrel and as these are Bronze Age we would be dealing with red squirrel (*Sciurus vulgaris*). They are clearly too spherical for rat which are elongate with pointed ends, and too big for mouse. Morphologically they are similar to water vole (*Arvicola terrestris* [amphibious]), whose pellets are this shape and are 8–12mm long and 4–5mm thick. Assuming a portion of shrinkage on charring by the removal of the moderately large water content this would seem to be a good match.

Two were fractured to examine their contents. The charred matrix is fine-grained and homogeneous and contained well-masticated mass with recognisable grass stems which were still visible under the microscope. No coarse material such as nuts or a ground-mass which is likely to be nuts was recognisable.

We can discount squirrel, rat and mouse on basic morphology and size, and rat on the contents. After comparison with numerous other faecal pellets the most similar is water vole though this can be confused with field vole (*Microtus agrestis*) which, although also native to Britain, leave much smaller droppings (at most 2mm wide compared with 4–5mm width for water vole). In summer and spring water voles leave their droppings in piles (latrines) sited near the water's edge but do migrate. They eat grass and in particular *Juncus* (rushes).

These droppings may be water vole, as although not immediately next to water the River Avon is only *c.* 200m away, and water voles inhabit wet ditches and channels feeding into rivers, lakes etc. Although the faecal pellets are full of grass stems, the vole(s) may have also have been attracted to, and fed on, the grain (prior to its carbonisation).

Water vole is native to Britain, but currently facing a fight against extinction in Devon as a result of predation by the introduction of American mink (*Neovison vison*). If verified this is an important (pre)historical reference for the water vole, and also indicates the likelihood of small water-filled ditches in close proximity to the structure in the Bronze Age.

Discussion of earlier prehistoric assemblages

Neolithic and Bronze Age

Arable agriculture and hand-collected foodstuffs

Plant macrofossils assemblages from the Mesolithic, Neolithic and Bronze Age periods are typically recovered in small numbers. The Devon pipeline assemblages largely follow this trend and consist of small numbers (one to three items per sample) of vetch/vetchlings, tubers, crab apple, cherry, grass, seeds and carbonised oat, emmer/spelt, bread wheat, rye and barley cereal grains. The exceptions to this pattern are the large numbers of hazelnut shells from both Neolithic and Bronze Age contexts, and the size and variety of seeds and other plant remains from the Middle Bronze Age structure at Beneknowle, Diptford (Site 30).

There were 9091 fragments of hazelnut shell from Neolithic features and 2306 from Bronze Age ones. There is a trend of decreasing amounts of hazelnut shell from the middle into the later Neolithic features, continuing into the Bronze Age (Fig. 6.2) perhaps indicating increased reliance on arable farming and more permanent settlements through the 3rd millennium BC. There are high hazelnut shell counts from the Bronze Age pit at Filham House, Ugborough (Site 34) which may indicate an atypical reliance on hand-collected foodstuffs, perhaps relating to a temporary occupation.

In the Neolithic period hunting and gathering of wild foodstuffs was combined with small-scale cereal cultivation (emmer wheat, hulled six-row barley and naked six- and two-rowed barley being dominant) and with animal husbandry (Darvill 2010, 88). Evidence for cereal cultivation is generally sparse on archaeological sites, large volumes of soil being required to obtain small numbers of grain and chaff (Fairbairn 2000b, 107). For example, the long enclosure at Castle Hill, Devon contained just three emmer wheat spikelet fragments (Clapham 1999a, 51). There was very limited evidence for cereal cultivation from sites on the present project. From Neolithic features there was one possible oat grain, two barley grains and one possible emmer/spelt grain. There was a little more evidence for cereals in the Bronze Age with three oat grains, eleven barley, one rye, one bread wheat and two emmer/spelt grains and two culm nodes and a palea identified. Counts are too low to determine the dominant crop in either of these periods, although from the Bronze Age samples barley is the most numerous. This trend is shown in Figure 6.2 where the Neolithic has the lowest percentage of crops and in the Bronze Age crops became slightly more important. The evidence is compatible with that from other sites in the region, such as Neolithic long enclosures and Bronze Age pits at Castle Hill, East Devon (Clapham 1999a, 51), a Neolithic pit at Long Range, East Devon (Clapham 1999b, 152), and Neolithic and Bronze Age pits at Hayes Farm, Clyst Honiton, Devon (Cobain forthcoming), which indicates the exploitation and consumption of wild food resources together with slight evidence for cereal cultivation.

Generally in southern England, emmer wheat was the main cereal cultivated, but the cultivation of spelt wheat expanded at the end of the Bronze Age and became more dominant in the Iron Age (Campbell and Straker 2003, 15). Until recently, bread wheat was not thought to have been cultivated in Britain until the Roman period (Hagan 2006, 32). It is possible that the bread wheat identified from Crablake Farm, Exminster (Site 15, pit 14.09.016) is an intrusive grain, but bread wheat has been recovered from Bronze Age features at Trethellan Farm, Cornwall (Straker 1991, 166), pits at Castle Hill, Devon (Clapham 1999a, 53) and pits at Hayne Lane, Devon (Clapham 1999c, 115) and there is mounting evidence that it was being grown during this period. Oats are rare in Neolithic and Bronze Age deposits (Campbell and Straker 2003, 15). The absence of oat floret bases from sites on the present project means that it is not possible to determine whether they were domesticated or wild.

Rye is a rare occurrence in Bronze Age deposits, but a single rye grain was recovered from Hood Ball, Rattery (Site 21) and radiocarbon dated to 1316–1127 cal. BC (NZA-36173; 88.4%: Table 2.8). Rye was present in the south of England and has been recorded from a settlement at Weir Bank Stud Farm, Bray (Clapham 1995, 36 cited in Campbell and Straker 2003, 22), but a large assemblage of rye grains, to the knowledge of the author, has yet to be recovered. It is entirely possible that rye was a cultivated crop, but it is perhaps equally likely to have been a crop contaminant.

At Beneknowle, Diptford (Site 30) the unusual number of seeds (849) comprised a range of crops, arable weeds, weeds of disturbed ground, hay grassland species, wetland species, and species of woodland or scrub. Interpretation of this deposit is tentative, but the assemblage appears to represent a collection of burnt fodder. This size and diversity of remains from Bronze Age Devon is particularly rare and to the knowledge of the author there are no comparable published examples. Vetch has been recorded, for example, at Flagstones, Dorset (Straker 1997c, cited in Campbell and Straker 2003, 15) but here only a few vetch, tare and pea legumes were found. Vetches are known to improve the quality of the soil by fixing nitrogen (Stone 2005, 107), and it is possible they were cultivated for this purpose as well as for food or fodder. There is also a high number of oak charcoal fragments within this deposit. It is possible that these originate from structural elements of the Bronze Age terraced building, 21.06.008.

Barley was more common than other cereals identified in the Bronze Age (Table 2.25), and this would be expected in Devon as it can tolerate heavier and more acidic soils than emmer wheat. This may be the reason for the dominance of barley over emmer wheat in the Bronze Age settlement at Trethellan Farm, Cornwall (Straker 1991, 176).

Hand-gathered fruits and nuts would have provided additional vitamins and minerals as well as making food more palatable (Pearson 1997, 14). Hazelnuts could have been roasted and eaten, added to stews, or processed into a type of biscuit for long term storage. Raspberry, blackberry, crab apples and cherry fruits may have been eaten raw, although crab apple and cherry are both very sour and it is likely they were processed for consumption and to preserve them for the winter months. Herbaceous taxa such as fat hen, vetches and cleavers are known to have been used raw as salad or boiled down as vegetables (Behre 2008, 67-8). Roasted cleavers seeds may have been used as a coffee-like drink (Mabey 2007, 70). There is little direct evidence for processing techniques although many 'recipes' have been proposed, such as juices, ciders, puddings and sauces (Wood 2001).

Fuel

Samples from Neolithic and Bronze Age features were all from deposits of waste material/waste firing debris within pits, with the possible exception of the Bronze Age cremation pit at Salston B, Ottery St Mary (Site 6) which probably related to pyre material. The broad characterisation of the Neolithic charcoal showed that it was dominated by alder/hazel and hazel, with smaller quantities of oak, ash and hawthorn/rowan/crab apple fragments. The Bronze Age charcoal also consists dominantly of alder, alder/hazel and hazel, with moderate counts of oak and smaller counts of gorse/broom, ash, cherry and willow/poplar. There are however variations with this. In particular at Hood Ball, Rattery (Site 21), pit 12.05.013 was dominated by alder/hazel species, and pits 12.05.009 and 12.05.019 by ash. It is possible that the difference reflects differing fire temperature requirements for whatever activities were carried out.

The Bronze Age assemblages are similar to those of the Neolithic (Figure 6.3), but there is a proportional decrease in alder/hazel and an increase in oak. This is due to the inclusion of the cremation at Salston B, Ottery St Mary, where the use of oak for fuel may not have been typical. If this feature is excluded it brings the percentages of oak to the levels found in the Neolithic. A similar trend is observed in the Iron Age assemblages where the high volume of oak results from the dominance of oak in the iron smelting furnaces at Tigley A (Site 26).

The broad characterisation of the charcoal shows similar species present in the Neolithic and Bronze Age (Fig. 6.3), although the full analysis (Fig. 6.4) shows an increase (albeit small) in the proportion of shrubby trees such as hawthorn/rowan/crab apple and blackthorn/sloe. The presence of gorse/broom for the first time in the Bronze Age is also notable. This is consistent with the increase in woodland clearance for settlement and agriculture over this period which introduced more open areas, allowing these lower level trees to establish in larger numbers (Rackham 2001, 35). However, it is possible that this variation results from the larger number of samples analysed from the Bronze Age, which would capture minor species present, or the presence of intrusive charcoal.

The majority of the oak and ash charcoal fragments did not exhibit curved growth rings, which may suggest that they originated from roundwood branches or trunk wood, although to confirm the use of larger roundwood branches fragments of charcoal greater than 5cm in diameter would be needed. The lack of curved growth rings on small charcoal fragments does, however, eliminate the use of oak twigs. By contrast, most fragments from the remaining species exhibited curved growth rings, suggesting that small branch wood and twigs from the alder/hazel, alder, hazel, hawthorn/rowan/crab apple, gorse/broom, cherry, blackthorn/sloe and willow/poplar were being utilised. In the absence of whole fragments of roundwood, however, this observation could not be supported further.

The varied selection of fuel woods may suggest a range of domestic uses. Both oak and ash are often chosen as the main fuel where a constant high temperature is required (Cutler and Gale 2000, 120, 205). Hazel, hawthorn/rowan/crab apple, gorse/broom, blackthorn/sloe and cherry are all also recorded as good fuel woods, although they do not burn for as long periods as oak or ash. Alder and poplar/willow are species which are ideal to use for kindling, because they are anatomically less dense than oak and ash, and burn very quickly at very high temperatures (Cutler and Gale 2000, 236, 260). Similar charcoal assemblages were found at Neolithic long enclosures and Bronze Age pits at Castle Hill, Devon (Gale 1999a, 59–61). As with the present project, gorse/broom and willow/poplar were not present until the Bronze Age.

The Early Bronze Age cremation pit at Salston B, Ottery St Mary (Site 6) showed oak charcoal dominant and a small amount of alder and alder/hazel. This is typical of cremation assemblages where there is usually one dominant species used to construct the pyre and between one and three additional species (kindling or the burnt remains of wooden objects/offerings made as part of the cremation ritual). The use of a single dominant fuel (usually oak or ash) for cremation pyres is found on other Bronze Age sites such as Shepton Mallet, Somerset (Barnett 2008, 5–6), Westhampnett, West Sussex (Gale 2006, 41) and Raunds, Northamptonshire (Campbell and Robinson 2007, 30–1). Oak, in particular, has been linked historically to myths and folklore and it has been suggested that these myths originated in prehistory and indicate an early ritual association and use for the tree (Cutler and Gale 2000, 204; Gale 2006, 41).

Local landscape

The narrow range of plant macrofossil remains from Neolithic features makes it difficult to reconstruct the local flora by this means. Hazelnut shells make up 99.9% of the plant macrofossil assemblage. A single crab apple seed indicates crab apple trees were established within scrub woodland areas and the scant cereal remains indicate areas of arable agriculture near Pixies' Parlour, Ottery St Mary (Site 4) and the Hems Valley, Staverton (Site 17) possibly on the lighter valley or valley edge soils. The presence of vetch/vetchlings and tuber seeds in the Neolithic assemblage indicate disturbed or arable environments, which would be expected in areas of woodland clearance for settlement and agriculture (Rose 2006, 282–4).

During the Bronze Age there is continued evidence for the presence of hazel trees in the landscape together with a single cherry pip suggesting the presence of cherry trees within scrub woodland. Cereal remains indicate areas of crop cultivation at or nearby Crabtree Farm, Exminster (Site 15), Hood Ball, Rattery (21) and Beneknowle, Diptford (Site 30). The diverse range of species from Beneknowle, with evidence of arable weeds such as cleavers, indicates areas of crop cultivation. Species such as buttercup, self heal and ribwort plantain indicate areas of grassland (Rose 2006, 380, 387) and species indicative of a disturbed environment, such as fat hen/goosefoot, black-bindweed, mustard/cabbage charlock, are also present (ibid., 130, 170, 201). This would be expected in areas where woodland had been cleared for settlement and agriculture. Vetch/vetchlings are known to grow in disturbed areas (ibid., 282–4) but were probably cultivated as a fodder crop. There was also evidence for wetland areas (most likely small streams/tributaries of the River Dart) indicated by fool's-water-cress (ibid., 163, 344).

Although it is not possible to use charcoal fragment counts to infer the percentage compositions of woodlands it is possible to give a 'presence/absence' indicator for species (Asouti and Austin 2005, 10–12). On this basis it can be assumed that the woodland during the Neolithic would have consisted mostly of oak primary woodland with secondary/scrub woodland consisting of large amounts of alder/hazel and hazel and smaller quantities of ash and hawthorn/rowan/crab apple (Cutler and Gale 2000, 88, 120, 183–4, 204). During the Bronze Age the primary woodland would have been similar, but with more secondary/scrub woodland including hawthorn/rowan/crab apple, cherry and blackthorn/sloe (Cutler and Gale 2000, 88, 120, 183–4, 196, 204). There was also heathland of gorse/broom (ibid., 260) likely to have been close to Crablake Farm (Site 15) and areas of wet woodland including alder and willow/poplar (ibid., 36, 190, 236) near Hood Ball (Site 21) which is close to the River Dart and its tributaries.

Cremated human remains from Salston B, Ottery St Mary

Harriet Jacklin

The cremated remains (deposits 205.012 and 205.005) from pit 205.004 at Salston B, Ottery St Mary (Site 6) represent a cremation burial unaccompanied by a vessel (Table 2.27). The burial was excavated in two

Table 2.27: Cremation burial from Salston B (pit 205.004). (Total bone weight 767g).

Fragment Size (mm)	Weight (g)	Colour (%)	Additional Notes
0<2mm	42g	White 99%, white-grey 1%	Unidentifiable human bone fragments mixed with bone dust.
2<5mm	36g	White 99%, white-grey 1%	Majority of the fragments unidentifiable consisting of long bone and trabacular bone. One fragment of a dental root.
5<10mm	314g	White 99%, white-grey 1%	Majority of fragments consist of long bone, trabacular bone and cranial fragments. Cranial fragments adult width and size (although slender) and include partially closed suture lines indicating a possible young adult. Three dental roots (fully formed), fragments of vertebral neural arches, a diaphysis of an unsided metacarpal (5) and a fragment of an unsided fully fused metacarpal (5) distal epiphysis (possibly the same), an unsided medial hand phalanx and fragments of proximal-medial hand phalanx have also been identified.
10mm+	375g	White 99%, white-grey 1%	Majority of fragments identifiable; epiphysis, cranium and long bone. Also two fully fused hand medial-distal epiphysis, five fragments of vertebral neural arches (including several cervical and thoracic facets) and one fragment of a lumbar body (including annular rim). No age-related changes or pathology, all fragments in good condition.
Epiphysis fragments (20g): Fragments of epiphysis and metaphysis including fragments of a distal femur (18+ years), proximal tibia (17+ years), femoral or humeral heads (16/17+ years), a proximal ulna fragment (14+ years) and an unsided metacarpal (1) proximal end. All of adult size and fully fused indicating 18+ years. No age-related changes or pathology, all fragments in good condition.
Cranial fragments (80g): Fragments of frontal occipital, parietal and temporal bone. Sutures visible and partially closed. All adult in size and width. Fragments include nuchal crest which scores '1' indicating a female, and left and right supra orbital ridges which both score '1', again indicating a female. Also a fragment of the right mandible but with no sockets or teeth, the left zygomatic arch and two fragments of the left maxilla consisting of dental sockets for premolars and molars; no avolar bone reabsorbtion (indicating ante-mortem loss) visible, loss of teeth are post-mortem. No age-related changes or pathology, all fragments in good condition.
Long bone fragments (220g): Fragments of humerus, ulna, radius, femur, tibia and fibula. No age-related changes or pathology found, all fragments in good condition.

sections and has no associated finds other than charcoal, identified as a mixture of oak, alder and hazel/alder (Table 2.24, SS 63). A radiocarbon measurement obtained on a sample of bone returned a date in the range 1948–1772 cal. BC (NZA-36660), placing it in the Early Bronze Age. A fragment of associated alder charcoal returned a date of 2137–1975 cal. BC (NZA-36711) (Table 2.4)

The cremated remains weighed 767g and there was no duplication of skeletal parts. The surviving cremated bone represents a possible female aged 18+ years. The age at death was based on the assessment of epiphyseal fusion and the estimation of sex based on assessment of the cranial fragments and overall size and robusticity. The majority of the identifiable skeletal elements represented within the cremation were the long bones and the cranium, which take longer to burn than other skeletal elements. The small quantity of the smaller skeletal elements such as the hands, feet and ribs is expected as these elements take a shorter amount of time to reduce effectively. The colour of the cremated remains reflects the degree of oxidisation (temperature) to which the bone was submitted. The majority of the cremated material reached a temperature in excess of *c.* 600 degrees Centigrade (full oxidisation).

Radiocarbon dating

Andrew Mudd

The radiocarbon dates from the sites described above are shown in Tables 2.2–2.11. All dates were on individual charred seeds and hazelnut shells where possible, and some were on wood charcoal of short-lived species. Excepting the date from the cremated human bone at Salston B (Site 6), none of the samples were ideal in the sense of being demonstrated primary *in situ* material. This is reflected in some of the dating of undoubtedly intrusive and residual material, and in other cases, what was probably old wood. Multiple dates from features were chosen where possible to avoid doubt. Three unacceptably early (Neolithic) dates from a pit east of Broad Oak (Site 7), the ring-ditch south-east of Broad Oak (Site 8) and a pit at Crablake Farm (Site 15) are most likely due to dating old wood. The large ditch at Hood Quarry (Site 23) also yielded an early date from short-lived wood species likely to have been redeposited, and a hazelnut shell from the Beneknowle terraced building yielded a Middle Neolithic date, presumably again redeposited. Despite these unhelpful results, there were a large number of mutually supporting dates, in many cases associated with pottery, flint and valuable charred assemblages. The unacceptably early dates, while not useful for interpreting the archaeology, do at least suggest early prehistoric burning at these sites, presumably related to woodland clearance.

Chapter 3
Later Prehistoric and Roman Periods

Introduction

No features or artefacts can be attributed to the early Iron Age but the scatter of Middle Iron Age features, dating from about 400 BC, conforms to the general increase in the number of sites and finds in the county from that date (Quinnell 1999). There was a significant group of iron smelting furnaces at Tigley A (Site 26), dated solely by radiocarbon. There also were pits and ditches from Slade Farm (Site 2), Pixies' Parlour (Site 4) and Crablake Farm (Site 15) in East Devon, and from Barton Hill Cross (Site 19), Springfield (Site 31) and Filham House (Site 34) in South Devon. The distinction between the Iron Age and Roman activity is not altogether clear due to the sparseness and conservative nature of the Iron Age wares and the continuing use of traditional architectural forms in the Roman period. Roman activity was dominated by settlement sites at Billany Farm (Site 24) and Springfield (Site 31), which yielded relatively large assemblages of pottery. There was another possible Roman settlement at Barton Hill Cross, and other features at Pixies' Parlour and Dun Cross, Dartington (Site 25). Undated iron furnaces at Lower Velwell, Rattery (Site 22) are likely to be Iron Age or Roman, while ditches at Exwell Barton, Powderham (Site 14) appear to be of a similar date.

Site descriptions
Stuart Joyce and Andrew Mudd

East Devon

Site 2, Slade Farm, Ottery St Mary

An isolated pit, 2.03.004, lay south-east of Slade Farm at 96m AOD on a gentle west-facing slope (Fig. 3.1). This pit, cut into the sandy substrate of Triassic mudstone, measured 0.8m wide and 0.34m deep with steep sides and a flat base (Fig. 3.2). The single, dark fill, 2.03.005, contained abundant charred remains including cereals such as oats, barley, rye and spelt wheat, and weeds (Table 3.16). There was also wood charcoal from a range of species (Table 3.17). The pit also contained six sherds of abraded pottery, three of which were positively identified as Peterborough Ware of the Middle Neolithic. These appear inconsistent with the charred plant remains and, due to this ambivalent dating, three radiocarbon determinations were obtained on grains of wheat and barley, and on hazelnut shell. These produced date ranges of 388–208 cal. BC (NZA-36305), 388–212 cal. BC (NZA-36320) and 392–212 (NZA-36304) cal. BC, placing the pit firmly within the Middle Iron Age and indicating that the Neolithic pottery is residual (Table 3.1). The remaining three sherds of pottery, while of a

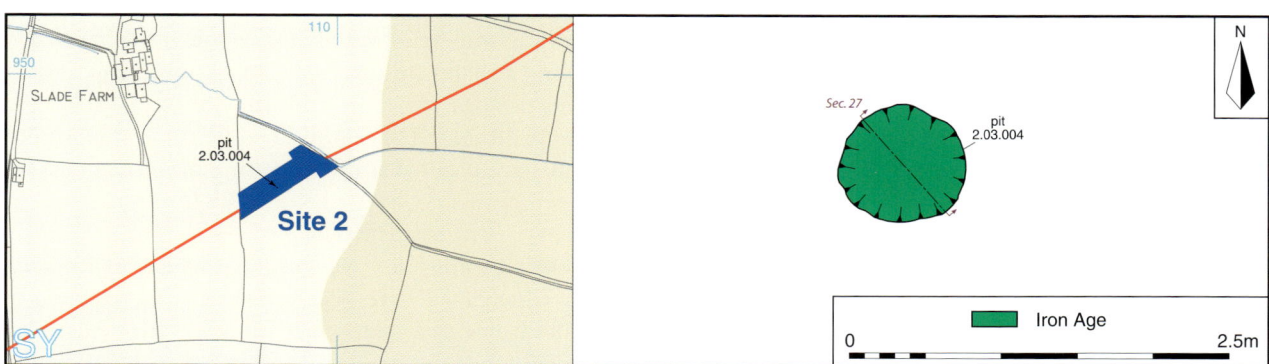

Fig. 3.1   Slade Farm (Site 2); plan of pit 2.03.004. Scales 1:50 and 1:10,000

Table 3.1: Radiocarbon dates from Slade Farm, Site 2 (OTA 2.03)

Feature	Context	Lab No.	Material	δ ^{13}C	Radiocarbon Age	Calibrated Age 95%	Calibrated Age 68%
Pit 02.03.004	02.03.005	NZA 36305	Wheat grain (*Triticum spp*)	-22.8‰	2249 ± 20 yr BP	388–349 BC (35.2%) plus 299–208 BC (59.9%)	382–355 BC (29.8%) plus 282–255 BC (26.6%) plus 246–233 BC (11.2%)
Pit 02.03.004	02.03.005	NZA 36320	Barley grain (*Hordeum vulgare*)	-20.7‰	2252 ± 15 yr BP	388–351 BC (42.3%) plus 291–228 BC (51.7%) plus 216–212 BC (1.0%)	383–357 BC (36.9%) plus 278–256 BC (24.9%) plus 241–234 BC (6.2%)
Pit 02.03.004	02.03.005	NZA 36304	Hazelnut shell (*Corylus avellana*)	-24.5‰	2263 ± 20 yr BP	392–352 BC (50.6%) plus 291–228 BC (43.3%) plus 216–212 BC (0.9%)	388–357 BC (46.4%) plus 277–257 BC (20.0%) plus 240–237 BC (2.2%)

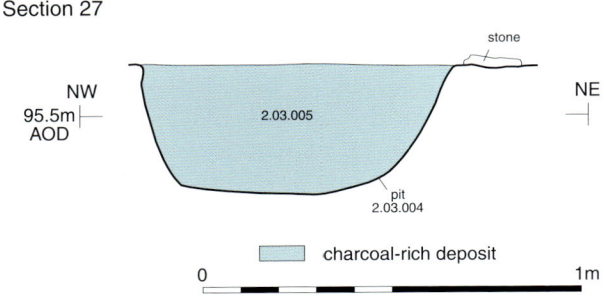

Fig. 3.2 Slade Farm (Site 2); section 27 through pit 2.03.004. Scale 1:20

similar local fabric, are perhaps more likely to date to the Iron Age (Quinnell, this chapter).

The function and wider context of this pit are not at all clear. It does not have the dimensions of a typical grain storage pit, but it was sharp-profiled and appears to have been filled shortly after it was dug. The range of plant remains, including cereal chaff and weeds, suggests that it was filled with burnt crop-processing waste which would imply a proximity to settlement, although there were no other features within the 14m-wide pipeline easement here. Alternatively, it is possible that the pit was located away from settlement, and had received material burnt through activities carried out in the fields.

Site 4, Pixies' Parlour, Ottery St Mary

The location of the site, above the floodplain of the River Otter, has been described above in relation to the earlier prehistoric flintwork and Neolithic and Bronze Age pits discovered here. The site was initially designated for excavation following the discovery of a large curving ditch in the preliminary geophysical survey (Archaeological Surveys 2006a; Fig. 3.3). The site was examined with a single trench (T206) to confirm its archaeological significance, and area excavation followed.

Two phases of Iron Age to Roman activity were identified. In the western part of the site a penannular ditch, 3.04.045, had an internal diameter of 8m, with an entrance gap to the south-east up to 2m wide. The ditch was 0.85m wide and 0.39m deep with symmetrical steep sides and a concave base. The primary fill, 3.04.042, a dark red-brown silt, contained a sherd of pottery from the eastern terminal, broadly dated to the Roman period on the basis of the fabric, and a Late Iron Age sherd. A soil sample from the secondary fill (03.04.088) produced only a very poorly preserved hazelnut shell fragment from the residue, and this may have been redeposited from the earlier prehistoric occupation on the site. The penannular ditch with its south-eastern entrance is typical of an eaves-drainage ditch around an Iron Age roundhouse. It is not closely dated as this native style of architecture may have been current into the 2nd or 3rd centuries AD. The potsherds support, but do not help refine, this dating.

Curvilinear ditch 3.04.004 cut the penannular ditch and ran the length of the site. It was between 1.75m and 2.25m wide, with a maximum depth of 1.1m. The ditch was initially examined with nine sections. It had a slightly asymmetrical profile with a south edge normally showing a shallow upper and steeper lower slope, while the north slope was more uniformly moderate (Fig. 3.4, sections 28–31). The reason for this is not obvious but it may have resulted from excavating from the northern side which would have been the slightly easier access. The base was normally flat or gently rounded and a narrower cleaning slot was recorded in one of the sections, which may have been a general characteristic of the ditch not easily identified since the slot was filled with clean redeposited sand. There was some variation to the ditch fills in section, but generally there was little anthropogenic input. Following the recording of

Later Prehistoric and Roman Periods 81

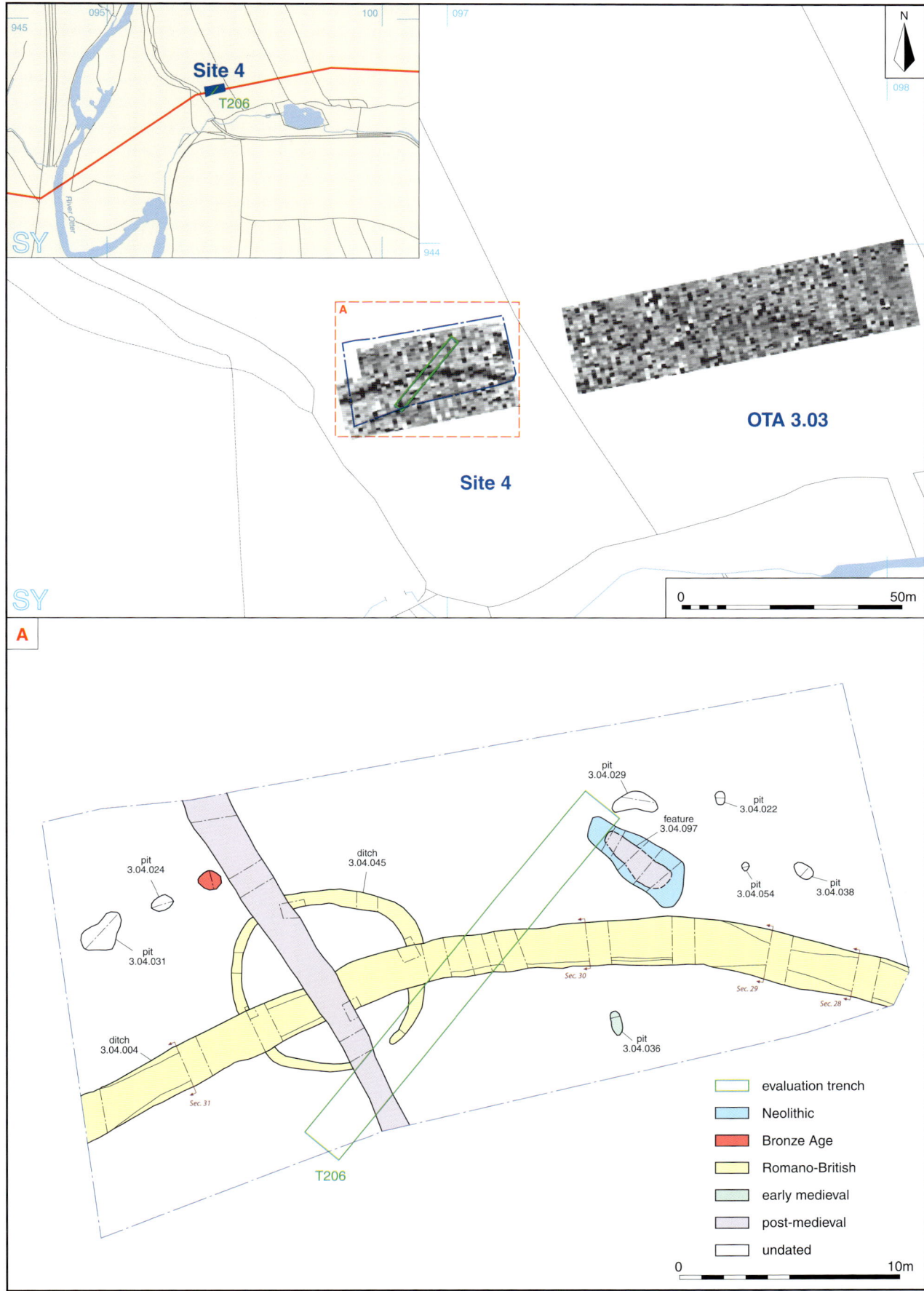

Fig. 3.3   Pixies' Parlour (Site 4); plan of geophysical anomalies and (A) Roman and later features. Scales 1:250, 1:1250, 1:10,000

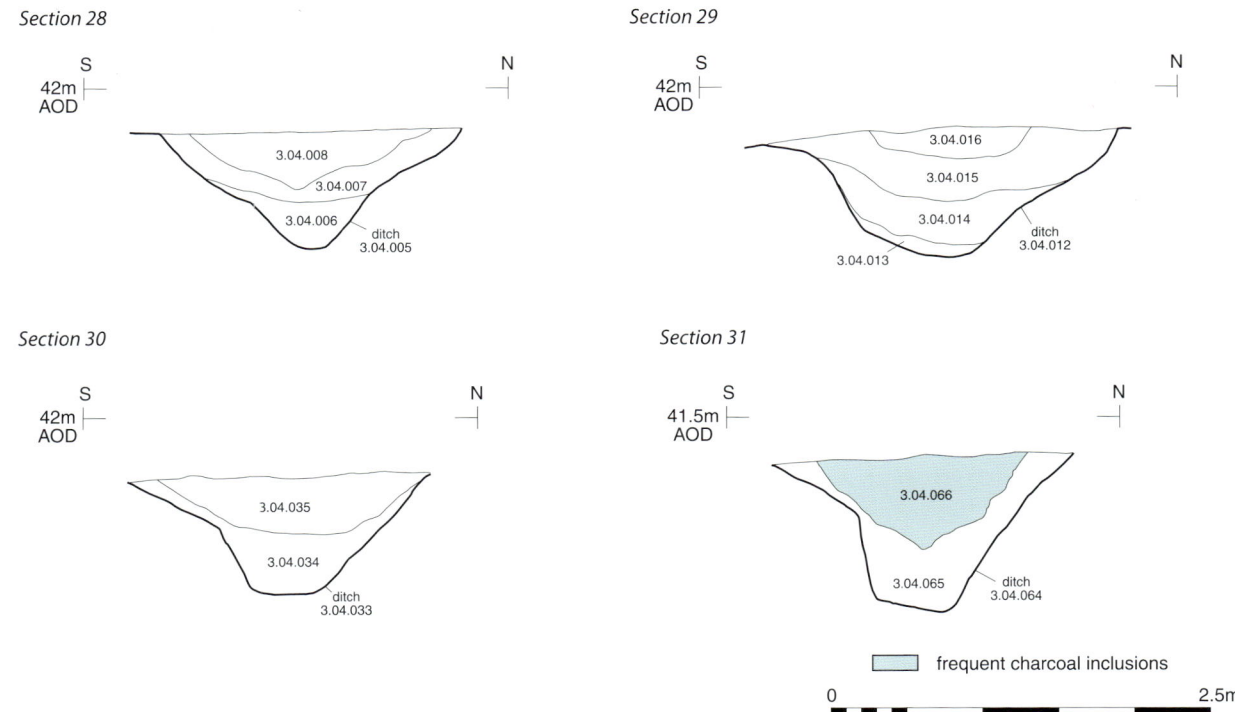

Fig. 3.4 Pixies' Parlour (Site 4); sections 28 to 31 through ditch 3.04.004. Scale 1:50

the sections the entire length of ditch was excavated to maximise the retrieval of finds (Fig. 3.5).

The primary fills comprised grey-yellow clay-sand from natural silting and initial collapse of unstable sides soon after the ditch was cut. The middle fills were pink-brown silty clay, presumably accumulating over a longer usage phase of the ditch. Fill 3.04.014 contained one sherd of Roman pottery and a worked flint, and middle

Fig. 3.5 Pixies' Parlour (Site 4); excavating ditch 3.04.004, looking west

fill 3.04.062 another sherd. A sherd of 12th to 14th-century pottery is believed to be intrusive. The upper fills tended to be darker greyish brown with charcoal flecks common in some places. A soil sample from fill 3.04.020 contained oak, hazel/alder and gorse/broom (Table 3.19, sample 78). This may indicate some form of domestic or agricultural activity in the vicinity during the final phases of ditch infilling. A cobble from the Budleigh Salterton Pebble Beds utilised as a polisher or whetstone was recovered from fill 3.04.015. Soil samples from primary ditch fill 03.04.095 and secondary ditch fill 03.04.064 were assessed and yielded only single emmer/spelt wheat grains from each. A further seven samples from basal fills were without remains.

There is a notable dearth of evidence for the date or function of ditch 3.04.004. A Roman date appears likely, although the Roman pottery could be residual in a later feature. Certainly by the medieval period the site was probably agricultural, as indicated by the strip fields fossilised in the post-medieval field boundaries. It is, however, worth drawing attention to the radiocarbon date on a barley grain from pit 3.04.036 which returned a date of AD 642–692 (91.6% confidence; NZA-36659) (Table 2.1) suggesting early medieval activity on the site (Chapter 4). Other pits may be of a similar date.

The curve of the ditch suggests that it formed the northern side of an enclosure, and there is just enough room to accommodate one, about 50m in diameter, on the spur of land here. The mirror curve of the southern field boundary may be telling. There is no firm evidence as to function of this putative enclosure, the shortage of material remains perhaps suggesting that a corral for livestock is more likely than an enclosed settlement. However, the evidence for a roundhouse in the first phase of occupation perhaps suggests that there was a tradition of occupation here, albeit materially poor, and the enclosure may have been part of a direct remodelling of an existing settlement.

Site 14, Exwell Barton, Powderham

The plot is situated south-west of Exwell Barton (Fig. 3.6). There is evidence of prehistoric occupation pre-

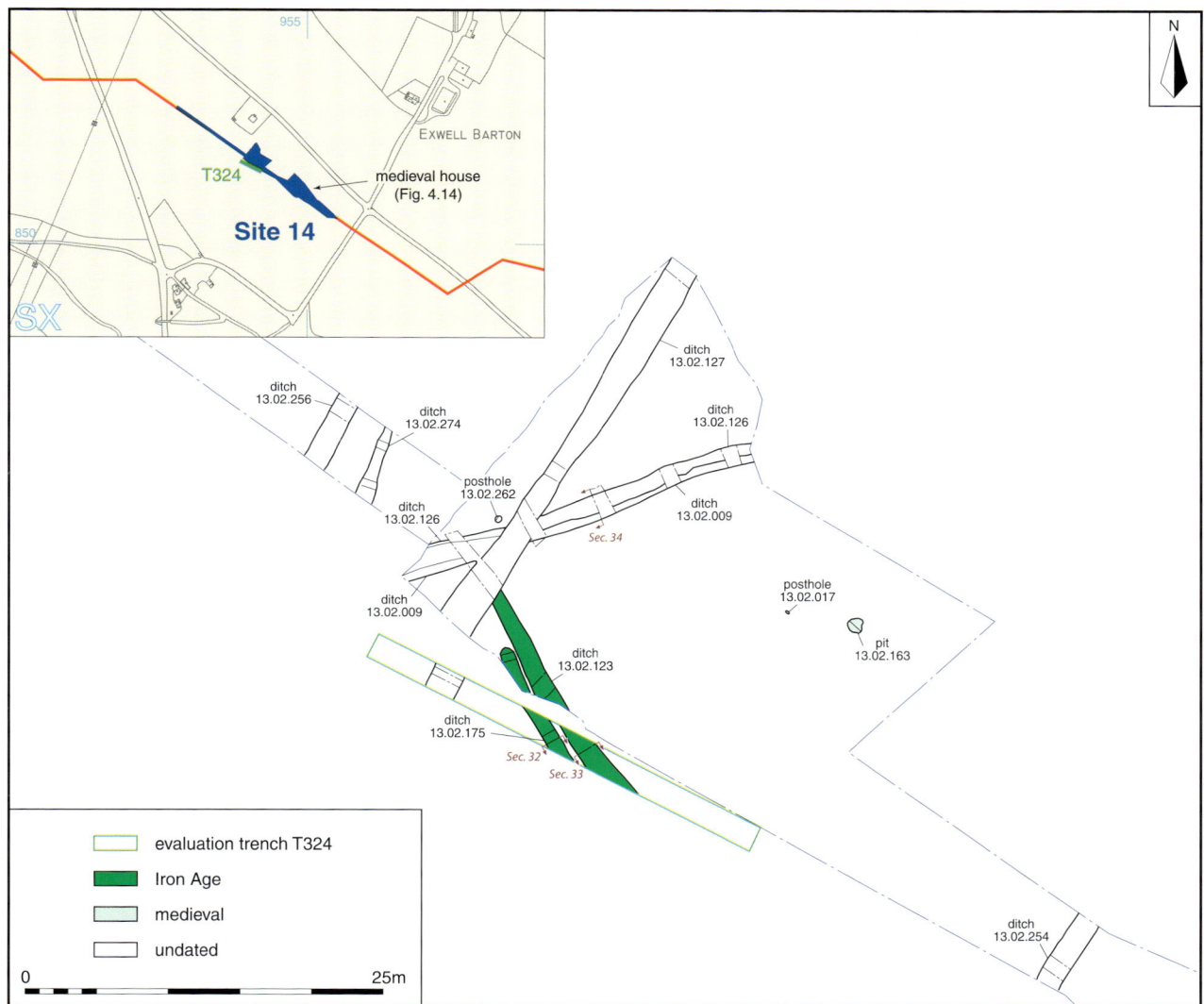

Fig. 3.6 Exwell Barton Iron Age ditches (Site 14); plan of excavated features. Scales 1:500 and 1:10,000

Table 3.2: Radiocarbon date from Exwell Barton, Site 14 (ATK 13.02)

Feature	Context	Lab No.	Material	δ ¹³C	Radiocarbon Age	Calibrated Date 95%	Calibrated Date 68%
Ditch 13.02.123	13.02.124	NZA 36578	Oak charcoal (heartwood) (*Quercus robur/petraea*)	-26.4‰	4127 ± 25 yr BP	2865–2802 BC (26.5%) plus 2775–2582 BC (68.4%)	2856–2830 BC (13.6%) plus 2819–2809 BC (5.1%) plus 2748–2721 BC (13.7%) plus 2698–2629 BC (35.6%)

dating the establishment of the medieval buildings on this site. This occupation took the form of ditches, two with dating evidence and a third without, that might form part of a rectilinear field system orientated north-west/south-east and north-east/south-west. North-west/south-east orientated ditch 13.02.123 was about 1.5m wide and 0.47–0.75m deep with moderately steep sides. Dark orange-brown fill, 13.02.124 (not illustrated), contained two sherds in Exeter volcanic fabric likely to be of Late Iron Age date. Parallel ditch 13.02.175, which terminated in the excavation area, was smaller. It was about 1m wide and 0.25–0.34m in depth (Fig. 3.7). The similarly coloured fill, 13.02.176 (not illustrated), contained one sherd of pottery in the same fabric as that from 13.02.124. A sample of oak charcoal from the primary fill, 13.02.124, of ditch 13.02.123 produced a radiocarbon date in the range 2865–2582 cal. BC (NZA-36578), but this is considered to be from residual or old material and both ditches are considered likely to be later Iron Age or Roman on the basis of the pottery (Table 3.2).

Ditch 13.02.123 terminated at its intersection with ditch 13.02.009 running at right-angles, although their relationship had been destroyed by ditch 13.02.127 (likely to be post-medieval). There is a case for supposing the two earlier ditches to have been contemporaneous, although 13.02.009 was without finds. It was about 1m wide and 0.6m deep with a single fill. It was subsequently cut on its northern side along its entire length by ditch 13.02.126. This was far less substantial, being less that 0.2m deep with a flat base (Fig. 3.7, Section 34). It was also without finds. It is possible that this sequence of cuts was replicated by the other two ditches, where the shallower ditch 13.02.175 may have been a recut of 13.02.123 since they appear too close to have been contemporary, enclosing a hedge or fence between them. If this were the case, the termination of ditch 13.02.175 seven metres short of ditch 13.02.126 implies that remodelling involved the creation of access between the eastern and western enclosures.

Site 15, Crablake Farm, Exminster

The site lies at approximately 38m AOD, on a gentle east-facing slope about 50m east of the group of Bronze

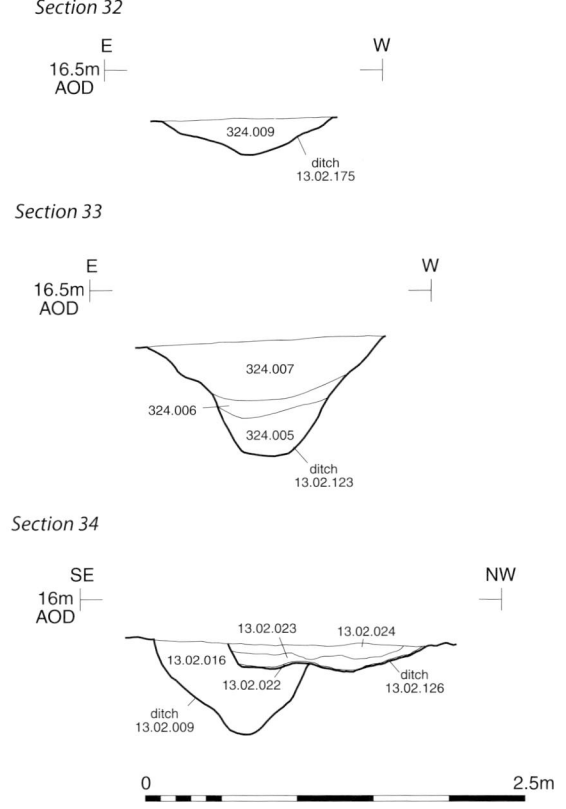

Fig. 3.7 Exwell Barton Iron Age ditches (Site 14); sections 32 to 34. Scale 1:50

Age pits (Chapter 2, Fig. 2.21). A single curvilinear gully 14.09.021, was revealed. It was shallow, 0.1m to 0.3m deep, 0.9m wide and broadly symmetrical, with even sides and a concave base. The primary fill, 14.09.021, was a grey-brown silty sand, probably a result of natural silting. The secondary fill, 14.09.023, was a darker charcoal-rich silty sand. A soil sample (sample 287) from this deposit produced an assemblage of crop processing waste, which contained spelt glume bases (Tables 3.16, 3.18). The final fill of the ditch comprised grey-brown silty sand, deposited by natural sedimentation. Two radiocarbon dates on grains of barley from the soil sample gave date ranges 347–95 cal. BC (NZA-36378) and 176–53 cal. BC (NZA-36268) (Table 2.7). The dates are consistent and despite the possibility that the dated material was redeposited the gully can readily be interpreted as an eaves-drainage feature defining an Iron Age roundhouse. The extrapolated gully would have enclosed a circle about 12m in diameter, which is compatible with a roundhouse about 10m across.

There is little clue as to the nature of the Iron Age settlement here, although the crop processing waste itself suggests a farmstead with an arable component to it. The absence of associated features probably indicates the focus of activity further to the north or south, and the settlement, of whatever size it was, does not appear to have been enclosed. The anomalous Iron Age radiocarbon date from one of the Bronze Age pits to the west can be noted, and may suggest a light scatter of activity in this direction, but there are no firm indications of this.

South Devon

Site 19, Barton Hill Cross, Littlehempston

The site comprised a series of pits, postholes and ditches situated on the flat summit of a hill at approximately 140m AOD just west of Barton Hill Cross (Fig. 3.8). These probably represent part of a Romano-British settlement with Iron Age antecedents. Most of the features are undated artefactually, but their association with dated features suggests many could be of a similar date. The site was not subjected to geophysical survey and the features were completely unexpected.

Iron Age

A series of intercutting features was located in the centre of the plot. Curvilinear ditch 7.01.068 was 0.37m deep and 1.9m wide at its widest revealed point (Fig. 3.9,

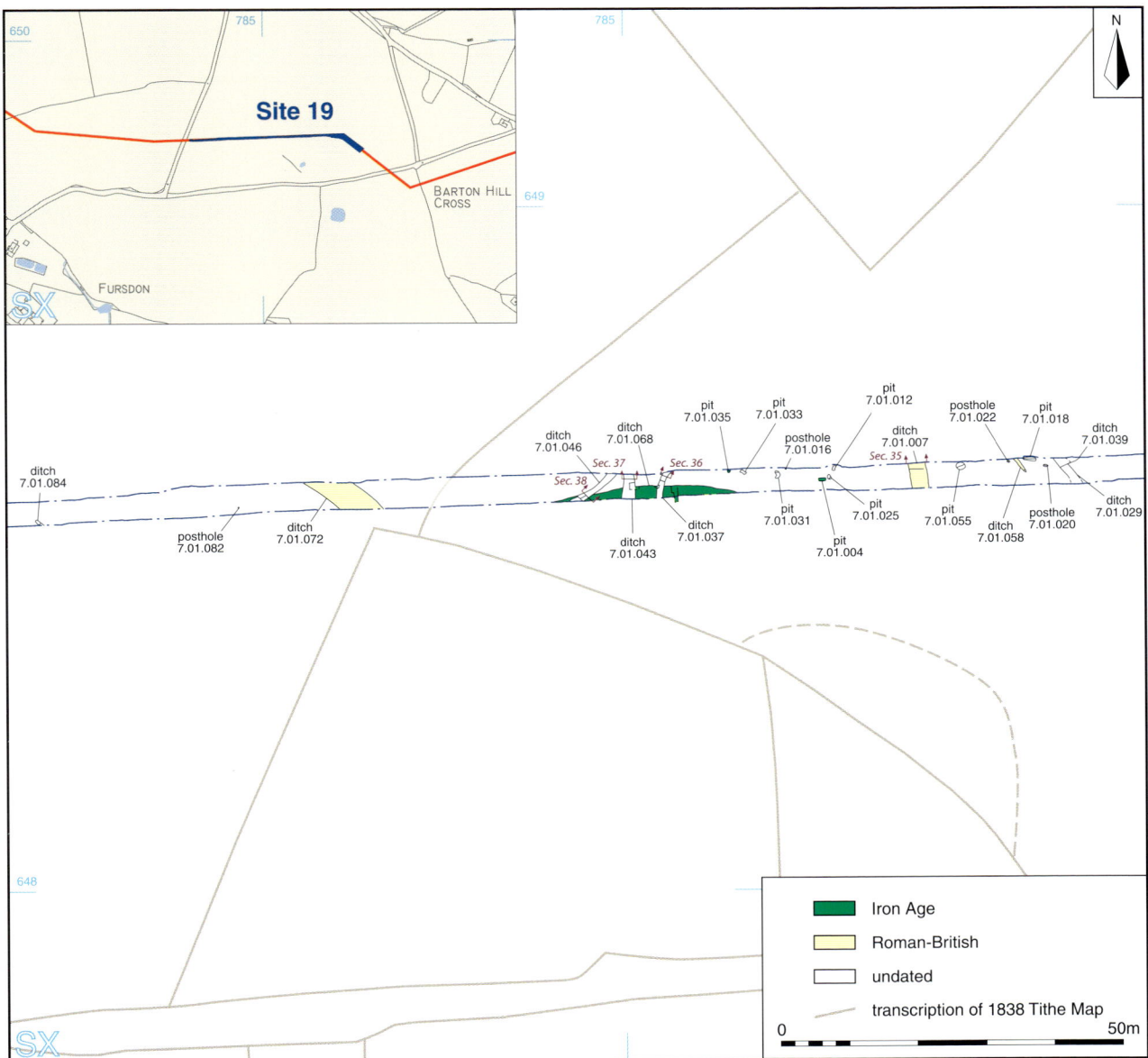

Fig. 3.8 Barton Hill Cross (Site 19); transcription of 1838 Tithe Map, showing excavated features. Scales 1:1250 and 1:10,000

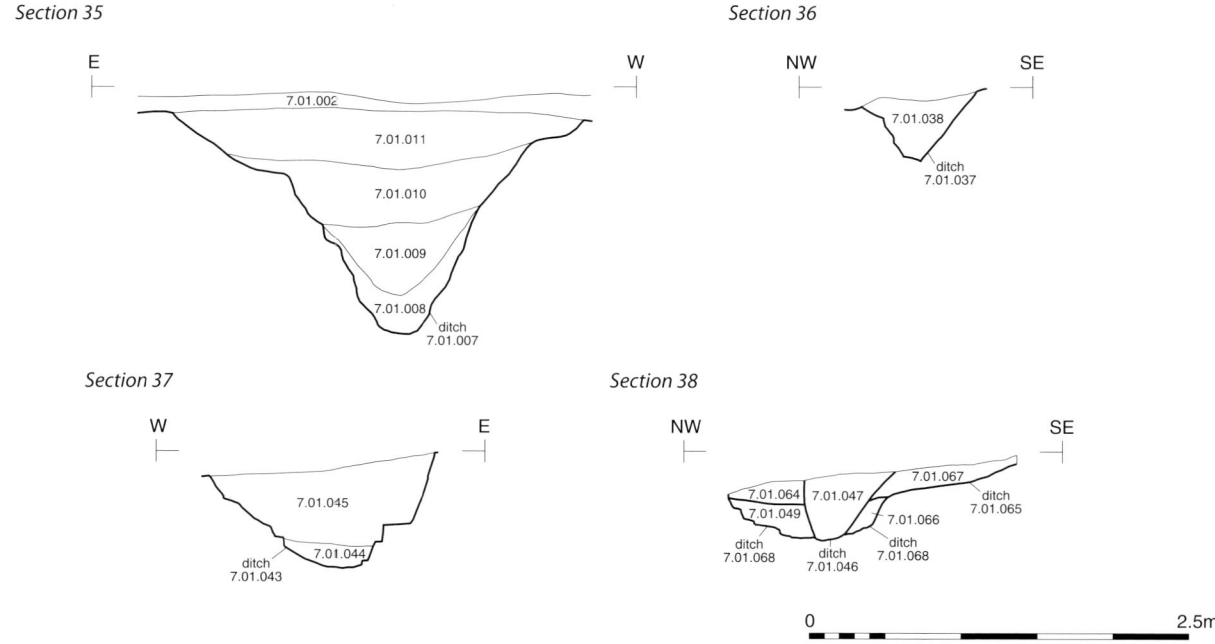

Fig. 3.9   Barton Hill Cross (Site 19); sections 35 to 38. Scale 1:50

section 38). The primary fill, 7.01.049/066, consisted of shale in a silty clay matrix, formed from weathering of the sides of the ditch. Secondary fill, 7.01.064/067, comprised yellow grey silty clay, formed from eroded clay from the underlying shale and clay natural. Deposit 7.01.071 (n.i.), the final silting of the ditch, contained a single sherd of pottery dating to the Iron Age. This was in turn cut by three (undated) ditches. Curvilinear ditches 7.01.037 and 7.01.046 which measured 0.7m and 1.1m wide and 0.40m and 0.48m deep respectively may have continued so as to form circular enclosures 15–20m across (Fig. 3.9, sections 36, 38). Straighter ditch 7.01.043 was 1.45m wide and 0.77m deep (Fig. 3.9, section 37). These may represent settlement features of later Iron Age or Roman date.

There were numerous small pits and postholes to the east of ditch 7.01.068, only two of which (7.01.035 and 7.01.004) contained any pottery. Posthole 7.01.035 contained post packing of redeposited shale natural, and a charcoal-rich silty clay deposit, which may represent the post-pipe. This fill contained two burnished sherds of Middle Iron Age pottery. Rectangular pit 7.01.004, with step sides and a flat base, was 1.08m long, 0.56m wide and 0.3m deep. The primary fill contained 17 sherds of Middle Iron Age pottery comprising the rim and upper part of a plain South Western Decorated vessel in a burnished granitic-derived fabric. The upper fill was without finds.

The remaining pits and postholes in this area did not contain any datable material; features 7.01.020, 7.01.022, 7.01.012, 7.01.025 and 7.01.016 had diameters of between 0.2m and 0.55m and depths of between 0.23m and 0.57m, while larger features 7.01.018, 7.01.055, 7.01.031 and 7.01.033 had diameters of between 1.2m and 1.95m and depths of between 0.15m and 0.40m. The form of the pits was not indicative of function and their primary use remains elusive. In the western part of the site was posthole 7.01.082, 0.22m wide and 0.15m deep, similar in size and form to Iron Age posthole 7.01.035.

Roman

Ditch 7.01.007, in the eastern part of the site, was the most substantial feature encountered; it was 2.5m wide and 1.30m deep with a steep V-shaped profile and a concave base (Fig. 3.9, section 35). The primary fill, 7.01.008, comprised light orange-brown clay silt, and was overlain by a similar fill, 7.01.009. The third fill, 7.01.010, contained frequent shale fragments perhaps from a collapsed bank. The upper fill, 7.01.011, contained dating evidence in the form of 12 sherds of Roman South Devon Ware pottery, as well as an iron blade fragment of possible Roman date but lacking diagnostic features to enable classification.

Also in the eastern area of the site was north-west/south-east orientated ditch 7.01.058. The fill, 7.01.059, contained two sherds of Roman South Devon Ware pottery. Toward the western end of the site was north/south-orientated ditch 7.01.072, which contained 13 sherds of late 2nd to 4th-century pottery, including sherds from an everted-rim jar within an upper fill, 7.01.073. Although all the pottery from this context was of the same Roman South Devon Ware fabric, it is unlikely that the pottery belongs to a single vessel and it may well be residual. The ditch was 3.2m across but only 0.28m deep and, while it is possible that ditches 7.01.007 and 7.01.072 were two boundaries of an enclosure about 80m across, their dissimilar forms suggest this is not the case. Ditch 7.01.072 has some of the character of a field boundary ditch, and it coincides approximately with a former boundary depicted on the Tithe Map (Fig. 3.8). The Roman finds come from the upper fills of both ditches and it is possible that their original construction was earlier, perhaps within the Late Iron Age and contemporary with some of the earlier features already discussed. Alternatively the Roman material may have been redeposited in later features.

Undated features of probable Roman/Iron Age date
At the eastern end of the site was north-east/south-west orientated ditch 7.01.039, which was 1.8m wide and 0.34m deep. It was cut at right-angles by ditch 7.01.029 which was 1.23m wide and 0.6m deep. Ditch 7.01.029 was parallel to, and 5m from, ditch 7.01.058, which contained Roman pottery. This suggests that they formed part of a coherent organisation of land. North-west/south-east orientated ditch 7.01.084 (0.43m wide and 0.25m deep) followed a similar alignment. It can be noted that the former rectangular field to the north has boundaries aligned with ditches 7.01.058 and 7.01.039. On current information it is a matter for speculation whether all these boundaries have medieval or later origins, or whether they owe their origin to a Roman agricultural pattern.

Site 22, Lower Velwell, Rattery

The shallow bases of two adjacent hearths or furnaces were found on gently sloping land on the south facing slope of Hood Ball at approximately 52m AOD. An area of 8m by 10m was stripped for pipe storage. The stripped area also ran for the length of the field from plot 12.05 but over most of this length only topsoil was removed and the field was not available for archaeological inspection (Fig. 3.10).

Furnace pit 12.05w.004, was 0.51m long, 0.48m wide and 0.12m deep and furnace pit 12.05w.005 was 0.49m long, 0.41m wide and 0.09m deep (Fig. 3.11). There was scorching of the surrounding silt-clay subsoil and underlying shale substrate indicative of *in situ* burning, and the fills of both features contained burnt material. A soil sample from pit 12.05w.004 was

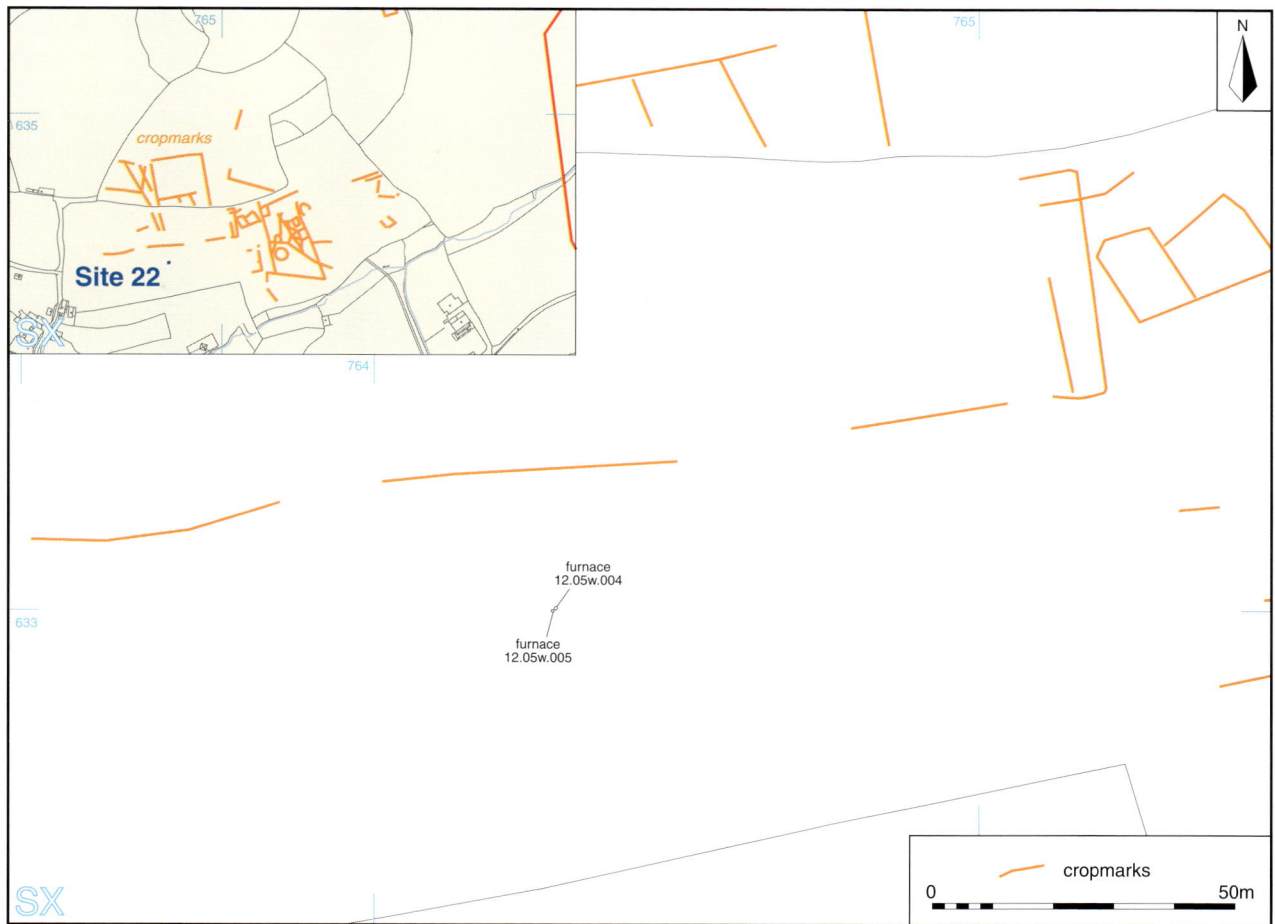

Fig. 3.10 Lower Velwell (Site 22); plan of cropmarks and excavated features. Scales 1:1250 and 1:10,000

Table 3.3: Radiocarbon date from Lower Velwell, Site 22 (FTC 12.05w)

Feature	Context	Lab No.	Material	δ ¹³C	Radiocarbon Age	Calibrated Date 95%	Calibrated Date 68%
Furnace 12.05w.004	12.05w.007	NZA 36247	Alder/hazel charcoal (*Alnus glutinosa/ Corylus avellana*)	-25.8‰	4179 ± 20 yr BP	2879–2839 BC (19.2%) plus 2812–2677 BC (75.8%)	2874–2859 BC (12.5%) plus 2806–2755 BC (44.0%) plus 2718–2703 BC (11.6%)

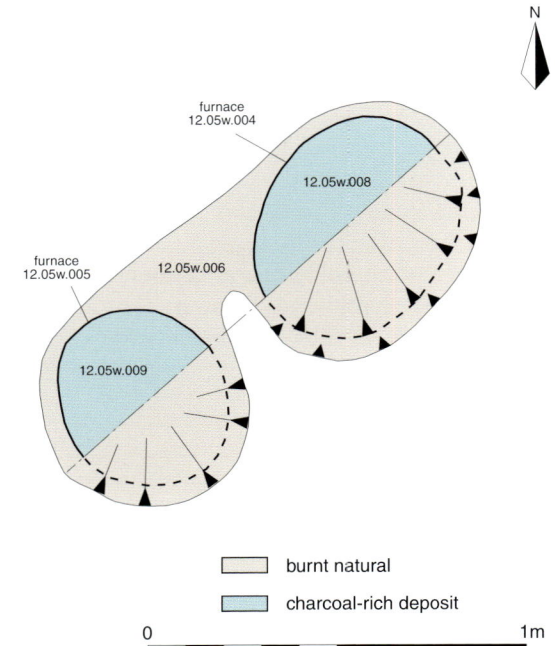

Fig. 3.11 Lower Velwell (Site 22); plan of furnaces. Scale 1:20

assessed and contained wood charcoal, identified as mostly oak heartwood, and over 2kg of metalworking debris. Most of this debris proved to be undiagnostic ironworking slag, but a possible smithing hearth bottom was identified, which suggests smithing taking place, although no hammerscale was present. The presence of fayalitic run slag is indicative of smelting, although the lack of any furnace lining is unusual (Starley, below). The presence of both smithing and smelting debris from the same feature is evidence that that both processes took place on the site, and possibly in the same furnace. The smelting, using a non-slag-tapping process, would appear to be at a similar technological level to that employed at Tigley A in the Middle Iron Age (Site 26, below), but it is possible that it was later in date. A sample of alder/hazel charcoal from furnace 12.05w.004 produced a radiocarbon date in the range of 2879–2677 cal. BC (NZA-36247), but this must have resulted from redeposited charcoal (Table 3.3). There are extensive cropmarks of enclosures in this plot just to the east, and further clearer cropmarks in the field to the north (Fig. 3.12). These would appear to relate to Iron Age and/ or Roman period settlement in the area to which these furnaces may have belonged.

Site 24, Billany Farm, Dartington

The site lay between 103m AOD in the north and 65m AOD in the south on a south-facing slope west of Billany Farm some 0.8km north-east of Westcombe. An enclosure known from cropmarks was confirmed by geophysical survey (Stratascan 2001; Archaeological Surveys 2006c). These indicated a roughly rectangular enclosure with a rounded south-western side and internal dimensions of 65m by 45m (Fig. 3.13). A trial trench confirmed the presence of the southern ditch and two further trial trenches on the hill top to the north of the enclosure revealed no archaeological features. Subsequent excavation in a strip 15m wide revealed two sides of the enclosure and a light scatter of internal features (Fig. 3.14). There was no indication of an entrance. Each ditch was examined with three sections and each appeared to have been cut in one continuous length through the slate substrate, which was loose and weathered at the top but became solid rock from a depth of c. 0.4m.

The northern enclosure ditch, 14.01.105, was 3.5m wide and 1.45m deep. The general profile, partially dictated by the geology, was steeply angular with a broad flat base, up to 1.2m wide (Fig. 3.15). The southern ditch, 14.01.106, was 2.9m wide and 2.35m deep with a more marked asymmetry and a tapered profile (Fig. 3.16, section 40). Because of its relative narrowness and constant flooding the base of this ditch was recorded in two sections during the subsequent summer watching brief (Fig. 3.17).

The primary fill in the northern ditch 14.01.105 (14.01.021/24/31/32), comprised brown silty clay deposits, representing an initial slump along the southern edge of the ditch. This is suggestive of a collapsed bank on the southern side of the ditch which must have happened soon after the ditch was excavated, or the ditch must have been regularly cleaned out before this event as no silting deposits lay beneath it. Next, a mixed shale and silty clay deposit (14.01.022/23) probably represented a gradual infilling by natural

Fig. 3.12 Lower Velwell (Site 22); aerial photograph showing cropmarks. (Devon County Council Ref. DAP VL.04)

processes with some admixture of occupation material. The subsequent fill (14.01.062) also appears to have resulted from natural silting. The uppermost fill, 14.01.033/14.01.063, contained four sherds of broadly Roman pottery, probably deposited after the enclosure was abandoned.

The primary fill (14.01.099) of the southern ditch was a thick (0.8m) deposit of redeposited natural silt-clay, which either represents rapid natural infilling or a deliberate deposit. It contained part of a carinated bowl or cup, dated to the middle 1st to 2nd-century AD. The secondary fill (14.01.072) was interspersed with silty lenses, suggesting the periodic collapse of a possible internal bank or more likely the unstable sides with periods of stabilisation. The final fill of the southern ditch (14.01.045/061/066) contained 30 sherds of broadly Roman pottery as well as a fragment of rotary quern of Cornish greisen. This final deposit could represent post-abandonment infilling by the plough.

The form of the southern ditch with its deep narrow base and pronounced asymmetry suggest that it was a palisade trench intended to hold a row of contiguous or closely spaced timbers. The shallower northern edge would have been an original design to facilitate sliding the timbers into position and up against the near-vertical southern edge. The absence of any indication of a packing around a post-pipe implies that the posts were at some stage withdrawn, and the recorded fills would therefore represent sediments that had accumulated after this particular form of boundary had been abandoned. By contrast, the broader and shallower northern boundary ditch seems unlikely to have been for a palisade.

Internal features

The total internal area of the enclosure is estimated to be 2750m²; of this, an area of 630m² was exposed for excavation. This represented 23% of the estimated internal area. Internal features were quite sparse. In the centre of the site was a terrace which had been cut into the slope to create a level platform, 14.01.107, 6m long, 2.5m wide and up to 0.7m deep at the back edge, although normally it was shallower (Fig. 3.18). At the eastern end of the platform was a possible revetment wall, 14.01.086, which appeared to form a dry-stone

Fig. 3.13 Billany Farm (Site 24); plan of geophysical anomalies and excavated features. Scales 1:1000 and 1:10,000

lining the eastern edge of the terrace. It was constructed of roughly shaped blocks, a single course high and a single course wide. An unstructured group of stones (14.01.089), lying directly on the floor of the platform, may belong to the usage phase of the platform. No specific use could be attributed to this deposit.

There was no clear evidence of a structure occupying the platform. Posthole 14.01.087, towards the front of the platform on the eastern side, was an isolated feature. Another posthole, 14.01.036, on the western side of the platform was similarly isolated and, cutting pit 14.01.034, was not of the first phase of use. There was no evidence of a floor or occupation layers. Intermittent scorching of the underlying slate across the area of the terrace is taken as evidence of a fire, and this may have destroyed any structure present.

Towards the front of the terrace, pit 14.01.034 was circular in plan with vertical sides and a relatively flat base sloping slightly to the east. Its single fill, 14.01.035, included fired clay hearth lining and possibly fragments of a collapsed oven 'hood', as well as slight charcoal remains and six sherds of late 1st to 2nd-century AD pottery. A soil sample yielded some charred flax seeds (Table 3.20, sample 38). The feature appears likely to have been a hearth or 'fire-pit' of unclear purpose. It was later cut by posthole 14.01.036. Nearby, pit 14.01.081

Fig. 3.14 Billany Farm (Site 24); plan of excavated features. Scale 1:250

Fig. 3.15 Billany Farm (Site 24): initial trench through terrace 14.01.107, looking east. Scale 1m

was oval in plan, with shallow sloping symmetrical sides. Its single fill, 14.01.082, contained 26 sherds of Roman pottery, probable hearth/furnace lining and a large fragment of quernstone of Cornish greisen (Fig. 3.31 no. 2). Pit 14.01.004 on the southern side of the enclosure, contained 29 sherds of Roman pottery (fill 14.01.008). These pits contained one third of all the pottery from the site and seem likely to relate to settlement. Pit 14.01.048 was without finds and more irregular in shape but is considered potentially Roman based on spatial association. None of the pits could be positively identified as storage pits and their primary functions remain unknown.

The partly scorched terrace floor was overlain by a charcoal-rich layer (14.01.046, 14.01.077, 14.01.084 and 14.01.092), and all subsequent layers (14.01.047, 14301.085 and 14.01.093) were related to the infilling of the terrace. The charcoal was assessed and seen to comprise a mixture of wood species. Within the abandonment fills, fragments of large storage jars with distinctive raised cordons and curved rims (deposits 14.01.046 and 14.01.084) and everted-rim jars with

Fig. 3.16 Billany Farm (Site 24); ditch 14.01.105, looking north-east. Scale 1m

Fig. 3.17 Billany Farm (Site 24); ditch 14.01.106, looking west. Scale 1m

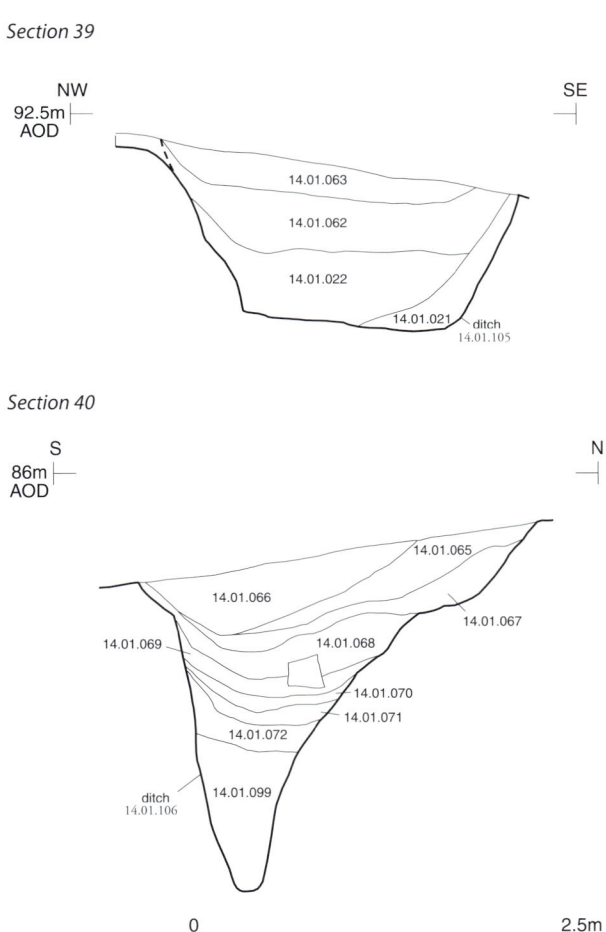

Fig. 3.18 Billany Farm (Site 24): Sections 39 and 40. Scale 1:50

grooved rim uppers (deposits 14.01.046 and 14.01.077), were found, which indicate domestic activity and are broadly dated to the late 3rd to 4th century AD. A fragmentary coin of Tetricus (AD 270–4) was recovered from deposit 14.01.046. These deposits represent the final phase of settlement and the abandonment of the settlement.

Pit 14.01.038 was the latest stratified feature and cut the fills of the terrace. It was relatively shallow and did not cut into the terrace floor to more than 0.16m. Its primary fill, 14.01.078/79, consisted of charcoal-rich silt, which appears to have naturally infilled from the surrounding soils of the terrace. The secondary fill, 14.01.039/14.01.080, contained 12 sherds of late 2nd to 4th-century pottery as well as a fragment of a granite rotary quern (Fig. 3.31 no. 1) and two 3rd-century coins. Of interest is the amount of charred flax seeds from soil samples from this feature, found together with smaller quantities of cereals and a range of wood charcoal (Table 3.20, samples 44, 53, 54). The feature is of unknown function. It post-dates the terrace abandonment and may represent post-Roman activity, although it is considered likely that all the finds within it are redeposited from the Roman occupation, including the charred flax from which two identical radiocarbon determinations were obtained falling within the range cal. AD 256–416 (SUERC-37345; -37346) (Table 3.4)

Table 3.4: Radiocarbon dates from Billany Farm, Site 24 (FTC 14.01)

Feature	Context	Lab No.	Material	δ ¹³C	Radiocarbon Age	Calibrated Date 95%	Calibrated Date 68%
Pit 14.01.038	14.01.079	SU-ERC-37345 GU-26123	Flax seeds (*Linum usitatissium*)	-25.4‰	1695 ± 30 yr BP	256–304 AD (23.0%) plus 314–416 AD (72.4%)	263–77 AD (9.8%) plus 330–99 AD (58.4%)
Pit 14.01.038	14.01.079	SU-ERC-37346 GU-26124	Flax seeds (*Linum usitatissium*)	-25.4‰	1695 ± 30 yr BP	256–304 AD (23.0%) plus 314–416 AD (72.4%)	263–77 AD (9.8%) plus 330–99 AD (58.4%)

Site 25, Dun Cross, Dartington

A group of pits and burnt areas were revealed on flat, valley bottom land at approximately 42m AOD to the south-west of Dun Cross, near Dartington (Fig. 3.19). Sub-oval pit 16.01.007 measured 0.48m by 0.67m and was 90mm deep. The fill, 16.01.008, comprised silty clay, containing abundant, mainly oak, charcoal (Table 3.21, sample 279). A sample of short-lived Maloideae species (hawthorn/rowan/crab apple) charcoal produced a radiocarbon date of 78–220 cal AD (NZA-36579), placing it firmly in the Early Roman period (Table 3.5). Irregular pit 16.01.009 was about 3.5m long, 1m wide and 70mm deep. The charcoal-rich fill, 16.01.010, produced a radiocarbon date of cal. AD 26–134 (NZA-

Table 3.5: Radiocarbon dates from Dun Cross, Site 25 (FTC 16.01)

Feature	Context	Lab No.	Material	δ ¹³C	Radiocarbon Age	Calibrated Date 95%	Calibrated Date 68%
Pit 16.01.007	16.01.008	NZA 36579	Hawthorn/rowan/crab apple charcoal (*Crataegus monogyna/ Sorbus* spp/*Malus sylvestris*)	-26.1‰	1869 ± 25 yr BP	78–220 AD (94.7%)	84–140 AD plus (47.4%) plus 153–70 AD plus (10.4 %) plus 195–210 AD (9.9%)
Pit 16.01.009	16.01.011	NZA 36580	Hawthorn/rowan/crab apple charcoal (*Crataegus monogyna/ Sorbus* spp/*Malus sylvestris*)	-27‰	1913 ± 25 yr BP	26–134 AD (95%)	68–93 AD plus (33.7%) plus 98–125 AD (34.7%)

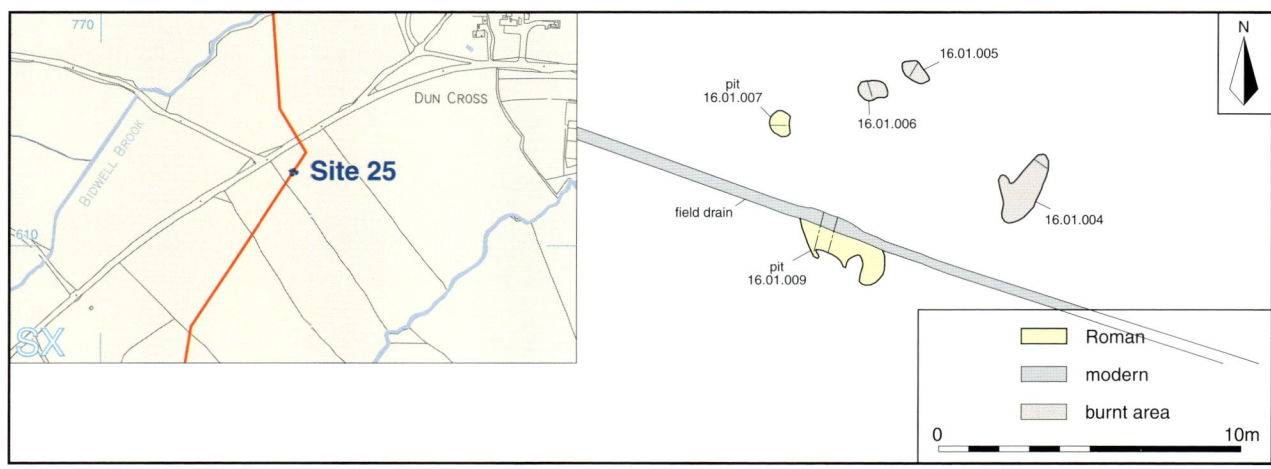

Fig. 3.19 Dun Cross (Site 25); plan of excavated features, showing burnt areas. Scales 1:250 and 1:10,000

36580) from Maloideae species charcoal, confirming the earlier Roman date. Areas of *in situ* scorched earth, 16.01.004, 16.01.005 and 16.01.006, were between 0.6m and 2.5m in length with negligible depths. All these features had charcoal-rich fills (where sampled, predominantly oak) and would seem to have been the bases of hearths of unknown purpose.

Site 26, Tigley A, Dartington

The site lies on a flat spur of land some 0.9km east of the village of Tigley on the border between the parishes of Dartington and Harberton at between 53m AOD in the east and 60m AOD in the west (Fig. 3.20). The underlying geology is mapped as Slate of the Middle Devonian era (BGS 1974b), although fieldwork showed this to consist of weathered shale fragments in a yellow-brown clay matrix. No preparatory geophysical survey,

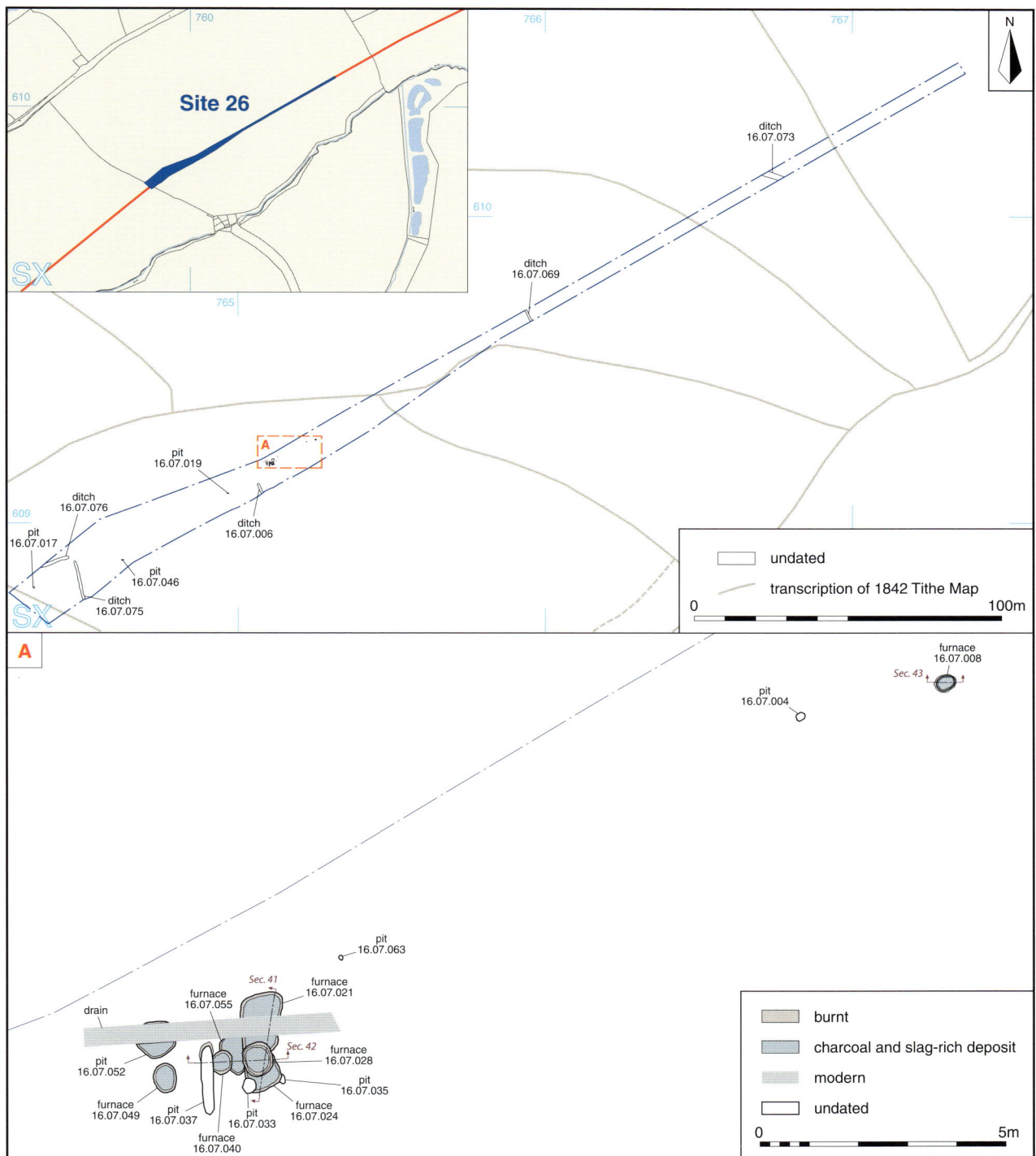

Fig. 3.20 Tigley A (Site 26); excavated features on transcription of 1842 Tithe Map. Scales 1:125, 1:2000 and 1:10,000

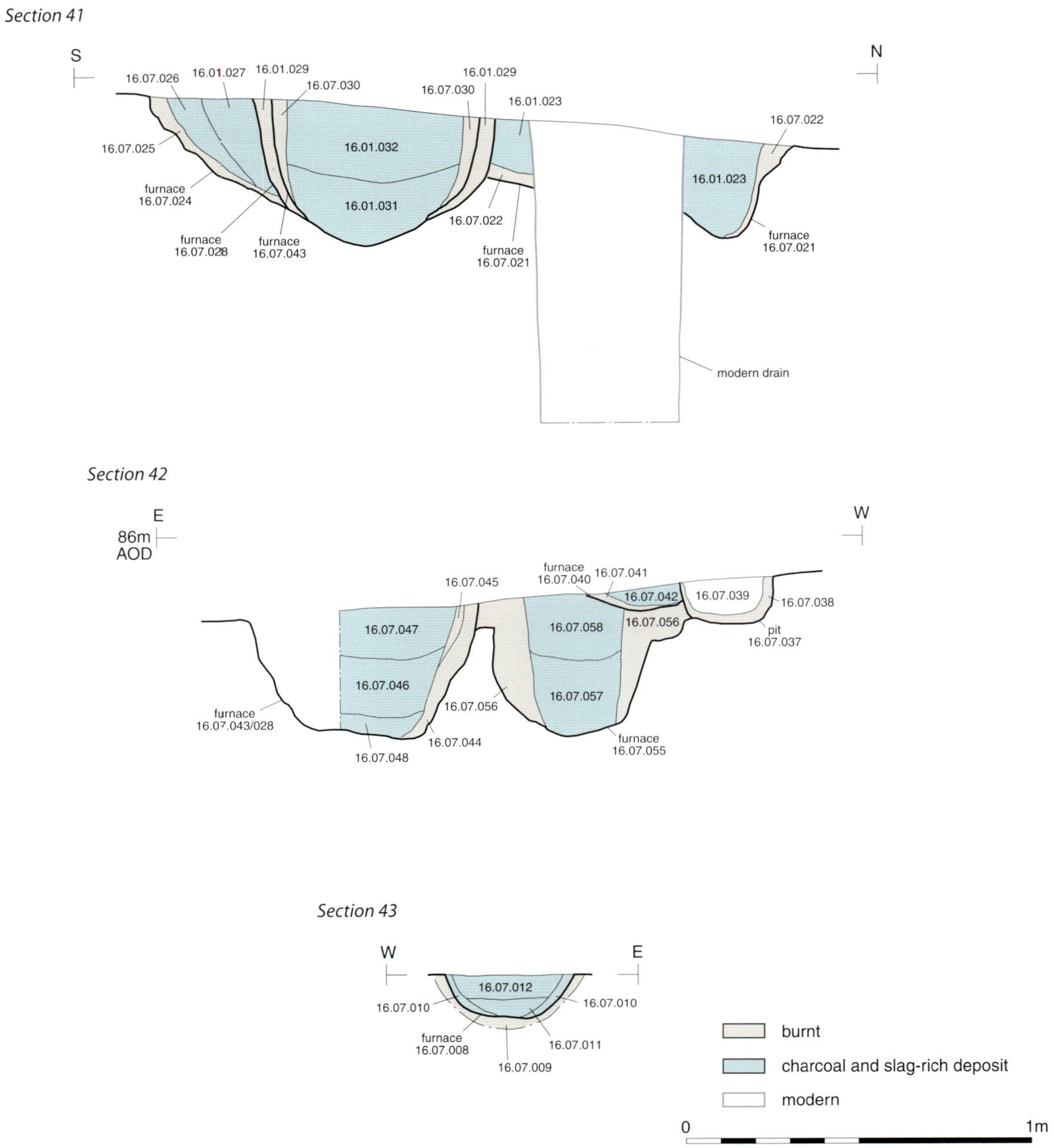

Fig. 3.21 Tigley A (Site 26); sections 41, 42 and 43. Scale 1:20

Fig. 3.22 Tigley A (Site 26); furnace cluster, pre-excavation, looking south-east. Scales 0.5m and 1m

fieldwalking or trial trenching had been undertaken in this plot.

The archaeological features on the site consisted of a group of iron-smelting furnaces and pits of less secure function, many containing abundant iron slag (Figs 3.22, 3.23). There were also three small ditches which may have been associated. The furnaces were not well preserved, surviving only as simple cut pits without evidence of their original above-ground forms, probably due to later agricultural truncation. In addition, a tight group of them were intercutting, leaving those of the earlier phases very fragmentary. No datable finds were present, but six radiocarbon determinations on charcoal from these furnaces gave dates in the general range 400–200 cal. BC (Table 3.6) and the complex therefore appears to be securely Middle Iron Age.

Isolated furnaces 16.07.008, 16.07.049 and pits 16.07.004, 16.07.052

In the north-eastern part of the site, oval pit 16.07.008 was interpreted during excavation as the remains of an iron smelting furnace (Fig. 3.25). It was 0.8m wide and 0.53m long and survived to a depth of 0.22m. A clay lining, 0.12mm thick, lined the whole pit. It was mid greyish brown colour, which is indicative of the reducing conditions required in a smelting furnace. Discolouration of the natural ground around the furnace also suggests prolonged high temperature running. In the base of the furnace (fill 16.07.010) a large piece of slag represented an *in situ* furnace bottom, confirming the interpretation of this feature. The upper fills contained charcoal and slag representing backfill of original furnace material after the feature had gone out of use. About half the

Fig. 3.23 Tigley A (Site 26); furnaces, looking north. Scale 0.5m

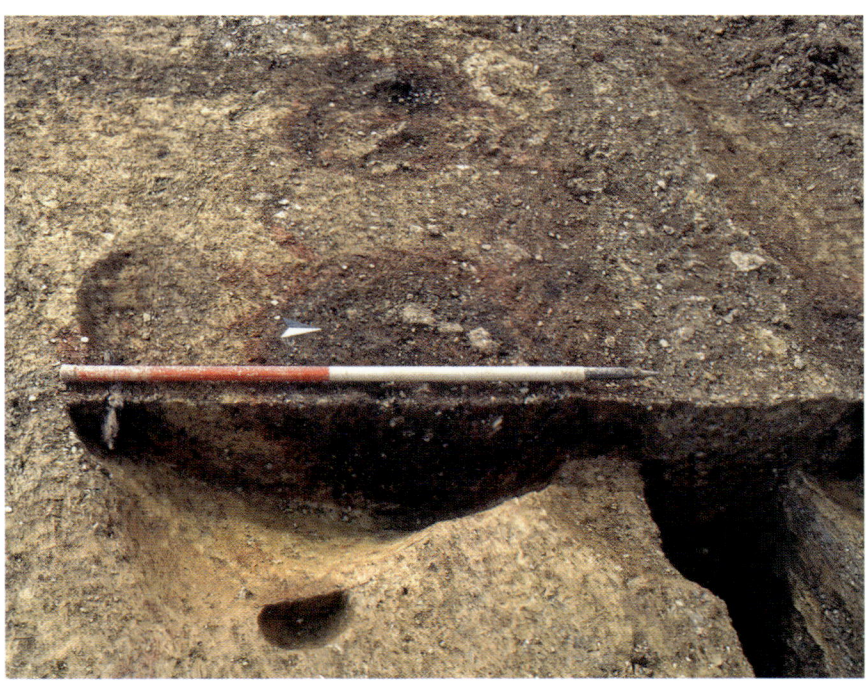

Fig. 3.24 Tigley A (Site 26); section 41, looking west. Scale 1m

Table 3.6: Radiocarbon dates from Tigley A, Site 26 (FTC 16.07)

Feature	Context	Lab No.	Material	δ ¹³C	Radiocarbon Age	Calibrated Date 95%	Calibrated Date 68%
Furnace 16.07.008	16.07.016	NZA 32531	Alder charcoal (*Alnus glutinosa*)	-24.0‰	2257 ± 20 yr BP	391–350 BC (43.8%) plus 293–227 BC (48.8%) plus 219–210 BC (2.3%)	386–356 BC (39.3%) plus 279–256 BC (23.2%) plus 241–234 BC (5.7%)
Furnace 16.07.021	16.07.022	NZA 36581	Ash charcoal (*Fraxinus excelsior*)	-24.9‰	2216 ± 25 yr BP	374–202 BC (95.0%)	359–348 BC (7.4%) plus 310–272 BC (25.0%) plus 259–207 BC (35.2%)
Furnace 16.07.021	16.07.022	NZA 36594	Elm charcoal (*Ulmus glabra*)	-24.7‰	2281 ± 25 yr BP	398-353 BC (64.5%) plus 290-229 BC (30.8%)	394-359 BC (60.0%) plus 270-261 BC (8.1%)
Pit 16.07.037	16.07.039	NZA 36640	Wheat spp grain (*Triticum* spp)	-22.3‰	651 ± 20 yr BP	1285–1318 AD (42.1%) plus 1353–1390 AD (53.0%)	1291–1307 AD (28.6%) plus 1363–85 AD (41.7%)
Pit 16.07.037	16.07.039	NZA 36701	Hazel charcoal (*Corylus avellana*)	-27.1‰	2282 ± 20 yr BP	397–356 BC (75%) plus 283–252 BC (15.9%) plus 247–233 BC (4.2%)	393–363 BC (68.1%)
Furnace 16.07.043	16.07.046	NZA 36655	Hazel charcoal (*Corylus avellana*)	-25‰	2280 ± 20 yr BP	396–355 BC (72.6%) plus 283–251 BC (17.6%) plus 247–233 BC (4.7%)	393–361 BC (67.7%) plus 265–264 BC (1.0%)
Furnace 16.07.043	16.07.046	NZA 36706	Hazel charcoal (*Corylus avellana*)	-24.1‰	2256 ± 20 yr BP	391–350 BC (42.7%) plus 294–209 BC (52.7%)	385–356 BC (37.5%) plus 279–256 BC (23.3%) plus 242–234 BC (6.6%)

Fig. 3.25 Tigley A (Site 26); furnace 16.07.008, looking north. Scale 0.5m

slag was diagnostic of smelting. The charcoal from soil samples from each of the three fills was overwhelmingly oak (Table 3.17, sample 242), although grains of emmer or spelt wheat were recovered. A radiocarbon date in the range 391–210 cal. BC (NZA-32531) was obtained on alder charcoal from upper fill 16.07.016 (Table 3.6). Nearby was small pit 16.07.004 which was without a burnt lining but contained some charcoal and slag identified as smithing hearth bottom from its single fill. The slag (154g) may have been redeposited rather than indicative of a smithing hearth here.

Furnace 16.07.049 lay close to a cluster of intercutting furnaces and pits in the western part of the site. It was circular and measured 0.53m in diameter and 0.15m deep. The scorched natural silt-clay indicated that heating of this feature had taken place but it was unclear whether the pit had been deliberately lined. The fill, 16.07.051, contained 1.19kg of undiagnostic iron slag, none of it *in situ*, and a small quantity of charcoal. It seems likely that this was the remains of another smelting furnace although the evidence is not conclusive.

Nearby, pit 16.07.052 was approximately circular, about 0.5m in diameter and 0.35m deep. Its exact form and dimensions could not be established due to its truncation by a modern land drain. The feature had a burnt lining which may have been inserted, although it is possible that it resulted from heating the natural clay subsoil. The dark-red purple colour of the lining suggests an oxidising process, such as roasting ore, rather than smelting. Debris examined from its two fills consisted entirely of vitrified hearth lining with no fayalitic smelting slags, and only traces of charcoal. The purpose of this pit remains unknown although likely to have been connected in some way with iron production or secondary working.

Intercutting pits and furnaces
The intercutting group of features in the western part of the site formed three stratigraphic phases.

Phase One: Furnace 16.07.055
Furnace 16.07.055 was almost circular in shape and, while partly truncated, had surface measurements of 0.7m long and 0.4m wide, and a depth of 0.4m (Fig. 3.21, section 42). Again, there is uncertainty as to whether the heat affected material lining the pit was deliberately applied clay or the natural clay-rich subsoil. The lower of the two fills, 16.07.057, contained a high proportion of smelting debris, while the upper, 16.07.058, contained some evidence for smithing (Starley, below), suggesting that after the removal of the bloom the structure was used to reheat and consolidate it. The furnace was subsequently cut by all three Phase Two furnaces, but no further mechanical damage to the lining of the furnace was identified, suggesting that bloom and slag had been removed from the furnace above the present ground level.

Phase Two: Furnaces 16.07.021, 16.07.024 and 16.07.040
Three furnaces are stratigraphically within Phase Two, but in view of their proximity it is unlikely they actually operated concurrently. Furnace 16.07.021 was almost subrectangular in shape and the largest of the furnaces, measuring in excess of 1.0m long and 0.7m wide but only up to 0.28m deep at the northern end (Fig. 3.21, section 41). The dark orange-brown lining extended all the way around and fill 16.07.023 contained a piece of slag classed as 'tap slag', together with fayalitic run slag from smelting, undiagnostic iron slag and small quantities of charcoal. Elm and ash charcoal from the lining, 16.07.022, produced radiocarbon dates of 374–202 cal. BC and 398– 229 cal. BC (NZA-36581; NZA-36594).

Furnace or pit 16.07.024 had been largely cut away by furnace 16.07.028 but it appeared to have been subrectangular or sub-circular in plan, about 0.70m across and a little over 0.30m deep. It had an orange heat-affected lining and the intact side was relatively gently sloping. Fills 16.07.026 and 16.07.027 contained very small amounts of fayalitic run slag and charcoal, but a high concentration of magnetic residue which was possibly a residue of the ore (Starley, this report).

Furnace 16.07.040 measured 0.28m in diameter and 0.07m in depth and contained *in situ* vitrified hearth/furnace lining (Fig. 3.21, section 42). The fill contained small quantities of run slag and undiagnostic ironworking slag, as well as a large quantity of charcoal consisting entirely of oak heartwood (Tables 3.17, 3.18, samples 263, 264).

Phase Three: Furnace 16.07.028 (16.07.043)
This furnace was the most complete of the group and was circular in plan, 0.5m in diameter and 0.4m deep (Fig. 3.21, sections 41, 42; Fig. 3.24). It showed two phases of burnt lining and so appears to have been cleaned out and reused as furnace 16.07.043. Two of the fills proved very rich in slag. In the second fill, 16.07.046, fayalitic run slag, diagnostic of smelting, dominated. The upper fill, 16.07.047, a disuse deposit, contained less run slag but contained hammerscale which suggests that the furnace had been used for bloom-smithing as well as smelting. The charcoal from both fills, and from lining 16.07.030, contained a range of wood species, but was dominated by oak (Tables 3.17, 3.18, samples 253, 267, 268). Paired radiocarbon dates obtained on hazel charcoal from fill 16.07.046 produced very similar date ranges of 396–223 cal. BC (NZA-36655) and 391–209 cal. BC (NZA-36706).

Other pits and ditches
Nearby, pit 16.07.035 was without metalworking debris and was cut by furnace 16.07.024; therefore it pre-dated the second phase of furnace construction. Cutting furnace 16.07.040, elongated shallow feature, 16.07.037, was 1m long and 0.16m deep. It contained

heat-affected (red oxidised) lining at its northern end. The function of this feature is unknown. It contained undiagnostic iron slag, and small quantities of charcoal, but these need not have been connected with the original use of the pit. Radiocarbon dates on hazel charcoal and a wheat grain from fill 16.07.039 produced dates in the range 397–233 cal. BC and cal. AD 1285–1390 (NZA-36701; NZA-36640). This second date (on the grain of wheat) is considered to have been obtained from intrusive material, and the feature is more likely to have been Iron Age and associated in some way with the iron production here. Pit 16.07.033 (also cutting furnace 16.07.024) contained a very small amount of undiagnostic ironworking slag and some burned stone but it too may be post-Iron Age. Pit 16.07.063, of unknown function, lay to the immediate north-west of this group of furnaces.

To the west of the group of intercutting features pits 16.07.017, 16.07.019 and 16.07.046, which form no clear pattern, may be unrelated to the furnaces. Pit 16.07.017 did not contain metalworking debris and is of uncertain date. Also to the west, ditches 16.07.075 and 16.07.076 were at right-angles to one another and may have formed the corner of an enclosure. Nearby ditch 16.07.006 was on a slightly different alignment.

The date of these ditches is not known. They were very shallow (0.06m–0.14m deep) and between 0.7m and 1.05m wide and it is possible that their wider extents had been lost to the plough.

Site 31, Springfield, Ugborough

The site at Springfield (near Fancy) was situated just off the crest of a hill, at approximately 140m AOD. The site lies on a south facing slope south of a large round barrow, which is a Scheduled Monument (No. 33756). Both plots were the subject of a geophysical survey, which identified several linear anomalies but nothing with much clarity due to magnetic disturbances (Figs 3.26, 3.27). Plot 24.02 was investigated with a trial trench and the subsequent excavation was undertaken a little way south of the original easement. Plot 24.03 went straight to excavation due to its proximity to the Scheduled area and the possibility of Bronze Age satellite burials being encountered. In both plots the excavations were undertaken within an easement *c.* 15m wide and the site treated as one. A pit containing fragments of an Early Bronze Age Beaker is described in Chapter 2. Most features on the site relate to Roman occupation and they consisted of a partial enclosure, and an unenclosed area of pits, postholes and ring gullies. The

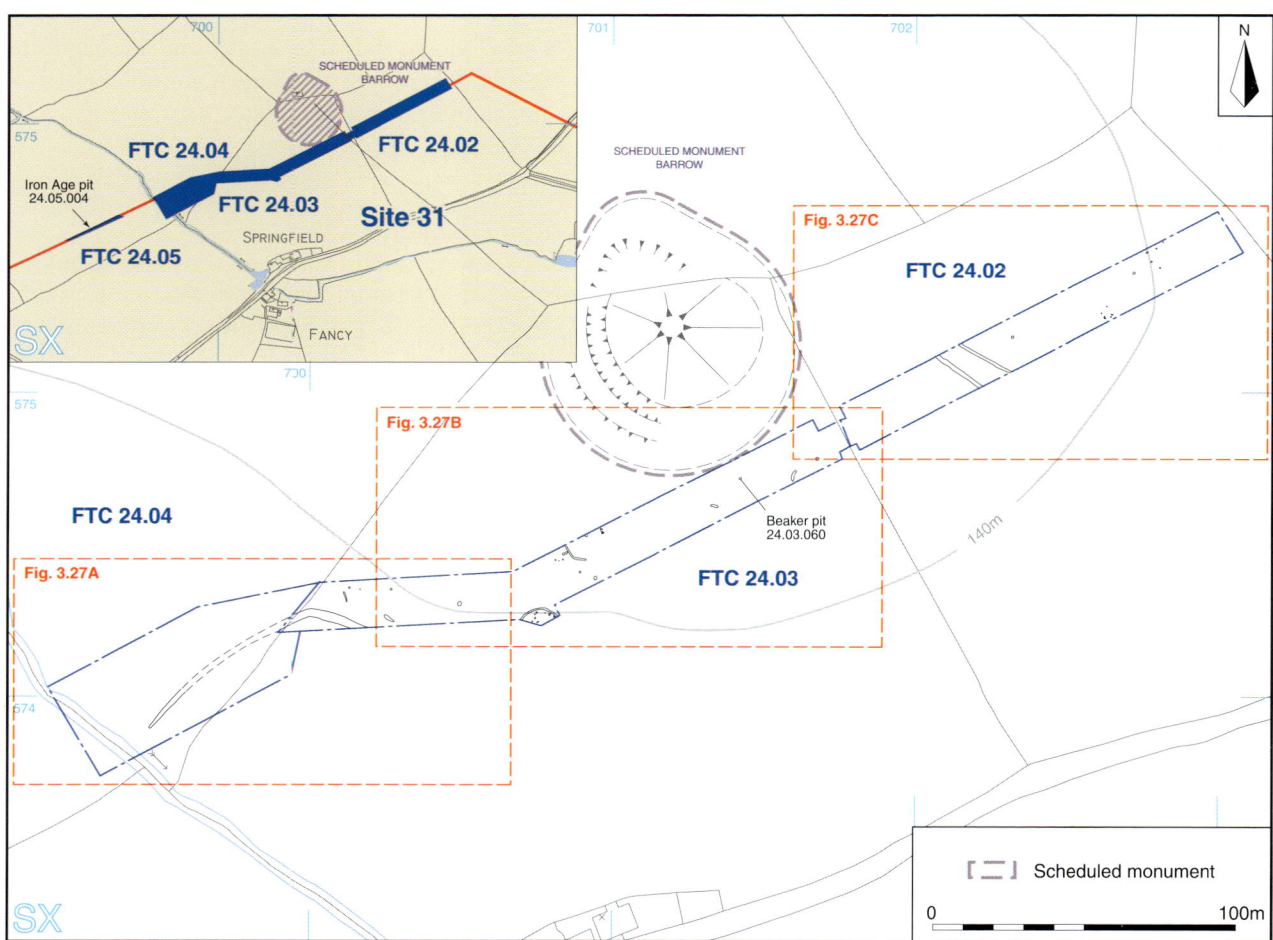

Fig. 3.26 Springfield (Site 31); plan of excavated features. Scales 1:2500 and 1:10,000

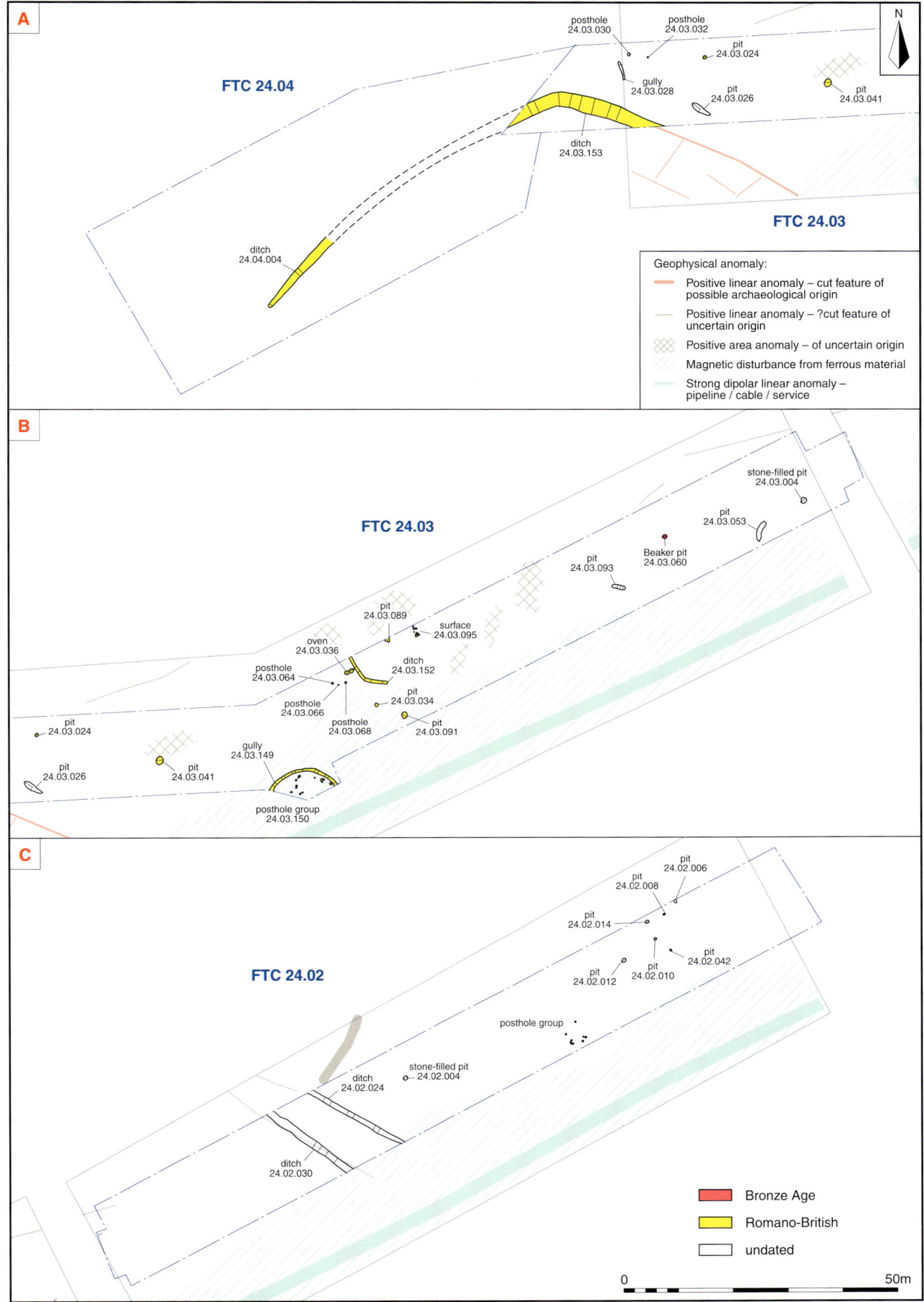

Fig. 3.27 Springfield (Site 31); plan of excavated features. Scale 1:1000

features appear to relate to a Roman period settlement although their scattered nature and the partial picture obtained within the excavation area makes the overall form of the settlement unclear. It was not possible to outline a chronological development of the site and, with the exception of a single Iron Age pit in the plot to the west, the following account describes features by group rather than by phase.

Iron Age pit 24.05.004
Lying 50m to the west of the Roman features on gently sloping land, circular pit 24.05.004 measured 0.9m in diameter and 0.26m deep (Fig. 3.26, inset). It had a single unremarkable fill which yielded two burnished sherds of pottery in granite-derived fabric, likely to be Iron Age. The feature is without immediate context and its significance is difficult to evaluate.

Enclosure ditch 24.03.153/24.04.004
Within the western area of plot 24.03 was a substantial curvilinear ditch 24.03.153/ 24.04.004, which is likely to have formed part of an enclosure (Fig. 3.27A). This ditch corresponds to the outer ditch of a double-ditched enclosure depicted by the geophysical survey, the inner ditch lying outside of the pipeline corridor. This outer ditch ran broadly from east to west in plot 24.03 before turning to the south-west and continuing for *c.* 55m to a terminal in plot 24.04. No features were identified within the area delineated by the enclosure and its purpose remains unknown. The ditch appeared to have been dug in one continuous length and was 2.6m wide and 0.7m deep. A similar sequence of fills was identified within each section. The primary fill (24.03.118/086/075) was derived from natural silting probably during the initial usage phase and did not contain any datable material. The secondary fill, 24.03.076/087/119, comprised light yellow-brown clay-silt which had probably accumulated during the life of the settlement and contained a relatively large assemblage of 60 sherds of late 3rd to 4th-century AD pottery. The tertiary fill, 24.03.077/088/120/147, comprised silty clay with unsorted shale fragments which contained 128 sherds of late 3rd to 4th-century AD pottery. It is possible that the deposit derives from a deliberate act of backfilling the ditch with nearby midden material and suggests there was significant occupation of this date nearby. Other finds of interest included a fragment of granite quern from the primary fill and two fragments of a stone mould for a pewter dish from the upper fill (Figs 3.32, 3.33).

Ring-gully 24.03.149 and internal posthole group 24.03.150
A gully, 24.03.149, comprising approximately one third of a circle, was partially revealed extending beyond the southern limits of the pipeline strip (Fig. 3.27B). Its projected internal diameter was c.13.7m. It was 0.5m in width and 0.3m in depth with moderately steeply sloping sides, a flat base and a shallow symmetrical profile, and was probably an eaves-drainage gully. The fill, 24.03.110, contained a single sherd of broadly Roman pottery.

The gully enclosed ten postholes (group number 24.03.150) and a small oval pit of unknown origin. The postholes, which had an average diameter of 0.3m and depths of between 0.1m and 0.3m, were generally steep-sided with flat bases. No dating evidence was recovered but they are likely to have formed a structure contemporary with the encircling gully. Four postholes appear to partially define a curving wall which would have formed a structure about 11m in diameter. The remaining postholes most likely relate to internal features and subdivisions but no clear patterns are evident. Other shallower postholes may have been lost to truncation. The absence of *in situ* post-packing and post-pipes may suggest that the posts were deliberately removed.

Ditch 24.03.152 and associated features
In the centre of the site was curvilinear ditch 24.03.152, which extended beyond the limits of the site (Fig. 3.27B). This feature, which measured 0.5m wide and less than 0.10m deep, was interpreted as part of a possible house ring-gully, which would have had a projected internal diameter of *c.* 10m. The single fill (24.03.057) contained one sherd of broadly Roman pottery. The very shallow nature of the feature made it difficult to define in plan and it probably originally extended further than the surviving part indicates. The only feature which may have lain within the projected area of the ring-gully was pit 24.03.089. The part of this pit within the site was 0.67m in diameter and 0.11m deep. Its single, charcoal-rich, fill (24.03.090) contained cinder, fayalitic run slag indicative of iron smelting and iron hammerscale, which strongly suggests that iron smithing was carried out here. The charcoal was identified as a mixture of oak and alder/hazel roundwood. A small yellow–brown cylindrical glass bead of probable Late Roman date was also recovered (Fig. 3.34 no. 2). To the north-west was part of a stone slab surface, 24.03.095, which is likely to have been more extensive originally. This would have lain immediately outside of the projected area delineated by gully 24.03.152, and may indicate the former entranceway to the building.

Oven 24.03.036
A possible oven, 24.03.036, lay immediately west of curvilinear ditch 24.03.152. It was ovoid in plan, measuring *c.*1m long, 0.7m wide and 0.17m deep (Fig. 3.28). Charcoal-rich deposit 24.03.037 lay within a shallow depression immediately outside the oven on its long axis and appeared to represent 'rakings' from the oven. None of the above-ground structure of the oven remained, but a partial clay lining of the pit sides 24.03.50 and 24.03.45 may represent remnants of the base of the clay hood superstructure. The feature

Fig. 3.28 Springfield (Site 31); view of oven 24.03.036, looking south-east. Scale 1m

contained substantial well-preserved charred plant remains from deposits 24.03.038 and 24.03.037 comprising a large range of cereals indicative of crop-processing waste (Table 3.22). Final deposit 24.03.040, consisting of partly burnt clay, represents the collapsed clay hood superstructure. A hazelnut shell from 24.03.038 produced a radiocarbon date in the range AD 140–326 (NZA-36393) with the greatest likelihood of it falling within the range AD 210–261 (61.1%) supporting the general dating of the pottery from the site (Table 3.7).

Pits and postholes near oven
Near oven 24.03.036 were shallow postholes 24.03.068, 24.03.066 and 24.03.064, which may have formed the posts of a windbreak or lean-to, shielding the oven. To the south, pit 24.03.034 measured 0.6m in diameter and 0.22m in depth. A fragment of elvan rotary quern stone (originating from the area to the north of Plymouth) came from the single fill, 24.03.035. Pit 24.03.091 to the east was of a similar form, 1.0m in diameter and 0.22m in depth. It is likely to be Roman, although without finds.

Pits and other features in the western part of the site
Pit 24.03.041 had a well-defined circular shape in plan, with steep sides and a flat base (Fig. 3.27B). It was 1.28m in diameter and 0.29m deep. The lower fill, 24.03.044,

Table 3.7: Radiocarbon date from Springfield, Site 31 (FTC 24.03)

Feature	Context	Lab No.	Material	δ ^{13}C	Radiocarbon Age	Calibrated Date 95%	Calibrated Date 68%
Pit 24.03.036	24.03.038	NZA 36393	Hazelnut shell (*Corylus avellana*)	-26‰	1784 ± 15 yr BP	140–55 AD (2.4%) plus 166–95 AD (6.2%) plus 210–61 AD (61.1%) plus 281–326 AD (25.4%)	225–57 AD (53.5%) plus 302–17 AD (15.1%)

was a deposit of carbon-rich material, which contained ironworking residues, including hearth/furnace lining, smelting slag (fayalitic run slag) and hammerscale. There was no evidence for this material having been burnt *in situ*, and it is considered more likely that it represents secondary deposition of waste from a furnace. The charcoal was identified as mostly oak, with some alder or hazel, consistent with ironworking. The secondary fill, 24.03.43/71, of red-brown silt, contained one sherd of Roman pottery and rare charcoal flecks. The final fill, 24.03.042, contained a piece of upper quern of fine-grained Dartmoor granite, as well as six sherds of broadly Roman pottery and quantities of burnt clay. It may be significant that a sample of black-glazed vitrified clay analysed by x-ray fluorescence showed high levels of tin. This is the only evidence of the working of tin alloys on the site, although the presence of part of a mould for a pewter dish from enclosure ditch 24.03.153 strongly suggests this possibility.

Another well-defined circular pit, 24.03.024, was 0.55m in diameter and 0.2m deep, with moderately sloping sides and a flat base. Its single fill, 24.03.025, contained 11 sherds of middle 3rd to 4th-century pottery as well as slag, vitrified hearth lining and an iron blade or strip. The original function of the pit is unclear, although it appears to have been deliberately backfilled with 'waste'.

In the western part of plot 24.03 were a group of features consisting of gully 24.03.028 and pits 24.03.026, 24.03.030 and 24.03.032. These were all 0.1m or less deep and of unknown origin. While undated these appear most likely to be Roman.

Pits and postholes in the eastern part of the site
Lozenge shaped pit 24.03.093 and more irregular pit 24.03.053 lay in the vicinity of the Beaker pit 24.03.060 (Fig. 3.27B). The recovery of ironworking slag from pit 24.03.093 indicates it is likely to be of Roman or later date. A group of 15 small undated pits or postholes were identified in the eastern part of plot 24.02 (Fig. 3.27C). They were 0.19–0.7m in diameter and 0.08–0.25m deep with similar sterile fills of dark red-brown clay-silt. They may have been a part of insubstantial structures here but their nature and date remain unresolved.

Stone-filled pits 24.02.004 and 24.03.004
Circular pit 24.02.004 measured 0.78m in diameter and 0.28m in depth. It contained a single deliberately placed fill of shale and quartz stone in a red silty clay matrix. Similar in size and form was circular pit 24.03.004; located *c*. 75m to the west it measured 0.9m in diameter and 0.2m in depth. It contained two fills: the primary fill, 24.03.016, consisted of dark red silty clay. The loose nature of the fill suggests a dumped deposit. The upper fill, 24.03.005, consisted of angular shale and quartz stone. No finds were recovered from either pit and their date, while assumed to be Roman, is not confirmed.

Site 34, Filham House, Ugborough

Lying south of Filham House, near Ivybridge, on flat land between the River Erme and Lud Brook at *c*. 53m AOD, were deliberately placed deposits of reddened clay 33.02.006 and 33.02.007, both displaying signs of *in situ* burning, but not to a high temperature (Fig. 3.29).

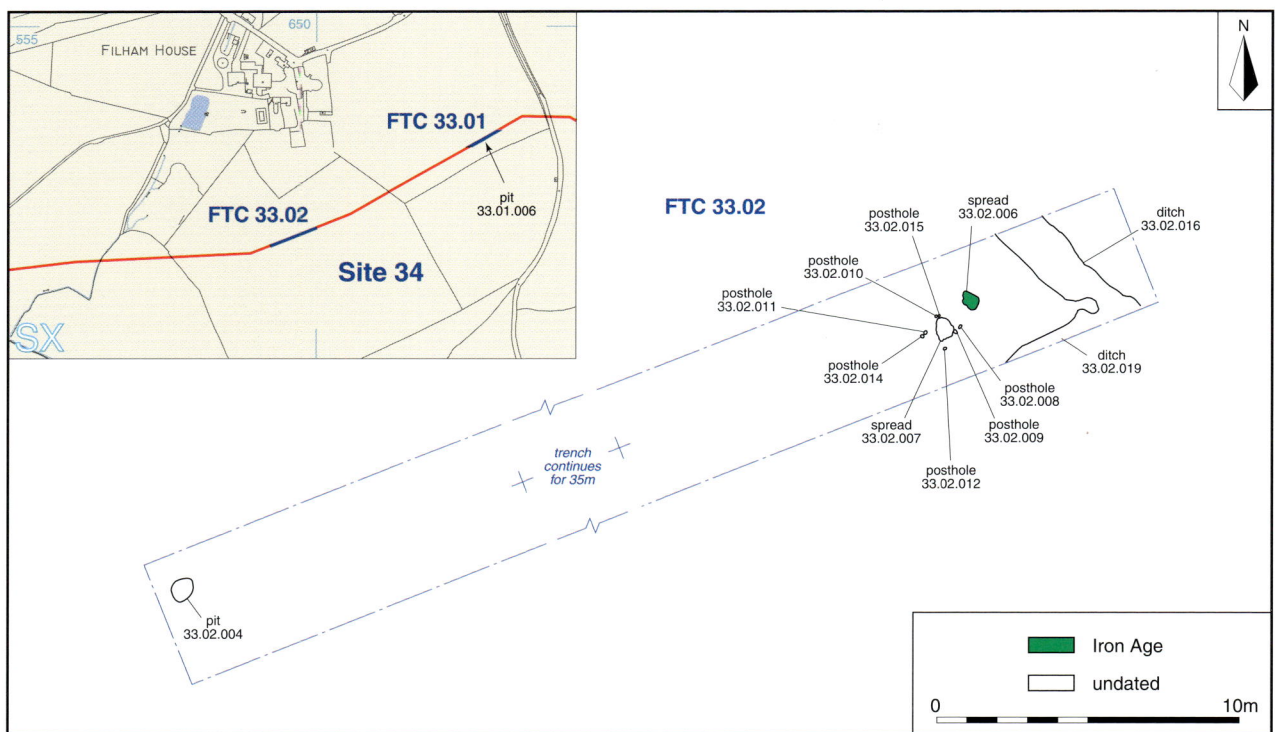

Fig. 3.29 Filham House (Site 34); plan of excavated features. Scales 1:250 and 1:10,000

Deposit 33.02.006 was 0.6m long by 0.45m wide and deposit 33.02.007 0.53m long by 0.58m wide. Both were of negligible thickness. The former was tentatively dated to the later Iron Age by two sherds of pottery in granite-derived fabric from within it. Assessed soil samples yielded only sparse charcoal. Associated with these spreads was a group of seven stakeholes, with pointed profiles driven to depths of between 0.08 and 0.19m. They displayed similar fills of dark brown silty clay with charcoal flecking. No dating evidence was recovered from the stakeholes, but they appeared to be associated with the burnt patches of clay. Deposits 33.02.006 and 33.02.007 are likely to have been hearths, but the fact that they were not heated to a high temperature might imply the existence of stone bases, now removed. The stakes may have supported a light and irregular superstructure around hearth 33.02.007. The poor quality of the archaeological evidence makes further conjecture futile. To the east, ditches 33.02.019 and 33.02.016 form a corner of an enclosure that appears to be shown on the tithe map and are therefore not likely to have been associated.

Later Iron Age pottery

Henrietta Quinnell

Introductory comment

The term 'Later Iron Age' is used to describe well-made fabrics with sparse, evenly sized inclusions often around 1mm in size. Such fabrics, as distinct from thicker wares with larger inclusions, appear part way through the Early Iron Age, probably from about 600 BC. In Cornwall this broad fabric is used for undecorated vessels termed the Plain Jar Group from the Early, as opposed to the Earliest, Iron Age (Quinnell 2011) and then through the Middle Iron Age with South Western Decorated Ware from around 300 BC. In Cornwall too it is used for the Late Iron Age Cordoned Ware style from around 100 BC. In Devon there are problems with the identification of a distinctive Late Iron Age style although it now appears that some Durotrigian style vessels were replacing South Western Decorated Ware from around the turn of the era (Quinnell in prep.).

The data from the present project show a long gap between the Middle Bronze Age and the Middle Iron Age (see radiocarbon overview, Fig. 6.1). This is consistent with the pattern of ceramic use in Devon, where pottery use seems to have been at a low level through this period, the Late Bronze Age and the Earliest Iron Age down to around 600/500 cal. BC (Quinnell 1999). The scatter of Later Iron Age sites reflects the general increase of pottery found in the county from that date. The granite-derived material from the South Devon sites is of considerable interest in providing a possible early start for the fabric source known as South Devon Ware which occurs in the Roman period (Bidwell and Silvester 1988) and for which a source in the upper Dart valley has been suggested. The total assemblage of Later Iron Age sherds, 32 sherds weighing 123 grammes, shows a consistent change in fabrics used, from chert inclusions around Ottery St Mary, through rock inclusions and Ludwell Valley in the Exeter area to granite-derived material on the South Devon sites skirting Dartmoor (Table 3.8).

East Devon

Site 2: Slade Farm, Ottery St Mary
(See also Chapter 2, Neolithic) Pit 2.03.004 (fill 2.03.005). The pit and four of the sherds, harder with a more even fracture, may be Later Iron Age in view of the three radiocarbon determinations from this pit: (NZA-36304) 392–212 cal. BC, (NZA-36305) 388–208 cal. BC and (NZA-36320) 388–212 cal. BC (all 95% confidence).

Site 4: Pixies' Parlour, Ottery St Mary
(See also Chapter 2, Early Neolithic, Bronze Age). Ring ditch 3.04.045. Fill 206.007 of ditch 3.04.045 contained a small abraded sherd.
Layer 03.04.002 (subsoil) contained four burnished abraded sherds.

Site 10: Hogsbrook Farm, surface find
Subsoil 4a.01.002 produced a moderately abraded base angle in Ludwell Valley fabric, generally Later Iron Age in character. Ludwell Valley fabrics originate on the east side of Exeter (Quinnell in prep.). This indicates some activity in the Later Iron Age here.

Site 14: Exwell Barton, Powderham
Ditch 13.02.123, fill 13.02.124, produced two abraded sherds in a thin fabric with rock inclusions. Ditch 13.02.175, fill 13.02.176, produced a single thicker bodysherd in the same faric.

South Devon

Site 19: Barton Hill Cross, Littlehempston
P12 (not illus.) 7.01.005 fill of pit 7.01.004. Seventeen moderately abraded sherds in a burnished fabric PS17 with some granitic derived inclusions: oxidised (5YR5/3) reddish brown with reduced (5YR4/1) dark grey core. Rim and upper part of plain vessel which belongs most probably to South Western Decorated Ware. The shape is illustrated in the assemblage at Milber Down (Fox *et al* 1949–50, fig. 9, nos 6 and 13).
7.01.036 fill of posthole 7.01.035: two fresh burnished sherds as 7.01.005.
7.01.071 fill of ditch 7.01.068: one fresh sherd as 7.01.005.

Site 23: Hood Quarry, Dartington
Ditch 13.03.04 fill 905 (evaluation trench 9): one sherd of abraded granite-derived fabric similar to those from Site 19.

Site 31: Springfield, Ugborough
Pit 24.05.004, fill 24.05.005: two fresh burnished sherds in fine granite-derived fabric.

Site 34: Filham House, Ugborough
Clay spread 33.02.006: two abraded sherds in granite-derived fabric.

Table 3.8: Later Iron Age ceramics; sherd numbers with weight in grammes

Context No.	Feature	Sherds	Wt	Ref.	Fabric
Pixies' Parlour, Site 4					
206.007	Fill, ring-gully 3.04.045	1	1	-	CH.3 Upper Greensand with chert
03.04.002	Subsoil	4	12	-	CH.3
Total		5	13	-	
Hogsbrook Farm, Site 10					
4a.01.002	Subsoil	1	4	-	PB.2 Permian Breccia, Ludwell Valley
Exwell Barton, Site 14 ditches					
13.02.124	Fill, ditch 13.02.123	2	7	-	RO.2 Exeter Volcanic, with basaltic rock inclusions
13.02.176	Fill, ditch 13.02.175	1	13	-	RO.2
Total		3	20	-	
Barton Hill Cross, Site 19, pits					
7.01.005	Fill, pit 7.01.004	17	45	P12	GN.4 Granite-derived, with quartz, feldspar and biotite
7.01.036	Fill, pit 7.01.035	2	9	-	GN.4
7.01.071	Fill, ditch 7.01.068	1	2	-	GN.4
Total		20	56		
Hood Quarry, Site 23					
905	Fill, ditch 13.03.004	1	8	-	GN.4
Springfield, Site 31					
24.03.002	Subsoil	1	6	-	GN.4
Filham House, Site 34					
33.02.006	Clay spread	2	6	-	GN.4

Roman pottery

Angela Aggujaro and E.R. McSloy

A total assemblage of 689 sherds (5552g) of Roman pottery was recovered from nine defined 'sites' in the East and South Devon sections. The bulk of this material was recovered by hand, but a proportion (58 sherds, 321g) came from soil samples.

Two groups from the South Devon sites at Billany Farm, Dartington (Site 24) and Springfield, Ugborough (Site 31) were considered of sufficient size to warrant publication. A summary for the remaining material is provided. The pottery was sorted by fabric and quantified according to sherd count, weight and rim EVEs per fabric. Regional or traded wares are defined using the National Roman reference collection codes (Tomber and Dore 1998). Local and unsourced wares were coded in a similar manner. Recording of vessel form, decoration and presence of carbonised or other residues was also undertaken.

The condition of the pottery is mixed; surface preservation varies according to fabric and typically the finewares are least well preserved. Rates of fragmentation are high for both sites. The mean sherd weight (for the hand-collected material) 8.3 grammes, is low for a Roman assemblage.

Assemblage Composition (Tables 3.9 and 3.10)

Local and unsourced

SOD RE South Devon (micaceous) reduced ware (Holbrook and Bidwell 1991, 177; Tomber and Dore 1998, 126).

LOC GW1 Greyware, grey throughout smooth feel. Dense and hard sandy fabric with well-sorted quartz and small particle of black grog (?) (smaller than 0.05mm).

LOC GW2 Greyware, pale orange outer surface and grey inner and core. Soft with powdery feel and finely irregular fracture. Moderate (1–2.5mm) grog inclusion.

LOC OX Oxidised fineware, orange-brown surfaces and grey core. Soft with powdery feel and finely irregular fracture. Sparse voids from burnt-out organic inclusions and sparse gold mica. Broadly consistent with Oxidised fabrics described from Exeter (Holbrook and Bidwell 1991, 181–8).

GT Grog-tempered, dark brown outside to pale grey inside. Slightly sandy feel, smooth fracture. Sparse fine grog (0.05mm) and sparse quartz, black mica and iron oxide.

BS Black Sandy. Dark brown throughout. Smooth feel and fine regular fracture. Fine silty fabric, which may contain very sparse slate inclusions (1.5–2mm).

Regional imported

NFO CC New Forest Colour-Coated Ware (Tomber and Dore 1998, 141).

DOR BB1 South-East Dorset (Poole Harbour) Black-Burnished Ware (Tomber and Dore 1998, 127).

Table 3.9: Roman pottery summary; Billany Farm (Site 24) and Springfield (Site 31)

Fabric	Billany Farm, Site 24			Springfield, Site 31			Total		
	Ct	Wt	EVE	Ct	Wt	EVE	Ct	Wt	EVE
SOD RE	148	2109	0.84	339	1818	1.68	487	3927	2.52
LOC GW1	-	-	-	2	24	-	2	24	-
LOC GW2	-	-	-	1	63	-	1	63	-
LOC OX	13	113	0.08	-	-	-	13	113	0.08
BS	4	32	-	-	-	-	4	32	-
GT	4	81	0.18	-	-	-	4	81	0.18
DOR BB1	12	133	0.04	56	637	1.13	68	770	1.17
NFO CC	1	4	0.05	2	6	0.15	3	10	0.2
LEZ SA	2	17	0.09	-	-	-	2	17	0.09
Total	184	2489	1.28	400	2548	2.96	584	5037	4.24

Continental imported wares
LEZ SA2 Central Gaulish (Lezoux) Samian (Tomber and Dore 1998, 32).

The comparative composition of the assemblage across the sites is presented in Table 3.9. South Devon micaceous reduced ware (hereafter termed South Devon Ware) is dominant from the two main sites Billany Farm and Springfield (83% of total sherd count; 59% by EVEs) and across the entire pipeline. South Devon Ware is commonly the dominant type among later Roman groups from the area, although its origins are seemingly earlier (Holbrook and Bidwell 1991, 178). The petrology and of this type distribution indicate an origin 'in or near one of the river valleys draining from Dartmoor' (ibid., 177). The second largest group comprises Dorset Black-Burnished Ware (12% of total sherd count from both sites; 27% by EVEs). This 'traded ware', originating from the Pool Harbour area is also well represented locally, and particularly abundant from Exeter (Holbrook and Bidwell 1991).

Reduced coarsewares (greyware, black sandy ware and a grog-tempered ware) makes up the bulk of the remaining assemblage and is presumed to be of relatively local origin. Oxidised coarseware fabrics occur only very sparsely: type LOC OX was recorded from three deposits (totalling 15 sherds from East and South Devon) and is characterised by a fine and powdery fabric. It compares in its description to types recorded from Exeter of probably local origin.

Roman finewares occur in very low levels across the pipeline. Two sherds of Central Gaulish Samian were identified from Billany Farm. A single vessel form in this type, a Dragendorff 33 cup, came from deposit 14.01.077 in terrace 14.01.107. Late Roman finewares are represented as three small beaker sherds in New Forest Colour-Coated Ware from Billany Farm and Springfield.

Discussion by site

Site 24: Billany Farm, Dartington
Pottery amounting to 185 sherds weighing 2490 grammes was hand-collected from 17 deposits, mainly ditch fills, deposits associated with terrace 14.01.107 and pit fills. This site produced some larger, well-preserved groups and the average sherd weight is moderately high at 13.5 grammes.

The range of fabrics present is narrow with the assemblage dominated by two types: South Devon Ware and Dorset Black-Burnished Ware (Table 3.9). Finewares were recorded from three deposits and consist of Central Gaulish Samian Ware, which is seemingly residual, and New Forest Colour-Coated Ware. A fine grog-tempered fabric occurs from a single deposit ditch fill 14.01.099 (ditch 14.01.106). The fabric and the form represent a carinated bowl or cup (Fig. 3.30 no. 1) suggestive of an Early Roman, probably 1st-century AD, dating. An unsourced but probably local (Exeter?) oxidised ware was recovered from one deposit (14.01.061), the upper fill of ditch 14.01.106. This occurs as large, joining sherds from a necked jar with curved rim (Fig. 3.30 no. 2).

Identifiable forms among South Devon reduced ware reflect the restricted range apparent for this type (Holbrook and Bidwell 1991, figs 71–2). Most common are globular (Fig. 3.30 no. 3) or slack-bodied jars with everted rim, sometimes with a shallow internal groove (as Fig. 3.30 no. 9). There also occur large storage jars (Fig. 3.30 nos 4–5), some with raised horizontal cordons, conical flanged bowls (Fig. 3.30 no. 6) and a small number of dishes with plain rim (Fig. 3.30 no. 7). Certain of the jars and dishes/bowls are clearly influenced by late forms in Black-Burnished Ware.

The chronological focus appears to be across the later 2nd to the 4th centuries AD, based on the abundance of South Devon Ware and the forms represented in this type and the Dorset Black-Burnished Wares. The presence of particular vessels forms among the common coarsewares, including conical flanged bowls and plain rimmed dishes, and of sherds of New Forest Colour-Coated Ware, indicate dating in some instances after *c.* AD 250. Such dating is also supported by three radiate coins from the site (McSloy, this report). There is limited evidence from the grog-tempered vessel (Fig. 3.30 no. 1) and the Samian for earlier activity.

Site 31: Springfield, Ugborough
Pottery amounting to 409 sherds, weighing 2571 grammes, was hand-collected from 19 deposits, mainly ditch, pit and gully fills. The assemblage exhibits a high level of fragmentation and the mean sherd is low at 6.4 grammes.

The large majority of the assemblage is made up of South Devon Ware. This type was ubiquitous across the site and represents 85% of the total (sherd count). Other coarsewares were Dorset Black-Burnished Ware (14% of the total) and a smaller quantity of greywares of probable local origin (types LOC GW 1 and 2). Two sherds in New Forest Colour-Coated Ware are the only finewares present.

Of the identifiable vessel forms, the majority are jars including those with everted and grooved/lid-seated rims in South Devon Ware (Fig. 3.30 nos 8 and 9) which are comparable to examples illustrated by Holbrook and Bidwell (fig. 71 no. 4.2). 'Open' vessel forms occur as conical bowls and plain-rim dishes in South Devon Ware and Dorset Black-Burnished Ware. There is a single beaker in New Forest Colour-Coated ware (Fig. 3.30 no. 10), which compares to indented beaker type 27 (Fulford 2000, 50–3). Based on the vessel forms represented dating is consistent with a focus in the 3rd to 4th centuries AD, with elements such as the New Forest indented beaker suggesting dating after *c.* AD 260.

Other sites (summaries)
East Devon

Site 4: Pixies' Parlour, Ottery St Mary
Single bodysherds of Roman pottery (in total 51g) were recovered from ditch 3.04.004 (fills 3.04.014, 3.04.062), penannular gully 3.04.045 (fill 3.04.042), and topsoil deposit 3.04.001. Broadly Roman dating of this material is indicated on the basis of the fabric alone.

Site 7: Land East of Broad Oak, Ottery St Mary
A single, small and abraded sherd in a black-firing sandy fabric from upper fill 4.10.023 (ditch 4.10.018), has been identified as of probable Roman date.

Site 9: New Nutwalls, Aylesbeare
Ditch 0.03.006 (fill 0.03.07) produced five sherds (16g) in a coarse sandy reduced fabric representing a single vessel (see Chapter 5 for site description). The vessel form is identifiable as a necked jar or bowl with out-curved rim and with a possible cordon at the junction of neck and shoulder. The surfaces are much degraded, due to a combination of the soils conditions and possibly also as the result of burning. There are traces of a carbonised deposit below the rim.

Site 14: Exwell Barton, Powderham
Two abraded bodysherds of Roman pottery (9g) were recovered from subsoil deposit 13.02.002. One sherd occurs in a hard sandy fabric with orange-firing outer surface and grey inner and core. The second is heavily weathered but is probably a sherd of Dorset Black-Burnished Ware.

South Devon

Site 19: Barton Hill Cross, Littlehempston
A small group of 27 (86g) sherds, entirely comprising heavily fragmented South Devon Wares, was recovered from ditches. A single vessel form, an everted-rim jar, was identifiable from deposit 7.01.073, the upper fill of ditch 7.01.072.

Site 23: Hood Quarry, Dartington
A single small chip (1g) of Black-Burnished Ware, broadly of Roman date, was recovered from ditch 13.03.011.

Plot FTC 22.03: Land south of Beneknowle, Diptford
Two sherds of Black-Burnished Ware and one of South Devon type (13g total) were recovered from subsoil deposit 22.03.002. The South Devon sherd is identifiable as from a flanged bowl of Late Roman type (mid 3rd to 4th centuries). No archaeological features were identified.

Plot FTC 20.03: Land north of Elwell, Diptford
One abraded rim sherd of South Devon ware weighing 9 grams was recovered from subsoil in an evaluation trench. The form is identifiable as a conical flanged bowl and this suggests a later 3rd to 4th-century date.

General discussion
The Roman pottery assemblage is of a very limited size and range. In its conservative character and dominance of South Devon Ware this group compares to others from the small native-style enclosures occurring from the area (Holbrook and Bidwell 1991, 3, fig. 7; Seager Smith 1999, 286–326). The nature of this material hinders appreciation of chronology. On the basis of the range of fabrics and forms represented among the two larger site groups, both belong primarily to the Late Roman Period. Good evidence for Early Roman activity is scarce, although a carinated vessel from Billany Farm (Site 24), which probably dates to the 1st century AD, is of interest in this respect.

The dominance South Devon Wares and other coarsewares among the smaller rural sites in the area is likely to be a reflection both of relatively lowly economic status and the chief requirement for 'utilitarian' pottery for cooking and storage. The very limited presence of finewares and absence of 'specialist wares' such as mortaria suggests a limited need for, or possibly restricted access, to such types. Evidence for vessel function from carbonised or other residues was largely absent, probably as the result of burial conditions. The dominance of jars and utilitarian dishes/bowls (Table

Table 3.10: Roman pottery forms; Billany Farm (Site 24) and Springfield (Site 31)

Form	Billany Farm, Site 24			Springfield, Site 31			
	Jar	Bowl	Dish	Beaker	Jar	Bowl	Dish
Fabric	No./EVEs	No./EVEs	No./EVEs	No./EVEs	No./EVEs	No./EVEs	No./EVEs
SOD RE	7/.62	2.16	1/.06	-	13/1.12	3/.56	-
GT	-	1/.18	-	-	-	-	-
LOC OX	1/.08	-	-	-	-	-	-
DOR BB1	-	2/.04	-	-	3/.25	2/.30	4/.58
NFO CC	-	1/.05	-	1/.15	-	-	-
LEZ SA	-	1/.09	-	-	-	-	-
Total	8/0.70	7/.52	1/.06	1/.15	16/1.37	5/.86	4/.58

3.10) suggests use for cooking and/or storage. The large handmade cordoned jars (Fig. 3.30 nos 4–5), which are a common component among South Devon Wares, were best suited to storage, possibly of dry foodstuffs.

Catalogue of illustrated vessels

Billany Farm, Dartington

1 Carinated bowl or cup; fabric GT; fill 14.01.099 (ditch 14.01.106)
2 Necked jar with curved rim; fabric LOC OX; fill 14.01.061 (ditch 14.01.106)
3 Globular jar with short everted rim; fabric SOD RE; fill 14.01.008 (pit 14.01.004)
4 Large storage jar; fabric SOD RE; fill 14.01.084 (terrace 14.01.107)
5 Cordoned sherd; fabric SOD RE; fill 14.01.084 (terrace 14.01.107)
6 Conical flanged bowl: fabric SOD RE; fill 14.01.080 (pit 14.01.038)

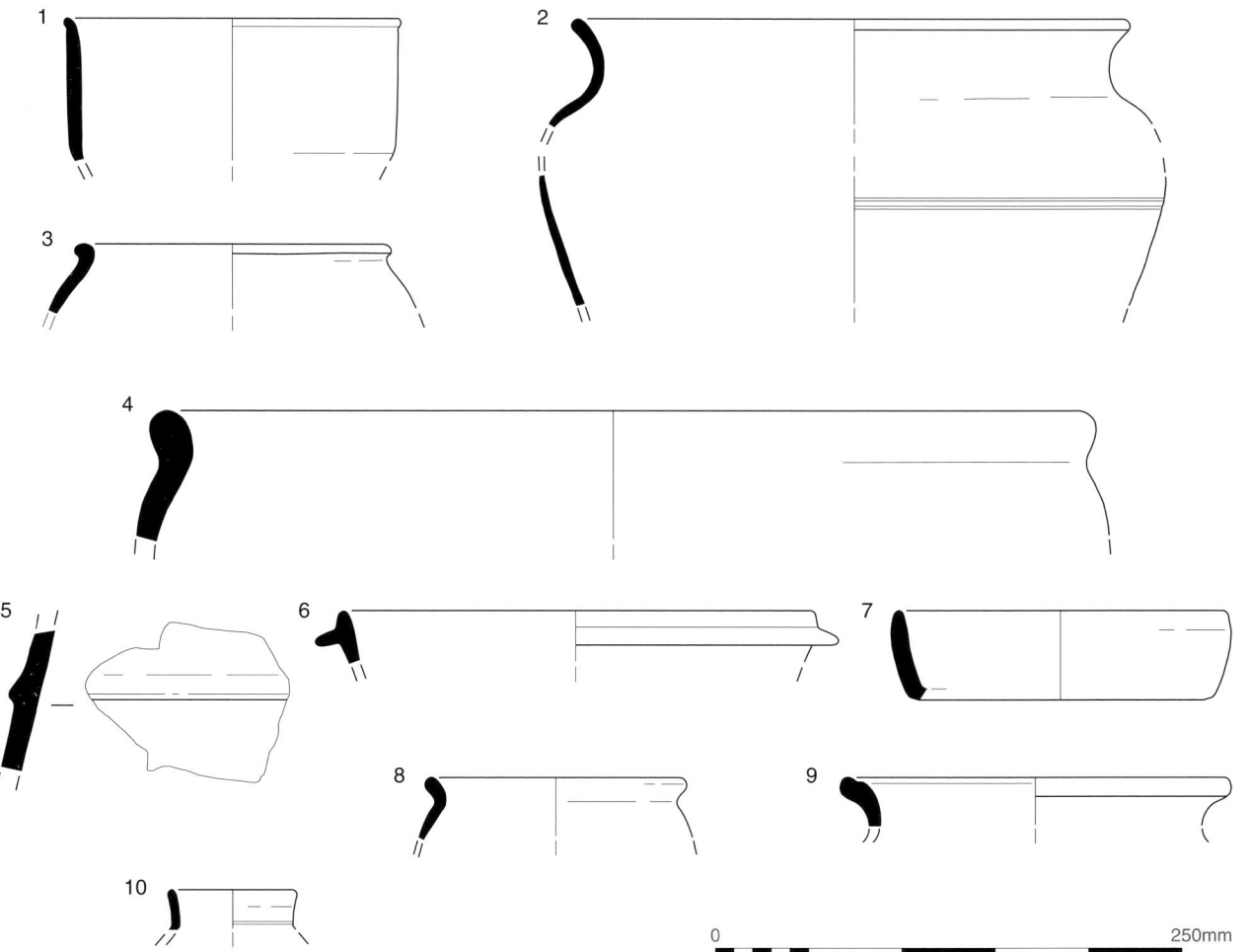

Fig. 3.30 Roman pottery from Billany Farm (Site 24) and Springfield (Site 31). Scale 1:4

Table 3.11: Pixies' Parlour (Site 4); worked and utilised stone

Ditch	Context	Stone Artefact
3.04.004	3.04.021, fourth fill	Two joining fragments of cobble from the Budleigh Salterton Pebble Beds. Burnt (623g)
3.04.004	3.04.066, fill	Budleigh Salterton Pebble Beds cobble used as a polisher or whetstone (884g) L159.0mm/W58.2mm/Th59.8mm

7   Plain rim dish; fabric SOD RE; fill 14.01.080 (pit 14.01.038):

Springfield, Ugborough

8   Slack jar with everted rim; fabric SOD RE; fill 24.03.011 (ditch 24.03.010, n. i.)
9   Jar with everted/grooved rim; fabric SOD RE; fill 24.03.119 (ditch 24.03.153)
10   Beaker; fabric NFO CC; fill 24.03.088 (ditch 24.03.153)

Worked and utilised stone

Susan Watts, with geological identifications by Roger T. Taylor

East Devon

Site 4: Pixies' Parlour, Ottery St Mary

Two utilised stones were recorded (Table 3.11). Two joining fragments of a burnt cobble and a cobble used as a polisher or whetstone were recovered from the fill of an enclosure ditch (3.04.004) possibly dated to the Roman period. Both cobbles derive from the Budleigh Salterton Pebble Beds and were probably imported to the site from the west.

Site 12: Lower Nutwell, Woodbury

A piece from a small, neat, rectangular whetstone of fine Carboniferous sandstone from Mid Devon was recovered from a collapsed medieval or post-medieval wall (Table 3.12). The whetstone is possibly residual from the prehistoric period.

Table 3.12: Lower Nutwell (Site 12); worked and utilised stone

Feature	Context	Stone Artefact
Wall collapse 12.01.034	325.002	Fragment of whetstone Mid Devon Carboniferous sandstone (14g) L35.8mm/W19.9mm/Th11.0mm

South Devon

Site 24: Billany Farm, Dartington

Quernstones

One fragment of lower stone and two fragments from upper stones of rotary querns were recovered from Roman contexts (Table 3.13). The two fragments of upper stone, S6 and S7, are of Cornish greisen, although probably from separate sources, while the fragment of lower stone, S5, is of Dartmoor granite. Querns from other Romano-British sites in south and east Devon, such as Pomeroy Wood near Honiton (Loader 1999, 281), Topsham (Montague 1938, 78), Lower Well Farm near Stoke Gabriel (Masson Phillips 1966, 26) and Clanacombe near Thurlestone (Greene and Greene 1970, 134), indicate that fairly local stone types were generally utilised for their manufacture. Notable exceptions are the lava querns from the Eifel region of Germany which were imported by the military and were found in the forts at Exeter and Pomeroy Wood (Bell and Bradshaw 1983, 128). Billany Farm, Dartington, lies close to the southern edge of Dartmoor and the fragment of a quern of Dartmoor granite appears to fit the general pattern of local quern supply and acquisition. However, the two upper stones of Cornish greisen, an altered form of granite, obviously come from much further afield. The main sources of Cornish greisen in the Roman period appear to have been within the Tregonning/Godolphin and St Austell granites, although small areas of greisen are also known in east Cornwall, on Bodmin Moor and St Agnes on the Isles of Scilly and, as S7 indicates, greisen from the Carnmenellis granite was also utilised (Quinnell 1993, 31, fig. 1). Although querns of Cornish greisen have been found on a number of Cornish sites such as at Carn Euny, Reawla, Trethurgy and Boden Vean (Christie 1978, 388; Quinnell 1992, 109; Quinnell and Watts 2004; Quinnell forthcoming (c)) they have not, to date, been identified in Devon. On current evidence, therefore, the presence of such querns at Billany Farm must be considered unusual, indicative of trade and/or particular contacts between Cornwall and South Devon.

Quern fragments S5 and S6 show little by way of diagnostic features but their general form appears typical of the flatter types of quern that were widely adopted during the Roman period (Watts 2002, 34). Fragment S7 on the other hand, which comprises a little over a quarter of a neatly made upper stone, has the remains of a collar around the central hole or eye and a concave grinding surface (Fig. 3.31 no. 2). The quernstone would originally have been *c.* 420mm in diameter, the collar forming a hopper around the eye of *c.*180mm diameter. The form and size of the stone with its concave grinding surface and collar is typical of querns of the later Roman period and is similar to

Table 3.13: Billany Farm (Site 24) and Springfield (Site 31); worked and utilised stone from Romano-British contexts

Site	Feature	Context	Stone Artefact
24	Ditch 14.01.105	Fill 14.01.021	Dolerite cobble possibly intended for use (696g)
	Pit 14.01.038	Fill 14.01.039	Quern fragment SF2 (see description) (S5)
	Ditch 14.01.106	Fill 14.01.061	Quern fragment (see description) (S6)
	Terrace 14.01.107	Fill 14.01.077	Half quartzite beach cobble. Brought to site from some distance away, possibly part of a hammerstone that split (446g)
	Pit 14.01.081	Fill 14.01.082	Quern fragment SF6 (see description) (S7)
31	Pit 24.03.041	Fill 24.03.035	Probable quern fragment (see description) (S8)
	Pit 24.03.041	Fill 24.03.042	Quern fragment (see description) (S9)
	Pit 24.03.041	Fill 24.03.042	Fragment of surface-derived vein quartz (38g)
	Gully 24.03.152	Fill 24.03.057	Small fragment of granite with some haematite. Possibly collected for pigment (24g)
	Ditch 24.03.153	Fill 24.03.084	Granite river pebble. Possibly from River Avon
	Ditch 24.03.153	Fill 24.03.086	Cobble of tourmalinised hornfels utilised as whetstone. Possibly from the River Avon. The smooth faces of the stone bear fine scratch marks (274g). L83.7mm/W63.9mm/Th34.6mm
	Ditch 24.03.153	Fill 24.03.086	Quern fragment (see description) (S10)
	Ditch 24.03.153	Fill 24.03.119	2 joining fragments of a mould stone (see description) (S11)
	Ditch 24.03.153	Fill 24.03.148	4 oval-shaped granite river pebbles of varying coarseness. Possibly from River Avon (44g, 53g, 73g, 84g)

examples from Shortlands Lane, Cullompton, Chew Park and Camerton, Somerset and also Trethurgy near St Austell, Cornwall (Wedlake 1958, 244; Rahtz and Greenfield 1977, 202; Watts 2002, 37; 2011; Quinnell and Watts 2004, 149). There is no evidence of how the handle was attached on the surviving fragment from Billany Farm but querns from elsewhere in Roman Britain indicate that several alternatives were possible. The stone may have had an L-shaped handle hole drilled from its top surface through to the side, or the handle may have fitted in a groove cut across the top surface. Alternatively, the handle was held in a loop on an iron band around the circumference of the stone, although the fragment shows no evidence of iron staining (see for example Budge 1903, 73; Welfare 1985, 159; Watts 2002, 37; Wright 2002, 274).

The pattern of wear exhibited on the grinding surface of S7 not only shows that the stone has been used quite extensively but it also indicates how the grain was ground as it passed between the grinding surfaces of the upper and lower stones. The inner *c*. 70mm of the grinding surface, where the initial breaking open of the grain took place, exhibits the least amount of wear. More wear, in the form of concentric wear rings and some glazing of high spots, is visible in the middle *c*. 90mm of the grinding surface. Secondary reduction occurred in this section, the fineness of the meal determined by the coarseness of the stone, the size of the gap between the upper and lower stones, the diameter of the stone and also by the speed with which the upper stone was turned. The most wear has occurred at the very periphery of the grinding surface. The grinding surfaces of the upper and lower stones would have been closest together at this point and the stone has worn quite smooth with the passage of the ground meal between the two stones as it exited the quern (after Jørgensen 2000, 189–91; Watts 2008, 9).

Other stone

Also found was half a quartzite beach cobble recovered from the fill of the late Roman terrace (14.01.107). Although the cobble shows no evidence of wear or use it was brought to site from some distance away and may perhaps have been part of a hammerstone that split. A dolerite cobble retrieved from ditch 14.01.105 may also have been intended for use, perhaps as a rubbing stone.

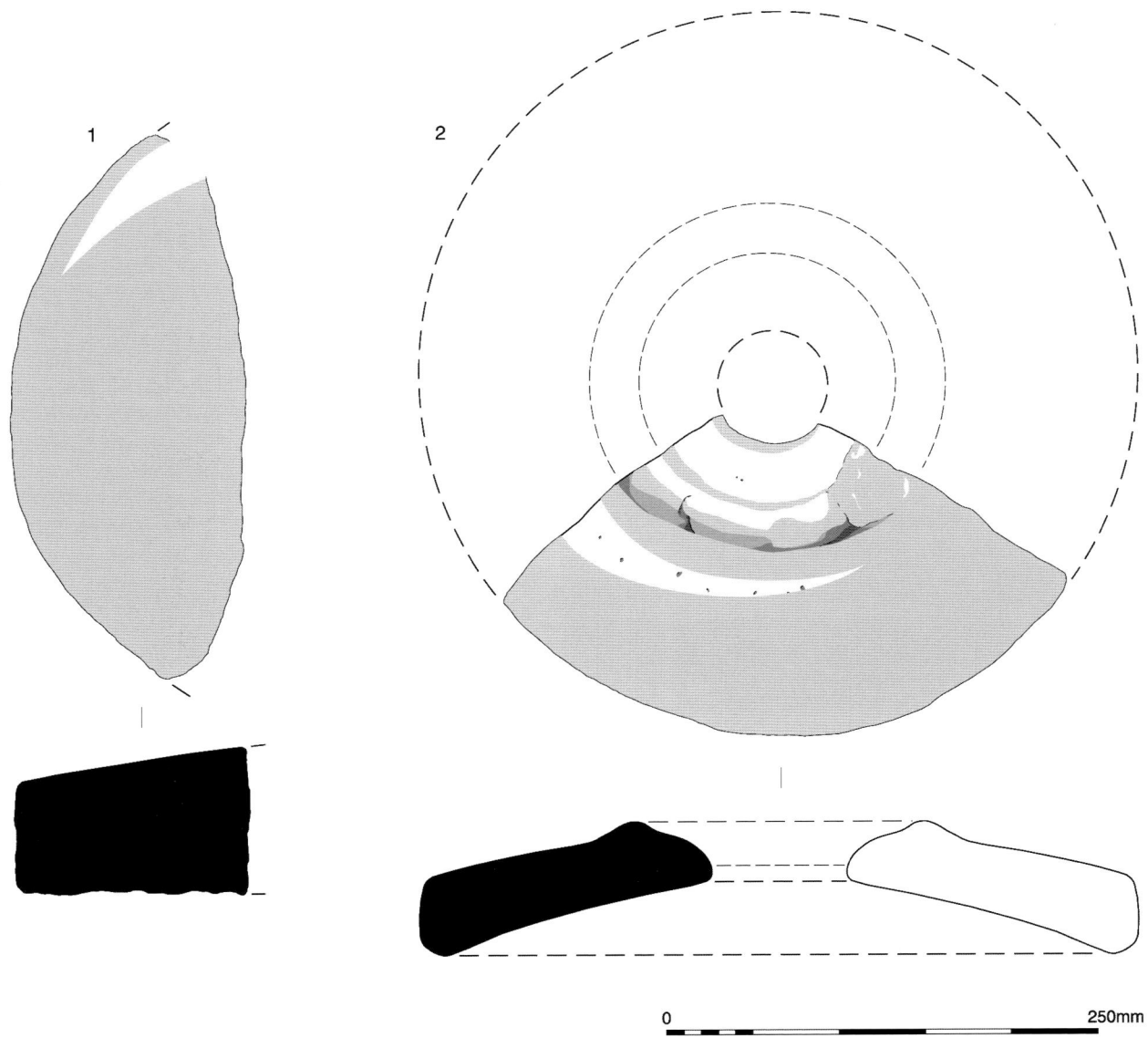

Fig. 3.31 Quern fragments from Billany Farm (Site 24). Scale 1:4

Catalogue

S5. 14.01.039 (RA2) (fill of pit 14.01.038) (Fig. 3.31 no. 1)
Large segment of lower rotary quernstone. Fine–medium-grained granite, probably from Dartmoor. Sloping, slightly concavo-convex grinding surface. Grinding surface worn. No remains of spindle hole. Underside of stone roughly flat.
L 318mm/W 139.5mm/Th 83.3mm centre, 68.8mm edge. Original diameter *c.* 380mm. Weight *c.* 4.0kg

S6. 14.01.061 (fill of ditch 14.01.106) (not illus.)
Fragment of upper rotary quernstone. Greisen with some black tourmaline, from Cornwall.
Flattened bun shape with flat grinding surface. The grinding surface is worn but was probably originally pecked. The stone now wears very easily. This is probably due to its sojourn in the ground as used in this condition it would impart numerous grains of stone into the ground meal.
L 129mm/W 101.1mm/Th 65.6mm. Weight 931g

S7. 14.01.082 (SF6) (fill of pit 14.01.081) (Fig. 3.31 no. 2)
Quarter of an upper rotary quernstone. Quartzite rich greisen with tourmaline clots, possibly from Carnmenellis, Cornwall. A neatly made quernstone with the remains of a collar around the central hole or eye. The collar stands *c.* 108mm high and forms a hopper, originally *c.* 160mm diameter which slopes down to the eye of *c.* 80mm diameter. The grinding surface is concave and originally pecked but the stone is now very worn, particularly towards the edge with concentric rings of wear and evidence of glazing around the periphery. L 316mm/W 186mm/Th 50.6mm edge, 18.5mm centre. Original *c.* 420mm. Weight c. 3.5kg

Site 31: Springfield, Ugborough

Twelve worked, utilised and collected stones were recorded from Romano-British contexts (Table 3.13) including several fragments of quernstone, two joining fragments of a stone mould for casting pewter and a number of small but attractive granite pebbles.

Mouldstone

Two joining fragments from a stone mould for a pewter dish (S11) were recovered from enclosure ditch 24.03.153, indicating the presence of a small-scale pewter casting industry in the vicinity (Figs 3.32, 3.33).

Although many pewter vessels have now been recorded from Romano-British sites, comparatively few moulds for casting the pewter have been found. In his 1980s analysis of the Romano-British pewter industry, Beagrie (1989) lists just 15 sites, and few have been found in more recent years. The fragments from Springfield are particularly important, therefore, at both national and local levels.

The mould, of a fine-grained granite probably from Dartmoor, is neatly made and carved on both sides, suggesting it comes from a nest of moulds designed for casting two or three dishes at the time (Beagrie 1989, 186, 187). The shape of the upper surface of the mould is similar to that of one of the moulds from St Just, Cornwall (Brown 1970, fig. 31). This would have formed the underside of a dish with a sharply defined up-turn for the start of the rim, a curving side or bouge and a flat base with concentric groove which would have formed a support ring on the bottom of the dish. Such support rings are typical of Romano-British pewter plates and dishes (Peal 1967, 24–5). The underside of the mould was for casting the upper surface of a larger dish or plate and also has the remains of two concentric grooves in a flat plane; two or three rings being usual for such tableware (ibid.). Both the grooves and the planes of the mould are sharply defined and the whole is friction polished to a smooth finish.

The majority of other pewter moulds found to date appear to be of limestone, although examples of Old Red Sandstone and silt-stone are also known. However, the two moulds from St Just are of greisen and another from Halangy Down, Isles of Scilly, is also of fine-grained granite (Beagrie 1989, 182–8; Brown 1970, 108; Ashbee 1970, 75). The distribution pattern of the moulds, including that from Springfield, very much suggests, therefore, that local sources of stone were utilised for their production. Pewter is thought to have been a cheap substitute for silver and the industry appears to have flourished widely in the later Roman period, *c.* AD 250–410 (Wedlake 1958, 55; Brown 1970, 108; Beagrie 1989, 175). The stone mould from Springfield sits comfortably within these dates.

Quernstones

Three fragments of quernstone were recovered from Romano-British contexts. A piece of upper stone of fine-grained granite was incorporated in the fill of pit 24.03.041 (S9), another fragment, of biotite granite, came from a fill of ditch 24.03.153 (S10) and a fragment from a quernstone of Elvan, a local term for quartz-porphyry (S8), was recovered from pit 24.03.034. Fragments S9 and S10 both derive from fairly local granite sources on Dartmoor. Fragment S8 originates from the Roborough area to the north of Plymouth. The suitability of this otherwise fine-grained rock for grinding comes from its porous surface, due to the weathering out of the felspars which together with the projecting quartz grains provide plentiful natural cutting edges (Quinnell and Watts 2004, 147). The quartz grains, however, would have gradually dropped out as the stone wore. While this would have caused occasional problems if the quernstone was used for milling grain for baking purposes, presumably necessitating the need for sieving the ground meal, the problem would have been of less import in grinding malted grain for brewing. Fragments of Elvan quern have also been found on the Iron Age/Romano-British site at Mount Folly above Bigbury Bay (Watts 2007). Roborough Elvan continued to be used for the manufacture of quernstones into the medieval period, its carvability making it eminently suitable for the manufacture of pot querns (Spooner and Russell 1967, 376–8).

Quern fragments S8 and S10 bear no diagnostic features to indicate whether they derive from upper or lower stones. Indeed the rather rounded shape of the latter suggests that it may have had a secondary use before deposition in the ditch. Fragment S9, from the edge of an upper stone, appears generally typical of the flatter types of Romano-British quern. Its flat upper surface has been polished to a smooth finish. Its concave grinding surface is also exceptionally smooth. This suggests that the stone has been excessively used, or rather was not repecked in the latter stages of its use life, making it a less effective milling tool, particularly for grain.

Other stone

Also found in ditch 24.03.153 was a local cobble of tourmalinised hornfels which had been used as a whetstone and five smooth granite river pebbles. Both cobble and pebbles probably derived from the River Avon nearby. The latter, of varying coarseness and textures, were perhaps picked up for use as slingstones or purely for their aesthetic qualities.

Catalogue

S8. 24.03.035 (fill of pit 24.03.034)
Three-sided pyramidal quern fragment of Elvan from the Roborough area to the north of Plymouth. One side is flatter than the other three and may be the remains of the grinding surface. The felspars within the Elvan have weathered out but the stone still contains numerous small quartz crystals.
L 80.9mm/W 63.6mm/Th 67.8mm. Weight 25g

S9. 24.03.042 (third fill of pit 24.03.041)
Fragment from edge of upper rotary quernstone. Fine-grained granite with tourmaline clots and quartz phenocrysts. Concave grinding surface worn smooth but was originally pecked. Upper surface is also flat and smooth, the side is flat but has been left rough.
L 204mm/W 123.2mm/Th 67.6mm. Weight *c.* 2.5kg

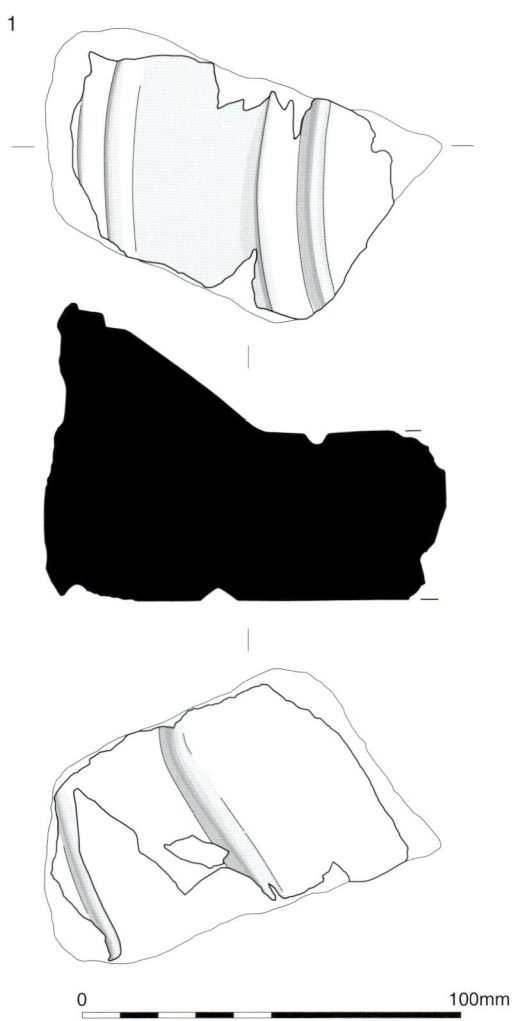

Fig. 3.32 Stone mould for pewter dish from Springfield (Site 31). Scale 1:2

Fig. 3.33 Stone mould for pewter dish from Springfield (Site 31).

S10. 24.03.086 (primary fill of ditch 24.03.153)
Rounded quern fragment of medium-grained biotite granite from Dartmoor. Two opposing worked faces, one of which continues slightly in a 'V' shape down the side of the stone which may possibly be the remains of an eye or spindle hole. Stone rather degraded.
L 88.4mm/W 81.1mm/Th 75.1mm. Weight 795g

S11. 24.03.119 (secondary fill of ditch 24.03.153) (Figs 3.32,and 3.33)
Two joining fragments of a double-sided stone mould for a dish, made of fine-grained granite. The mould faces are smooth. The upper side is dish-shaped with two well-defined circular grooves. The inner groove is 6.6mm wide by 3.2mm deep, the outer is more L-shaped, *c.* 4mm wide. The underside is for a larger plate or dish and bears the remains of two circular grooves; the mould has broken along the inner groove. The outer groove was *c.* 6.9mm wide.
L 97.6mm/W 54.6mm/Th 76.9mm. Weight 565g

Other artefacts

E.R. McSloy

Glass beads from Springfield, Ugborough (Site 31) and Hems Valley, Staverton (Site 17)

At Springfield a small segmented bead in translucent yellow glass (Guido 1978, 91–2) came from pit 24.03.089 (fill 24.03.090). Most examples date to the Late Roman period (later 3rd to 4th centuries) and similar dating is likely for this example. Diameter 4mm; thickness 3.5mm (Fig. 3.34 no. 2)

From Hems Valley came an unstratified globular bead of translucent cobalt blue glass. It accords with Guido's Group 7(iv), a type with pre-Roman ancestry, but thought to be most common in the Roman period (Guido 1978, 70). Diameter 15mm; thickness 8–10mm (Fig. 3.34 no. 1)

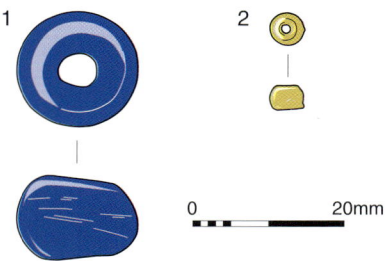

Fig. 3.34 Roman glass beads. Scale 1:1

Roman coins from Billany Farm, Dartington (Site 24)

Catalogue (not illus.)

1   AR radiate (Antoninianus), likely to be Postumus AD 259–68. Fragment, details uncertain. Reverse shows emperor standing right with spear and globe. RIC 83? Pit 14.01.038, fill 14.01.039.
2   Tetricus I radiate. Fragment, details uncertain. Reverse: Virtus standing left, holding spear. AD 270–4. RIC 148? Pit 14.01.038, fill 14.01.039.
3   Tetricus I radiate. Fragment, details uncertain. Reverse: Pax standing left with transverse sceptre. AD 270–4. Terrace 14.01.107, fill 14.01.046.

Metalworking

David Starley

Analysis overview

Significant metalworking debris was recovered from four sites, all in South Devon. These were the middle Iron Age furnaces at Tigley A, Dartington (Site 26), a pair of undated, but probably Iron Age or Roman furnaces at Lower Velwell, Rattery (Site 22), a hearth in the Roman enclosure at Billany Farm, Dartington (Site 24) and a group of metalworking features on the Roman settlement at Springfield, Ugborough (Site 31). Debris from other sites was sparse, not in primary contexts and frequently not diagnostic as to process and, following assessment, was not considered further.

Visual examination of all bulk metalworking debris was followed by a programme of physico-chemical analysis, including scanning electron microscope (SEM)-based microanalysis undertaken with the aim of understanding in greater depth both the manufacture and working of iron, and providing clearer identification of the spatial and temporal distribution of the processes. Analysis also aimed to determine whether the magnetic burned shale recovered in substantial quantities from soil samples related to the iron smelting process. Portable x-ray fluorescence (XRF) was also used to provide a link between debris and the find of a pewter mould fragment from Springfield.

Metalworking from South Devon

Table 3.14 shows the mineral identifications from SEM-based analysis and in Table 3.15 the bulk debris from the South Devon pipeline is grouped by activity and by phase. Magnetic residues from 117 contexts, totalling 6484g, were also examined, of which only two, both from Springfield (24.03.044 and 24.03.090) produced hammerscale.

Tigley A, Dartington (Site 26)

Site 26, to the east of Tigley, produced the most striking and important evidence of metalworking on the project, with structural evidence, debris identification and unambiguous radiocarbon dating combining to provide one of the best recorded examples of an iron smelting site from the Middle Iron Age. The ironworking remains, amounting to over 18kg, came from eight furnaces and other features in two spatial groups (Fig. 3.20).

Furnace 16.07.008

In the easternmost site, oval pit 16.07.008, with a vitrified clay lining, is identified as the remains of an iron smelting furnace (Fig. 3.25). The colouration of the lining is mid greyish brown, indicating low oxygen conditions, as required in the reduction zone of a smelting furnace. Discolouration of the natural silt around the furnace also suggests prolonged high temperature op-

Table 3.14: SEM-based analysis of metallurgical samples. Mineral composition (%) from Tigley A (Site 26) and Lower Velwell (Site 22)

Site	Context	Material	Na_2O	MgO	Al_2O_3	SiO_2	P_2O_5	SO_3	K_2O	CaO	TiO_2	MnO	FeO
26	16.07.016	furnace bottom	0.47	1.59	6.36	21.73	0.22	0.25	1.37	0.72	0.37	1.96	64.96
22	12.05w.007	fayalitic run slag	0.59	0.41	9.49	26.30	0.88	0.20	2.50	3.79	0.28	0.83	54.73
26	16.07.011	fayalitic run slag	0.44	0.87	9.78	29.70	0.03	0.21	1.59	0.92	0.38	1.45	54.62
26	16.07.016	fayalitic run slag	2.34	0.23	12.94	28.13	0.52	0.21	0.47	1.43	0.54	1.17	52.01
26	16.07.046	fayalitic run slag	0.14	3.95	6.74	22.81	0.16	0.33	0.00	0.65	0.56	1.84	62.82
26	16.07.047	fayalitic run slag (?)	1.18	1.28	10.46	50.89	0.18	0.10	4.01	0.81	0.13	0.70	30.26
26	16.07.057	fayalitic run slag	0.21	0.26	2.63	6.76	0.26	0.08	0.46	1.35	0.05	1.36	86.58
26	16.07.023	tap slag	0.61	1.31	9.81	26.89	0.09	0.02	1.82	0.63	0.28	1.20	57.34
26	16.07.057	Undiag. ironworking	0.47	0.27	7.67	20.58	0.29	0.04	1.71	2.83	0.21	1.56	64.36
26	16.07.058	Undiag. ironworking	0.14	0.34	10.00	25.39	0.38	0.13	0.07	2.93	0.56	2.60	57.45
22	12.05w.007	smithing hearth bottom	0.43	0.56	7.97	19.81	1.11	0.19	1.39	1.44	0.26	0.65	66.19
26	16.07.058	smithing hearth bottom	0.48	0.46	7.62	19.26	0.31	0.24	1.11	2.31	0.16	1.60	66.45
26	16.07.026	magnetic shale 2	0.49	0.36	19.13	30.12	0.46	0.00	2.56	0.22	0.79	0.11	45.75
26	16.07.026	magnetic shale 1	0.51	0.33	20.67	64.30	0.29	0.15	4.23	0.11	0.97	0.02	8.41

eration. The fills contained charcoal and metallic slag. Examination of the nearly 4kg of debris from these fills found more than 2kg to be classified as fayalitic run slag. In the base of the furnace (layer 16.07.016) was one of the largest pieces of slag found on the project; a furnace bottom which had remained *in situ* following the final operation of the furnace. The size of this piece (972g, 190 x 140 x 80mm) is modest compared to slag block technology, best known from eastern counties of England in the Saxon period, but is entirely in accordance with Iron Age non-slag-tapping furnaces. Associated with the fills of the furnace were quantities of magnetic residues recovered from soil samples.

Dating from roundwood alder charcoal from fill 16.07.016 provided a confirmatory radiocarbon date of 391–210 cal. BC (Table 3.6). The surviving furnace remains closely parallel to other UK examples of Middle Iron Age date, as discussed below, although this structure and most others are clearly heavily truncated.

Three samples were examined by SEM-based microanalysis to determine whether the type and source of ore could be identified: the furnace bottom from 16.07.016, a fragment of run slag from the same context and another piece of run slag from 16.07.011 (Table 3.14). None of these samples provided closely similar compositions, though all three were notably high in alumina (almost 13% in the case of the 16.07.016 run slag), possibly an indication of the composition of the ore, but also possibly of the materials of furnace construction. The phosphorus content was low. On balance, it would seem more likely that a 'rock' ore was used rather than a redeposited bog ore. The furnace bottom was distinguished by its higher iron oxide content (65% compared to 55% and 52%), but such relatively low iron contents suggest good efficiency for a furnace type which has been reported to be relatively inefficient (Salter 1989, 266).

Furnace cluster Phase One. Furnace 16.07.055
This comprised an elongated pit (0.70m x 0.60m x 0.40m deep). There is uncertainty as to whether the heat-affected material lining the pit was deliberately applied clay, or the natural clay-rich subsoil. The lower fill, 16.07.057, contained a high proportion of clear smelting debris, while the upper, 16.07.058, contained some smithing evidence in the form of a possible smithing hearth bottom and hammerscale. This raises the possibility that, after the initial removal of the bloom, the same structure was used to reheat and consolidate the slag-rich spongy iron. Both fills and the lining contained the ubiquitous magnetic residues.

To explore any difference between smithing and smelting products, four samples were examined: run slag and undiagnostic slag from the lower layer 16.07.057, and undiagnostic and possible smithing hearth bottom from the upper, 16.07.058. The run slag from the base of the furnace proved the most distinctive comprising 90% wustite in its usual dendritic form and an analysed composition of 87% ferrous oxide, a composition which, if typical, would only allow metallic iron to be smelted from the richest of iron ores. The other three samples are less dominated by iron oxide but are otherwise of very similar composition, having the high levels of alumina which are characteristic of the site, but not of the heterogeneity typical of smithing slags. On balance they probably all derive from smelting or possibly from bloom-smithing, the slag from which will compositionally resemble that from smelting. Certainly the presence of hammerscale in the upper layer shows that smithing or bloom-smithing was carried out in the vicinity of the smelting furnace, after the smelting operation was completed.

Phase Two. Furnaces 16.07.021, 16.07.024 and 16.07.040
Furnace 16.07.021 was the largest, although relatively shallow. Although cut through by the later furnace 16.07.028 and a modern drain, its subrectangular form was still evident, with dark orange-brown lining containing charcoal and slag. Fill 16.07.023 includes the only piece of slag on the site classed as tap slag, together with fayalitic run slag and undiagnostic ironworking slag totalling 433g. The importance of a single piece of slag resembling the waste product from a tapping furnace in an assemblage of debris typical of non-tapping should not be overstated and in this context is thought not to be significant. SEM-based examination showed a typical tap slag microstructure of wustite dendrites, fayalite laths, hercynite and a glassy matrix and a bulk composition close to that of fayalite, which would help maintain fluidity. As with most other slags from this project high alumina values are evident.

Furnace 16.07.024 had been largely cut away by furnace 16.07.028. It had either been lined or the natural had been heat-modified, turning a distinctive orange colour. It contained only a very small amount (4g) of fayalitic run slag in fill 16.07.026, but one of the highest concentrations of magnetic residue was recovered from soil sample 256 (fill 16.07.026) (Table 3.14).

Magnetic residue was very much a feature of the site. It has the appearance of small pink coloured shale-like stone flakes and is readily attracted to a magnet. The question of whether this contained sufficient iron to be a viable ore was addressed by SEM analysis. Examined under backscattered electron imaging, which highlights atomic number contrast, dense, iron-rich regions, were visible. A first sample analysed gave a bulk analysis of only 8.4% FeO (in fact the iron may be present as magnetite, Fe_3O_4) – way below the percentage of iron needed for smelting, which must exceed that of the slag (Table 3.14, magnetic shale 1). However, the iron-rich phase within the sample contained a promising 65% FeO. Examining a second sample with a higher concentration of iron-rich phase gave a bulk iron oxide content of 46% (Table 3.14, magnetic shale 2). This is again too low to be viable, but does at least approach the richness needed. Also of significance was the notable level of alumina (20–21%) within the samples. The difficulty in interpreting this material lies in the question as to whether this material really is the residue of the ore used, perhaps after some selection to remove richer material, or is simply the remains of local stone from an iron-rich material used in the construction of the furnaces, or even a component of the natural soil of the site.

Furnace 16.07.040 (0.28m dia. x 0.07m deep) was a shallow cut feature containing burned clay lining, largely *in situ*, of which over 1.7kg was examined and classed as vitrified hearth/furnace lining. Smaller quantities of run slag and undiagnostic ironworking slag were found within the lining 16.07.041 and fill 16.07.042 as well as the usual burned shale-like stone.

Phase Three. Furnaces 16.07.028 and 16.07.043
Furnace 16.07.28 was apparently cleaned out and reused as 16.07.43 with a new lining, or heat modified natural clay. The base survived to a depth of 0.35m with a diameter of 0.4 m (Fig. 3.21, sections 41, 42). Two of the fills of this furnace proved very rich in slag. In the lower, 16.07.046, fayalitic run slag, diagnostic of smelting, dominated the nearly 1.4 kg total weight of debris. The upper fill, 16.07.047, contained 2.3kg of debris, of which a smaller proportion was run slag but more was hearth/furnaces lining and undiagnostic ironworking slag. Significantly, it also contained some hammerscale, suggesting, as for furnace 16.07.055, that this smelting furnace was also used for smithing, perhaps to consolidate the bloom immediately after its removal

from the furnace. Both fills contained burned shale and the lower one also spheroidal debris. Analysis and examination showed the microstructures to be typical of bloomery slag. Fayalitic run slag from 16.07.046 showed a typically high (62%) iron oxide content, while 16.07.047 showed a similar microstructure. Typically for the site, both were high in alumina.

Isolated furnace 16.07.49

Furnace 16.07.049 was delineated by an orange clay lining. Some small slag fragments had become embedded in this lining but it also produced 100g of magnetic residue, suggesting that this material is a component of the natural subsoil. The fill (16.07.051) contained 1.19kg of undiagnostic ironworking slag.

Pits thought not to be furnaces (16.07.052, 16.07.017, 16.07.033, 16.07.035, 16.07.037)

Pit 16.07.052 had a dark red-purple lining suggesting an oxidising process, such as ore roasting rather than smelting, despite the depth of the feature. Debris examined from its two fills (0.5kg) consisted entirely of vitrified hearth lining, with no fayalitic slags, but the usual burnt shale in both the fill and heat-affected natural. It would seem likely that the vitrified lining found in the fill derived from a furnace, not related to the pit in which it was found.

Pit 16.07.017 contained no metalworking debris, only a few grams of burned shale and some quartz of unknown purpose. It does not serve any obvious purpose associated with iron smelting. Two small pits, 16.07.033 and 16.07.035, within the furnace cluster showed no evidence of lining or heating and appear not to have been furnaces. Feature 16.07.037 was a narrow, elongated, shallow feature (0.75m x 0.25m x 0.16m deep), with heat-affected (red oxidised) lining at the north end, and might have functioned as an ore-roasting pit. It contained 0.5kg of undiagnostic ironworking slag which may have originated in one of the adjacent furnaces. A relatively modest amount of burnt shale was also recovered.

Lower Velwell, Rattery (Site 22)

The fill, 12.05W.007, of undated pit 12.05W.004 included over 2kg of ironworking debris, suggesting that the function of this isolated feature was ironworking. The context also produced a concentration of magnetic residue. Identifying the specific activity was not unambiguous. Most of the debris proved to be undiagnostic ironworking slag. Visual examination of the bulk slag identified a possible smithing hearth bottom although no hammerscale was found. The presence of fayalitic run slag probably provides the key to identifying this feature as the base of a non-tapping smelting furnace, similar to those found at Tigley A, but the lack of any lining material or heat-altered substrate is unusual.

A piece of fayalitic run slag and the possible smithing hearth bottom were analysed by SEM. The microstructure of the smithing hearth bottom proved more heterogeneous than that of the run slag and had higher iron content, some unreacted constituents and an additional phase, the aluminium-rich mineral hercynite. To some extent this supports its visual identification as a product of smithing. The compositions of the two types of debris were otherwise very similar, yet distinctly different from other slag analysed from the project, having a significantly higher phosphorus content (Table 3.14). On balance, it would seem that the feature here does relate to the smelting of iron using a non-slag-tapping bloomery furnace technology typical of the Middle Iron Age. The smelting is likely to have been followed by some consolidation of the iron bloom produced. The compositional distinctiveness almost certainly results from a different ore source to that exploited at Tigley A, the higher phosphorus content elsewhere having been found to be associated with the use of bog ores.

Billany Farm, Dartington (Site 24)

The small quantity of debris from this Roman enclosure limits any interpretation of the metalworking undertaken. While clearly relating to ironworking, none of the debris is diagnostic of smelting or smithing, although the latter would seem more probable. It may also be significant that no magnetic residues were recovered from this area.

Springfield, Ugborough (Site 31)

Two Roman pits, 24.03.041 (fill 24.03.044) and 24.03.089 (fill 24.03.090), yielded the only two magnetic residues to contain unambiguous evidence of smithing in the form of flake hammerscale. Another feature, 24.03.095, was a possible metalworking surface although no slag or residues were available to confirm this. Several pits, including those containing the hammerscale, yielded a scattering of slag, which, while undiagnostic, was probably from smithing. Burnt magnetic shale was fairly widely distributed in hearths and the fills of pits and ditches.

One particular find, a pewter mould fragment, raises the possibility that the site may also have been involved in the manufacture of pewter artefacts or the smelting of tin from the ore. To investigate this further, a series of samples from the metalworking debris found in the vicinity was analysed using X-ray fluorescence. In almost all instances no trace of non-ferrous metals was found, although zinc traces were just above minimum detectible levels in three instances and lead once. More certain, however, were the low levels (0.20% and 0.17% with an error of 0.04%) for tin on a black-glazed fragment of vitrified hearth lining from 24.03.42, another fill of pit 24.03.041 that had already produced hammerscale. Tin is an element that volatilises easily during melting, and absorption of this element (not the lead) is not surprising where tin alloys are being worked. In can therefore be suggested that some mixed metalworking took place on this site, including the working of iron and tin alloys, but the limited quantities of data prevent us learning more about the scale or nature of the work.

Discussion

A significant amount of metalworking debris was associated with Iron Age and Roman occupations at Tigley A (Site 26), Billany Farm (Site 24) and Springfield (Site 31), together with a small amount of comparable material from Lower Velwell (Site 22), which is probably of similar date (Table 3.15). This material is not entirely unambiguous, but generally confirms the excavators' interpretation for iron smelting furnaces of Middle Iron Age date at Tigley A, together with further evidence of iron smelting at Lower Velwell, of iron smithing from these sites and also of Roman-period smithing at the other sites. The smelting furnaces are bloomeries, that is, they directly produce a malleable 'bloom' of iron or steel and are of the 'non-tapping' type. Given the rarity of evidence for Middle Iron Age iron smelting, Tigley A is highly significant. The XRF analysis suggests that Springfield was the site of tin alloy working in the Roman period, which is also a significant finding.

Eight of the burnt pits at Tigley A were confirmed

Table 3.15: Origin of metalworking residues by mass (in grammes) (Nq = present but not quantified)

Activity	Material	Site / Tigley A	Springfield	Billany Farm	Lower Velwell	Total
		Iron Age	Roman	Roman	Undated	
Smelting	tap slag	179	-	-	-	179
	fayalitic run slag	3673	16	-	109	3798
	furnace bottom	972	-	-	-	972
	possible ore	-	-	-	-	-
Smithing	flake hammerscale	nq	nq	-	-	nq
	poss. smithing hearth bottom	1399	-	-	169	1568
	poss. spheroidal hammerscale	nq	nq	-	-	nq
Non-diag.	dense slag	-	428	-	-	428
	undiagnostic ironworking slag	8757	175	74	1811	10817
	iron-rich cinder	55	14	-	-	69
Other	burned stone	12	1	-	-	13
	cinder	100	15	9	-	124
	fired clay	203	-	-	-	203
	vitrified hearth/furnace lining	2696	155	123	-	2974
Non slag	iron concretion	-	1	8	-	9
	stone	-	-	-	-	-
Total		**18046**	**805**	**214**	**2089**	**21154**

to have been smelting furnaces by the examination of slag from them, but it seems likely two other features, 16.07.052 and 16.07.037, were used for the roasting, or at least storage, of iron ore, a process which reddened the lining but produced no fayalitic slags. However, this identification is made less certain by a lack of recovery of any surviving ore from these putative roasting hearths, nor indeed from the furnaces themselves.

No purpose-built smithing hearths were identified, but there is evidence from smithing debris and hammerscale that two smelting furnaces, 16.07.055 and 16.07.057, were used for bloom consolidation, presumably after the furnace superstructure had been compromised by the recovery of the bloom. At least one other furnace base was identified at Lower Velwell where the slags yielded evidence for both smelting and smithing. There was also clear evidence for iron smithing, likely to be of Roman date, at Springfield. XRF analysis of a piece of hearth lining detected tin, which, combined with the finding of a stone pewter-dish mould, provides the only evidence of non-ferrous metalworking on site.

While the Tigley A furnaces have been traditionally referred to as 'bowl furnaces', this terminology has largely gone out of favour, not least because experimental archaeology has demonstrated the difficulty, compared to other metals such as lead, copper or tin, of smelting iron ore in an equiaxial space. A vertical shaft provides greater separation for the major chemical reactions required, including the conversion of ore to metal which requires a high-temperature, highly reducing region away from the combustion zone. Unfortunately, it is very rare indeed for any of this superstructure to survive. Important exceptions were the late Iron Age and Roman furnaces at Priors Hall, Corby (Hall 2008); some of these 'sunken shaft furnaces' remained intact up to a height of 0.7m. However, their construction differs significantly from the Tigley A furnaces. At Priors Hall the shaft occupied only one end of the construction pit and the front base was broken away after smelting to allow bloom and slag to be dragged out into the part of the pit that remained open. In the Tigley A furnaces, despite surviving depths of up to 0.4m, there is no suggestion that any part of the surviving furnace wall was ever unburied or pierced to allow air in or slag and iron bloom out. The Tigley A furnaces do have some parallels with later British and continental 'slag-pit furnaces' where a below-ground pit was dug to accumulate a large block of slag. However, the Tigley A furnaces produced only one small 'furnace bottom' type slag block. Given the early date (391–210 cal. BC) and the small quantities of slag it is likely that the furnaces were relatively modest structures for which the above ground superstructure and provision for inputting air have now been lost, and that slag largely collected within the furnace with the metal being extracted, as a solid bloom, from above. A more appropriate term, as coined by Cleere (1972), is 'non slag-tapping furnace', characterised by a basal pit into which slag collected.

Some minor variations in construction and operation are detectable nationally, judging by the portions of the furnace pits and slag that survive (Paynter 2007). Very frequently the slag retains the impressions of chopped wood, with which the pit appears to have been initially filled, but occasionally straw impressions are found instead. The sizes of the furnaces at Tigley can only be judged by the surviving pits which, for the eight identified as furnace bases, average 0.63m on the major axis (which is generally aligned north/south) and 0.45m on the minor axis, with a surviving depth of 0.26m. There is, however, considerable variety and the original height can only be conjectural. The sizes are very similar in range to those at Brooklands, near Weybridge, Surrey, for which the 'very probable' furnace pits typically range from 0.35m to 0.8m and exceptionally 1m in diameter, often with slight elongation (Cleere 1977).

The Tigley A furnaces clearly belong to a reasonably consistent and widespread tradition of non-tapping furnace, one which was superseded from the late Iron Age by the tapping furnace, with the characteristic rope-like flows of fayalitic slag that were released from the furnace periodically, enabling a greater throughput of ore. This has been argued to result in greater efficiency and its ability to operate using leaner ores (Salter 1989), but in other respects the operation of the different furnace types in terms of temperatures and reducing (redox) conditions achieved was little different (Paynter 2007).

The question concerning the type and source of the iron ore used has been difficult to resolve. For a bloomery smelting furnace to produce metallic iron there needs to be a higher proportion of the element in the ore than in the slag waste products. No ore has been identified by visual examination, nor as inclusions within the samples examined by SEM. A possible answer lies in the large quantities of magnetic residues from the soil samples. This burnt, shale-like stone clearly has significant iron content in the form of magnetite, to allow it to be collected by magnet. Analysis showed that it comprised almost 50% iron oxide, not viable as ore, but more than might have been expected. It could be speculated that the material found was only the tailings of richer ores. On the other hand one might argue that the post-excavation processing, which including extracting the material with a magnet, artificially selects that material richer in iron in a way that was not possible for an Iron Age metalworker and therefore overemphasises its presence. Three factors relating to the distribution of the burned shale might also be significant. First, the greatest concentrations occur in features associated with metalworking. This may be countered by the argument that metalworking, particularly iron smelting, provides exposure to greater temperatures over longer periods than any other domestic activity. Second, while the greatest concentrations are found near iron smelting features, a small amount are to be found far from any known metalworking. Moreover, examination of contexts consisting of heat-affected natural substrate, the 'linings' of the furnaces, found these to contain concentrations approaching those of the furnace fills, yet it is hard to see how such material entered these contexts unless it was part of the natural subsoil in the first place. Finally, two features which may be associated with the roasting or storage of roasted ore do not appear particularly rich in this material.

On balance, it is considered that the burnt shale-like material has not been brought to the site as a source of ore but is a constituent of the soil which has been incidentally chemically altered by heating, particularly metalworking. The Mineral Reconnaissance Programme shows soils in the region to contain up to 34% iron (Leake and Norton 1993, table 4).

Paynter (2006) has compared slag analyses for Iron Age and Roman sites across England. Although these do not include any from Devon, they do allow regional groupings to be identified, with distinctive compositions deriving largely from the ore used. However, Paynter also emphasises the significant input of the elements in the materials from which the furnace is constructed. As the most distinctive component of the slag from Tigley A is the high alumina content, we must be cautious in case this also derives from the furnaces rather than the ores.

Aside from the shale on the site, there is a wide range of possible iron ore sources in the immediate region around Tigley. The Higher Ludbrook iron ore deposits just a few miles from the site are of sufficient importance to be included on the 1:1 500 000 metallogenic map of Britain and Ireland (BGS 1996). These deposits include pyrite and weathered carbonate ores, although the former can be discounted, as the sulphur content would have been evident in the slag. Historically, brown haematite was mined at Bulkamore only a couple of miles to the north. However, the area around Tigley is geologically heterogeneous, with the interaction of Middle Devonian Volcanic Belt and sedimentary rocks (Leake and Norton 1993) again giving rise to various possible mineral sources (Figs 2.43, 2.44). To these can be added the possible use of weathered minerals and redeposited material such as bog ores, both of which can be richer in iron than the parent rock and, due to their high porosity, relatively easy to smelt. Ancient iron producers needed rich ores and were often able to make use of very localised sources of no interest to commercial mining operators of recent times. It would seem likely that rich ores suitable for the furnace could have been found in close proximity to the site.

In terms of composition, smithing slags were found to be little different from smelting slags, possibly because they were associated with the consolidation of the bloom and therefore contained a high proportion of the smelting slag released from the spongy iron bloom. Such similarity between the composition of smithing and smelting slags was also noted for the Richard Lander School and Truro College assemblage by Young (2007b). In terms of size, two smithing hearth bottoms were relatively small at 154g and 169g, the third being a more massive 1245g. Interestingly, a comparable size differential was visible at Crawcwellt West, Gwynedd (Crew 1989) and Richard Lander School/Truro College Cornwall (Young 2007b) which both had small 'cakes' of 100–150g and larger ones of 300–400g. For the first site, Crew suggested that the smaller related to the final stages of smithing, the larger to bloom smithing.

Two other resources should be mentioned. First, clay was required for the construction of the furnace superstructure. Nearly three kilos of this material was recovered, which will have derived from those parts of the furnace most strongly fired during the smelting and smithing processes. It is still unclear whether the basal pits of the furnaces were normally lined with clay. In many cases the evidence was ambivalent because of the similarity between the natural clay substrate and the sides of the furnaces, but it would appear that the 'lining' often generally consisted of the heat affected substrate which contained sufficient clay to be baked to a crusty consistency, in addition to its colour being changed due to the oxidation of iron minerals within it. The second resource is the fuel for raising the temperature and generating the carbon monoxide required to reduce the iron oxide to metallic iron. Many of the fragments of the run slag retained impressions of charcoal, or more probably chopped wood, with which the bases of these furnaces appear to have been packed.

The importance of the ironworking evidence from the South Devon Pipeline

The Iron Age saw a progressive increase in the number, size and diversity of ferrous artefacts from across Britain, but sites known to have manufactured iron are few and have been given relatively little attention. In his synthesis of the scientific investigation of the iron industry in Iron Age Britain, Salter (1989) identified south-west England as a likely origin for much of the iron used in southern and central Britain. His reasoning derived partly from the results of provenancing studies of ironwork from Danebury hillfort and elsewhere, but also on the assumption that the non-tapping furnaces in use at this date would have required particularly rich ore, such as that from the south-west. Additionally, he argued that the south-west's close links with the continent, and the local population's longstanding experience of smelting non-ferrous metals, would have provided the technical knowledge to utilise their resources.

At the time of Salter's writing, clear archaeological evidence for smelting sites in this region was meagre. A 'bowl furnace' at Kes Tor, Dartmoor had only 2kg of slag associated with it (Fox 1954) and its Iron Age date is now thought to be suspect (Peter Crew, pers. comm.), while at Trevelgue Head, Cornwall, no furnaces were identified, and the amount of iron slag discovered is less than previously publicised (Dungworth 2011a). From Gussage All Saints, Dorset, 700kg of debris was recorded, but this apparently derived from later, slag-tapping, furnaces. The limited, even dwindling, evidence from the south-west can be contrasted with a growing recognition of early non-tapping furnaces elsewhere in the British Isles. Three sites have produced more than one tonne of slag: Crawcwellt West and Bryn y Castell, both in North Wales, and Moore's Farm, East Yorkshire (Halkon 2008, 169). At Brooklands in Surrey (Cleere 1977) an iron smelting area with five non-tapping furnaces was separated from a second area for the smithing of the blooms. The dating of these features is imprecise, but it is suggested that the first iron smelting was carried out in the Early Iron Age. This site has proved to be only the first of a number in the locality, including Thorpe Lee Nurseries (Starley 1998), St Anne's Heath School (Starley 2009) and Littlewater, a site apparently producing several tonnes of iron smelting slag (Paynter, pers. comm.). More recently the possibility of a similar tradition of non-tapping furnaces has been inferred from geophysical and surface collection at Caerau hillfort in South Wales (Tim Young, pers. comm.), but this has yet to be confirmed by excavation.

The record for the south-west is, however, beginning to change, although identifications of furnaces are still rare. The retrospective report on Trevelgue Head, including Dungworth's discussion of the ironworking, has now been published (Nowakowski and Quinnell 2011). The slag (183kg) has been confirmed as being of non-tapping type, described as prills and slag lumps with impressions of charcoal. The fuel was oak charcoal, and the ore has been shown by analysis to be low in phosphorus. Another site with very strong similarities is Richard Lander School/Truro College Cornwall (Young 2007b). This site produced 13kg of smelting and smithing slag, very similar to that from Tigley A, but only one tentative furnace base. Of considerable interest was 2kg of goethite ore recovered containing 81% Fe_2O_3, a rich ore. A very limited amount of slag from a non-tapping furnace was also recovered at Berry Ball, Crediton Hamlets, Devon (Young 2007a).

The multiple furnaces at Tigley A are also supported by radiocarbon dating, which although relatively imprecise due to the flat region of the calibration curve at this time, do unambiguously place the furnaces within the 3rd to 4th centuries BC. In terms of scale of activity the presence of eight furnaces at Tigley A clearly represents continuity of iron smelting on the same site. Reuse of furnaces, unproven except for 16.07.043/.028, might further increase potential output. The quantity of slag recovered, while not massive, is considerably greater than the 2kg found at Kes Tor, which Halkon (2008, 169) notes was once thought typical, before recent larger finds. It would also seem likely that, given the number of furnaces surviving in the narrow site under investigation, further evidence is to be found beyond the excavation area, making this one of the larger and more significant sites of this date nationally.

Plant macrofossils and charcoal

Sarah Cobain

Results of assessment and analysis

The samples of plant macrofossils and charcoal were well preserved but not prolific overall except in a handful of cases. The results form a significant addition to information for the Iron Age and Roman periods in Devon, with particularly important remains coming from the Roman enclosure at Billany Farm, Dartington (Site 24). This section summarises the results from the assessed and analysed botanical samples. The detailed results of analysis are presented in Tables 3.16–3.22.

Table 3.16: Iron Age plant macrofossil identifications; Slade Farm (Site 2), Pixies' Parlour (Site 4), Crablake Farm (Site 15)

Habitat Codes: *A = Arable weed; D = Opportunistic weed from a disturbed environment; DC = Opportunistic weed but may have been consumed; P = Grassland species (possible pasture); E = Economic species (plants deliberately cultivated for economic use); H = Heathland species; HSW = Hedgerow, scrub, woodland species; M = Marsh/wetland species; WF = Wild Food*
Identifications: ** = modern; hw = heartwood (old wood); sw = sapwood (young wood)*

Habitat code			Site	2	4	15
			Context number	02.03.005	03.04.088	14.09.023
			Feature number	02.03.004	03.04.045	14.09.021
			Sample number	174	72	287
			Sample volume (L)	30	12	11
			Flot volume (ml)	175	14	33
	Family	**Species**	**Common Name**			
DC	Amaranthaceae	*Chenopodium album*	Fat hen	5	-	2
DC		*Chenopodium album*	Fat hen *	3	-	-
DC		*Chenopodium* spp	Fat hen/goosefoot spp	-	-	15
WF	Betulaceae	*Corylus avellana*	Hazelnut	9	5	-
DC	Caryophyllaceae	*Stellaria media*	Common chickweed	1	-	-
P	Lamiaceae	*Prunella vulgaris*	Self heal	1	-	-
D	Plantaginaceae	*Plantago lanceolata*	Ribwort plantain	5	-	-
E	Poaceae	*Avena* spp	Oat	47	-	2
E		*Hordeum vulgare*	Hulled barley	16	-	-
E		*Secale cereale*	Rye	1	-	1
E		*Triticum* spp	Wheat	8	-	-
E		*Triticum aestivum/turgidum/ durum*	Bread-type wheat	5	-	3
E		*Triticum spelta*	Spelt	7	-	-
E	*Poaceae*	*Triticum spelta*	Spelt glume base	49	-	-
E		*Triticum dicoccum/spelta*	Emmer/spelt	40	-	-
E		Poaceae	Indet. cereal grain	66	-	41
E		Poaceae	Cereal chaff – Culm node	5	-	18
E		Poaceae	Cereal chaff – Culm base	-	-	2
E		Poaceae	Cereal chaff – Palea	-	-	1
D		Poaceae	Grass	1	-	-
D	Polygonaceae	*Fallopia convolvulus*	Black-bindweed	9	-	9
A		*Persicaria amphiba*	Amphibious bistort	-	-	5
D		*Persicaria lapathifolia*	Pale persicaria	9	-	-
D		*Rumex* spp	Dock	1	-	-
D		*Rumex* spp	Dock *	1	-	-
			Total macrofossils identified	288	5	198

Iron Age

East Devon

Slade Farm, Ottery St Mary (Site 2)
Pit 02.03.004 (Table 3.16, SS 174) contained a large assemblage of carbonised crop remains which was dominated by oat and spelt wheat (since emmer/spelt wheat grains and spelt glume bases were found in an almost 1:1 ratio is can be assumed the cereals are spelt wheat rather than emmer), with smaller amounts of barley, rye and bread wheat and some carbonised culm nodes. Pale persicaria was identified and is known as an arable weed. Weeds from a disturbed environment were represented by species such as fat hen, common chickweed, ribwort plantain and black-bindweed. The charcoal from this pit was fully analysed and consisted of moderate amounts of alder/hazel, hazel and oak together with smaller amounts of gorse/broom, blackthorn/sloe and elm fragments (Table 3.17). This material would represent crop-processing waste possibly raked out from a hearth/oven used to parch the spelt.

Pixies' Parlour, Ottery St Mary (Site 4)
The secondary fill 3.04.088 of penannular gully 03.04.045 (Table 3.16, SS 72) contained small numbers of carbonised hazelnut shells. These are most likely to be residual from earlier activity nearby.

Powderham medieval settlement (Site 14)
The charcoal recovered from fill 13.02.016 of possible Iron Age/Roman ditch 13.02.009 (Table 3.18, SS 139) was broadly characterised and consisted dominantly of cherry together with smaller amounts of ash, and blackthorn fragments.

Crablake Farm, Exminster (Site 15)
Secondary fill 14.09.023 (Table 3.16, SS 287) of ring ditch 14.09.021 was dominated by carbonised indeterminate cereal grains with small numbers of oat, rye and bread wheat that could be identified together with relatively high numbers of culm nodes and smaller numbers of culm bases and a palea. Weed species were represented by moderate quantities of carbonised fat hen, fat hen/goosefoot, black-bindweed and amphibious bistort seeds. The charcoal from this fill was broadly characterised and consisted dominantly of alder/hazel with smaller amounts of willow/poplar charcoal fragments (Table 3.18).

South Devon

Tigley A, Dartington (Site 26)
Fill 16.07.011 of furnace 16.07.008 (Table 3.17, SS 242) was fully analysed and contained purely oak charcoal fragments. The charcoal from pit 16.07.017 (Table 3.18, SS 250) was broadly characterised and was dominated by alder/hazel and hazel with a single fragment of oak and hawthorn/rowan/crab apple charcoal. The clay lining 16.07.041 (SS 263) (fully analysed) and fill 16.07.042 (SS 264) (broadly characterised) of furnace 16.07.040 contained purely oak charcoal fragments.

Three samples were retrieved from the fill of furnace 16.07.028/043. The clay lining 16.07.030 (Table 3.17, SS 253) was fully analysed and contained purely oak charcoal fragments, secondary fill 16.07.046 (SS 267) and tertiary fill 16.07.047 (SS 268) were broadly characterised and contained dominantly oak with smaller amounts of alder/hazel, hazel, gorse/broom and ash charcoal fragments. The primary fill 16.07.057 of furnace 16.07.055 was fully analysed and contained dominantly oak charcoal with a single alder/hazel and three ash charcoal fragments (Table 3.17, SS 274).

Roman

East Devon

Pixies' Parlour, Ottery St Mary (Site 4)
The charcoal from the third fill 03.04.020 of ditch 03.04.004 (Table 3.19, SS 78) was broadly characterised and consisted dominantly of oak with smaller numbers of alder/hazel and gorse/broom fragments.

Table 3.17: Iron Age charcoal identifications (full analysis); Slade Farm (Site 2) and Tigley A (Site 26). (For Key see Table 3.16).

		Site	2	26	26	26	26
		Context number	02.03.005	16.07.011	16.07.041	16.07.057	16.07.030
		Feature number	02.03.004	16.07.008	16.07.040	16.07.055	16.07.028
		Sample number	174	242	263	274	253
		Sample volume (L)	30	1	4	22	8
Family	**Species**	**Common Name**					
Betulaceae	*Alnus glutinosa/Corylus avellana*	Alder/hazel	15	-	-	1	-
	Corylus avellana	Hazel	28	-	-	-	-
Fabaceae	*Ulex* spp/*Cytisus* spp	Gorse/broom	14	-	-	-	-
Fagaceae	*Quercus robur/petraea*	Sessile/pedunculate oak	24	-	42	24	30
	Quercus robur/petraea hw	Sessile/pedunculate oak h/w	2	100	27	72	5
	Quercus robur/petraea sw	Sessile/pedunculate oak s/w	14	-	-	-	-
Oleaceae	*Fraxinus excelsior*	Ash	-	-	-	3	-
Rosaceae	*Prunus spinosa*	Blackthorn/sloe	2	-	-	-	-
Ulmaceae	*Ulmus glabra*	Elm	1	-	-	-	-
		Total fragments identified	100	100	69	100	35

Table 3.18: Iron Age charcoal identifications (broad characterisation); Exwell Barton (Site 14), Crablake Farm (Site 15) and Tigley A (Site 26). (For Key see Table 3.16).

Family	Species	Common Name	Site 14	Site 15	Site 26	Site 26	Site 26	Site 26	Site 26
		Context number	13.02.016	14.09.023	16.07.018	16.07.042	16.07.046	16.07.047	
		Feature number	13.02.009	14.09.021	16.07.017	16.07.040	16.07.043	16.07.043	
		Sample number	139	287	250	264	267	268	
		Sample volume (L)	5	11	8	5	9	7	
Betulaceae	*Alnus glutinosa*	Alder	-	2	-	-	-	-	
	Alnus glutinosa/Corylus avellana	Alder/hazel	-	13	6	-	1	1	
	Corylus avellana	Hazel	-	4	12	-	2	-	
Fabaceae	*Ulex* spp/*Cytisus* spp	Gorse/broom	-	-	-	-	4	-	
Fagaceae	*Quercus robur/petraea*	Sessile/pedunculate oak	-	-	1	16	8	5	
	Quercus robur/petraea hw	Sessile/pedunculate oak h/w	-	-	-	4	5	10	
	Quercus robur/petraea sw	Sessile/pedunculate oak s/w	-	-	-	-	-	3	
Oleaceae	*Fraxinus excelsior*	Ash	3	-	-	-	-	1	
Rosaceae	*Crataegus monogyna/Sorbus* spp/*Malus sylvestris*	Hawthorn/rowan/ crab apple	-	-	1	-	-	-	
	Prunus avium/padus	Wild/bird cherry	13	-	-	-	-	-	
	Prunus spinosa	Blackthorn/sloe	4	-	-	-	-	-	
Salicaceae	*Salix* spp/*Populus* spp	Willow/poplar	-	1	-	-	-	-	
		Total fragments identified	20	20	20	20	20	20	

Table 3.19: Roman charcoal identifications (broad characterisation); Pixies' Parlour (Site 4), Billany Farm (Site 24), Springfield (Site 31). (For Key see Table 3.16).

		Site	4	24	24	24	24	24	31	31
		Context number	03.04.020	14.01.008	14.01.037	14.01.079	14.01.080	24.03.044	24.03.078
		Feature number	03.04.004	14.01.004	14.01.036	14.01.038	14.01.038	24.03.041	24.03.036
		Sample number	78	35	39	53	54	11	13
		Sample volume (L)	5	8	7	22	16	8	5
Family	Species	Common Name								
Betulaceae	*Alnus glutinosa*	Alder	-	4	-	2	-	-	-
	Alnus glutinosa/Corylus avellana	Alder/hazel	1	5	3	-	-	6	7
	Corylus avellana	Hazel	-	7	10	-	4	-	4
Fabaceae	*Ulex* spp/*Cytisus* spp	Gorse/broom	1	1	-	-	-	-	-
Fagaceae	*Quercus robur/petraea*	Sessile/pedunculate oak	5	2	-	9	7	9	4
	Quercus robur/petraea b/w	Sessile/pedunculate oak b/w	13	-	-	8	7	4	-
	Quercus robur/petraea sw	Sessile/pedunculate oak s/w	-	-	-	-	-	1	-
Oleaceae	*Fraxinus excelsior*	Ash	-	-	-	-	-	-	2
Rosaceae	*Crataegus monogyna*/*Sorbus* spp/*Malus Sylvestris*	Hawthorn/rowan/ crab apple	-	1	3	1	2	-	1
Salicaceae	*Salix* spp/*Populus* spp	Willow/poplar	-	-	4	-	-	-	-
Ulmaceae	*Ulmus glabra*	Elm	-	-	-	-	-	-	2
		Total fragments identified	20	20	20	20	20	20	20

Table 3.20: Roman plant macrofossil identifications; Billany Farm (Site 24). (For Key see Table 3.16).

Habitat code	Family	Species	Common Name	Site 24 Context number 14.01.035 Feature number 14.01.034 Sample number 38 Sample volume (L) 10 Flot volume (ml) 20	24 14.01.039 14.01.038 44 24 467	24 14.01.079 14.01.038 53 15 558	24 14.01.080 14.01.038 54 8 377
DC	Amaranthaceae	*Chenopodium album*	Fat hen *	-	2	-	8
DC		*Chenopodium* spp	Fat hen/goosefoot	-	-	1	1
DC	Caryophyllaceae	*Stellaria media*	Common chickweed	-	-	1	-
DC	Fabaceae	*Vicia* spp/*Lathyrus* spp	Vetch/vetchlings	-	-	-	1
E		*Vicia cf sativa*	Common vetch	-	-	-	4
E		*Vicia faba var minor*	Celtic bean	-	2	-	-
E	Linaceae	*Linum usitatissimum*	Flax seed	7	73	127	79
E		*Linum usitatissimum*	Flax seed concreted together in capsule	3	11	2	2
E		*Linum usitatissimum*	Flax perianith	-	-	1	-
D	Malvaceae	*Malva* spp	Mallow	-	1	-	-
E	Poaceae	*Avena* spp	Oat	-	2	4	5
E		*Hordeum vulgare*	Hulled barley	-	-	-	1
E		*Triticum dicoccum*	Emmer	-	-	-	3
E		*Triticum dicoccum/spelta*	Emmer/spelt	-	4	cf 1	3
E		Poaceae	Indet. cereal grain	-	9	19	19
D	Polygonaceae	*Fallopia convolvulus*	Black-bindweed	-	-	1	-
DC		*Rumex* spp	Dock	-	3	-	-
			Total macrofossils identified	10	107	157	126

Billany Farm, Dartington (Site 24)
Four samples came from two features on this site. Pit 14.01.034 (Table 3.20, SS 38) contained a small number of carbonised flax seeds. Three fills (14.01.039, 14.01.079 and 14.01.080; SS 44, SS 53, SS 54) from pit 14.01.038 contained a broadly similar plant macrofossil assemblage consisting dominantly of carbonised flax seeds. There were also small numbers of cereal grains consisting of oat, emmer and emmer/spelt grains and a

Table 3.21: Roman charcoal identifications (full analysis); Billany Farm (Site 24) and Dun Cross (Site 25). (For Key see Table 3.16).

Family	Species	Common Name	Site 24 Context number 14.01.039 Feature number 14.01.038 Sample number 44 Sample volume (L) 32	25 16.01.008 16.01.007 279 6
Betulaceae	*Alnus glutinosa/Corylus avellana*	Alder/hazel	6	1
	Corylus avellana	Hazel	16	-
Fagaceae	*Quercus robur/petraea*	Sessile/pedunculate oak	45	70
	Quercus robur/petraea hw	Sessile/pedunculate oak h/w	24	13
	Quercus robur/petraea sw	Sessile/pedunculate oak s/w	-	12
Rosaceae	*Crataegus monogyna/Sorbus* spp/ *Malus sylvestris*	Hawthorn/rowan/ crab apple	4	4
	Prunus avium/padus	Wild/bird cherry	2	-
Salicaceae	*Salix* spp/*Populus* spp	Willow/poplar	3	-
		Total fragments identified	100	100

Table 3.22. Roman plant macrofossil identifications; Springfield (Site 31). (For Key see Table 3.16).

Habitat code	Family	Species	Common Name	Site							
				31	31	31	31	31	31	31	31
			Context number	24.03.037	24.03.037	24.03.038	24.03.036	24.03.040	24.03.080	24.03.081	24.06.036
			Feature number	24.03.036	24.03.036	24.03.036	24.03.036	24.03.036	24.06.036	24.06.036	24.03.036
			Sample volume (L)	8	13	7	9	15	16		
			Flot volume (ml)	6	5	8	6	6	12		
				10	25	19	10	20	25		
WF	Adoxaceae	*Sambucus nigra*	Elder	-	-	-	-	1	-
DC	Amaranthaceae	*Chenopodium album*	Fat hen *	-	-	-	-	1	2
A	Asteraceae	*Tripleurospermum inodorum*	Scentless mayweed	-	-	1	-	-	-
WF	Betulaceae	*Corylus avellana*	Hazelnut	3	-	15	2	6	-
DC	Brassicaceae	*Brassica/Sinapsis* spp	Mustard/cabbage/charlock	-	-	2	-	-	-
A		*Raphanus raphanistrum*	Wild radish perianith	-	2	-	-	-	-
H	Fabaceae	*Ulex* spp	Gorse	-	-	1	-	-	-
E	Poaceae	*Avena* spp	Oat	3	6	40	-	8	4
A		*Bromus sect bromus*	Chess	10	8	7	8	17	9
E		*Hordeum vulgare*	Hulled barley	1	3	7	-	-	-
E		*Hordeum vulgare*	Naked barley	-	-	1	-	-	-
E		*Secale cereale*	Rye	1	-	-	-	2	-
E		*Triticum* spp	Wheat	-	4	9	2	2	-
E		*Triticum dicoccum*	Emmer glume base	-	-	-	-	1	-
E		*Triticum dicoccum/spelta*	Emmer/spelt	2	27	4	3	6	2
E		*Triticum*	Wheat – spelt glume base	-	5	1	1	2	1
E		Poaceae	Indeterminate cereal grain	8	-	25	2	11	7
E		Poaceae	Cereal chaff – culm bases	3	-	-	-	-	-
E		Poaceae	Cereal chaff – glume bases	-	-	-	-	3	-
DC		*Rumex* spp	Dock	-	1	-	-	1	-
D	Solanaceae	*Solanum nigrum*	Black nightshade	1	-	-	-	-	-
			Total macrofossils identified	32	56	113	16	61	25

small number of weed seeds including fat hen/goosefoot, vetches/vetchlings, black-bindweed and dock. The charcoal from fill 14.01.039 was fully analysed and was dominated by alder, alder/hazel, oak, hawthorn/rowan/crab apple, cherry and willow/poplar fragments (Table 3.21, SS 44). Fills 14.01.079 and 14.01.080 were broadly characterised and contained the same species as fill 14.01.039 with the exception of cherry and willow/poplar (Table 3.19, SS 53, 54).

Broad characterisation of the charcoal was also undertaken for pit 14.01.004 and posthole 14.01.036. Pit 14.01.004 (Table 3.19, SS 35) was dominated by alder, alder/hazel and hazel with smaller amounts of gorse/broom, oak and hawthorn/rowan/crab apple charcoal. Posthole 14.01.036 contained alder/hazel hazel, hawthorn/rowan/crab apple and willow/poplar charcoal. The mixture of species within this fill indicates that the post was not burnt *in situ*.

Dun Cross, Dartington (Site 25)
The fill 16.01.008 from pit 16.01.007 (Table 3.21, SS 279) was fully analysed and was dominated by oak charcoal fragments with smaller amounts of alder/hazel and hawthorn/rowan/crab apple fragments.

Springfield, Ugborough (Site 31)
Six samples came from fills 24.03.038, 24.03.037, 24.03.040, 24.03.078, 24.03.080 and 24.03.081 of oven 24.03.036 (Table 3.22, SS 7, SS 8, SS 9, SS 13, SS 15 and SS 16). The plant macrofossil assemblages from all these fills were broadly similar and represent cereal-processing waste which was subsequently burnt. The most important crops appear to have been oats and emmer/spelt, with smaller amounts of barley and rye. Cereal chaff, including spelt glume bases and culm bases, was also present. Arable weed species included large numbers of chess and smaller numbers of scentless mayweed and wild radish. Weeds indicative of disturbed environments were represented in smaller numbers by dock and black nightshade. Woodland/scrub/heath species were indicated by hazelnut shells, elder seeds and a gorse seed. The charcoal from fill 24.03.078 was broadly characterised and consisted of alder/hazel, hazel, oak, ash, hawthorn/rowan/crab apple and elm fragments (Table 3.19, SS 13). The charcoal from pit 24.03.041 was broadly characterised and consisted dominantly of oak with a smaller amount of alder/hazel.

Discussion of later prehistoric and Roman plant macrofossil assemblages

Iron Age

Arable agriculture and hand-collected foodstuffs
In the Iron Age wild foods were far less important compared to the Neolithic and Bronze Age and the results from the present project show a large increase in the number of seeds associated with crop cultivation and processing (Fig. 6.2). The only hand-collected foodstuffs identified in the Iron Age assemblages was carbonised hazelnut shells and these may have been redeposited from an earlier occupation, or may have become incorporated from odd hazelnuts attached to branches that were burnt as fuel. Elsewhere in Devon, small quantities of hazelnuts were found in a penannular gully at Langland Lane (Clapham 1999d, 135) and penannular gullies at Long Range, both in East Devon (Clapham 1999b, 153). If not residual, in all these cases hazelnuts may have been used to augment the diet, providing additional vitamins and minerals.

The cereals identified from the Iron Age phases of activity at Slade Farm (Site 2), consisted dominantly of emmer/spelt (most likely spelt) and oat, with smaller quantities of barley, rye, unspecified wheat and bread wheat. These types of cereal assemblages are typical of the Iron Age. From the end of the Bronze Age and into the Iron Age period in southern England there were two major changes in the types of crops being cultivated. There was, first, a switch from emmer to spelt wheat and, second, a gradual increase in the cultivation of bread wheat towards the end of the period (Campbell and Straker 2003, 18; Fitzpatrick 2008, 139). From the evidence from Slade Farm, spelt wheat appears to be more dominant than emmer; this is slightly different to the trend observed at Langland Lane, Devon (Clapham 1999d, 135), Long Range, Devon (Clapham 1999b, 153) and Blackhorse, Devon (Clapham 1999e, 184–7), where emmer was a dominant crop. There was a moderate assemblage of oats and, although the absence of floret bases made it impossible to distinguish wild from cultivated oats, the common presence of oats together with the general paucity of weeds suggests that the oats were cultivated.

The assemblages from Slade Farm (Site 2) and Crablake Farm (Site 15) contained relatively large amounts of cereal chaff, suggesting that crops were cultivated and processed close to these sites. The cereal chaff from Slade Farm contained high numbers of spelt glume bases and emmer/spelt cereal grains. This can be attributed to the processing techniques used for hulled/glume cereals. Unlike free threshing cereals, such as oat, barley and bread-type wheat, hulled emmer and spelt wheat are usually stored as bulk spikelets and require parching in order to make the cereal chaff brittle and allow grains to be released from their spikelets (Hillman 1981, 133–4). This means that emmer and spelt wheat grains and chaff has a higher likelihood of becoming accidentally burnt, thereby having a higher representation in carbonised cereal assemblages. As a consequence it is difficult to determine whether small quantities of barley, bread wheat and rye mean that they were weeds of the oat, emmer and spelt crops, or were crops that are under-represented due to their non-exposure to fire.

The weed seeds from Slade Farm allow some interpretation of crop harvesting methods. All, with the exception of self heal and ribwort plantain, are particularly tall weeds (0.5–2m in height) (Rose 2006, 130, 150, 163–8, 170, 380, 387), and the general absence of seeds from shorter weeds suggests that crops were harvested high up on the plants. The assemblage from Crablake Farm is made up dominantly of culm nodes with some culm bases and palea and few weed seeds. Interestingly, the presence of culm bases suggests that crops were being uprooted rather than cut. This may indicate a different stage in crop harvesting where the ears have already been removed and the straw is being cut/uprooted, perhaps for tinder, bedding or thatch.

Fuel
The charcoal samples from Slade Farm (Site 2), Exwell Barton (Site 14) and Crablake Farm (Site 15) were all characterised as deposits of fuel waste from crop processing. The eight samples from Tigley A (Site 26) were associated with furnaces 16.07.008, 16.07.028, 16.07.040 and 16.07.055, and pit 16.07.017. These samples have been characterised as waste associated with ironworking.

The dominant tree species varied between sites (Tables 3.17, 3.18). Oak dominated at Tigley A, attributable to the deliberate selection of fuels for use in the iron furnaces. The remaining sites had similar assemblages to those of the Bronze Age. Alder/hazel and hazel dominated at Slade Farm Exwell Barton and Crablake Farm, but overall there is an increase in percentage of cherry, blackthorn/sloe and willow/poplar, and a decrease in alder/hazel species, perhaps indicating a continued expansion (and use) of scrub woodland associated with clearings for settlement and agriculture (Figure 6.3).

Full analysis of charcoal from Slade Farm and Tigley A has shown an interesting assortment of sizes of fuel wood used. The majority of the fragments from Slade Farm (including oak) exhibit curved growth rings and, in particular, there is a large number of twig and small roundwood fragments, indicating the use of small branches/brushwood. In contrast, the oak used in furnaces at Tigley A did not exhibit curved growth rings, although the species identified in smaller percentages, such as alder/hazel, gorse and ash, did. This may indicate a selective use of woodland resources, with smaller scrappy fragments being used for kindling and small domestic fires, and larger oak branches and timbers being saved for use in furnaces, where they would have been suitable for maintaining a high temperature (Cutler and Gale 2000, 205).

At Slade Farm, pit 2.03.004 was also dominated by oak but, in contrast to Tigley A, over half of the identified oak exhibited curved growth rings indicating it originated from smaller twigs and branches. The remaining fuel consisted of alder/hazel, alder, hazel and gorse. The dominance of oak still indicates it was a main fuel, and it would have provided a steady temperature required for parching crops, although the increased use of small branches and twigs suggests a less specialised nature for the fire. The scrub woodland species would have been used as kindling. A similar assemblage was found with settlement activity at Long Range, Devon (Gale 1999b, 155–8) where assemblages consisted of maple (*Acer* spp), holly (*Ilex* spp), hazel, alder, birch, oak, hawthorn/rowan/crab apple, cherry, blackthorn, gorse/broom and willow/poplar. As with Slade Farm, the Long Range assemblage contained lots of small twiggy and roundwood fragments, indicating a similar approach to fuel wood collection from woodlands and hedges.

Local landscape
The majority of the weeds from Slade Farm and Crablake Farm, species such as fat hen/goosefoot, common chickweed, black-bindweed and dock, are opportunistic species (Rose 2006, 130, 150, 170, 163–8) but are known to have established on arable ground, whose presence can also be inferred from the cereal remains at these sites. The remaining species, self heal and ribwort plantain, although not recorded in arable fields today (Rose 2006 380, 387) will establish in disturbed areas such as cleared ground and hedgerows or banks around fields and seeds might therefore have easily dispersed into nearby cleared arable fields.

Palaeoenvironmental sequences in the South West tend to show that lowland Devon was largely cleared of woodland by the middle of the Iron Age (Rippon 2012, 232 and table 11.6). The trend of woodland clearance increased dramatically with the increase in both arable and pastoral farming. The varied selection of fuel woods from these Iron Age sites suggests that wood was normally gathered from the local area but that the oakwood fuel used in furnaces at Tigley A was more carefully selected. It may have been collected from further afield, or the furnaces located close to the source of suitable fuel. It appears that the woodland available at the East Devon sites Slade Farm, Exwell Barton and Crablake Farm consisted of a mosaic of primary oak woodland and secondary/scrub woodland of hazel, ash, elm, hawthorn/rowan/crab apple, cherry and blackthorn/sloe (Cutler and Gale 2000, 88, 120, 183–4, 196, 204, 264). Areas of heath with gorse/broom (ibid., 260) are likely to have been close to Slade Farm and areas of wet woodland including alder and willow/poplar (ibid., 36, 190, 236) were found near the sites at Exwell Barton and Crablake Farm, both of which are not far from streams. These sites are in areas now characterised by lowland heaths. In Devon, heathland containing gorse/broom started establishing locally from the Neolithic period once woodlands started to be cleared and agriculture caused the fertility of sandy soils to be depleted (Brown *et al.* 2008).

It is more difficult to interpret the woodland composition at Tigley A but it is likely that the oak originated from woodlands relatively close to the site, as would be expected for an industry requiring large amounts of fuel. The landscape probably included oak primary woodland, with secondary/scrub woodland of ash, hazel and hawthorn/rowan/crab apple, and heathland represented by gorse/broom.

Roman period

Arable agriculture and hand-collected foodstuffs

The main crops cultivated in Britain throughout the Roman period were oat, barley and emmer, spelt and bread wheats (Cool 2006, 69), and all, with the exception of bread wheat, were recovered from the South Devon Roman settlements at Billany Farm (Site 24) and Springfield (Site 31). These crops are also typical of Roman sites further west in Cornwall, such as the 3rd/4th-century settlement at Penhale Round (Scaife 1998–9, 96) and the settlement at Reawla (Straker 1992, 90). Generally in west Devon and Cornwall barley and oats were more common than wheat in the Roman period, and crop husbandry regimes appear to have had a different pattern to those further east (Rippon 2012, 269).

Cereal remains from pit 14.01.038 and pit 14.01.034 at Billany Farm were found in small numbers. At Springfield the cereal assemblage from oven 24.03.036 contained a much larger carbonised grain assemblage together with cereal chaff suggestive of crop-processing waste. The oven may have been a domestic type perhaps temporarily used for drying grain. The dominant crops here were oats and spelt (identification of spelt glume bases suggest the emmer/spelt cereal grains identified are likely to be spelt than emmer wheat). The identification of oats, which are not thought to be a dominant crop in the Roman period (Cool 2006, 70–1) suggest a mixed arable landscape with cereals perhaps cultivated both for fodder and for domestic consumption. It is also possible oats were being used to supplement a poor harvest which is a suggestion also made by Pearson (1987, 6) where frequent oat grains came from the 3rd-century square enclosure at Hayes Farm, Clyst Honiton.

The arable weeds from Springfield include chess, scentless mayweed and wild radish. There were also some opportunistic species known to establish in arable areas, including black nightshade and dock. The arable weeds were mainly from medium to tall growing plants, with the exception of scentless mayweed, but the evidence of culm bases suggests that the crops were uprooted rather than cut higher up the plant. It is possible that the ears were harvested first and the straw bases uprooted in a second phase of harvesting with both practices contributing to the charred remains recovered.

Cereal crops had a wide range of uses in Roman times. Barley was used to produce bread, porridge, pottages, for animal fodder and to produce beer. Oats were used as fodder but were also known to be used to make porridge, unleavened bread or oat cakes. Spelt wheat was used to bake bread and emmer wheat, which had a lower gluten content (therefore did not rise as well), was more often used for making porridge and cakes (Cool 2006, 70–1). Other plants of economic importance included Celtic bean and cultivated vetch at Billany Farm, and mustard/cabbage/charlock and hazelnut at Springfield. Celtic bean, cultivated vetch and mustard/cabbage/charlock are rare in plant macrofossil assemblages as food preparation would not have required exposure to fire. Celtic beans have also been recorded on Hayes Farm, Clyst Honiton (Pearson 1987, 6) and could have been utilised as vegetables as well as in soups/pottages (Cool 2006, 126–8). Vetches and Celtic beans are known for their ability to fix nitrogen to the soil thereby fertilising fields (Stone 2005, 107). Hazelnut had been exploited since the Mesolithic and is known to have been utilised in the Roman period, albeit in smaller quantities. They would have been roasted and eaten or placed in long term storage (Cool 2006, 126).

Another species of economic importance recovered from Billany Farm was flax, a collection of 279 carbonised seeds coming from the three fills sampled from pit 14.01.038 and the one from nearby pit 14.01.034. The identification of flax in the Roman period appears to be very rare. Comparative material across the country shows that flax is present in Roman assemblages but only one or two seeds are ever recovered, which suggests either that it was not usually exposed to fire, or that it was present as a background weed rather than a cultivated crop. One exception is ditches from Renny Lodge, Milton Keynes where charred seeds, capsules and stems of flax were found and thought to have been utilised for linen production or linseed oil extraction (Stevens 2009, 118–24).

Flax is known to have been used to produce linen and rope from the plant fibres and linseed oil from the seeds (Cutler and Gale 2000, 152-3) and, specific to the Roman period, linen is recorded as being used in military clothing as well as everyday clothing such as shirts and tunics (Bishop and Coulston 1993, 141). It is difficult to determine whether flax processing was taking place on the site as it is a destructive process. The flax was recovered as individual carbonised seeds as well as parts of flax capsules, together with black melted vitrified fragments. In order to produce linen the flax seeds and leaves are removed from the plant and the stems placed in retting pools to extract the fibres. It is possible that this waste represents seeds/pods that had been removed and subsequently burnt.

Fuel

There was a wide variety of wood charcoal from Billany Farm and Springfield and a more restricted range form Dun Cross (Site 25) and Pixies' Parlour (Site 4).

As shown on Figures 6.3 and 6.4, there were slight but perhaps not significant changes in the relative proportions of tree species compared with the Iron Age, with oak still dominant. The slight increase in shrubby species such as hazel, hawthorn/rowan/crab apple and willow/poplar may be attributed to increased pressure on woodlands with species from hedgerows being utilised more often for fuel.

The highest fragment counts were of oak with smaller

numbers of alder, alder/hazel, hawthorn/rowan/crab apple and, in pit 14.01.038 at Billany Farm, cherry and willow/poplar. The majority of oak fragments did not exhibit curved growth rings, which suggests the use of large branch or trunk wood (a trend also seen in the Iron Age). Most of the remaining species exhibited curved growth rings indicating small roundwood branches and brushwood was being utilised possibly as kindling, or for smaller, temporary fires. There were a couple of fragments of hazel from Billany Farm which appeared to exhibit fast growth (wide growth rings), suggesting coppiced stands, but as the charcoal was highly fragmented this is difficult to confirm with any certainty. Similar assemblages were also found at Penhale Round, Cornwall (Gale 1998–9, 111) where they consisted of hazel, oak, hawthorn/rowan/crab apple, blackthorn and gorse/broom, used as fuel for domestic purposes.

Local landscape

The cereal remains and arable weeds from Billany Farm and Springfield indicate an arable landscape close to these sites (Rose 2006, 201, 202, 282–4, 455). Opportunistic species such as fat hen, dock, black nightshade, mallow and black-bindweed may have established on disturbed areas within the settlements (Rose 2006, 130, 163–8, 170, 180, 354). Hazelnut and elder suggest scrub/woodland and the gorse seed together with gorse charcoal indicates heathland nearby (Rose 2006, 268). The evidence from South Devon may suggest a greater presence of oak than other trees, but hazel, ash, hawthorn/rowan/crab apple and cherry were also prevalent. Alder and willow/poplar would have been found relatively close to streams and gorse/broom on heathland, perhaps on the higher ground.

Radiocarbon dating

Andrew Mudd

Radiocarbon dating in the Iron Age and Roman periods is often not considered worthwhile because the plateau in the calibration curve in the later first millennium BC gives imprecise calibrated dates, and because pottery dating in the later Iron Age and Roman period normally gives a better resolution than radiocarbon. The results of the radiocarbon dating on this project, however, show the value of even imprecise dating where there is no other evidence. Six consistent and valuable dates came from wood charcoal from the Tigley A furnaces (Table 3.6) although, paradoxically, the best potential sample, a grain of wheat, was shown to be intrusive. A group of three dates from Slade Farm also convincingly show that the deposit of charred plant remains is Iron Age, despite the Neolithic pottery found (Table 3.1). Consistent Roman dates came from flax seeds at Billany Farm, removing all doubt that this is a Roman deposit even though stratigraphically late (Table 3.4). Two consistent dates also came from Dun Cross (Table 3.5). Less useful (later Neolithic) dates from Exwell Barton and Lower Velwell can be attributed to old wood and reinforce the need for good samples and confirmatory dating where available.

Chapter 4
Medieval and Later Periods

Introduction

The principal discovery from the medieval period was part of an unsuspected house, with an adjacent sunken oven house or corn drying building, south of Exwell Barton, Powderham (Site 14). While little survived of the form of the house, the sunken building showed a sequence of hearths or ovens with abundant charred cereal remains and appears to be a unique find in Devon. The settlement confirms to the general dating of deserted settlements to between the 12th and 14th centuries. Cereal remains also came from an apparently isolated pit at Coldharbour, Ottery St Mary (Site 1), and there was a pit of slightly earlier date in South Devon at Bluepost, Harberton (Site 29). There were still earlier pits, dating from the immediate post-Roman period, at Pixies' Parlour, Ottery St Mary (Site 4), Tigley B, Harberton (Site 27) and Moore Farm, Harberton (Site 28), all unsuspected and dated exclusively by radiocarbon. Slight and less conclusively medieval remains were investigated at White House, Powderham (Site 13: a trackway) and Forder Cross, Ugborough (Site 32: several ditches and pits). Post-medieval remains included a cob building at Lower Nutwell, Woodbury (Site 12), and the remains of a brick clamp at Salston A, Ottery St Mary (Site 5), both probably dating to the 18th century.

Site descriptions
Stuart Joyce and Andrew Mudd

Post-Roman/Early medieval

East Devon

Site 4: Pit at Pixies' Parlour, Ottery St Mary
Pit 3.04.036 lay within the area enclosed by Roman ditch 3.04.004 (Fig. 3.3). This pit was oval in plan, with steeply sloping symmetrical sides and a concave base. It measured 1.15m long, 0.45m wide and 0.28m deep, with an unremarkable fill, 3.04.036, of grey-brown sandy silt, with occasional charcoal flecks. It was originally considered to be prehistoric, based on association with nearby features, but a radiocarbon determination on a charred grain of barley (Soil Sample 70) produced a date of cal. AD 642–692 (91.6%; NZA-36659) (Table 2.1). At face value this appears to be a 7th-century pit, although it is possible that the grain was intrusive in a feature associated with the prehistoric or Roman occupations. Pit 3.04.036 is similar in form to undated pits 3.04.038 and 3.04.024 on this site and it is possible that activity of this date was more widespread than an apparently isolated pit.

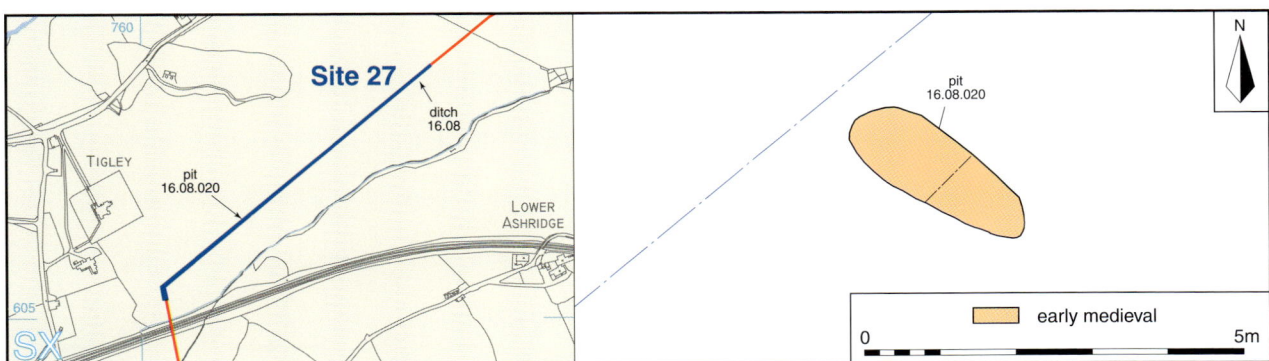

Fig. 4.1   Tigley B (Site 27); plan of pit 16.08.020. Scales 1:100 and 1:10,000

Table 4.1: Radiocarbon date from Tigley B, Site 27 (FTC 16.08)

Feature	Context	Lab No.	Material	δ ^{13}C	Radiocarbon Age	Calibrated Date 95%	Calibrated Date 68%
Pit 16.08.020	16.08.021	NZA 36702	Hazelnut shell (*Corylus avellan*a)	-28.1‰	1462 ± 20 yr BP	566–643 AD (94.8%)	583–632 AD (68.5%)

South Devon

Site 27: Pit at Tigley B, Harberton

Large oval pit 16.08.020 lay at the south-western area of the field east of Tigley (Fig. 4.1). It was 2.56m long, 0.87m wide and 0.48m deep with moderately sloping even sides and a slightly concave base. The single fill, 16.08.021, was a dark, charcoal-rich clay silt containing charred oats, barley and indeterminate grains, and a range of wood species (Tables 4.4, 4.5, sample 299). A radiocarbon date of cal. AD 566–643 (NZA-36702) was obtained from a hazelnut shell (Table 4.1). The remains appear to indicate a dump of burnt harvested 'waste' in a pit deliberately dug to receive it (as well as, perhaps, material that has not survived). The 6th/7th-century date is not out of place with the nature of the remains, but it is possible the hazelnut was intrusive in an earlier feature, or residual in a later one.

Site 28: Pit at Moore Farm, Harberton

The site lies at approximately 115m AOD (Fig. 2.9). Among the scatter of earlier prehistoric features on the hill crest here, circular pit 18.12.015, 1.5m in diameter and 0.38m deep, contained carbonised remains identified as barley, oats and wood charcoal consisting mainly of oak and hazel (Tables 4.4, 4.5, sample 303). A radiocarbon assay on a grain of wheat returned a date in the range cal. AD 394–534 (NZA-36703), placing it in the very late Roman or immediate post-Roman period (Table 2.3). The purpose of this pit is unclear but it may be indicative

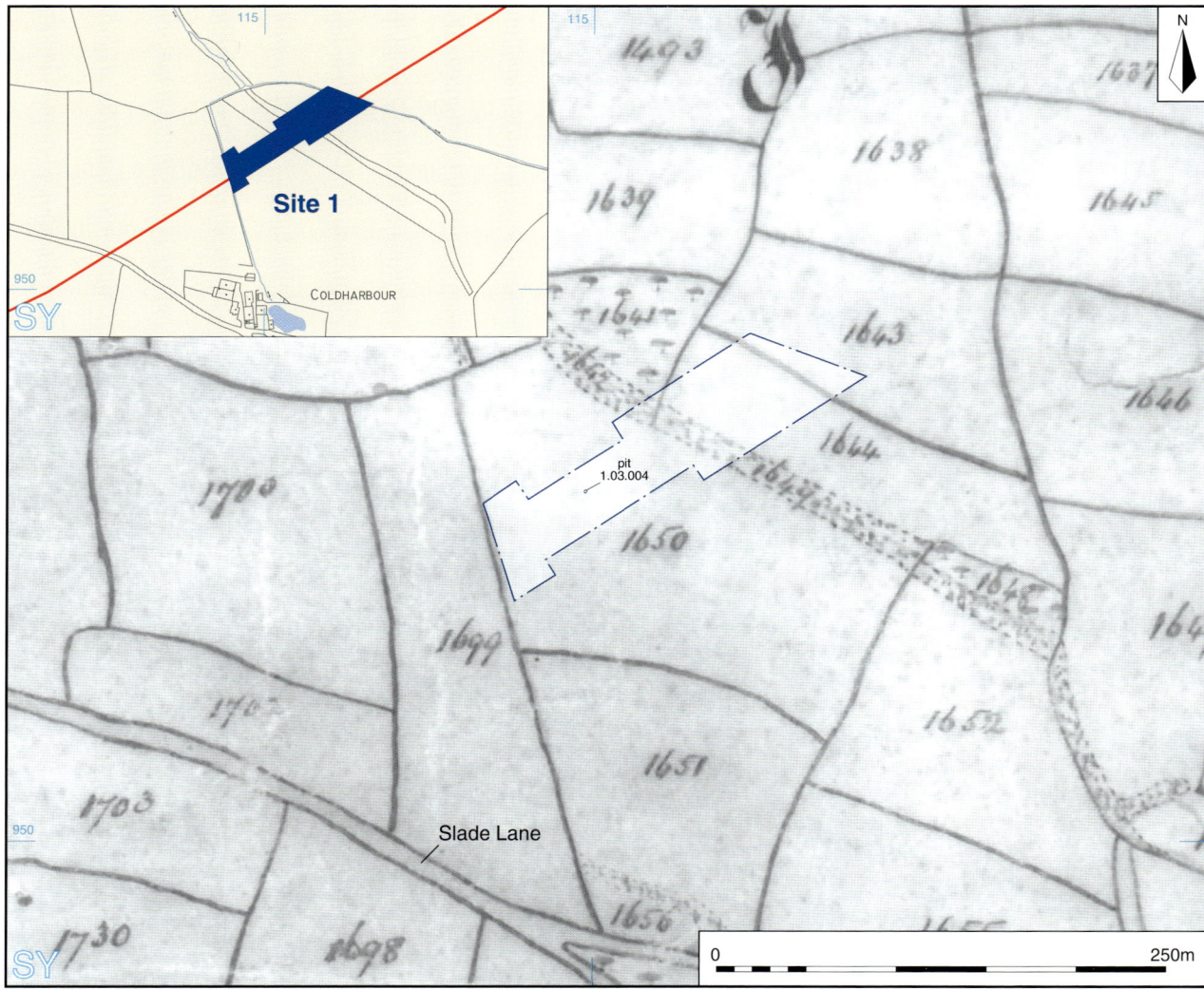

Fig. 4.2   Coldharbour (Site 1); extract from 1845 Tithe Map, showing excavated feature. Scales 1:4000 and 1:10,000

of more general occupation in this plot of this date to which some of the undated features may belong. Nearby, undated pit 18.12.013 was kidney-shaped with steeply sloping sides and a flat base, its single fill consisting of slightly silty clay. Pit 18.12.022 was sub-circular with shallow uneven sides and base and a similar fill.

Post-Conquest medieval and later

East Devon

Site 1: Pit at Coldharbour, Ottery St Mary

Lying about 200m north of Coldharbour, south-east of Ottery St Mary, at the western end of the plot was a well defined sub-circular pit 1.03.004 (Fig. 4.2). It was 1.78m in diameter and 0.41m deep with moderately sloping, symmetrical sides and a slightly concave base. The fill, 1.03.005, consisted of charcoal-rich silt with inclusions of large stones, deliberately placed within the pit. It contained nine sherds of 12th to 13th-century pottery and significant amounts of charred oat and rye grains (Table 4.6, sample 173). The assemblage appears to represent processed grain either from two crops, or from a mixed rye/oat maslin. The pit itself could be an indicator of nearby settlement in the medieval period, although it lies isolated from any other remains within the 35m-wide and 200m-long strip undertaken here. It is also *c.* 400m from Rill Farm and *c.* 500m from Great Well Farm and distant from existing lanes as shown on the 1845 Tithe Map (Fig. 4.2). The feature may, alternatively, relate to activities carried out in the fields as part of the agricultural cycle.

Site 4: Pit at Pixies' Parlour, Ottery St Mary

A post-medieval pit (3.04.097) is interpreted as cutting the Early Neolithic tree-hole 3.04.096, although it was not recognised in the field and its presence only deduced following the examination of the charred plant remains and the associated radiocarbon date (Figs 2.1, 2.2, sections 1, 2; Table 2.1). The pit was about 3m long and 1m wide, with a depth of up to 0.45m. The lower fill in the central part (3.04.092) contained a deposit of charred remains which included sparse wheat and oats and a range of wood charcoal (Tables 4.10 and 4.11). The radiocarbon determination on a grain of wheat returned a date in the range cal. AD 1523–1664 (NZA-36306). The purpose of this pit is not known but it falls within a category of off-site features of medieval and later date that may relate to activities undertaken in the fields.

Site 5: Brick clamp, Salston A, Ottery St Mary

Peter Davenport

The site lies on the floodplain of the River Otter south of Salston (Fig. 4.3). The watching brief at this site recorded an area (*c.* 6m by 6m) of intense heat discolouration of the natural alluvium, associated with spreads of wood ash/carbonised wood and brick fragments. The plan

Fig. 4.3 Salston A (Site 5); location on extract from 1845 Tithe Map. Scale 1:7500

of the discoloured area was not completely retrieved, as it extended beyond the observed area except for the western side. Here the wood ash had a nearly straight edge. There was no depth to the deposits which overlay the silt-clay substrate and had been truncated by closely spaced furrows (Fig. 4.4).

Fig. 4.4 Salston A (Site 5); excavation in progress, looking west. Scales 1m

The burnt material can be interpreted as the remains of a brick clamp. The burning was clearly intense and the presence of brick fragments, including some that have vitrified faces, and signs of over-firing internally as well, make this fairly clear. The brick fragments found are in a light orangey-red, well-mixed fabric with brick grog and sparse very fine quartz and iron oxide tempers (identified by E.R. McSloy). There is the occasional larger pebble fragment. The external faces are sanded, suggesting palette moulding (Brunskill 1990, 24). No brick fragment survived to even a quarter of the likely original length, but all were consistently 2½ inches thick and 4¼ inches wide. The size and method of moulding and the lack of a frog suggest a pre-19th century date, as does the lack of any indication of a brickfield on the Tithe Map (although there is a field name 'Brick Plot' some 500m away). The dating from type is very imprecise, but brick making on site (itinerant brick making) is likely to have died out with the coming of improved transport during the 19th century.

The clamp itself is evidenced by the area of intense heating, which is a minimum of 5m square. Nothing survives of the structure of the clamp, which would have consisted almost entirely of the brick to be fired, and the lowest levels would have been largely fuel (wood or charcoal). There was no sign of a bed of bricks, but this could be raised on a mound of ash and this may be all that survives here (Hammond 1984), or the distribution of ash and heat discolouration may suggest the clamp was built directly on the cleared ground. Over-fired bricks found may represent this floor but the rest of the bricks at the base of a clamp would usually be over-fired as well (Hammond 1984; Brunskill 1990, 8). The over-fired bricks are vitrified on what seem to be the ends and top and bottom faces, indicating these examples were stacked on edge with gaps either side. Apart from the few flues in the base, bricks were generally packed tightly together in a clamp, so these bricks may be from the sides of the flues.

Site 12: Cob building at Lower Nutwell, Woodbury

The site lay south of Exton on flat land described by the BGS as first terrace river deposits overlying Exmouth Sandstone and Mudstone (BGS 1976) (Fig. 4.5). In the south-east corner of plot 12.01 was a partially upstanding cob-walled building, 12.01.01, with an internal area measuring 12m by 4.7m. The south-west gable wall survived in part to a height of a little over 2m and part of the north-western wall survived to a similar height (Figs 4.6, 4.7). The building had three apparent entrances, two 1.8m wide at either end of in its long walls and a narrower central one (1.3m) in the north-western wall.

The building was excavated in a series of trenches, recovering a partial floor plan and a sequence of construction. Five trenches were excavated to examine the details of construction, and extended beyond the building footprint to reveal the external sequence. This was followed by a partial removal of the internal overburden to reveal the floor plan more completely. The excavations revealed comparable sequences of deposits in each trench enabling an overall narrative of the construction. The building itself had a single phase of construction, although there appeared to have been a remodelling of the interior floor using cobbles and brick edging, which may have been of a later date rather than part of the original design.

The natural geological substrate, 12.01.011, consisting of sandy clay with rounded and sub-angular pebbles, was encountered in the external trenches at a depth of 0.81m (25.36m AOD). This was in turn overlain by subsoil 12.01.012, identified both internally and externally, which was without finds. The subsoil was cut by wall construction trench 12.01.013, measuring 0.78m wide and 0.78m deep. This was filled by hardcore/bedding layer 12.01.014, consisting of large rounded cobbles (0.16m in depth), overlain by limestone cement foundations, 12.01.015, 0.3m in depth. This was in turn overlain by a limestone cement plinth 12.01.010 (0.3m in depth) (Fig. 4.8), on top of which, cob walls were constructed, which, at the time of the fieldwork survived to a maximum height of 2.1m. The walls were of identical construction. The cob was built up in 'lifts', identified from the shuttering marks in the layered construction, and the walls were bonded to one another. No dating evidence was recovered from these contexts and no architectural features were present. Within the structure was a rammed earth corridor, 12.01.036, consisting of firm orange-brown silty clay, which may have extended across the whole building to form the original floor surface. There were no finds from this layer. The narrowest of the three entrances was precisely central on the north-western side. Two large openings (*c.* 1.8m in width) within the north-western and south-eastern walls appear to be part of the original design as, in common with the central doorway, the limestone footings did not extend across them.

There appears to have been a second phase of building involving resurfacing the interior. Overlying the beaten floor surface in the north-eastern and south-western parts of the building was dark orange-brown gritty bedding layer 12.01.018, up to 0.1m in thickness. This contained fragments of shell, and also of tile, which has been identified as roof pantile and therefore probably of later 17th- or early 18th-century date. It is possible that these were from the original roof. Set in the bedding layer was cobble floor surface, 12.01.019, constructed of rounded cobbles, averaging 0.10m to 0.15m in diameter within lime cement (Fig. 4.8). Small, Flemish, handmade edging bricks, 12.01.023/12.01.027, butted the cobbles and delineated a central uncobbled passageway *c.* 2.5m wide. At the north-eastern end of the building the cobble surface formed a mud-and-cobble entrance ramp, 315.020. This was not solidly mortared and was considerably eroded. Stone post-pads, 12.01.024, appear to have been inserted through the cobble floor and probably relate to a modification or repair of the door

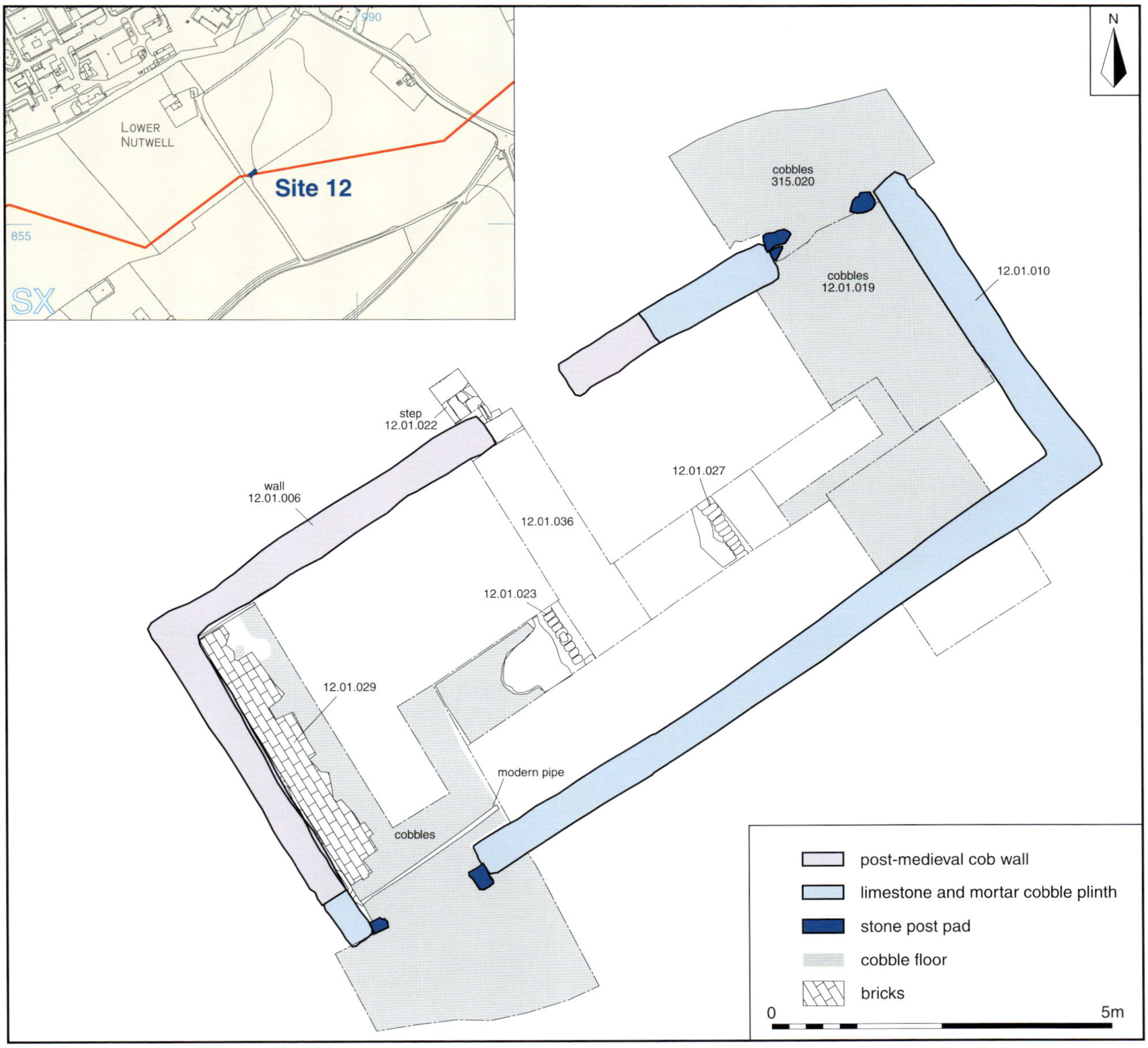

Fig. 4.5 Lower Nutwell (Site 12); plan of building. Scales 1:100 and 1:10,000

Fig. 4.6 Lower Nutwell (Site 12); view of building, looking west. Scale 1m

Fig. 4.7 Lower Nutwell (Site 12); view of interior of wall 12.01.006, looking north-west. Scale 1m

Fig. 4.8 Lower Nutwell (Site 12); view of cobbles 12.01.019 and plinth 12.01.010, looking south-west. Scale 1m

jamb of this entrance. Leading from the central entrance were two steps (12.01.021, 12.01.022) made from hand-made bricks bonded with hard, creamy-pink mortar.

On the cobble surface against the south-western wall was a layer of hand-made, unbonded, Flemish bricks, 12.01.029 (Fig. 4.9). It is difficult to envisage a function for these and it is probable that they were simply stored in the building. These bricks, and the remainder of the interior, were overlain by a layer of debris, 12.01.030, deriving from the disuse and eventual collapse of the building. It consisted of cob-silt and decomposed organic material; similar deposits lay outside the building. These abandonment layers yielded a range of finds including, notably, 13kg of tile, including pantile, suggesting that the building had been roofed with this material. The pantiles are of the typical form, s-shaped in profile with a nib on the underside. The fabric is hard, of orange firing, sandy and with evidence for coarse moulding sand. However, fragments of slate –

Fig. 4.9 Lower Nutwell (Site 12); bricks 12.01.029 and cobbles 12.01.019, looking north-west. Scale 1m

both from South Hams in Devon and Cornish Delabole – were identified, suggesting that these had been used as roofing materials at some time. There were also a few fragments of (modern) window glass and lead strips which may have been window flashing, so it is possible that a glass window had been inserted at one time. More enigmatically the only pottery retrieved comprised 27 sherds from a medieval chert-tempered cooking pot and two sherds from a 16th-century jug. It is unclear why these should have been deposited here, but it is possible that the building was used to store various assorted material after its primary function had ceased.

It is not known when the building fell into disuse, but it appears to have been standing and roofed in 1946 when it appears on a vertical aerial photograph. The image is small but the roof appears to be in two separate parts, both hipped (NMR library ref. 250).

Interpretation
There was no clear indication as to the date or function of this building, but it appears to have been constructed in one phase with three original doorways, one central one on the north-west side and two wider side-entrances, one facing north-west and the other south-east. This is plausibly explained as providing access for people (from the farm at Lower Nutwell) and for animals to and from the fields on either side. The Woodbury Tithe Map (1849) depicts the building in the corner of the field here before the field boundary on the long axis of the building had been removed, and shows that a break in the boundary provided a funnel for the north-eastern entrance to the building (Fig. 4.10). There is no indication from the tithe map, or from the geophysical survey and trial trenching in this plot, of any associated structures here, and it seems likely that it was an isolated, purpose-built animal shelter. Reflooring with cobbles and Flemish bricks can be dated to the late 17th or 18th centuries (Allan, below), unless the bricks had been reused, in which case it could have been slightly later. Fragments of pantile from beneath the cobbles suggest

Fig. 4.10 Lower Nutwell (Site 12); extract from 1849 Tithe Map showing cob building. Scale 1:2500

a similar date for the roofing on the earlier structure, although these need not have been the original roofing material. That the cobble surface with brick edging is not original is suggested both by the inclusions of roof pantile in the bedding layer, and also by the fact that it was not quite symmetrical in relation to the central doorway. The effect was to create (or recreate) a three-celled structure, the two end cells (4.0m and 4.5m wide) with cobble floors, and a central cell 2.5m wide retaining an earthen floor. The building is readily interpreted as a field barn or linhay for cattle (sheep did not normally need winter shelter), with a central feeding passage. The feeding passage would have been divided from the cattle by low partitions against which would have been placed mangers or troughs, although there is no evidence for these internal structures. There is also no evidence of internal drains, which perhaps would be expected in a building for cattle. There is also likely to have been a hay loft, probably reached by ladder from the feeding passage. There is no difficulty with envisaging a building of sufficient height since the walls were well founded.

Linhays (and cow houses elsewhere) were often provided with openings or pitching eyes at loft level for loading hay from carts (Barnwell and Giles 1997, 112–14).

Site 13: Trackway at White House, Powderham

The route of the pipeline rose from the Exe estuary and crossed a small dry valley behind 'Round House' (Fig. 4.11). Aerial photographs of this plot, taken in January 1988 (DCC: DAP JM08, DAP JM09) show the land under pasture with faint linear earthworks running from the Powderham road and crossing the dry valley (Fig. 4.12). These form an approximately rectangular pattern and may represent the boundaries of agricultural or building plots. Their date is not clear but there are no plots depicted on the tithe map (1838) and they seem likely to be of medieval or early post-medieval date. At the time of fieldwork the land was under arable and these features were not visible. Similar cropmarks are visible extending to the north and north-east (NMR library ref. 9496). Geophysical survey along the pipeline route showed the corner of an apparent rectangular enclosure,

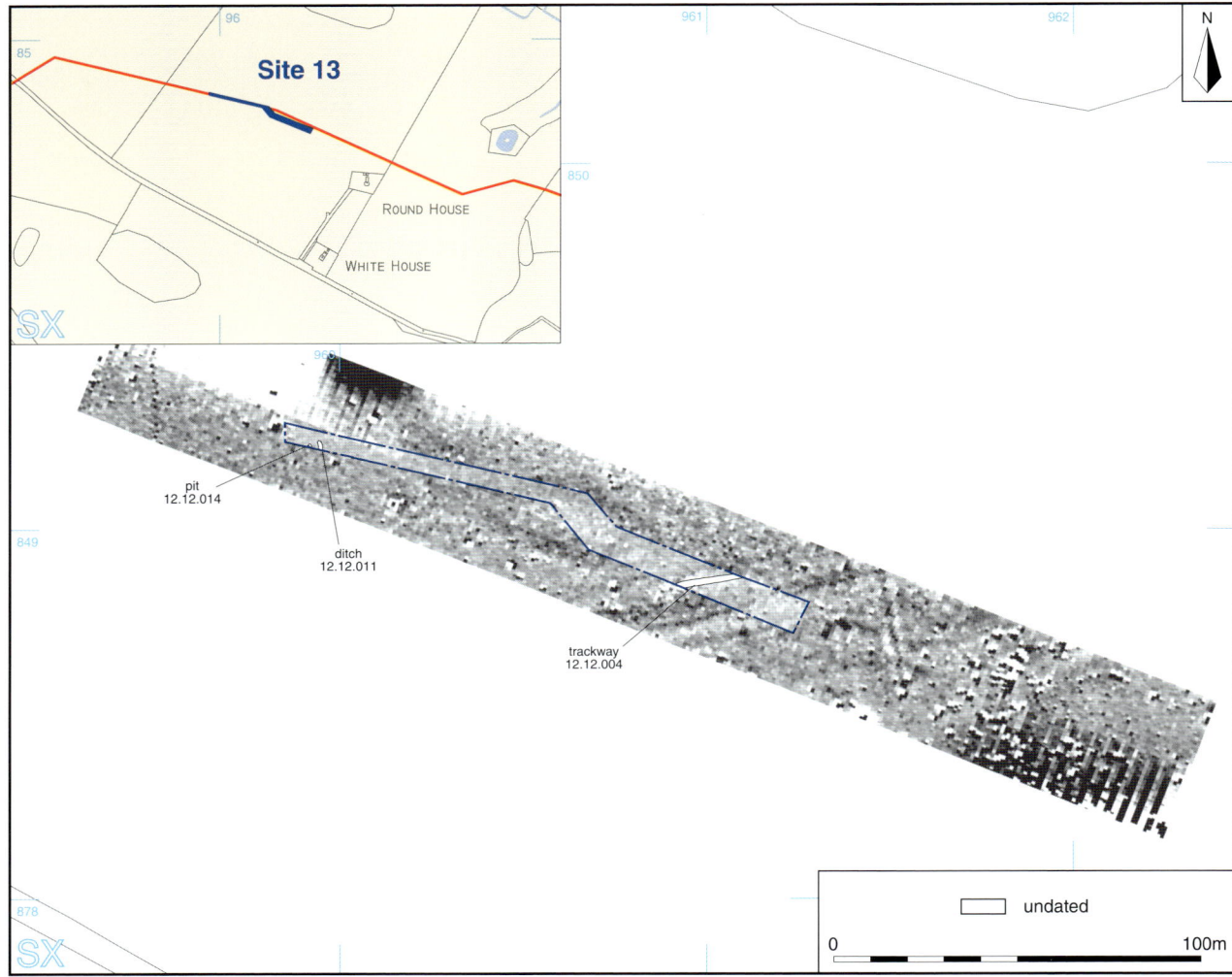

Fig. 4.11 White House (Site 13); plan of excavated features, showing geophysical survey results. Scales 1:2000 and 1:10,000

Fig. 4.12 White House (Site 13); aerial photograph of earthworks showing location of excavated area, looking south-east (Devon County Council Ref. DAP JM.08)

and other linear and discrete anomalies which may not be archaeological (Fig. 4.11).

At the centre of the site was an east/west orientated trackway 12.12.004, 2m wide, which consisted of angular stones, which cut the underlying natural substrate (Fig. 4.13). No dating evidence was recovered. It corresponds to a faint positive anomaly, depicted on the geophysical survey plot, which lies immediately adjacent to the enclosure ditch. It is not clear why the ditch was not uncovered, although it is possible (but not clear from the geophysical survey) that there was a gap in the ditch here. There is no clear association between the earthworks visible on the aerial photographs and the enclosure ditch or the trackway, but the evidence does indicate elements of a pre-modern agricultural landscape here.

In the western part of the site was curving ditch terminus 12.12.011, which was 0.82m wide and 0.47m deep and extended for *c.* 2m into the excavation area. Immediately west of this was pit 12.12.014, 0.80m in diameter and 0.21m deep. No dating evidence was recovered. There was nothing intrinsically significant about these features, but it is possible that they related to the pre-modern landscape indicated by the combined field and desk-based investigations. They may form a constituent part of dispersed medieval/early post-medieval settlement, fronting the Powderham road. An east/west orientated ditch, 12.10.004, was identified in plot 12.10, along with a small pit, 12.10.006 (not illustrated). Although undated they would seem to fit with the general background activity identified for the medieval or early post-medieval period.

Site 14: Medieval house and sunken outbuilding at Exwell Barton, Powderham

The site lies at 16m OD on the flat land south-west of Exwell Barton, some 2 km south-east of the town of Exminster (Fig. 4.14). The underlying geology is mapped as Dawlish Sandstone which fieldwork showed to comprise a silty sand. An aerial photograph taken in April 1969 shows faint linear cropmarks parallel with and at right-angles to the Powderham road to the north (NMR library ref. 9496). Geophysical survey was not, however, undertaken because of crop cover. Fieldwork

Fig. 4.13 White House (Site 13); trackway 12.12.004, looking west. Scale 1m

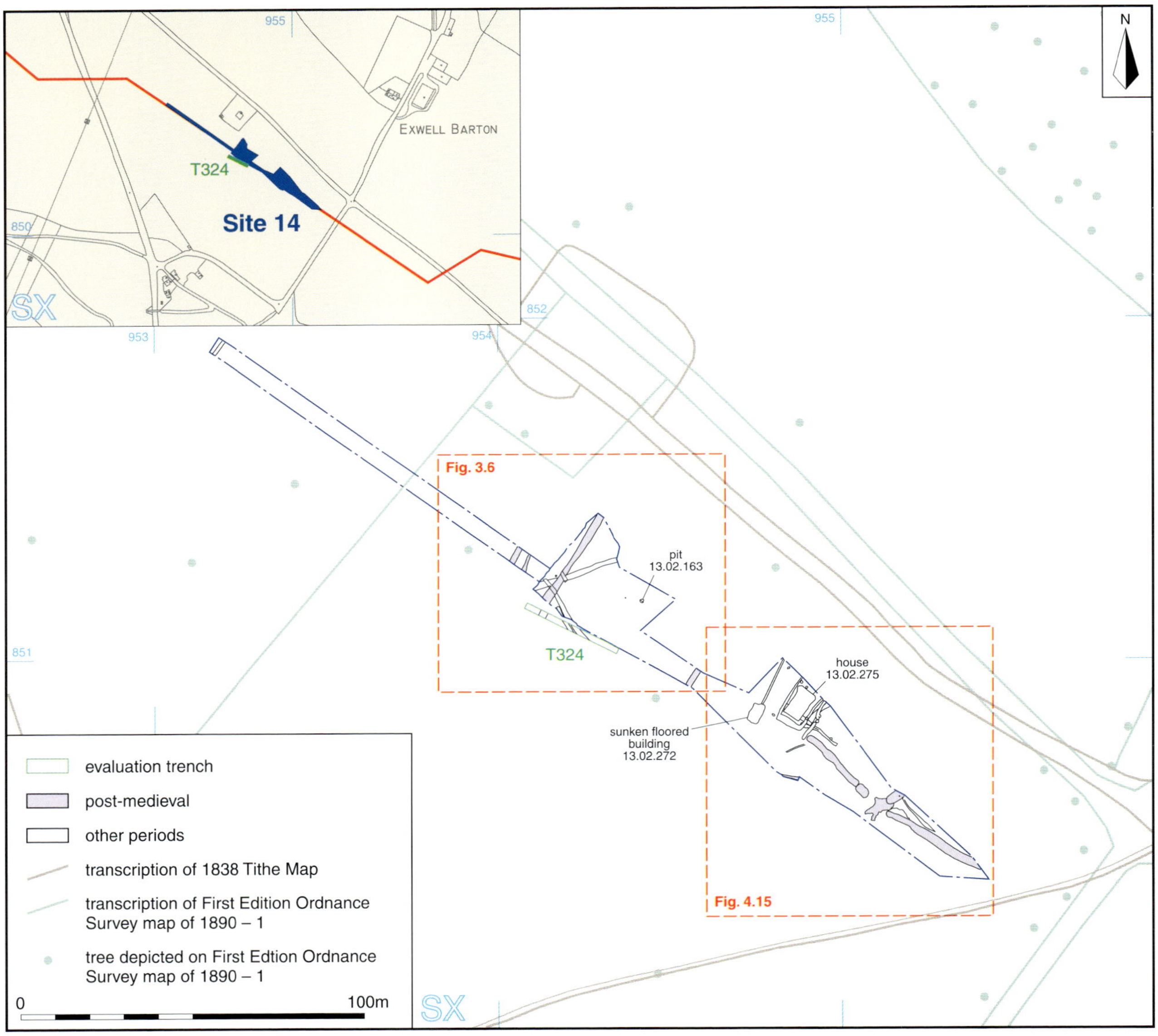

Fig. 4.14 Exwell Barton medieval settlement (Site 14); plan showing transcription from 1838 Tithe Map and First Edition Ordnance Survey map of 1890–1, and excavated features. Scales 1:2000 and 1:10,000

entailed the initial excavation of two trial trenches across the plot, and this was followed by area excavation where archaeological features had been identified.

The earliest features identified were ditches of probable Iron Age date, which are described above (Chapter 3). The principal occupation, however, related to the medieval period and comprised part of a domestic dwelling defined by a shallow gully with a floor and hearth surviving, and an adjacent sunken outbuilding which included the remains of two ovens/hearths in the base of the sunken area (Fig. 4.15). The main period of occupation is quite tightly defined by the pottery assemblage to the period AD 1250–1350, although the earliest phases of activity may have commenced in the late 12th or early 13th century. Later ditches and pits to the south-east of the dwelling have more limited dating evidence, generally of the 16th–18th centuries, although it appears that there was continuity in the general alignment of features. Cartographic evidence from the 19th century shows no trace of these earlier arrangements (Fig. 4.14: Tithe Map, Powderham 1838; OS first edition 1890–1).

?12th to 14th-century activity
There were features stratigraphically pre-dating the house and sunken building which may represent domestic occupation of a slightly earlier phase (Fig. 4.15). Ditches 13.02.067 and 13.02.270 were followed closely by the gullies of the later house, to the extent of providing a template for the later construction. It is possible that they defined house plots for which no real evidence of buildings remained. Nine sherds of pottery were recovered, two sherds of pottery were recovered from 13.02.270 and represent part of a green-glazed Saintonge jug, with seven sherds of pottery retrieved from 13.02.067, in a calcareous-tempered coarseware. These date generally to the 12th–14th centuries and provide the only dating evidence from these ditches. To the north-west the extremely straight narrow ditch 13.02.244 was also stratigraphically early and contained similar dating evidence. To the southeast, ditch 13.02.251 was stratigraphically early and in alignment with ditch 13.02.067. Underlying the house ditches and deposits was sub-oval pit 13.02.222, measuring 1.4m long, 1m wide and 0.37m deep. Its single fill, 13.02.223, contained two sherds of 12th to 14th-century pottery and it was cut by circular pit 13.02.228, measuring 0.5m in diameter and 0.18m deep. This contained a sequence of deliberately placed soils (13.02.229, 13.02.232, 13.02.233, 13.02.234) and was capped by stone deposit 13.02.224. Fills 13.02.232 and 13.02.233 contained a good assemblage of charred

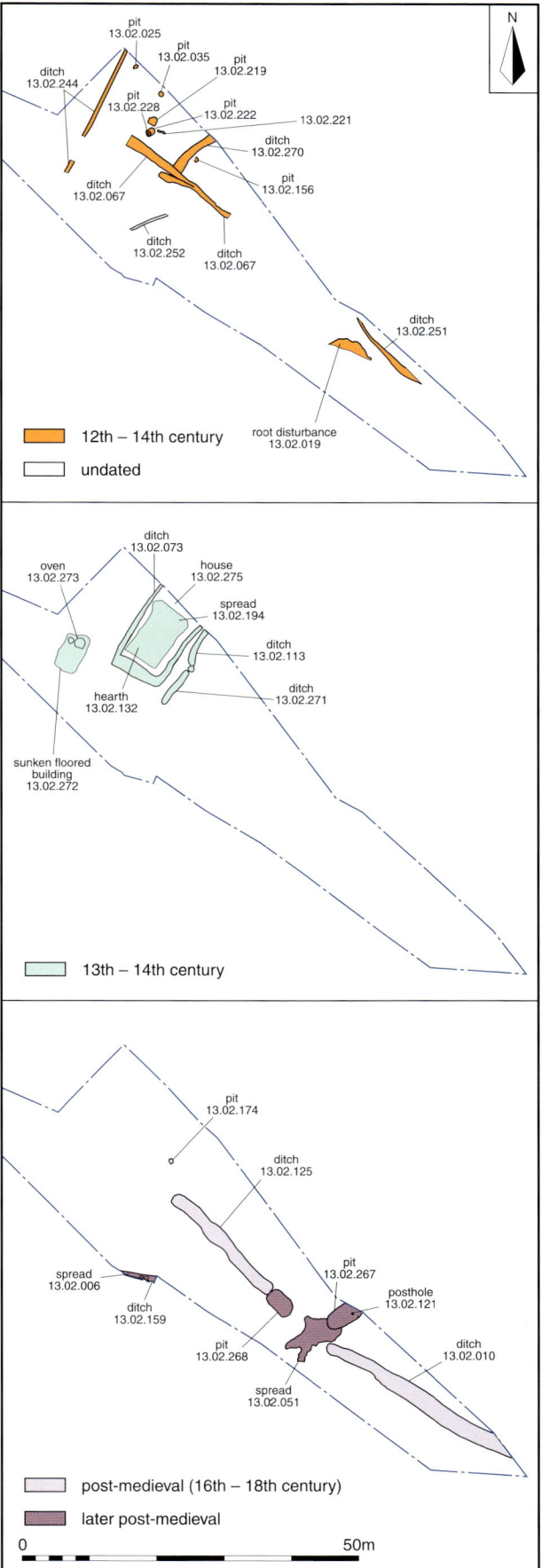

Fig. 4.15 Exwell Barton medieval settlement (Site 14); phased plan of excavated features. Scale 1:1000

crop waste, consisting of abundant amounts of rye, with some oats, barley, bread-type wheat and a possible large legume such as Celtic bean (Table 4.7, samples 163 and 164 respectively). Pit 13.02.219, nearby posthole 13.02.210 (not illustrated) and charcoal layer 13.02.221 also underlay the house, while pits 13.02.025 and 13.02.035, without stratigraphic relationships, may also be early. There is, therefore, the suggestion of a structure pre-dating the medieval house, but this cannot be defined with any precision.

13th to 14th-century construction and use of house and sunken outbuilding

The location of a house (13.02.275) was defined by a gully enclosing a rectangular area over 11m long and about 7m wide containing a beaten earth floor and a

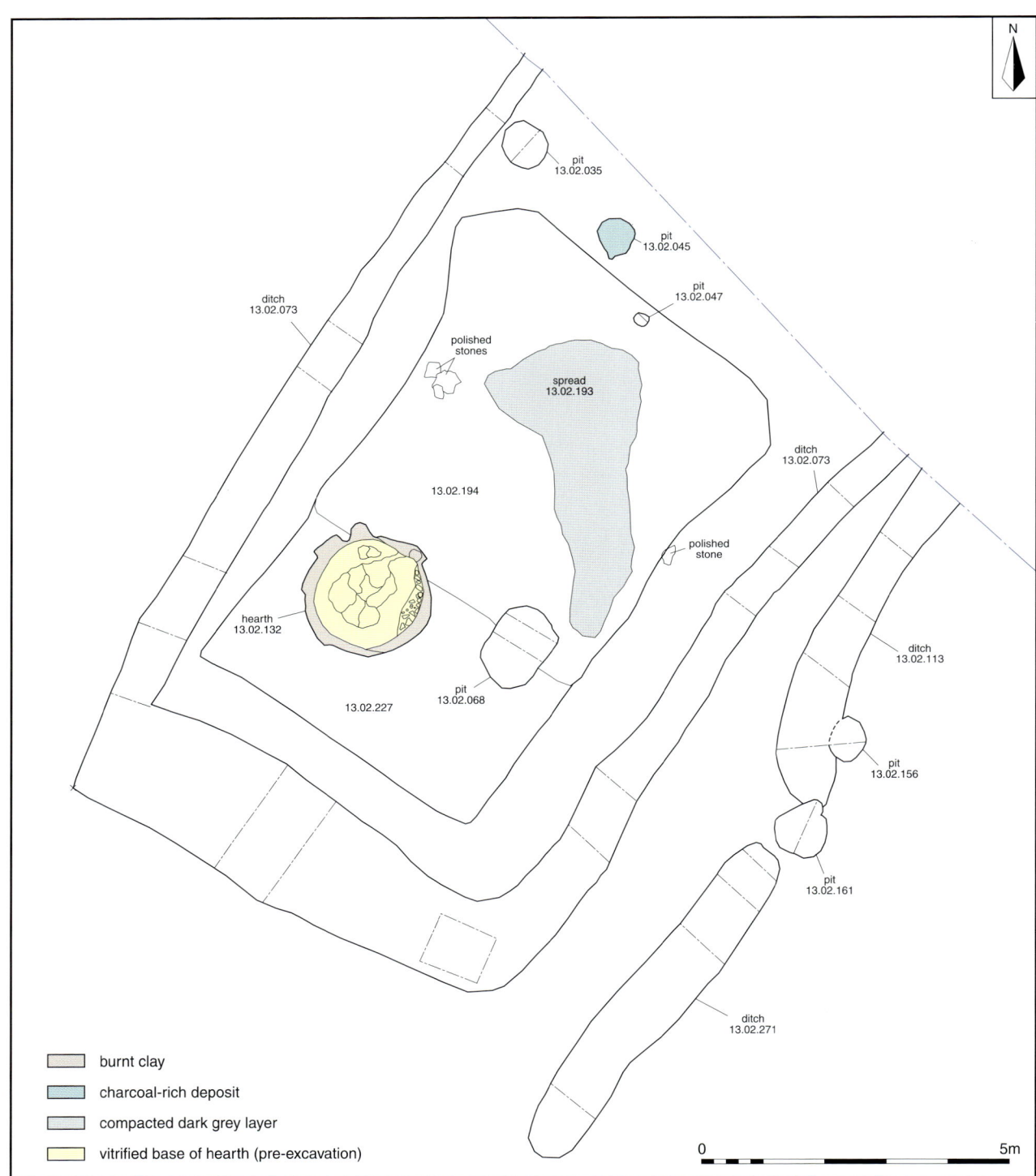

Fig. 4.16 Exwell Barton medieval building (Site 14); plan of excavated features. Scale 1:100

Fig. 4.17 Exwell Barton medieval building (Site 14); hearth 13.02.132, looking north-east. Scale 1m

large circular hearth (Fig. 4.16). The gully (13.02.073) varied in size from 0.4m to 2.0m wide and 0.1m to 0.3m deep. The widest section was at the western end of the feature, where its width may relate more to destruction activity than construction processes, although the regular profile would suggest otherwise. It may have been dug as an eaves drainage ditch, although in places it lay very close to the edge of floor 13.02.227 leaving little room for a wall. There was no evidence at all for the wall structure which may have been of cob laid directly on the subsoil or geological substrate, or on a low plinth which has since been truncated. The gully was contained on the south-east side by a linear arrangement of ditches 13.02.113 and 13.02.271, and pits 13.02.161 and 13.02.156.

Defined by the gully was a subrectangular area of compacted silty clay (13.02.194) and a slightly looser clay (13.02.227) which probably formed the original beaten earth floor. It lay within a slight hollow, about 0.25m deep, which may mean that it was deliberately constructed, although it is possible that the floor area had eroded through use forming a hollow. The floor may have been repaired and raised as needed, but there was no indication of successive repair horizons. The straight edges to the floor on its shorter sides suggest there may have been internal partitions here, thereby creating a room about 9m long. The width was generally about 5m although slightly wider at the northern end perhaps indicating the presence of a doorway here. Two pits, 13.02.035 and 13.02.045, have no stratigraphic association with the floor, but their position suggests they may have been part of an internal structural division. Pit 13.02.035 was 0.7m in diameter, 0.17m deep, circular in plan, with near vertical sides and a flat base. Pit 13.02.045 was 0.6m in diameter, 0.23m deep, circular in plan with steep sides and a relatively flat base. These two features may represent postholes but the evidence is not strong.

Towards the southern end of the room was a large circular hearth (13.02.132), 1.85m in diameter (Fig. 4.17). It had been carefully constructed in a pit 0.19m deep into which had been placed a layer of quartz rock (13.02.169). This was partly overlain by an outer ring of stones (13.02.168 and 13.02.190) which contained 193 sherds of 12th to 14th-century pottery as part of the make up. The stones were overlain by baked clay deposits 13.02.165 and 13.02.189 containing a further 1021 sherds of 13th to 14th-century pottery between them, weighing 6.78kg. It seems clear that broken pottery had been used as part of the structure of the hearth. This was covered by a layer of compact silt, 13.02.158. Another ring of stones, incorporating 115 sherds of 13th to 15th-century pottery, appears to represent a rebuilding of the hearth. This was sealed by

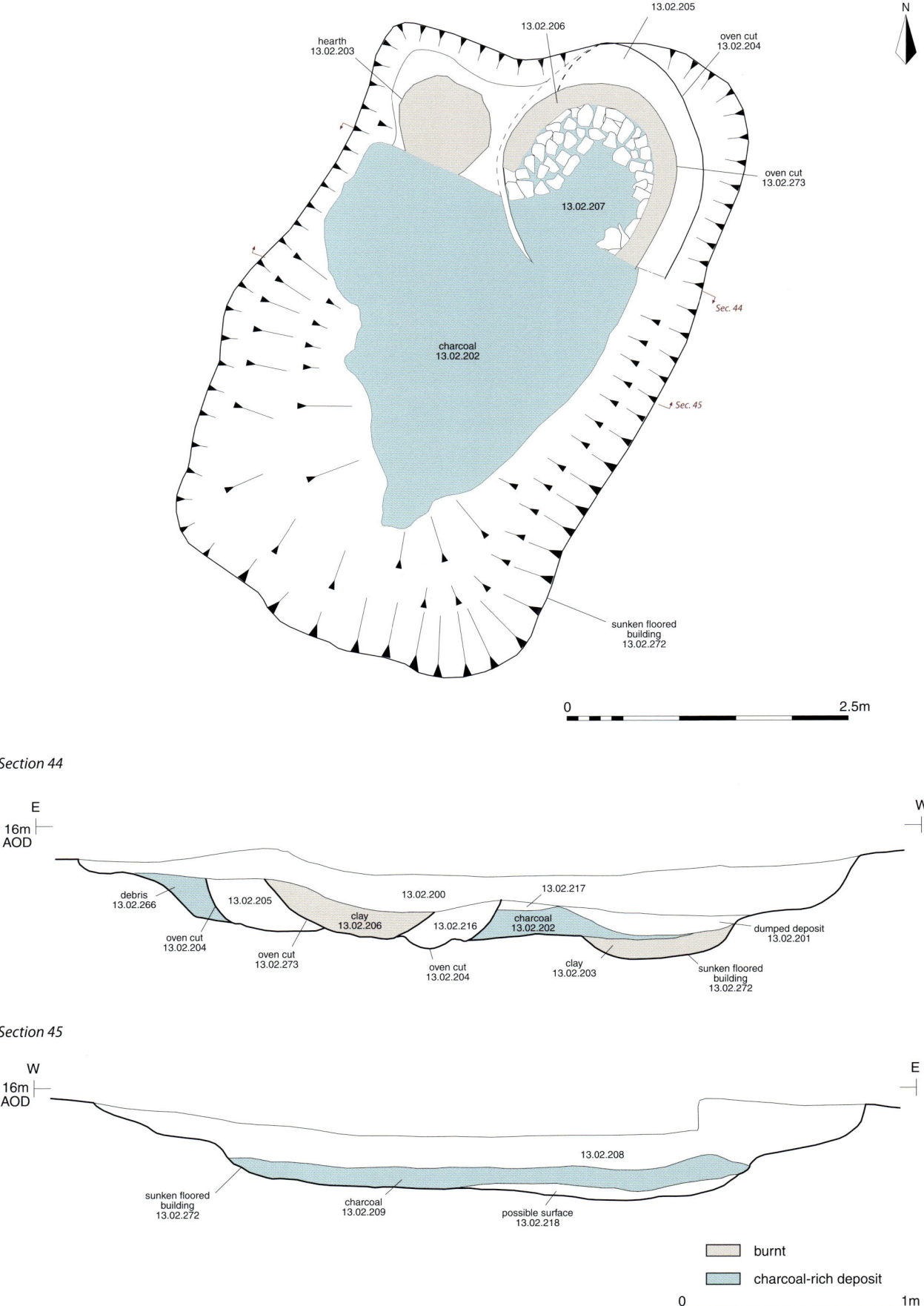

Fig. 4.18 Exwell Barton medieval settlement (Site 14); plan and sections of sunken-floored building 13.02.272. Scales 1:50 and 1:25

a baked clay layer 13.02.134/13.02.185, with a further 78 sherds of pottery, forming the functional surface of the hearth. The final hearth deposit was a mixed and degraded clay layer, 13.02.133, from the hearth's usage and abandonment.

To the side of the hearth was a lozenge-shaped pit 13.02.068, 0.18m deep with gently sloping sides and a flat base. No datable material was recovered from the single sandy silt fill. It did not have any distinctive characteristics and its function remains unknown. North of the hearth, layer 13.02.193 was a dark red brown silty sand representing the eroded floor layer mixed with occupation debris.

To the west of the medieval house was sunken building 13.02.272 (Fig. 4.18). Although no walls survived, the footprint and remains of a building dating from the later 13th to 14th centuries AD were apparent. Three possible phases of construction were identified. The first phase construction of the building took the form of a shallow rectangular pit 6m long, 4m wide and up to 0.4m deep. The sides were steep, but not vertical, and had a gentle break of slope suggesting a degree of weathering of the pit sides. Also belonging to this first phase of construction, and cut into the base of the pit, the earliest feature identified within the kitchen was hearth 13.02.203. This consisted of a localised area of burnt orange clay and charcoal, 0.68m in diameter. The lack of evidence for a superstructure, despite its location in the base of the pit, suggests that it was a simple hearth. To the south of the hearth, charcoal-rich layer 13.02.202 was probably an associated rake-out deposit. Overlying this was silty levelling deposit 13.02.217 and sandy silt deposit 13.02.201 (Fig. 4.18, section 44). The later deposit was seemingly deliberately placed in order to seal hearth 13.02.203, perhaps in preparation for the second phase of construction.

A possible floor surface, 13.02.218, comprising silty clay, partially survived in the centre of the building and belongs to this second phase of construction. It appears to have overlain the charcoal-rich spread, but this was barely evident in section (Fig.4.18, section 45). During this phase the building appears to have been enlarged in its north-eastern corner to accommodate a second phase hearth or oven (13.02.204). From the bulge the oven makes in the plan of the sunken building there is the suggestion that the entire footprint of the building was enlarged during this phase, but there was no other evidence for this. Little evidence for hearth/oven 13.02.204 survives, beyond the original cut. The structure appears to have been deliberately removed and no layers could be definitively attributed to its usage. Deposits 13.02.205 and 13.02.215 fill the void which would have been left after the hearth removal, and may represent redeposited layers associated with either hearth 13.02.203 or 13.02.204.

Located in the north-eastern corner of the building, and partially superimposed upon the footprint of hearth 13.02.204, was an almost circular oven (13.02.273), c. 1.7m in diameter (Fig. 4.19). This represents a third phase of construction or alteration within the building. The oven was cut into the floor of the pit and also cut through charcoal deposits 13.02.205, and 13.02.215 (not illustrated). The oven was constructed upon a floor of small local stones (13.02.235) which overlay fire-reddened natural sand. The clay oven wall (13.02.206), comprising heat-affected clay, had been raised on the edge of the stone floor and survived to a height of 0.25m. It is probable that the newly constructed oven was deliberately placed away from the building wall, with deposit 13.02.205 either left or deliberately placed to act as insulation between the oven and the edge of the structure/walls. The transference of heat from the oven to the walls may have been the reason for the short-lived nature of the second hearth/oven, 13.02.204. The charcoal from deposit 13.02.205 (Table 4.9, Sample 161) showed that oak and hazel wood were the main

Fig. 4.19 Exwell Barton medieval settlement (Site 14); view of hearth 13.02.203 (far) and oven 13.02.273 (near), looking north-west. Scale 0.5m

fuels, with gorse, alder and birch also present and perhaps used as kindling. The charred seeds were dominated by oats and corn marigold, with smaller amounts of rye and barley, as well as other weeds. Covering the oven, deposit 13.02.207 contained fragments of fired clay probably from the collapsed superstructure of the oven, or possibly representing the eroded base of the oven. The earlier hearth, 13.02.203, was of a different form and presumably of different function to the oven, although the range of charred plant remains was very similar (Table 4.7, samples 161, 157). Charcoal-rich silty deposit 13.02.209 probably represents the rake-out from the oven. An orange-brown sandy silt layer (13.02.200/13.02.208) overlay all the deposits within the footprint of the building and represented the disuse phase.

There appeared to be no features or finds relating to the superstructure of the building and the construction materials and methods are not clear. It is possible that the building was of cob, although there was no evidence for this in the backfill, and it is perhaps just as likely that the walls were of wood and constructed on a shallow plinth or beam slot that has since been lost to the plough. There was no indication of a wall within the pit and the closeness of the oven to the pit edge indicates that the wall line can be assumed to have lain outside. Similarly, there was no indication of a doorway.

Interpretation
There is no doubt that structure 13.02.275 is a house and the large quantity of pottery, particularly from hearth 13.02.132, indicates a date of use in the later 13th to 14th centuries AD. While the complete plan of the building was not present in the excavation area, it may be suggested that the area uncovered would have been the domestic end of a longhouse, with the shippon lying to the north, which is slightly downhill from the domestic area, as is typical for this type of building, allowing animal waste to be channelled away from the living area. The form of construction is not clear as the walls did not survive. It is possible that there was a cob wall between the floor and the outer gully, but this would have been narrow (*c*. 0.3m) on the western side, and perhaps even narrower than shown, factoring in a degree of vertical truncation of the gully and floor edge. Alternatively, it is possible that the gully was a foundation trench for wooden posts, or a horizontal beam supporting timber uprights, and thus represents the wall line. It is difficult to account for the variation in gully dimensions if it were a foundation trench, although it can be noted that, since it was without evidence for post emplacements, the ultimate form of the trench may well have undergone modifications at its demise, for example, had the posts been withdrawn rather than left to rot *in situ*.

The sunken outbuilding 13.02.272 (Fig. 4.20), with evidence for two adjacent ovens/hearths, is similar to examples from elsewhere in the county which are sometimes termed corn drying buildings. It is possible that hearth 13.02.203 was actually a demolished oven and the stratigraphic evidence shows that it was earlier than oven 13.02.273, although it is not entirely clear that it was replaced by it. It is very similar in plan to other dual-featured buildings where it is suggested or assumed that both hearths/ovens were in use together for different purposes (Henderson and Weddell 1996,

Fig. 4.20 Exwell Barton medieval settlement (Site 14), sunken-floored building 13.02.272, looking south-west. Scale 1m

fig. 9). There is no clear indication of their functions. The charred material from the features was quite similar in composition, although it can be noted that the weeds from layer 13.02.202 in particular (sample 161) associated with the first phase of hearth or oven 13.02.203 perhaps indicates primary crop processing being undertaken. Otherwise it is possible that the building was used mostly to dry already cleaned grain to preserve it and harden it for milling (Cobain, this report). In this case the oven would probably have been heated with wood and once the fuel had been burnt the ash would have been swept out and the grain put inside to dry.

Outlying field boundary ditches and pits

There was one medieval pit, 13.02.163, which lay at distance north-west of the medieval dwelling (Figs 3.6, 4.14). It contained pottery of general 13th to 15th-century date and cereal remains similar to those from the house and sunken kitchen (Table 4.6, sample 103).

An approximately rectilinear pattern of field ditches is apparent, several of them undated (Fig. 3.6; ditches 13.02.256, 13.02.274, 13.02.127 and 13.02.254), but those south-east of the medieval house containing post-medieval pottery (Fig. 4.15; ditches 13.02.125, 13.02.010). The ditches ranged in width from 1m to 2.5m, with concave profiles 0.25m to 0.5m deep, and clean sandy fills. A relatively small finds assemblage, comprising six sherds of 16th to 18th-century pottery and two sherds of residual medieval pottery, was recovered from the ditches, associated pits 13.02.268, 13.02.267 and clay spread 13.02.051. It is entirely possible that elements of this field system have their origins in the medieval or earlier periods.

Ditch 13.02.159, dated to the 18th century or later by two sherds of pottery, does not appear to be part of this pattern but is of interest as it contained a large deposit of cockle shells, as well as small pieces of animal bone in its upper fill (13.02.006) (Geber, Warman and Taylor, below).

Site 29: Pit at Bluepost, Harberton

The site lies on a south-facing slope at 118m OD, 0.4km south-west of Bluepost Farm and 0.6km north-west of the hamlet of Kerswill (Fig. 4.21). The only feature encountered was a small sub-circular pit 19.07.004, surviving to dimensions of 0.42m in diameter and 0.1m deep. The single fill, 19.07.005, was a charcoal-rich red-brown silty clay. A soil sample (Table 4.7, sample 312) contained an assemblage of oats and rye, together with gorse spines, bracken fragments and burnt twine. This may have been a bale of livestock fodder that had been burnt and buried. A radiocarbon date in the range of cal. AD 1018–1155 (NZA-36171) was returned from a sample of rye grain (Table 4.2).

There were no other features within the 6m-wide strip across this field and the feature does not appear to be related to settlement. It lies within an area of landscape characterised by medieval enclosures (Devon County Council/English Heritage Historic Landscape Characterisation) close to the historical parish boundary between Harberton and South Brent, which is formed by an unnamed brook to the south-west, and at distance from present or historical settlement. A similar, but

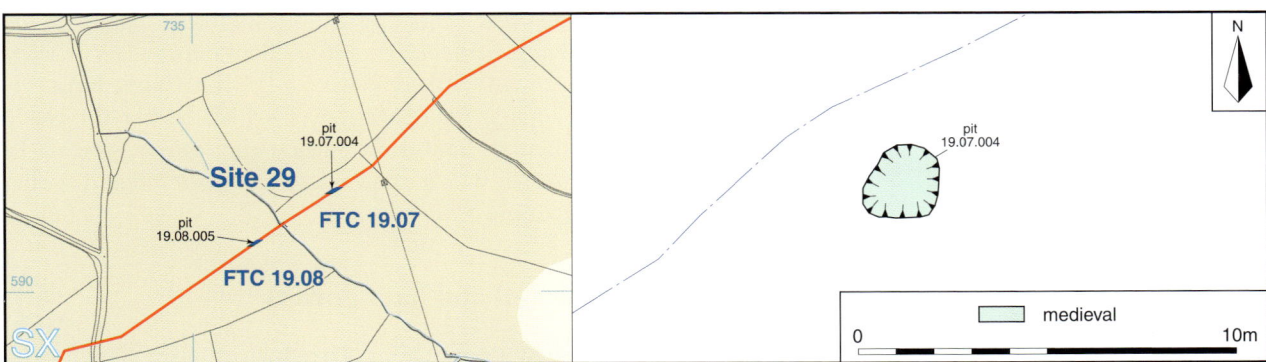

Fig. 4.21 Bluepost (Site 29); plan of pit 19.07.004. Scales 1:50 and 1:10,000

Table 4.2: Radiocarbon date from Bluepost, Site 29 (FTC 19.07)

Feature	Context	Lab No.	Material	δ ^{13}C	Radiocarbon Age	Calibrated Date 95%	Calibrated Date 68%
Pit 19.07.004	19.07.005	NZA 36171	Rye grain (*Secale cereale*)	-21.7‰	970 ± 25 yr BP	1018–58 AD (38.4%) plus 1070–1155 AD (56.6%)	1022–46 AD (31.8%) plus 1093–1121 AD (28.9%) plus 1141–8 AD (6.7%)

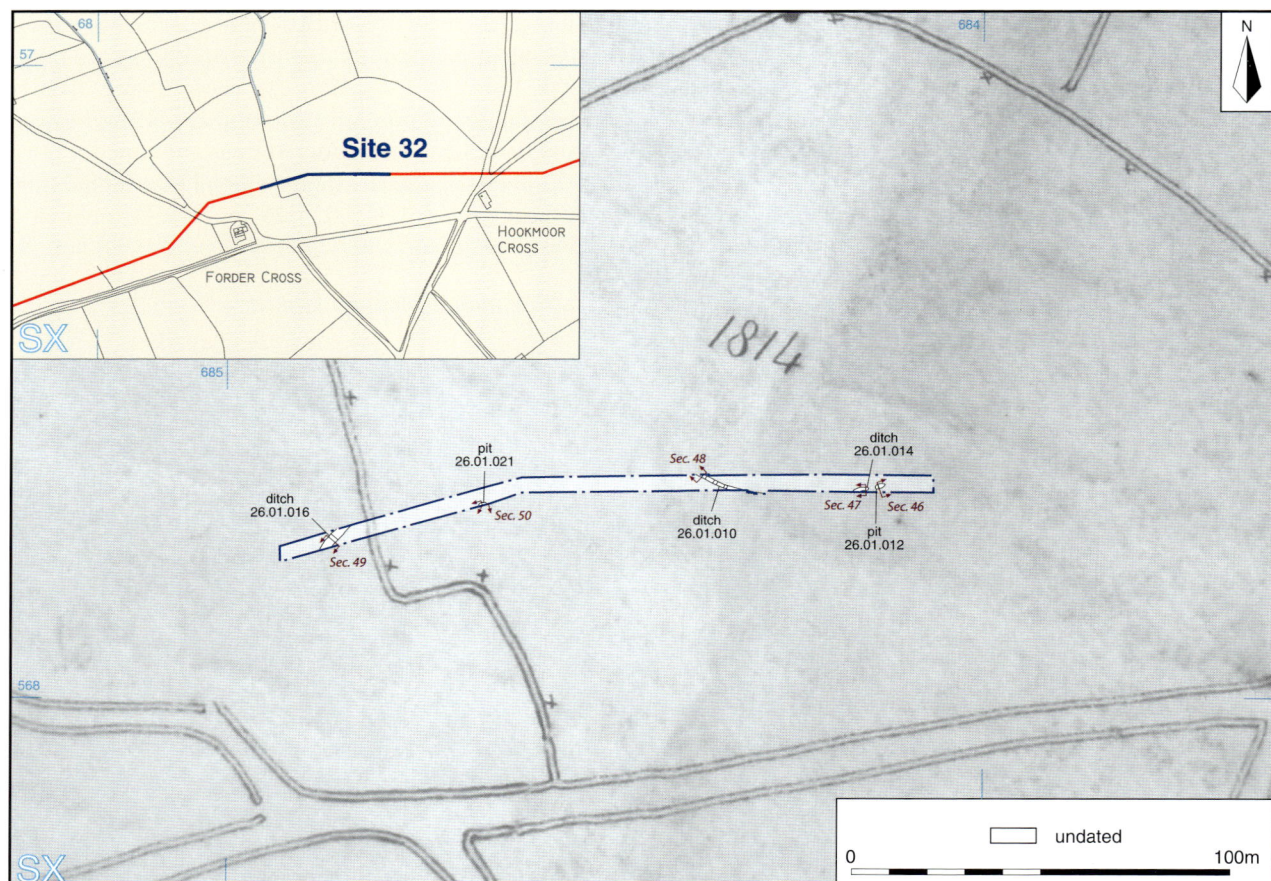

Fig. 4.22 Forder Cross (Site 32); extract from 1843 Tithe Map, showing excavated features. Scales 1:2000 and 1:10,000

undated, pit on the other side of the brook (FTC 19.08, pit 19.08.005) contained charred remains that included gorse and sloe/plum charcoal but was without cereal remains. This would also appear to relate to agricultural activities carried out in the fields, perhaps related to weed or brash clearance.

Site 32: Occupation at Forder Cross, Ugborough

The site lay on high ground between Hookmoor Cross and Forder Cross on the ridge south of Lud Brook (Fig. 4.22). The 3m-wide soil strip through this plot revealed a number of pits and ditches, most of which remain undated. Near the centre of the plot, however, curving ditch 26.01.010, which was 1.10m wide and 0.33m deep, contained 41 sherds (64g) of medieval pottery and a single sherd of 16th–17th century pottery from single fill 26.01.005 (not illustrated). This suggests occupation of some form nearby. To the east, curvilinear ditch terminus 26.01.014 was 0.8m wide and 0.32m deep with an irregular profile while nearby pit 26.01.012 was 1.2m wide and 0.18m deep (Fig. 4.23, sections 46, 47). In the western part of the site pit 26.01.021 was only partly revealed, but was 2.0m across and 0.5m deep (Fig. 4.23, section 50). Further west still, ditch 26.01.016 was a substantial 2.0m wide and 0.85m deep (Fig. 4.23, section 49).

A plot of these features on the 1843 Tithe Map of Ugborough shows that they are not accounted for by the mapped fields and it appears likely that there are surviving elements of a pre-modern occupation or series of occupations here (Fig. 4.22). The mapped curving and angular field boundaries, which largely survive in the modern landscape, suggest the former presence of enclosures which may relate to medieval and earlier occupation.

Medieval and later pottery

John Allan, with a contribution from Roger T. Taylor

Introduction

The medieval and later ceramics from all three lengths of the pipeline were submitted to the author for reporting. The most significant assemblage by far is that from the small medieval house and sunken outbuilding near Exwell Barton (Site 14), which is the most substantial sample of the ceramics of a medieval lowland rural site excavated so far in Devon. It offers interesting comparisons both with the broadly contemporary urban assemblages from nearby Exeter and with the pottery

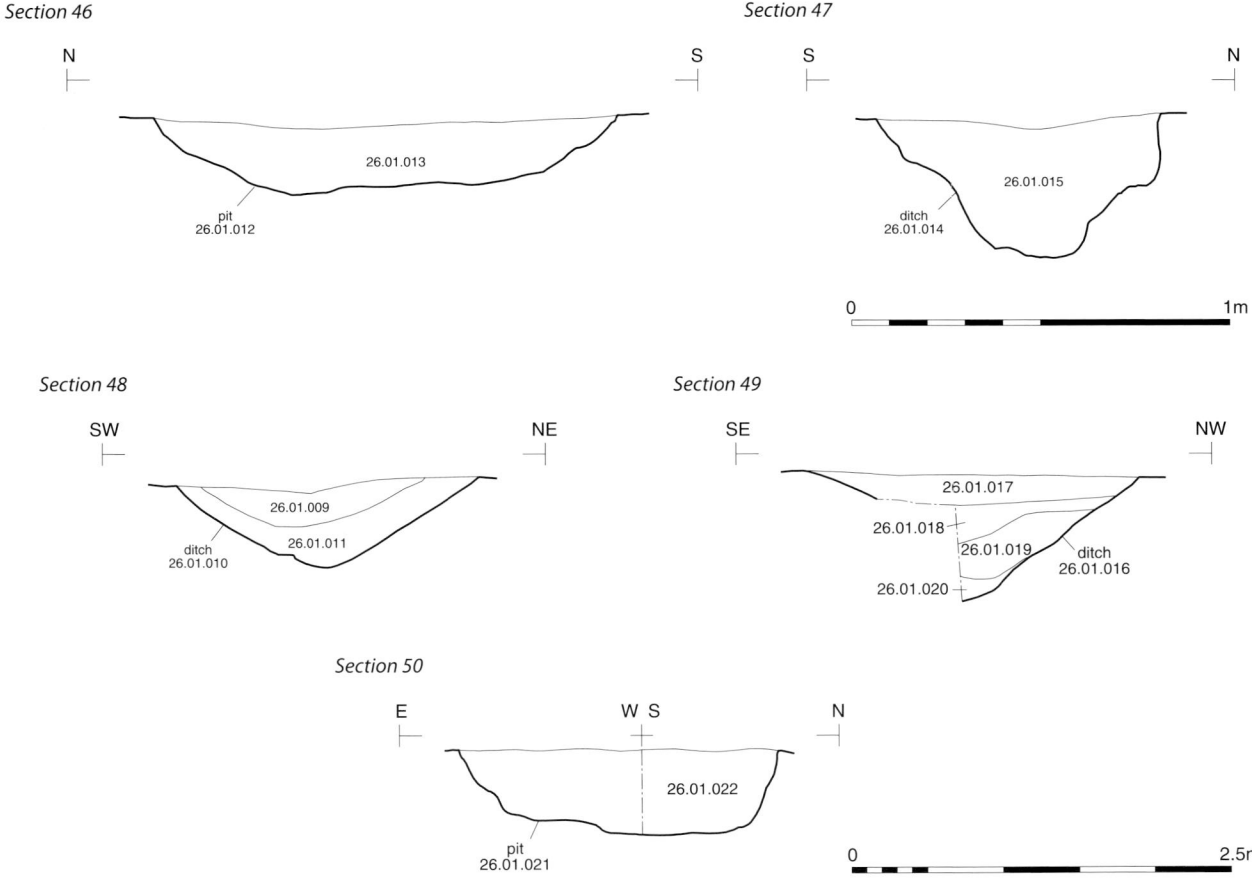

Fig. 4.23 Forder Cross (Site 32); sections 46 to 50. Scales 1:20 and 1:50

from deserted medieval settlements on Dartmoor and Exmoor which, like the Exwell Barton house, probably represent the peasantry.

The sherds from the other sites consist largely of unstratified fragments recovered during initial fieldwalking and topsoil stripping. The fact that they are unstratified limits their value, but the material is nevertheless of interest since it includes a scatter of late medieval and early modern imported ceramics, with a few unusual vessels in local pottery.

Methodology

Sherd counts, weights, minimum vessel numbers and forms were recorded for each fabric and each context; an MS Excel spreadsheet listing the entire collection is deposited in the site archive. In the case of the Exwell Barton finds, Dr Taylor has once more undertaken petrological analyses; his work is steadily building up a database of the petrology of the region's pottery which is throwing much new light on this material.

The medieval house at Exwell Barton, Powderham (Site 14)

This important assemblage, scattered among many contexts within, around and over the small medieval house, amounts to 3160 sherds. No chronological distinctions were detected among the finds from different contexts; therefore the material is discussed in its entirety.

Fabrics
The following fabrics are represented in the collection:
- *Fabric 1.* Upper-Greensand-Derived (UGSD) ware. The standard unglazed hand-made medieval coarseware of South Somerset and East Devon, with inclusions of flint, chert, silicified shell, soft red limonite and polished quartz. This fabric has been the subject of much recent research, which has shown that it was made on the fringes of the Blackdown Hills and was widely distributed in south-west England (Allan *et al.* 2010; forthcoming).
- *Fabric 2.* 'Membury-type' ware, as defined in Allan and Langman 2002: hand-made unglazed coarseware, typically with mid-brown surfaces, the fabric with numerous vesicles, almost certainly representing the former presence of much limestone, alongside the range of Upper Greensand-Derived inclusions seen in fabric 1. Visual matching to the Membury material is confirmed by Dr Taylor's petrological study (below).
- *Exeter fabrics 40 and 42.* The two most common fabrics of wheel-thrown jugs in the Exeter area, the first a very fine sand-tempered ware, the second with rather coarser inclusions, both usually fired red or orange-red. Defined in Allan 1984a, 4–6; described in thin-section by Brown and Vince (1984) and by Taylor (below).

- *Possible Bristol sherd.* A single small sherd from a wheel-thrown jug, with a light grey fabric and mottled pale green glaze is not a local South Devon ware and may be from Bristol.
- *French wares.* Sherds from several Saintonge green-glazed jugs and a single probable Breton vessel, described individually below.

The quantities, proportions and forms of these wares are shown in Table 4.3.

Table 4.3: Total quantities of pottery from the Exwell Barton medieval settlement (Site 14)

Fabric	No. of Sherds	Min. No. Vessels	Forms
Saintonge green-glazed	78 (2.5%)	5+	Jugs
Basic igneous, Breton?	2 (0.06%)	1	–
Exeter fabric 40	14 (0.4%)	2+	Jugs
Exeter fabric 42	23 (0.7%)	3+	Jugs
?Hampshire	1	1	Jug
Bristol?	1 (0.03%)	1	Jug
Fabric 1: Upper Greensand	2507 (79%)	?30+	Jars
Fabric 2: 'Membury-type'	534 (17%)	?10+	Jars
Total	**3160**	**c. 52++**	

Dating

The ware forming most of the collection (fabric 1) has a very wide date range; it was first produced in the late 10th century and continued little changed into the mid-14th century or later (e.g. Allan 1984a, 4–90). Over this long period there was little technological change, and thus featureless bodysherds are assignable only to a very wide date range. Some typological developments have been distinguished, however, both in the overall vessel form (evident only when vessels are more complete than the Exwell Barton specimens) and in some rim forms, notably the widespread use of the cupped jar (i.e. cooking pot) rim after the mid-13th century. The presence of several examples of these rims at Exwell Barton indicates that a sizeable fraction of the coarsewares belongs in the period *c.* 1250–1350. The presence of many other examples of cupped rims in fabric 2 points to the same conclusion; these too have been found in association with wares of *c.* 1250–1350 (Allan and Langman 2002). By the late 14th century these long-lived types apparently lost their dominance as new forms and fabrics were introduced (see for example the Exeter group Trichay Street 169: Allan 1984a, 87–9). These are absent from the Exwell Barton assemblage; it therefore seems unlikely that the assemblage dates after 1350.

All the finewares but one belong to the period after the mid-13th century. The Saintonge wares arrived in England from *c.* 1250; the main period of their importation was the following century. The local jug fabrics 40 and 42 came into circulation at the same time, and likewise continued in circulation into the 15th century. The possible exception is the Breton sherd. All the other examples of this fabric recorded so far from Exeter have come from deposits of *c.* 1200–50 (Allan 1984a, 7); it is unknown whether importation of this type of pottery was restricted to this period.

A further suggestion that some of the pottery is earlier than *c.* 1250 is the presence of oxidised sherds of fabric 1 (catalogue nos 5 and 12 below). Towards the end of the 12th century oxidised vessels become much less frequent in this material, and the typical appearance of pottery is grey. Inevitably there were exceptions, so their presence is not a firm pointer to an earlier date.

In summary, then, the house was certainly occupied in the period 1250–1350, and a starting date for the settlement in the late 12th or early 13th century is possible. There is, however, no sign of the distinctive Saxo-Norman forms or decorative styles of the late 10th, 11th and early 12th centuries, nor of tripod pitchers or other wares distinctive of the mid-12th to early 13th century. The pottery would be consistent with abandonment of the settlement at the Black Death, or in one of the preceding calamities of the early 14th century.

Discussion

Fully 96% of the assemblage (by sherd count) consists of hand-made coarsewares made around the fringes of the Blackdown Hills. The striking rarity of glazed wares (3.7% of sherds) contrasts markedly with the picture at nearby Exeter, where such wares are seven or eight times more common in a large sample of contemporary ceramics (28% by sherd count in a total of 2774 sherds in the seven largest published pit groups of *c.* 1250–1350: Allan 1984a, 79–88, groups GS 135, 215, 256; TS 215; QS 112; NS 11–12; for quantification of data see Allan and Langman 1997b). In this regard the Exwell Barton assemblage is typical of rural sites in the South West; glazed wares form 1% or less of many assemblages on or around the fringes of Dartmoor (the largest Okehampton Park 0.5% of 10,187 sherds: Allan 1978, 234; Sourton Down 0.3% of 6243 sherds: Allan and Langman 1997a, 83; for other sites see Allan 1994, 141–4), although there are some exceptions such as the Dinna Clerks longhouse where they are more plentiful. This pronounced contrast between rural and urban finds suggests that at this date there was a basic distinction between the households they represent. Since the most likely use of most of the unglazed coarseware was for cooking, a likely explanation is that many or most urban households had already adopted the use of metal cooking pots, whereas most peasants, whether near Exeter or on Dartmoor, continued to use pottery.

Among the coarseware sherds the predominance of fabric 1 will occasion little surprise, since this ware made up almost all the hand-made pottery of contemporary deposits in Exeter, and was very common throughout east Devon. The strong showing of Membury-type ware – more than 500 sherds forming 17% of the assemblage – is however remarkable, since this fabric is far less common on other local sites. For example, in the Exeter groups of *c.* 1250–1350 quoted above, Membury-type ware forms 1.7% of coarsewares and 1.2% of all sherds – less than a tenth of the proportion at Exwell Barton (Allan and Langman 1997b). This is unlikely to be a matter of chance or of personal preference. Since Exwell Barton enjoyed easy access to the shore nearby, a likely explanation is that the Membury-type ware was brought in by boat; some other low-value goods shipped by coast, such as some building stones and the Dutch bricks discussed below, were likewise far more common around the Exe Estuary than they were in Exeter. Membury ware appears to have been made on the east Devon side of the Blackdowns, perhaps close to Membury itself. It seems likely that this ware was transported to Exwell Barton by coastal shipping, perhaps from the Axminster area, just as Donyatt pottery was brought overland to Lyme Regis in the 17th and 18th centuries for transport by sea to Plymouth (Allan 1983, 41).

Although the glazed jugs form a relatively small proportion of the total assemblage, they too indicate the significance of maritime trade at Exwell Barton. This is apparent from the contrast between the rural house and Exeter, only 8km inland from Exwell Barton. Saintonge wares imported from south-western France are represented in all substantial pit groups of this period from the city, but in every instance they are strongly outnumbered by locally made jugs, which are almost four times more common than imports in the groups cited above. It is difficult to determine quite how many vessels are represented among the 78 Saintonge sherds scattered around the Exwell Barton house, but there are probably appreciably more than the five vessels distinguished here. By sherd count, Saintonge jugs are about twice as common at the settlement as the local jugs of the Exeter area. Since Saintonge wares, with their associations with the Bordeaux wine trade, have commonly been claimed as evidence of the exalted status of the occupants of sites where they are found, the humble form of the Exwell Barton house is an interesting reminder that these wares may have been common in some coastal locations simply because transport by sea was cheap. A parallel may be drawn with the Saintonge wares on most sites on the Isles of Scilly, whose inhabitants were clearly poor but where Saintonge wares were used in considerable quantities (Allan 1991).

Illustrated catalogue (Fig. 4.24)

1 Sherds from the base, lower and upper body, wheel-thrown handle and rim of a Saintonge jug or jugs (almost certainly several vessels). Usual fine white fabric with some very fine white mica inclusions, some with clear water-worn quartz and iron oxide pellets; mottled green glaze on each sherd except the handle. The rim displays one edge of an applied beak spout; the body has an applied vertical thumbed strip, and the lower part of a graffito is scratched on the handle after firing. The last feature is seen on many Saintonge jugs (e.g. the fine collection from Wood Quay, Dublin: McCutcheon 2006, 114–19; others from Southampton, Hull and Exeter: Platt and Coleman-Smith 1975, 144, Nos 1036, 1043, 1046; Watkins 1978; Allan 1984a, 84, 90, 94, nos 1381, 1464, 1567). It has been proposed (McCutcheon 2006, 114–15) that such graffiti were 'owners' marks', but since they are a distinctive feature of Saintonge jugs and are hardly ever seen on other types of medieval pottery, it seems more likely that they were added prior to arrival in Britain – perhaps, for example as batch marks representing the output of a particular kiln. Although this baluster form, with thumbed vertical strips, was made over a long period (*c.* 1250–1450), Watkins (1983, 249–50) noted evidence from Hull and Southampton that it was especially common in the late 13th century. (Handle: 13.02.002, subsoil. Base: layer 13.02.054. Rim: 13.02.112: group 8, final fill of ditch 13.02.270; layer 13.02.242)

2 Two unglazed bodysherds from the lower part of a vessel, uncertain whether wheel-thrown, perhaps a jar. Pale orange-buff surfaces and core, the fabric containing much fine white mica and a few glistening golden plates, characteristic of mica schists, described by Taylor below. The sherds offer a good visual match to Exeter fabric 103 (Allan 1984a, 7) for which a Breton source has seemed probable – a conclusion reinforced by Dr Taylor's discussion (below). Internal sooting towards the bottom of the pot, perhaps indicating some specialist form of vessel usage. (13.02.002, subsoil)

3 Jug rim and handle, Exeter fabric 40, with traces of green-brown glaze. Flat handles with knife-stabbing are typical of this fabric; the triple rows of stabbing are less common than single rows, and are a feature of the wide, thick handles used on especially large jugs (e.g. Allan 1984a, 89, No. 1451). (13.02.062, fill of ditch 13.02.073)

4 Rod handle, redware with fine quartz sand temper, with traces of thin mid-green glaze. Perhaps a regional import from south-central England. (13.02.136, hearth 13.02.132)

5 Fabric 1 with oxidised surfaces and simple upright rim, possibly 12th- or early 13th-century. (13.02.202, group 10, use of oven 13.02.273)

6–15 Rims of fabric 1 from central hearth 13.02.132 of house. (6, 9–11, 15 from baked clay of central hearth 13.02.189; 7–8 from 13.02.190, preceding deposit of stones around hearth; 12, oxidised, from pit 13.02.035, set 50; 13 from 13.02.148, fill of ditch 13.02.127; 14 from 13.02.054, unstratified)

16–18 Rims of fabric 2 (Membury ware), with pitted surfaces resulting from weathering out of calcareous inclusions; all sooted externally. (16 from 13.02.168; 17–18 from 13.02.189, both baked clay of central hearth 13.02.132)

Pottery from other sites

East Devon: Aylesbeare to Kenn pipeline
A total of 124 sherds, including post-medieval imports, come from sites close to the Exe Estuary.

Catalogue (Fig. 4.24)

19 Rim of a small tin-glazed bowl, the soft cream fabric without gross inclusions, and with plain white glaze. Seville plain ware *escudilla*, 16th or early 17th-century. There are many similar bowls in the town refuse deposit at Castle Street, Plymouth, which dates mainly to the period after *c.* 1580 (Allan 1995, 310, nos 84–7 with slightly straighter sides). (Plot ATK 12.09, unstratified)

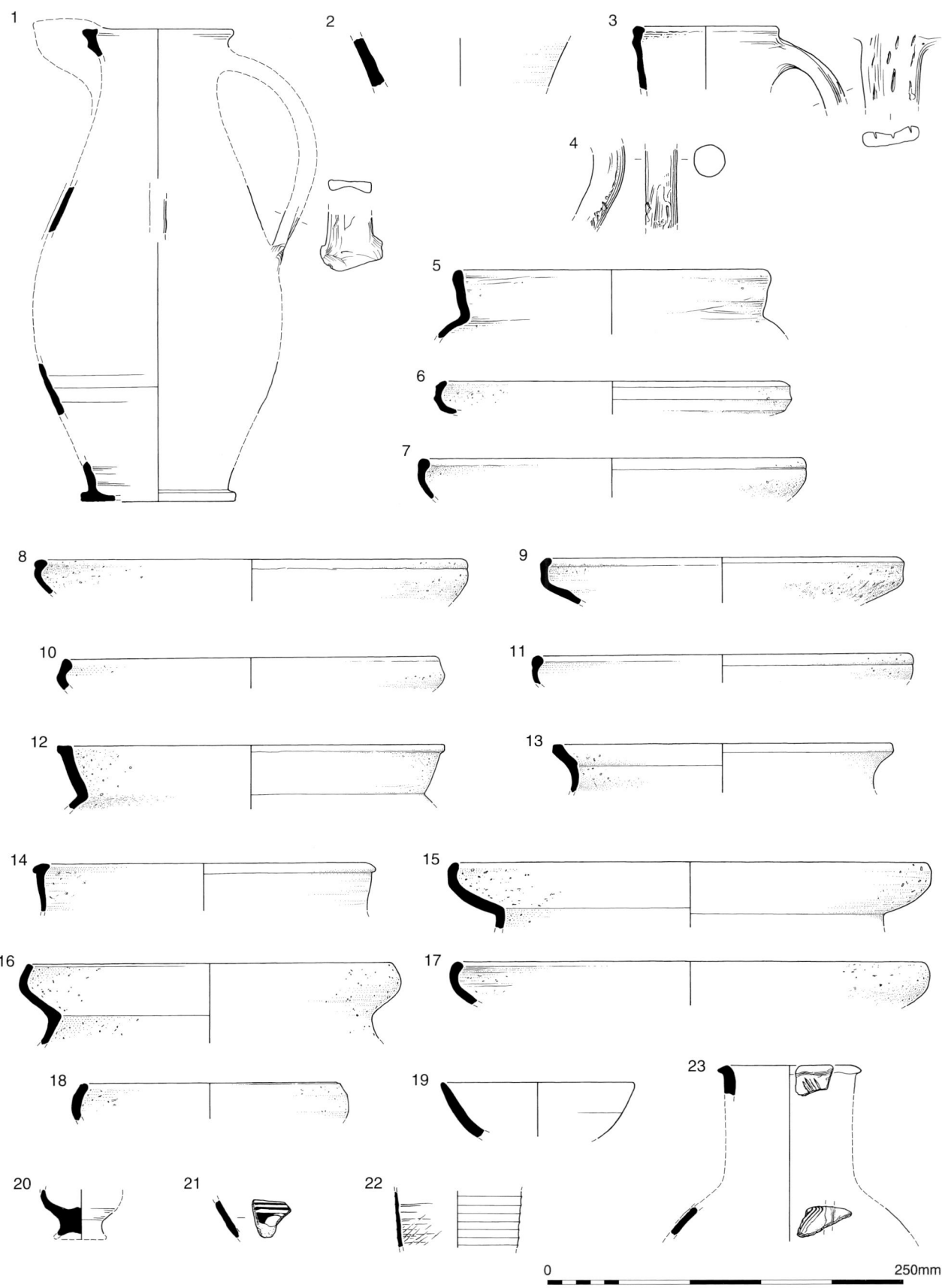

Fig. 4.24 Medieval and later pottery. Scale 1:4

20 Fine unglazed white ware vessel with a few fine iron oxide inclusions. Unclear whether a lid or a base. Source uncertain, possibly a Saintonge import, although the fabric contains no visible mica. (ATK 13.02.002, subsoil)

21 Werra slipware sherd, from a small bowl rather than the more common dish. Fine red-fawn fabric with very fine mica inclusions, distinctive parallel slipware bands above trailed slip motif outlined with sgraffito line, glazed orange-brown over body, greenish-yellow over slip, c.1570–1630. For discussion of the type and its distribution on 175 sites in the British Isles see Hurst and Gaimster 2005. (ATK 13.02.002, subsoil)

Not drawn: Granite-derived micaceous coarseware, perhaps Breton or Portuguese, perhaps 16th-century (ATK 13.02.002, subsoil); sherd from the bowl of a Saintonge type 1A chafing dish (Hurst 1974, 239–43) with the edge of a yellow-glazed face mask (the glaze confined to the mask) and the stub of the handle descending to the bowl, late 15th- or early 16th-century (ATK 12.12.000, unstratified); Normandy stoneware (ATK 13.02.002, subsoil); Raeren stoneware, 1470–1560 (ATK 13.02.002, subsoil); Cologne stoneware drinking jug sherd, 1500–50 (ATK 12.09.000, unstratified); Saintonge chafing dish sherd (ATK 13.02.000, unstratified)

East Devon: Ottery St Mary to Aylesbeare pipeline

A minor collection of 59 sherds, nearly all post-medieval, but with one 12th-century context (Site 1). As expected in this part of Devon, all the coarsewares are South Somerset products.

Catalogue (Fig. 4.24)

22 Sherd from the narrow neck of a delicate Siegburg or Beauvais stoneware jug or tall beaker. Cream-fawn body, unglazed surfaces with traces of grey-brown ash glaze. (Site 4, 3.04.21, upper fill of ditch 3.04.004)

Although this vessel would cause no surprise in eastern England, it is an unusual find in a regional context, since late medieval stonewares are very rarely seen in Devon and Cornwall prior to the arrival of mass-produced Raeren stonewares towards the end of the 15th century.

23 Rim and bodysherd of a typical Upper Greensand-Derived tripod pitcher with dark grey core, light grey-fawn surfaces, usual combing on rim and body, also with applied roughly thumbed strip on body and traces of thin decayed glaze, now green-brown. Sherds of a chert-tempered comb-decorated cooking pot of the mid to late 12th century came from the same context. (Site 1, pit 1.03.004)

Not drawn: Martincamp flask sherd, late 15th- or early 16th-century. (OTA 3.03.001, topsoil)

South Devon: Fishacre to Choakford pipeline

A total of 185 sherds came from 32 contexts. The earliest material (FTC 3.01.001 and 13.02 unstratified) includes hand-made South Devon granite-derived ware and Upper Greensand-Derived ware of the 13th/14th century. Elsewhere there is a scatter of single sherds of late medieval wheel-thrown South Devon granite-derived wares.

The post-medieval collection is dominated by coarsewares whose inclusions are derived from the granite. Many of these match closely the finds from Totnes which were probably made in the kilns at Bridgetown Pomeroy, but other centres making very similar material have recently been recognised at Plympton and Bere Ferrers. North Devon pottery makes a limited showing (nine sherds from six vessels, one sgraffito-decorated), as does St Germans-type calcareous (probably shell-tempered) ware. A single featureless bodysherd with a dense red fabric and glossy brown glaze may be a Spanish *Melado* ware, a distinctive 'honey-coloured' red earthenware, rarely recognised in this country.

Catalogue (Fig. 4.25)

24 Lower part of a ?candlestick in a granite-derived fabric, probably Totnes-type ware or from a related kiln such as Dodbrooke or Plympton. Wheel-thrown dark grey fabric with granite-derived inclusions and slate fragments, black-spotted dark green glaze in bowl, unglazed dark fawn surfaces below. (FTC 37.01.002)

25 Stem of a chill in Totnes-type ware (Allan 1984b, 79–91), the fabric with black mica inclusions, with glaze on bowl interior and with patch of glaze on stem. Dark grey discolouration below the glaze of the bowl, probably from use. Chills were a distinctive West Country vessel type; fish oil was burnt in the bowl as an alternative to candles. Probably 17th-century, cf. the examples of this form known in North Devon gravel-tempered ware (Allan *et al.* 2007, 161, nos 226–30), but an unusual find in this fabric. (FTC 25.01.007, fill of ditch 25.01.006)

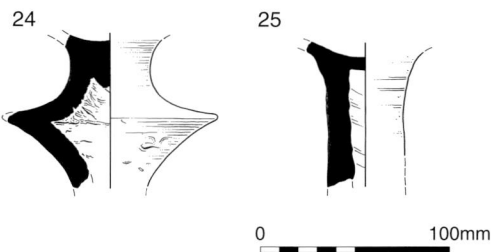

Fig. 4.25 Post-medieval pottery. Scale 1:4

Petrology of some pottery from the small medieval house at Exwell Barton

Roger T. Taylor

The writer was invited to examine the petrology of the temper of three fabrics identified in hand specimen; since the principal fabric grouping represented in the collection (fabric 1) has been the subject of much recent work (Allan *et al.* 2010; forthcoming), it was not included in the study.

Fabric 2: vesicular coarseware

Numerous sherds were examined, all of a very similar fabric but representing several vessels, with variations among the rim profiles. Most sherds have oxidised surfaces and a reduced core but few sherds are completely oxidised. They are *c.* 4.1–5.6mm thick and moderately hard to moderately soft fired. Abrasion 2, surface erosion 1–2. Temper forms *c.* 5% of the fabric. In descending order of frequency the inclusions are:

> Quartz: transparent to translucent, colourless angular to well-rounded and polished grains, 0.1–1.3mm
> Chert: sparse light grey to white mottled and white bleached, angular to sub-angular fragments, 1–3mm
> Tourmaline: very rare, black sub-angular to sub-rounded grains, 0.2–0.5mm
> Shell: rare white silicified thin, curved fragment, 0.8–1.5mm
> Mica: rare muscovite flakes, 0.1–0.3mm
> Sandstone: silicified angular, 0.6mm
> Matrix: smooth very finely micaceous clay

Comment

The surfaces and cores of all the sherds are vesicular, with many sub-rounded cavities which are undercut when they are open at the surface. They range in size from 0.2 to 3.5mm across and tend to be unevenly distributed. The cavities may represent a substantial tempering addition of limestone fragments which have been dissolved out and are now represented by cavities. The fabric is now completely non-calcareous, with no evidence of any carbonate content on freshly broken surfaces. If the cavities represent a lost tempering component, the temper percentage would be 25–30%.

The presence of chert/flint fragments with the quartz sand suggests that these components were mixed in sand which had moved downslope from the Greensand outcrop or were obtained from a stream or streams flowing from the outcrop. It is difficult to distinguish flint from chert, although some chert grains can be distinguished by a grey and white mottled texture or a porous appearance resulting from the removal of glauconite grains. The more uniform grains are white, grey or bluish-grey, but these colours can occur in both weathered flint and chert. A few grains have a finely botryoidal form but again this can occur in both flint and chert.

The fabric closely resembles the wares from Haycroft Farm, Membury, east Devon (Taylor 2002), although cavities are mostly somewhat smaller. The temper components indicate derivation from the Upper Greensand outcrop of the East Devon/Dorset area, with possible flint being derived from the overlying flint-rich early Tertiary residual deposits. The soft white grains in some sherds, also seen in Iron Age pottery with similar temper, may also be derived from the matrix of the Tertiary gravels. They are too soft to have been transported any distance.

Exeter fabric 40

This distinctive fine redware fabric, used in the production of wheel-thrown jugs, has been described in thin-section in the past (Brown and Vince 1984, 33); the most abundant inclusions are angular to sub-angular quartz (up to 0.4mm but mainly much smaller), but clay pellets and muscovite are also typical features. Although the concentration of finds of this type in the Exeter area had suggested that production somewhere near the city was likely, Brown and Vince thought that a source well to the east of the city was implied by the presence of glauconite in the fabric.

Two vessels were examined by the writer alongside many comparable sherds from Exeter. Inspection of this wider range of samples under the binocular microscope shows that, although the fine sand inclusions appear to be a common factor, the relative proportions of the components of the temper vary considerably from vessel to vessel. Sparse inclusions of coarser angular quartz and ?igneous grains are discernible in some samples; these keep tending to tie this ware to the Exeter area, where there are potential source rocks for such material, particularly in the Permian breccias in the hinterland of the estuary. They could be associated with the Exe Estuary, where the Permian breccias outcrop, extending into the hinterland. Many vessels also contain beach sand, and the presence of shell fragments in some specimens may also point to a source in the lower estuary, where the mussel (oyster) and other estuarine molluscs would provide a source. Some vessels contain coarse rounded quartz grains associated with the fine-grained sand. The implication is that these come from a source higher up the estuary where some coarse river-founded sand is present. The overall implications are that, rather than being made in east Devon/south Somerset, Exeter fabric 40 wares were produced in the Exeter area, although with no direct indication that they were produced in the city itself. The base clays could either be the Permian marls or possibly clays weathered from the Carboniferous shales, although there are no indications of residual sandstone fragments or vein quartz which might be likely from this source.

The possible Breton vessel

Two sherds from a single vessel (no. 2) have been recognised in hand specimen as examples of Exeter fabric 103, a ware first distinguished by Allan (1984a), who thought a Breton source was likely in view of its high quality, early 13th-century date and its distribution. Alongside the Exwell Barton find, sherds from eight vessels in this fabric from Exeter were examined by the writer; they display a very consistent appearance and temper. The fabric is generally pale creamy-buff to very pale-pink, and all the specimens examined are oxidised; an overall petrological description is offered here.

Temper

> Muscovite: abundant white mica flakes, commonly *c.* 0.1mm but reaching *c.* 0.2mm
> Quartz: some small white grains among the mica, 0.1–0.2mm. Larger angular composite grains tending to be elongated possibly metamorphic/metasedimentary up to 0.5mm
> Biotite: possible small flakes, *c.* 0.1mm
> Rock fragments: some very fine-grained quartz-biotite schist grains, *c.* 0.2mm. Quartz-muscovite schist grains up to *c.* 0.5mm. Some other dark schistose fragments

The abundance of mica and schistose rock fragments points to a metamorphic terrain. Areas in the South West previously considered as possible sources (Williams 1984), such as the Lizard, the Dodman and Start Point, seem unlikely to provide such material. The Armorican metamorphic terrain of Brittany, where there are extensive tracts of metasedimentary schists, is a much more likely source. The high proportion of muscovite is unusual. The low iron content of the clay giving the pale firing colour could also be the result of kaolinisation. The fine grain size of the quartz and mica and the presence of metamorphic fragments tend to preclude a greisenised granite source for the mica and quartz.

Flemish bricks

John Allan

A collection of distinctive small bricks was excavated at the cob building at Lower Nutwell, Woodbury (Site 12). Six examples (edging bricks from contexts 12.01.028 and 12.01.027) were examined by the writer. All display the typical features of imported Flemish bricks: their small size (*c.* 35–45 by 80 by 165–180mm, or 1½–2 by 3¼[1] by 6½–7½ inches), yellow or pale pink fabrics (mainly pink in this case) and irregularity, which no doubt reflected their hurried manufacture. All the specimens examined retain remains of their lime mortar bedding.

The importation of Flemish bricks is recorded in the customs accounts for the port of Exeter from 1478 until 1756 (Allan 1984a, 228–32), and these bricks could in theory date to any stage in this period of almost 200 years. It is most likely, however, that they were imported between *c.* 1670 and 1730, since imports reached their peak at that time (ibid.). The bricks which were brought into the port of Exeter came almost entirely from Rotterdam, although a few late examples were sent from Amsterdam. They were often imported in the return journeys of ships carrying Devon cloth to the Low Countries. It is sometimes claimed that they were carried as ballast, but this is not strictly true: bricks were a dutiable commodity, albeit a low-value one.

Many examples of such bricks survive in the late 17th and early 18th-century buildings of Topsham, especially in chimneys but sometimes in party walls, garden walls and outbuildings. They are also to be seen in other settlements around the Exe Estuary which would have been readily accessible to Topsham quay, such as Exton, Woodbury Salterton and Exmouth (*in situ* examples at Exton Farm, Exton; finds in Exeter City Museums collection from Woodbury Salterton and Exmouth excavations) but they are appreciably less common in Exeter and other places only a few kilometres from the port.

Worked and utilised stone

Susan Watts, with geological identification by Roger T. Taylor

Cob building at Lower Nutwell, Woodbury (Site 12)

A number of pieces of roofing slate were found in association with the partly collapsed post-medieval agricultural building. The slate derives from quarries in both the South Hams in Devon, and Cornwall, including Delabole. The use of slate from different quarries not only suggests several phases of reconstruction and repair of the roof of the building but is also indicative of the greater movement of Cornish slate following the development of the railway network in the 19th century (Beacham 1995, 23).

Medieval house at Exwell Barton, Powderham (Site 14)

Several fragments of Dartmoor granite and local sandstone formed part of the structure or repairs to a large 13th–14th-century hearth (13.02.132) within the medieval house. Pieces of roofing slate from the South Hams found on the site are also likely to have derived from the house. South Devon was an important producer of slate from the 12th/13th century until the 19th century, with Dartmouth and Totnes being the main centres for export (Beacham 1995, 23).

Other artefacts

E.R. McSloy

Metal objects

In total 225 items, comprising 210 of iron, four of copper alloy and 13 of lead were recorded from the route of the three pipeline sections. The largest proportion (167 items) related to the Aylesbeare to Kenn section, and in particular to the cob building at Lower Nutwell (Site 12) and to the post-medieval activity identified. The bulk of recovered materials comprise iron nails, structural fittings and unidentifiable fragmentary items. A catalogue recording all such items is contained in the archive. Of the entire collection, two items of individual note are described and drawn for publication, one of these being the Bronze Age pin described in Chapter 2. X-ray fluorescence (XRF) analysis, undertaken for the two described objects, was carried out by David Dungworth. The full results of this analysis are contained in the archive.

The published object of medieval and later date is an iron knife which comes from the medieval house site at Exwell Barton, Powderham (Site 14). It was recovered from a pit together with pottery broadly of 12th to 14th-century date. Whittle-tang knives are common throughout this period, the length of the tang and possibly the use of a decorated shoulder plate are possible indications for dating late on in this range, probably after 1200/50.

Catalogue (Fig. 4.26)

2   Iron whittle-tang knife with decorative copper-alloy mount at the shoulder. The tang is central to the blade, the back and cutting edge tapering towards the point. The blade is broken; its projected total length being less than *c.* 100mm. The decorative plate is of thin sheet metal, its back edge bent upwards to meet the edge of the handle. It features two lines of tooled 'rope' patterned decoration. Parallel grooves on the opposing indicate that the presence of a second (now missing) plate. The means of attachment is unclear although soldering seems most likely. The use of decorated shoulder plates would appear to be unusual and the best parallels occur with later scale-tang knives (Cowgill *et al.* 1987). The XRF analysis of the decoration indicates the use of brass (Dungworth 2011b). Surviving length 108mm; width at shoulder 22mm. Pit 13.02.161, fill 13.02.162

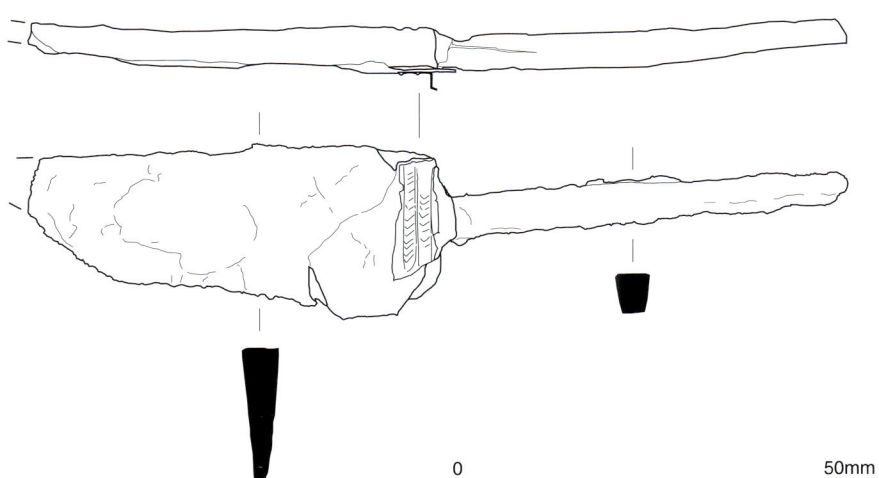

Fig. 4.26 Iron whittle-tang knife from Exwell Barton (Site 14), pit 13.02.161. Scale 1:1

Glass beads

Two glass beads were recovered, one from Tigley B (Site 27) and one from Exwell Barton (Site 14). They are described below.

2 'Chevron' bead probably of Venetian manufacture (Fig. 4.27). Composed of six alternating layers (white/blue/white/terracotta red/white/cobalt blue) of glass; the bead ends being chamfered to reveal a repeated 12-point star-shaped pattern. Beads of this type were produced from the late 15th century and widely exported. Manufacture has continued into modern times and in isolation no. 2 cannot be dated. Length 6mm; diameter 6.5mm. Site 27, Ditch 16.08.006, fill 16.08.007. Unphased

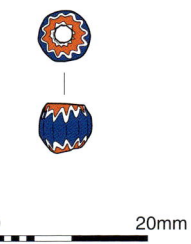

Fig. 4.27 Post-medieval bead from Tigley B (Site 27), ditch 16.08.006. Scale 1:1

4 Small annular bead in opaque black glass. The use of glass for beads in the medieval period is unusual. The size of no. 4 is such that it might easily be a re-deposited find or a later intrusion. It is significantly smaller than would be expected for the kind of small segmented beads which occur in 'appearing black' glass from the Late Roman and earlier Anglo-Saxon periods. Comparably small beads are however known, more commonly in blue and bottle green, which date to the 17th century and later and were intended for use with clothing (Noël Hume 1969, 54). Diameter 2mm; thickness 1mm. Site 14, sunken outbuilding 13.02.272, fill 13.02.203. *Not illustrated*

Plant macrofossils and charcoal

Sarah Cobain

Results of assessment and analysis

The samples of plant macrofossils and charcoal were exceptionally prolific and well preserved from deposits associated with the 13th–14th-century sunken outbuilding at Exwell Barton, Powderham (Site 14). Elsewhere, useful assemblages were retrieved from isolated pits at Coldharbour, Ottery St Mary (Site 1) and Bluepost, Harberton (Site 29) giving insights into medieval crop husbandry. Smaller groups of material came from Tigley B, Harberton (Site 27) and Moore Farm, Harberton (Site 28). This section summarises the results from the assessed and fully analysed botanical samples. The detailed results of analysis are presented in Tables 4.4–4.11.

Post-Roman/Early medieval

South Devon

Tigley B, Harberton (Site 27)
Pit 16.08.020 (Table 4.4, SS 299) contained carbonised oat, barley and indeterminate cereal grains. The charcoal was broadly characterised and consisted of alder, alder/hazel, hazel, oak, ash and hawthorn/rowan/crab apple fragments (Table 4.5, SS 299).

Moore Farm, Harberton (Site 28)
Pit 18.12.015 (Table 4.4, SS 303) contained carbonised oat, barley and indeterminate cereal grains. The charcoal was broadly characterised and consisted of alder/hazel, hazel and oak fragments (Table 4.5, SS 303).

Medieval

East Devon

Coldharbour, Ottery St Mary (Site 1)
Pit 01.03.004 contained an assemblage rich in evidence for cereal crop waste (Table 4.6, SS 173). The dominant crop appears to be bread wheat, closely followed by oat with smaller values of barley and rye. Arable weeds are represented through small numbers

Table 4.4: Early medieval plant macrofossil identifications; Tigley B (Site 27) and Moore Farm (Site 28)
Habitat Codes: A = Arable weed; D = Opportunistic weed from a disturbed environment; DC = Opportunistic weed but may have been consumed; P = Grassland species (possible pasture); E = Economic species (plants deliberately cultivated for economic use); H = Heathland species; HSW = Hedgerow, scrub, woodland species; M = Marsh/wetland species; WF = Wild Food
Identifications: * = modern; hw = heartwood (old wood); sw = sapwood (young wood)

Habitat code	Family	Species	Common Name	Site	27	28
			Context number		16.08.021	18.12.017
			Feature number		16.08.020	18.12.015
			Sample number		299	303
			Sample volume (L)		7	10
			Flot volume (ml)		300	75
	Family	Species	Common Name			
E	Poaceae	*Avena* spp	Oat		13	11
E		*Hordeum vulgare*	Hulled barley		5	26
E		Poaceae	Indet. cereal grain		12	12
			Total macrofossils identified		30	49

Table 4.5: Early medieval charcoal identifications (broad characterisation); Tigley B (Site 27) and Moore Farm (Site 28) (For Key see Table 4.4).

			Site	27	28
			Context number	16.08.021	18.12.017
			Cut number	16.08.020	18.12.015
			Sample number	299	303
			Sample volume (L)	7	10
Family	Species		Common Name		
Betulaceae	*Alnus glutinosa*		Alder	1	-
	Alnus glutinosa/Corylus avellana		Alder/hazel	7	5
	Corylus avellana		Hazel	1	8
Fagaceae	*Quercus robur/petraea*		Sessile/pedunculate oak	4	1
	Quercus robur/petraea hw		Sessile/pedunculate oak h/w	5	2
	Quercus robur/petraea sw		Sessile/pedunculate oak s/w	-	4
Oleaceae	*Fraxinus excelsior*		Ash	1	-
Rosaceae	*Crataegus monogyna/Sorbus* spp/*Malus sylvestris*		Hawthorn/rowan/ crab apple	1	-
			Total fragments identified	20	20

of corn marigold and wild radish seeds. The charcoal was broadly characterised and consisted of gorse/broom, oak and hawthorn/rowan/crab apple fragments (Table 4.8).

Medieval settlement at Exwell Barton, Powderham (Site 14)
The earliest feature sampled was the 12th–14th-century pit 13.02.228 (Fig. 4.15). Two samples from fills 13.02.232 and 13.02.233 contained similar plant macrofossil assemblages (Table 4.7, SS 163, 164). The dominant crop was rye with moderate quantities of oat and smaller numbers of barley, bread wheat, spelt and emmer/spelt wheat. Cereal chaff consisted of small amounts of rye rachis and culm nodes. Arable weeds were represented by corn marigold, annual knawel, corn spurrey and chess seeds. Hedgerow/scrub species were indicated by small numbers of elder and alder seeds and weed species indicative of disturbed environments were represented through small numbers of fat hen, fat hen/goosefoot, hawkweeds and sheep's sorrel seeds.

From pit 12.03.228 full analysis was undertaken on charcoal from fill 13.02.229 and broad characterisation from fills 13.02.232, 13.02.233 and 13.02.234 (SS 159, SS 163, SS 164, and SS 165). Fill 13.02.229 contained dominantly gorse/broom charcoal with moderate amounts of ash and hawthorn/rowan/crab apple, and smaller numbers of alder/hazel, hazel, and cherry fragments (Table 4.9). Fills 13.02.232, 13.02.233 and 13.02.234 were dominated by cherry with smaller amounts of alder/hazel, hazel, gorse/broom and hawthorn/rowan/crab

Table 4.6: Medieval plant macrofossil identifications; Coldharbour (Site 1) and Exwell Barton (Site 14). (For Key see Table 4.4).

Habitat code	Family	Species	Common Name	Site 1 Context 01.03.005 Feature 01.03.004 Sample 173 Volume (L) 8 Flot (ml) 106	14 13.02.164 13.02.163 103 13 99	14 13.02.193 N/A 146 50 15	14 13.02.212 13.02.272 152 16 27	14 13.02.213 13.02.272 153 6 10	14 13.02.209 13.02.272 154 15 44
DC	Amaranthaceae	*Chenopodium album*	Fat hen *	3	-	6	9	3	4
A	Asteraceae	*Anthemis cotula*	Stinking chamomile	-	-	-	-	-	2
A		*Centaurea cyanus*	Cornflower	-	1	-	-	-	-
A		*Chrysanthemum segetum*	Corn marigold	11	-	3	11	2	77
A	Brassicaceae	*Raphanus raphanistrum*	Wild radish perianth	1	-	-	-	-	-
A	Caryophyllaceae	*Agrostemma githago*	Corncockle (fragments)	-	-	-	1?	-	-
DC		*Stellaria media*	Common chickweed *	-	-	-	3	-	3
A		*Spergula arvensis*	Corn spurrey	-	-	2	-	-	-
DC		*Vicia spp/Lathyrus spp*	Vetches/vetchlings	-	1	-	-	-	1
E	Poaceae	*Avena spp*	Oat	49	22	4	12	2	100
A		*Bromus sect bromus*	Chess	-	-	-	-	-	-
E		*Hordeum vulgare*	Barley hulled	12	-	-	2	-	1
E		*Secale cereale*	Rye	13	3	1	10	4	17
E		*Secale cereale*	Rye rachis	-	-	-	5	-	4
E		*Triticum spp*	Wheat	1	-	-	-	-	-
E		*Triticum aestivum/turgidum/durum*	Bread-type wheat	59	3	-	1	-	4
E		*Triticum dicoccum/spelta*	Emmer/spelt	-	2	-	-	-	1
E		Poaceae	Indeterminate cereal grain	54	20	8	10	6	43
E		Poaceae	Cereal chaff – culm node	-	-	-	1	-	1
D		Poaceae	Grass spp	1	-	-	-	-	-
DC	Polygonaceae	*Rumex spp*	Dock	-	-	-	-	-	1
A	Rubiaceae	*Galium aparine*	Cleavers	-	1	-	2	3	-
			Total macrofossils identified	204	53	24	66	20	259

Table 4.7. Medieval plant macrofossil identifications; Exwell Barton (Site 14) and Bluepost (Site 29). (For Key see Table 4.4).

Habitat code	Family	Species	Common Name	Site: 14	14	14	14	14	29
			Context number	13.02.203	13.02.202	13.02.232	13.02.233	13.02.207	19.07.005
			Feature number	13.02.272	13.02.272	13.02.228	13.02.228	13.02.273	19.07.004
			Sample number	157	161	163	164	166	312
			Sample volume (L)	17	62	5	6	17	5
			Flot volume (ml)	33	80	100	316	20	285
WF/HSW	Adoxaceae	*Sambucus nigra*	Elder	-	-	2	-	-	-
D	Amaranthaceae	*Atriplex patula*	Common orache	-	-	1	-	-	-
DC		*Chenopodium album*	Fat hen	4	-	4	8	-	-
DC		*Chenopodium album*	Fat hen *	4	-	-	-	9	-
A	Asteraceae	*Anthemis cotula*	Stinking chamomile	-	-	-	-	-	2
A		*Centaurea cyanus*	Cornflower	-	-	-	1	-	-
A		*Chrysanthemum segetum*	Corn marigold	37	267	3	17	4	1
D		*Hieracium* spp	Hawkweeds	-	-	-	1	-	-
A		*Hypochaeris glabra*	Smooth cat's ear	-	-	2	-	-	-
HSW	Betulaceae	*Alnus glutinosa*	Alder	-	-	-	2	-	-
WF		*Corylus avellana*	Hazelnut	-	5	-	-	-	1
A	Brassicaceae	*Raphanus raphanistrum*	Wild radish perianth	-	4	-	-	-	1
A	Caryophyllaceae	*Scleranthus annus*	Annual knawel	-	-	2	1	-	-
DC		*Stellaria media*	Common chickweed	-	3	-	-	-	-
A		*Spergula arvensis*	Corn spurrey	-	4	4	6	-	-
G	Fabaceae	*Medicago lupulina*	Black medick	1	1	-	-	-	-
HSW/H		*Ulex* spp/*Prunus spinosa*	Gorse/blackthorn spines	-	-	-	-	-	554
DC		*Vicia* spp/*Lathyrus* spp	Vetches/vetchlings	2	4	-	-	-	-
E	Poaceae	*Avena* spp	Oat	92	343	8	43	9	67
A		*Bromus* sect *bromus*	Chess	-	-	-	3	1	1
E		*Hordeum vulgare*	Hulled barley	10	32	10	17	2	-
E		*Hordeum vulgare*	2-row hulled barley	-	-	2	1	-	-
E		*Secale cereale*	Rye	17	68	15	102	1	96

Table 4.7 (cont.): Medieval plant macrofossil identifications; Exwell Barton (Site 14) and Bluepost (Site 29). (For Key see Table 4.4).

Habitat code	Family	Species	Common Name	Site						
				14	14	14	14	14	14	29
			Context number	13.02.203	13.02.202	13.02.232	13.02.233	13.02.207	19.07.005	
			Feature number	13.02.272	13.02.272	13.02.228	13.02.228	13.02.273	19.07.004	
			Sample number	157	161	163	164	166	312	
			Sample volume (L)	17	62	5	6	17	5	
			Flot volume (ml)	33	80	100	316	20	285	
E		*Secale cereale*	Rye rachis	3	2	3	1	2	2	
E		*Triticum* spp	Wheat	-	3	2	2	-	-	
E		*Triticum aestivum/turgidum/durum*	Bread-type wheat	3	8	6	63	-	-	
E		*Triticum spelta*	Spelt	-	-	5	6	-	-	
E		*Triticum spelta*	Spelt glume base	-	-	-	-	1	-	
E		*Triticum dicoccum/spelta*	Emmer/spelt	2	-	-	8	-	-	
E		Poaceae	Indeterminate cereal grain	41	94	7	34	-	78	
E		Poaceae	Cereal chaff – culm node	-	-	-	3	-	-	
E		Poaceae	Cereal chaff – culm node	-	-	-	-	-	1	
E		Poaceae	Cereal chaff – Palea	-	-	-	-	-	1	
D		Poaceae	Grass spp	1	1	2	12	8	-	
D	Polygonaceae	*Persicaria lapathifolia*	Pale persicaria	-	1	-	-	-	-	
D		*Polygonum aviculare*	Knotgrass	-	-	-	-	1	-	
DC		*Rumex* spp	Dock	3	2	-	-	1	-	
DC		*Rumex acetosella*	Sheep's sorrel	-	-	-	4	1	-	
WF	Rosaceae	*Fragaria vesca*	Wild strawberry	-	-	-	-	-	cf 1	
A	Rubiaceae	*Galium aparine*	Cleavers	1	-	-	-	-	-	
E			Burnt string	-	-	-	-	-	2	
			Total macrofossils identified	221	842	78	335	40	814	

Table 4.8: Medieval charcoal identifications (broad characterisation); Coldharbour (Site 1), Exwell Barton (Site 14), Bluepost (Site 29). (For Key see Table 4.4).

Site	1	14	14	14	14	14	29	29
Context number	01.03.005	13.02.221	13.02.212	13.02.232	13.02.233	13.02.234	19.07.005	19.08.005
Cut number	01.03.004	N/A	13.02.272	13.02.228	13.02.228	13.02.228	19.07.004	19.08.004
Sample number	173	151	152	163	164	165	312	311
Sample volume (L)	18	2	16	5	6	5	5	3

Family	Species	Common Name								
Betulaceae	*Alnus glutinosa*	Alder	-	4	-	-	-	-	-	-
	Alnus glutinosa/Corylus avellana	Alder/hazel	-	3	-	-	-	-	6	-
	Corylus avellana	Hazel	-	1	1	-	-	-	1	-
Fabaceae	*Ulex* spp/*Cytisus* spp	Gorse/broom	6	5	3	1	13	-	3	20
Fagaceae	*Quercus robur/petraea*	Sessile/pedunculate oak	9	-	12	1	4	-	-	-
	Quercus robur/petraea hw	Sessile/pedunculate oak h/w	1	-	3	-	1	-	-	-
	Quercus robur/petraea sw	Sessile/pedunculate oak s/w	-	-	-	-	2	-	-	-
Oleaceae	*Fraxinus excelsior*	Ash	-	1	-	2	-	-	-	-
Rosaceae	*Crataegus monogyna/Sorbus* spp/ *Malus sylvestris*	Hawthorn/rowan/ crab apple	4	-	1	1	-	-	-	-
	Prunus avium/padus	Wild/bird cherry	-	-	-	15	-	-	10	-
Salicaceae	*Salix* spp/*Populus* spp	Willow/poplar	-	6	-	-	-	-	-	-
		Total fragments identified	20	20	20	20	20	20	20	20

Table 4.9: Medieval charcoal identifications (full analysis); Exwell Barton (Site 14). (For Key see Table 4.4).

Family	Species	Common Name	Site	14	14	14
		Context number		13.02.209	13.02.229	13.02.202
		Feature number		13.02.272	13.02.228	13.02.272
		Sample number		154	159	161
		Sample volume (L)		15	8	62
Betulaceae	*Alnus glutinosa*	Alder		-	-	1
	Alnus glutinosa/Corylus avellana	Alder/hazel		-	3	9
	Corylus avellana	Hazel		7	1	1
Fabaceae	*Ulex* spp/*Cytisus* spp	Gorse/broom		63	63	7
Fagaceae	*Quercus robur/petraea*	Sessile/pedunculate oak		-	-	48
	Quercus robur/petraea hw	Sessile/pedunculate oak h/w		22	-	34
	Quercus robur/petraea sw	Sessile/pedunculate oak s/w		4	-	-
Oleaceae	*Fraxinus excelsior*	Ash		1	12	-
Rosaceae	*Crataegus monogyna/Sorbus* spp/*Malus sylvestris*	Hawthorn/rowan/ crab apple		3	19	-
	Prunus avium/padus	Wild/bird cherry		-	2	-
		Total fragments identified		**100**	**100**	**100**

apple (Table 4.8). Charcoal layer 13.02.221 (Table 4.8, SS 151) pre-dated the construction of the long house. It was broadly characterised as alder, alder/hazel, hazel, gorse/broom, ash and willow/poplar. Floor layer 13.02.193 within medieval house 13.02.275 contained small numbers of carbonised oat, rye and indeterminate cereal grains, and carbonised corn marigold, corn spurrey and (modern) fat hen seeds (Table 4.6, SS 146).

Six samples were taken from the sunken outbuilding 13.02.272, all of which were dominated by cereal-processing remains. Hearth 13.02.203 was dominated by oats with smaller amounts of barley, rye, bread wheat and emmer/spelt wheat grains, and occasional carbonised rye rachis (Table 4.7, SS 157). Arable weeds were represented by large numbers of corn marigold and a single cleavers seed. Weeds of disturbed areas included fat hen/goosefoot, fat hen, grass, dock and vetch/vetchlings seeds. A single black medick seed indicates grassland.

Charcoal spread 13.02.202 (rake-out from hearth 13.02.203) had a similar assemblage to the hearth/oven base and was dominated by oat grains with moderate amounts of rye and smaller numbers of barley and bread wheat (Table 4.7, SS 161). A small quantity of rye rachis (cereal chaff) was also present. Arable weeds were dominated by corn marigold seeds and smaller numbers of wild radish and corn spurrey seeds. Species indicative of a disturbed environment were represented by small numbers of common chickweed, pale persicaria, dock and vetch/vetchlings seeds. A black medick seed was also present indicating grassland. Carbonised hazelnut shells indicate woodland or scrub nearby. The charcoal from this sample was fully analysed and consisted dominantly of oak with smaller amounts of alder, alder/hazel, hazel and gorse/broom.

Disuse fill 13.02.207 from oven 13.02.273 contained small numbers of carbonised oat, hulled barley and rye cereal grains, carbonised rye rachis and spelt glume base (cereal chaff), carbonised corn marigold, chess, grass, knotgrass, dock and sheep's sorrel seeds (Table 4.7, SS 166).

The fills 13.02.212, 13.02.213 and 13.02.209 of sunken outbuilding 13.02.272 were dominated by crop-processing waste (Table 4.6, SS 152, SS 153, SS 154). The crops were mainly oats with moderate amounts of rye and small quantities of barley, bread wheat and emmer/spelt wheat. Carbonised rye rachis and culm nodes (cereal chaff) were also present. Arable weeds included large numbers of corn marigold and smaller numbers of stinking chamomile, corncockle and, cleavers. Weeds from disturbed environments included small numbers of vetch/vetchlings and dock. The charcoal from 13.02.209 was fully analysed and was dominated by gorse/broom with moderate amounts of oak and smaller numbers of hazel, ash and hawthorn/rowan/crab apple (Table 4.9). Fill 13.02.212 was broadly characterised and contained hazel, gorse/broom, oak and hawthorn/rowan/crab apple fragments (Table 4.8).

Isolated pit 13.02.163 contained carbonised oat, rye, bread wheat, emmer/spelt and indeterminate cereal grains, and cornflower, vetch/vetchlings, cleavers and ribwort plantain seeds (Table 4.6, SS 103).

Bluepost, Harberton (Site 29)
A sample from fill 19.07.005 of pit 19.07.004 (Fig. 4.21) was dominated by rye with moderate counts of oat grains (Tables 4.7 and 4.8, SS 312). Rye rachis, culm node and palea were present. Small numbers of arable weeds including stinking chamomile, corn marigold, wild radish and chess were present. Woodland/scrub/heath species were represented by small numbers of carbonised hazelnut shells and possible wild strawberry seeds, and large numbers of gorse/blackthorn spines (most likely to be gorse owing to large amounts of gorse/broom charcoal identified). There were also two fragments of carbonised twine/string from this sample. The charcoal was broadly characterised and consisted dominantly of gorse/broom with smaller amounts of oak (Table 4.8, SS 312). A similar dominance of gorse/broom with some oak came from undated pit 19.08.004 in the neighbouring field, but it contained no plant macrofossil material (Table 4.8, SS 311).

Post-medieval

East Devon

Pixies' Parlour, Ottery St Mary (Site 4)
The fill of 16th–17th-century pit 3.04.097 (Table 4.10, SS 73) contained a possible carbonised oat and emmer/spelt wheat grain. Broad characterisation of the charcoal was carried out and the species identified consisted dominantly of oak with smaller quantities of alder/hazel, oak, ash, wild/bird cherry and blackthorn/sloe (Table 4.11). As there was no cereal chaff identified, it is difficult to interpret whether this is cereal processing waste or domestic waste.

Medieval settlement at Exwell Barton, Powderham (Site 14)
Pit 13.02.174 (Fig. 4.15) contained carbonised rye and indeterminate cereal grains and carbonised corn marigold and modern fat hen seeds (Table 4.10, SS 93).

Discussion

Early medieval

Arable agriculture
The pits at Moore Farm (Site 28) and Tigley B (Site 27), Harberton, both contained oats, barley and indeterminate cereal grains. The national trend for early medieval cereal assemblages is a change from hulled cereals, such as emmer and spelt wheat, to free-threshing cereals such as bread wheat. The shortage of well-dated deposits in the South West means that the date of this development is uncertain (Straker 2008a, 163), and what evidence there is indicates that a mixture of crops was cultivated. For example, 5th–6th-century hearth deposits, a ditch and buried soils

Table 4.10: Post-medieval plant macrofossil identifications; Pixies' Parlour (Site 4) and Exwell Barton (Site 14). (For Key see Table 4.4).

Habitat code	Family	Species	Common Name	Site: 4	Site: 14
			Context number	03.04.092	13.02.097
			Feature number	03.04.097	13.02.174
			Sample number	73	93
			Sample volume (L)	29	9
			Flot volume (ml)	29	25
D	Amaranthaceae	*Chenopodium album*	Fat hen *	-	10
C	Apiaceae	*Glebionis segetum*	Corn marigold	-	2
A	Poaceae	*Avena* spp	Oat	cf 1	-
A		*Secale cereale*	Rye	-	1
E		*Triticum dicoccum/spelta*	Emmer/spelt wheat	cf 1	-
E		*Poaceae*	Indeterminate cereal grain	1	8
			Total macrofossils identified	3	21

Table 4.11: Post-medieval charcoal identifications (broad characterisation); Pixies' Parlour (Site 4)

Family	Species	Common Name	Site: 4
		Context number	03.04.092
		Feature number	03.04.097
		Sample number	73
		Sample volume (L)	29
Betulaceae	*Alnus glutinosa*	Alder	1
	Alnus glutinosa/Corylus avellana	Alder/hazel	2
Fagaceae	*Quercus robur/petraea*	Sessile/pedunculate oak	6
Oleaceae	*Fraxinus excelsior*	Ash	8
Rosaceae	*Prunus avium/padus*	Wild/bird cherry	2
	Prunus spinosa	Blackthorn/sloe	1
		Total fragments identified	**20**

at Bantham Ham, Kingsbridge, contained carbonised bread wheat, oats and hulled barley (Jones 2002, 3). Samples from 5th–6th-century settlement at Tintagel Island, Cornwall, contained barley and oats, which were more common than free-threshing wheat (Straker 1997a, 97). The 3rd/4th-century pit/hearth and rubbish layers at Duckpool, Morwenstow, Cornwall indicated a dominance of oats, with wheat and barley also represented (Straker 1995, 155). The presence of oats and barley and the lack of wheat is notable and the pits at Moore Farm and Tigley B appear typical of this pattern in the South West west of the Blackdown Hills (Rippon 2012, 255). A similar trend was found in 5th/6th-century pits at South Petherton, Somerset (Cobain 2012)

Further afield, a low frequency of bread-type wheat was also found in the early and mid Saxon phases of activity at West Heslerton, North Yorkshire, where barley was the predominant cereal cultivated (Carruthers and Hunter 2001, 9). It is suggested by Carruthers and Hunter (ibid.) that this was because bread wheat, being a free-threshing cereal unlike oats or barley, would not have required heat to release the grains, thereby reducing the numbers of accidentally carbonised cereal grains. It also must be considered that, as wheat was viewed as a more valuable crop, more care would have been taken to prevent accidental losses of cereals (ibid.). It is also possible that local arable communities varied regionally and the damper climate experience in the South West together with heavy clay soils in the South Devon region meant that a variety of more hardy cereals such as barley and oat were cultivated in case bread wheat crops failed.

It is difficult to interpret these assemblages as they are based on just 30 (Site 27) and 49 (Site 28) grains, and the pits appeared isolated from settlement. It is possible that bread wheat was being cultivated and processed in the area, but for reasons discussed above no evidence has survived. As there were no floret bases present it was not possible to ascertain whether the oats were the cultivated or wild forms, although the absence of other weed species does suggest the oats were cultivated. The mixture of cultivated oats and barley may be indicative of 'spring sown dredge', which was used as fodder, perhaps indicating a pastoral form of agriculture being undertaken within this area as well as use for ale, pottage and bread (Stone 2006, 13).

Fuel
The charcoal fragments from pits at Tigley B and Moore Farm were characterised as fire debris. The purpose of the fires is not entirely clear, although the cereal grains may indicate the burning of cereal waste, field clearance or domestic cooking. The charcoal shows a variety of local wood used from these two features.

Local landscape
The cereal grains indicate an arable landscape in the vicinity of these plots, but there was no further information about the local flora. The charcoal shows that scrub woodland and/or hedgerows would have contained oak, ash, alder, hazel and hawthorn/rowan/crab apple. The charcoal gives no indication of coppicing (curved growth rings showing fast growth), so it not known whether woodlands were being managed (Rackham 1994, 9).

Medieval

Arable agriculture and hand-collected foodstuffs
Cereal crops played an important part in medieval diets, oats, free-threshing wheat (bread/rivet wheat), barley and rye making up the bulk of the calorific intake (Stone 2006, 11–12). In general, cereal composition was characterised by a dominance of bread wheat, as was the case for the 12–13th-century pit at Coldharbour, Ottery St Mary (Site 1), where it was closely followed by oats, and smaller quantities of barley and rye. Similar assemblages came from the 11th–13th-century ditch and burnt deposits at Church Field's, Shapwick Heath, Somerset (Campbell *et al.* 2007, 879).

More commonly on the present project, sites show a dominance of oats and rye, followed by smaller numbers of barley, bread and emmer/spelt wheat. The early phase (12th/14th-century) pit at Exwell Barton, Powderham (Site 14, pit 13.02.228) and the 11th-century pit at Bluepost, Harberton (Site 29, pit 19.07.004) contained higher amounts of rye compared to oats, whereas the 13th/14th-century features associated with the medieval house and sunken kitchen at Exwell Barton contained a larger proportion of oats compared to rye. The contribution of hand-gathered foodstuffs in the medieval period was minimal (Fig. 6.2).

The general picture at the Exwell Barton medieval house is the small quantity of cereal chaff and weed seeds from the samples (Tables 4.6 and 4.7). This suggests that these cereals were already processed/cleaned and were possibly being heated to harden the grain prior to pounding/milling or to preserve for future use. If this were the case, the low proportion of bread wheat would reflect the real balance of crops processed, rather than factors of taphonomy, and it can be assumed that oats and rye, rather than bread wheat, were the dominant crops. They may have been grown as mixed oat/rye maslin. A dominance of oats has also been recorded at the medieval settlement at Sourton Down, near Okehampton (Straker 1997b, 115), and this is common in West Devon and Cornwall generally (Rippon 2012, 256). Oats and rye were often favoured as they have higher yields than free-threshing wheat and also are known to be able to tolerate the more acidic soil, such as that experienced on the silty sand soil at Exwell Barton, and damp climatic conditions experienced in south-west England (Moffett 2006, 48; Straker 2008b, 189). The presence of barley, emmer/spelt and bread wheat may indicate secondary cultivated crops, but the small quantities of each suggest they could be contaminants growing in oat and rye fields. Since oats and rye are not considered premium crops it is also possible that they were being cultivated for fodder to support pastoral farming. The oats and rye may have been exposed to fire while being dried for long-term storage. For human consumption, oats would have been used for porridges, pottages, bread and ale. Rye was used to produce bread, barley to produce bread and ale, and free-threshing wheat was used for the best quality bread and ale (Stone 2006, 13).

Only small numbers of weed seeds were recovered from the Exwell Barton medieval house with the exception of charcoal-rich deposit 13.02.202 associated with the early phase hearth 13.02.203 which is mirrored by the sample from the feature itself (Table 4.7, SS 161, SS 157). This included large numbers of corn marigold seeds, suggesting that the batch of grain had not undergone the final stages of cleaning, the crop perhaps having been spoilt and burnt. Many of the weed seeds do not have specific preferred habitats, but corn marigold is indicative of an acidic sandy soil and corn spurrey, smooth cat's ear and annual knawel suggest a sandy soil type. Stinking chamomile indicates a more clay rich soil (Rose 2006, 156, 158, 448, 455, 474), but this was only present in very low numbers. These types of weeds would be expected on the silty sand soil at the site.

There were also small numbers of carbonised hazelnut shells, carbonised elder and one possible wild strawberry seed. It is possible they were hand-collected foodstuffs, although they may have been attached to fuel wood or dropped by birds.

Fuel
The charcoal from Coldharbour, Ottery St Mary (Site 1) and Exwell Barton, Powderham (Site 14) may be characterised as fuel for cereal drying, but if the sunken building had been used as a general kitchen, it may have included fuel for baking and other forms of cooking. Most abundant were oak and gorse/broom, with smaller amounts of alder, alder/hazel, hazel, oak, ash and hawthorn/rowan/crab apple, cherry, blackthorn/sloe and willow/poplar. The dominant fuel was oak in layer 13.02.202 and gorse/broom in the later charcoal layer 13.02.209 in the sunken kitchen, and also in early phase pit 13.02.228. The fully analysed samples from the Exwell Barton settlement indicate that the majority of oak fragments did not exhibit curved growth rings, which suggests the use of large branches/trunk wood. The majority of the remaining fragments did exhibit curved growth rings indicating that small roundwood branches were being utilised. Where curved growth rings were not recorded, it is possible that larger stem wood/trunk wood was being utilised, however, in the absence of larger charcoal fragments this cannot be confirmed.

The broad characterisation of charcoal (Fig. 6.3) indicates that there is a decrease in the percentage of alder/hazel and oak and an increase in hawthorn/rowan/crab apple and cherry compared to the early medieval period, although the medieval assemblage is based on a larger number of samples and the comparison should be treated with caution. On the broader scale, the high fragment counts of gorse/broom and increase in hawthorn/rowan/crab apple and cherry compared to earlier periods suggests that woodland resources were becoming more scarce and different types of wood were being exploited. Gorse/broom establishes in areas of poor soil fertility and may have been common locally, reflecting soil impoverishment. It may, however, have been deliberately selected. It is known to be very good for bread ovens as it burns at a high temperature. Together with oak these would be ideal species for cereal drying and bread baking (Cutler and Gale 2000, 260). Similar charcoal assemblages were also found within the clay floor of a 12th/13th-century building at Shapwick House moat, Somerset (Gale 2007, 892) where they consisted of oak, blackthorn, hawthorn/rowan/crab apple and willow/poplar used for fuel for domestic purposes, although there was no gorse/broom.

There were also a large number of gorse/broom spines and charcoal found in the sample from Bluepost, Harberton (Site 29) along with two fragments of carbonised twine/string. This string may have been used to tie up the thin gorse/broom branches to use as brushwood bundles within the fire. Gorse is a shrub with large numbers of thin branches, and the high numbers of small twig/roundwood fragments found is to be expected.

Local landscape
The large number of carbonised cereal remains from Coldharbour, Ottery St Mary, Exwell Barton, Powderham and Bluepost, Harberton, together with arable weeds, reflect the arable component of the landscape at these locations in East and South Devon. There were also weeds of disturbed ground and grassland, although in the context of crop-processing waste, these could have been present as opportunistic species in marginal areas/hedgerows surrounding the fields, or growing within newly ploughed soil on the fields, rather than in areas of pasture. There were also alder and elder seeds, hazelnut shells and gorse/broom spines. The alder seeds from Exwell Barton indicate a wetland environment which would have existed on the nearby River Kenn floodplain, if not more locally. The willow/poplar charcoal reflects a similar environment. Gorse/broom indicates the presence of heathland, possibly nearby common lands for grazing and areas of scrub woodland.

Generally, obtaining wood for fuel became more difficult by the medieval period. Woodlands had become increasingly depleted and their exploitation was governed by ownerships and rights woven into the fabric of the rigidly hierarchical social system (Rackham 2001, 62). They were intensively managed with coppicing and pollarding (although there was no evidence of this from the charcoal recovered due to its highly fragmentary nature). The fuel wood utilised on these sites may have been locally harvested from common land or hedgerows, rather than woodland, as suggested by the quantity of gorse/broom together with increased roundwood fragment counts of cherry and hawthorn/rowan/crab apple charcoal which give an indication of the landscape at the time.

Post-medieval

Arable agriculture

The plant macrofossil remains were found in small quantities with 11 seeds (excluding modern fat hen) found in 16th–18th-century pit 13.02.174 at Exwell Barton, Powderham and three seeds from pit 3.04.097 at Pixies' Parlour, Ottery St Mary. The cereals consisted of oat, indeterminate wheat, cf emmer/spelt wheat and rye. There have been few studies of the post-medieval cereal remains in the south-west of England (Straker 2008c, 211), although these are all crops that are known to have been cultivated during the 16th–18th-century period. As so few cereal remains were recovered the activities associated with this pit are uncertain. It is possible that they are waste from domestic cooking or processing, but are not closely associated with settlement. There is nothing from the arable crop or weed remains that adds to the picture of the farming or the wider environment here at this time.

Pit 3.04.097 at Pixies' Parlour, which cut an Early Neolithic tree-hole, was initially considered to be Early Neolithic, but the botanical assemblage suggests that this is not the case. Elsewhere, Early Neolithic pits contained mostly hazelnut shell, which was entirely absent from Pixies' Parlour. In addition the charcoal analysis reveals a wide range of wood species including wild/bird cherry, blackthorn/sloe and larger amounts of ash, which is different to other Early Neolithic samples. Taken together this suggests a later date for the feature and this is supported by the radiocarbon date (Table 2.1).

Animal bones and sea shells

Jonny Geber with Sylvia Warman and Victoria Taylor

Exwell Barton, Powderham, medieval settlement (Site 14)

The fills of medieval pits and ditches contained a total of 34 fragments of animal bone, of which fragments of ulna from both cattle *(Bos taurus)* and horse *(Equus caballus)* were identified.

Small fragments of, in total, a minimum of only one edible cockle was found within part of debris of hearth 13.02.204 in the sunken kitchen building. Cockles *(Cerastoderma edula)* occur in great quantities in sandy bays, as well as in mud and gravel (McMillan 1968, 10; Tebble 1966, 95), and have throughout history been a greatly exploited source of food; however, the find of only one specimen from medieval deposits makes any interpretation with regard to diet uncertain.

Large quantities of cockles were, however, present in a post-medieval ditch 13.02.159 (fill 13.02.006), a feature that contained a minimum of 801 cockles and three oysters (Fig. 4.15). Cockles are in season between the autumn and the spring (Donovan 1802), and it is likely that these were consumed during that period. The majority of the shells measured between 18 and 30mm in greatest valve length, with a few larger outliers, and would indicate ages of probably around four years and above (see Cardoso 2007, fig. 9.2.; Franklin 1972, 4). In a crude estimation of meat yield, based on a presumed average of 14.5% per total weight (Crowley 1973), the cockles found in deposit 13.02.006 would only generate approximately 420g in wet meat. Considering the fact that marine molluscs were only found within one context, it may be suggested that they represent the food waste from a single event.

Lower Nutwell, Woodbury, cob building (Site 12)

Two species of marine molluscs were encountered from post-medieval contexts. One fragment of periwinkle was noted in a disuse spread (315) within the building. This is a common edible intertidal species (McMillan 1968, 30), but in this case it may primarily have been used as part of the mortar fabric of the structure itself. This is further indicated by the find of two oyster shell fragments within a collapsed cob wall (12.01.034) of the same structure. Possible structural use of mussel shells was also noted with seven fragments identified within the levelling/bedding layer 12.01.018.

Radiocarbon dating

Andrew Mudd

The chief significance of the radiocarbon dating programme for the post-Roman period was the discovery of three pits dated to around the 5th, 6th and 7th centuries from Moore Farm, Tigley B and Pixies' Parlour respectively (Tables 2.3, 4.1 and 2.1). These were without artefacts and were not otherwise datable. It is not known what sort of site they relate to, although it appears significant that sites of this date are present if difficult to identify and not possible to characterise with such limited interventions. An 11th-century pit at Bluepost was of similar character (Table 4.2). Another radiocarbon date from Pixies' Parlour has indicated an intrusive 16th/17th-century pit in an Early Neolithic deposit (Table 2.1).

Chapter 5
Enclosures and Field Systems

Introduction

In addition to the sites and 'off-site' features of more or less secure date, more than 150 undated ditches were recorded in the East Devon and South Devon pipeline sections. Most are likely to be medieval and later field boundaries and many correlate with former field boundaries as depicted on tithe maps. No analysis has been undertaken of most of these features, but there was a small number whose alignments were at variance with the existing field patterns and do not seem to correspond to boundaries on early mapping. These are considered as being of possible prehistoric or Roman date. The remainder are of less intrinsic significance and are only summarised here. Although some extant and recently extant field boundaries may have much earlier origins, the archaeological evidence for this was lacking almost everywhere.

Undated ditches of possible prehistoric or Roman date

Stuart Joyce and Andrew Mudd

East Devon

Site 3: Knightstone Farm, Ottery St Mary

This pair of fields (plots OTA 2.06 and OTA 3.01) lies on gently undulating land on both sides of Sidmouth Road at between 56m and 62m AOD (Fig. 5.1). Ditches

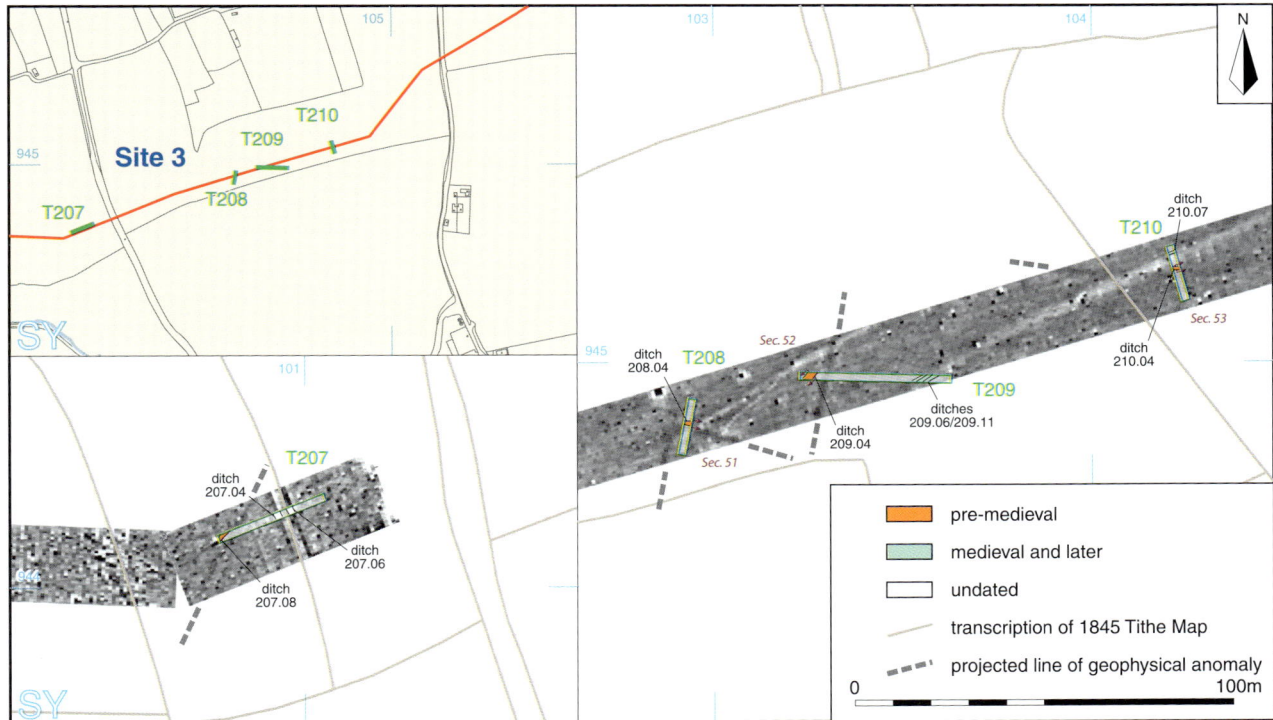

Fig. 5.1 Knightstone Farm (Site 3); geophysical anomalies and excavated features on transcription of 1845 Tithe Map. Scales 1:2000 and 1:10,000

were identified in both plots by geophysical survey and their locations confirmed by trial trenches (T207–210). Only two of these ditches correspond to former field boundaries as depicted on the 1845 Tithe Map (Fig. 5.1, Plot 3.01, ditches 207.04 and 207.06). Ditch 207.04 was asymmetrical in profile, with a shallow sloping south-west side and a steeply sloping north-west side. Its single fill consisted of dark brown silty sand. Ditch 207.06 was V-shaped in profile with moderately steep sides and a tapering concave base. Its single fill comprised dark orange brown silty sand. These ran parallel, about 1m apart, and resemble ditches flanking a narrow hedgebank, or alternatively a pair of ditches on one side of a field boundary within a pattern of medieval strip fields. In Plot 2.06 parallel ditches 209.11 and 209.06, also about 1m apart, are probably of a similar date. While there is no known former field boundary here, and both ditches were very shallow, they appear to be related to the strong positive linear magnetic anomaly, which seems likely to indicate a former bank although this was not recognised in this trench. This positive anomaly appears to coincide with ditch 210.07, which, unusually, was 0.7m deep with near-vertical sides and a flat base, and had upcast banks on each side buried by subsoil. Its stratigraphic position cutting a lower deposit of subsoil, and the preservation of earthen banks, suggest that it is relatively modern. Its absence from historic maps suggests that it is pre-19th century in date, but a field boundary (pre-dating the present one but in a similar location) is shown on an early vertical aerial photograph and the feature may date to the early 20th century. Its depiction as a positive magnetic anomaly may relate to the larger of the two banks (that lying on the northern side of the ditch). Another linear positive anomaly, running approximately parallel to these features, lies 20m to the north. This coincides with a cropmark on the vertical photographic coverage (NMR: library ref. 13310), but the interpretation of both these features is problematic.

Aside from these relatively modern features, there was a series of ditches on a different alignment, which, while undated, bear no relationship to the tithe map field boundaries and are likely to represent a pre-medieval layout of fields. The corner of an enclosure in T208 was found to be formed by ditch 208.04, 1.4m wide and 0.78m deep, buried by at least 0.4m of subsoil (Fig. 5.2, section 51). On an alignment at right-angles was ditch 209.04, 1.9m wide and 0.64m deep (Fig. 5.2, section 52). To the east ditch 210.04 (Fig. 5.2, section 53) seemed to be part of this ditch 'system'. While it was just 0.2m deep its burial beneath 1.3m of subsoil (making it stratigraphically earlier than ditch 210.07) indicates that it is pre-modern. It coincided with an east/west-aligned magnetic anomaly which was partly obscured by the positive signal from the later bank.

To the west of Sidmouth Road (Plot 3.01) ditch 207.08 corresponds to a magnetic anomaly on a north-

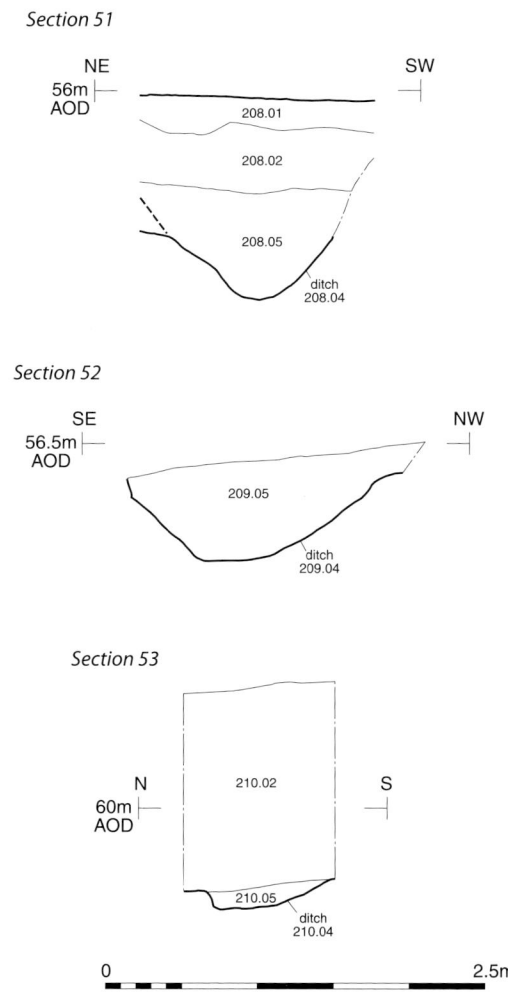

Fig. 5.2 Knightstone Farm (Site 3); sections 51 to 53. Scale 1:50

west/south-east alignment. It was 1.9m wide and 0.3m deep and, although it yielded a fragment of clay tobacco pipe, its post-medieval date may be doubted as it appears to pre-date the medieval strip field pattern in a similar way to the ditches to the east in Plot 2.06. There is therefore the suggestion of an orthogonal pattern of pre-medieval fields aligned north-west/south-east.

Site 9: New Nutwalls, Aylesbeare

A curvilinear gully, 0.03.004, was identified extending from the southern limit of excavation for *c.* 5m before returning outside the excavation area (Fig. 5.3). No dating evidence was recovered from the feature, although it may represent a small prehistoric enclosure or ring-gully. It was 0.9m wide and 0.07m deep, with a symmetrical profile. The single fill, 0.03.005, comprised mid yellow-orange slightly silty clay derived from the surrounding subsoil and clay natural substrate. Sixty-five metres to the west, ditch 0.03.006 was 0.7m wide and 0.19m deep, with gently sloping sides and a slightly concave base. The single fill was orange-grey clay and contained five small sherds (16g) of Roman pottery. It is not

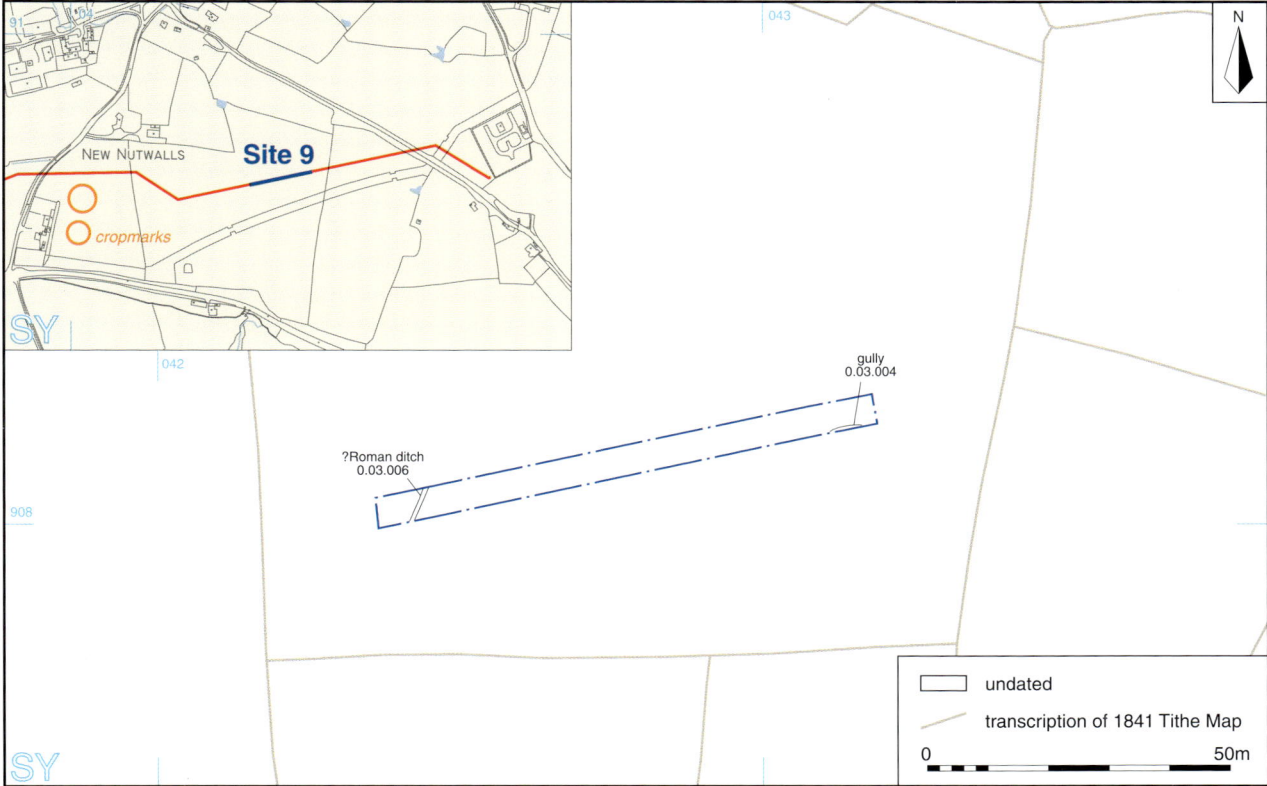

Fig. 5.3   New Nutwalls (Site 9); excavated features on transcription of 1841 Tithe Map. Scales 1:1250 and 1:10,000

clear if these sherds are redeposited and, while there is no strong reason to indicate that these features are archaeologically significant, they do not correspond to boundaries depicted on the Aylesbeare Tithe Map (Fig. 5.3) and are likely to be pre-19th century, if not later prehistoric or Roman. There are substantial circular cropmarks in the field to the west (NMR: library ref. 13550), whose date and significance are likewise unclear. These were avoided by the pipeline route.

Site 11: The Nutwell Lodge, Woodbury

The site lies on a gentle west-facing slope in the field adjacent to Exmouth Road (Fig. 5.4). The magnetometer survey revealed a poorly defined negative anomaly which subsequent soil stripping showed to be a sharply turning curve of a presumed circular ditch, 11.04.028, cutting the underlying Triassic mudstone and sandstone substrate. The feature was only partly revealed but had a projected internal diameter of *c.* 5m. A single 1m-wide section was excavated through the ditch, which measured 2.9m in width. Its projected depth was about 1.5m, although it was not fully excavated because of the high watertable and unstable soil, and it had symmetrical, moderately steep sides (Fig. 5.5, Section 54). The lowest fill encountered, 11.04.029, consisted of mid red-brown clay derived from the surrounding natural, and probably represents initial collapse of the ditch sides. The secondary fill, 11.04.030, comprised dark red-brown sandy silt and resulted from gradual natural silting. The final infilling phase of the ditch is represented by light yellow-brown deposit 11.04.031. There were no finds of any sort and the date and purpose of this feature remains enigmatic. Twenty-five metres to the north-east, ditch 11.04.004 also remained undated, but is comparable in scale. It measured 4.7m in width and 1.3m in depth and may represent part of a boundary ditch (Fig. 5.5, section 55).

The features have been mapped against the 1849 Tithe Map (Fig. 5.4) but do not correspond to any features depicted nearby. To the north-west, the map depicts a large complex of buildings at Ashtrees, presumably a farm, now reduced to a single building called The Nutwell Lodge.

Site 16: Soloman's Farm, Exminster

The site lies on an east-facing slope on the Dawlish Standstone ridge between the Exe valley at Exminster and the River Kenn, between 40m and 55m OD (Fig. 5.6). Ditch 15.02.018 extended southwards for 3m from the northern baulk of the site, and turned east for 13m before terminating. The ditch lay beneath 0.5m of topsoil and subsoil. Three 1m-wide sections were excavated which showed the ditch to be between 0.53m and 0.72m wide and 0.17m and 0.21m deep, with moderately sloping asymmetrical sides and a slightly concave base. Approximately 50m to the west lay a group of four pits, 15.02.019, which may have formed a four-post structure about 1.2m by 0.8m in size. None of

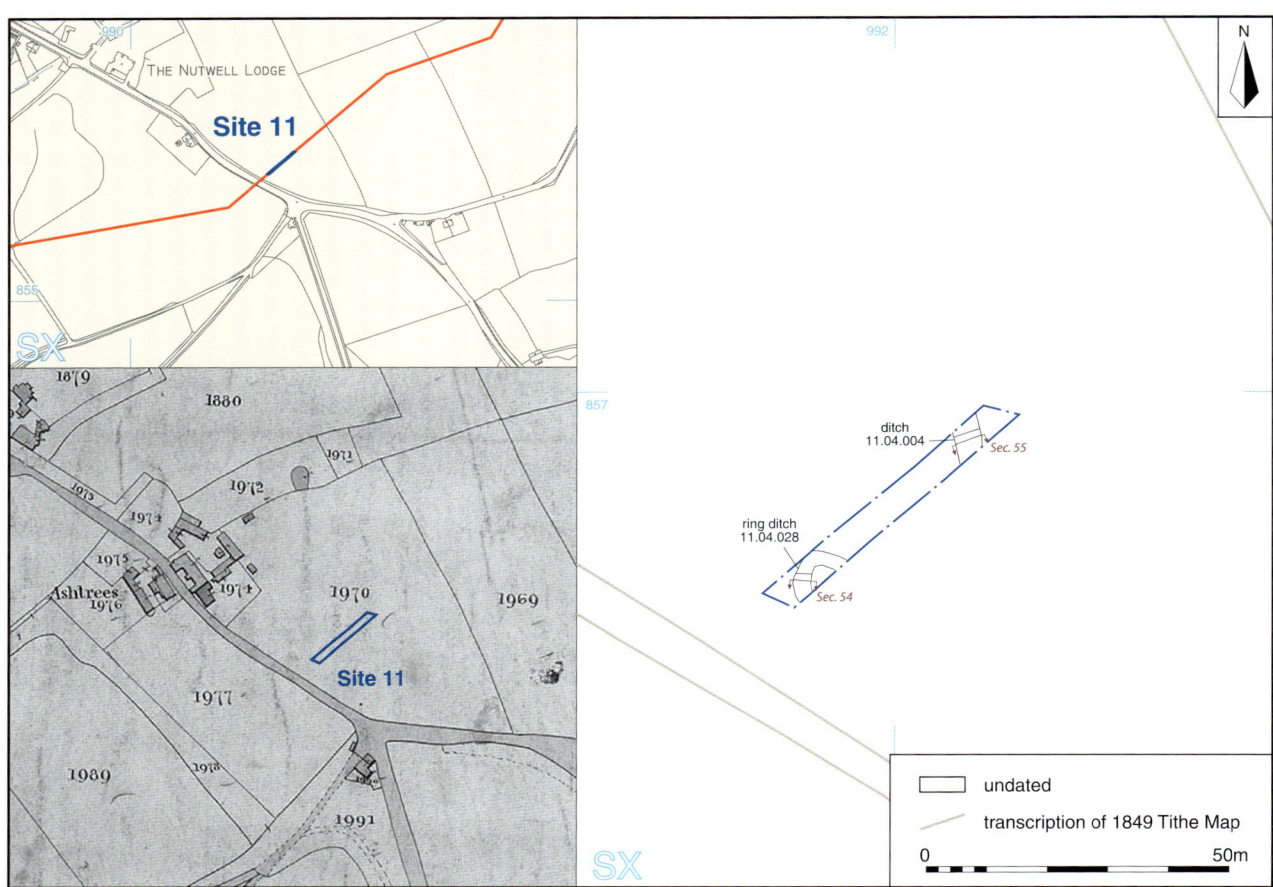

Fig. 5.4   The Nutwell Lodge (Site 11); excavated features on transcription of 1849 Tithe Map. Scales 1:1250, 1:5000 and 1:10,000

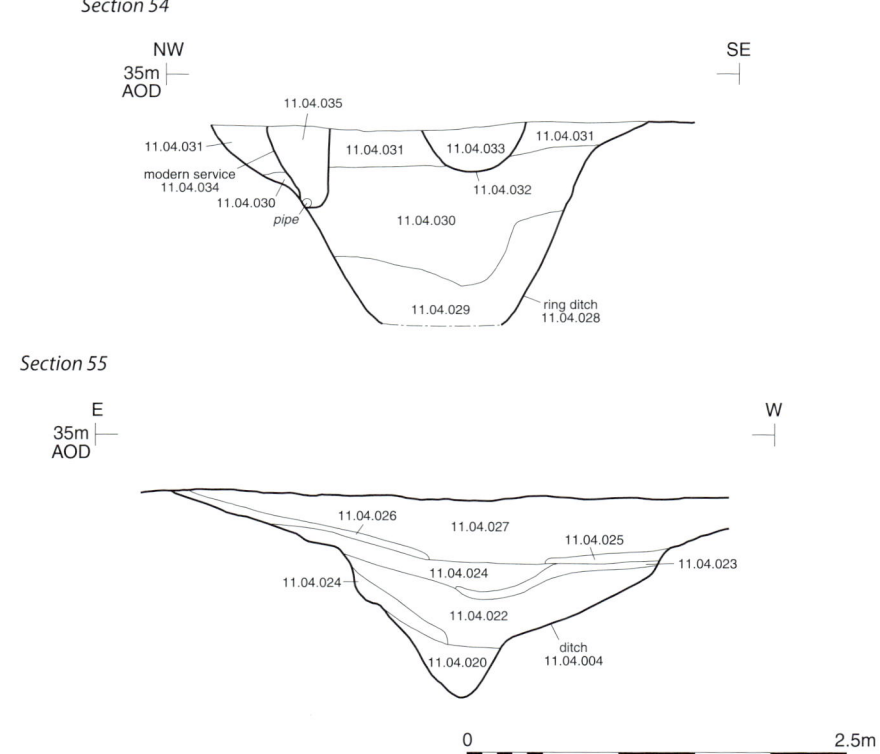

Fig. 5.5   The Nutwell Lodge (Site 11); sections 54 and 55. Scale 1:50

Fig. 5.6 Soloman's Farm (Site 16); excavated features on transcription of 1838 Tithe Map

these features contained any dating evidence. The ditch does not correspond to any recent field boundaries and the features may be elements of a somewhat dispersed prehistoric or Roman settlement.

The site lies 0.5km west of the group of Bronze Age pits and the Iron Age gully at Crablake Farm (Site 15) which would seem to attest to the suitability of the sandy ridge for scattered prehistoric occupation. The site is about 0.5km north of the early post-Roman cemetery at Long Stone Field, Kenn, potentially in use between the 5th and 8th centuries AD (Weddell 2000). The location and nature of associated settlement remains unknown (ibid.,117-18) and there would seem to be the potential for the characteristically artefact-poor remains to be represented among the types of features found at Soloman's Farm.

South Devon

Site 18: Moothill Cross, Staverton

The site lies about 0.5km east of Moothill Cross on the east-facing slope of the ridge between the rivers Dart and Hems, at approximately 70m AOD (Fig. 5.7). Slightly curving ditch 4.02.015 ran for 45m within the site and turned northwards at the present field boundary. Two 1m-long sections were excavated. The ditch, which was sealed by subsoil, was about 1m deep with moderately steep symmetrical sides and a concave base (Fig. 5.8). A broadly similar stratigraphic sequence of infilling was identified within each section. The primary deposit, 4.02.010, represents an initial collapse of unstable sides, presumably occurring soon after the feature was originally created. The secondary fill 4.02.011, a mid brown-grey silt, represents natural silting while the ditch was in use. The middle dark silt, 4.02.012, may have derived from the contemporaneous topsoil and subsoil. A thin stabilisation layer, 4.02.013 appears to have formed before the final silting of the ditch, 4.02.0014. The purpose of this feature is unknown but it appears to have belonged to an enclosure partly underlying the eastern hedgebank boundary of this field.

The wider context of this plot is intriguing. The name 'Moothill' suggests the location of a Saxon hundredal meeting and the north/south lane of the 'cross' is recorded as a possible pre-Roman route ('Goat Path'), although this interpretation is unsubstantiated (NMR: site ref. 1008349). The location of ditch 4.02.015 coincides with the location of another putative ancient

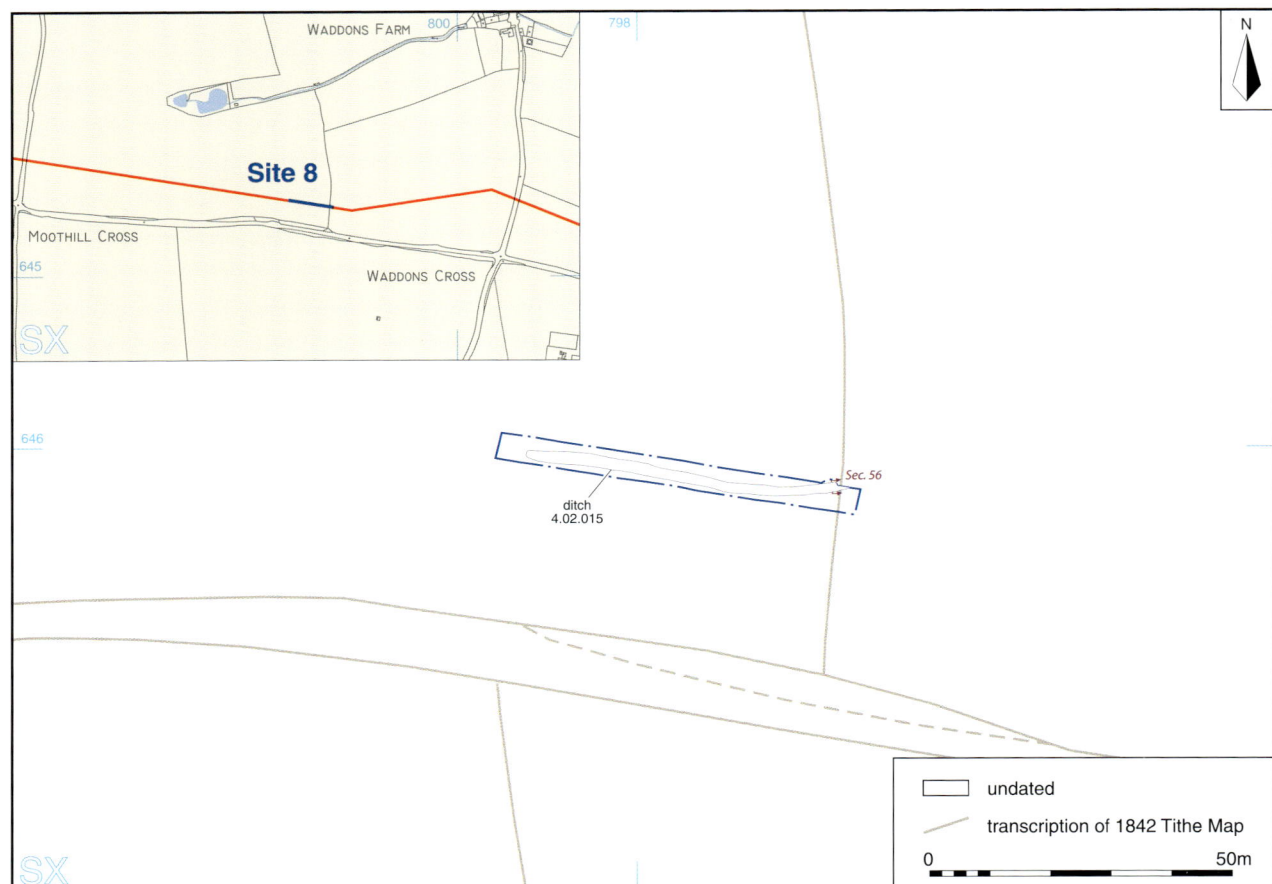

Fig. 5.7 Moothill Cross (Site 18); excavated features on transcription of 1842 Tithe Map. Scales 1:1250 and 1:10,000

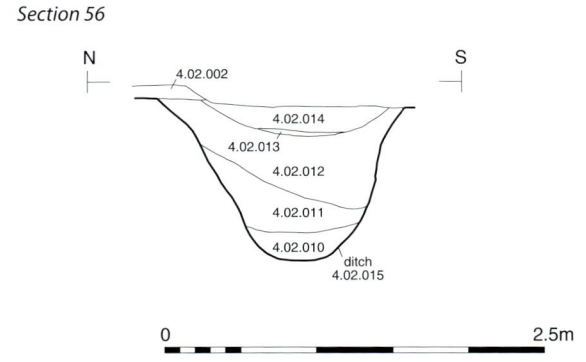

Fig. 5.8 Moothill Cross (Site 18); section 56. Scale 1:50

north/south routeway "Old Straight Track", although again the origins of this record are obscure (NMR: site ref. 1342008). Neither name is found on the early Ordnance Survey maps.

Site 33: Wood Farm, Ugborough

The series of northwest/southeast-aligned field boundaries east of Earlscombe Farm and south of Wood Farm follow their alignments over substantial distances and are considered possible extensions of the Bronze Age reave system on Dartmoor across the Lyd Valley to the north (DHER ref. SX65NE317) (Fig. 5.9). Archaeological investigations in 1991 in connection with the South Devon Spine Main had suggested their possible prehistoric origin (Turton and Weddell 1989, 8; Reed 1991). There was no evidence of prehistoric origins to the present hedgebanks when they were breached, but the geophysical survey of this block of plots (FTC 31.02–31.07), and the subsequent watching brief during soil removal, recorded evidence of ditches on different alignments to the present field boundaries. None of these features yielded dating evidence, but it appears they pre-date the present boundaries and may be prehistoric.

Ditch 31.05.004 was 1.2m wide and 0.6m deep with moderately steep sides and a concave base. It appeared approximately parallel to the current boundary between Plots 31.05 and 31.06, but the wider geophysical survey shows that it runs under it and must be therefore be earlier (Fig. 5.9). No dating evidence was retrieved. Ditch 31.07.004 was 0.5m wide and 0.17m deep with a slightly stepped profile, due to the underlying shale natural. Within the 5m-wide stripped easement it appeared to be rectilinear, but the geophysical survey shows the feature curving under the present boundary and apparently returning in Plot 31.06 to form a semicircle about 14m in diameter. The feature

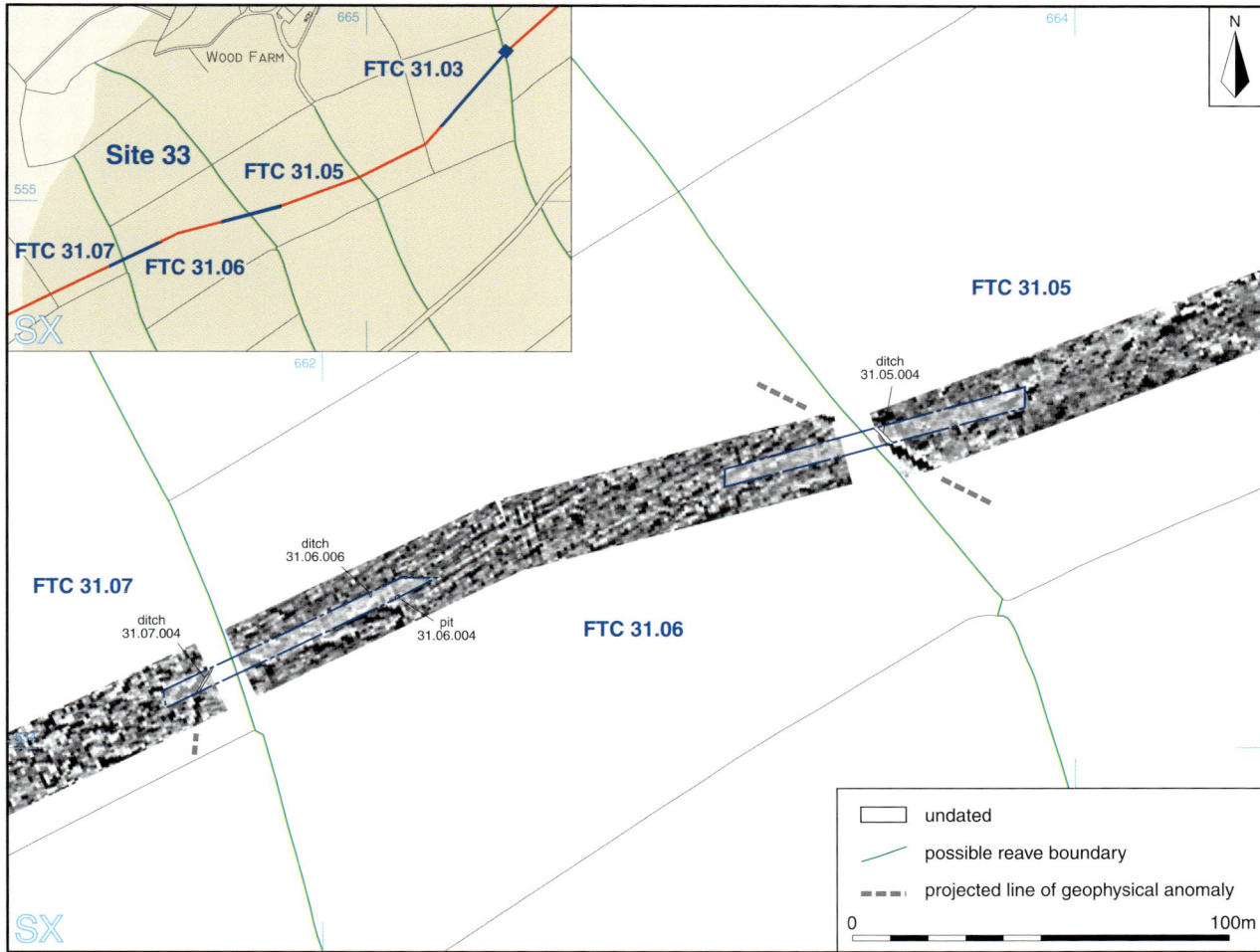

Fig. 5.9 Wood Farm (Site 33); plan of geophysical anomalies and excavated features. Scales 1:2000 and 1:10,000

was not recorded in Plot 31.06 and the reliability of the interpretation of the geophysical survey may be doubted, but ditch 31.07.004 does appear to pre-date the present field pattern. Pit/ditch terminus 31.06.006, 0.4m wide and 0.9m deep, was located 45m to the east of ditch 31.07.004, and contained a similar silty clay fill from which no finds were recovered. Pit 31.06.004, 5m to the south-east, measured 0.59m wide and 0.3m deep, contained a reddish brown, silty clay fill, with redeposited natural shale fragments and again without dating.

Medieval and later ditches and boundaries

Stuart Joyce and Andrew Mudd

The majority of the remaining undated ditches were isolated but some parallel ditches were also present. Most are assumed to have flanked an earthen hedgebank of traditional Devon form, which were constructed until recent times. A description of the process was given by Charles Vancouver in his report to the Board of Agriculture at the beginning of the 19th century. This quote related to North Devon and, in ideal practice at least, this entailed: 'raising a mound on a 9 feet base, with a ditch 3 feet wide on each side, (making the whole site of the fence 15 feet), facing the mound 4 feet high with stones, sodded 3 feet higher above the stone-work, and leaving 4½ feet broad upon the top …' (Vancouver 1808).

Forty-seven ditches in the parallel-ditch group (including three triple-ditched sites) were between 1m and 4m apart, which appears to be within the range of a hedgebank. A further eight were 5m to 7m apart, and these may represent trackway ditches. Of the 47 parallel-ditched field boundary ditches, 29 coincided with boundaries depicted on tithe maps. The triple-ditched boundaries presumably relate to the recutting of one of the ditches, perhaps as the hedgebank was widened, or where the single ditch was replaced by a hedgebank flanked by ditches. The remaining 88 ditches were single ditches. Any of these may not have been field boundaries, but may have been deep cultivation furrows or have been dug as drains within fields. There were no indications of patterns of ridge-and-furrow cultivation.

Recently extant field boundaries were examined at Hogsbrook Farm, Woodbury (Site 10). The land is now

174 *The Archaeology of the South-West Reinforcement Gas Pipeline, Devon: Investigations in 2005–2007*

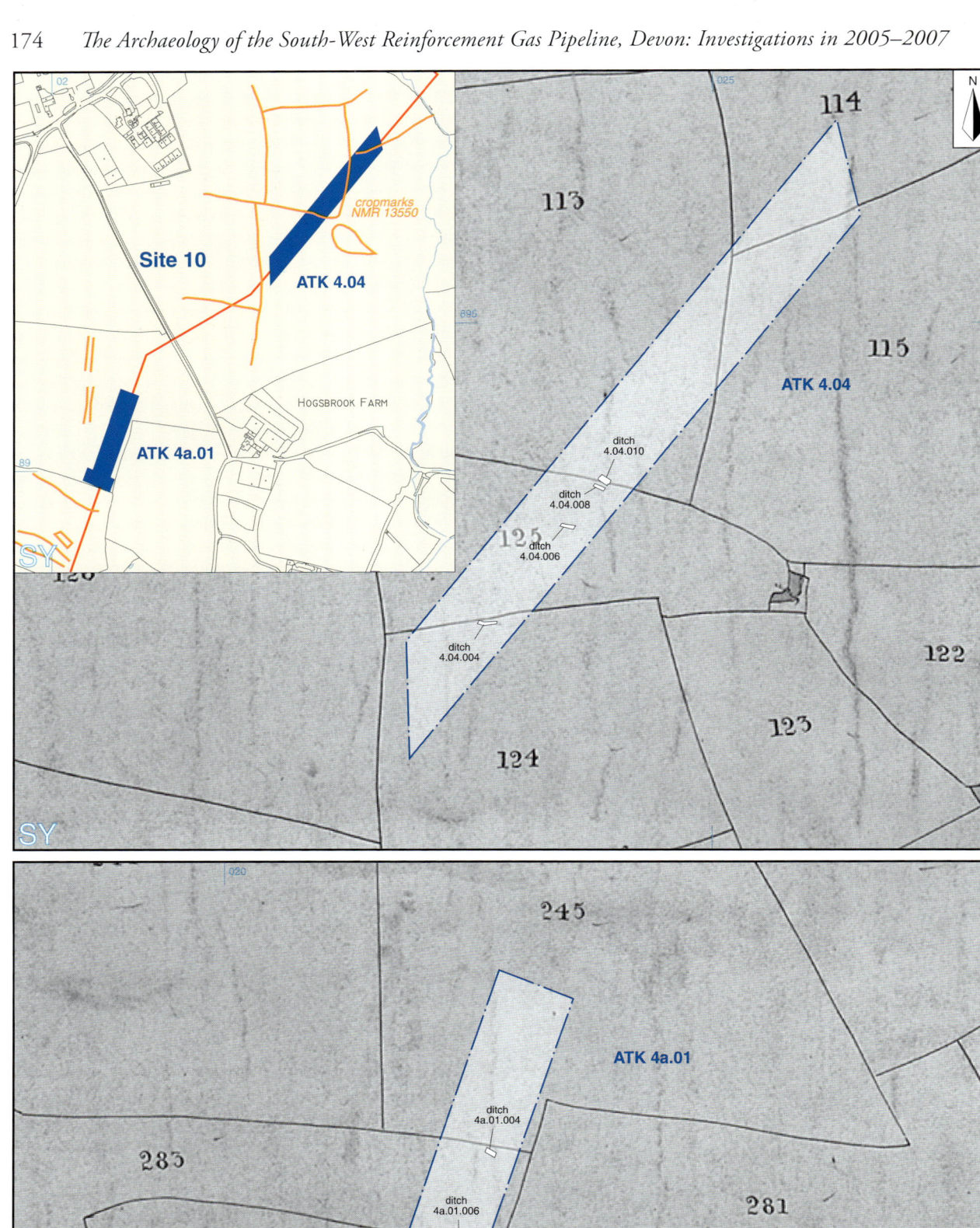

Fig. 5.10 Hogsbrook Farm (Site 10); extract from 1849 Tithe Map, showing excavated features. Scales 1:2500 and 1:10,000

open and 'modern' in historic landscape terms, but the 1849 Tithe Map shows the former field boundaries which now show only as cropmarks (Fig. 5.10). The historic landscape character suggests that the northern part was enclosed with hedgebanks in the late medieval period, probably from strip fields, while the southern part has more of the character of Barton Fields, enclosed between the 15th and 18th centuries. The investigations showed the character of the ditches, none of which contained finds. A series of three parallel approximately east/west-orientated ditches were identified in plot 4a.01, which broadly correlate with the field pattern shown on the tithe map. They were between 1.1m and 1.75m wide and 0.21 and 0.35m deep. Each had moderately sloping symmetrical sides and a relatively flat base and was filled with orange-brown silty clay. To the north-east a similar group of four parallel east/west orientated ditches was identified, correlating or broadly coinciding with those shown on the tithe map. These had a similar shallow profile, moderately sloping symmetrical sides and a relatively flat base and measured between 0.55m and 1m in width; all measured roughly 0.15m in depth. The slightness of these features appears to be typical of ordinary field boundaries in the medieval and later period, although no doubt many exceptions could be found. This may relate to the normal need to dig earth purely to construct the boundary bank, rather than provide a barrier or drainage. The slightness of these features appears typical of ordinary field boundaries in the medieval and later period, and has led to the tendency, in the earlier part of this chapter, to draw attention to particularly deep undated ditches as potentially being pre-medieval.

Most of the 404 field boundaries breached in the three sections of pipeline were earthen banks. Their cross sections did not show indications of rebuilding or later enhancement, such as heightening to form stock proof hedges. A few modern fencelines were recorded, either replacing earlier hedgebanks or forming new field subdivisions. In the South Devon section a total of 23 field boundaries had stone revetments on either one or both faces. No stone-revetted hedgebanks were identified on the pipeline sections in East Devon.

In the Ottery St Mary to Aylesbeare section most (65) of the 74 field boundaries breached did not have associated ditches and the other nine had only one ditch. No extant field boundaries had two flanking ditches, although seven such relict field boundary features were identified during soil stripping. The majority (80) of the 107 field boundaries in the Aylesbeare to Kenn section did not have any signs of ditches, 26 had one associated ditch and only one field boundary had a pair of flanking ditches. Seven double-ditched former field boundaries were identified during soil stripping. On the Fishacre to Choakford section, 192 of the 223 field boundaries breached were without flanking ditches, 27 had one associated ditch and just four had flanking ditches. This general absence of flanking ditches on the existing boundaries fits with the findings on the project as a whole, which revealed only nine sets of double ditches, interpreted as removed field boundaries. From the foregoing it appears that it would be impossible to reconstruct historical field patterns from archaeological evidence alone. In many cases it seems that hedgebanks would have been constructed from topsoil and subsoil alone without the need to dig much deeper, and therefore would leave no archaeologically identifiable traces.

Chapter 6
Discussion

Introduction

This chapter provides a discussion of the evidence of past human activity recovered from this project, and its wider archaeological context. Notwithstanding the limitations of archaeological understanding imposed by the very narrow transect of the pipeline, several significant discoveries have been made, and the examination of 'off-site' archaeology has offered a counterpoint to 'settlement-focused' excavations, which miss the totality of activities undertaken by past individuals and communities in the inhabited landscape of this part of the country. The value of the project has been shown to lie in the cumulative gain of information from individually small-scale excavations – the scatters of pits and ditches, often yielding few finds and difficult to place in their contemporary context. The less obvious sites include, in particular, those lacking ditched enclosures, and the work has helped to counter the bias in much archaeological work, which takes the 'settlement enclosure' as the unit of study. This has led to the discovery of individual pits and pit clusters of prehistoric and early medieval date, unenclosed Iron Age, Roman and medieval settlement, and rural industry in the form of Iron Age iron production and Roman-period pewter making. There are also suggestions that land division in the Otter Valley and South Devon was more prevalent in the Middle Bronze Age than in the Roman period – a contrast to patterns found in other parts of the country. The shortage of evidence for Romano-British fields in Devon has become more apparent with the accumulation of archaeological information in the county (Rippon 2012, 299–300) and the present project confirms this observation.

The programme of radiocarbon dating has supported and augmented the scant artefactual evidence considerably (Fig. 6.1; Table 6.1). Although few of the samples of material dated would be considered ideal in terms of their contextual integrity, the cumulative pattern is of interest, reflecting as it does the broad trend of past activity across this transect of land. It is perhaps relevant that even the dates from redeposited material, providing five of the earlier Neolithic dates, can be taken as indications of activity in the landscape at this time notwithstanding an absence of associated features.

Mesolithic (9500 to 4000 BC)

The Mesolithic covered a long time span, from c. 9500 BC to c. 4000 BC, depending on the definition used, and was arguably a major formative stage for both the environment and cultures of the British Isles but, despite this, the record for the South West is thinly spread and that for Devon in particular 'relatively minor' and dominated by surface scatters of flint and occasional small pits (Hosfield *et al.* 2008, 53). Mesolithic material from the present project appears typical of this trend. The only identified Mesolithic feature was a small pit containing charred oak and hazelnut shell at Moore Farm, Harberton (Site 28). A piece of hazelnut was radiocarbon dated to 5017–4847 BC, putting it in the same general Late Mesolithic date range as the Westward Ho! shell midden site and Three Holes Cave, Torbryan (ibid.). The pit was without flintwork, but small collections of diagnostically Mesolithic flintwork came from five plots along the 56km of the pipeline sections, all from residual contexts. The only potentially significant group would seem to be that from Pixies' Parlour, Ottery St Mary (Site 4) where the lithics included an obliquely blunted bladelet (Fig. 2.45, 1). Two core-rejuvenation flakes (one illustrated, Fig. 2.45, 2) are potentially Mesolithic or Early Neolithic. Mesolithic flintwork (27 blades) had previously been recorded from this area (DHER ref. SY09SE/1). The scale of this occupation is unclear, partly because of the difficulty of distinguishing Mesolithic from Early Neolithic knapping debris and also because of the limited area examined. It should be noted that the recovery of unstratified flintwork on this project was opportunistic rather than systematic and therefore cannot be directly compared with excavations

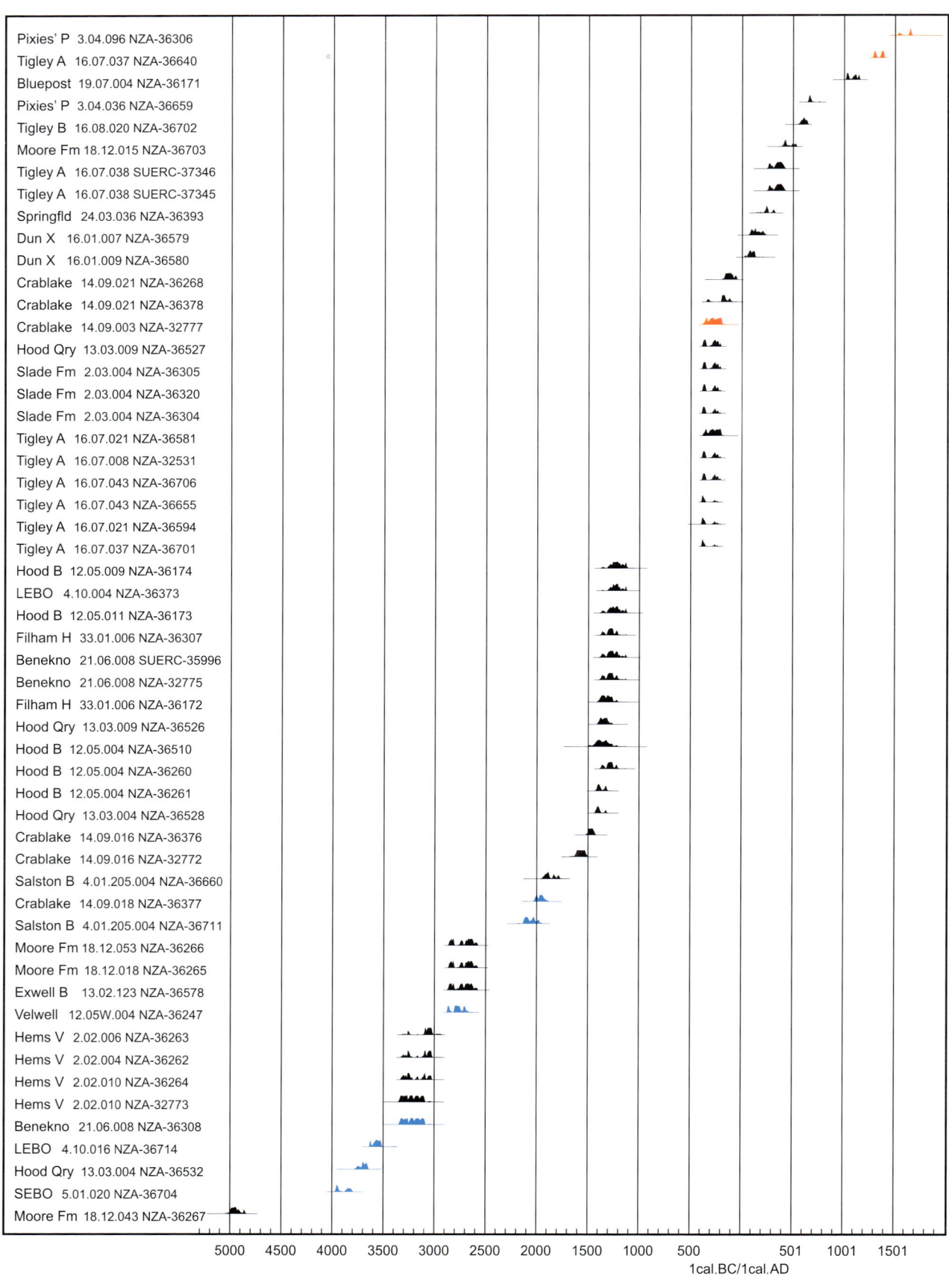

Fig. 6.1 Radiocarbon dates calibrated using OXCal 4.1.7 (Bronk Ramsey 2009) and the Incal09 dataset (Reimer et al. 2009). Distributions in blue are for samples which were redeposited in their contexts and/or consisted of old wood; distributions in red are for samples which were intrusive in their contexts

Table 6.1: Key to scheme-wide radiocarbon dating plot

Feature No.	Site No.	Site Name
OTA 3.04.096	4	Pixies' Parlour, Ottery St Mary
FTC 16.07.037	26	Tigley A, Dartington
FTC 19.07.004	29	Blue Post, Harberton
OTA 3.04.036	4	Pixies' Parlour, Ottery St Mary
FTC 16.08.020	27	Tigley B, Dartington
FTC 18.12.015	28	Moore Farm, Harberton
FTC 16.07.038 (2 dates)	26	Tigley A, Dartington
FTC 24.03.036	31	Springfield, Ugborough
FTC 16.01.007	25	Dun Cross, Dartington
FTC 16.01.009	25	Dun Cross, Dartington
ATK 14.09.021 (2 dates)	15	Crablake Farm, Exminster
ATK 14.09.003	15	Crablake Farm, Exminster
FTC 13.03.009 (2 dates)	23	Hood Quarry, Dartington
OTA 2.03.004 (3 dates)	2	Slade Farm, Ottery St Mary
FTC 16.07.021 (2 dates)	26	Tigley A, Dartington
FTC 16.07.008	26	Tigley A, Dartington
FTC 16.07.077 (043) (2 dates)	26	Tigley A, Dartington
FTC 16.07.037	26	Tigley A, Dartington
FTC 12.05.009	21	Hood Ball, Rattery
OTA 4.10.004	7	Land East of Broad Oak, Ottery St Mary
FTC 12.05.011	21	Hood Ball, Rattery
FTC 33.01.006 (2 dates)	34	Filham House, Ugborough
FTC 21.06.008 (3 dates)	30	Beneknowle, Diptford
FTC 12.05.004 (3 dates)	21	Hood Ball, Rattery
FTC 13.03.004 (2 dates)	23	Hood Quarry, Dartington
ATK 14.09.016 (2 dates)	15	Crablake Farm, Exminster
OTA 4.01.205.004 (2 dates)	6	Salston B, Ottery St Mary
ATK 14.09.018	15	Crablake Farm, Exminster
FTC 18.12.053	28	Moore Farm, Harberton
FTC 18.12.018	28	Moore Farm, Harberton
ATK 13.02.123	14	Exwell Barton, Powderham
FTC 12.05W.004	22	Lower Velwell, Rattery
FTC 2.02.006	17	Hems Valley, Staverton
FTC 2.02.004	17	Hems Valley, Staverton
FTC 2.02.010 (2 dates)	17	Hems Valley, Staverton
OTA 4.10.016	7	Land East of Broad Oak, Ottery St Mary
OTA 5.01.020	8	South-East of Broad Oak, Ottery St Mary
FTC 18.12.043	28	Moore Farm, Harberton

deliberately targeting Mesolithic materials. The location, on a sandy knoll above the floodplain of the River Otter, would seem to be an ecotonal boundary, chosen to exploit a variety plant and animal resources, and typical of Mesolithic occupations, while its location between coastal and upland sites of this period invite comparison with the late Mesolithic occupation at Three Holes Cave, where marine shell beads and a beach pebble rubber demonstrate coastal contacts (Hosfield *et al.* 2008, 53). It is possible that the occupation at Pixies'

Parlour fitted a seasonal migration pattern, although this cannot be confirmed and there is little that can be deduced about activities undertaken.

The findspots of prehistoric flintwork on Figures 2.41–2.44 show a varied but not random distribution. These figures conflate lithics from a wide chronological range, but there are notable clusters on ground above the Otter Valley and some of the minor tributaries in this section of pipeline (Fig. 2.41). Sites with over 20 pieces are presented as pie charts. The significance of Pixies' Parlour (Site 4) in the overall quantification is overwhelming, as is the proportion of earlier prehistoric forms (blades and blade cores) which are uncommon elsewhere. There is not a particularly dense distribution across the sandstone geology of East Devon (Figs 2.41–2.42), although there is a minor cluster on the ridge between the Exe Estuary and the River Kenn west of Powderham (Sites 13 and 14) without a great number of diagnostically early pieces. The distribution of flint is not notably less on the slate-dominated geology of South Devon (Figs 2.43–2.44), although some bias in introduced by the systematic surface collection in 2001 from Site 17 and FTC plots 3.03, 3.04, 7.01, 27.02, 27.03 and 27.04.. There are early forms on the interfluve above the Dart Valley (plots FTC 3.04–FTC 9.05), by an upper tributary of the Avon at Springfield (Site 31) and between the River Erme and Ludd Brook (Site 34). It is likely that the distribution of Mesolithic and Early Neolithic flint was connected with the seasonal movements of hunting and gathering, and perhaps pastoralism, so that locations on or overlooking routeways and water sources was more of a determining factor than the nature of the underlying geology and its implication for soils, which would have been more important once land clearance had made tillage and more permanent grazing possible. It may be significant that the concentration of flintwork between the Erme and Ludd Brook (Site 34) lies on the edge of lighter soils which developed on the river gravels, and it is possible that this area was cleared for grazing and cultivation relatively early, maintaining its significance as an area of occupation through earlier prehistoric times.

Early Neolithic (4000 to 3300 BC)

The increased number and range of finds over the previous period appear typical of lowland Devon, although the narrow corridor of investigation makes overall site, let alone landscape-wide, interpretations rather speculative. There was Early Neolithic occupation in East Devon at Pixies' Parlour (Site 4) as shown by a probable tree-throw hole containing pottery and flint, as well as a large group of unstratified and redeposited flint, which includes at least some Early Neolithic material. The pottery is not closely datable, but the carinated bowls are closely comparable with those from Carn Brea in Cornwall (R.J. Mercer 1981) which suggests a date perhaps as early as 3700 BC (Quinnell, Chapter 2). While the form of the feature suggests it was a tree-throw, the material from it does not suggest a random accumulation and it appears that the pottery and flint were deliberately deposited. The range of pottery fabrics (six types identified) includes granite-derived fabrics from the Dartmoor area and a Permian breccia fabric likely to be from the Exe valley. The flint is also non-local, the east Devon coast and/or the Blackdown Hills being the most likely sources, and the chert may also have come from the latter region. The range of sources of material from just one feature is further evidence of the network of contacts maintained by societies at this time. This may reflect continuing aspects of movement undertaken in the Mesolithic period and indicate similar social and economic motives. Early Neolithic features are relatively rare in the region; a pit group from approximately 2km to the west, on the western side of the River Otter, has been published (Fitzpatrick *et al.* 1999). Although these pits were of a smaller size (*c.* 0.41m in diameter), they contained Early Neolithic pottery from three separate vessels. A further four sites containing Early Neolithic pits with pottery are recorded within the vicinity (Leverett and Quinnell 2010)

The possible ditch terminal at Croft Cottages, Staverton (Site 20), containing fragments of Early Neolithic carinated bowl, is also of uncertain form. The suggestion that it formed part of an interrupted ditch feature is speculative but cannot be ruled out, particularly in view of the faint but intriguing suggestion of curving cropmarks in this plot. The ditch does not have the characteristic broad profile of causewayed enclosures, which are not known this far west in any case. In plan form there is the suggestion of postholes which may have formed a palisade, but these were not clear enough to be defined or commented upon during excavation. South Devon is a region where the nature of Early Neolithic occupation sites is obscure and the presence of enclosures of this date still a matter of debate. Possible tor enclosures lie at Whittor and Dewerstone on the western side of Dartmoor, while Hazard Hill (south-west of Staverton) has been identified as a possible causewayed enclosure without conclusive evidence being forthcoming from any of these sites (Griffith 2001; Whittle *et al.* 2011, 476–8, fig. 10.1).

Middle to Late Neolithic (3300 to 2400 BC)

Securely identified later Neolithic and Early Bronze Age sites are poorly represented in Devon compared with counties further east despite the number of monuments on Dartmoor (such as stone circles, stone rows and cairns) that are thought to be of these periods (Pollard and Healy 2008, 77). Four late 4th millennium BC radiocarbon dates from the group of pits in the Hems Valley, Staverton (Site 17), confirm the presence of occupation associated with Peterborough Ware, which is rare in Devon. The pottery itself was abraded (and provisionally identified as Grooved Ware before radiocarbon dating), but was associated with charred hazelnut shells, hazel charcoal and with what appeared to be deliberate deposits of natural and utilised rubbing stones. The group exhibits a clear instance of intentional deposition, as found elsewhere in the South West (Pollard and Healy 2008, 82), and falls within a pattern of pit deposition recorded on a number of sites in Devon and Cornwall such as the late Neolithic pits at Tremough, Cornwall (Gossip and Jones 2007). It also has similarities with a general pattern identified for the Neolithic in eastern England, where pit deposits often consist of redeposited midden material, with pottery sherds invariably representing less than a quarter of the original vessel (Garrow *et al.* 2005, 139; Garrow 2007, 11–16).

At Moore Farm, Harberton (Site 28), the date of pits and a curving gully containing Grooved Ware pottery was confirmed by two virtually identical radiocarbon determinations (in the range 2860–2579 BC: NZA-36265, -36266) on associated hazelnut shells from separate pits. Sites of this date are rare in Devon. The pottery was abraded but included conjoining sherds so may have been deliberate placements comparable to the more 'formal' Grooved Ware pits found further east (Webster 2008a, 82). The inclusion of an oyster shell fragment in pit 18.12.032 is noteworthy, and it may be significant that the pottery from this feature was of gabbroic fabric from Cornwall, another indicator of distant contacts. The oyster shell may have been an ornament or acquired for other non-dietary reasons, but it was too incomplete to ascertain whether it had been modified. A perforated oyster shell, found on the chest of the Early Bronze Age 'Amesbury Archer', had probably been worn as a pendant (Wyles 2011, 163–4). Oyster has been also been found as an ingredient of Grooved Ware pots from Ratfyn, Woodlands and Chalk Plaque Pit in the Amesbury area (Wiltshire), while scallop shells have come from pits at Ratfyn and Woodlands (ibid.).

The nature of the Moore Farm site is unclear, but the gully may form part of a small circular monument comparable to ring-ditches or 'hengiform' enclosures known from other parts of the region in the later Neolithic. It can be emphasised that there were a number of undated pits and gullies along the 250m strip on this ridge, any number of which may have been associated with the Late Neolithic activity. There appears, however, to be a time depth to activity here with two radiocarbon samples from pits returning dates as divergent as the late Mesolithic (pit 18.12.043, Chapter 2) and the late or sub-Roman period (pit 18.12.015, Chapter 4). The observation that both late Mesolithic and Grooved Ware activity was found at Three Holes Cave, Torbryan (the late Mesolithic date of 5290–4840 BC (OxA-4492) overlapping with the date from the pit at Moore Farm) poses questions about just how persistent these patterns of movement around the landscape were. In the present state of knowledge perhaps not too much should be made of coincidences of material remains. Late Mesolithic flintwork has been found beneath Neolithic sites elsewhere in the South West (Webster 2008a, 76) without demonstration of a relationship between the two. However, the complete absence of cultivated plants among the charred hazel wood and hazelnuts from the Moore Farm pits (Table 2.20) makes the suggestion that settled agriculture was not the only option available to the inhabitants of the region, even as late as the mid third millennium BC. The evidence from Moore Farm and Hems Valley is compatible with the concept of a 'punctuated transition' from wild to cultivated foods in the Neolithic, a model that envisages a general lessening or abandonment of cereal cultivation from *c.* 3350 BC for about a thousand years, a trend that has been indicated nationally by an increasing number of closely targeted radiocarbon dates (Stevens and Fuller 2012). It is possible therefore that pastoralism and wild resources were more important than arable farming in Devon at this time. The broad picture provided by pollen sequences in the Exe Valley and Exmoor suggests that local areas of oak-hazel woodland persisted into the Neolithic. At Brightworthy in the upper Exe the local pollen signal can be extrapolated to suggest clearance in the early Bronze Age, and more generally woodland clearance on Exmoor is dated from about 2000 BC, more or less synchronous with the expected date for clearances on Dartmoor prior to the establishment of the reaves from *c.* 1500 BC (Fyfe *et al.* 2003, 178). In the Exe Valley lowland deforestation of the more mixed elm-lime-oak-hazel woodland started in the late Mesolithic, and cereal pollen is present from *c.* 3500 BC, strongly suggesting established clearances which can be related to the developing ceremonial and domestic use of the valley (ibid., 178–9). It should be mentioned that the major Early Neolithic site on Hazard Hill lies just 2km east of Moore Farm, although the nature of this occupation, including the presence or otherwise of an enclosure, is still uncertain (Griffith 2001) and its relationship with Moore Farm, and indeed other Neolithic sites in South Devon, remains a subject for future research.

The emphasis on hazelnuts among the charred remains from both Neolithic and Bronze Age features can be gauged from Figure 6.2 although the statistics need treating with caution. The overall quantities of cereals and hazelnuts are not directly comparable since they derive from different taphonomies leading to different chances of preservation (Jones 2000). They cannot be used to suggest the relative importance of gathered and cultivated plants in any period. It is possible that all the hazelnut shells derived from relatively few burning events, such as when caches of hazelnuts were consumed and their discarded shells used as fuel. Processing cereals for consumption need not have left much charred grain, even if cereals had been the dietary mainstay.

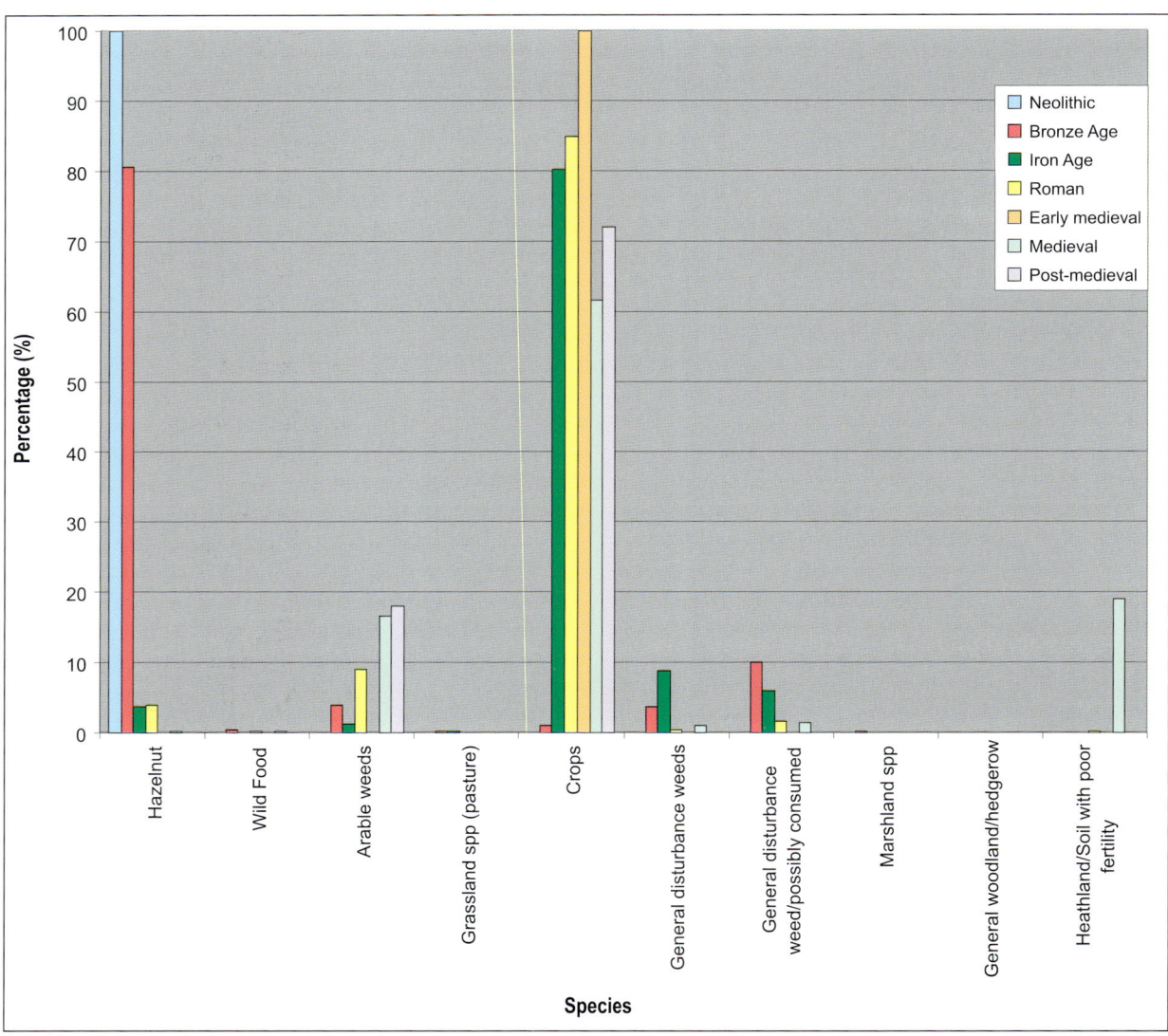

Fig. 6.2 Percentage of wild food, cultivated crops and weed species

Notwithstanding this caveat, it seems clear that the practices involving the consumption of wild foods, while broadly similar in the Neolithic and Bronze Age, had changed by the Iron Age. There appears to have been a decisive shift in subsistence strategies by the mid 1st millennium BC which made wild foods of marginal significance in the archaeological record. The relative proportions of tree species, shown by the charcoal identifications, also show a marked decline in hazel, which dominates the Neolithic assemblages (Figs 6.3 and 6.4). The Bronze Age assemblages show a greater variety of species, including gorse/broom, oak, ash and cherry, which is consistent with a greater variety of habitats resulting from the clearance of closed canopy forest.

Early Bronze Age (2400 to 1800 BC)

Two sites had evidence of Early Bronze Age activity; the Beaker pit at Springfield, Ugborough (Site 31) and the unaccompanied cremation at Salston B, Ottery St Mary (Site 6). The ring-ditch or barrow south-east of Broad Oak, Ottery St Mary (Site 7) yielded virtually nothing by way of dating evidence, although the few flints recovered may be more indicative of the early rather than middle Bronze Age. The virtual indestructibility of flint means that small quantities can easily become redeposited in later contexts and are not reliable for dating purposes even when intrinsically datable.

The partially complete All-Over-Cord Beaker from Springfield is an early form but is not itself datable with any precision, lying within the range 2500–2000 BC (Quinnell, Chapter 2; Fig. 2.37). It is the first of its type to be found in Devon or Cornwall and as such may be a relatively late introduction. It would appear to have been associated with the round barrow, perhaps as a marker for its construction, but nothing is known about the date or sequence of activity involved in the barrow's construction and usage, and it is perhaps

Discussion 183

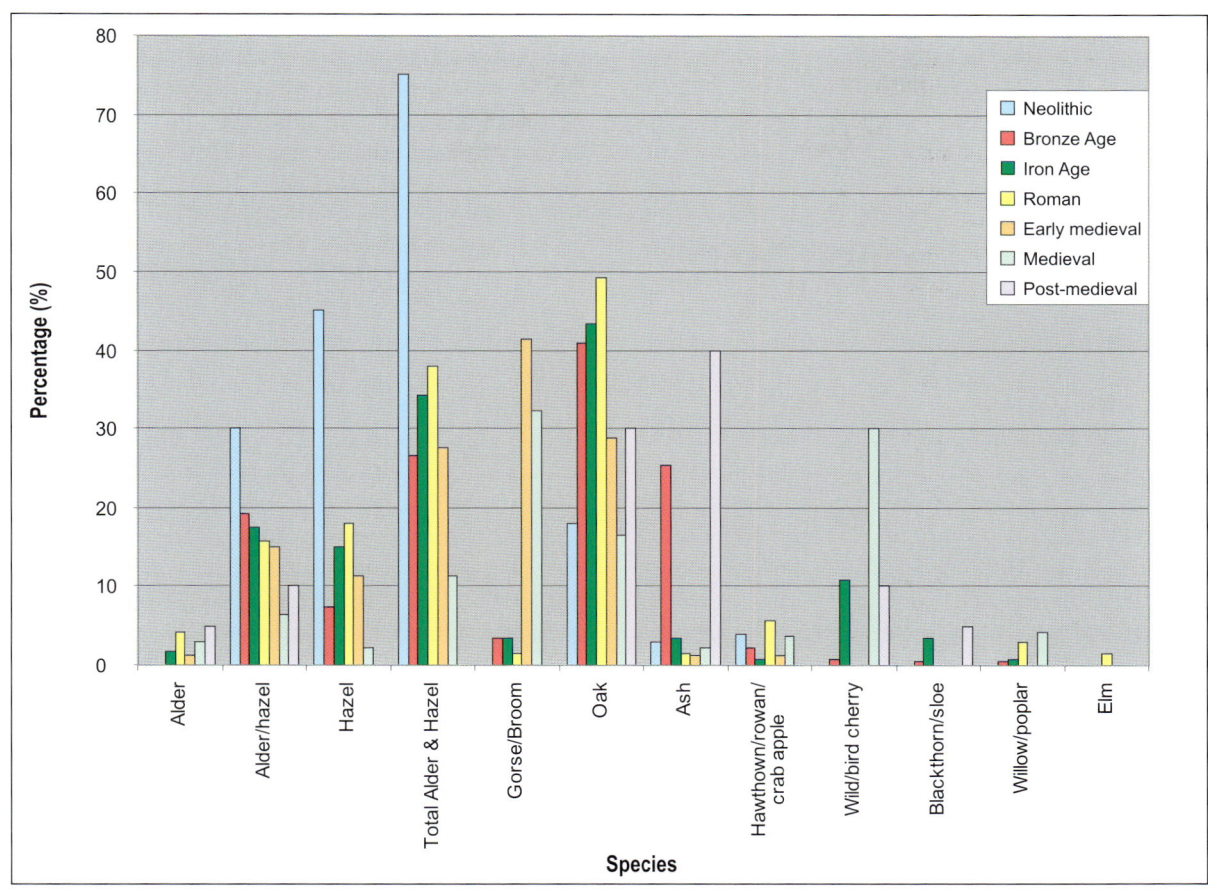

Fig. 6.3   Broad characterisation of charcoal species fragments identified from the Neolithic to post-medieval periods

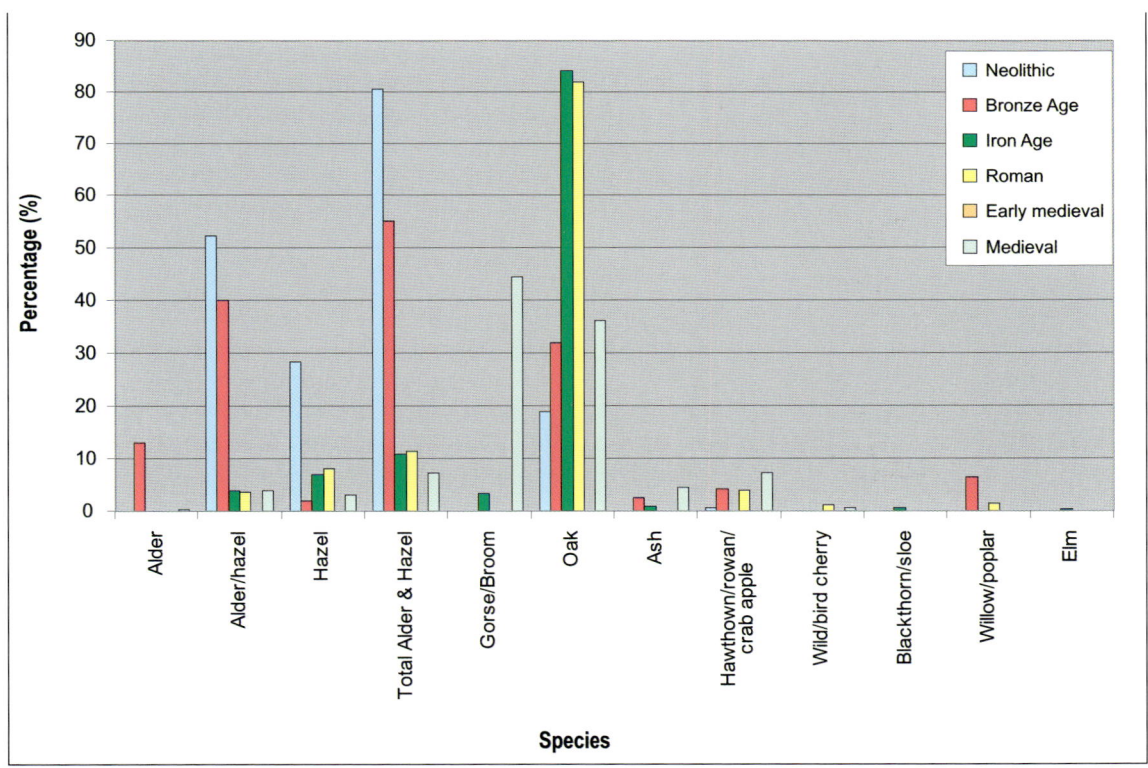

Fig. 6.4   Full analysis of charcoal species identified from the Neolithic to medieval periods

equally possible that its deposition was coeval with the early elements of the barrow. Recent research shows that the construction of round barrows begins in the Early Neolithic and the Neolithic forms are often larger and more elliptical in shape than the later, rounder and smaller 'Beaker' barrows (Woodward 2002, 37, 139–42). It therefore remains uncertain whether the Beaker vessel was positioned in relation to the earlier monument or whether it represents a significant location upon which the later barrow was focused. Nonetheless the association of large mound and early Beaker is of interest in the continuing debate about the nature of the 'Beaker phenomenon' (e.g. Sheridan 2012).

A common theme of Bronze Age barrow studies in recent years has been the emphasis on sequences of activity, many non-funerary, preceding the construction of the barrow mound, which is sometimes seen as the final act of closure (Last 2007). Nowhere is this more apparent than in the south-west peninsula, where the term 'ritual barrow' has been coined to emphasise the need to understand the use of space, and the sequence and meaning of actions, rather than to assume that the monument was only a place of burial (Nowakowski 2007). Quinnell (2003, 1) has made the point that, nationally, only 9% of Beaker pottery has any association with burials and that fragmentary vessels from pits is typical for Devon (ibid., 17). Springfield Barrow itself was not surveyed as part of the current project, and there is no detailed record of its form. The schedule describes it as a bowl barrow, although said to be oval in form and with an outer bank partly surviving outside the ditch (Fig. 2.13). This makes it unusual for a bowl barrow and in English Heritage's own lexicon it should perhaps be classified as a 'fancy barrow', a term accommodating unusual or elaborate features (English Heritage 2011). The 'pear-shaped' (rather than oval) plan of the Scheduled area may reflect the influence of the quarry on its northern side. Whatever its present appearance, classification of the final outward form of the barrow is an insufficient basis for understanding the structural sequences and deposits which provide the evidence for the wider meaning of these monuments and the way they developed over time.

The original form of the ring-ditch south-east of Broad Oak (Site 8) is not clear, although it does appear to have contained a central mound, much eroded by cultivation, composed of several discrete layers of sediment, including redeposited sand from the ditch and darker soil that may have been topsoil or turf (Fig. 2.20). There was no evidence of a burial of any sort, but little of the interior was examined and it is not possible to arrive at a definitive conclusion about the monument's purpose. The ditch fills were indicative of natural infilling over the long term with a final infill of ploughsoil. The presence of clay fill in the central part of the ditch appears natural but is not immediately explicable as being derived from the neighbouring sandstone geology and its presence does recall the widespread occurrence of imported material for filling ditches of Cornish barrows reported by Nowakowski (2007). These examples apparently included 'dumps' of yellow clay at Little Gaverigan, Indian Queens (ibid., 101–2).

The Salston B cremation was that of an adult woman whose remains had been placed in a small pit without a surviving container or accompanying grave goods (Fig. 2.12). The later of the two dates (c. 1900 BC) on the bone itself is early for flat grave, unaccompanied cremations. In the South West, Early Bronze Age burial is normally linked with monuments such as round barrows or ring-ditches, and sometimes flat graves are associated with standing stones, although this is not invariably the case (Webster 2008a, 101). The Early Bronze Age cremation cemetery at Elburton, Plymouth, appears to have been a satellite to a barrow although the precise relationship is uncertain (Watts and Quinnell 2001, 32). The burial at Salston B may have been associated with the other features here, but there is no indication that this was the case and all were without finds. It is possible to speculate that other pits contained uncremated human remains or, along with the possible 'trapezoidal enclosure', were elements of a mortuary monument of some kind whose structure has largely been lost, but on the current evidence this is unconvincing. The burial adds to the range of Early Bronze Age burial practices in the region but provides little scope for further insight.

Middle Bronze Age (1800 to 1300 BC)

The Middle Bronze Age is here defined through the presence of Trevisker Ware pottery and/or radiocarbon dates falling in the middle centuries of the 2nd millennium BC. The number of sites and finds of this period was larger than any other prehistoric period, partly reflected in the number of radiocarbon dates falling in this range (Fig. 6.1). The variety of evidence was also wide. This included part of a terraced structure at Beneknowle, Diptford (Site 30), a group of pottery-filled pits at Crablake Farm, Exminster (Site 15), a scatter of charcoal pits at Hood Ball (Site 21), a large boundary ditch at Hood Quarry and assorted ditches and pits elsewhere (Sites 4, 7, 8 and 34).

The group of five pits at Crablake Farm, Exminster (Site 15) yielded the largest group of Middle Bronze Age pottery from the project. This site was recorded in the field as a possible cremation cemetery, although subsequent soil processing revealed no bone to be present. The palaeobotanical remains from pit 14.09.016 include bread-type wheat and barley grains, suggesting the site of a farming settlement and the site can be interpreted as a domestic one, although there was no evidence for buildings and it is difficult to justify any specific interpretation of the features. Of great interest was the recovery of a portion of a large *in situ* Trevisker vessel (Figs 2.38, 2.39). The pot had been positioned upright but was missing both its rim and base, so it had never been buried complete. The interior, while containing dark soil, was without finds. Decorated sherds, found apart from the vessel and not joining it, appear likely to have been from the upper body, but this is not certain. The recovery of semi-complete vessels is not uncommon in the region. Part of a Trevisker vessel was found in a pit in the hillslope enclosure at Holworthy Farm, Parracombe, although, with the base preserved, there it is possible to suggest that the pot functioned as a storage vessel. The bed of hazel charcoal upon which the Parracombe pot sat may, however, indicate some related act of symbolism. It is noteworthy that this plough-truncated site showed few readily interpretable features, just a scatter of small pits, postholes and gullies, while the enclosure itself was defined only by a low bank without a ditch (Green 2009, fig. 17). On some plough-truncated sites it is clear that evidence of settlement would be very hard to elucidate. Parts of vessels are also known from more clearly non-domestic contexts such as the Little Gaverigan Barrow, where part of an inverted Collared Urn was found centrally under the mound. Devoid of contents, it is suggested that the vessel was concerned with an act of commemoration (Nowakowski 2007, 101). Likewise, in another apparently funerary context, the Early Bronze Age cremation cemetery at Elburton included a charcoal-filled Collared Urn without trace of cremated bone (Watts and Quinnell 2001, 32). Such deposits could have been appropriate to a range of sites and contexts, and, as with Beakers, parts of vessels (and perhaps other items of material culture) would appear to have been used as metaphors or metonyms in commemorative or other ritual activities. At Lockington, Leicestershire, it was suggested that the missing sherds from the (grog-tempered) Beakers buried near the Barrow VI may have been used as tempering for new pots, which thereby inherited the identity and associations of the old vessel (Hughes 2000, 98).

The scatter of seven shallow pits containing charred food remains at Hood Ball (Site 21) would seem to be another aspect of Bronze Age occupation. The series of five radiocarbon determinations were reasonably consistently in the range 1400–1200 cal. BC and were clearly the only means of dating this type of slight and fragile evidence. It remains unclear whether these pits were in any way associated with the wider pattern of ditches to the west visible as cropmarks.

More evidence for settlement of some form came from Beneknowle (Site 30), where the sunken pit is seen as part of a building terraced into the hillside (Figs 2.30, 2.32). Two of the three radiocarbon dates are consistent and within the range *c.* 1400–1100 BC. The excavated evidence strongly suggests that the structure was a Middle Bronze Age building similar in design to those excavated at Trethellan Farm, Newquay (Nowakowski 1991). The form seems unique so far in Devon. The comparisons include the tradition of construction within a hollow, the south-east-facing entrance ramp, and the construction, in some cases at least, of a stone kerb. At Trethellan Farm there was evidence from internal postholes that the roofs were supported on a ring of wooden posts and that the walls were likely to have been of wattle and daub. This seems likely to have been the case at Beneknowle as well, although, except for the clear posthole on the left side of the doorway, which has an exact counterpart in House 2222 at Trethellan (Nowakowski 1991, figs 15a, 18), there was considerably less evidence for the structure's architecture. Too little of the structure was revealed to extend these comparisons much further, but from the area exposed it appears that it would have been rather smaller than the Trethellan examples (which were *c.* 8–9m) and was perhaps an ancillary building rather than a residence. This interpretation may be supported by the complete absence of artefacts from the structure. It can be added that the evidence for the demise of the building, with the withdrawal of the post some time prior to the deposition of a layer of charcoal, and a fairly rapid infilling of the hollow, is compatible with a model that sees a systematic abandonment of the building at the end of the occupation (Nowakowski 1991, 2001). The range and quantity of charred botanical remains from the layer of charcoal are exceptional for this period, but found within a single deposit do not suggest an obvious origin (Tables 2.24, 2.25). The quantity of vetch, *Chenopodium* and *Brassica/sinapsis* species may indicate a predominance of arable weeds, although they may have been harvested as fodder or even food for humans or thatching. Other plants comprise mainly species of disturbed ground (black-bindweed, greater plantain, dock) compatible with arable land, but there are also 'hedgerow' species (blackberry, raspberry) and species of grassland (grass, buttercup, self heal). There was a low presence of cereals. The charred faecal pellets of water vole suggest that vegetation may have been collected from stream edges. If the conflagration is seen as a deliberate act of closure, it is possible to see these remains as a deliberate gathering of vegetation from the land around, rather than material that happened to be near or in the building, and perhaps analogous to the large depositions of artefactual materials in the demolition deposits of some of the Trethellan houses (Nowakowski 2001, 141–3). The variety of wood charcoal is similarly wide and may have been largely structural, or alternatively gathered from various sources (Table 2.28).

It is clear that by the Middle Bronze Age the division and apportionment of land was extensive in Devon, but the evidence is almost exclusively limited to Dartmoor and its landscape-wide system of reaves. There is the expectation that Dartmoor was not a special case, the 'moor' and 'off-moor' landscapes being largely historical constructs, and that such land division and associated patterns of settlement ought to be evident elsewhere (Griffith 1994). Set against this is the recognition that the landscapes of the Bronze Age have been shown to vary across the southern England, with extensive land divisions recognisable in some areas of both upland and lowland, but absent in others (Yates 2007). In Devon there have been patchy discoveries of ditched field boundaries in the Exe Valley (Barber 2000), at Castle Hill, Feniton, above the Otter valley (Butterworth 1999a) and elsewhere, and there is the suggestion that patterns of land division may have been widespread in southern Devon, from Dartmoor to the coast (Yates 2007, 66–7).

The boundary ditch at Hood Quarry, Dartington (Site 23) appears to have been a massive feature, clearly identified by magnetometer and with a straight length of about 450m westwards visible as a cropmark (Fig. 2.26). There is the suggestion from the vertical aerial photographic coverage that the ditch curved southwards (Fig. 2.29) but it cannot be traced much further and there was no suggestion from the pipeline fieldwork that it completed an enclosure. The ditch was filled with largely sterile sediments and dating is not secure. The sparse material recovered gives us a choice of three dates: Early Neolithic from a radiocarbon date on Maloideae charcoal in the primary fill; Middle Bronze Age, from a date on ash charcoal also in the primary fill; and Iron Age, from a potsherd in an upper fill of the evaluation trench. The Early Neolithic date is unlikely in the extreme and must be from old wood. Although an earthwork of this size would not be out of place in the Iron Age, either as a defensive 'dyke' or hilltop enclosure, there is nothing comparable in the region. The Iron Age potsherd, moreover, is not from a primary fill and appears likely to relate to later infilling. As a Middle Bronze Age feature the ditch is remarkable, but 'monumental' landscape division has a precedent only 8km to the west on the moors above South Brent where the mapped reave system has its most southerly extent (Fleming 1988). In its directness and 'terrain obliviousness' in crossing the headwaters of the stream in Hood Copse to the west, and its apparent aim to demarcate the high land between streams draining into the Dart, the Hood Quarry ditch has aspects in common with the long, terminal reaves on Dartmoor whose purpose seems to have been to delimit and control upland grazing land (Fleming 1988; 1994; Herring 2008). As with the reaves, there may have been no need to completely enclose the grazing land, so the ditch need not have completed a circuit in order to have served its purpose.

The possibility that reaves extended onto the lower ground south-east of Dartmoor was examined when the pipeline breached the hedgebanks at Wood Farm, Ugborough (Site 33, plots FTC 31.02–31.07). Four of these hedgebanks, whose alignment follows the north-west/south-east grain of the present boundaries coming off the moor and appears to mirror that of the parallel reaves on Ugborough Moor, have been identified as potential reaves (DHER: ref. SX65NE317). The hedgebanks did not, however, contain any internal stone structure or other indications of a prehistoric origin, and only one (that between plots 31.01 and 31.02) sealed a ditch on the hedgebank alignment. The presence of ditches underlying and on different alignments to the hedgebanks, as identified by the magnetometer survey and confirmed by excavation, does however indicate pre-modern, potentially Bronze Age, occupation here about which little more can be said (Fig. 5.9).

At least one ditch of Bronze Age date was discovered east of Broad Oak, Ottery St Mary (Site 7, ditch 4.10.008), here associated with two small pits, one containing Bronze Age pottery and the other yielding a radiocarbon date in the range c. 1300–1100 BC (NZA-36373). The interest in this site lies in how the Bronze Age ditch related to the wider pattern of ditches found in this plot, at least one of which (ditch 4.10.018) was of a similar steep-sided and broad-based profile (Fig. 2.16). There is no clear pattern of early ditches here, and it is surprising that Bronze Age ditch 4.10.008 coincided quite precisely with a recent east/west-aligned field boundary (Fig. 2.15 on the tithe map background) with the characteristic aratral (or reversed 's') curve of the medieval strip field. At face value it would appear that this particular field boundary has Bronze Age origins (and the ditch profile indicates possible recutting in the top accounting for this longevity), but it is not a major axis of land division and it is not clear that any other field boundaries here show such distant origins. It is entirely possible that the location is coincidental and a wider picture might confirm this. The most likely ancient boundary here is the curving 'terminal' boundary bounding the stream, and ditch 4.10.016 may be the Bronze Age version of this. A probable Bronze Age gully south-east of Broad Oak (Site 8), with a larger but undated ditch running approximately at right-angles to it, hints at more Bronze Age land division in this area to the west of the River Otter. This fragmentary pattern of Bronze Age activity appears to corroborate the suggestion of extensive settlement and farming in the River Otter corridor (Yates 2007, 66) the main evidence for which still comes from the sites at Castle Hill and Patteson's Cross on the Honiton to Exeter A30 road project (Fitzpatrick *et. al.* 1999). More speculative Bronze Age fields have been described at Knightstone Farm east of the Otter (Site 3). There is no dating evidence for these, and the ditches are not particularly distinctive in form, but they pre-date the post-medieval pattern here and a Roman or Bronze Age date seems likely.

Iron Age and Roman (400 BC to AD 400)

The shortage of evidence for occupation in the first half of the 1st millennium BC is noteworthy (Fig. 6.1) and appears to be a phenomenon common to Devon as a whole. It was noted on the Honiton to Exeter A30 road project (Fitzpatrick *et al.* 1999, 219), where the Late Bronze Age date from Hayne Lane extends to 800 BC at the latest (Butterworth 1999b, table 33) and, with the exception of a single date from the post-built roundhouse at Blackhorse, which lies within the range 700–370 cal. BC (ibid., table 53), there is a gap to the Middle (or Later) Iron Age sites, which are probably no earlier than 400 BC (Fitzpatrick *et al.* 1999, fig. 97). It was suggested that this reflects a general decline in pottery, although the visibility of sites may also be a factor. The question was posed by Quinnell (1994b) as to whether the lack of evidence for settlement at this time on Dartmoor was a reflection of population movement away from the upland, and the answer from the present project is that this does not appear to be the case; arguably both upland and lowland areas had very similar trajectories of settlement change leading to fewer archaeologically detectable remains. This is not simply a reflection of largely aceramic modes of living as the radiocarbon dates from this project, which came from a number of aceramic features (such as those of 5th to 7th-century date), show; the absence of evidence for any form of activity, settled or transient, would seem to indicate that settlement is either genuinely sparse (perhaps concentrated in relatively few sites) or (perhaps more probably) is not detectable because subsurface features were not commonly dug, or at least not filled with datable material. The wider picture provided by pollen sequences from sites in central Devon indicates a 'growing intensity' of agricultural exploitation (Rippon 2008, 112), with woodland clearance and increasing pasture from the 10th to 9th centuries BC, and the appearance of wheat, oats and rye from the sixth to fifth centuries (ibid.) shown on Broadclyst Moor. Pollen from Nymet Barton showed an open landscape with very little tree pollen around 300 BC (Caseldine *et al.* 2000) and there is a similar picture from Mosshayne (West Clyst), Hares Down near Rackenford in mid Devon and the southern fringe of Exmoor (Fyfe *et al.* 2003; Rippon 2008). It is possible that the extensive woodland clearances recorded by pollen diagrams, with the poverty of material in the archaeological record, is a signature of agricultural regimes dominated by extensive grazing.

The dating and characterisation of Iron Age features was generally imprecise. At Pixies' Parlour (Site 4) the roundhouse penannular gully, cut by the ditch of a possible ovoid enclosure, contained virtually no finds or other dating material from either feature (Fig. 3.3). This is remarkable given the extent of the site examined by excavation, and the fact that the ditch did contain Roman pottery which in other contexts can be moderately common (including the Billany Farm and Springfield settlements on the present project). It is therefore not clear what sort of site this represents, or its date. The roundhouse gully is typologically broadly 'Later Iron Age/Roman' and the enclosure (or perhaps cross-dyke to cover another possibility) probably Roman. Attention has been drawn to the 7th-century radiocarbon dates from one of the pits on the site, and a post-Roman date for the ditch is a possibility.

Iron Age occupation at Crablake Farm (Site 15) is suggested by two radiocarbon dates from the curving gully which was otherwise without finds (Fig. 2.21). This is plausibly part of an eaves drainage gully and the absence of enclosure ditches in this section of the pipeline suggests part of an open and perhaps quite dispersed settlement. The poorly defined site at Barton Hill Cross (Site 19) appears to be part of an Iron Age settlement succeeded by a Roman enclosure, but the evidence from the scattered and for the most part poorly dated features is not strong (Fig. 3.8).

The iron smelting furnaces at Tigley A (Site 26) yielded unambiguous Middle Iron Age dating from six radiocarbon dates (Fig. 3.20). The dates, from a group of furnaces as well as an isolated one, suffer from the imprecision due to the plateau in the calibration curve, but they are very similar and place the whole group in the early 4th to late 3rd centuries BC. The analysis of the ironworking residues, together with the characteristics of the features, suggests the presence of seven smelting furnaces, and there was also hammerscale from some of them, probably from the consolidation of the bloom. There was no indication of ore preparation, nor the working of other metals, although it is possible that ore roasting was carried out in a least two of the fire-reddened pits. There were few other (non-metallurgical) features present and no suggestion of a settlement, so it is probable that the iron production took place at some unquantifiable distance from a habitation. It is possible that the location was determined by proximity to a source of ore, although the type of ore used and its source are questions that could not be resolved in the analysis. However, it is highly likely that small sources of iron ore could have been found quite locally. Wood for fuel was probably readily available in the locality. It has been suggested that, in the medieval period, large-scale bloomery iron production was always concentrated where ores and woodland were in close proximity because of the weight of ore and the volume of charcoal required (Foard 2001, 70). For the smaller-scale industry in the Iron Age similar, if somewhat less imperative, considerations may have applied and both iron ore and oak woodland were probably found close by. The intercutting nature of one group of furnaces is a curious aspect of the site that suggests that their precise locations were prescribed by factors not evident in the archaeological record.

The furnaces all appear of the simple non-slag-tapping shaft type. There was some variety in size and shape but it is clear by the way the whole circumference of each pit was affected by heat that the shape of the pit defined the shape of the furnace shaft. There was no adjacent slag-tapping or 'rake-out' pit to remove slag or bloom and is assumed both were extracted from above. It is not clear why different shapes and sizes of furnaces were built, but it suggests that iron was produced on an *ad hoc* basis for immediate and varied needs. The extraction of the iron bloom seems to have been accompanied by a disturbance to the contents of the furnace as a whole as there was little *in situ* slag found. Furnace 16.07.008 was the only one with furnace-bottom slag at the base of the pit, the other furnace-bottom slags presumably having been removed for other purposes. This serves to underline the danger of assuming that the presence of slag on a site implies ironworking close by. Slag could have been transported any distance if needed although the reasons why this might have been done are obscure.

Two adjacent hearth or furnace bases found at Lower Velwell (Site 22) contained both iron smelting and smithing debris, but the radiocarbon measurement on hazel/alder charcoal produced an erroneous (3rd millennium BC) date and the context of the features is unclear. They seem likely to be later Iron Age or Roman and perhaps associated with the cropmark enclosures to the north, although absence of settlement evidence immediately nearby may be more apparent than real given their recording under watching brief conditions.

Although the identification of Iron Age settlement was problematic, and suggests no more than scattered activity, some insight into subsistence activities at this time came from isolated features. The pit containing charred plant remains at Slade Farm (Site 2) shows that the principal crops were spelt wheat and oats, together with a range of other cereals, including barley, bread wheat and rye (Table 3.16). The range is similar to the Iron Age assemblages from Langland Lane, Long Range and Blackhorse west of Honiton (Fitzpatrick *et al.* 1999), except that the quantity of oats from Slade Farm indicates that it was a crop rather than an occasional weed. This shows a form of farming adaptation through diversification, which has a resonance in the historical period in the county (below). The gully at Crablake Farm (Site 15) contained fewer identifiable remains, and the context is potentially less secure, but oats, rye and bread wheat were present here. There is an interesting point of contrast in the detail of these two sites, the lack of short weeds and basal culm nodes at Slade Farm suggesting that cereals were harvested high on the stalk, while the basal culm nodes at Crablake Farm may indicate that crop (or perhaps the straw) was uprooted. There is perhaps the suggestion of a two-stage harvest, but the contrast may be no more than a vagary of these particular samples and requires much more research. The way farming was organised is still a subject lacking information to evaluate and there is no good evidence of fields or other land allotment at this time. The Iron Age sites on the Honiton–Exeter project consisted for the most part of penannular gullies and postholes or small pits, with a subrectangular enclosure at Blackhorse (Fitzpatrick *et al.* 1999, 161). Grain storage seems to have been undertaken in four-post structures, and there was not the density of pits or the tight ordering of settlement sometimes found in other parts of southern England. The rectilinear boundary ditches at Blackhorse and Langland have, at best, unconvincing dates and none need be Iron Age (ibid., figs 66, 81). It can readily be appreciated that a narrow corridor of investigation through this kind of landscape would produce for the most part scatters of small features and occasional, probably undated, ditches. There were dated features of this nature at Barton Hill Cross (Site 19), Springfield (Site 31) and Filham House (Site 34) and a number of possible sites of this such as The Nutwell Lodge (Site 11), Soloman's Farm (Site 16) and Wood Farm (Site 33). In broader terms the farming landscape must have been highly varied, but apparently without the degree of demarcation and organisation seen approximately a millennium earlier.

The botanical remains suggest that the landscapes of the Bronze Age were not dissimilar to those of the Iron Age, with a broadly comparable range of trees and shrubs. Allowing for the overwhelming predominance of oak wood used in the Tigley A iron furnaces, which has the effect of lowering the representation of other species, the charcoal profiles from these two periods are more similar to each other than the Bronze Age profile is to that of the Neolithic (Figs 6.3–6.4). The food species, however, show a different trend, with crops more important in the Iron Age than they had been in the Bronze Age (Fig. 6.2). The contrast is exaggerated by the deposit of hazelnut shells from Filham House (Site 34), but at face value there is the suggestion of different groups of burnt material in Iron Age features as compared with Bronze Age ones, perhaps relating to complex processes of taphonomy and deposition as much as to differences in economic strategies. The pattern is worth observing and may be found more widely. The Iron Age trend of cereal domination continues into the Roman and later periods.

The Billany Farm settlement (Site 24) is of a type classified at a hillslope enclosure, known to be relatively numerous in Devon but not well understood (Webster 2008a, 134–5). This was the only instance on this project where the pipeline was not diverted around a known archaeologically significant site, and it was clearly defined by extensive geophysical survey before the excavation (Fig. 3.13). Although the dating of the later phases of occupation on the terrace platform is securely 3rd–4th century AD, the little evidence that there is from the enclosure ditch suggests a 1st or 2nd-century date deriving from pottery in the primary fill. The contrast in dating makes it possible to suggest that the enclosure was earlier than most of the occupation within it, and it seems entirely possible that the ditches had ceased to be functional by the 3rd century. The suggestion that the southern (downslope) ditch was dug to contain a wooden palisade adds further complexity to the interpretation, although it lacks supporting evidence of structural detail such as post impressions and packing. There is, however, a comparable feature at the hillslope enclosure at Rudge, Morchard Bishop, where a timber palisade of probable late 1st-century AD date formed the inner ditch, 'facing' downslope to the south-east (Todd 1998). The palisade did not complete the perimeter circuit and it was remarked that it could have served no defensive purpose. Like the Billany Farm palisade, it seems to have been deliberately dismantled. In both cases the features may have been intended principally to be stock-proof, but the Billany Farm enclosure appears to have been bounded by a mixture of ditch and palisade, an inconsistency not easily explicable in purely practical terms. It is possible that, in both cases, the palisades were built primarily for display, since they would have been highly visible from below (the side where security in itself would have been a less significant concern because of the natural slope) and would also have had the effect of preventing a view into the interior. Any impediment to the view from the interior outward could presumably have been mitigated by the height and spacing of the timbers. A similar form of sharp, asymmetrical ditch was recorded on the multivallate hillslope enclosure at North Hill Cleeve, Bittadon. Here the ditch on the downslope side had an almost vertical, and occasionally undercut, outer edge (Reed and Manning 2000, fig. 5, sections 1, 5). Like Billany Farm, there was nothing in the sediment sequence to suggest a palisade and, had timbers been present, it must be assumed they had been withdrawn. The ditch itself (2.3m wide and 1.6m deep) was smaller than the Billany Farm ditch, and in other contexts is within the range of enclosure ditches for which no defensive function is proposed. Had this multivallate enclosure any defensive purpose, a palisade on the lip of the steep slope here would have improved it considerably. However, in common with most hillslope enclosures, the defensive function appears to be undermined by its siting, overlooked by higher ground, and the motives behind the form of perimeter definition therefore appear to be not straightforward.

Interior features at Billany Farm were sparse, but indicate some level of occupation from the 1st/2nd century until the later 3rd century (the coin of Tetricus, AD 270-4, being the latest closely datable find). It appears that much of the interior was not occupied, and may have been for corralling stock and/or storage, but it must be admitted that the degree of plough truncation and its effects on shallow cut features are unquantifiable. The terrace platform provided a local patch of stratified archaeological deposits, but despite the strong probability of it having been occupied by a structure, perhaps most likely a domestic dwelling, there was no clear evidence of one. The natural shillet surface contained no evidence of a floor and there was no hearth or recognisable pattern of postholes. It can be surmised that that much of the interior could have been occupied by 'structures' of this kind which, without terraces to identify their locations, would have been lost to the archaeological record. The finds included a small range not out of place in a domestic setting, including quernstones and charred grain and arable weeds. Of most significance was a large collection of burnt linseed and capsules, indicating that flax processing was almost certainly undertaken. Two radiocarbon dates on the seeds themselves confirm a 3rd–4th century AD date, and the fact that they also came, in small quantities, from an early pit, dated by pottery to the 1st–2nd century, indicates a persistent local industry. It is not clear how the flax seeds came to be charred, although the plant as a whole may have been artificially dried after harvesting. It seems possible that the seeds and capsules were simply waste used as fuel. The rarity of evidence for flax in this period is difficult to evaluate. It may have been cultivated quite widely but, without normally needing to be near fire, the evidence would not survive. It is one of the very few plants found along with emmer wheat, free-threshing wheat and barley on Neolithic sites in Britain (Fairbairn 2000b, 109) and presumably had been present since that time. On the other hand it may have been a rare crop in Roman Britain, conceivably part of the local diet. Pliny recounts that linseed was parched and mixed with barley and ground to make polenta (Pliny 1855). In the present context it was probably an aspect of a broad-based farming economy producing a range of crops for subsistence and exchange. The presence of querns made from Cornish greisen give an indication of contacts, probably reflecting the continuing tradition of coastal trading. Burning of the substrate within the area of the terrace, as well as large quantities of wood charcoal within the lower fills of this feature, may suggest destruction by fire immediately prior to abandonment.

Little can be said of the form of the late Roman settlement at Springfield (Site 31) which does not appear to have been enclosed overall and displays little evidence of internal structuring. The dating indicated by the pottery, which is dominated by South Devon and Black-Burnished Wares, places the site in the later 3rd to 4th centuries AD. There is evidence that spelt wheat was the principal cereal grown, with some oats and barley but, as elsewhere, animal bone did not normally survive. The evidence for metalworking is particularly notable. This includes iron production (both smelting and smithing residues were found, but no furnaces) and the manufacture of pewter, the evidence for which is part of a stone mould for a dish, and traces of tin in a fragment of vitrified clay. Ditch 24.03.152 might have marked the location of a smithy since hammerscale came from an 'internal' pit 24.03.089. No detail of the structure of this building survived. To the south-west curving gully 24.03.149, together with a group of internal postholes, is convincing evidence of a circular building, but there was little associated material and the form of construction is also unclear. If the dating of this structure conforms to the general Late Roman date of the site (a supposition which is not assured) the roundhouse form would be unusual, perhaps suggesting it was not a domestic building. At Pomeroy Wood, west of Honiton, roundhouses were constructed in the 2nd or 3rd centuries AD but not thereafter, and this is common to much of southern England (Fitzpatrick and Grove 1999, 401–2). Aspects of structural detail which are absent or ambiguous include support for the roof and the nature of the wall. The preferred interpretation sees the gully as a drainage feature surrounding a post-and-wattle wall but, alternatively, it is possible that the gully was a bedding trench for wall of close-set timbers (as interpreted at Pomeroy Wood), although this would have made the structure quite large (*c.* 13m in diameter). The lack of interpretable detail is common, particularly on plough-damaged sites, and this building can add little to knowledge of vernacular architecture in this period. The groups of postholes in the north-eastern part of the site are even less interpretable of form or date.

The site at Barton Hill Cross (Site 19) is also of undefined form. It showed features containing pottery dating to the Iron Age and Roman period, although the lack of secure dating for most features and an absence of any clear patterning makes the site difficult to characterise. The features included many elements considered to be indicative of settlement, such as curvilinear ditches, pits and postholes. One interpretation is that an unenclosed Iron Age settlement later became defined by ditches 7.01.007 and 7.01.072 or 7.01.043 (or perhaps both) forming an enclosure 40m or 80m across. There is, however, little suggestion of a continuity of use for the site, as the only pottery recovered, prior to the South Devon Roman wares of the 2nd to 4th centuries, was of middle Iron Age date, and the Roman pottery suggested a more likely range of the 3rd to 4th centuries AD.

It is significant that the Roman period activity identified on the pipeline routes is largely devoid of field boundary ditches, which are common and sometimes ubiquitous in counties further east. The one instance where Late Iron Age or Roman ditches appear to have been present is at Exwell Barton (Site 14), but even here the dating, based upon three sherds of pottery, is not secure. Land division of uncertain extent has also been suggested at Barton Hill Cross (Site 19) in South Devon, but there is no conclusive dating, while near Lower Velwell (Site 22) the cropmark enclosures are thought likely to have been later Iron Age or Roman purely because of their form and scale but are also undated. Pre-medieval (possibly Roman) fields have been recorded at Knightstone Farm (Site 3) and there was a ditch containing Roman pottery at New Nutwalls (Site 9), but this is a paltry list of features from an investigation of this distance. The evidence as a whole appears to conform to the emerging picture of the Roman South West whose unique character includes a notable shortage of the outward signs of Roman influence (towns, villas, Romano-Celtic temples, 'Roman' material culture) together with a general absence of land apportionment in the form of fields defined by ditches (Rippon 2008, 115-17). This is not to say that ditched fields were absent everywhere, and many archaeological investigations show an insufficient view of the landscape to be sure of the pattern or date of any ditches found, but the evidence on the present project has been slight. Significantly, the more extensive area excavations on the A30 Honiton to Exeter road (Fitzpatrick 1999) and those at Hayes Farm, Clyst Honiton, were also devoid of Romano-British field boundaries; the ditches present at Hayes Farm (in a total of a little over 4ha. excavated) were either Middle–Late Bronze Age or relatively modern (Hart *et al.* forthcoming).

This character of settlement fits alongside the pollen record from several sites that shows a very open landscape with both pasture and cereal cultivation present, and the overall impression is one of agricultural intensification throughout the Roman period (Rippon 2008, 117–18). It is, however, difficult to correlate pollen sequences with agricultural regimes with any degree of precision, and it may be possible to model the combined evidence as very extensive but fundamentally low intensity of land exploitation, with the landscape retaining an unenclosed mosaic of uses, rather than being formally demarcated by fields. It is possible that this reflected a strongly pastoral farming emphasis with relatively small areas of arable close settlement appropriate to small domestic mode of production and the wide-ranging grazing of livestock throughout the year.

Alternatively, enclosure may have been achieved by banked and hedged boundaries, ditches being reserved for enclosing only the settlements themselves, and then not in every instance. The evidence for enclosure may therefore be archaeologically invisible in most cases. The implication of this type of land management may be that the landscape started taking on its modern character of small hedged fields and sunken lanes in the Roman period or earlier. Such a view is familiar from counties in the east, where there are claims that the pattern of modern fields in parts of East Anglia can be traced back to pre-Roman times (Drury and Rodwell 1980; Williamson 1987). While it may be wrong to claim that this represents a planned landscape, it seems reasonable to suggest that the framework of the principal landscape elements was established by the use of traditional agricultural routeways with likely pre-Roman origins, and that the boundary pattern became more deeply established over time. In Devon, however, there is little evidence of continuity between the Romano-British landscape and the medieval one. In repeated instances

Romano-British rural settlements show no continuity with the medieval patterns of fields and enclosures and, conversely, medieval settlements have no elements that can be traced as far back as Roman times. There is therefore a strong indication that Roman settlements were not in the same places as the medieval ones. Concluding a lengthy examination of the historical landscape of Devon, Rippon writes:

> Overall there seems to have been a significant discontinuity in the landscape some time between the sixth century, when archaeological evidence for the continued use of what was essentially still the late prehistoric and Romano-British landscape ceases, and the tenth and eleventh centuries, being the date back to which we can trace the medieval landscape. Crucially, neither archaeological nor documentary sources can say whether this discontinuity was a sudden or a gradual process, or precisely when it occurred. (Rippon 2008, 132).

The archaeological evidence from the present project unfortunately has little to contribute to this enquiry, being extremely sparse between the 4th and 13th centuries.

Post-Roman and Medieval (AD 400 to 1500)

Of the numerous individual pits discovered in the course of fieldwork, three selected for radiocarbon dating, purely on the basis of suitable material and the lack of any other means of dating them, yielded dates in the 5th to 7th centuries AD. There was no other evidence for occupation in this period, where a notorious shortage of datable material makes settlements difficult to identify even where research is directed specifically to this end (Gerrard and Aston 2007). The South West has a distinctive character of post-Roman settlement, sometimes occupying (or continuing to occupy) enclosures of Roman (and earlier) date (Webster 2008a, 71). There is no strong suggestion that the 5th–7th-century pits on the present project are indicative of settlement location, or were linked to Roman occupation, despite the fact they each contained some material interpreted as cereal-processing waste. However, the location of 7th-century pit 3.04.036 at Pixies' Parlour (Site 4), within the possible Roman enclosure, is intriguing. This may represent an occupation taking advantage of an extant earthwork, if not a continuity or, given the shortage of Roman material from this ditch, it is possible that the enclosure is actually post-Roman. The ditch is similar in dimensions to the early post-Roman enclosure ditch at Hayes Farm, Clyst Honiton (Simpson *et al.* 1989) which had a similar lack of material to date it. The enclosure at Hayes Farm is large (*c.* 90m east–west) but of uncertain status (ibid., fig.1, 24–5). The site at Moore Farm, Harberton (Site 28) is another possible candidate for settlement, where the sub-Roman pit 18.12.015 lay among a group of small undated pits which may be of a similar date (Fig. 2.9). There was no indication of Roman occupation in this plot, although a scatter of undated small features were present in the 120m stretch of pipe-easement, and subrectangular cropmark enclosures to the east and north-west are suggestive of Roman origins. At Tigley B (Site 27) the apparently isolated pit 16.08.020 was similar to pit 18.12.015, containing a mixture of oats, barley and assorted wood charcoal. Whether these cereal remains need be by-products of human diet, or were perhaps fodder, is debatable. Essentially it is unclear whether fodder would have needed heating and therefore be exposed to the risk of being burnt, or why it should have been disposed of in this manner if it had.

The charred remains from the 13th–14th-century house at Exwell Barton (Site 14) showed that cultivated crops here were dominated by oats and rye, which are a typical 'maslin' of the South West, chosen for hardiness as an insurance against poor harvests. They were found mainly and prolifically in the sunken, purpose-built corn drying building (which may have been used as a bakehouse), making it likely that they were the mainstay of human diet. A similar combination of crops came from the isolated 11th-century pit at Bluepost (Site 29). The common presence of oats on medieval sites in the south-west peninsula, together with the presence of rye, is typical, and contrasts with the more common dominance of bread wheat further east. Bread wheat dominated in the isolated 12th/13th-century pit at Coldharbour, Ottery St Mary (Site 1), where there was also a strong presence of oats, suggesting a slightly different adaptation. It is less than certain how these apparently isolated pits should be interpreted. At Coldharbour, the wide area of overburden removal emphasises its character as apparently unrelated to settlement despite its 'domestic' contents (Fig. 4.2). Pit 13.02.163 at Exwell Barton also may have lain isolated, although there may have been settlement not far to the north (Fig. 4.14). Rather than being an indication of settlement nearby, it is possible that they relate to activities undertaken in the fields, such as field clearance or harvesting. The pit at Bluepost may be related to this kind of practice and the presence of twine indicates some intentional gathering of vegetation (Fig. 4.21). There is a pit in the adjacent field (FTC 19.08.005) which, like pit 19.07.004, contains gorse charcoal and may be of a similar date. Both may be related to weed and scrub clearance. Medieval 'convertible husbandry' involved preparing arable fields that had previously been under grass by burning the turf and spreading ashes across the field. As Charles Vancouver noted in his report to the Board of Agriculture:

> When spading or paring and burning the surface of a field is mediated, it is pared off clean to the depth of three-fourths to one inch in thickness; these slices are set edgeways, and when dry, they are collected into heaps, or what are provincially termed beat bar-

rows, and with the assistance of furze fern, heather, hedgerow or copse faggots, the whole pared surface is reduced to a mass of ashes; these ashes when cool are generally spread together with 80 Winchester bushels of lime per acre mixed with twice the quantity of hedge-row mould, road scrapings, or other fresh soil most convenient to be procured. (Vancouver 1808, 139–40)

Pits containing crop remains may have been a product of temporary camps set up at harvest time. The excavation of pits specifically to hold burnt crop waste appears, however, to be an unnecessarily fastidious undertaking for essentially practical agricultural tasks, and, alternatively, may have been linked to agricultural rituals for which no records now survive. Possible contexts are found in the 'first fruits' festivals, which in the English context relate to the Lammas ('loaf mass') festival of 1 August known to have been practised since Anglo-Saxon times (Hutton 1996, 330). As far as is known, these lacked activities specifically in fields, although an elaborate harvest ritual, sometimes involving the perambulation of fields, was recorded from the Hebrides by Alexander Carmichael as recently as the late 19th century, and it seems possible that similar activities were once more widespread.

> The Feast Day of St Mary the Great is the 15th day of August. Early in the morning of this day the people go into their fields and pluck ears of corn, generally bere, to make the 'Moilean Moire'. These ears are laid on a rock exposed to the sun, to dry. When dry they are husked in the hand, winnowed in a fan, ground in a quern, kneaded on a sheep-skin, and formed into a bannock which is called the 'Moillean Moire', the fatling of Mary. The bannock is toasted before a fire of rowans or some other sacred wood ... While singing (thus), the family walk sunwise round the fire, the father leading, the mother following and the children following according to age. After going round the fire, the man puts the embers of the fagot-fire with bits of old iron into a pot which he carries sunwise round the outside of his house, sometimes round his steadings and his fields, and his flocks gathered in for the purpose. (quoted in MacNeill 1962, 361)

The medieval house discovered at Exwell Barton is likely to have been a peasant dwelling, as shown by the limited and utilitarian range of pottery and other finds, although its overall form and method of construction were not resolvable. The surviving dimensions are compatible with those of the medieval longhouses on Dartmoor, which have general internal dimension of 12–14m by 4.0–4.5m, roughly half of which comprises the living area and the rest the shippon. There is no indication of eaves drainage channels having been provided. The living area normally contained a central hearth, laid on a granite base, about 1.5m from the end wall (Henderson and Weddell 1996, 123). It is interesting to note that the hearth at Exwell Barton incorporated broken pottery above the quartzite base, perhaps as a method to retain heat as much as to provide a solid foundation. The Exwell Barton house would have had at least two rooms and possibly more, although it may not have been a longhouse in the strict sense of a dual-purpose farm building (ibid.). 13th–14th-century farmhouses up to 18m in length are known from Devon but all appear to be of a recognisable regional plan form, 'a continuum of types suggestive of diversification within a common building tradition' (ibid., 135). There is little evidence for superstructures of these houses. Earth-fast cruck roof trusses have been identified at Okehampton Park and Sourton, but on most sites roof trusses do not seem to have extended to ground level and may have been set in the walls or on padstones, as shown by a small number of standing examples (ibid., 137–8). There is insufficient evidence from Exwell Barton to add to the discussion of medieval vernacular structures, and the question as to whether the walls were entirely of cob, or timber-framed, is open to debate. A few pieces of South Hams roofing slate suggest that it was so roofed. It can be noted that, had the gable end gully been for drainage rather than a wall trench, this would indicate that the roof was likely to have been hipped.

The sunken 'corn drying building' similarly gives little indication of how it was constructed. A cob or timber wall around the perimeter of the sunken area seems likely. Although the form of building appears to be so far unique in Devon, there are examples from Kent that are similar both in size and in the detail of having adjacent ovens. The similarity of form in such different parts of the country is remarkable but without obvious explanation. The entrances, where evident, were on the long axis at a distance from the ovens (Andrews *et al.* 2009, figs 1.8, 3.4). The sunken 'kitchen' building at Fulston Manor, Sittingbourne in Kent lacked charred cereals and the building was interpreted as a bakery which would have used flour produced elsewhere (ibid., 183). The hearth at Fulston Manor was thought to have been for a different process, such as boiling water in the process of brewing ale (ibid.). A similar purpose may be envisaged for the hearth at Exwell Barton, although a number of functions for both the open and enclosed types of heater are possible.

On Dartmoor outbuildings with pairs of ovens, sometimes described as a kiln and an oven, are thought to have been for barns for crop storage and drying (Henderson and Weddell 1996, 123). The Exwell Barton building had a useable floor area of about 5m by 3m and so seems to have been rather small for storage, although a loft is entirely possible and may have been intentionally facilitated by having the floor at a sunken level. The charred cereal remains indicate that crop drying took place, but it seems inherently likely that the ovens were for a range of uses at other times, including baking bread. A separate kitchen building has comparisons with dwellings of high status, and the containment of fire risk is often cited as a sound reason for this.

The wider context of the Exwell Barton buildings is not known. They may have been an individual farmstead or part of a larger hamlet. Both types of deserted settlement are known on Dartmoor. The dating in the 13th–14th centuries is typical of the pattern seen widely in the county and is attributed to an increase in population and agriculture in the 13th century, followed by a decline a century or so later (Henderson and Weddell 1996, 135). Deserted medieval settlements are common on Dartmoor but, like so much earlier archaeology, this reflects the high visibility of remains on the moor, rather than factors specific to it, and the pattern of settlement founding and abandonment is likely to have been similar elsewhere. At Exwell Barton there was some indication of nearby settlement in the post-medieval period from deposits of charred cereals in a boundary ditch, and an unrelated dump of seafood (mainly cockle shells) in a 17th-century or later ditch on the edge of the site. This may be indicative of more widespread settlement in this plot in medieval and later times. In the 18th century Powderham deer park was extended and landscaped (English Heritage 2001) and the site then probably took on the form shown on the Tithe Map (1838), an undivided field with extensive plantations to the south.

Concluding remarks

The investigations of these long transects through Eastern and Southern Devon have added to the sum of information hard won from the archaeological subtleties of the South West landscape. The corridor of investigation was a narrow one and, despite the limitations that can be put upon interpretations of many of these sites and scattered features, the presentation and interrogation of much base-line information show that in many respects the prehistoric and early historical landscape was inhabited in the same manner as other parts of England. These common themes include Neolithic and Bronze Age occupations defined mainly by scattered pits that are difficult to place in a context of settlement or other activity and whose locations are impossible to predict. The dominance of hazelnuts in the food remains is also typical of the wider pattern. By the Middle Bronze Age occupation, still often difficult to characterise, had become relatively dense and the landscape appears to have become divided in a similar manner to that found in other parts of southern England but, away from Dartmoor, this may not have been ubiquitous in southern or eastern Devon. In other respects the distinctiveness of Devon has been underlined. Iron Age and Roman sites were surprisingly elusive and the Early Iron Age was entirely invisible on the project. At this time there was less concern with ditched settlement or field enclosure and little interest in durable material culture, in contrast to the picture found over most of southern England, phenomena running through the Roman and Early medieval periods. It appears likely that unenclosed settlement was at least as common as the enclosed sort (of the archaeologically visible variety), and little Roman material either made its way into Devon or was copied locally. Radiocarbon dating helped fill material voids, in particular in the Iron Age and early post-Roman periods. The presence of metal production west of the Exe valley in the Iron Age and Roman periods has received some confirmation and suggests the basis for its importance in historical times. The lack of bone from almost all sites, a consequence of the acidic soil, limited what could be said about farming but, nonetheless, there was widespread evidence of cereal cultivation from the Iron Age and a variety (viz. oats, barley, rye, emmer, spelt and bread wheat) suggesting that the distinctive mixed crop regimes of the medieval period in the South West had a long tradition. Whether there was any strong distinction between east and south Devon in prehistory or early historical times has not been apparent from these results, but they do appear to show common trends which make them different to the trajectories of development found to the east of the Blackdown Hills, and give a time depth to the historic and current landscapes of the county.

Appendix: Technical methodologies

Charred plant macrofossils and charcoal

Sarah Cobain

A total of 247 bulk soil samples were processed and assessed for plant macrofossil and charcoal remains. Following assessment, 49 of these samples were selected for full analysis of the plant remains, 17 for full analysis of the charcoal and 43 for broad characterisation of the charcoal. Full analysis of charcoal was undertaken on a relatively small number of samples, the larger number of identified fragments allowing an insight into dominant fuels used and additional species present. Broad characterisation, encompassing a larger number of samples, provided more comparative information on the general environment and wood selection, and trends through time. The samples were chosen on the basis of the intrinsic quality of the material, and also to address specific questions concerning crop and fuel selection, the functions of features sampled and the composition of the local woodlands and flora (Carruthers 2010, 228; Challinor 2010, 201–2).

The charred remains were retrieved by standard flotation using a 250micron sieve to collect the float and 1mm mesh to retain the residue. The residue was dried and sorted by eye and the floated material scanned. Seeds were identified using a low power stereomicroscope (Brunel MX1) (x10-x40). Identifications were carried out with reference to images and descriptions by Bekker et al. (2006), Berggren (1981) and Anderberg (1994). Nomenclature follows Stace (1997).

For the charcoal analysis, up to 100 charcoal fragments of the >2mm sieve fraction were fractured by hand to reveal the wood anatomy on radial, tangential and transverse planes. For broad characterisation of the assemblage, 20 charcoal fragments from two sieve sizes, (2mm and 4mm) were selected for full identification. In every case the pieces were identified using an epi-illuminating microscope (Brunel SP400) (x40-x400). Identifications were carried out with reference to images and descriptions by Cutler and Gale (2000), Heller *et al.* (2004) and Baas *et al.* (1989). Nomenclature follows Stace (1997).

The species have been assigned habitat codes based on their preferred environment. The following codes have been assigned:

- A = Arable weed
- D = Opportunistic weed from a disturbed environment
- DC = Opportunistic weed but may have been consumed
- P = Grassland species (possible pasture)
- E = Economic species (plants deliberately cultivated for economic use)
- H = Heathland species
- HSW = Hedgerow, scrub, woodland species
- M = Marsh/wetland species
- WF = Wild Food

Some species have been assigned two or three habitat codes because they can establish in a variety of habitats.

Metalworking debris from South Devon

David Starley

Visual examination of bulk debris

Twenty-two kilogrammes of bulk slag was visually examined and classified into categories used by the former English Heritage Ancient Monuments Laboratory. Visual observation of the exterior was supported by examination of fresh fracture surfaces and by the use of a geological streak plate and magnet. The samples derive from four sites; Tigley A, Billany Farm (both Dartington), Lower Velwell, Rattery, and Springfield, Ugborough.

Only a relatively small proportion of the debris was visually diagnostic of metallurgical process and could be classified in this way. By far the majority of the debris was less distinctive and it was not always possible to be certain which metallurgical, or other high temperature process, individual pieces derived from. Some categories such as 'undiagnostic ironworking slag' may equally derive from smithing or smelting. Visual examination identified no clear evidence for non-ferrous metalworking, but some debris may have derived from other high temperature processes.

Evidence from magnetic residues

Residues from soil samples had a magnet passed through them and a total of 7.1kg of magnetic material was visually examined for the presence of spheroidal and flake hammerscale. These residues contained a high proportion of small flat platelets which adhered strongly to a magnet and resembled flake hammerscale. However, close examination suggested that they consisted almost entirely of strongly heated, natural shale-like material, together with some burned clay. As a result, the naturally present iron had been converted to magnetite, giving the material's magnetic qualities. (Among the burned natural shale, however, two samples from Roman pits at Springfield, Ugborough, were found to contain a proportion of true hammerscale.)

SEM-based microanalysis and back-scattered electron imaging of debris

Scanning electron microscope (SEM)-based energy dispersive X-ray (EDX) microanalysis was carried out to help understand the smelting processes undertaken. Twelve samples from Tigley A and two from Lower Velwell were selected, including six fragments of the fayalitic run slag, two fragments of the magnetic shale, one furnace bottom, two smithing hearth bottoms, a fragment of tap slag and two pieces of undiagnostic ironworking slag. Cut sections from the interior of the pieces were mounted in cold-setting epoxy resin and the samples were ground and polished using standard techniques.

The advantages of SEM-based EDX analysis lie in the ability of the technique to undertake analysis at high magnifications on selected small areas such as specific phases or mixtures of phases. The method is therefore highly suitable for heterogeneous archaeological materials. The sample may be viewed in back-scattered mode prior to analysis. This mode enhances atomic number contrast, rather than topography, allowing mineralogical phases in the flat, polished specimen to be differentiated. EDX measures elemental presence. The quoted figures, which refer to the weight percentage of oxide, are derived from assumptions about the stoichiometry (i.e. the combining tendency) of each element. The "bulk" data in Table 3.14 relates to the analysis of typical areas of the sample.

Cremated human remains

Harriet Jacklin

The analysis of the cremated human remains from Salston B, Ottery St Mary, included the assessment of age, sex and pathology. The results were recorded using a standardised recording form created by Jacklin (2005), in line with standards advocated by Brickley and McKinley (2004). References used included: McKinley (1994), McKinley (2000a), McKinley (2000b), McKinley and Roberts (1993) and McKinley and Bond (2001). All fusion data is based on Scheuer and Black (2000) and all sex data is based on Buikstra and Ubelaker (1994). The details of the analysis are presented in Table 2.27.

References

Primary references

DHER (Devon Historical Environment Record)
    SY09SE/1 collection of worked flint from Pixies' Parlour, Ottery St Mary
    SX65NE317 linear pattern of field boundaries near Wood Farm, Ugborough

DCC (Devon County Council) aerial photographs
    BS.10A–12 cropmarks west of Hood Quarry, Dartington, 11 July 1984
    FE.09–10 cropmarks at Hood Ball, Rattery, 18 July 1985
    MH.07–09 cropmarks at Hood Ball, Rattery, 23 June 1989
    RG.01–02 cropmarks at Hood Ball, Rattery, 4 June 1990
    VL.03–06 cropmarks at Hood Ball, Rattery, 7 July 1992
    JM.08–09 earthworks at The White House, Powderham, 11 January 1988

DRO (Devon Record Office) Tithe Maps
    Aylesbeare 1841
    Dartington 1840
    Diptford 1839
    Ermington 1841
    Exminster 1838
    Harberton 1842
    Kenn 1841
    Little Hempston 1838
    Ottery St Mary 1845
    Powderham 1838
    Rattery 1843
    Staverton 1842
    Ugborough 1843
    Woodbury 1849

NMR (National Monuments Record) aerial photographs
    Library ref. 250 13 April 1946, W of Woodbury, Woodbury
    Library ref. 430 12 July 1946, cropmark W of Hood Quarry, Dartington
    Library ref. 543 10 December 1946 soil marks N of Fursdon, Staverton
    Library ref. 9496 6 April 1969, features at Exwell Barton, Powderham
    Library ref. 12637 4 July 1984, cropmarks N of Moore Farm, Harberton
    Library ref. 13310 22 June 1988, cropmarks NW of Knightstone and SE of Broad Oak, Ottery St Mary
    Library ref. 13550 14 June 1989, cropmarks near New Nutwalls, Aylesbeare

Bibliography

Allan, J.P. 1978 'The pottery', in Austin, D., 'Excavations in Okehampton Deer Park, Devon, 1976–1978', *Proc. Devon Archaeol. Soc.* **36**, 226–34

Allan, J.P. 1983 'Some post-medieval documentary evidence for the trade in ceramics', in Davey, P. and Hodges, R. (eds), *Ceramics and trade: the production and distribution of later medieval pottery in north-west Europe* Sheffield, Department of Prehistory and Archaeology, University of Sheffield, 37–45

Allan, J.P. 1984a *Medieval and post-medieval finds from Exeter, 1971–1980* Exeter Archaeology Report **3**

Allan, J.P. 1984b 'The pottery; the glass', in Griffiths, D.M. and Griffith, F.M., 'An excavation at 39 Fore St, Totnes', *Proc. Devon Archaeol. Soc.* **42**, 79–95

Allan, J.P. 1991 'Medieval and post-medieval pottery', in Ratcliffe, J., *Lighting up the past in Scilly: Archaeological results from the 1985 electrification programme* (Truro, Inst. Cornish Studies and Cornwall Archaeol. Unit), 93–9

Allan, J.P. 1994 'Medieval pottery and the dating of deserted settlements on Dartmoor', *Proc. Devon Archaeol. Soc.* **52**, 141–7

Allan, J.P. 1995 'Iberian pottery imported into South-West England, *c.* 1250–1600', in Gerrard, C. *et al.* (eds), *Spanish medieval ceramics in Spain and the British Isles,* Brit. Archaeol. Rep. Int. Ser. **610**, 299–314

Allan, J.P. and Langman, G. 1997a 'The pottery', in Weddell and Reed 1997, 81–5

Allan, J.P. and Langman, G. 1997b *Inventory of medieval and post-medieval pottery from sites excavated in Exeter, 1971–80* Exeter Archaeology Report **97.66**

Allan, J.P. and Langman, G. 2002 'A group of medieval pottery from Haycroft Farm, Membury', *Proc. Devon Archaeol. Soc.* **60**, 59–73

Allan, J.P., Cramp, C. and Horner, B. 2007 'The post-medieval pottery at Castle Hill, Great Torrington, North Devon', *Proc. Devon Archaeol. Soc.* **65**, 135–81

Allan, J.P., Hughes, M.J. and Taylor, R.T. 2010 'Saxo-Norman pottery in Somerset: some recent research', *Somerset Archaeol. Natur. Hist.* **154**, 165–84

Allan, J.P., Hughes, M.J. and Taylor, R.T. forthcoming 'The post-Roman pottery', in Smart, C., 'Excavations at the Roman fort and later settlement at Calstock, Cornwall', *Archaeol. J.*

Anderberg, A-L. 1994 *Atlas of seeds: part 4* Swedish Museum of Natural History, Uddevalla, Risbergs Tryckeri AB

Andrews P., Egging Dinwiddy, K., Ellis, C., Hutcheson, A., Phillpotts, C., Powell, A.B. and Schuster, J. 2009 *Kentish sites and sites of Kent: a miscellany of four archaeological excavations* Wessex Archaeology Report 24

Appleton-Fox, N. 1992 'Excavations at a Romano-British round; Reawla, Gwinear, Cornwall', *Cornish Archaeol.* **31**, 69–123

Archaeological Surveys 2006a *Ottery St Mary to Aylesbeare, Devon, gas pipeline: magnetometer survey*, ref. no. **137** (Apr/May 2006)

Archaeological Surveys 2006b *Aylesbeare to Kenn. Devon, gas pipeline: magnetometer survey part 1*, ref. no. **147** ((July/Aug. 2006)

Archaeological Surveys 2006c *Fishacre to Choakford, Devon, gas pipeline: magnetometer survey*, ref. no. **128** (Dec. 2005/Jan. 2006)

Archaeological Surveys 2007 *Sections 20.04 to 20.06, Fishacre to Choakford, Devon, gas pipeline: magnetometer survey*, ref. no. **128** (Dec. 2005/Jan. 2006)

Ashbee, P. 1970 'Excavations at Halangy Down, St. Mary's, Isles of Scilly, 1969–1970', *Cornish Archaeol.* **9**, 69–76

Asouti, E. and Austin, P. 2005 'Reconstructing woodland vegetation and its exploitation by past societies, based on the analysis and interpretation of archaeological wood charcoal macro-remains', *Environmental Archaeology* **10**, 1–18

Baas, P., Gasson, P.E. and Wheeler, E.A. 1989 'IAWA list of microscopic features for hardwood identification', *IAWA Bulletin new ser.* **10**, 219–332

Barber, A. 2000 *Hayes Farm, Clyst Honiton, near Exeter, Devon, archaeological excavation phase 1 (1999)* Cotswold Archaeological Trust Report **001127**

Barnett, C. (neé Chisham) 2008 'IV. Charcoal', in McKinley, J.I. 2008 *Beacon Hill Wood, Shepton Mallet, Somerset (BHN07/W67060) Middle Bronze Age urned cremation burial* Unpublished Wessex Archaeology Report **5–6**

Barnwell, P.S. and Giles, P. 1997 *English farmsteads 1750–1914* London, Royal Commission on the Historical Monuments of England

Beacham, P. (ed.) 1995 *Devon building* Tiverton, Devon Books

Beagrie, N. 1989 'The Romano-British pewter industry', *Britannia* **20**, 161–91

Behre, K-E. 2008 'Collected seeds and fruits from herbs as prehistoric food', *Vegetation History and Archaeobotany* **17**, 65–73

Bekker, R.M., Cappers, R.T.J. and Jans, J.E.A. 2006 *Digital seed atlas of the Netherlands* Groningen Archaeological Studies 4, Eelde, Barkhuis Publishing, www.plantatlas.eu

Bell, M. and Bradshaw, R. 1983 'Roman lava querns from Exeter', *Proc. Devon Archaeol. Soc.* **41**, 128–30

Bellamy, P.S. 1999 'Flaked stone', in Butterworth 1999a, 37–43

Berggren, G. 1981 *Atlas of seeds: part 3* Swedish Museum of Natural History, Arlöv, Berlings

BGS (British Geological Survey) 1974a *Geological survey of Great Britain (England and Wales) sheet 326 and 340: Sidmouth* 1:50,000

BGS (British Geological Survey) 1974b *Geological survey of Great Britain (England and Wales) sheet 349: Ivybridge* 1:50,000

BGS (British Geological Survey) 1976 *Geological survey of Great Britain (England and Wales) sheet 339: Newton Abbot* 1:50,000

BGS (British Geological Survey) 1995 *Geological survey of Great Britain (England and Wales) sheet 325: Exeter* 1:50,000

BGS (British Geological Survey) 1996 *Metallogenic Map of Britain and Ireland*, 1:1 500 000

Bidwell, P.T. and Silvester, R.J. 1978 'The Roman pottery', in Cunliffe, B. *Mount Batten, Plymouth. A prehistoric and a Roman fort* Oxford University Committee for Archaeology Monograph **26**, 42–9

Bishop, M.C. and Coulston, J.C.N. 1993 *Roman military equipment* London, Batsford

Brickley, M. and McKinley, J.I. 2004 *Guidelines to the Standards for Recording Human Remains*, Southampton/Reading, BABAO/ IFA Paper No. 7

Bronk Ramsey, C. 2009 'Bayesian analysis of radiocarbon dates', *Radiocarbon,* **51(1)**, 337-360

Brown, A., Fyfe, R., Jones, J. and Straker, V. 2008 'Romano-British environmental background', in Webster 2008a, 145–50

Brown, D.H. and Vince, A.G. 1984 'Petrological aspects: the medieval pottery of Exeter under the microscope', in Allan 1984a, 32–4

Brown, L. 2003 *The prehistoric pottery from Bow* Archive report lodged with Bath Archaeological Trust

Brown, P.D.C. 1970 'A Roman pewter mould from St. Just in Penwith, Cornwall', *Cornish Archaeol.* **9**, 107–10

Brunskill, R.W. 1990 Brick building in Britain London, Victor Gollancz

Budge, E.A.W. 1903 *An account of the Roman antiquities preserved in the museum at Chesters, Northumberland* London, Gilbert and Rivington

Buikstra, J.E. and Ubelaker, D.H. 1994 *Standards for Data Collection from Human Skeletal Remains*, Arkansas Archaeological Survey Research Series, Fayetteville, Arkansas Archaeological Survey No. **44**

Butterworth, C.A. 1999a 'Castle Hill', in Fitzpatrick, Butterworth and Grove 1999, 18–69

Butterworth, C.A. 1999b 'Hayne Lane', in Fitzpatrick, Butterworth and Grove 1999, 91–129

CA (Cotswold Archaeology) 2001 *Fishacre to Lyneham natural gas pipeline: archaeological fieldwalking and field reconnaissance survey* Cotswold Archaeological Trust Job **1224**, Nov.

CA (Cotswold Archaeology) 2005a *Aylesbeare to Kenn, Devon, gas pipeline: archaeology and heritage survey* Cotswold Archaeology Report **05113**

CA (Cotswold Archaeology) 2005b *Fishacre to Choakford, Devon, gas pipeline: archaeology and heritage survey* Cotswold Archaeology Report **05125**

CA (Cotswold Archaeology) 2006 *Ottery St Mary to Aylesbeare, Devon, gas pipeline: archaeology and heritage survey* Cotswold Archaeology Report **05108**

CA (Cotswold Archaeology) 2010 *Ottery St Mary to Aylesbeare, Aylesbeare to Kenn, Fishacre to Choakford gas pipelines, Devon: post-excavation assessment and updated project design, three volumes* Cotswold Archaeology Report **09106**

Campbell, G. and Robinson, M. 2007 'Environment and land use in the valley bottom', in Harding, J. and Healy, F., *The Raunds Area Project – a Neolithic and Bronze Age landscape in Northamptonshire* Swindon, English Heritage, 18–36

Campbell, G. and Straker, V. 2003 'Prehistoric crop husbandry and plant use in southern England: development and regionality', in Robson Brown, K.A. (ed.), *Archaeological Sciences 1999. Proceedings of the Archaeological Science Conference, University of Bristol, 1999* Brit. Archaeol. Rep. Int. Ser. **1111**, 14–30

Campbell, G., Smith, W. and Straker, V. 2007 'The charred plant macrofossils', in Gerrard and Aston 2007, 869–888

Cardoso, J.F.M.F. 2007 'Growth and reproduction in bivalves: an energy budget approach', doctoral dissertation, Rijksuniversiteit Groningen

Carruthers, W. 2010 'Appendix 15: the charred plant remains', in Collard, Joyce and Mudd 2010, 203–28

Carruthers, W. and Hunter, J. 2001 *West Heslerton: the plant remains* Unpublished palaeobotanical report

Caseldine, C., Coles, B.J., Griffith, F.M. and Hatton J.M. 2000 'Conservation or change? Human influence on the Mid-Devon Landscape', in Nicholson, R.A. and Connor, T.P. (eds) *People as an Agent of Environmental Change,* Symposia of the Association for Environmental Archaeology no. 16, Oxford: Oxbow Books, 60-70

Challinor, D. 2010 'Appendix 14: charcoal', in Collard, Joyce and Mudd 2010, 192–202

Christie, P.M.L. 1978 'The excavation of an Iron Age souterrain and settlement at Carn Euny, Sancreed, Cornwall', *Proc. Prehist. Soc.* **44**, 309–433

Clapham, A.J. 1995 'Plant remains', in Barnes, I., Boismier, W.A., Cleal, R.M.J., Fitzpatrick, A.P. and Roberts, M.R., *Early settlement in Berkshire: Mesolithic–Roman occupation sites in the Thames and Kennet Valleys*, Wessex Archaeology Report 6, 35–45

Clapham, A.J. 1999a 'Charred plant remains', in Fitzpatrick, Butterworth, and Grove 1999, 51–9

Clapham, A.J. 1999b 'Charred plant remains', in Fitzpatrick, Butterworth, and Grove 1999, 152–5

Clapham, A.J. 1999c 'Charred plant remains', in Fitzpatrick, Butterworth, and Grove 1999, 113–19

Clapham, A.J. 1999d 'Charred plant remains', in Fitzpatrick, Butterworth, and Grove 1999, 134–5

Clapham, A.J. 1999f 'Charred plant remains', in Butterworth, Fitzpatrick and Grove 1999, 184–8

Clarke, D.L. 1970 *Beaker pottery of Great Britain and Ireland* Cambridge, Cambridge University Press

Cleal, R. 1999 'Introduction: the what, where, when and why of Grooved Ware', in Cleal and MacSween 1999, 1–8

Cleal, R. and MacSween, A. 1999 *Grooved Ware in Britain and Ireland* Oxford, Oxbow Books

Cleere, H. 1972 'The classification of early iron-smelting furnaces', *Antiq. J.* 52, 8–23

Cleere, H. 1977 'Comments on the iron-working activities', in Hanworth, R. and Tomalin, D., *Brooklands, Weybridge: The excavation of an Iron Age and medieval site 1964–5 and 1970–71* Research Volume **4**, Guildford, Surrey Archaeological Society, 19–22

Cobain S.L. 2012 'Plant macrofossils and charcoal', in Mudd, A. and Brett, M., 'A Neolithic and Bronze Age monument complex and its early medieval reuse: excavations at Netherfield Farm, South Petherton, Somerset, 2006', *Archaeol. J.* **169**, 50–9

Cobain, S.L. forthcoming 'Plant macrofossils and charcoal', in Hart *et al.* forthcoming

Cole, D. and Jones, A.M. 2002–3 'Journeys to the rock: archaeological investigations at Tregarrick Farm, Roche, Cornwall', *Cornish Archaeol.* **41–2**, 107–43

Coleman, T. *et al.* 1996 *Metallogenic map of Britain and Ireland* Keyworth, Nottingham, British Geological Survey

Collard, M., Joyce, S. and Mudd, A. 2010 *South-West Reinforcement Project. Ottery St Mary to Aylesbeare, Aylesbeare to Kenn, Fishacre to Choakford gas pipelines, Devon, post-excavation assessment and updated project design, issue 2* Cotswold Archaeology Report **09106**

Cool, H.E.M. 2006 *Eating and drinking in Roman Britain*, Cambridge, Cambridge University Press

Cowgill, J., de Neergaard, M. and Griffiths, N. 1987 *Medieval Finds from Excavations in London 1: Knives and Scabbards,* London, Museum of London

Crew, P. 1989 'Crawcwellt West excavations 1986–1989. A late prehistoric ironworking settlement', *Archaeology in Wales* **29**, 11–16

Crowley, M. 1973 *Shellfish survey of Castlemaine harbour (Cromane)* Fishery Leaflet 46, Dublin, Department of Agriculture and Fisheries

Cutler, D.F. and Gale, R. 2000 *Plants in archaeology, identification manual of artefacts of plant origin from Europe and the Mediterranean* Kew, Westbury Scientific Publishing

Darvill, T. 2010 *Prehistoric Britain* Oxford, Routledge

Devaney, R. 2005 'Ceremonial and domestic flint arrowheads', *Lithics: The Journal of the Lithic Studies Society* **26**, 9–22

Devon County Council/English Heritage (n.d.) *Historic landscape characterisation* http://www.devon.gov.uk/index/environment/historic_environment/landscapes/landscape-characterisation.htm

Donovan, E. 1802 *The natural history of British shells* London, Bye and Law

Drury, P.J. and Rodwell, W. 1980 'Late Iron Age and Roman settlement', in Buckley, D.G. (ed.), *The archaeology of Essex to AD 1500* London, Counc. Brit. Archaeol., 59–75

Dungworth, D. 2011a 'The metalworking', in Nowakowski and Quinnell 2011, 220-244

Dungworth, D. 2011b 'XRF analysis of Cu alloy objects', project archive report for Cotswold Archaeology

English Heritage 2001 'Pastscape – detailed result: Poderham Park, Monument No. 1346465', http://www.pastscape.org.uk/hob.aspx?hob_47995&sort=4&search=all&criteria=powderham&rational=q&recordsperpage=10

English Heritage 2011 *Introductions to heritage assets: prehistoric barrows and burial mounds* Swindon, English Heritage

Fairbairn A.S. (ed.) 2000a *Plants in Neolithic Britain and beyond, Neolithic Studies Group Seminar Papers 5* Oxford, Oxbow Books

Fairbairn, A.S. 2000b 'On the spread of plant crops across Neolithic Britain, with special reference to southern England', in Fairbairn 2000a, 107–22

Fasham, P., Johnstone, D. and Moore, C. 1998–9 'Excavations at Penhale Round, Fraddon, Cornwall 1995/6', *Cornish Archaeol.* **37–8**, 72–120

Fitzpatrick, A. (ed.) 2008 'Later Bronze Age and Iron Age', in Webster 2008a, 117–44

Fitzpatrick, A.P. 1999 'A summary', in Fitzpatrick, Butterworth and Grove 1999, 213–22

Fitzpatrick, A.P. and Grove, J. 1999 'Discussion of the Roman sites', in Fitzpatrick, Butterworth and Grove 1999, vol. 2, 396–403

Fitzpatrick, A.P., Butterworth, C.A. and Grove, J. 1999 *Prehistoric and Roman sites in East Devon: The A30 Honiton to Exeter Improvement DBFO Scheme, 1996–9,* 2 vols, Salisbury, Wessex Archaeology Report **16**

Fleming, A. 1988 *The Dartmoor reaves: investigating prehistoric land divisions* London, Batsford

Fleming, A. 1994 'The reaves reviewed', *Proc. Devon Archaeol. Soc.* **52**, 63–74

Foard, G. 2001 'Medieval woodland, agriculture and industry in Rockingham Forest, Northamptonshire', *Medieval Archaeol.* **45**, 41–95

Fox, A. 1952 'Hill-slope forts and related earthworks in south-west England and Wales', *Archaeol. J.* **109**, 1–22

Fox, A. 1954 'Excavations at Kes Tor', *Trans. Devonshire Assoc.* **86**, 21–62

Fox, A., Radford, C.A.R., Rogers, E.H. and Shorter, A.H. 1949–50 'Report on the excavations at Milber Down, 1937–8', *Proc. Devon Archaeol. Ex. Soc.* **IV**, 2/3, 27–66

Franklin, A. 1972 *The cockle and its fisheries* Laboratory Leaflet 26, Burnham on Crouch, Ministry of Agriculture, Fisheries and Food

Fulford, M.G. 2000, *New Forest Roman pottery, manufacture and distribution, with a corpus of the pottery types* Brit. Archaeol. Rep. Brit. Ser. **17**

Fyfe, R.M., Brown, A.G. and Coles, B.J. 2003, 'Mesolithic to Bronze Age vegetation change and human activity in the Exe Valley, Devon, UK', *Proc. Prehist. Soc.* **69**, 161–81

Gale, R. 1998–9 'Charcoal', in Fasham, Johnston and Moore 1998–9, 106–12

Gale, R. 1999a 'Charcoal', in Fitzpatrick, Butterworth, and Grove 1999, 59–62

Gale, R. 1999b 'Charcoal', in Fitzpatrick, Butterworth, and Grove 1999, 155–8

Gale, R. 2006 'Charcoal', in Chadwick, A.M., *Bronze Age burials and settlement and an Anglo-Saxon settlement at Claypit Lane, Westhampnett, West Sussex* Sussex Archaeol. Collect. **144**, 7–50

Garrow, D. 2007 'Placing pits: landscape occupation and depositional practice during the Neolithic in East Anglia', *Proc. Prehist. Soc.* **73**, 1–24

Garrow, D., Beadsmoore, E. and Knight, M. 2005 'Pit clusters and the temporality of occupation: an Earlier Neolithic Site at Kilverstone, Thetford, Norfolk, *Proc. Prehist. Soc.* **71**, 139–57

Garwood, P. 1999 'Grooved Ware in southern Britain: chronology and interpretation', in Cleal and MacSween 1999, 145–76

Gent, T.H. and Quninnell, H. 1999a 'Excavation of a causewayed enclosure and hillfort on Raddon Hill, Stockleigh Pomeroy', *Proc. Devon Archaeol. Soc.* **57**, 1–75

Gent, T.H. and Quinnell, H. 1999b 'Salvage recording on the Neolithic site at Haldon Belvedere', *Proc. Devon Archaeol. Soc.* **57**, 77–104

Gerrard, C. and Aston, M. 2007 *The Shapwick Project, Somerset: A rural landscape explored* Society for Medieval Archaeology Monograph **25**

Gibson, A. 1992 'The excavation of an Iron Age settlement at Gold Park, Dartmoor', *Proc. Devon Archaeol. Soc.* **50**, 19–46

Gibson, A. and Kinnes, I. 1997 'On the urns of a dilemma: radiocarbon and the Peterborough problem', *Oxford J. Archaeol.* **16**, 65–72

Gossip, J. and Jones, A.M. (eds) 2007 *Archaeological investigations of a Later Prehistoric and a Romano-British landscape at Tremough, Penryn, Cornwall* Oxford, Brit. Archaeol. Rep. Brit. Ser. **443**

Green, H.S. 1980 *The flint arrowheads of the British Isles* Oxford, Brit. Archaeol. Rep. Brit. Ser. **75**

Green, T. 2009 'Excavation of a hillslope enclosure at Holworthy Farm, Parracombe, displaying Bronze Age and Iron Age activity', *Proc. Devon Arch. Soc.* **67**, 39–97

Greene, J.P. and Greene, K.T. 1970 'A trial excavation on a Romano-British site at Clanacombe, Thurlestone, 1969', *Proc. Devon Archaeol. Soc.* **28**, 130–6

Griffith, F.M. 1985 'Some newly discovered ritual monuments in mid Devon', *Proc. Prehist. Soc.* **51**, 310–15

Griffith, F.M. 1994 'Changing perceptions of the context of Prehistoric Dartmoor', in Griffiths 1994, 85–100

Griffith, F.M. 2001 'Recent work on Neolithic enclosures in Devon', in Darvill, T. and Thomas, J. (eds), *Neolithic enclosures in Atlantic northwest Europe* Oxford, Oxbow Books

Griffiths, D. (ed.) 1994 'The archaeology of Dartmoor: perspectives from the 1990s', *Proc. Devon Arch. Soc.* **52**

Guido, M. 1978 *The glass beads of the Prehistoric and Roman periods in Britain and Ireland* London, Reports of the Research Committee of the Society of Antiquaries of London **35**

Hagan, A. 2006 *Anglo-Saxon food and drink* Ely, Anglo-Saxon Books

Halkon, P. 2008 *Archaeology and environment in a changing East Yorkshire landscape* Brit. Archaeol. Rep. Brit. Ser. **472**, Oxford, Archaeopress

Hall, R. 2008 'Putting the iron into Iron Age', *British Archaeology* **Jan–Feb**, 44–7

Hammond, M.D.P. 1984 'Brick kilns: an illustrated survey – II: clamps', British Brick Society Information **33**, http://www.arct.cam.ac.uk/personal-page/james/bbs/bbs_33.pdf (accessed 6 October 2011)

Hart, J., Wood, I., Barber, A., Brett A. and Hardy, A. forthcoming 'Prehistoric land use in the Clyst Valley: excavations at Hayes Farm, Clyst Honiton 1996–2012', *Proc. Devon Archaeol. Soc.*

Heller, I., Kienast, F., Schoch, W. and Schweingruber, F.H. 2004 *Wood anatomy of Central European species*, www.woodanatomy.ch (accessed 2 May 2014)

Henderson, C.G. and Weddell, P.J. 1994 'Medieval settlements on Dartmoor and in West Devon: the evidence from excavations', *Proc. Devon Arch. Soc.* **52**, 119–40

Herring, P. 2008 'Commons, fields and communities in prehistoric Cornwall', in Chadwick A. (ed.), *Recent approaches to the archaeology of land allotment* Oxford, BAR Int. Ser. **1875**, 70–96

Hillman, G. 1981 'Reconstructing crop husbandry practices from charred remains of crops', in Mercer 1981 *Farming practice in British Prehistory*, 123–62

Holbrook, N. (ed.) 2008 'Roman', in Webster 2008a, 151–61

Holbrook, N. and Bidwell, P.T. 1991 *Roman finds from Exeter* Exeter Archaeological Reports **4**

Hosfield, R., Straker, V. and Gardiner P. 2008 'Palaeolithic and Mesolithic', in Webster 2008a, 23–62

Houlder, C.H. 1963 'A Neolithic settlement on Hazard Hill, Totnes', *Proc. Devon Archaeol. Exploration Soc.* **21**, 2–30

Hughes, G. 2000 *The Lockington gold hoard: an Early Bronze Age barrow cemetery at Lockington, Leicestershire* Oxford, Oxbow Books

Hurst, J.G. 1974 'Sixteenth- and seventeenth-century imported pottery from the Saintonge', in Evison, V.I., Hodges, H. and Hurst, J.G. (eds), *Medieval pottery from excavations: studies presented to Gerald Clough Dunning, with a bibliography of his works* London, John Baker, 221–55

Hurst, J.G. and Gaimster, D.R. 2005 'Werra ware in Britain, Ireland and North America', *Post-Medieval Archaeol.* **39**/2, 267–93

Hutton, R. 1996 *The stations of the sun: a history of the ritual year in Britain* Oxford, Oxford University Press

Jacklin, H. A., 2005 *A New, Fully Standardized Skeletal Recording Form Following BABAO and IFA Guidelines*, unpublished

Johnson, N. and Rose, P. 1994 *Bodmin Moor: an archaeological survey. Volume 1: the human landscape to c. 1800* London, English Heritage Archaeological Report **24**

Jones, A.M. and Quinnell, H. 2006 'Cornish Beakers: new discoveries and perspectives', *Cornish Archaeol.* **45**, 31–70

Jones, A.M. and Reed, S.J. 2006 'By land, sea and air: an Early Neolithic pit group at Portscatho, Cornwall, and consideration of coastal activity during the Neolithic', *Cornish Archaeol.* **45**, 1–130

Jones, G. 2000 'Evaluating the importance of cereals in Neolithic Britain', in Fairbairn 2000a, 79–84

Jones, J. 2002 *Charred plant remains from Bantham Ham Surf Club* Unpublished Exeter Archaeology Report

Jørgensen, A.B. 2000 'Investigations of Danish rotary querns from the Iron Age: archaeological evidence and practical experiments', in Procopiou, H. and Treuil, R. (eds), *Moudre et Broyer* **2**, Paris, CTHS, 183–96

Laidlaw, M. 1999. 'Pottery', in Fitzpatrick, Butterworth and Grove 1999, 148–52

Laidlaw, M. and Mepham, L. 1999 'Pottery', in Fitzpatrick, Butterworth and Grove 1999, 43–51

Last, J. 2007 'Covering old ground: barrows as closures', in Last, J. (ed.) *Beyond the grave: new perspectives on barrows* Oxford, Oxbow Books, 1–13

Leake, R. and Norton, G. 1993 *Mineralisation in the Middle Devonian volcanic belt and associated rocks of South Devon* Mineral Reconnaissance Programme Report **129**, British Geological Survey Technological Report WF/93/6, Keyworth, Nottingham, British Geological Survey

Leverett, M. and Quinnell, H. 2010 'An Early Neolithic assemblage from Wayland's, Tiverton', *Proc. Devon Archaeol. Soc.* **68**, 1–14

Loader, E. 1999 'Worked stone', in Fitzpatrick, Butterworth and Grove 1999, 281–2

Longworth, I.H. 1971 'The Neolithic pottery', in Wainwright, G.J. and Longworth, I.H., *Durrington Walls: excavations 1966–1968* London, Society of Antiquaries, 48–155

Longworth, I.H. and Cleal, R. 1999. 'Grooved Ware gazetteer', in Cleal and MacSween 1999, 177–206

Mabey, R. 2007 Food for Free London, HarperCollins

Masson Phillips, E.N. 1966 'Excavation of a Romano-British site at Lower Well Farm, Stoke Gabriel, Devon', Proc. Devon Archaeol. Exploration Soc. **23**, 2–29

MacNeill, M. 1962 *The festival of Lughnasa: a study of the survival of the Celtic festival of the beginning of harvest* Oxford, Irish Folklore Commission

McCutcheon, C. 2006 *Medieval pottery from Wood Quay, Dublin* Royal Irish Academy ser. B **7**

McKinley, J.L., and Roberts, C.A. 1993 *Excavation and Post-Excavation Treatment of Cremated and Inhumed Human Remains*, IFA Technical Paper. No. **13**

McKinley, J.L. 1994 'Bone Fragment Size in British Cremation Burials and its Implications for Pyre Technology and Ritual', *Journal of Archaeological Science* **21.3**, 339-342

McKinley, J.L. 2000a 'Putting Cremated Bone into Context'. In S. Roskams (Ed) *Interpreting Stratigraphy; Site Evaluation, Recording Procedures and Stratigraphic Analysis,* Brit. Archaeol. Rep. Int. Ser., Oxford, Archaeopress No. **910**, 135-140

McKinley, J.L. 2000b 'The analysis of cremated bone', In M. Cox and S. Mays (Eds.) *Human Osteology* London, Greenwich Medical Media, 403-421

McKinley, J.L. and Bond, J. M., 2001 'Cremated Bone', In D.R. Brothwell and A.M. Pollard (Eds) *Handbook of Archaeological Sciences* Chichester, Wiley, 281-292

McMillan, N.F. 1968 *British shells* London, Frederick Warne

Mercer, R. 1981 *Farming practice in British prehistory* Edinburgh, Edinburgh University Press

Mercer, R.J. 1981 'Excavations at Carn Brea, Illogan, Cornwall 1970–73', *Cornish Archaeol.* **20**, 1–204

Moffett, L. 2006 'The archaeology of medieval plant food', in Serjeantson, Waldron and Woolgar 2006, 41–55

Montague, L.A.D. 1938 'The finds', in Morris, P., Montague, L.A.D. and Goodchild, R., 'A Romano-British building at Topsham', *Proc. Devon Archaeol. Exploration Soc.* **3**/2, 70–9

Munsell 1975 *Munsell Soil Colour Charts 1975* Munsell Colour, MacBeth Division of Kollmorgen Corp., Baltimore, USA

Needham, S. 2005 'Transforming Beaker culture in north-west Europe: processes of fusion and fission', *Proc. Prehist. Soc.* **71**, 171–218

Newberry, J. 2002 'Inland flint in prehistoric Devon: sources, tool-making quality and use', *Proc. Devon Archaeol. Soc.* **60**, 1–36

Noël Hume, I. 1969 *A guide to artifacts of colonial America* Philadelphia, University of Pennsylvania Press

Nowakowski, J. 1991 'Trethellan Farm, Newquay: the excavation of a lowland Bronze Age settlement and Iron Age cemetery', *Cornish Archaeol.* **30**, 5–242

Nowakowski, J. 2001 'Leaving home in the Cornish Bronze Age: insights into planned abandonment processes', in Brück, J. (ed.), *Bronze Age landscapes: tradition and transformation* Oxford, Oxbow, 139–48

Nowakowski, J. 2007 'Digging deeper into barrow ditches: investigating the making of Early Bronze Age memories in Cornwall', in Last, J. (ed.), *Beyond the grave: new perspectives on barrows* Oxford, Oxbow Books, 91–112

Nowakowski, J. and Quinnell, H. 2011 *Trevelgue Head, Cornwall: the importance of CK Croft Andrew's 1939 excavations for Prehistoric and Roman Cornwall* Truro, Cornwall Council Historic Environment

Paynter, S. 2006 'Regional variations in bloomery smelting slag of the Iron Age and Romano-British period', *Archaeometry* **48**/2, 271–92

Paynter, S. 2007 'Innovations in bloomery smelting in Iron Age and Romano-British England', in La Niece, S., Hook, D. and Craddock, P. *Metals and mines: studies in archaeometallurgy* London, Archtype Publications in association with the British Museum, 202–10

Peacock, D.P.S. 1969 'A contribution to the study of Glastonbury Ware from south-western Britain', *Antiq. J.* **49**, 41–61

Peal, C.A. 1967 'Romano-British pewter plates and dishes', *Proc. Cambridge Antiq. Soc.* **60**, 19–37

Pearson, K.L. 1997 'Nutrition and the early-medieval diet', *Speculum* **72**/1, 1–32

Pearson, T. 1987 *The Hayes Farm, Clyst Honiton, Devon 1987, carbonised plant remains* English Heritage Ancient Monuments Laboratory Report **31**/89

Platt, C.P.S. and Coleman-Smith, R. 1975 *Excavations in medieval Southampton 1953–1969* **2**, Leicester, Leicester University Press

Pliny 1855 *The Natural History of Pliny the Elder,* trans. Bostock, J. and Riley H.T., *Book 18, Ch. 14*, Perseus Digital Library http://www.perseus.tufts.edu/hopper/text;jsessionid=9CC9AFC0596A5245D2456FD8F038028F?doc=Perseus%3atext%3a1999.02.0137

Pollard, J. 2001 'The aesthetics of depositional practice', *World Archaeol.* **33**/2, 315–33

Pollard, J. and Healy, F. (eds) 2008 'Neolithic and early Bronze Age', in Webster 2008a, 75–115

Prehistoric Ceramics Research Group 2010 *The study of prehistoric pottery: general policies and guidelines for analysis and publications*. Occasional Paper 1 and 2. 3rd revised online edition, http://www.pcrg.org.uk/News_pages/PCRG%20Gudielines%203rd%20Edition%20(2010).pdf

Quinn, G.F. 1995 'A new survey of the prehistoric field system on Kerswell Down and Whilborough Common', *Proc. Devon Archaeol. Soc.* **53**, 131–4

Quinnell, H. 1991 'The late Mrs EM Minter's excavation of hut circles at Heatree, Manaton in 1968', *Proc. Devon Archaeol. Soc.* **49**, 1–25

Quinnell, H. 1992 'Stone objects', in Appleton-Fox 1992, 106–13

Quinnell, H. 1993 'A sense of identity: distinctive Cornish stone artefacts in the Roman and Post-Roman periods', *Cornish Archaeol.* **32**, 29–46

Quinnell, H. 1994a 'New perspectives on upland monuments – Dartmoor in earlier prehistory', *Proc. Devon Archaeol. Soc.* **52**, 49–62

Quinnell, H. 1994b 'Becoming marginal? Dartmoor in later prehistory', *Proc. Devon Archaeol. Soc.* **52**, 75–83

Quinnell, H. 1999 'Pottery', in Gent and Quinnell 1999a, 38–53

Quinnell, H. 2003 'Devon Beakers: new finds, new thoughts', *Proc. Devon Archaeol. Soc.* **61**, 1–20

Quinnell, H. 2007 'A Peterborough sherd from the beach at Westward Ho!', *Proc. Devon Archaeol. Soc.* **65**, 231–3

Quinnell, H. 2008 *The pottery from the Sidmouth Donkey Sanctuary* Unpublished report for South West Archaeology lodged with Devon HER

Quinnell, H. 2011 'The pottery', in Nowakowski and Quinnell 2011, chapter 7

Quinnell, H. forthcoming (a) 'The pottery', in Gossip, J., 'The evaluation of a multi-period prehistoric site at Boden Vean, St Anthony in Meneage, Cornwall 2003', *Cornish Archaeol.*

Quinnell, H. forthcoming (b) 'The prehistoric pottery' in Farnell, A., 'Multi-period settlement, burial, industry and agriculture: archaeological excavations 2007-2012 at Twin Yeo Quarry, Chudleigh Knighton', *Proc. Devon Archaeol. Soc.*

Quinnell, H. forthcoming (c) 'The stonework', in Johns, C.A. and Gossip, J., 'Excavations at Boden Vean fogou and enclosure, St. Antony-in-Meneage', for submission to *Cornish Archaeol.*

Quinnell, H. in prep. 'The pottery from sites excavated by Exeter Archaeology at Digby, Exeter', *Proc. Devon Archaeol. Soc.*

Quinnell, H. and Taylor R. 2002–3 'Stone artefacts', in Cole and Jones 2002-3, 41–2, 121–3

Quinnell, H. and Watts, S. 2004 'Rotary querns', in Quinnell, H., *Trethurgy. Excavations at Trethurgy Round, St. Austell: community and status in Roman and post-Roman Cornwall* Truro, Cornwall County Council, 145–51

Rackham, J. 1994 *Environment and economy in Anglo-Saxon England: a review of recent work on the environmental archaeology or rural and urban Anglo-Saxon settlements in England. Proceedings of a conference held at the Museum of London, 9–10 April, 1990* Counc. Brit. Archaeol. Res. Rep. **89**

Rackham, O. 2001 *Trees and woodland in the British landscape: the complete history of Britain's trees, wood and hedgerows* London, Phoenix Press

Rahtz, P.A. and Greenfield, E. 1977 *Excavations at Chew Valley Lake, Somerset* Department of Environment Archaeological Report **8**

Reed, S.J. 1991 *Archaeological recording on the SWW South Devon Spine Main (Roborough to Littlehempston)* Exeter Museums Archaeological Field Unit Report **91.36**

Reed, S.J. and Manning, P.T. 2000 'Archaeological recording of a hillslope enclosure at North Hill Cleeve, Bittadon, North Devon', *Proc. Devon Archaeol. Soc.* **58**, 201–14

Reimer, P.J., Baillie, M.G.L., Bard, E., Bayliss, A., Beck, J.W, Blackwell, P.G., Bronk Ramsey, C., Buck, C.E., Burr, G.S., Edwards, R.L., Friedrich, M., Grootes, P.M., Guilderson, T.P., Hajdas, I., Heaton, T.J., Hogg, A.G., Hughen, K.A., Kaiser, K.F., Kromer, B., McCormac, F.G., Manning, S.W., Reimer, R.W., Richards, D.A., Southon, J.R., Talamo, S., Turney, C.S.M., van der Plicht, J. and Weyhenmeyer, C.E. 2009 'IntCal 09 and Marine09 radiocarbon age calibration curves, 0-50,000 years cal BP', Radiocarbon **51** (**4**), 1111-1150

Rippon, S. 2008 *Beyond the medieval village: the diversification of landscape character in southern Britain* Oxford, Oxford University Press

Rippon, S. 2012 *Making sense of an historic landscape* Oxford, Oxford University Press

Rippon, S. and Croft, B. (eds) 2008 'Post-conquest medieval', in Webster 2008a, 195–208

Rose, F. 2006 *The wild flower key* London, Warne

Rosenfeld, A. 1964 'Excavations in the Torbryan Caves', *Proc. Devon Archaeol. Soc.* **22**, 3–26

Salter, C. 1989 'The scientific investigation of the iron industry in Iron Age Britain 250–273', in Henderson, J. (ed.), *Scientific analysis in archaeology* Oxford University Committee for Archaeology, Monograph **19** and UCLA Institute of Archaeology, Archaeological Research Tools **5**

Scaife, R.G. 1998–9 'The charred seed remains', in Fasham, Johnstone and Moore 1998–9, 96–106

Scheuer, L. and Black, S. 2000 *Developmental Juvenile Osteology* Academic Press, London

Seager Smith, R. 1999 'Romano-British pottery', in Fitzpatrick, Butterworth and Grove 1999, 286–326

Serjeantson, D., Waldron, T. and Woolgar, C.M. 2006 *Food in medieval England: diet and nutrition* Oxford, Oxford University Press

Sheridan, A. 2012 'A Rumsfeld reality check: what we know, what we don't know and what we don't know we don't know about the Chalcolithic in Britain and Ireland', in Allen, M.J., Gardiner, J. and Sheridan, A. (eds), *Is there a British Chalcolithic? People, place and polity in the later 3rd millennium* Prehistoric Society Research Paper **4**, Oxford and Oakville, Oxbow Books

Sheridan, A., Schulting, R., Quinnell, H. and Taylor, R. 2008 'Revisiting a small passage grave tomb at Broadsands, Devon', *Proc. Devon Archaeol. Soc.* **66**, 1–27

Simpson, S., Griffith, F.M. and Holbrook, N. 1989 'The prehistoric, Roman and early post-Roman site at Hayes Farm, Clyst Honiton', *Proc. Devon Archaeol. Soc.* **47**, 1–28

Smith, I.F. 1965 *Windmill Hill and Avebury: excavations by Alexander Keiller 1925–1939* Oxford, Oxford University Press

Smith, I.F. 1975 'Neolithic pottery', in Jarvis, K. and Maxfield, V., 'The excavation of a first century Roman farmstead and a Late Neolithic settlement, Topsham, Devon', *Proc. Devon Archaeol. Soc.* **33**, 249–51

Smith, I.F. 1981 'Stone artefacts and Neolithic pottery', in Mercer R.J. 1981, 153–79

Sorenson, M.-L.S. 1996 'Sherds and pot groups as keys to site formation process', in Needham, S. and Spence, T., *Refuse and disposal at Area 16 East, Runnymede* London, British Museum Press, 1–74

Spooner, G.M. and Russell, F.S. (eds) 1967 *Worth's Dartmoor* Newton Abbot, David and Charles

Stace, C. 1997 *A new British flora* Cambridge, Cambridge University Press

Starley, D. 1998 *The analysis of metalworking debris from Thorpe Lee Nurseries, near Egham, Surrey 1990–1994* English Heritage Ancient Monuments Laboratory Report **1/98**

Starley, D. 2009 *The assessment of Iron Age ironworking debris from St Ann's Heath School, Virginia Water, Surrey* Unpublished David Starley Archaeometallurgy Report **08/09**

Steinmetzer, M. and Quinnell, H. forthcoming 'Prehistory activity in the area of the Royal Naval Stores Depot, Topsham', *Proc. Devon Archaeol. Soc.*

Stevens, C.J. 2009 'Charred plant remains', in Budd, C. and Crockett, A.D., 'The archaeology and history of Renny Lodge: Romano-British farmstead, workhouse, hospital, houses', *Records of Buckinghamshire* **49**, 118–24

Stevens, C.J. and Fuller, D.Q. 2012 'Did Neolithic farming fail? The case for a Bronze Age agricultural revolution in the British Isles', *Antiquity* **86**, 707–22

Stone, D.J. 2005 *Decision-making in medieval agriculture* Oxford, Oxford University Press

Stone, D.J. 2006 'The consumption of field crops in late medieval England', in Serjeantson, Waldron and Woolgar 2006, 11–26

Straker, V. 1991 'Charred plant macrofossils', in Nowakowski 1991, 161–79

Straker, V. 1992 'Charred plant macrofossils', in Appleton-Fox 1992, 89–91

Straker, V. 1995 'Plant macrofossils', in Ratcliffe, J., 'Duckpool, Morwenstow: a Romano-British and early medieval industrial site and harbour', *Cornish Archaeol.* **34**, 155–7

Straker, V. 1997a 'The ecofactual assemblage', in Harry, R. and Morris, C.D., 'Excavations on the Lower Terrace Site C, Tintagel Island 1990–94', *Antiq. J.* **77**, 82–107

Straker, V. 1997b 'Sourton Down medieval settlement: assessment of charred plant macrofossils from bulk samples', in Weddell and Reed 1997, 115–17

Straker, V. 1997c 'Charred plant remains', in Allen, M.J., Barnes, I. Healy, F., Morris, E.L., Smith, R.J.C. and Woodward, J., *Excavations along the route of the Dorchester by-pass, Dorset, 1986–8* Wessex Archaeology Report **11**

Straker, V. 2008a 'Early medieval environmental background', in Webster 2008a, 163–8

Straker, V. 2008b 'Post-conquest medieval environmental background', in Webster 2008a, 189–94

Straker, V. 2008c 'Post-medieval to modern environmental background', in Webster 2008a, 209–12

Stratascan 2001 *A report for Cotswold Archaeological Trust on a geophysical survey carried out at Fishacre-Lyneham pipeline trials, Devon* Ref. No. **1629**, Dec.

Taylor, R.T. 2002 'The petrology of the temper of the Haycroft Farm pottery', in Allan and Langman 2002, 65–7

Tebble, N. 1966 *British bivalve seashells: a handbook for identification* London, British Museum (Natural History)

Thomas, J. 1999 *Understanding the Neolithic* London, Routledge

Tingle, M. 2006 'Excavations of a possible causewayed enclosure and Roman site at Membury 1986 and 1994–2000', *Proc. Devon Archaeol. Soc.* **64**, 1–52

Tomber, T. and Dore, J. 1998, *The National Roman fabric reference collection, a handbook* MoLAS Monograph 2

Todd, M. 1998, 'A hillslope enclosure at Rudge, Morchard Bishop', *Proc. Devon Archaeol. Soc.* 56, 133–53

Turner, S. 2007 *Ancient country: the historic character of rural Devon* Devon Archaeol. Soc. Occas. Pap. **20**

Turton, S.D. and Weddell, P.J. 1989 *An archaeological assessment of the South Devon Spine Main (Roborough to Littlehempston)* Exeter Museums Archaeological Field Unit unpublished report **89.15**

Vancouver, C. 1808 *General view of the County of Devon; with observations of the means for its improvement. Drawn up for the Board of Agriculture and Internal Improvement* London, Macmillan

Watkins, G. 1978 'Pottery from excavations in Hull', *Medieval Ceram.* **2**, 43–50

Watkins, G. 1983 'North European pottery imported into Hull, 1200–1500', in Davey, P. and Hodges, R. (eds), *Ceramics and trade: the production and distribution of pottery in north-west Europe* Sheffield, Sheffield University, 244–53

Watts, M. 2002 *The archaeology of mills and milling* Stroud, Tempus Publishing

Watts, M. 2008 *Corn milling* Oxford, Shire Publications

Watts, M.A. and Quinnell, H. 2001 'A Bronze Age cremation cemetery at Elburton, Plymouth', *Proc. Devon Archaeol. Soc.* **59**, 11–43

Watts, S. 2007 *Querns from Mount Folly, Bigbury, Devon* Unpublished report for E. Wilkes, Bournemouth University

Watts, S. 2011 *Quern from Shortlands Lane, Cullompton* Unpublished report for SouthWest Archaeology

Webster, C.J. (ed.) 2008a *The Archaeology of South West England: south west archaeological research framework, resource assessment and research agenda* Taunton, Somerset Heritage Services

Webster, C.J. (ed.) 2008b 'Early medieval', in Webster 2008a, 169–88

Weddell, P.J. 2000 'The excavation of a post-Roman cemetery near Kenn, South Devon', *Proc. Devon Archaeol. Soc.* **58**, 93–126

Weddell, P.J. and Reed, S.J. 1997 'Excavations at Sourton Down, Okehampton 1986–1991: Roman road, deserted medieval hamlet and other landscape features', *Proc. Devon Archaeol. Soc.* **55**, 39–147

Wedlake, W.J. 1958 *Excavations at Camerton, Somerset* Camerton, Camerton Excavation Club.

Welfare, A.T. 1985 'Milling stones', in Bidwell, P.T., *The Roman fort of Vindolanda at Chesterholm, Northumberland* London, Historic Buildings and Monuments Commission for England, 154–64

Whittle, A., Bayliss, A., Healy, F., Mercer, R., Jones, A.M. and Todd, M. 2011 'The south-west peninsula', in Whittle, A., Healey, F. and Bayliss, A. *Gathering Time: dating the Early Neolithic enclosures of Southern Britain and Ireland* Oxford, Oxbow Books, 476–82

Williams, D. 1984 'The petrology of the possible Breton sherds', in Allan 1984a, 37

Williamson, T. 1987 'Early co-axial field systems on the East Anglian Boulder Clays', *Proc. Prehist. Soc.* **53**, 419–31

Willock, E.H. 1936 'A Neolithic site on Haldon', *Proc. Devon Archaeol. Exploration Soc.* **2**, 244–63

Wood, J. 2001 *Prehistoric cooking* Stroud, Tempus Publishing

Woodward, A. 2002 *British Barrows: a matter of life and death* Stroud, Tempus Publishing

Woodward, A. and Cane, C. 1991 'The Bronze Age pottery', in Nowakowski 1991, 103–31

Woodward, A. and Williams, D. 1999 'The prehistoric pottery', in Simpson, Griffith and Holbrook 1999, 14

Wright, M.E. 2002 'Querns and millstones', in Wilson, P.R., *Cataractonium: Roman Catterick and its hinterland: excavations and research, 1958–1997, part 2* York, Counc. Brit. Archaeol. Res. Rep. **129**, 267–80

Wyles, S. 2011 'Oyster shell', in Fitzpatrick, A.P., *The Amesbury Archer and the Boscombe Bowmen: burials on Boscombe Down, Amesbury, Wiltshire* Salisbury, Wessex Archaeology Report **27**, 163–4

Yates, D.T. 2007 *Land, power and prestige: Bronze Age field systems in southern England* Oxford, Oxbow Books

Young, T. 2007a *Evaluation of archaeometallurgical residues from Berry Ball, Devon* Unpublished GeoArch report **2007/21**

Young, T. 2007b *Archaeometallurgical residues from Richard Lander School (RLS04) and Truro College (TCF05)* Unpublished GeoArch report **2007/22**

Index

Page numbers in italics refer to illustrations.

agricultural rituals, medieval 192
Anglo-Saxon period 12
animal bone, Exwell Barton (Site 14), medieval and later 147, 166
arable agriculture (and hand-collected foodstuffs) 10
    Mesolithic and Neolithic 73-4, 76, 77, 181, 182
    Bronze Age 73-5, 76
    Iron Age 74, 127-8, 188, 193
    Roman 74, 129, 190-1
    early medieval 156, 157, 163-4, 165
    medieval 12, 156-62, 164-6, 190-1, 193
    post-medieval 163, 166
    see also plant remains *under site names*
arrowheads
    Early Neolithic
        (FTC 3.03) 62
        Pixies' Parlour (Site 4) 17, 58, 62, *63*
    Early Bronze Age (Site 14) 58-9, 62, *63*
ATK Aylesbeare to Kenn (= East Devon) 1, *2*, 3, 4, *6-7*, 14
    field boundaries 175
    flint 55, *57*, 58-9, 62
    metal objects 155
    pottery, medieval and later 151, *152*, 153
ATK 0.02, flint *57*
ATK 0.03 *see* New Nutwalls (Site 9)
ATK 1.03, flint *57*
ATK 2.03, flint *57*
ATK 4.04 & 4a.01 *see* Hogsbrook Farm (Site 10)
ATK 5.01, flint *57*
ATK 7.01 *see* Deepway Farm
ATK 7.02, flint *57*
ATK 8.02, flint *57*
ATK 10.03, flint *57*
ATK 11.04 *see* Nutwell Lodge (Site 11)
ATK 12.01 *see* Lower Nutwell (Site 12)
ATK 12.09, flint *7, 57*
    pottery 151, *152*, 153
ATK 12.10, ditch and pit, ?medieval/early post-medieval *7*, 139
ATK 12.12 *see* White House (Site 13)
ATK 12.13, pottery, Bronze Age *7*, 35, 52, 53
ATK 13.01, flint and chert *7, 57*, 59
ATK 13.02 *see* Exwell Barton (Site 14)
ATK 14.01, .04, .09, flint *57*

ATK 27.02, .03, .04, flint 55, 62
Aylesbeare *2*, 4; *see also* ATK *and* OTA *plot numbers*; Livermore Farm; New Nutwells

barrows
    Neolithic 11, 24
    Bronze Age 15, 24, 27, 184, *and see* Springfield (Site 31)
    Middle Bronze Age *see* Broad Oak (Site 8)
Barton Hill Cross, Littlehempston (Site 19; FTC 7.01) *2*, 3, *8*, 13, 14
    prehistoric flint (FTC 7.01) *8*, 19, *60*, 180
    Iron Age/Roman (RB) settlement 13, 14, 79, 85-7, *85*, 187, 188, 190
        iron blade, Roman 86
        pottery, Iron Age/MIA 86, 105, 106, 190, Roman 86-7, 108, 190
    land division/boundaries, undated 87, 190
beads, glass
    Roman
        Hems Valley (Site 17) 114, *114*
        Springfield (Site 31) 102, 114, *114*
    early medieval (Site 27) 156, *156*
    medieval (Site 14) 156
Beaker pit *see* Springfield (Site 31)
Beneknowle (village) *9*, 10
Beneknowle, Diptford (Site 30; FTC 21.06), Middle Bronze Age terraced timber structure (pit) *2*, 4, *9*, 13, 14, 15, 41-4, 184, 185
    ditches 41, 44
    flint *60*
    hazelnuts 44, 73, 74, 77
    Middle Neolithic radiocarbon date on hazelnut 44, 74, 77, 178-9
    plant remains and charcoal 41, *42*, 44, 69, 70-1, 73, 74, 76, 185
    radiocarbon dating 44, 178-9, 185
    water-vole faecal pellets 73, 185
Billany Farm, Dartington (Site 24; FTC 14.01), Romano-British settlement (enclosure) *2*, 3, *8*, 13, 14, 79, 88-94, 188-9
    cobbles, as hammerstone and rubbing stone 111
    coins, Roman 93, 108, 115, 189
    flax (processing, linseed) 90, 93, 94, 125, 129, 130, 189
    fuel waste 189

Billany Farm, Dartington (cont.)
  hearth/furnace lining, fired clay 90, 92
  metalworking (iron) hearth or 'fire-pit' 90, 115, 117, 118, 194
  palisade? and ditch 89, 189
  plant remains and charcoal 90, *91*, 92, 93, 121, 124, 125, 127, 129-30, 189
  pottery 89, 90, 92-3, 106, 107-8, 109-10, *109*, 188
  querns 89, 92, 93, 110-11, 112, *112*, 189
  radiocarbon dating 93, 94, 130, 189
Black Death 150
blades, iron, Roman 86, 104
Bluepost, Harberton (Site 29; FTC 19.07-08), medieval pit *2, 4, 8, 9*, 13, 131, 147-8, *147*, 191
  hazelnut 162
  pit in field (FTC 19.08), with charcoal 191
  plant remains and charcoal 147, 148, 156, 159-60, 161, 162, 164, 165, 191
  radiocarbon dating 147, 166, 178-9
  twine/string, burnt 147, 162, 165, 191
bone 13, 193
  human remains *see* Salston B (Site 6)
  see also animal bone
brick clamp *see* Salston A (Site 5)
bricks *see* Flemish bricks
Broad Oak, land east of (Site 7; OTA 4.10)
  Middle Bronze Age ditches and pits *2, 3, 5*, 13, 14, 27-30, 52, 58, 182, 184, 186
    charcoal 28, 69
    flint *56*, 58
    land boundaries 15, 186
    Neolithic radiocarbon date on charcoal 28, 29, 77, 178-9
    pottery 28, 52, 54, 58, 186
    radiocarbon dating 28, 29, 178-9, 186
  Roman
    ploughsoil 29
    pottery 28, 108
  medieval ditches 28
Broad Oak, land south-east of (Site 8; OTA 5.01/5.02), Middle Bronze Age *2, 3, 5*, 13
  charcoal 32
  flint, Neolithic/EBA 32, *56*, 58, 182
  Neolithic radiocarbon date 32, 77
  pottery 33, 52, 53
  radiocarbon dating 32, 77, 178-9
  ring-ditch (barrow) and ditches 14, 15, 30-3, *30*, 52, 53, 58, 77, 182, 184
Bronze Age, Early/Beaker 13, 14, 15, 24-7, 180, 182-4
  Beaker pit and EBA pottery *see* Springfield (Site 31)
  cremation burial, EBA *see* Salston B (Site 6)
  plant remains (charcoal) and radiocarbon dating 17, 24, 68
  see also pottery
Bronze Age, Middle 11-12, 13, 14, 15, 27-45, 184-6, 193
  field systems and land/field boundaries 11-12, 15, 186, *and see* Broad Oak (Site 7); Hood Quarry (Site 23)
  flint and chert, Neolithic/EBA/MBA 27, 32, 34, 38, 44, 55, 56-62, 182
  pits *see* Crablake Farm (Site 15); Filham House (Site 34); Hood Ball (Site 21); Pixies' Parlour (Site 4)
  plant remains 27-45 *passim*, 68-76, 182, 183, 184-6, 188
  radiocarbon dating 27-45 *passim*, 74, 184, 185, 186
  ring-ditch/barrow *see* Broad Oak (Site 8)
  terraced building *see* Beneknowle (Site 30)

and see under site names; see also arrowheads; barrows; hedgebanks; pin shaft fragment; pottery
buildings *see* structures and buildings

Choakford 1, *2, 4, 10, 10; see also* FTC *plot numbers*
clay
  Neolithic, fired clay in pit 22
  MIA, as furnace superstructure/lining, Tigley A (Site 26) 99, 116, 120, 122
  Roman, fired clay hearth lining (hood), Billany Farm (Site 24) 90, 92, *and see* Springfield (Site 31)
  medieval, fired clay as oven superstructure, Exwell Barton (Site 14) 146
clay tobacco pipe 168
cobbles, utilised, Roman
  Billany Farm (Site 24), hammerstone and rubbing stone 111
  Pixies' Parlour (Site 4), as whetstone/polisher 83, 110
  Springfield (Site 31), as whetstone 111, 113
  see also rubbing stones
cob building *see* Lower Nutwell (Site 12)
cockles *see* marine shells
coins, Roman, Billany Farm (Site 24) 93, 108, 115, 189
Coldharbour (Site 1; OTA 1.03), medieval pit *2, 3, 5*, 13, 131, *132*, 133, 191
  plant remains and charcoal 131, 133, 156-7, 158, 161, 164, 165, 191
  pottery 133, *152*, 153
copper-alloy objects 155
corn-drying structure *see* Exwell Barton (Site 14)
Crablake Farm, Exminster (Site 15; ATK 14.09) *2, 3, 7*, 13, 171
  Middle Bronze Age pits 13, 14, 33-5, *33*, 53-4, 69, 73, 85, 184
    cereal processing 73
    flint 34
    pin shaft fragment 35, 66, *66*
    plant remains and charcoal 34-5, 54, 69, 70-1, 73, 74, 76, 77, 184
    pottery 34, *34*, 35, 52, 53-4, *53*, 55, 66, 184, 185
    radiocarbon dating 34, 35, 54, 66, 73, 77, 85, 178-9
  Iron Age ditch/gully [.021] (roundhouse) 13, 14, *33*, 79, 84-5, 171, 187, 188
    crop-processing 84, 85, 127, 128, 188
    plant remains and charcoal 84, 85, 121, 122, 123, 127-8, 188
    radiocarbon dating 73, 84, 85, 178-9, 187
cremated human remains 194, *and see* Salston B (Site 6)
cremation pits 68, *and see* Pixies' Parlour (Site 4); Salston B (Site 6)
Croft Cottages, Staverton (Site 20; FTC 8.02), (Early) Neolithic ditch terminal *2, 3, 8*, 13, 14, 15, 18-19, 180
  postholes (?palisade) 180
  pottery 18, 46, 47, 180
crop-processing (fuel waste)
  Neolithic 181
  Middle Bronze Age 73
  Iron Age/Roman 128, 162, *and see* Crablake Farm (Site 15); Exwell Barton (Site 14); Slade Farm (Site 2)
  Roman *see* Springfield (Site 31)
  medieval *see* Coldharbour (Site 1); Exwell Barton (Site 14)
  post-medieval *see* Pixies' Parlour (Site 4)

Dartington *see* Billany Farm (Site 24); Hood Quarry (Site 23); Tigley A (Site 26); Tigley B (Site 27)
Deepway Farm, Woodbury (ATK 7.01), Late Neolithic/EBA flint *6*, 55, *57*, 58, 62
deserted medieval settlements 131, 149, 193
ditches, *see under site names; see also* field systems
Dumnonii 12
Dun Cross (Site 25; FTC 16.01), (early) Roman pits *2, 3, 8*, 13, 79, 94-5, *94*
  hearths 95
  plant remains and charcoal 94-5, 125, 127, 129, 130
  radiocarbon dating 94-5, 130, 178-9

enclosures
  undated (?prehistoric or Roman) 168, 171
  Iron Age/Roman *see* Billany Farm (Site 24); Hood Quarry (Site 23); Lower Velwell (Site 22)
  Roman *see* Hood Ball (Site 21); Pixies' Parlour (Site 4); Springfield (Site 31)
  medieval or later 138, 147, 190-1
  see also field systems
Exminster *see* Crablake Farm (Site 15); Soloman's Farm (Site 16)
Exwell Barton, Powderham (Site 14; ATK 13.02) *2, 3, 7*, 191, 192-3
  Mesolithic flint 15, *57*, 58-9, 62, *63*, 180
  Early Bronze Age, arrowhead 58-9, 62, *63*
  Late Iron Age/Roman, ditches and pits (field boundaries) 14, 79, 83-4, *83, 84*, 105, 141, 147, 190, 191
    crop-processing (fuel waste) 128, 162
    plant remains and charcoal 84, 122, 123, 128, 130
    pottery 84, 105, 106, 108
    radiocarbon dating 84, 130, 178-9
    pre-house features: 12th-14th century pit (and ditches) 141-2, *141*
    crop waste, charred 141-2
    knife (whittle-tang), iron 155, *156*
    plant remains 157, 162, 164
    pottery 141, 155
  medieval (settlement) 13, 14, 131, 139-47
    field boundary ditches and pits (including animal bone) 147, 166
    house (gully and hearths) 3, *83, 84, 140*, 141, *141*, 142-7, *142*, 164-5, 191
      as peasant dwelling 149, 192
      flint, Mesolithic 58
      hearth repairs of granite and sandstone 155
      hearths *141, 142, 143*, 145, 165
      plant remains 164-5, 191
      pottery 143, 145, 146, 148-51, 155-6, 192
      roofing slate 155, 192
    pit [.163], with pottery and crop remains 140, 147, 191
    pottery 141, 143, 145, 146, 147, 148-51, *152, 153*, 192
      Breton? 150, 151, *152*, 154
      petrology 155-6
      Saintonge 141, 150, 151, *152*, 153
    sunken (out)building (kitchen) *83, 84*, 131, *140*, 141, *141, 144*, 145-7, *146*, 165
      as ?bakehouse 191
      bead, glass 156
      charcoal as fuel 145-6, 162, 165
      cockle shell 166
    corn-drying 131, 146, 147, 191, 192
    crop-processing waste 147, 162, 164-5, 191
    fired clay, oven superstructure 146
    flint, Mesolithic 58
    hazelnut 162, 165
    hearth (?oven), earliest [.203] 145, *145*, 146-7, 165
    ovens/hearths 141, *141, 142*, 143, *143, 144*, 145, *145*, 146-7, 162, 165, 192
    plant remains 146, 147, 156, 157-62, 164-5, 191
  post-medieval, ditches and pits 84, 141, *141*, 147, 193
    animal bone 147
    cockles and oysters in ditch 147, 166, 193
    plant remains 163, 166, 193
    pottery 147, 153, *153*

field systems (boundaries) 14, 167-75, 190-1
  ?prehistoric or Roman, ditches and enclosures (undated), 14, 33, 44, 84, 167-73, 186, 190, 191
  medieval and later ditches and boundaries 12, 147, 167, 173-5, 190-1
  and see under site names; see also enclosures; hedgebanks
Filham House, Ugborough (Site 34; FTC 33.01-02) *2, 3, 4, 9, 10*
  Mesolithic flint 15, *61*, 62, 180
  Late Neolithic/Bronze Age worked flint 44
  Middle Bronze Age pit 13, 14, 15, 44, 59, 73, 184
    flint 44, 55, 59, *61*, 62, *63*
    hazelnut 44, 73, 74
    plant remains and charcoal 44, 45, 70-1, 72, 73, 74
    radiocarbon dating 44, 45, 59, 178-9
  Iron Age hearths 13, 14, 79, 104-5, *104*, 188
    charcoal 105
    hazelnut 188
    pottery 105, 106
fired clay *see* clay
Fishacre Above Ground Installation (AGI) *2, 4, 8; see also* FTC *plot numbers*
Fishacre Barton 1, 10
flax (processing, and linseed) *see* Billany Farm (Site 24)
Flemish bricks (Site 12) 134, 136, 137, 155
flint, worked *see under periods and site names*
fodder 74, 76, 129, 164, 165, 185
Forder Cross (Site 32; FTC 26.01), medieval? pits and ditches *2, 4, 9*, 13, 131, 148, *148, 149*
  flint (FTC 26.01) *61*
  pottery 148
FTC Fishacre to Choakford (= South Devon) 1, *2*, 3-4, 8-9, *10*, 14
  field boundaries 175
  flint 55, 59, *60, 61*, 62
  pottery, medieval and post-medieval 153, *153*
FTC 2.02 *see* Hems Valley (Site 17)
FTC 3.01 *8*, flint *60*
  pottery 153
FTC 3.03, Hems valley *8*
  arrowhead 62
  flint 55, *60*, 62, 180
FTC 3.04, Hems valley, flint *8*, 55, *60*, 62, 180
FTC 4.02 *see* Moothill Cross (Site 18)
FTC 7.01 *see* Barton Hill Cross (Site 19)
FTC 8.01 flint and Mesolithic bladelet *8*, 15, 19, *60*
FTC 8.02 *see* Croft Cottages (Site 20)

Index

FTC 8.03, undated pits *8*, 18-19
FTC 9.02, .03, .05, flint *60*
FTC 12.05 *see* Hood Ball (Site 21)
FTC 12.05w *see* Lower Velwell (Site 22)
FTC 13.02, pottery *8*, 153
FTC 13.03 *see* Hood Quarry (Site 23)
FTC 14.01 *see* Billany Farm (Site 24)
FTC 16.01 *see* Dun Cross (Site 25)
FTC 16.07 *see* Tigley A (Site 26)
FTC 16.08 *see* Tigley B (Site 27)
FTC 18.11, *8*
FTC 18.12 & 18.13 *see* Moore Farm (Site 28)
FTC 19.07 & 19.08 *see* Bluepost (Site 29)
FTC 20.03, Roman pottery *9*, 108
FTC 20.07, flint *60*
FTC 21.06 *see* Beneknowle (Site 30)
FTC 22.03, Roman pottery *9*, 108
FTC 23.04, flint *60*
FTC 24.02-05 *see* Springfield (Site 31)
FTC 24.10, .11, flint *61*
FTC 25.01, pottery 153, *153*
FTC 26.01 *see* Forder Cross (Site 32)
FTC 27.01, *9*
FTC 27.02, .03, .04, flint *9*, 55, *61*, *62*, 180
FTC 31.02-04, *9*
FTC 31.05-07 *see* Wood Farm (Site 33)
FTC 32.01, flint *61*
FTC 33.01-02 *see* Filham House (Site 34)
FTC 33.03 south-west of Filham House, flint *10*, *61*, *62*
FTC 34.08, flint *61*
FTC 35.01, flint *61*
FTC 37.01, flint *61*
  pottery 153, *153*
FTC 42.01, flint *61*
fuel (charcoal) 22, 193
  Neolithic 22, 75
  Bronze Age 75
  Early Bronze Age, cremation pit pyre *see* Salston B (Site 6)
  Middle Bronze Age, crop-processing *see* Hood Ball (Site 21)
  Iron Age 75, 128; for crop-processing waste *see* Crablake Farm (Site 15); Exwell Barton (Site 14); Slade Farm (Site 2)
  Middle Iron Age furnace waste *see* Tigley A (Site 26)
  Roman 129-30, *and see* Billany Farm (Site 24); Dun Cross (Site 25); Pixies' Parlour (Site 4); Springfield (Site 31)
  early medieval 164, *and see* Moore Farm (Site 28); Tigley B (Site 27)
  medieval 165, 166, *and see* Exwell Barton (Site 14)
  hazelnuts used as 181
  see also metalworking
furnaces
  Middle Iron Age iron smelting *see* Tigley A (Site 26)
  Late Iron Age/Roman ironworking *see* Lower Velwell (Site 22)

glass *see* beads; Lower Nutwell (Site 12), window

hammerscale 102, 104, 115, 117, 118, 189, 194
hammerstones 20, 55, 59, 62, *63*, 111
Harberton *see* Bluepost (Site 29); Moore Farm (Site 28)
Hazard Hill 11, 181

hazelnuts
  Mesolithic 15, 23, 66, 129, 177
  Neolithic 20, 22, 23, 24, 66-7, 74, 77, 166, 181, 193
  Bronze Age 35, 44, 70, 73, 74-5, 77, 181, 193
  Iron Age 79, 80, 122, 127, 188
  Roman 103, 129, 130
  medieval 132, 162, 165
  used as fuel 181
  and see under site names
hearths
  Neolithic 22, 63
  Iron Age *see* Filham House (Site 34)
  Roman/Romano-British metalworking *see* Billany Farm (Site 24)
  Roman (early), Dun Cross (Site 25) 95
  medieval *see* Exwell Barton (Site 14)
hedgebanks (earthen)
  Bronze Age 172, 186
  medieval and later 12, 173, 175
Hems Valley, Staverton (Site 17; FTC 2.02)
  Mesolithic flint 16, 59, *60*, 180
  Neolithic pits *2*, *3*, *8*, 13, 14, 15, 19-23, *19*, 63-5, 66, 180-1
    fired clay 22
    flint 19, 20, 22-3, 48, 55, 59, *60*, *62*, *63*
    hazelnut shells 20, 22, 66, 181
    hearth 22, 63
    plant remains and charcoal 20, 22, 66, 67-8, 75
    pottery 15, 19, 20, 22, 47, 48, 180-1
    radiocarbon dating 20, 22, 48, 178-9, 180
    rubbing stones, cobbles and pebbles 19-20, 63-5, *66*, 181
  Roman, glass bead 114, *114*
hillslope enclosures, Iron Age/Roman 188-9
Hogsbrook Farm, Woodbury (Site 10; ATK 4.04 & 4a.01) *2*, *3*, *6*
  Bronze Age pottery 35, 52, 53, 54
  Late Iron Age pottery 105, 106
  medieval/post-medieval? 13
  undated ditches and field boundaries 3, 173, *174*, 175
Hood Ball, Rattery (Site 21; FTC 12.05) *2*, *3*, *8*
  Mesolithic flint 15, 62, *63*
  Middle Bronze Age pits 13, 14, 15, 35-7, *36*, 62, 73, 184, 185
    food preparation (cereal processing) 35, 73, 75
    hazelnut 35, 73
    plant remains and charcoal 35, 69, 70-1, 72, 73, 74, 75, 76, 184, 185
    radiocarbon dating 35, 62, 74, 178-9, 185
  undated (?Roman) cropmarks and enclosures 35, *36*, 37
Hood Quarry, Dartington (Site 23; FTC 13.03) *2*, *3*, *8*
  Middle Bronze Age ditches 13, 14, 37-41, *37*, 62, 186
    Early Neolithic, radiocarbon dating 38
    flint 38, *60*, *62*, *63*
    land boundaries and boundary ditch 15, 40-1, 184, 186
    plant remains and charcoal 38, 40, 41
    pottery 38, 186
    radiocarbon dating 38, 40, 41, 77, 178-9, 186
  Late Iron Age/Roman, enclosures *37*, 40
    pottery 38, 186, LIA 105, 106, Roman 40, 108
  post-medieval, field boundary ditches (recent) *37*, 40
human remains, EBA cremation burial *see* Salston B (Site 6)

Iron Age/Middle-Late Iron Age 12, 13, 14, 79, 186-9, 193
    crop-processing *see* Crablake Farm (Site 15); Exwell Barton (Site 14); Slade Farm (Site 2)
    fuel 75, 128
    hearths *see* Filham House (Site 34)
    iron smelting furnaces, MIA *see* Tigley A (Site 26)
    ironworking hearth/furnace *see* Lower Velwell (Site 22)
    pits and ditches 79, *and see* Slade Farm (Site 2); Springfield (Site 31)
    plant remains and charcoal 74, 121-2, 123, 127-8, 182, 183, 187, 188, *and see under site names*
    radiocarbon dating 12, 130, 187, *and see under site names*
    roundhouses *see* Crablake Farm (Site 15); Pixies' Parlour (Site 4)
    settlement, IA/Roman *see* Barton Hill Cross (Site 19); Billany Farm (Site 24)
    and see under site names; see also pottery
iron objects 155
iron ore, and sources *60, 61*, 118, 119, 187
ironworking (smithing, smelting) *see* Billany Farm (Site 24); Lower Velwell (Site 22); Springfield (Site 31); Tigley A (Site 26); *see also* metalworking

Kenn, terminal 1, *2*; *see also* ATK *plot numbers*
knife (whittle-tang), iron, medieval 155, *156*
Knightstone Farm, Ottery St Mary (Site 3; OTA 2.06/3.01) *2, 3, 5*, 13
    clay tobacco pipe 168
    ditches (fields), pre-medieval? 167-8, *167*, 186, 190
    Early Neolithic curving ditch 16
    flint (OTA 3.01 & 2.06) *56*

lead objects 155
linen, Roman 129
linhays 138
Littlehempston *see* Barton Hill Cross (Site 19)
Livermore Farm, Aylesbeare (OTA 9.02) *5*
    Early Neolithic pottery, in field boundary ditch 17-18, 46, 47
    flint *56*
Lower Nutwell, Woodbury (Site 12; ATK 12.01)
    prehistoric
        flint and chert *57*, 59
        whetstone 110
    post-medieval, 18th-century cob building *2, 3, 6, 7*, 13, 131, 134-8, *135*
        as a linhay (or field barn) 138
        Flemish bricks 134, 136, 137, 155
        glass window and lead strip 136-7
        marine shells used in construction 166
        metal objects 155
        pottery 137
        roof pantile 134, 136, 137-8
        slate roofing 136, 155
Lower Velwell, Rattery (Site 22; FTC 12.05w), Iron Age/Roman *2, 3, 8*, 13, 87-8, *87*
    cropmark enclosures 88, *89*, 190
    iron furnaces (hearths) 79, 87-8, *88*, 115, 117, 118, 188
    plant remains and charcoal 88, 130, 188
    radiocarbon dating 88, 130, 178-9, 188
    Roman 88
    slag 88, 115, 117, 118, 194

smithing hearth bottoms 88, 115, 117, 118, 194

marine shells 166, 181
    cockles 147, 166, 193
    oyster 23, 166, 181
    used in cob construction (Site 12) 134, 166
medieval, early (5th-7th centuries) pits 131, 166, 191
    plant remains and charcoal 131, 132, 156, 157, 163-4, 165, 183, 191
    radiocarbon dating 23, 24, 83, 131, 132, 166, 178-9, 187, 191
    and see Moore Farm (Site 28); Pixies' Parlour (Site 4); Tigley B (Site 27)
medieval 13, 14, 131-75, 191-3
    agriculture and rituals 192, 193
    enclosures 138, 147, 190-1
    field systems, ditches and boundaries 12, 147, 167, 173-5, 190-1
    house and sunken (out)building *see* Exwell Barton (Site 14)
    pits *see* Bluepost (Site 29); Coldharbour (Site 1); Forder Cross (Site 32)
    plant remains 156-62, 164-6, 183, 191-3
    radiocarbon dating 131, 166, 191
    trackway *see* White House (Site 13)
    and see under site names; see also arable agriculture; medieval, early; pottery
Mesolithic (flint) 11, 13, 14, 15-16, 55, 56, 58, 59, 62, 177-80, 181
    plant remains 23, 66, 73, 129
    see also Moore Farm (Site 28); Pixies' Parlour (Site 4)
metalworking 115-20, 194
    fuel (charcoal) 75, 116, 120, 128, 187, 188
    Middle Iron Age iron smelting *see* Tigley A (Site 26)
    Iron Age/Roman ironworking *see* Billany Farm (Site 24); Lower Velwell (Site 22)
    Roman ironworking, pewter casting (mould), and tin-alloy working *see* Springfield (Site 31)
    see also clay; iron ore
Moore Farm, Harberton (Site 28; FTC 18.12 & 18.13) *2, 4, 8*, 13, 14, 15, *60*
    Mesolithic pit, with radiocarbon-dated hazelnut 15, *22*, 23, 51, 66, 177, 178-9, 181
    Late Neolithic pits and ditch 13, 14, 15, *22*, 23-4, 66, 181
        hazelnuts 23, 24, 66-8, 181
        oyster shell 23, 181
        plant remains and charcoal 15, 23, 24, 66, 67, 68, 181
        pottery 15, 23, 24, 47, 49-51, *49, 50*, 54, 181
        radiocarbon dating 15, 23, 24, 50-1, 178-9, 181
        ring-ditch? 24, 181
    Roman cropmark enclosures to east and north-west 24, 191
    sub-Roman/post-Roman (early medieval) pit [.015] 13, *22*, 24, 131, 132-3, 191
        fire debris (charcoal) 164
        plant remains and charcoal 24, 132, 156, 157, 163-4
        radiocarbon dating 23, 24, 132, 166, 178-9, 181
Moothill Cross, Staverton (Site 18; FTC 4.02) *2, 3, 8*, 13
    ditch (?routeway), undated 171-2, *172*
    flint (FTC 4.02) *60*
    'Old Straight Track' 172
    placename 171
mould, stone, for casting pewter dish 102, 104, 111, 112, 113, 114, *114*, 117, 118, 189

nails, iron 155
Neolithic 13, 14, 193
    heathland 128
    plant remains and charcoal 17, 73-4, 75-6, 166, 189
Neolithic, Early 11, 16-19, 180, 181
    flint 16, 17, 19, 55, 56, 58-9, 177, 180
    radiocarbon dates from ?old wood 28, 29, 32, 34, 77, 178-9, 186
    see also Croft Cottages (Site 20); Livermore Farm; Pixies' Parlour (Site 4); pottery
Neolithic, Middle to Late 11, 13-14, 19-24, 180-2
    flint 19, 20, 22, 55, 56, 58, 59, 62, 181
    hazelnut 74
    pit deposits, ritual 64-5, 181
    plant remains and charcoal 73-6, 128, 181-2, 183, 189, *and see Sites 17 and 28*
    radiocarbon dating 17, 77, 130, 177, 178-9, 180, 181, *and see Sites 17 and 28, and* Beneknowle (Site 30)
    and see Hems Valley (Site 17); Moore Farm (Site 28); *see also* pottery; rubbing stones
New Nutwalls, Aylesbeare (Site 9; ATK 0.03) 2, 3, 6, 13
    gully, ?prehistoric 168-9, *169*, 190
    Roman pottery 108, 168-9, 190
Nutwell Lodge, Woodbury (Site 11; ATK 11.04), ditches, undated 2, 3, 6, 13, 169, *170*, 188

'Old Straight Track' 172
OTA Ottery St Mary to Aylesbeare (= East Devon) 1, 2, 3, 4, 5, 14
    field boundaries 175
    flint 55, 56, *56*, 58
    pottery, medieval and later *152*, 153
OTA 1.01, .02, flint *56*
OTA 1.03 *see* Coldharbour (Site 1)
OTA 2.01, flint *56*
OTA 2.03 *see* Slade Farm (Site 2)
OTA 2.04, flint *56*
OTA 2.06/3.01 *see* Knightstone Farm (Site 3)
OTA 3.02 field to east of Pixies' Parlour, flint 5, 55, 56, *56*
OTA 3.03, flint *5, 56*
OTA 3.04 *see* Pixies' Parlour (Site 4)
OTA 3.07 *see* Salston A (Site 5)
OTA 3.08, flint *56*
OTA 4.01 *see* Salston B (Site 6)
OTA 4.06, .08, .09, flint *56*
OTA 4.10 *see* Broad Oak, land east of (Site 7)
OTA 4.11, flint *56*
OTA 5.01/5.02 *see* Broad Oak, land south-east of (Site 8)
OTA 5.03, flint *56*
OTA 7a.04, flint *56*
OTA 9.01, flint *5*, 15, *56*, 58, 62, *63*
OTA 9.02 *see* Livermore Farm
Ottery St Mary 2, 4; *see also* Knightstone Farm (Site 3); Pixies' Parlour (Site 4); Salston A (Site 5); Salston B (Site 6); Slade Farm (Site 2)
ovens
    Roman *see* Springfield (Site 31)
    medieval *see* Exwell Barton (Site 14)
oyster shell 23, 166, 181

Palaeolithic 11
pantiles 134, 136, 137-8

pebbles, utilised (Site 31) 111, 112, 113
pewter casting industry 113, *and see* mould
pin shaft fragment, MBA 35, 66, *66*
pit deposits (deliberate, ritual)
    Neolithic 64-5, 181
    Middle Bronze Age, Trevisker pottery 34, 54
Pixies' Parlour, Ottery St Mary (Site 4; OTA 3.04) 2, 3, 5, 13, *16*
    Mesolithic flint 15, 16, 56, 177, 179-80
    Early Neolithic 14, 16-17, *16, 17*, 80, *81*, 180
        arrowhead 17, 58, 62, *63*
        flint 17, 46, 55, 56, *56*, 62, *63*, 180
        knapping debris 17, 177
        plant remains (dated to 16th/17th centuries) 17, 166
        pottery 15, 16, 17, 45-6, *46*, 180
        radiocarbon dating 17, 46, 166, 178-9
        tree-throw hole (sub-oval feature) 16-17, 133, 166, 180
    Bronze Age/Middle Bronze Age pits 14, *16*, 27, 80, *81*, 184
        charcoal 27, 68, 69
        cremation pit, BA? 68
        flint 27, 58
        plant remains 27, 75
        pottery, MBA 15, 27, 52, 56
    Late Iron Age/Roman 14, *16*, 79, 80-3, *81*
    Late Iron Age penannular ditch [.045] (ring-ditch, ?roundhouse) *16*, 55, 58, 79, 80, *81*, 83, 187
        as cross-dyke 187
        hazelnut 80, 122
        pottery, LIA 80, 105, 106, Roman 80, 108, 187
        plant remains and charcoal 121, 122
    Roman features *16*, 79, 187
        curving ditch [.004] (enclosure) *16*, 27, 55, 56, 58, 80, 82-3, *82*, 187, 191
        cobbles (polisher or whetstone) 83, 110
        flint 58, 82
        plant remains 83, 122, 124, 129
        pottery 80, 82, 83, 108, 187
    early medieval (7th century), pit *16*, *81*, 83, 131, 191
        plant remains 131
        radiocarbon dating 83, 131, 166, 178-9, 187
    medieval pottery 83
    post-medieval pit and field boundaries *16*, *81*, 83, 133
        plant remains and charcoal (?processing waste) 133, 163, 166
        pottery *152*, 153
        radiocarbon dating 133, 166
placename, Moothill 171
plant remains and charcoal (including local landscape) 13, 66-76
    analysis 193-4
    and see under periods and site names; see also arable agriculture; crop-processing; fuel
Plot numbers *2-10, 4*
polisher or whetstone, cobble 83, 110
post-medieval 193
    brick clamp *see* Salston A (Site 5)
    cob building *see* Lower Nutwell (Site 12)
    plant remains 163, 166, 183
    radiocarbon dating 166
    and see under site names; see also pottery
post-Roman/early medieval *see* Moore Farm (Site 28); Pixies' Parlour (Site 4); Tigley B (Site 27); *see also* medieval, early

pottery (*fabric names only*)
　dating 13
　Early Neolithic 15, 16, 17, 18, 45-7, 180
　　CH.1 Upper Greensand-derived 45, 46, 47
　　CH.2 Upper Greensand with chert 45, 46
　　GN.1 & GN.2 granite-derived 45, 46, 180
　　IV.1 fabric with voids 45, 46
　　PB.1 Permian breccia 45, 46, *46*, 180
　　VQ.1 vein quartz in granite-derived matrix 45, 46, *46*, 47
　Middle Neolithic
　　Peterborough Ware 15, 19, 20, 47-8, 59, 79, 180-1
　　QU.1 rare rounded quartz 47-8
　　VQ.2 sparse vein quartz 47, 48
　Late Neolithic
　　GA.1 gabbroic (Lizard gabbroic) 47, 48, 49, 181
　　GR.1 grog in local clay 47, 48, 49
　　Grooved Ware 15, 23, 24, 47, 48-51, 54, 181
　　QU.2 sparse quartz 47, 48, 49, *49*, 54
　　QU.3 sparse quartz 47, 48, 49, *49*, 54
　　VQ.3 vein quartz 47, 48, *49*, 54
　Bronze Age 28
　　Beaker 184
　　grog- and rock-tempered 28
　Early Bronze Age/Beaker 51-2, *51*
　　GN.3 granite-derived All-Over-Cord style 15, 27, 51-2, *51*, 54, 182
　Middle Bronze Age 52-5, 184-5
　　GR.2 grog, chert, quartz 52, 53
　　GR.3 grog, vein quartz 52
　　grog-tempered 27, 33
　　RO.1 Exeter volcanic 52, 53-5, *53*
　　Trevisker (RO.1) 12, 15, 28, 34, *34*, 35, 52, 53-4, *53*, 55, 66, 184, 185
　Iron Age, granitic 38
　Middle Iron Age, South Western Decorated 86, 105
　Late Iron Age
　　CH.3 Upper Greensand with chert 105, 106
　　GN.4 granite-derived fabric 102, 105, 106
　　PB.2 Permian breccia, Ludwell Valley fabric 105, 106
　　RO.2 Exeter volcanic fabric 84, 105, 106
　Roman
　　Black Sandy (BS) 106, 107
　　Black-Burnished ware 40
　　Central Gaulish Samian (LEZ SA2) 107, 108
　　greyware (LOC GW1) 106, 107, 108
　　greyware (LOC GW2) 106, 107, 108
　　grog-tempered (GT) 106, 107, 108, 109, *109*
　　New Forest Colour-Coated ware (NFO CC) 106, 107, 108, 110
　　oxidised fineware (LOC OX) 106, 107, 109, *109*
　　South Devon (micaceous) reduced ware (SOD RE) 106, 107, 108-9, *109*, 110
　　South Devon ware 86, 105, 189, 190
　　South-East Dorset Black-Burnished (DOR BB1) 106, 107, 108, 109
　medieval 148-54
　　Breton? 150, 151, *152*, 154
　　Bristol? 150
　　calcareous-tempered 141
　　chert-tempered 137, 153
　　Exeter fabric 40: 149, 150, 151, *152*, 154
　　Exeter fabric 42: 149, 150
　　fabric 1 Upper Greensand 149, 150, 151, *152*, 153
　　fabric 2 'Membury-type' 149, 150-1, *152*, 153-4
　　?Hampshire fabric 150
　　handmade South Devon granite-derived ware 153
　　petrology 153-4
　　redware 151, *152*
　　Saintonge 141, 150, 151, *152*, 153
　　Seville plain ware 151, *152*
　　wheel-thrown South Devon granite-derived ware 153
　post-medieval 151, 153
　　Cologne stoneware 153
　　fine unglazed white ware (?Saintonge) *152*, 153
　　granite-derived micaceous coarseware 153
　　Martincamp flask 153
　　Normandy stoneware 153
　　North Devon 153
　　Raeren stoneware 153
　　St Germans-type calcareous ware 153
　　Siegburg or Beauvais stoneware *152*, 153
　　Spanish *Melado* ware 153
　　Totnes-type ware 153, *153*
　　Werra slipware *152*, 153
　see also under site names
Powderham 4
　deer park 193
　see also Exwell Barton (Site 14)

quernstones *see* Billany Farm (Site 24); Springfield (Site 31)

radiocarbon dating 13, 177, 178-9, 180-93 *passim; see also under periods and site names*
Rattery *see* Hood Ball (Site 21); Lower Velwell (Site 22)
ring-ditches 11, *and see* Broad Oak (Site 8); Moore Farm (Site 28); Pixies' Parlour (Site 4)
Roman (Romano-British) 12, 13, 14, 79, 189-91, 193
　ditches (field boundaries) 190, *and see* Barton Hill Cross (Site 19); Exwell Barton (Site 14); Knightstone Farm (Site 3); Lower Velwell (Site 22); New Nutwells (Site 9)
　enclosure/settlement *see* Billany Farm (Site 24)
　fuel 129-30
　furnaces, Iron Age or Roman *see* Lower Velwell (Site 22)
　landscape 190-1
　LIA/R *see* Exwell Barton (Site 14); Pixies' Parlour (Site 4)
　linen 129
　metalworking and settlement, Late Roman *see* Springfield (Site 31)
　pits, early Roman *see* Dun Cross (Site 25)
　plant remains and charcoal 74, 122, 124-7, 129-30, 183, 189, 190-1
　radiocarbon dating 130
　settlement, Romano-British *see* Barton Hill Cross (Site 19)
　see also beads; blades; cobbles; coins; pottery; whetstones
roundhouses, Bronze Age to Roman 11, 12, 190; *see also* Crablake Farm (Site 15); Pixies' Parlour (Site 4)
rubbing stones
　Neolithic, pebble (Site 17) 19-20, 63-5, *66*, 181
　Roman, cobbles (Site 24) 111

Salston A, Ottery St Mary (Site 5; OTA 3.07), post-medieval brick clamp *2, 3, 5*, 13, 14, 131, 133-4, *133*
　charcoal 133
　flint *56*

Salston B, Ottery St Mary (Site 6; OTA 4.01), Early Bronze Age/Beaker cremation pit 3, *5*, 13, 14, 15, 24, *26*, 68, 182, 184
    charcoal (fuel) 24, 68, 69, 75
    ditches and pits 24, *25*
    flint *56*
    human bone 15, 24, 76-7, 194
    radiocarbon dating 24, 77, 178-9
site names and numbers *2-10*, 4
Site 1 *see* Coldharbour (OTA 1.03)
Site 2 *see* Slade Farm (OTA 2.03)
Site 3 *see* Knightstone Farm (OTA 2.06/3.01)
Site 4 *see* Pixies' Parlour (OTA 3.04)
Site 5 *see* Salstone A (OTA 3.07)
Site 6 *see* Salston B (OTA 4.01)
Site 7 *see* Broad Oak, land east of (OTA 4.10)
Site 8 *see* Broad Oak, land south-east of (OTA 5.01/5.02)
Site 9 *see* New Nutwalls (ATK 0.03)
Site 10 *see* Hogsbrook Farm (ATK 4.04 & 4a.01)
Site 11 *see* Nutwell Lodge (ATK 11.04)
Site 12 *see* Lower Nutwell (ATK 12.01)
Site 13 *see* White House (ATK 12.12)
Site 14 *see* Exwell Barton (ATK 13.02)
Site 17 *see* Hems Valley (FTC 2.02)
Site 18 *see* Moothill Cross (FTC 4.02)
Site 19 *see* Barton Hill Cross (FTC 7.01)
Site 20 *see* Croft Cottages (FTC 8.02)
Site 21 *see* Hood Ball (FTC 12.05)
Site 22 *see* Lower Velwell (FTC 12.05w)
Site 23 *see* Hood Quarry (FTC 13.03)
Site 24 *see* Billany Farm (FTC 14.01)
Site 25 *see* Dun Cross (FTC 16.01)
Site 26 *see* Tigley A (FTC 16.07)
Site 27 *see* Tigley B (FTC 16.08)
Site 28 *see* Moore Farm (FTC 18.12 & 18.13)
Site 29 *see* Bluepost (FTC 19.07 & 19.08)
Site 30 *see* Beneknowle (FTC 21.06)
Site 31 *see* Springfield (FTC 24.02-05)
Site 32 *see* Forder Cross (FTC 26.01)
Site 33 *see* Wood Farm (FTC 31.05-07)
Site 34 *see* Filham House (FTC 33.01-02)
Slade Farm, Ottery St Mary (Site 2; OTA 2.03) *2, 3, 5*
    Neolithic pottery 47-8, 79, 130
        radiocarbon dating 48
    Iron Age pits and ditches 13, 14, 79-80, *79*, 188
        crop-processing 14, 15, 80, 122, 127, 128, 130
        hazelnut 79, 80
        plant remains and charcoal 14, 15, 79, 80, 121, 122, 127, 128, 130, 188
        pottery 79-80, 105
        radiocarbon dating 79, 80, 105, 130, 178-9
slag *see under* Lower Velwell (Site 22); Springfield (Site 31); Tigley A (Site 26)
slate, roofing 136, 155, 192
smithing hearth bottoms 119-20
    Middle Iron Age *see* Tigley A (Site 26)
    Iron Age or Roman *see* Lower Velwell (Site 22)
Soloman's Farm, Exminster (Site 16; ATK 15.02), ditch and pits (four-post structure) *2, 3, 7*, 13, 169, 171, *171*, 188, 190
Springfield, Ugborough (Site 31; FTC 24.02-05) *2, 4, 9*
    Mesolithic flint 59, 180
    Bronze Age 13, 24, *26*, 27, *101*
        barrow 15, 24, *26*, 27, 51, 52, 100, 182, 184
        Beaker pit 27, *27*, 51-2, *51*, 100, 182, 184
        flint 59, *61*
        pottery 15, 27, 51-2, *51*, 182, 184
    Iron Age pit 13, 79, 102, 188
        pottery 102, 105, 106
    Roman settlement 13, 79, 100-4, *100*, *101*, 189-90, 194
        blade or strip, iron 104
        crop-processing 103, 127, 129
        enclosure ditch 100, *101*, 102
        glass bead 102, 114, *114*
        hammerscale 102, 104, 117, 118, 189, 194
        hazelnut 103, 129
        hearth/furnace lining 104
        ironworking 102, 104, 117, 118, 189
        metalworking 115, 117, 118, 189, 194
        mould (stone) for pewter dish 102, 104, 111, 112, 113, 114, *114*, 117, 118, 189
        oven, with clay lining (hood) 102-3, *103*, 127, 129
        pebbles 111, 112, 113
        pigment on granite 111
        pits 103-4
        plant remains and charcoal 102, 103, 104, 124, 126, 127, 129-30, 189
        pottery, Roman 79, 102, 103, 104, 106, 107, 109, *109*, 110, 189
        querns 102, 103, 104, 111, 112, 113-14
        radiocarbon dating 103, 178-9
        ring-gully and postholes [.149] (circular building?) 100, 102, 189-90
        slag 102, 104, 117, 118
        smithy? (ditch [.152]) *101*, 102, 189
        stone-filled pits *101*, 104
        stone (other) 111, 112-14, *and see* mould *above*
        tin alloy (working) 104, 117, 118, 189
        whetstone, cobble 111, 113
Staverton *see* Croft Cottages (Site 20); Hems Valley (Site 17); Moothill Cross (Site 18)
stone (worked and utilised)
    prehistoric 63-6, *66*
    Late Iron Age/Roman 110-14
    flint *see under* periods and site names
    see also cobbles; mould; pebbles; quernstones; rubbing stones; slate, roofing; whetstones
structures and buildings
    MBA terraced building *see* Beneknowle (Site 30)
    Iron Age, four-post structure 188
    undated (?prehistoric/Roman) four-post structure (Site 16) 169, *171*
    Roman ring-gully and smithy? *see* Springfield (Site 31)
    medieval house and sunken outbuilding *see* Exwell Barton (Site 14)
    post-medieval
        brick clamp *see* Salston A (Site 5)
        cob building *see* Lower Nutwell (Site 12)
    see also furnaces; hearths

Tigley A, Dartington (Site 26; FTC 16.07), Middle Iron Age iron smelting furnaces *2, 3, 8*, 13, 14, 79, 88, 95-100, *95*, 187-8
    charcoal (fuel) 75, 97, 98, 99, 100, 116, 123, 128, 130, 187

Tigley A, Middle Iron Age iron smelting furnaces (cont.)
  clay lining 99, 116, 120, 122
  ditches 97, 100
  furnace bottom 115, 116, 118, 188
  furnaces, metalworking 115-20
  hammerscale 99, 116, 118, 187
  pits 97, 98, 99-100, 117
  plant remains 98, 99, 100, 122
  radiocarbon dating 79, 97, 98, 99, 100, 115, 116, 120, 130, 178, 179, 187
  slag 97, 99, 100, 115, 116-17, 118, 119, 188, 194
  smithing hearth bottoms 99, 115, 116, 194
Tigley B, Dartington (Site 27; FTC 16.08), early medieval pit (6th/7th century) 2, 4, 8, 13, 131, *131*, 132, 191
  charcoal (fire debris) 132, 164, 191
  glass bead 156, *156*
  hazelnut 132
  plant remains (dump of harvested waste) 132, 156, 157, 163-4, 191
  radiocarbon dating 132, 166, 178-9
tin alloy working, Roman *see* Springfield (Site 31)
trackway *see* White House (Site 13); *see also* Moothill Cross (Site 18)
twine or string, medieval 147, 162, 165, 191

Ugborough *see* Filham House (Site 34); Springfield (Site 31); Wood Farm (Site 33)
Ugborough Moor 186

water-vole faecal pellets 73, 185
whetstones
  prehistoric, sandstone, Lower Nutwell (Site 12) 110
  Roman, cobbles
    Pixies' Parlour (Site 4) 83, 110
    Springfield (Site 31) 111, 113
White House (Site 13; ATK 12.12)
  Mesolithic flint *57*, 58, 180
  medieval/early post-medieval
    ditch terminus and pit (ATK 12.12) 139
    pottery 153
    trackway 2, 3, *7*, 13, 131, 138-9, *140*
Woodbury *see* Deepway Farm; Hogsbrook Farm (Site 10); Nutwell Lodge (Site 11)
Wood Farm, Ugborough (Site 33; FTC 31.05-07), ?prehistoric ditches (hedgebanks) 2, 4, *9*, 13, 172-3, *173*, 186, 188
woodland clearance, prehistoric 75, 76, 77, 128, 181, 182, 187
woodlands 193
  Mesolithic 181
  Neolithic 76, 181
  Bronze Age 76
  Iron Age 128, 187
  Roman 129, 130
  early medieval 164
  medieval 162, 165-6